Introduction to Business

Introduction to Business:
Concepts and Careers

F. T. HANER
STEPHEN K. KEISER
DONALD J. PUGLISI

University of Delaware

MARGARET PYLE HASSERT, *Editor*

WINTHROP PUBLISHERS, INC.
Cambridge, Massachusetts

Library of Congress Cataloging in Publication Data

Haner, Frederick Theodore.
    Introduction to business.

    Includes index.
    1. Business.   2. Vocational guidance.   I. Keiser,
Stephen K., joint author.   II. Puglisi, Donald J.,
joint author.   III. Title.
HF5351.H256   658.4   75–41457
ISBN 0–87626–392–9

© 1976 by Winthrop Publishers, Inc.
    17 Dunster Street, Cambridge, Massachusetts 02138

All rights reserved. No part of this book may be reproduced
in any form or by any means without permission in writing
from the publisher. Printed in the United States of America.

10   9   8   7   6   5   4   3   2   1

Text design by Sandra Rigney.
Cover design by Donya Melanson Associates.

To my father,
Fred L. Haner

and

To our wives,
Barbara Keiser and
Anita Puglisi

Contents

Preface   xi

PART ONE: The Nature of Business   1

1   Business: Definition and Perspective   3

The American Business System   3
Developments Affecting American Business   8
Careers and Jobs   13
Chapter Summary   15

2   People in Business: The Workers   19

Jobs and Levels in an Organization   20
The Changing Composition of Workers in Business   27
Some Aspects of a Manager's Life   30
The Role of Labor Unions in Business   33
Careers and Jobs   40
Chapter Summary   41

PART TWO: The Environment of Business   45

3   The Role of Government   47

The Regulator Role   48
The Buyer Role   64

The Dispenser of Funds, Goods, and Services Role 68
The Setter of Policy Role 70
Government Careers 71
Chapter Summary 74

4 Business and Society   77

Public Demands from Business 77
Perspective on Business Responsibilities in the United States 84
Problems with Social Response 87
Resolution of Problems 90
Impact of New Responsibilities on Careers 97
Chapter Summary 99

5 The Economic Framework for Business   103

The American Economic System 103
Comparison with Other Economic Systems 108
Evaluation of the American Economic System 109
International Trade and Investment 114
A Perspective on Economic Problems 119
Careers and Jobs in Economics 126
Chapter Summary 127

PART THREE: Parts of a Typical Business   131

6 Introduction to Management   133

Part 1: Management Fundamentals 133
Part 2: Organization and Leadership 141
Careers and Jobs 151
Chapter Summary 152

7 Forms of Business Organization   159

The Proprietorship 159
The Partnership 161
The Corporation 163
Other Forms of Business Organization 173
Choosing a Specific Form of Business Organization 174
Chapter Summary 175

8 Producing Goods and Services   179

Materials and Components for Production 180
Plant and Equipment for Production 189
Management of the Production Process 197
Career Opportunities in Industrial Management 205
Chapter Summary 206

Contents

9 Marketing Concepts — 213

What Does Marketing Do? 213
The Impact of Marketing on the Firm 224
Historical Change in Importance of Marketing 226
The Consumerism Movement 228
Marketing as a Job 233
Chapter Summary 237

10 Promotion — 241

Promotion Objectives 241
Promotion Budget 247
Promotional Balance 250
Promotion Activities 253
Promotional Effectiveness 258
Promotion Jobs 260
Chapter Summary 266

11 Channels of Distribution — 271

Planning Title Transfer 271
Planning Physical Movement 288
Jobs in Distribution Channels 291
Chapter Summary 293

12 Employing, Developing, and Administering Personnel — 297

The Personnel Function in the Organization 297
The Employment Process 299
Training and Development 303
Labor Relations 309
Personnel Administration 314
Careers and Jobs 320
Chapter Summary 321

13 Accounting and Control Systems — 325

The Purpose and Need for Accounting 325
Accounting Fundamentals 328
Financial Accounting 333
Management Accounting 343
The Controller and Staff 348
Career Opportunities in Accounting 350
Chapter Summary 353

14 Finance and Capital for Business — 357

What Is Finance? 357
The Uses of Funds 358
The Sources of Funds 365

The Dividend Decision 372
External Growth 374
Career Opportunities in Finance 375
Chapter Summary 377

15 Risk and Insurance for Business 381

The Nature of Risk and Insurance 381
Kinds of Insurance Companies and Insurance 385
Trends in the Impact of Insurance on Business 397
Careers and Jobs in Insurance 399
Chapter Summary 400

16 The Computer in Business 405

Information 405
Systems to Provide Information 411
Computers and People 416
Successful Computer Use 419
Future Business Use of Computers 425
Jobs in the Computer Industry 427
Chapter Summary 430

17 Modern Quantitative Methods 433

The Quantitative Approach to Problem Solving 433
Business Statistics 436
Techniques and Terminology in Quantitative Methods 445
Bridging the Management Gap 451
Careers in Management Science 453
Chapter Summary 454

PART FOUR: Pulling Together Business Functions: The Company 459

18 General Management: Direction, Coordination, and Growth 461

Responsibilities of General Management 462
The General Manager's Role in Planning and Strategy 465
Sources of Growth 469
Plans, Strategies, and Reality 477
International Operations 480
Careers and Jobs 483
Chapter Summary 483

19 Establishing and Managing a Small Business 489

Definition of a Small Business 489
The Entrepreneur 490
Part 1: Establishing a Small Business 494

Part 2: Managing the Small Business 503
Careers and Jobs 509
Chapter Summary 510

20 Your Future Career in Business 515

Business Developments and Career Directions 515
Career Planning 519
Chapter Summary 531

Glossary 533

Index 553

Preface

The objective of this textbook is to introduce business as a course of study to students who have little or no background in the field. We hope that this introduction will generate the student's continuing interest leading to both a college degree and a satisfying and rewarding career in business. In the event that this book is the student's last formal learning experience about business, the knowledge gained, ranging from company operations to the overall effects of business on society, should result in a better understanding of the field and a more successful life in our capitalistic system.

The business environment is experiencing significant changes in the 1970s. Increasingly, decision makers in business and industry are being influenced by the impact of global competition, organized action by consumers, social pressures, the depletion of American resources, technological innovations, and government intervention in free enterprise. Discussion of these and other factors should make students realize that the environment of business is both awesome and exciting, requiring a thorough understanding of its many dynamic components.

As teachers and authors, we recognize the changing attitudes of both faculty and students toward an "introduction to business" course. Various methods of increasing the student's comprehension are being examined constantly. One approach involves stimulating students to take issue with controversial topics in addition to remembering facts and figures. We have started and ended each chapter with Provocative Statements by young people, business executives, politicians, labor leaders, and others to present contrasting viewpoints on important issues such as profits and social responsibility, government controls, worker rights, and discrimination.

Too, many students are anxious to learn as much information as possible which is relevant to their futures. Discussion of career selection and job opportunities in specific areas of business is provided at the end of each chapter. The reader is introduced to jobs in both the government and private firms, including careers in fields such as accounting, production, retailing, advertising, and selling.

The objective of producing an interesting and stimulating text was not achieved at the expense of content. We offer students and teachers the expertise of professionals who have both taught and worked in various areas of business. Each author has written about the field in which he has had current and practical knowledge.

Realizing that students using this book would have a wide range of reading ability and background, we retained Editor Margaret Pyle Hassert to assist us in writing a text understandable to students on all levels. This resulted in a controlled vocabulary, short sentences, key terms clearly outlined and identified, and a Glossary of terms at the end of the text. Each chapter was evaluated by experts for reading level, and college students with varied skills and abilities critiqued the content. The tables and figures were carefully prepared to facilitate student understanding. The many business examples and cartoons were selected to help the reader learn the basic concepts of the text.

We have divided the book into four basic parts. Part One introduces the student to the nature of business and compares the American system with other approaches. It also discusses some aspects of life inside a business organization.

The demands of the environment are dealt with in Part Two. Business must successfully interact with government, society, and the world economic system. Possible solutions to environmental problems are also suggested, from the American point of view.

The major concepts of business are discussed in Part Three. The functions of management, marketing, personnel, accounting, and finance are included. Our contemporary view of business also led to the inclusion of other areas vital to business. These include chapters on forms of business organization, insurance, computers, and quantitative methods.

Part Four integrates the concepts and components of company operations and clarifies the need for plans and strategies in realizing the fundamentals of small business. Finally, a chapter on career directions supplements the material presented in the other parts of the book.

We would like to acknowledge the contributions of reviewers, particularly Richard D. Brown, Andrew Lonyo, Thomas J. Nolan, and Kenneth R. Schock. Also, the Dean of Academic Affairs of Brandywine College, William M. Polishook, was immensely helpful in arranging for the testing of chapters as class projects. In addition, research assistance was received from Tres Birdsall, Daniel Jordan, and Eric Shimp. Finally, Nancy Bange coordinated permissions, composed the Index, and arranged for typing of manuscripts for the textbook, *Student Guide*, and *Instructor's Manual*.

The Nature of Business

PART ONE

Chapter Outline

The American Business System
   Definition of Business
   The Nature of American Business
   Business under Controls
   Social Progress with Privately Owned Business

Developments Affecting American Business
   Foreign Competition
      Some Specific Problems
      Some American Advantages
   Shortages of Energy and Other Materials
      Long-range Implications
      Government Cooperation
   Rapidly Changing Technology

Careers and Jobs
   Some Suggestions on the Approach to Choosing a Career

Chapter Summary

Provocative Statement 1: A Shift from Volume to Profits

Provocative Statement 2: Public Opinion about the Business Community

Key Terms

System
Capital
Per capita
Devaluation
Backward integration
Strategies for supply
Nationalization
Introverts
Extroverts
Full-line concept
Logistics

Business: Definition and Perspective

THE AMERICAN BUSINESS SYSTEM

1

The definition of a system is:

> A logical grouping of distinct yet interdependent components assembled for the purpose of achieving a predetermined objective.

When applied to American business, the objective of both individuals and privately owned firms supplying money is *profits*. The government plays a role in making the common objective of these two different groups workable within the American economy by regulation, guidance through policies, protection, and participation through purchases and sales.

It is important to understand the place of a business firm in our complex economy. The parts illustrated in Figure 1-1 (see p. 4) depend on each other for survival and growth. Companies that manufacture products as well as companies that provide services, such as retailers or plumbers, are considered. If a small regional firm goes under, the impact is negligible because a new company can replace the failure. However, the health of the economy is directly involved when a very large corporation fails, such as the Penn Central railroad, or when federal policy is changed in regard to level of government purchases, supply of dollars, or interest rates.

The attitude of managers, the people who make the decisions, is extremely important to the system. If these executives are confident, the economy grows and is healthy. If they are unsure of and worried about the future, the economy loses momentum and stalls. Actions by the government strongly influence management's level of confidence.

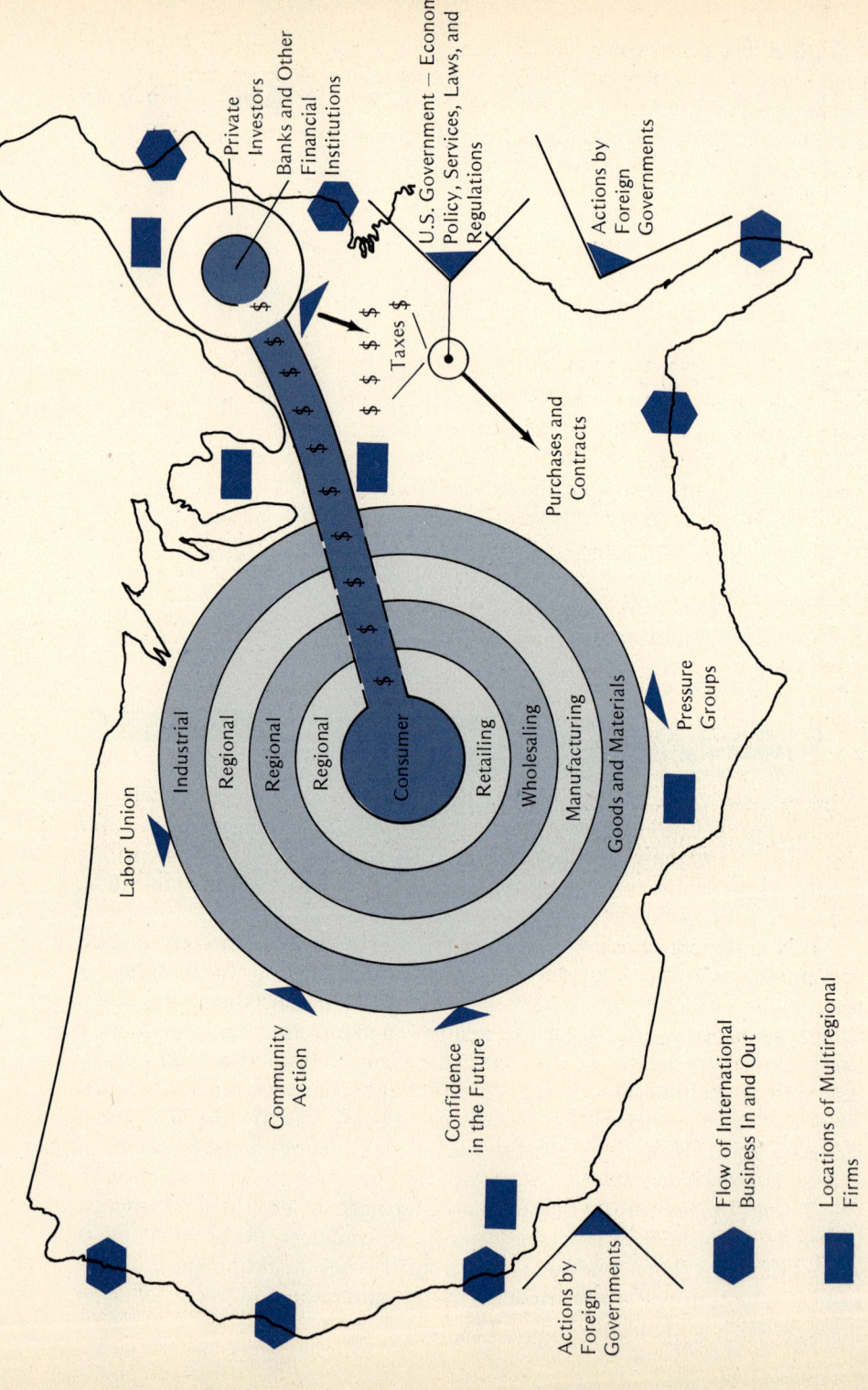

Figure 1-1. Simplified Model of the American Economy

Other factors can also influence the system. These are shown in Figure 1-1, also. They include labor availability and cost, the policies of labor unions, money for credit and loans, competition from outside the country, supplies and prices of items purchased outside the country, and pressures from nonbusiness sources, such as minority races and community organizations.

The Nature of American Business

A business can exist when people want something, and an individual or company can earn a profit by supplying what is wanted. Mass production and huge markets have helped industry to grow in this country. A high volume of sales from specializing in specific product lines has enabled **capital** to be invested in labor-saving machinery. Greater output per person permits higher salaries and wages. This has been followed by more demand from customers who have been earning more money in their own jobs.

The American business system is based on highly efficient large-scale facilities and on private capital. It now has about 90 million people working only 30 to 40 hours per week and earning 3 times as much as the average European.[1] It is equally important to note that a large part of the capital invested in American business comes from the employees themselves, rather than from a few powerful families.

In the United States and some other countries in the world, a person can freely go into business and compete against others in the same industry. There is paperwork to obtain licenses, zoning approvals, and so on to form the company and to set up operations. However, most of the time the new enterprise can begin without interference from the government or the community.

After it is formed, the firm sells its goods and services in competition with others in a similar business. This is good from the consumer's viewpoint because it means:

1. *A reasonable price.* Companies offering the same items tend to resist raising prices in fear of losing customers. Often they are forced to lower prices when competitors, seeking to increase their share of the market, lower theirs.

2. *Adequate quality.* Companies, when kept from raising prices, are sometimes tempted to reduce quality to maintain good profit margins. To prevent such companies from pretending they are offering the same product, we have laws, regulations, and customer action groups. Also, competitors gain an advantage when a deception on the part of a company is uncovered.

3. *Volume to meet needs.* Generally, there are adequate supplies of everything from food to luxuries. This situation occurs under the American business system because, when there is scarcity, there is economic opportunity. People enter business until there is abundance and some tendency for too much

---

[1] American income per capita was $5,160 in 1973, as compared to weighted estimates of $1,750 per capita for 17 European countries.

competition and price cutting. Only occasionally does a patent, limited raw materials, or other reason restrict entry of competition and result in unusual profits at the expense of the customer.

4. *Convenience.* Healthy competition provides greater convenience for customers in the form of (a) locations near their company or home and (b) improved service. Each supplier wants the business, and reaches out to the buyer through variations of free delivery, guaranteed performance, past-purchase service, and branches in suburban areas.

In our role as buyer, we benefit from competition. However, in our other roles as investor or worker, we are sometimes hurt by the freedom to start a business. Too many firms entering an industry can result in bankruptcy and loss of capital and jobs. Usually, the effects of intensive competition are not that bad, and the return on money invested can be what was expected. In a few cases, however, the capital might have earned more by drawing interest in a safe bank than by being put into a business.

All investors in business are confronted with several possibilities for earning a return on their capital, some of which are shown in Figure 1-2. The relationship to risk is generally proportional, that is, the higher the risk, the higher the profits. The ultimate objective of an investor is to have a business that has low risk and high return.

Figure 1-2. *Some Options for Use of Capital*

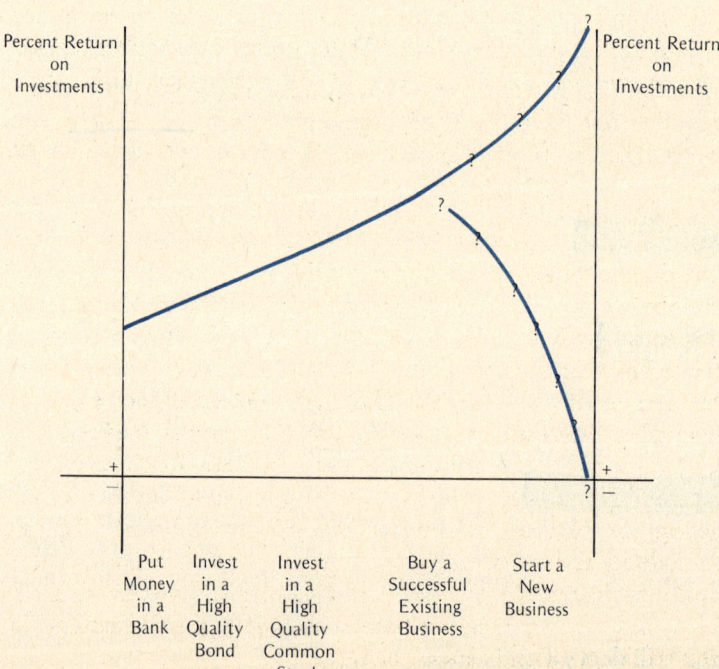

Business under Controls

In many countries, such as India, Morocco, and Peru, resources are limited and the people are poor. Governments must plan carefully the use of what is in the country and restrict the freedom to enter business enterprise. They give permission based on whether the proposed operation fits a development plan.

The profits may be controlled directly or indirectly after permission is granted. Prices can be fixed. Company paid benefits, including social security and health insurance, can be high. Authorities may insist on more workers than are necessary for efficiency in order to create employment. The amount of profits may even have a maximum so that benefits are distributed to the general public rather than to a few investors.

Business in such cases is a tool of government policy. If policies are too restrictive, capital and technology needed in the country go to other places where they can earn more profits and where management is freer to make decisions. Ireland and Korea are examples of countries that have laws and policies designed to attract foreign investors and to permit above average profits as an incentive to business expansion and growth.

Social Progress with Privately Owned Business

Some political systems strive toward having equal social benefits for all the people through laws and regulations and components of the economy owned by the state. Private ownership in the United States results in more benefits for those who are successful, but the general objective is adequate social progress for everyone. The U.S. government has taken steps to improve the condition of minorities and the poor through use of tax dollars from individuals and corporations.

Social legislation that results in equal job opportunities and improved distribution of wealth is obviously good. Elimination of misery among the poor and the aged, of disease, of insecurity about having a job, and of bad living conditions should be major objectives of government. The American approach toward achieving social goals is partly dependent on individuals with talent to organize businesses, take risks, and work hard. Success means more jobs, higher levels of income, and better work security. If the government does not tax the successful individual or company excessively, privately owned business can produce the needed social benefits without restrictions on personal initiative.

Social responsibility has become a major issue in business. Companies are taking steps to clean up pollution, to hire and train minorities, to stand behind statements on products and services, and to apply some company resources toward community problems. Federal, state, and local governments are prodding companies to move faster. Gaining both economic and social success in the United States will depend on balance among:

8 *The Nature of Business*

1. Business having sufficient freedom to make decisions that enable them to compete successfully against companies from other countries.
2. Government laws, regulations, and policies that support business but provide sufficient tax revenues to eliminate the extremes of poverty, disease, discrimination, crime, drug abuse, and other social problems.
3. Public confidence in government and business leaders based on decisions that actually lead to social progress rather than self-interest.

The early 1970s in this country saw the period of Watergate, alleged "deals" between business and government, and a growing lack of public confidence in leadership. A distrust arose from misuse of authority. Continued public dissatisfaction could lead to a shift toward regulated social progress rather than the present voluntary system.

DEVELOPMENTS AFFECTING AMERICAN BUSINESS

Important things are happening to American business. The newness of these factors has made some companies less effective than they were in the early 1970s, while some are more prosperous than ever before. The key points are:

1. Powerful foreign competitors.
2. Shortages of energy and other materials at a reasonable price.
3. Rapidly changing technology.

In addition, the rate of inflation has increased in the United States and other countries around the world. The reasons and their implications for business are discussed in Chapter Five.

Foreign Competition

In the 1960s, companies based in other countries became not only economically competitive but also very aggressive in world trade. In many cases, traditional sellers and buyers were by-passed in their efforts to penetrate markets in the United States.

Some Specific Problems

The United States had the highest annual output *per capita* in the world until recently. Now this country is second to Switzerland ($6,700 to $6,515) and just ahead of Sweden ($6,505). Significant improvement to regain first place in the future is in doubt because of complications that are becoming apparent in the 1970s.

First, economic growth and our high standard of living are consuming energy and other resources at a rate that cannot be sustained. The resources of the North American continent give us more potential than Japan or the European powers. However, the competitive advantage we have had is now less than before. The United States must search for oil, ores, and other raw materials as do many of our foreign competitors.

Second, the dollar has devalued officially. This means we can buy less in other countries when we change to their money, but they can buy more from us when they change to the dollar. Unfortunately, the dollar's position as the foundation of world trade has weakened because people are uncertain of its value when buying or selling. The American competitive position is improved because these goods and services are cheaper when purchased in the more valuable foreign money. However, it also creates opportunities for foreign investors to establish business within the United States, and it makes oil, raw materials, and so on, more expensive for us. As a result, competition everywhere gets more intense.

Third, our technology has been superior to firms from other countries up until recently. It is simple economics that, if an American firm is competing with companies from other nations on an equal price basis and pays its workers much more than these countries, the workers have to produce more products to make up the difference. Today, firms around the world have significantly narrowed the American technological advantage in many fields. This advantage was one basis of us gaining a better standard of living.

Some American Advantages

After you hear "It's impossible" or "It will take months" in other countries and see Americans do it quickly and easily, you start to understand something about what we have that few others possess. Given a challenge, Americans are tough competitors. Problem solving is a continuing need within a company, and Americans excel at it. The result is consistently better performance in business than that achieved by firms in other countries as measured by profits.

Also, the United States gained immense power after the conclusion of World War II, when most other countries were weak. This provided an opportunity for us to have investments outside our country. These investments have been called the third greatest economic force after the American domestic output and Russia. Certainly the European countries and the growth of Japan are forces to consider, but our present position is very strong.

We have the most extraordinary technological foundation in the world. It has been constructed from:

1. $7 billion[2] being spent by the U.S. government for projects including space and defense programs. Commercial possibilities not yet fully developed are being created, and need is accelerating the flow of these ideas into industry.

[2] 1973 statistics.

2. $20 billion[3] being spent by business on research. This level of effort is 20% greater than the average of research expenditures in the European Common Market and Russia. Reasonable results in the form of new ideas will generate an advantage for the United States.

3. $3 billion[4] in research at universities and nonprofit institutions (nonfederal government funds). New ideas are coming from scholarly research which supplements other programs.

The output from these three areas may maintain this country's remaining technological advantage despite gains by foreign competition.

Another important factor is that other countries are confronted with sharply increasing costs in wages and salaries. In the 1967–73 period, wages in Japan rose 163%, and inflation has greatly increased this total in recent years. In West Germany they rose 88% from a higher base in the same 1967–73 period. In Sweden wages increased 85%. In the same period identical statistics for the United States showed a rise of 47%. It is true that American workers were originally being paid much more than workers in other countries. However, these totals indicate that the disadvantages of past decades may be much less in future years. Perhaps in the 1980s we will see the time when the competitive difference between industrialized nations will be based only on technology and productivity.

Finally, primary competitors in global competition purchase more energy from sources outside their countries than the United States does. Independence from Arabs and others will give industry in this country an advantage as long as American oil and coal are as cheap as other sources. At present, there is a favorable difference in price.

Shortages of Energy and Other Materials

Until the mid-1970s it had always been assumed that companies could purchase adequate supplies at an economic price. Now this is not true. Some energy and materials cost more than they are worth to a firm, and substitutes are justified on the basis of both cost and performance.

In a period of shortages, business must consider:

1. Availability of what is needed for periods well into the future.
2. Price trends on materials and components normally used.
3. Substitutes that can serve the purpose and improve the net cost.

This means having enough information to know what is going on in each instance. Companies are appointing task forces and special buyers to assure supplies. Cost analysts are examining all the possibilities. Management is judging whether or not the company should enter buying cooperatives to in-

---

[3] 1973 statistics.
[4] Ibid.

crease purchasing power or seek other alternatives to remain competitive and grow.

Long-range Implications

In periods of sustained shortages, management must secure the future of the company. In addition to the steps just described, more fundamental solutions may be necessary to avoid losses or slowing of growth.

DROP THE LOSERS Businesses are identifying products or groups of products severely affected by shortages and an upward price spiral. This has led, in some companies, to *thinning* and elimination of those products with narrow profit margins. Sometimes whole groups of products are terminated. Such decisions are often complicated by one product depending on another and by inadequate supplies of energy and/or materials for products with similar profit margins.

DIVERSIFY INTO LESS AFFECTED PRODUCTS AND SERVICES Future profitability can be gained from either acquiring existing businesses or starting new operations in fields less affected by problems facing the company. In each case, a major factor is adequate management with experience in the unfamiliar industry. Frequently, personnel must be hired away from competitors.

INTEGRATE Some large corporations have acquired companies to secure needed supplies. The *Los Angeles Times* met its need for newsprint by buying forest lands and building its own pulp and paper mills. This method is called **backward integration**. It is directed toward acquiring supplies of basic items as compared to forward integration, which involves acquiring firms for distributing finished products.

ESTABLISH NEW MARKETS Another way companies are attempting to improve their situation is by opening new market areas and more aggressively identifying new customers in existing areas. Increased volume lowers costs per unit on one hand, and increases buying power, on the other. Also, prices to the new customers can be based on current conditions rather than restricted by past practices.

Government Cooperation

Competition for supplies of energy, materials, and components comes from four sources:

1. American companies, either individually or in groups, buying together.
2. Foreign companies acting independently in a manner similar to the American companies.
3. Foreign governments acting on behalf of the public and private industry in their own countries.
4. Groups of governments acting to assist public and private industry in several countries by acting jointly.

The U.S. government will be called upon to take an active role in making strategies for supply. For many materials it will act directly to obtain supplies through formal contracts with foreign countries and through informal agreements in which the United States exercises political power.

The government will also encourage American companies to join together in: (1) risk sharing in projects to develop resources in parts of the world where the possibility of nationalization (being taken over by the country), or where adverse changes in business conditions can occur; (2) buying cooperatives that could be formal or informal in their organization, short- or long-term in duration, and more effective in securing scarce supplies at a reasonable price than individual forms; and (3) trade missions to Eastern Bloc countries such as Poland or Rumania, to tap this source of supply. In these situations the U.S. government would act as a catalyst and coordinate the political aspects of each arrangement.

Some of these steps, if done without government approval, would bring investigations by the Justice Department and other federal agencies discussed in Chapter Three. These organizations protect the American public by prosecuting firms attempting to take unfair advantage of shortages and/or market conditions. Also, the U.S. government plays a direct role in shaping both agreements made with foreign parties and measures to conserve resources in this country.

Rapidly Changing Technology

The present position of American technology compared to that of foreign competitors is generally good. The immense advantage we had in the 1950s no longer exists for most goods and services. The loss of this advantage, along with other factors, caused a problem for this country in the 1960s and early 1970s when we began importing more goods than previously. This resulted in some countries such as Japan accumulating large amounts of dollars because we bought more of their products than they bought of ours. While the overall situation was quite complicated, the narrowing of our technological advantage had a direct bearing on the devaluations of the dollar in 1971 and 1973.

Despite these difficulties, a technological advantage still exists in most fields. It is the basis of our still superior standard of living. There are three business principles behind American affluence.

1. Products and services that do a better job of satisfying the customer's needs will get the business if the price asked for superiority is less than the value gained in the mind of the buyer.

2. Equipment and production ideas that increase output of the existing workforce or reduce the workforce while maintaining the output or both increase output and reduce the workforce are the bases of remaining competitive despite payment of high salaries, wages, and benefits.

3. Problem solving in the extracting and handling of raw materials (*preproduction*), and in the methods used to distribute goods after they have been made (*postproduction*), has maintained the flow of products to market with an adequate profit margin. It has in some cases expanded the scope of markets available to a firm.

Let us analyze the net effect of the three points. Assume that the price and the cost of an American product are the same as those of foreign competitors; in this instance, the profit margins are identical. The situation resulting for the firm in this country is likely to be:

1. Investment in plant and equipment is more efficient. In a study of the 20 largest American companies doing worldwide business and an equal number of large foreign companies, it was determined that the American firms invested $.89 for each dollar of sales while the foreign companies invested $1.27 for the same dollar of sales.

2. Return on investment is significantly greater for the American shareholder, probably 50% ± more than the average foreign experience.

3. Management of American companies is superior.[5] It is also the best paid when compared to averages in other countries. Despite this expense, which is a greater percentage of total costs than for foreign competition, operations are more efficient.

4. The number of workers in the American plant is substantially less, and the percentage of cost represented by labor is also less. These workers are more skilled than foreign labor because they are normally handling more sophisticated assignments using advanced equipment.

The effect of superior technology put into action by well-trained managers is the basis on which Americans can hope to improve their standard of living in the future. When the technological base described on pages 9 and 10 is considered, the outlook is very hopeful.

CAREERS AND JOBS

In the business environment foreseen in this chapter, American companies will have some problems to overcome. However, management should be able to succeed in achieving both acceptable profit performance and social progress. The future will actually depend in large part on the career choices made by young people in the 1970s.

The quality of personnel in key vocations will be more important than simply filling quotas. One aspect of quality is technical ability in the field.

---

[5] This statement is based on analysis of performance which led to published reports. While shortcomings exist when American managers are placed in an overseas environment, they usually achieve superior results.

Another is the enthusiasm of the individuals for this work, and the satisfaction they obtain from working. Behavioral scientists agree that the probability of achieving superior performance is greatly increased when the people are not only good but also enjoy what they are doing.

Choice of a career has always been important to the individual. He or she will spend 25%± of his or her life at work or work related activities such as commuting. Boredom, dissatisfaction, or even dislike of this portion of life can be terrible. An interesting job has always been important to every individual. Now, however, it is important to the country as well. Talent cannot be wasted.

Some Suggestions on the Approach to Choosing a Career

Many people in their 30s and 40s say, "I wish I knew in my 20s what I know now about working." This type of comment highlights the fact that young people are asked to make career decisions long before they have sufficient experience to know everything needed for the "right" choice. Luck plays a part, but it is essential that each person do everything possible to decrease the chance of a bad choice. Some fundamentals are suggested here.

1. *Establish a career file.* Collect newspaper pictures, articles in magazines, brochures, and so on, describing interesting jobs, and place them in a file folder on a regular basis. Keep this backlog of ideas current. Review the material periodically to see if there is a common factor in the jobs such as working with mathematics, or solving mechanical problems, or building structures, and so on.

2. *Follow up on possibilities.* Find out what a person actually does each day in the fields that appeal to you. You may find that glamorous-appearing jobs are boring, and the reverse. Find out the facts as far as you can, and make your own decision. This could mean taking tours sponsored by companies, working at summer jobs, and/or taking extended time away from school to be certain about your preliminary career choice.

3. *Learn about your capabilities.* Take advantage of any test or professional evaluation of your abilities offered by reliable sources, such as your school district or community. The objective is to find out how well you are matching career choice with ability to do a good job in a specific field. For example, being a doctor might seem appealing after a summer as an orderly in a hospital, but you might not be able to get the grades in college to get into medical school (nearly a straight "A" average is required).

4. *Take a good look at yourself.* In addition to finding out your capabilities, you should match your career with your personality. For example, **introverts** usually dislike sales positions, and **extroverts** feel confined by a laboratory and hours working with no people around. You must take an honest look at yourself and select a career that is compatible with your personality traits. Also, determine whether any flaws in your makeup can be corrected. It may be worth the hard work to make these corrections if an interesting career is at stake.

5. *Check your choice against changes in your life.* People change, especially as they grow older. Circumstances change, also. More facts about a job may affect your opinion on how you want to spend your working life. It is wrong to shift from one career choice to another too often. However, it is equally wrong to continue with something that does not suit you. Take time about every six months to be sure you are on the right path. If you are not, get out the career file and start the process over.

These five steps require some effort and time. However, leaving a career to luck may have serious results in the future. You should consider more than job security and the amount of money you can earn. You should find satisfaction that 25% of your life is being spent on a job that means something and that you are contributing something of value.

CHAPTER SUMMARY

Business is defined as producing, selling, and buying goods and services to earn an acceptable return on the capital employed, with people in roles as investors, management, workers, and customers. The use of some business resources for the needs of the community is an obligation that is being more widely recognized.

The American business system is composed of distinct yet interdependent components privately owned. The objective of business for the investor is achieving profits. The general public feels that the objective is satisfying their needs through products and services offered at a reasonable price. The government's role is regulation, guidance through policies, protection, and participation through purchases and sales. Specialization and mass production of specific product lines have resulted in highly efficient large-scale operations.

Social progress in the United States generated from business will depend on: (1) companies having sufficient freedom of decision making and profit incentives to compete successfully against foreign firms; (2) laws, regulations, and policies supporting social programs without excessive taxation; and (3) public confidence that government and business are truly working toward social progress.

Developments seriously affecting American business are the strength of foreign competition, shortages of energy and other materials, rapidly changing technology, and inflation. The outlook for companies in this country is quite good. While foreign firms have some advantages, the balance is in favor of American business, particularly because of our superior technology. The U.S. government will be cooperating in strategies for supply to secure resources purchased from abroad and to conserve those in this country.

Selection of a career will be critically important in the years ahead. It is suggested that young people: (1) establish a career file; (2) find out details about interesting jobs; (3) learn about their capabilities through testing and other professional evaluations; (4) keep personality and career selection in balance; and (5) update choices to reflect changes in their lives.

PROVOCATIVE STATEMENT

A Shift from Volume to Profits

1 "American business has moved a long way from the marketing philosophy of the 1950s and 1960s, dominated by the so-called **full-line product concept.** In those days, many companies, caught up in the growth fever that hit its peak in the mid-1960s, acquired new product lines or entire companies and put their emphasis on sales rather than profits. . . .

Lower-margin products are being dropped or deemphasized in favor of those that offer higher margins. Often this means cutting back on commodity products to concentrate on higher-margin specialty items, or deferring big investments in products of limited potential while stressing longer-range products. . . .

Many companies finally are measuring the high cost of overhead involved in going after some of those product segments. One by one companies are chopping out marginally profitable products and redirecting their efforts.

The implications are vast, not only for the product mix itself but also for broader corporate marketing strategies and the total buyer/seller relationship:

1. Products will become more functional and sport fewer frills, reflecting the narrowing of product lines and substitutions, compromises, and other efforts to conserve dwindling resources of raw materials. . . .
2. Cartons for liquor and perfume don't have to cost 50¢ each. Nor do match packs or even Christmas cards have to be coated with tinfoil and other flashy laminations. We have overengineered our products, and our clients have grown accustomed to 90 GE brightness (a General Electric numeral scale) when 80 GE brightness is perfectly adequate.
3. Product strategies will become more flexible and marketing timetables will be speeded up, as raw-material logistics gain equal importance with how well a company reads its markets.
4. New-product development will suffer. Raw-material uncertainties, rising costs, and the deemphasis or elimination of smaller market segments will make management far more critical of new-product ideas."

Excerpt from:
"The Squeeze on Product-Mix,"
Business Week,
January 5, 1974

PROVOCATIVE STATEMENT

Public Opinion about the Business Community

2 "For more than a decade now, the business community as a whole has been declining in public favor. Business has failed to do an effective job in communicating its point of view to the general public. As a result, its critics have grown stronger. The public has grown more receptive to proposals for more government intervention into and regulation of business. Substantial support is being gathered for the passage of legislation which eventually could lead to the reorganization and restructuring of many of our most basic American industries. Let there be no mistake: an attack is being mounted on the private enterprise system in the United States. The life of that system is at stake.

But business has not been alone in its fall from public favor. It has been joined, to greater or lesser extent, by virtually every other large institution in American society. This includes the federal government—both the Administration and the Congress—the military, the media, the educational community, and even the church."

M. A. Wright
Chairman and Chief Executive
Exxon Company, U.S.A.

REVIEW QUESTIONS

1. What does business involve? What are its objectives?
2. Competition plays a major role in the American business system. What advantages does this offer the consumer?
3. Name the major developments affecting American business and identify their impact on the firm.
4. Take a position on government intervention in business giving degrees of intervention you would accept. Cite specific examples to clarify your position.
5. What advantages do American businesses have in competing against foreign companies? How do these advantages affect the standard of living in the United States?
6. Will shortages of raw material in this country affect business if we can buy the materials from other countries? Defend your answer.
7. Would you take a summer job where you could learn about a business if you got paid less than another job which was straight labor? Explain.

Chapter Outline

Job Levels in the Organization
    Some Important Job Characteristics
    Factors in Job Security and Income

The Changing Composition of Workers in Business
    An Important Point in History
    Women as Workers
    Progress by Blacks

Some Aspects of a Manager's Life
    Business Travel
    Business Commuting
    Business Entertainment
    Community Obligations

The Role of Labor Unions in Business
    The Place of Employees in the Division of Profits
    The Issues in Labor Relations
    Brief History and Present Strength of Unions
        Union Membership and Influence
    Management Implications

Careers and Jobs

Chapter Summary

Provocative Statement 1: The Viewpoint of a Small Business Owner

Provocative Statement 2: A Woman's Viewpoint in Developing a Career

Key Terms

Mutual funds
Pension funds
Dividends
Bargaining
Social responsibility
International business
Cost of living
Foreman
Seniority
Controller

Company politics
Sexual complications
Double standards
Feminist movement
Fixed assets
Capital
Inflation
Closed shop

People in Business: The Workers

"Good or bad, you got no one to blame for a decision but yourself if you're both the owner and the manager."
—Small Business Owner

Years ago most people who owned a business worked as managers. They hired laborers for factories and skilled personnel for special jobs. When sales decreased or there was a seasonal slowdown, the owner/manager fired or laid off many of these people. This resulted in more profits for those who invested the money to start and operate the business, but some workers had to endure periods of time when they had no income.

Today this situation has improved. Most Americans can count on a substantial and steady income. Only a few workers—those with limited skills, with capabilities no longer required as technology progresses, or with skills possessed by large numbers of other people—experience problems keeping a steady job. Since there are a relatively small number of these workers, the economy has been helped by those people having steady jobs. Banks and finance companies can lend money to those with jobs at a reasonable cost. As a result, these workers can buy conveniences they might never have had. The subsequent demand for goods creates more jobs and more consumers.

Some important reasons for this improved situation are described here.

1. *Ownership* of business now involves: (a) many individuals investing small amounts of money ($500 to $10,000), who have very little to say about day-to-day decisions; or (b) organizations investing money accumulated from individuals, such as mutual and pension funds and insurance companies.

2. *Management* is now made up of employees. Even the top executives are hired workers. Those in management only keep their jobs if performance of the company is according to expectations. Today it is easier to fire a manager than other workers since most of management is not organized into unions.

3. *Worker organizations* have been successful in channeling some of the

money earned by business into benefits for the employees instead of into dividends for the owners or bonuses for top management. Bargaining for such advantages has often involved bitter battles. However, the net effect of worker organizations, rather than individuals, dealing with management is steadier employment and increasing participation in company earnings for the worker.

4. *Social responsibility* in business has resulted from several developments. While there is still contention between owner, manager, and laborer, standards for acceptable settlements and behavior have improved. Management is more aware of worker problems and less frequently treats workers as units of production instead of people. More resources of companies are being applied to community problems that are not their direct social responsibility.

5. *International business* has exposed decision makers to the ways workers are treated in other countries. While this is more often an example of what not to do, constructive ideas practiced in Japan, West Germany, and so on have led to better conditions and more security for employees in the United States.

These developments have contributed to greater acceptance of the attitude that there is little difference between management and the workforce. Each employee in the organization must be productive, or the performance of the whole company suffers. The achievement of a worker's personal goals in business usually depends on accomplishing company goals. Profits and progress happen most frequently, according to behavioral scientists, when employees have: (1) knowledge of company goals; (2) understanding of what attaining the goals means to the individual worker; and (3) a feeling that the division of earnings is fair.

Battles between management and unions usually result from disagreement about the benefits labor should receive from increased profits and how large raises should be to cover the higher cost of living. Managers who succeed in communicating company goals and the importance of accomplishing the goals to the worker, however, often find that they have also created an attitude of confidence in employees that distribution of earnings will be fair.

JOBS AND LEVELS IN THE ORGANIZATION

There are two fundamental reasons for working: (1) earning an adequate income for a full life outside of work and (2) obtaining sufficient satisfaction from the job to feel the time is well spent. Take a look at Figure 2-1. What are the differences between people at one level as compared to another? As a student you want to know: (1) who makes what amount of money? and (2) what does each person have to do for it? When you combine the answers to these questions with the kind of person you are, it makes the decision on how to earn a living an easier one. Let us look at some examples. Perhaps you know people with jobs described in the following paragraphs.

Figure 2-1. Organization of a Large Firm

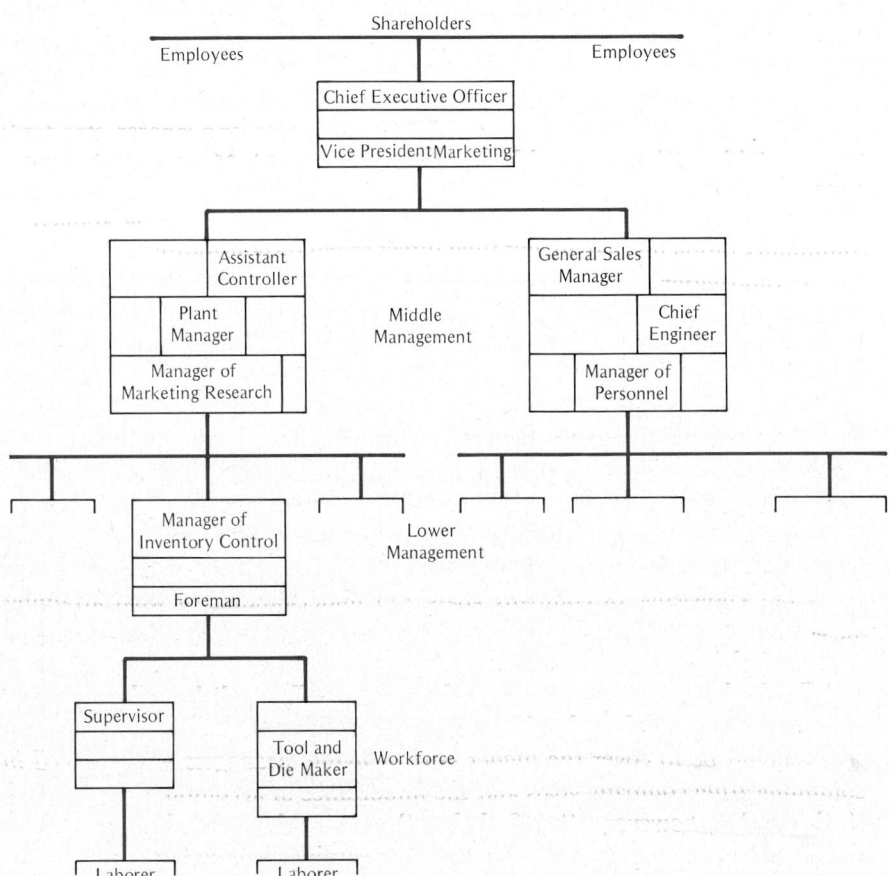

ASSEMBLY LINE WORKER This person is an integral part of the production line. One may tighten bolts on a wheel, attach a compressor, fit a door to a frame, and so on. This worker repeats the job for eight hours with scheduled breaks in the morning and afternoon and a half-hour for lunch. Very little skill is required to do most of the jobs on an assembly line. As a result, many people are qualified for the millions of these jobs that exist in American industry. There is little challenge, and some people will not apply.

Their lack of an important skill makes such workers vulnerable to management decisions. For instance, many workers lost their jobs in 1974–75 when management decided to close auto assembly plants for several months. However, unions have stepped in to improve job security and benefits, and today there are paid vacations, paid time for shut downs, procedures for layoffs and terminations, and so on. Assembly line workers may earn $12,000 per year. In time an individual may have a chance to become supervisor of a group of similar workers. A few will get even better jobs if they show abilities to manage people as well as to develop a skill.

Since most of these workers have no formal training in management or special skills, they must compete against workers who do have these skills for the more challenging jobs, and they usually lose out.

SKILLED TOOL AND DIE MAKER   This person makes precise pieces for the production line through use of a particular skill to complete specific assignments. Occasionally, he has the opportunity to think independently and develops a solution to a problem not considered by the engineers. This initiative can lead to assignments with greater responsibility and more income from higher job ratings. After a few years such a person may supervise a department making special tools and dies.

Certainly the level of advancement on the organizational chart in Figure 2-1 is not very high, but this type of worker can feel important and express ideas in work that is less routine than that of the assembly line worker. The business depends on these individuals for more than physical work. Their annual incomes could range from $12,000 to $18,000 because they have taken the time to learn skills most other workers do not know how to do. If they become interested in more than the skill and learn something about the "why" behind the skill, they add potential to their futures.

It is important to point out that skills required in business change over time, and a machine or computer might completely replace a skill. This is a major reason why 17 million Americans with and without college degrees are going to school after work. Some are preparing themselves for better jobs because the experience of working has given them a clearer picture of what they want to do. Others are investing time and money in education and training because the skill they have to offer can be done better another way.

FOREMAN   This person fills an important position. The foreman's job can be a very significant one in a large corporation. Often it is earned by a college graduate after the individual has spent time as a supervisor and assistant foreman with responsibilities for a specific part of the plant operation. The foreman's position can also be filled by promotion of a person in the shop who has demonstrated an ability to handle workers in the business and who has knowledge of the required skills. This position is usually the dividing line between management and wage earners, and commands a salary of $12,000 to $25,000 per year, depending on the size of company, the scope of the responsibilities involved and the length of seniority.

At this level in the organization a person has tasks that are not always routine. Problems that never occurred before need to be solved. The individual must maintain composure under pressure and not only handle the regular day-to-day aspects of the job, but also (1) motivate other employees to do their jobs to the best of their abilities and (2) innovate to fulfill all responsibilities.

This kind of position usually challenges individuals and leads them to think about solutions to work problems even when they are at home, on the golf course, or other places far removed from the plant. Figure 2-2 illustrates the sources of pressure on the foreman. A few people react with pleasure from daily confrontations with each of the four areas, won or lost. At the other end of the scale, some get ulcers, hypertension, and other symptoms of having a job that is too much for them.

ASSISTANT CONTROLLER The **controller** is professionally trained. The individual has invested four years in college and learned accounting, and is ready for a junior job in the controller's department. The person might be an analyst, observing and reporting on payments by customers, or a supervisor in the automated bookkeeping group.

Promotion will depend on the individual's effectiveness in: (1) applying the professional skills learned in college; (2) adapting to business situations not

Figure 2-2. *Typical Pressures on the Foreman*

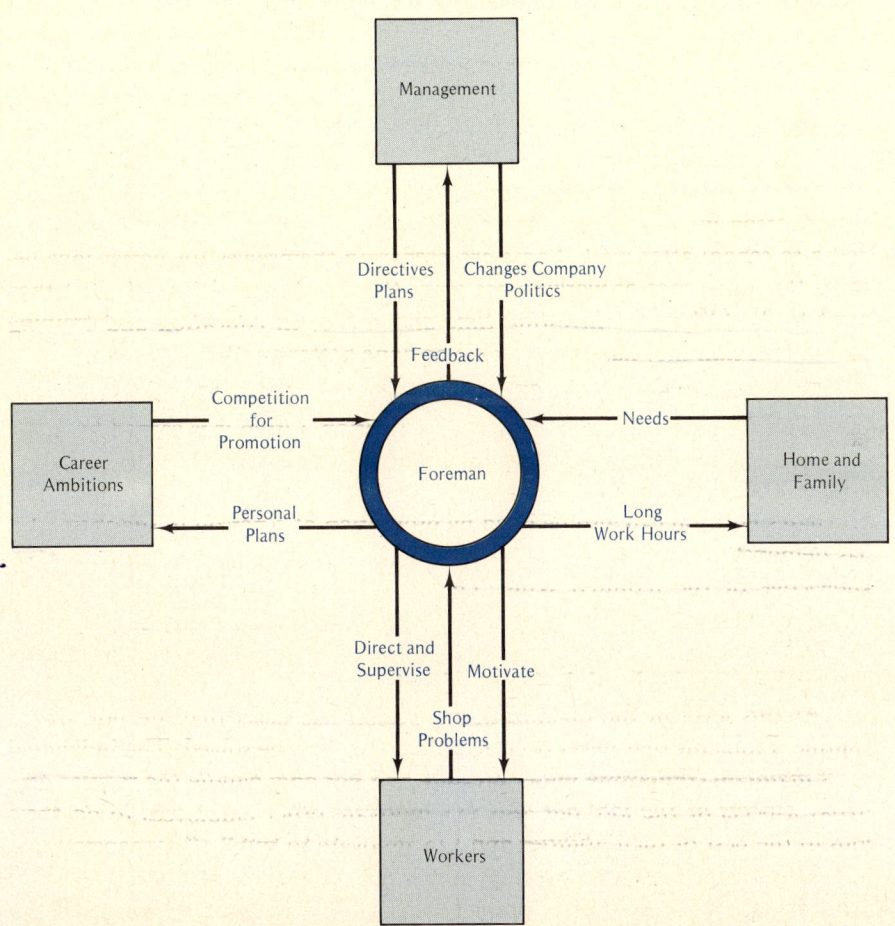

taught in college; and (3) getting along with people in the organization. Often an assistant controller remains in a low-level job, but has reasonable security at a salary of about $15,000 a year.

Still, outstanding success in the three factors can lead to advancement to the next level shown in Figure 2-1. An assistant controller can earn $25,000 per year or more in some companies. Creative management of the firm's cash will justify higher income. Eventually, "Mr./Ms. Success" could become controller, administrative vice president, or another high position.

By noting these examples at various levels in the organization, you will be able to gain more from points in the remainder of the book. We spend a major portion of our life working. It is logical to be careful about what we choose to do.

There are hundreds of types of jobs. Few people make a career being a secretary, although some become indispensable to their bosses. Sales representatives are often the reason for their company's success. Their contribution can be recognized through a salary that assures them of a regular income; however, some sales representatives receive only a commission on sales which at times could mean a very high income, perhaps more than some of the officers, but at other times an income much lower than a salary. Other workers try to build their seniority and job rating to assure themselves and their families of a prosperous future.

Some Important Job Characteristics

Key words can describe some people's feelings about work. *Boredom* is one. It is linked with routine. Psychologists have found that poor mental health can result from spending eight hours a day for several years doing something that is not interesting and is empty of challenge. Boredom is not limited to assembly lines. Men and women with great potential can be trapped in a routine office job as well as in a plant.

Satisfaction is the opposite of boredom. The workers like what they do to earn a living. The work day does not seem a hundred hours long. In fact, they look forward to returning the next day. This attitude can even be developed in workers doing a routine job if management can successfully communicate the importance of what they are doing and compensates them for their contribution. Employees want to feel a sense of accomplishment. Work then becomes a place where they can add to their lives instead of only putting in time.

Responsibility is a word critical to achieving business success. Not everybody wants it because, while increased income and status can result from having responsibility, it also means more work and greater pressure. Many workers would prefer to stay with jobs in which they can perform a valued skill and avoid getting involved with decision making. Those who will accept responsibilities and can handle them consistently well can significantly improve their standard of living.

Pressure is built into almost every job. "Time is money." "That work station has to put out ten an hour, not eight." "The report has to be completed by Friday morning." Tight schedules, the demand for better quality, conflicting opinions, company politics, and so on build a feeling within workers that they will have difficulty surviving, much less handling ordinary business situations. A few strong people welcome pressure and see it as a means of sorting out the "weak of heart." The vast majority of employees copes with it uneasily, wondering whether they have the abilities to perform at a satisfactory level.

Other words can be used to describe important job characteristics such as "stimulating," "technical," and "exhausting." However, the four just given briefly summarize the experience of working.

Factors in Job Security and Income

The factors listed here have an impact on job security and how much people will receive for their work.

1. *Supply and demand* must be considered. The number of openings (demand) and applicants (supply) affect the market place for managers and workers. A period of scarcity for skills and talents allows people to improve their income either through a raise or a change in company. When the number of applicants greatly exceeds openings, a period of long unemployment can result for many people.

2. *Training* is an important factor. Scarcity of a particular skill or talent is usually related to the amount of time and money invested in acquiring the added capability. It is a matter of (a) venturing to try and (b) picking the training that will offer a career for a reasonable number of years. Counseling and investigation are vital to choosing the most salable skill or talent to develop.

3. *Getting along with people* is essential. For the employee it means improving the chances of success and more income. It also results in a higher degree of contentment from the time spent at work; a joke, a friend, a tip about the boss, lead to greater job satisfaction. Some people do not bother about the feelings and rights of others. A few try too hard and fail. Most workers have to make a serious effort to get along with others to succeed in business.

4. *Risk* plays a role. It is occasionally necessary to sacrifice the security and benefits of an existing job to try something having greater potential. The new position is often a genuine opportunity for the particular worker because the change is made after investigation of both the job and firm. Not everyone will take a risk and accept more responsibility, but chances to climb higher in an organization frequently depend on doing so.

5. *Luck* is a factor. Outside events can lead to success or failure. For example, a sharp increase in the demand for air conditioners because of a heat wave could create a career opportunity for workers with a required skill. Luck, however, is sometimes blamed for problems that can be traced to the individual's lack of judgment, deficient characteristics for the job, inadequate training, poor performance, or a combination of these reasons. In any case, it helps to be at the right place at the right time.

Some people do not have the desire and determination to do what is necessary to succeed in advancing up the organizational ladder. These individuals must be prepared to accept a lower standard of living than successful managers. Sometimes it is the experience of working as a laborer in boring jobs that motivates a person to try harder and acquire skills to improve his life. Figure 2-3 shows the factors. The individual must decide how these relate to personal goals.

Figure 2-3. *Forces on Worker Income*

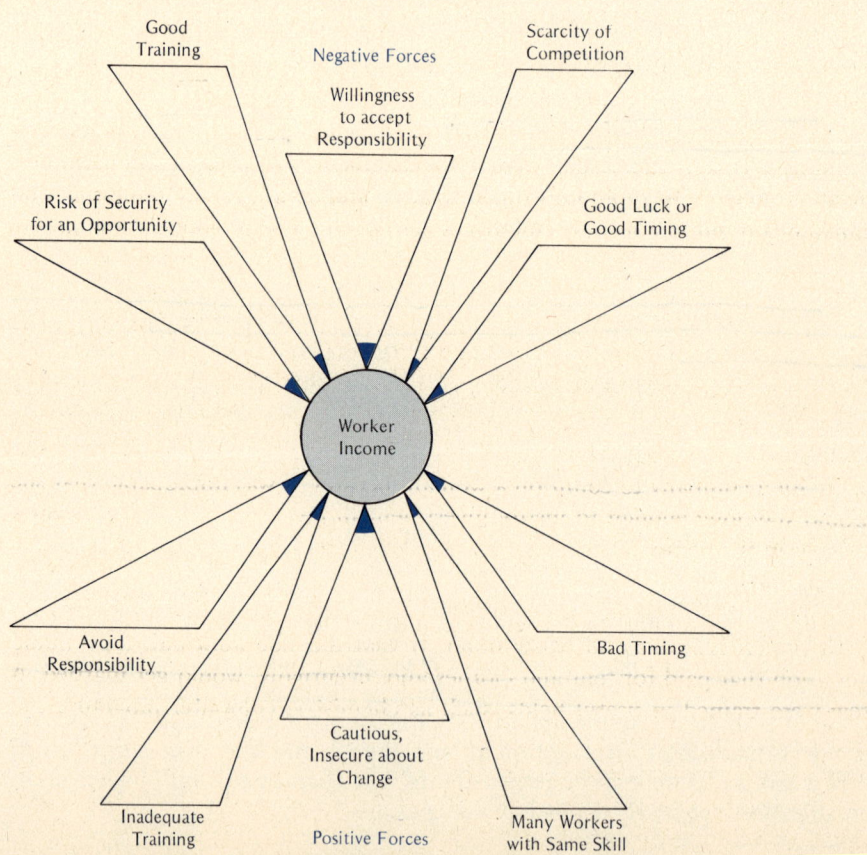

THE CHANGING COMPOSITION OF WORKERS IN BUSINESS

In the mid-1960s two laws were passed by the federal government, initiating changes in who works in the upper levels of an organization. The Equal Pay Act of 1963 requires equal pay for equal work by women and minority group members. In 1964 the Civil Rights Act was signed, eliminating discrimination on the basis of sex or race, requiring that all men and women be given equal consideration for a job.

An Important Point in History

A landmark decision was made in 1972, when American Telephone and Telegraph agreed to pay about $15 million in restitution and equal pay claims to 13,000± women and 2,000± male minority race employees. Even more important, the agreement specified that women and minorities would get credit towards seniority for time spent on all jobs with the company. Before this was resolved, ATT work rules discouraged these workers from seeking promotion. In the past, those taking a new job would be the first to be laid off because they had lost the seniority gained in the former job.

The momentum of progress leading to better positions for women and minorities is now increasing. Senior management will occasionally admit to needing pressure to promote women, blacks, and so on, to key positions. Fortunately, promotion of these employees has become much more commonplace.

Women as Workers

In the past, secretaries, nurses, school teachers, dieticians, and actresses were the stereotype jobs for women. Male employers usually assumed that female workers would get married, have children, and quit. To many it made no sense for a company to count on a woman, because it was improbable that she would stay long enough to justify investment in her future. This "a-woman's-place-is-in-the-home" attitude is still prevalent in a large portion of the male population.

Before 1970 business thought women went to college to find a husband with similar interests and background. If that did not work out, they would get a job that paid for rent and clothes and, eventually, would get married. A few were trained in useful fields, such as chemistry, computer programming, and languages. However, a woman seriously undertaking a business career was a sufficiently rare person to be generally ignored.

In addition to the probability of marriage and motherhood, the points usually cited by antifeminists are:

1. Sexual complications in the office and when traveling.
2. Emotional reactions to business problems.
3. Lack of stamina and physical strength.
4. Lack of mobility due to a husband's job and other family complications.

Women who want business careers must overcome these obstacles, double standards, and biases. The primary method for changing employer attitude is consistently good job performance. In addition, the 1970s have seen women handling obstacles in a number of other ways.

1. *Medical advances.* Today, it is possible to plan a family. As a result, a woman's career need not be affected by her capacity to bear children. Some employers claim, however, that this does not change the fact that the woman has the baby when a couple decides on parenthood, while a man is not subject to work interruption. To overcome this reservation by employers, a female job candidate has to generate confidence that her life is adequately planned to avoid career interruptions.

2. *Professional behavior.* Successful female managers work with facts, make unbiased judgments, and consider the opinions of other qualified workers. They retain their composure. The fundamental point is that women have to be extraconscious of professional behavior at this stage in the feminist movement.

3. *Training.* It is usually true that a woman has to be very well qualified to compete for an opening normally filled by a man. For management candidates this usually means attending a respected graduate school. Otherwise, excuses are used such as: (a) "She was not as qualified," and (b) "Her credentials weren't as good." This possibility should motivate women to get the best training from the most respected schools.

Attitudes towards women are changing among the people who influence our thinking, such as sociologists. These specialists now write more frequently about the absence of maladjustment in children of working mothers, the potential of successful marriages in which both partners have a career, and similar research projects. As the second Provocative Statement in this chapter says, "You have a chance, not an inside track." Figure 2-4 summarizes factors in the feminist movement.

Progress by Blacks

Many of the same comments regarding women in business apply to blacks. Laws, regulations, community pressure, and direct bargaining by organizations such as the Congress on Racial Equality (CORE) have resulted in progress. However, black managers are wondering how many generations must pass for employer attitudes to change completely and for blacks to achieve general acceptance in upper management.

Within today's job market, there are some practical points for the black students to help them get more out of a business firm:

Figure 2-4. *Getting Off the Ground with Progress for Women in Business*

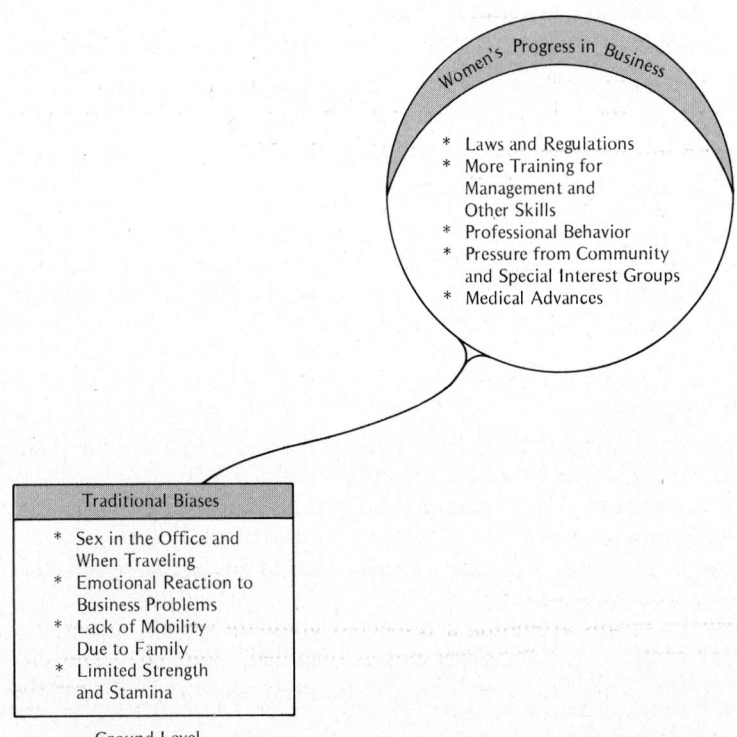

AVOID OVERSENSITIVITY After years of prejudicial treatment some black workers see a white racist behind every water cooler. It is equally human to react when racial prejudice is obvious in day-to-day affairs. Black workers must be patient. If they are going to succeed in a white-dominated business environment, oversensitivity to its behavior will lead to problems.

CHOOSE AN ISSUE CAREFULLY The legal and organizational framework exists for black managers to submit a grievance about treatment on the job. The safe driving ad that says, "Don't be dead right" often applies to individual complaints. If black workers want to develop a career with a company, they should be cautious about raising racial issues to avoid labels such as "agitator" or "chronic trouble maker."

GET ADEQUATE TRAINING Reread the section on women. Aside from a few words, the comments apply almost exactly. However, one additional point is important. Because of pressure on companies to meet racial quotas set by judges and other sources of authority, many blacks are currently being promoted to opportunities beyond their training and experiences. This will not

The Nature of Business

Figure 2-5. *Getting Racial Prejudice Out of Business*

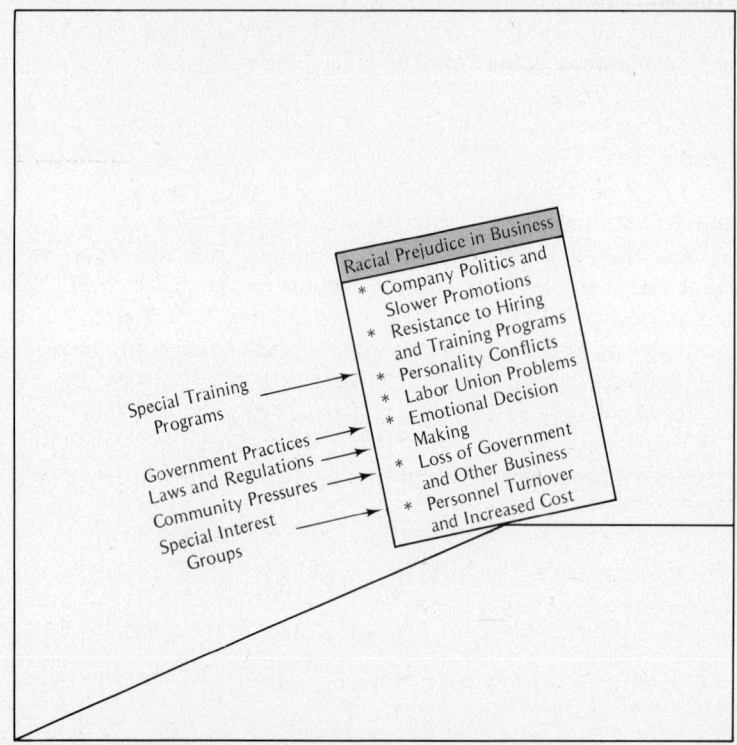

continue into the 1980s. A lifetime of working together with ambitions for steadily better incomes makes persevering with training and career planning critically important.

The creation of better job opportunities for minority race members is progressing more rapidly than the disappearance of racial prejudice, as shown in Figure 2-5. Performance by these workers, both on the job and in getting along with other workers, will be that basis on which myths are exploded.

SOME ASPECTS OF A MANAGER'S LIFE

At one extreme, men and women view their careers as a means to an end—a means of earning sufficient cash to enjoy life outside of business. At the other extreme are the people who become consumed by business life. They enjoy the challenge of work assignments, and the rewards of status and more money drive them deeper into their jobs. Somewhere between these two extremes is the normal manager who enjoys the job and is advancing up the organizational ladder, yet at the same time leads a satisfying life outside of work hours. It is a struggle, however, to balance the time devoted to an expanding career and that required by a demanding home life.

Business Travel

Some business executives travel about one or two days in a normal week. Normally, this rate of travel does not create pressure. It is the occasional extended trip that builds the backlog at the office and at home. Accumulated work, important decisions, delayed meetings, and so on require long hours upon return. Evenings and weekends are consumed by the task of catching up.

A high living standard is customary for managers when traveling. It is easy to become accustomed to extra luxuries and the pleasure of feeling important. Some of these conveniences cannot be duplicated at home. When this aspect of travel is combined with time-consuming trips, family relationships can be jeopardized.

"What do you mean, you're tired and you want to go home? This is our party. You are home!"

Drawing by W. Miller; © 1974 The New Yorker Magazine, Inc.

Business Commuting

Seldom do managers live within walking distance of the office or plant. Most have to commute distances requiring a half-hour or more, especially if they work in a big city.

As a result, two distinct lives develop. Home is in a suburb with activities completely unrelated to work in the city. Most people in business are either forced to drive or to dangle from handstraps in public transportation. Near-accidents, parking problems, and frustrating delays can start and end the day with tension and dissatisfaction. Workers have even changed jobs to eliminate these problems and to improve their lives.

Business Entertainment

Another aspect of business is entertainment of customers, suppliers, sources of financing and information, employees from other locations, and so on. When combined with travel, commuting, and family life in the suburbs, it can seriously stress an individual. The situation is further complicated: the more successful the person is, the more others in the organization measure their success by the amount of time that individual is willing to give them.

Figure 2-6. *Balancing a Business Executive's Life*

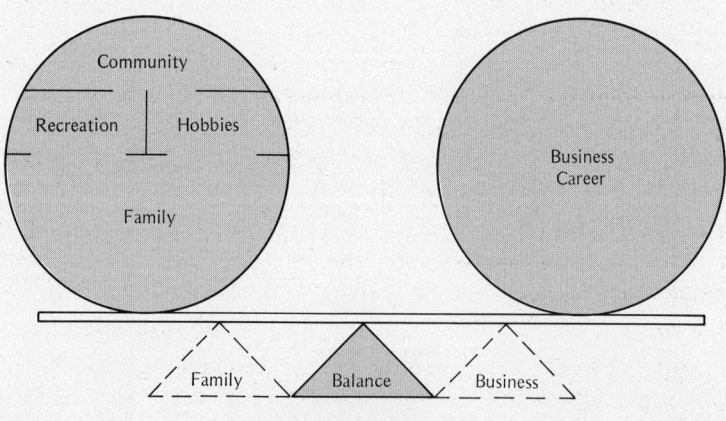

Community Obligations

A person accumulates obligations in the community. Little leagues and scouts must be kept going. Needed changes in the school system might be implemented sooner if added talent joined the pressure group pressing for change. Charity drives, pollution issues, good government campaigns, and scores of other organizations could use the help of people in business.

Most managers are parents. Few want to embarrass the family or themselves by doing a poor job as a parent for lack of time. Yet business obligations, including travel and entertainment, often prevent involvement in children's programs and campaigns. As a result, selection of community obligations is important to success at the office and at home.

One indication that business executives have the skills to be successful is the ability to plan. An important application of this ability is arranging their lives so that company, family, and community obligations can be fulfilled with a high standard of performance. Figure 2-6 summarizes the objective and includes the obligation such individuals have to themselves in recreation and hobbies.

THE ROLE OF LABOR UNIONS IN BUSINESS

The primary purpose of labor unions is to give employees strength in their bargaining with management. Because the company has growth and profits as its primary objectives, there can be a tendency to view workers as units of cost rather than as human beings with desires and needs. The pressures on decision makers from shareholders, the financial community, the government, competitors, and so on usually result in efforts to reduce costs. The collective strength of unions is necessary to make sure that these objectives do not become excessive from the workers' viewpoint.

Figure 2-7 illustrates the balance needed in the bargaining between management and unions. If companies do not treat their employees fairly, three things can happen.

1. Talent will flow to companies and industries offering better conditions.
2. Buying power will be decreased in areas vacated by talent, and the markets for products and services are potentially less.
3. Growth and profits will decline in the long run because of 1 and 2.

On the other hand, if unions exert too much power and obtain excessive benefits for their members, three other things can happen.

1. The company will earn lower profits and will have trouble attracting investors to buy its shares.

Figure 2-7. *Maintaining a Balance between Management and Unions*

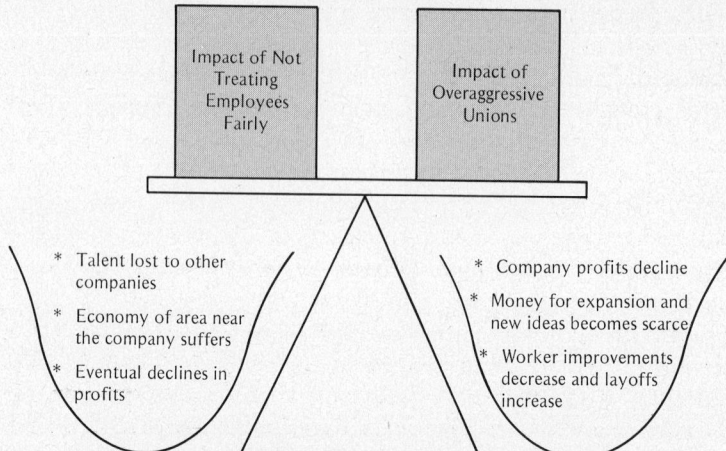

2. Less money will be available for expansion and research to find better ways to do things.
3. Future improvements for workers will be less likely because of the high level of company cost.

A balance is not always achieved, because the strengths of management and unions are rarely equal. Let us look at some examples of situations in which each side can gain the upper hand.

A boom is in progress, and the company has a large backlog of orders. Any work stoppage would lead to a large portion of the business shifting to competitors. History shows that many customers would be permanently lost. Management realizes that it cannot risk a strike. The union takes full advantage of the situation, stating that immediate gains would merely make up for the inequalities of previous years.

Now reverse the economic conditions. Growth and profits are threatened, and the union can see clearly that adding costs would threaten the long-run strength of the company. Management will usually strive toward the most efficient organization possible, including terminations and layoffs. The union attempts to minimize the impact on its membership and retain the benefits gained in past bargaining rather than pushing for new concessions.

Consider the different conditions when there is a large national union and a small company, or a big corporation with many plants and a local union. Shortages of labor or particular skills strengthen a union's position, while surpluses weaken it. The ability of leadership in management and unions to bargain is an important factor in balance and unbalance. Changing technology and shifting requirements for talents in business will also play a role. Finally, the history of the bargaining process in a company—for example, bitter battles, deception, and strikes as compared to compromise, cooperation, and personality rapport—has a bearing on the outcome.

The Place of Employees in the Division of Profits

The fundamentals needed for company operations are: (1) money; (2) human power; and (3) machinery and other fixed assets. After taxes are paid, cash is available to distribute to investors as dividends and to plow back into the business for growth and improved financial strength. Unions (even governments in other parts of the world) feel that after a fair return on capital and sufficient reinvestment to assure the future, workers should share in the prosperity of the firm.

Some sharing has occurred in the United States. Management has received incentive bonuses based on profit performance. However, very few firms have permitted employees earning wages to share in after-tax profits.

The traditional position of the investor has been one of risking the loss of capital or receiving a low rate of return on the money put into a business. The investor is willing to give incentives to decision makers because this tends to improve profit performance. The hope is to have both increasing dividends and value added to capital in the business. Until recently, the idea of dividing profits with the workforce has been regarded as radically socialistic in nature.

In a few instances, however, investors have been convinced that sharing with all employees is a reasonable decision. The concessions result in peaceful labor relations, availability of needed skills, and overall efficiency. In a period of global competition and increasingly complex technology in business, more investors and companies may see advantages in sharing after-tax earnings with all employees.

The right to a portion of profits is another question. Owners feel that all employees from president to custodian offer their services to the firm and are paid a salary or wage, the amount depending on factors described earlier in the chapter. Both parties have the right to terminate the relationship. However, because only the investors are risking capital, only they have the right to receive the return on this capital.

Another point of view is that the employees are risking their careers by working for that firm, and because human power is needed for operations just as much as capital, they have a right to some portion of the profits. All but the most radical observers agree that any participation by employees in profits must be limited to an amount that does not discourage growth from new capital from flowing into business.

The Issues in Labor Relations

Salaries and wages, specific rates and amounts for a coming period, are included in almost every contract between management and labor unions. They are a very serious issue during inflation because a distinction must be made between merit increases and those enabling a person to keep an adequate standard of living despite higher prices for goods purchased.

For example, if a person made $10,000 in 1971 and received a 5% per year increase in pay in 1972, 1973, and 1974, the resulting income would be $11,575. Would the individual be better off? No! In the same years the cost of living rose 4.9%, 8.8%, and 12.1% respectively. This means that this person would have to be earning $12,795 to buy the same things bought in 1971.

One of the problems faced by business is that concessions on salary and wages, which permit employees to keep their standard of living, may cut into profits. The market may not allow companies to ask higher prices for their products and services. Another way to avoid loss of profits from higher salaries and wages is to increase the output of each worker so that there is more to sell for each dollar paid to employees.

The impact of inflation added to the normal issue of real increases in income will likely cause considerable friction between management and unions in the 1970s.

<u>Benefits</u> are involved in all labor negotiations. Vacations, insurances, holidays, pension plans, layoff pay, subsidized lunches, and various other issues are part of the bargaining. Transportation to cover the crunch of gasoline prices is a new concern of unions. Benefits sometimes become a primary issue when the union believes that the company cannot afford major increases in wages.

<u>Work rules</u> are often a fundamental point with the company. For example, it might be possible to concede a substantial wage increase if the speed of the assembly line could be increased or if two workers could handle a job instead of three. Boredom on the job has become a sufficiently important factor to unions. Therefore, bargaining has begun for rules that permit worker rotation and other changes in assignment.

Procedures for determining seniority, terminations, layoffs, grievances, and transfers are detailed in the contract between a company and a union. Conveniences, such as a cafeteria or cleanup rooms and minimum tools to do the work, may be an issue. Safety is a constant concern to both management and the union. However, the cost of preventive devices could influence a company to delay installing them without the pressure of bargaining.

Brief History and Present Strength of Unions

To conclude this introduction to the role of unions in business, it is appropriate to give a brief summary of events in the labor movement in the United States.

The history of American unions began in 1792 when the shoemakers organized in Philadelphia. Seven years later they struck for the first union contract. In 1825 women tailors organized the first female union, and the first countrywide federation came into being in <u>1834 with the formation of the National Trader Union.</u> The legality of such groups was tested in 1842 in Massachusetts, when the state confirmed the right of workers to organize. Finally, the first truly national labor organization was formed in 1866.

After this beginning, unions continued to grow. The garment workers founded the Knights of Labor in 1869, and in 1886 the American Federation of Labor (AFL) was formed. The government recognized the importance of these groups by establishing the Bureau of Labor in 1884 in the Department of the Interior. Later it was moved into the Department of Commerce. Congress made Labor Day a national holiday in 1894, and in 1913 the Department of Labor was created as a separate entity.

Major strikes occurred in 1877 (railroad), 1892 (steel), and 1894 (railroad equipment). In 1919 after World War I, strikes idled 4 million workers, and the Boston Police Strike in that year was the first by government employees.

The Depression led to some important developments: (1) In 1932 the Norris–La Guardia Act limited use of federal court injunctions in strikes. (2) The National Labor Relations Act was passed in 1935 to protect union rights; it also created the National Labor Relations Board. (3) In the same year the Committee for Industrial Organization (CIO) was formed in Washington D.C.

In 1947 the Taft–Hartley Act was passed by Congress over President Truman's veto. It substantially strengthened management's position in bargaining with unions.

The Act (1) banned the closed shop, which forbade the hiring of non-union workers; (2) permitted employers to sue unions for broken contracts or damages inflicted during strikes; (3) required unions to abide by a 60-day "cooling-off period" before striking; (4) required unions to make public their financial statements; (5) forbade union contribution to political campaigns; (6) ended the "check-off system," in which the employer collected union dues; (7) required union leaders to take an oath stating they were not members of the Communist Party. The Taft–Hartley Act was amended on October 22, 1951 to permit union-shop contracts without first polling all employees involved.

Eight years later the AFL and the CIO merged, a major consolidation and an important step toward unified union positions in dealing with management and government. Figure 2-8 shows the organizational structure of the AFL–CIO. In 1959 the Taft–Hartley Act was amended, but the basic principle of a worker's right not to join a union was retained. The amendment also outlawed the closed shop (only union workers). Also in 1959, the Landrum–Griffin Act was passed, requiring unions to submit regular financial statements to the Secretary of Labor.

In recent years there have been important labor legislation and contract concessions. The 1963 Railroad Arbitration Act called for compulsory arbitration between companies and unions. Coordinated bargaining by eleven unions won a contract against General Electric in 1966 after the concept was tested in court. However, its legality was not fully proven due to early settlement. In 1967 the United Auto Workers won a 90%± of annual wage rate for workers when laid off.

Figure 2-8. *Organizational Structure of the AFL–CIO*

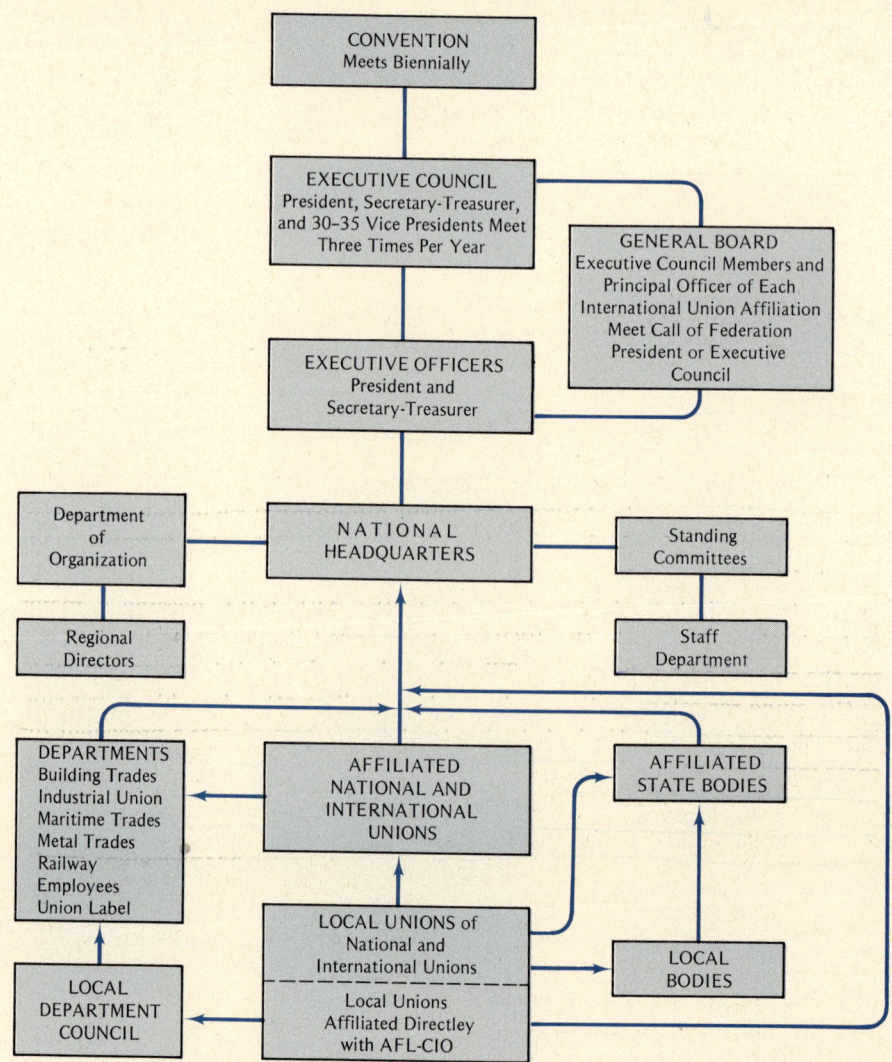

Union Membership and Influence

Table 2-1 gives statistics on the numerical strength of unions.

The true strength of unions cannot be measured in the 23% of the workforce shown in the statistics. Worker organizations involving teachers, government employees, and others up to about 4 million workers are not included in the numbers.

The AFL–CIO, Teamsters, and other unions have a major influence on elections. Propaganda is distributed by the unions to their members, who often vote for the man recommended by labor leaders.

Table 2-1. *Strength of Unions*

	MILLIONS OF WORKERS				
				LABOR UNIONS	
	CIVILIAN EMPLOYMENT	UNEMPLOYMENT TOTAL	%	MEMBERSHIP	% OF WORKFORCE*
1974	86.8	5.5	6.0	21.7	22.7
1973	84.9	4.6	5.1	21.4	23.0
1972	81.7	4.8	5.6	21.3	23.8
1971	79.1	5.0	5.9	21.5	24.7
1970	78.6	4.1	4.9	20.8	25.8
1965	73.8	3.4	4.5	18.5	28.5
1960	54.3	3.9	5.5	18.1	31.4

* All agricultural workers and government employees.

In addition to a political role, the unions have an important impact on the financial community. Millions of dollars are invested each year to manage cash and provide funds for pensions. For example, the Teamsters Union, founded in 1899, expelled from the AFL–CIO in 1957, and still functioning as the largest independent union outside the AFL–CIO, became a major factor in the economy in the 1960s as it expanded its power. Indirect power for the unions comes from nonaffiliated workers who look to organized labor as the guide for salary and wage demands as well as other benefits in bargaining with management. Each strike, contract, or concession sets a precedent for these independent employees.

Management Implications

With regard to unions, the basic things managers must know are: (1) grievance procedures and other contract details affecting day-to-day relations with employees; (2) the current positions of their companies on union relations and bargaining strategies so that they can effectively deal with employees; (3) the likely impact of union contracts on future plans of their companies.

Policies on how to deal with unions are basic to maintaining productive relationships with workers. Rather than waiting for something to happen and then reacting to a problem, companies set formal guidelines for decisions concerning employees and bargaining about wages, benefits, and so on. Usually this policy can smooth labor relations and improve output.

Some important issues from management's point of view are:

1. Technology leading to lower labor costs through fewer workers, changes in the type of skills needed, or a lower level of skills.
2. Changes in location for operations resulting in fewer employees at one plant and greater employment at another.

3. Flexibility in adding and laying off workers during busy and slow times.
4. Cooperation to adjust work rules to meet emergency requirements or allow for permanent changes in conditions.

The company needs the freedom to respond to changes in the market, new approaches by competitors, laws passed by government, and similar developments in business. The position of a union can have a very important effect on the success of management attempts to perform at levels expected by the shareholders.

CAREERS AND JOBS

This chapter gives some indications of what working is like. Details about jobs in business, for example, being a sales representative or accountant, come in Parts III and IV. This material should start you thinking about the following points.

1. *Level of organization.* What are your business ambitions? Do you want to be at the top, despite responsibility, pressures, travel, and so on? Is there a talent or skill you should develop? Where will it lead you? Are you content being a worker on the line or in the office bullpen?

2. *Self-analysis.* Are you prepared to be bored most of the working day in exchange for avoiding responsibility? Can you get along with people? Does job pressure turn you into jelly or a thrashing monster? What are the work factors that turn you on? Bother you? Can you persevere to finish college or other training or projects you start?

3. *Income and security factors.* Are your ambitions, talents, and personality in balance with desires for income? How scarce will your area of interest be when you look for the first job in your career choice? Are you prepared to sacrifice security for new opportunities? Is college or vocational training financially possible?

4. *Impact of changes.* Are there more opportunities for you as a woman or minority race member in the field you are thinking about these days? Can you go higher? Can you really use your skills and talents with minimum prejudice in this field? Has another field opened which you had discounted? Do the changes mean problems for white males?

Don't expect to have all the answers at this stage, but these are questions that should be answered before you start your career. During the course, look for information that will help you make decisions about your future. Put related news clippings in your *job file* (suggested in Chapter One). Identify references in this book which will help with the questions. Look for details about jobs. Fill in the missing pieces about what it is like. This will increase the likelihood you will make a good choice.

CHAPTER SUMMARY

Firing or laying off people without notice or unemployment benefits occurs rarely. This is because: (1) ownership is in the hands of many individuals rather than a few powerful people; (2) management is made up of professionals who clearly understand the impact of such decisions; (3) worker organizations have gained greater security and benefits for their memberships; (4) social responsibility has made decision makers more sympathetic toward the welfare of workers; and (5) international business has exposed management to the ways workers are treated in other countries.

There are two reasons for working: (1) income; and (2) satisfaction from time well spent. People try to avoid boring, routine jobs and strive for a sense of accomplishment from their work. Avoiding routine often means greater responsibility, more work, and greater pressure as well as higher income and satisfaction.

Factors in job security and income include the number of openings (demand) and the number of applicants (supply). Training is an important factor in being selected for and keeping a job. The scarcity of a skill or talent is usually related to the amount of time and money invested in acquiring the added capability. Getting along with people is also essential. In addition, taking a risk to try something with greater potential is sometimes necessary. It is also a fact that events outside the control of the individual can lead to success or failure.

The Equal Pay Act of 1963 and the Civil Rights Act of 1974 were major steps toward eliminating discrimination on the basis of sex or race. Women have been aided by the option to plan a family. In recent years they have also improved their professional qualifications for advancement within organizations through increased training. Blacks have also gained stature within many organizations by avoiding oversensitivity about their race, choosing racial issues carefully, and increasing their training to qualify for better jobs.

Labor unions give employees strength in their bargaining with management and reduce the tendency of management to view workers as units of cost rather than human beings with needs. In the United States, unions have not sought a division of after-tax profits for their memberships, nor have they tried for a role in top-level decision making as in socialistic countries. The tendency in this country is to treat employees from president to custodian as people offering their services for a salary or a wage. Only investors have a right to receive a return on this capital because they are risking capital.

The major issues in labor relations are salary and wages, benefits, and work rules, including seniority, grievances, and transfers.

The history of American unions began in 1792 and is summarized briefly in the chapter. Today, the membership of labor unions is just under 22 million.

Regarding a career in business, the individual should consider his or her ambitions and determine the level of organization to which he or she aspires. Self-analysis will help to identify the most desirable occupation. Income and security may be important, and the individual may be assisted by the changes that are giving greater opportunities to women and minorities.

PROVOCATIVE STATEMENT

The Viewpoint of a Small Business Owner

1 "Being your own boss is important to me. I guess I have to say things once in a while that aren't too smart for a career in a big company. When you have to say, 'that's misrepresenting the facts,' and the reply is, 'it's part of our strategy,' I'm in the wrong company.

They say you can lose your shirt in a small business. I think you can make good money if you run it right. That doesn't change in any business, but once in a while you can make it big in a small business. Choosing what and where to invest in is the first step to make sure of.

My main interest is being able to see what happens when I make decisions. You don't have to go through a bunch of committees and executives who know less and less about the situation as you go up the organization. Good or bad, you got no one to blame for a decision but yourself if you're both the owner and the manager.

Maybe sometimes you have to substitute 'psychic-income' for the real thing and put in some 20 hour days, but being a number in a big company is not my style. For example, once I couldn't have a picture on the wall or a bookcase, even if I bought the stuff, because I didn't have the right title and needed another promotion before I was qualified.

It just adds up to doing it yourself, or letting a lot of other people tell you what to say and how to act. Risking my savings, and worrying if I'd ever break even, was worth it to me."

John E. Dillon,
President,
Dillon Maintenance Services, Inc.
Detroit, Michigan

People in Business: The Workers

PROVOCATIVE STATEMENT

A Woman's Viewpoint in Developing a Career

2 "Today a woman has a better chance for a career in business. I'm not a feminist or a member of a woman's lib organization, but I have to admit they've made progress. My boss said the other day that the best thing you can be to get a good job is a black woman. That's pure bunk—lip service to laws and pressure groups. You have a chance, not an inside track.

Before the 1970s most men thought a woman was working long enough to get married. Those who stuck it out were spinsters who became executive secretaries or second rate 'assistant to's.' Once in a while a woman would stand out as a lawyer or designer or something special.

Now I'm being considered for Manager of Administration in St. Louis. It would be a big promotion. They asked me if my husband could move and whether we planned more children. Since he can transfer and the two children are enough, I've got a chance. In fact, I think I'll get it because I've managed the Dallas office staff successfully with no male/female complications.

The sex thing is still a problem. Traveling overnight on business is always good for a joke or two. Single girls sometimes don't get a promotion they're qualified for because of the travel. One thing that upsets me is that pretty girls get positions over better qualified women.

Despite the problems, you can find women in positions they would never have had before. Management isn't a barrier anymore. Women interview with men, and there's a much better possibility of actually getting the job instead of the company going through the motions and giving it to a man."

> Ms. Betty Schneider
> Manager, Office Services
> Dufore Company, Inc.
> Dallas, Texas

REVIEW QUESTIONS

1. Describe a job you have had and the characteristics of the typical worker holding that job. Where in Figure 2-1 was your position located?
2. What are some of the factors an employee would consider in judging job security?
3. Why is planning ability in and out of the office important for today's business executive?
4. Name examples of traditional biases that keep members of minorities from progressing in business organizations. Include those affecting women.
5. Discuss the statement, "Business executives make poor parents."
6. What is the primary purpose of labor unions? Cite a current example of labor/management bargaining and your opinion on the merits of the issues involved.
7. Can you cite a situation, real or imaginary, in which wages or salaries would not be involved in the bargaining?

The Environment of Business

PART TWO

Chapter Outline

The Regulator Role
   Taxation
      Major Federal Taxes
      Types of State and Local Taxes
   Legislation
      Labor Laws
      Environmental Protection Laws
      Antitrust Laws
      Legislation Protecting Consumers
      Miscellaneous Governmental Regulations

The Buyer Role
   Size
   Initiative by Buyers
   Methods of Purchase
      Bidding Procedures
      Negotiation
   Number of People
   Legal Requirements

The Dispenser of Funds, Goods, and Services Role
   Funds
   Goods and Services

The Setter of Policy Role

Government Careers
   Nature of Jobs
   Required Background
   Reward System

Chapter Summary

Provocative Statement 1:
   The Government Regulates Too Many Business Activities

Provocative Statement 2:
   Business Executives Can Break Laws as Long as They Do Not Get Caught

Key Terms

Income taxes
1040 form
Social security taxes
Excise taxes
Customs duties
Documentary stamp taxes
Occupational stamp taxes
Use taxes
Property taxes
Real property
Personal property
Sales taxes
Licenses
Fair Labor Standards Act
Occupational Safety and Health Act
National Environmental Policy Act

Antitrust laws
Trust
Sherman Act
Clayton Act
Tying arrangement
Exclusive dealing agreement
Federal Trade Commission Act
Interlocking directorates
Federal Trade Commission
Lanham Act
National Commission on Public Safety
Bidding
Subsidies
Federal Reserve Banking System
Wage and price controls

The Role of Government

"Although in America we have what is described as a free-enterprise economy, our government today regulates more business practices than most other democracies."
—Chairman, Citicorp

Business, today more than ever, must understand the influence of government on its operations. Just as society has demanded more from business, so has the influence of government expanded. Many of the taxes, laws, and other government actions we shall discuss in this chapter have been around only a short time. Few laws regulating pollution existed before the 1960s. A U.S. president recently instituted wage and price controls.

The major purpose of this chapter is to investigate the role of government in four business activities. These activities are:

1. Acquiring money for assets and working capital.
2. Buying goods and services.
3. Producing goods and services.
4. Selling goods and services.

Government has been established at all levels of society, ranging from local governing bodies through state agencies to the federal level. The impact of government on business results from government acting in one of its four roles. These roles, discussed in this chapter, are:

1. Regulator of business behavior through taxes and laws.
2. Buyer of business-produced goods and services.
3. Dispenser of funds, services, and goods to business and citizens.
4. Setter of policy for the economy of business.

THE REGULATOR ROLE

The control of economic activity, in some form, is necessary to make group life possible. Government in the United States has regulated business in two major ways—taxes and laws. This section discusses the nature and effect of taxes relating to business and of major business laws.

Taxation

Taxation generally refers to a government levy placed on some activity or item. Many types of taxes are levied on businesses by all levels of government. Taxes generally have two purposes: (1) to regulate behavior and (2) to provide income for government services. Any one type of tax is not restricted to only one purpose; the amount of the tax affects its purpose. For example, a high tax on the sale of gasoline will regulate and restrict the sale of gas because people cannot afford to buy as much. On the other hand, a low tax may have very little effect on the number of gallons of gasoline bought by consumers. The government may receive more money per gallon from the low tax. Taxes collected by the federal government are paid by all businesses. They are discussed in more detail than are state and local taxes.

Major Federal Taxes

The major federal taxes are as follows:

1. Income taxes.
2. Social security taxes.
3. Excise taxes.
4. Customs duties.
5. Miscellaneous taxes.

Income Taxes

The federal government places a tax on the income of all businesses. The taxable income is the difference between their total dollar sales and the expenses incurred in obtaining those sales.

Businesses are subject to one of two different tax rates. If the business operates as a proprietorship or a partnership (proprietorships and partnerships are defined in Chapter Five), it will have to pay **income taxes** according to the rates established for all citizens. This rate, ranging from 0 to 70% increases as incomes grow higher. Each year, proprietors (or partners) must tell the government how much they have made by filling out a **1040 form**. The 1040 form, shown in Figure 3-1 is the same form employees submit.

Figure 3-1. *The 1040 Individual Income Tax Form*

Form **1040** US Department of the Treasury—Internal Revenue Service
Individual Income Tax Return **1974**

For the year January 1–December 31, 1974, or other taxable year beginning ...., 1974, ending ...., 19.......

Please print or type

Name (If joint return, give first names and initials of both)	Last name	COUNTY OF RESIDENCE	Your social security number
Present home address (Number and street, including apartment number, or rural route)			Spouse's social security no.
City, town or post office, State and ZIP code		Occupation	Yours ▶ / Spouse's ▶

Filing Status (check only one)

1 ☐ Single
2 ☐ Married filing joint return (even if only one had income)
3 ☐ Married filing separately. If spouse is also filing give spouse's social security number in designated space above and enter full name here ▶
4 ☐ Unmarried Head of Household (See Instructions on page 5) ▶
5 ☐ Widow(er) with dependent child (Year spouse died ▶ 19)

Exemptions Regular / 65 or over / Blind

6a Yourself . . . ☐ ☐ ☐
b Spouse . . . ☐ ☐ ☐ Enter number of boxes checked ▶
c First names of your dependent children who lived with you ______ Enter number ▶
d Number of other dependents (from line 27) . . . ▶
7 Total exemptions claimed . . . . ▶

8 **Presidential Election Campaign Fund** . . ▶ Do you wish to designate $1 of your taxes for this fund? . . ☐ Yes ☐ No
If joint return, does your spouse wish to designate $1? . . ☐ Yes ☐ No
Note: If you check the "Yes" box(es) it will not increase your tax or reduce your refund.

Please attach Copy B of Forms W-2 here

Income

9 Wages, salaries, tips, and other employee compensation (Attach Forms W-2. If unavailable, see instructions on page 3.) . . . **9**
10a Dividends (See Instructions on pages 6 and 13)$................, 10b Less exclusion $.............., Balance ▶ **10c**
(If gross dividends and other distributions are over $400, list in Part I of Schedule B.)
11 Interest income. [If $400 or less, enter total without listing in Schedule B / If over $400, enter total and list in Part II of Schedule B] . **11**
12 Income other than wages, dividends, and interest (from line 38) **12**
13 Total (add lines 9, 10c, 11, and 12) **13**
14 Adjustments to income (such as "sick pay," moving expenses, etc. from line 43) . **14**
15 Subtract line 14 from line 13 (adjusted gross income) **15**

- **If you do not itemize deductions and line 15 is under $10,000, find tax in Tables and enter on line 16.**
- **If you itemize deductions or line 15 is $10,000 or more, go to line 44 to figure tax.**
- CAUTION. If you have unearned income and can be claimed as a dependent on your parent's return, check here ▶ ☐ and see Instructions on page 7.

Tax, Payments and Credits

16 Tax, check if from: ☐ Tax Tables 1–12 ☐ Tax Rate Schedule X, Y, or Z ☐ Schedule D ☐ Schedule G OR ☐ Form 4726 **16**
17 Total credits (from line 54) **17**
18 Income tax (subtract line 17 from line 16) **18**
19 Other taxes (from line 61) **19**
20 Total (add lines 18 and 19) **20**
21a Total Federal income tax withheld (attach Forms W-2 or W-2P to front) **21a**
b 1974 estimated tax payments (include amount allowed as credit from 1973 return) . . . . . **b**
c Amount paid with Form 4868, Application for Automatic Extension of Time to File U.S. Individual Income Tax Return **c**
d Other payments (from line 65) . . . . . . **d**
22 Total (add lines 21a, b, c, and d) **22**

Pay amount on line 23 in full with this return. Write social security number on check or money order and make payable to Internal Revenue Service.

Please attach Check or Money Order here

Balance Due or Refund

23 If line 20 is larger than line 22, enter **BALANCE DUE IRS** . . . . ▶ **23**
(Check here ▶ ☐, If Form 2210, Form 2210F, or statement is attached. See instructions on page 7.)
24 If line 22 is larger than line 20, enter amount **OVERPAID** . . . . ▶ **24**
25 Amount of line 24 to be **REFUNDED TO YOU** . . . . ▶ **25**
26 Amount of line 24 to be credited on 1975 estimated tax. ▶ **26**
If all of overpayment (line 24) is to be refunded (line 25), make no entry on line 26.

Sign here

Under penalties of perjury, I declare that I have examined this return, including accompanying schedules and statements, and to the best of my knowledge and belief it is true, correct, and complete. Declaration of preparer (other than taxpayer) is based on all information of which he has any knowledge.

▶ Your signature Date
▶ Preparer's signature (other than taxpayer) Date
▶ Spouse's signature (if filing jointly, BOTH must sign even if only one had income)
Address (and ZIP Code) Preparer's Emp. Ident. or Soc. Sec. No.

The federal government has established a much simpler tax rate structure for corporations. Corporations are taxed 22% on the first $25,000 of earnings. A 48% rate is paid for earnings over $25,000. For example, a corporation with taxable earnings of $10,000 pays 22% of earnings, or $2,200, for income taxes. Corporate earnings of $100,000 result in a federal income tax bill of $41,500 (22% of $25,000 plus 48% of $75,000). As a result, the corporation with $10,000 income pays an average rate of 22%, while the corporation with 10 times the earnings ($100,000) pays a higher average rate (41.5%).

EFFECT OF INCOME TAXES   The federal income tax affects business as a whole by requiring all non-tax-exempt businesses to file an annual tax return. Moreover, quarterly (four times a year) estimates of taxes must be sent to the government. Employees must be provided with a yearly statement of total taxes withheld (W-2 form). In addition, the federal income tax has a major impact on business activities of acquiring money, buying, producing, and selling as shown in Table 3-1.

ACQUIRING MONEY   The federal income tax tends to reduce the amount of money that people have to invest in businesses. This is especially true if the sliding scale of the income tax rate is considered. The people most likely to invest are those with high incomes—those who pay the highest tax rates.

Federal income tax encourages the use of borrowed money instead of that of owners. The interest expense paid for borrowed money can be deducted from the amount of business income before taxes are computed. Payments to owners (dividends) are not tax-deductible. However, as discussed in Chapter Fourteen, the choice of the source of business money depends on other factors besides tax treatment of the cost involved.

BUYING   Income tax laws influence whether equipment is bought or leased (rented). If equipment is bought, part of the cost of machines and other equipment can be deducted from the yearly income. This deduction, called *depreciation expense*, is discussed in Chapter Thirteen. If, however, a firm leases equipment, the money paid for the use of the equipment is subtracted from earnings before taxes are calculated. This lease payment may be higher than the depreciation expense. Thus, leasing of equipment may be preferred to buying because lower income taxes are paid.

Income taxes may affect not only the manner in which goods are purchased but also the timing of such purchases. In years of high revenue, businesses are more willing to buy needed equipment because these expenditures will help reduce the taxable income base.

PRODUCING   Income tax primarily affects the producing activity through its impact on employees. People may be less willing to work more hours if the increased pay places them in a higher tax bracket. Therefore, labor may be in shorter supply.

In response to this possible dampening effect of personal income taxes, businesses may pay their workers at some time after they actually earned the

Table 3-1. *Federal Tax Impact*

BUSINESS ACTIVITY	TYPE OF TAX			
	INCOME	SOCIAL INSURANCE	EXCISE	CUSTOMS
Acquiring Money	Encourages borrowing because interest expense, but not dividends is tax-deductible.			
Buying	Encourages production facilities to be leased, rather than bought.			Affects which suppliers are considered.
Producing	Decreases willingness of people to work.	Increases cost of production.	Increases cost and requires paperwork.	Affects items available for production and their costs.
Selling	Affects amount of customer purchases. Affects timing of expenditure for promotion, since expenses are tax deductible.	May increase consumer buying as monies are given to less thrifty people.	May reduce sales as taxes may require higher prices for goods.	Reduces competition. A higher selling price may be possible and necessary.

money. Payments in the form of retirement benefits allow workers to receive their money when they are no longer working. Therefore, they pay less taxes than if the money had been given to them before they retired.

SELLING Income taxes affect how much money people have to spend. The more money they have to spend, the better it is for businesses in general. Income taxes on businesses also influence the selling activity. Firms may try to make up their payments to the government by passing the cost on to consumers.

However, although a majority of firms are concerned with the increasing cost of income taxes, they may not be able to pass it on to consumers because of price competition. The more intense price competition is, the more likely

Social Security Taxes

The Social Security Act of 1935, amended in 1965, requires business payment of taxes for three types of employee benefits: OASDI, Medicare, and unemployment compensation. **Social security taxes**, or payroll taxes, are levied according to the amount of wages paid to employees. Both employers and employees pay into the social security fund to provide OASDI and Medicare benefits. The payroll deduction from employee wages (5.85% of the first $13,200 earned in 1974) is called Federal Insurance Contribution (FICA). The unemployment compensation program is funded by the employer alone.

OASDI (Old Age, Survivors, and Disability Insurance)—commonly known as Social Security—provides payments to retired persons, to disabled workers, or to the family of a deceased worker.

Medicare provides money for hospital bills of people 65 and over. Payment for medical bills is optional under the program; there is no cost to business.

Unemployment compensation pays money to willing and able workers who have lost their jobs (are laid off) and cannot find new employment.

EFFECT OF SOCIAL SECURITY TAX Like income tax, the social security tax adds to the general paperwork of a business and requires the business to send the money collected to the government. The major impact of the tax is on the business activities of producing and selling, as shown in Table 3-1.

PRODUCING The cost of the tax to business increases the cost of producing goods. The cost will rise as the number of employees working for the business grows.

SELLING Employees as well as employers must pay for OASDI and Medicare. These FICA taxes are withheld by employers. Selling is affected because less income is taken home by employees. Therefore, they buy less. However, business may benefit from this tax because the government gives social security benefits to people with low incomes. Generally, people with low incomes save less money than people with higher incomes. The unemployed person, for example, will probably need to spend all the money government gives him to live. Some workers who pay the social security tax may not need the money to live. They might have saved it if there were no social security tax.

Excise Taxes

The excise tax is a levy on the manufacture, sale, or purchase of selected goods.

It may be paid by businesses or consumers. For example, businesses selling tobacco, liquor, gasoline, and automobiles pay an excise tax on those items.

Excise taxes are also collected from consumers on the sale of furs, jewelry, and telephone bills.

EFFECT OF EXCISE TAX   The major effects of excise taxes are on producing and selling.

PRODUCING   Excise taxes on the manufacture of goods raise production costs. Production activities are also affected by the paperwork required for excise tax purposes. Detailed records of quantity and value of goods manufactured and sold are necessary.

SELLING   Excise taxes may influence the ability of a business to sell its products, since the tax is passed on to the consumer by increasing the price of the product. The higher price may discourage consumers from buying.

Customs Duties

Customs duties, commonly called *tariffs*, are taxes placed on goods as they enter or leave a country. The tax may be based on the volume of goods moved, such as ten cents a pound, or on the value by percentage, commonly called *ad valorem*. Most tariffs have been passed to protect American business from foreign competition.

EFFECT OF CUSTOMS DUTIES   Customs duties on goods imported to the United States have two opposite effects on business. The buying and selling activities are hindered by the cost of the taxes; on the other hand, the producing activity is helped by the protection they offer. Customs duties increase the price of imported goods. American businesses that use dutiable foreign commodities (goods upon which duties are levied) in the production of industrial products have higher costs of production because of the tariff. Businesses that own factories abroad are also adversely affected, because their imports into the United States are taxed.

Tariffs may reduce the market for American-produced goods in other countries. These other countries may depend on sales to the United States for dollars to buy American goods. If these sales to the United States are reduced by tariffs, fewer dollars will be available for purchase of American goods. In addition, foreign countries may strike back against American tariffs. They may charge tariffs on goods brought into their countries from the United States. Thus, the price of American goods exported abroad will be higher, and fewer of these goods will be demanded abroad.

PRODUCING   Many businesses have demanded tariffs as protection from foreign competition. In the past, producers of dyes, chemicals, textiles, fabrics, pottery, cameras, toys, bicycles, baseballs, gloves, and aluminum have demanded that the U.S. government pass tariffs to give them protection. Generally, these businesses have argued that foreign wages and other costs of production are so much lower than American costs. Therefore, foreign producers could undersell American producers in the American market if it were not for tariff protection. Government protection through tariffs may enable some businesses to stay in business. Others, protected from foreign competition, will be able to raise their prices, and hence, to make higher profits.

Miscellaneous Taxes

Business is also influenced by other taxes or charges imposed by the federal government. Businesses are liable for: (1) **documentary stamp taxes** on many items, such as bonds, deeds, and insurance policies; (2) **occupational stamp taxes** on such assorted pursuits as gambling, selling marijuana, or selling oleomargarine; and (3) **use taxes** on heavy motor vehicles.

EFFECT OF MISCELLANEOUS TAXES The diverse nature of miscellaneous taxes prohibits a detailed listing of their effects on business in this text. In general, these effects are similar to those of the previously discussed federal taxes.

Types of State and Local Taxes

Like federal taxes, taxes levied by state and local governments have a profound effect on the business activities of acquiring money, buying, producing, and selling. Although some of the types of taxes are levied by only one level of government, many are used by several or all units of government. The major revenue-producing state and local taxes are:

1. Property taxes.
2. Sales taxes.
3. Income taxes.
4. Licenses.

Other taxes levied at the state and local level include corporation taxes, unemployment taxes, special business taxes, and inheritance and estate taxes. These state and local taxes are described here. However, the specific effects of these taxes, similar to those of previously discussed federal taxes, are beyond the scope of the text. Their major effects are summarized in Table 3-2.

Property Taxes

Property taxes are levied on the assessed value of land, buildings, equipment, and goods in storage (inventories) owned by businesses. Generally, the property tax rate is stated as so much for each $1,000 of assessed value. These assessed values, set by government employees, are based on some percentage of marketable value of the property. A tax rate of $50 per thousand on a building assessed at $100,000 will result in a total tax bill of $5,000.

Property taxes may be on land or anything attached permanently to the land, such as buildings. This type of property, called **real property**, includes everything below or above the land's surface.

Governmental units may also tax **personal property**. Personal property is

Table 3-2. *State and Local Taxes*

Business Activity	Type of Tax		
	Property	Sales	License
Acquiring money	Reduces amount of funds available.		
Buying	Influences timing of property additions.		Affects availability of goods and services.
Producing	Influences rate of production and depletion of inventories. Encourages choice of areas with lowest rate or assessments.	Encourages location where there is no tax or where neighboring states have higher tax rates.	Restricts those who are allowed to produce.
Selling	May result in higher selling price, lower consumer purchasing power. Influences timing of property deletion.	Requires higher price to consumer.	May restrict sellers or prohibit some from selling.

any property not classified as real property and includes merchandise inventory, bonds, and equipment like cash registers.

Sales Taxes

The state and local equivalent of the federal excise tax is the sales tax. This tax is charged as a percentage of the selling price of goods or services. It is levied either on all sales or on the sale of selected products by all 50 states, many cities, and some counties.

Most states (excluding Alaska, Delaware, Montana, New Hampshire, and Oregon) have placed a general sales tax on most goods sold at retail; the general rates are shown in Figure 3-2.

About half of the states rely upon a use tax to back up the sales tax. That is, in order to prevent purchasers from avoiding the state sales tax by purchasing goods in other states not having a sales tax, levies are placed upon the use, consumption, or storage of goods so purchased.

All states levy sales taxes on liquor and gasoline. A number of states tax other products, such as cigarettes. These selective sales taxes were enacted to discourage the sale of certain goods.

Income Taxes

Income taxes, in addition to those charged by the federal government and a majority of the states, are also levied by local governments.

56 The Environment of Business

Figure 3-2. *State Sales Taxes*

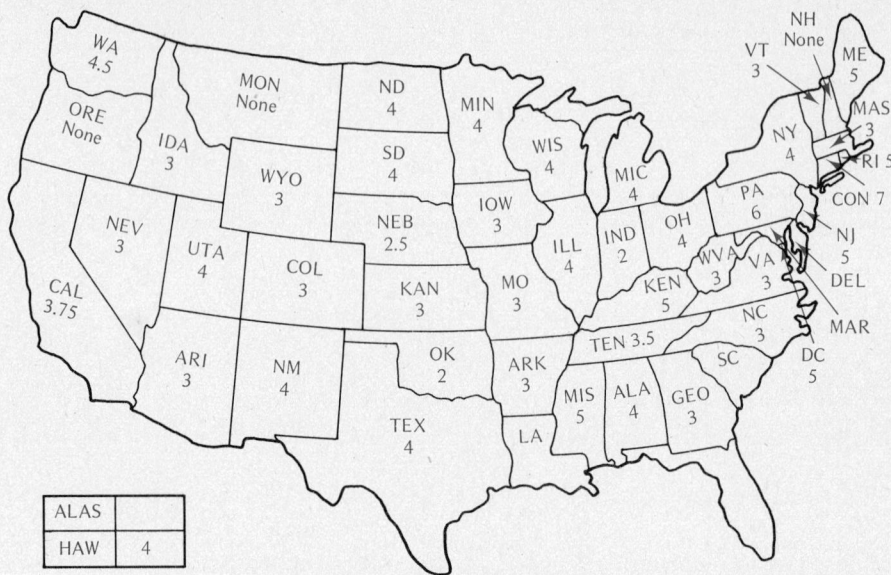

Most state and local income taxes on personal income are set up on a rising scale, like the federal income tax. The rate increases as taxable income increases. However, the rate does not change for state-levied corporate income taxes. Most states and local governments require corporations to pay a fixed rate, such as 4%, on all corporate net profit.

Licenses

State and local governments often require that examinations be passed before allowing a business or profession to initiate operations. Doctors, lawyers, and accountants are subject to such regulations. Upon satisfaction of the requirements, a license is granted.

Licenses are also issued to limit the number of firms in operation, such as liquor stores. Other businesses frequently required to be licensed include restaurants, hotels, movie theaters, pool halls, and street markets.

Although licenses are required primarily for regulating purposes, state revenues from sale of license plates for automobiles have proven substantial.

Other State and Local Taxes

Several other taxes levied by states or local governments are important to business. These taxes are discussed here. However, their specific effects on business are not detailed since they are similar to federal taxes, broad in nature, or related to a limited type of business.

CORPORATION TAXES A fee is required from a corporation when it secures a charter from the state in which it is incorporated. It must also pay an annual *franchise*, or license tax, to continue to operate in its state of incorporation. The amount of this tax is based on the amount of money invested in the company.

Corporations that wish to do business in a state other than where they were incorporated are also charged fees. A business incorporated in the state of Delaware must pay an entrance tax to carry on business in other states (where it would be considered foreign). Furthermore, an annual *privilege tax* must be paid for the privilege of continued operation in other states.

SPECIAL BUSINESS TAXES State and local governments have enacted tax laws that affect only certain industries. These industries, including railroads, public utilities, insurance companies, and banks, may be taxed on the basis of value of their income or property. Banks, for example, are frequently taxed on the basis of total deposits on hand on a specific date.

Legislation

Taxation has a profound effect on business, but it is only part of government's regulatory role. In addition, government has used its constitution-given power to regulate interstate commerce by passing and enforcing many laws designed to regulate business behavior. The major federal laws passed to regulate business are summarized here with emphasis on their major impact on business activities.

Federal laws influence many areas of business simultaneously. For example, the major laws influencing the business activity of producing may also affect buying, selling, or acquiring money. Because of the complexity of laws, five major groups of federal laws are discussed:

1. Labor laws.
2. Environmental protection laws.
3. Antitrust laws.
4. Consumer protection laws.
5. Miscellaneous government laws.

Labor Laws

Initial legislation passed to protect workers was intended to insure humane treatment of workers. Laws passed by the states prevent employment of children in mines and factories and correct abuses concerning unsafe and unhealthful working conditions. These early laws, now standard in all states, establish minimum standards for working conditions which any business must provide.

Another set of minimums and maximums was established for business by the Fair Labor Standards Act. This act, commonly called the *Minimum Wage Law*, requires businesses employing workers in occupations in or affecting interstate commerce to pay a prescribed minimum hourly wage and to pay overtime if a worker works over 40 hours per week. The minimum hourly wage is constantly being changed by Congress, as witnessed by a wage of $.25 an hour in 1938, $.40 in 1945, $1.25 in 1966, and $2.00 in 1973. Business owners, unless their business is exempt, must adhere to these limits or run the risk of a fine of $10,000 or a six-month prison term.

Most of the other labor laws discussed in Chapter Two, shown in Table 3-3, have their major impact on how business deals with workers and unions bargaining for workers. These laws require businesses to bargain with unions in good faith. However, unions are not allowed to force businesses to hire only union members. Furthermore, these laws protect workers from union pressure and illegal practices by officers.

Not only has governmental protection of workers' right to unionize come a long way since the 1930s, but also government protection of workers' right to safe and healthful working conditions has progressed. The federal government took a bold and broad stand against job-caused accidents and illnesses in the Occupational Safety and Health Act (OSHA). This act has resulted in thousands of inspections by Department of Labor inspectors, and in such requirements as that safety nets be used on high-rise construction where planking or scaffolding is not practical. It is estimated that the many regulations of

Table 3-3. *Major Labor Laws*

Law	Year Passed	Description of Content
Norris–LaGuardia Act	1932	Establishes legality of unionization and collective bargaining.
Wagner Act	1935	Requires employers to recognize and bargain with labor unions.
National Labor Relations Act	1938	Sets minimum wages and maximum weekly working hours, and prevents employment of children in hazardous occupations.
Taft–Hartley Act	1947	Prohibits unfair labor practices by labor unions.
Landrum–Griffin Act	1959	Protects members of unions against improper conduct by their officers.
Civil Rights Act	1964	Prohibits discrimination in matters affecting employment because of race, color, religion, sex, or national origin.
Occupational Safety and Health Act	1970	Requires industry to eliminate all conditions in plants and warehouses that could possibly contribute to disabling injury of either immediate or cumulative nature.

Table 3-4. *Federal Environmental Protection Laws*

Law	Year Passed	Description of Content
Rivers and Harbor Act	1899	Prohibits dumping of refuse in navigable waterways.
Water Pollution Control Act	1948	Encourages local governments to construct sewage treatment plants and to stop water pollution.
Clean Air Act	1963	Provides money and power to study impact of air pollution on human health and property and to control air pollution.
Water Quality Act	1965	Requires state and local governments to establish standards of quality for interstate waters.
National Environmental Policy Act	1969	Directs federal agencies to consider the environmental effects of existing and proposed programs.
Resource Recovery Act	1970	Provides money for research into solid waste disposal systems.

OSHA will increase the construction costs of buildings by 10 to 35%. Increased worker safety is going to increase the costs of production of all businesses.

Environmental Protection Laws

Production activities generally require the use of natural resources. Frequently, such activities result in waste materials that have no value. For many years, governmental restrictions on resource use and waste disposal were minimal. Apparently, the abundant resources in the United States suggested very little need for concern about their destruction. Legislation enacted to protect resources was not enforced. However, in recent years, concern about resource depletion has brought about new laws and regulatory agencies. A brief description of acts passed to regulate pollution is presented in Table 3-4. Most of these acts indicate the desire of government to reduce pollution and waste of natural resources.

The intent of the federal government to control all pollution is made concrete in the National Environmental Policy Act. This act declares that the continuing policy of Congress is "to use all practicable means . . . to create and maintain conditions under which man and nature can exist in productive harmony and fulfill the social, economic, and other requirements of present and future generations of Americans." Federal agencies are required, as a result of the act, to consider the environmental effects of existing and proposed programs. The act has also created a three-member Environmental Quality Council to assist the president in making environmental studies and policies. The existence of this council, with power to police the environmental behavior of other agencies of the federal government, clearly indicates that business will be required to control pollution with less regard to cost than in the past. No longer will the standard of the cost of pollution control be the issue. Now business will be forced to consider the dangers to society of all pollution.

In addition, business will have to learn about all present and future environmental laws. The rate of new legislation in this area of prime importance to society requires constant business updating of knowledge.

Antitrust Laws

Early in American history the predominant feeling of government was that if sellers compete with each other, they would offer the best goods and services at the lowest possible price. Federal laws to insure competition were not necessary as long as courts provided the needed protection by prohibiting all contracts that involved such practices as division of territories and fixing of prices. However, court enforcement of unwritten laws (*common law*), which prevent agreements among buyers or sellers to restrict trade, was not adequate for cases where all competitors agreed to limit competition. Fear of retaliation by large firms also encouraged injured firms to remain silent. Furthermore, court interpretation was not necessarily consistent among states. The growth of restraints preventing competition during the late 1800s brought about a public outcry for federal legislation to control these trade restraints.

The resultant federal laws to help competitors, called antitrust laws, are summarized in Table 3-5. The laws designed to prohibit anticompetitive practices are so named because the original business practice they were designed to stop was called a trust. The trust is a form of organization, first used by Standard Oil Company and John D. Rockefeller in 1879, which places the control of several companies in the hands of a group of people called *trustees*. These trustees have full power to decide on all business activities of all

Table 3-5. *Major Antitrust Laws*

Law	Year Passed	Description of Content
Sherman Antitrust Act	1890	Prohibits contracts, combinations, or conspiracies in restraint of trade and attempts to monopolize trade.
Clayton Act	1914	Prohibits discrimination in prices, exclusive dealing and tying contracts, intercorporate stockholdings, and interlocking directorates, if any of these practices tend to substantially lessen competition.
Federal Trade Commission Act	1914	Prohibits unfair methods of competition.

Figure 3-3. *The Oil Trust*

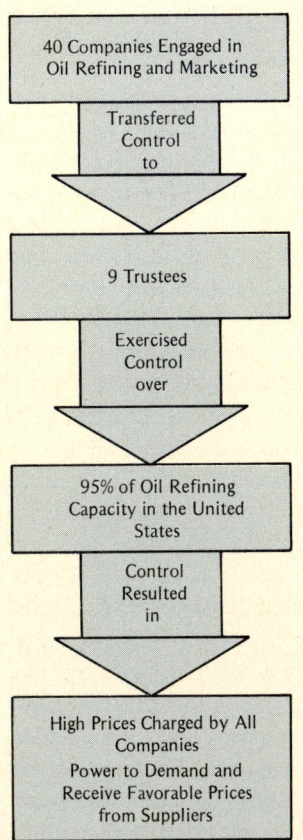

organizational members of the trust. The impact of the trust set-up is visible in the case of the Oil Trust depicted in Figure 3-3.

The Sherman Act was the first major antitrust law passed by the federal government. Through this law, businesses are not allowed to combine together to restrain or monopolize trade. Also, the Sherman Act makes it illegal for companies to join together to fix prices or divide markets.

The Clayton and Federal Trade Commission Acts were passed in 1914 when experience with court enforcement of the Sherman Act showed that business practices harmful to competition were not being stopped. The Clayton Act specifically outlaws four business practices if the effect of the practices "may be to substantially lessen competition."

First, the Clayton Act prohibits sellers from charging buyers of the same goods, under similar conditions, two different prices. This provision was further spelled out by an amendment (Robinson–Patman Act of 1936) to the

Clayton Act. The major purpose of the amendment is to protect small retailers from the price-cutting practices of large chains with big buying power.

Second, sellers are prohibited from making arrangements under which a buyer must buy another product to get a product (a **tying arrangement**) or forcing a buyer to agree not to buy the same good from another seller (an **exclusive dealing agreement**). Under this provision of the Clayton Act, the Standard Oil Company of California was stopped from requiring its service station dealers to buy gasoline and accessories only from Standard. International Salt Company was also stopped from requiring users of its salt dispensing machine to purchase only its salt.

The third practice prohibited by the Clayton Act is a business's ownership of the stock of other businesses with which it competes. This prohibition was broadened by amendment (the Celler–Kefauver Act of 1950) to include acquisition of assets and to prevent any mergers which may lessen competition.

Finally, the Clayton Act prohibits **interlocking directorates**, a situation in which a director or official of one corporation is also a member of the board of directors of another corporation. These interlocking directorates are now prohibited if one of the companies involved has capital of more than $1 million and if the interlocked companies are competitors.

It was felt by Congress in the early 1900s that the Sherman Act had failed to stop anticompetitive practices of business because no special governmental body was established to enforce the law. Subsequently, the Federal Trade Commission Act of 1914 was passed and established an administrative enforcement agency called the **Federal Trade Commission (FTC)**. The FTC, a five-person, president-appointed administrative agency, is charged with enforcement of the Clayton Act, the FTC Act, and several acts passed to protect consumers, such as the Wool Products Labeling Act. The provision of the FTC Act states that "unfair methods of competition in interstate commerce are hereby declared illegal." Under this provision, Atlantic Refining Company was stopped from forcing its dealers to buy Goodyear tires, batteries, and accessories. This act was also used by the FTC to force the major hospitals in Kansas City to accept blood from two properly licensed commercial blood banks in the Kansas City area.

Legislation Protecting Consumers

During experience with the antitrust laws, it became evident that more restrictions had to be placed on selling activities of businesses. Such activities may persuade consumers to purchase articles that are harmful, dangerous, or worthless. Without specific provisions to protect consumers, the only business practices stopped under antitrust legislation were those that injured competitors and a substantial part of public interest. For instance, under antitrust laws, a retailer could not be stopped from misleading customers by copying a competitor's store name, nor could a company be stopped from selling a worthless weight-reducing medicine.

Before legislation to protect consumers from sellers was passed, consumers were given some protection. They could get out of a contract signed because they were tricked by false claims, because goods did not perform as represented, or because the seller had not revealed to them known defects of the product. However, this protection was only afforded if a consumer was harmed, could prove harm, and was willing to bear the cost of bringing the court suit.

Consumer protection legislation, summarized in Table 3-6, has brought increased restriction of business activity. The specific impacts of major consumer legislation, discussed in Chapter Nine, have been on products, advertisements, and packages. Products harmful to health, such as soft drinks containing cyclamates, cannot be sold. Furthermore, advertisements promising untrue benefits, such as an improved sex life, have been stopped. Package regulations now require disclosure of contents and the size of one serving of the product.

Miscellaneous Governmental Regulations

The regulation of business by government covers a wider area than that covered in the preceding discussion. Government regulates business through patent laws by restricting use of inventions for seventeen years to those who patent them. Trademarks are also regulated by a law, the Lanham Act (1946).

Table 3-6. *Legislation Protecting Consumers*

Law	Year Passed	Description of Content
Pure Food and Drug Act	1906	Forbids adulteration and misbranding of foods and drugs sold in interstate commerce.
Meat Inspection Act	1907	Requires that meat be inspected and approved before it can be offered for sale.
Wheeler–Lea Act	1938	Amends Clayton Act to prevent unfair acts or practices.
Wool Products Labeling Act	1939	Requires executives who regularly make loans to content proportions for new, reprocessed, and reused wool.
Fair Packaging and Labeling Act	1966	Provides for establishment of rules on package disclosure regarding product identification, quantity of contents, and weight.
National Traffic and Motor Vehicle Safety Act	1966	Directs establishment of safety features and standards for new motor vehicles and tires.
Consumer Credit Protection Act	1968	Requires executives who regularly make loans to consumers to disclose the actual cost of credit in writing before giving credit to consumers.
Public Health Cigarette Smoking Act	1971	Prohibits the advertising of cigarettes on radio and television.

Trademark protection is given to registered names, symbols, and marks. Another area of recent regulation has been instituted by establishment of the **National Commission on Public Safety**. Because of this commission, new safety features are required on lawnmowers, color television sets, bicycles, and toys. Federal legislation prohibiting the manufacture and sale of fireworks is also in the not-too-distant future of business.

Much of existing legislation mainly affects certain industries. Because of their nature, public utilities that provide necessities to the public (transportation companies and common carriers of messages transmitted by wire and wireless) have been carefully regulated. In most cases, the government has decided that these businesses operate most satisfactorily if there is no competition from other businesses. If two water companies try to serve the same community, inefficient use of resources may result, especially since a huge outlay of money is needed to provide the necessary services. To cover this cost, a very large volume of sales is needed if selling prices are to be reasonable. Therefore, the government only allows one company to operate in the community.

The resultant monopolies that have been created in the utility, transportation, and communication industries are strictly regulated by law and administrative agencies. The Federal Power Commission, for example, regulates the transmission of natural gas. The rates and method of operation of transportation carriers are regulated by the Interstate Commerce Commission. The rates of telephone and telegraph companies are regulated by the Federal Communications Commission.

Many other laws regulate firms selling only to the U.S. government. These laws are discussed as part of government's buyer role.

THE BUYER ROLE

The government also affects business in its role as a buyer. More than 78,000 governmental units buy goods and services accounting for about one-third of the total value of goods and services produced in the United States. In 1970 government units paid $332.98 billion to American companies for their goods and services.

Government purchases cover a wide range of goods and services. A selection of goods purchased for the military services by the federal Defense Supply Agency is shown in Table 3-7. This agency uses a staff of over 50,000 workers to buy more than $3 billion worth of goods and services.

These purchases are important to many businesses. For instance, in 1963 Lockheed Aircraft Corporation depended on government purchases for three-fourths of its total sales. General Electric Company received 18% of its total

Table 3-7. *Some Defense Supply Agency Commodities*

> Meat
> Fruits
> Coffee
> Sugar
> Air conditioning equipment
> Laundry and dry cleaning equipment
> Industrial sewing machines
> Insecticides
> Kitchen equipment and appliances
> Drums and cans

revenue from government contracts. The size of purchases of military goods from selected other companies are shown in Table 3-8.

The government market provides problems as well as opportunities to many businesses. Potential sellers must be aware of differences in government markets compared to other potential customers. The differences concern:

1. Size of purchases.
2. Initiative by buyer.
3. Method of purchase.
4. Number of people who influence the buying decision.
5. Legal requirements for doing business.

Size

The number of units of goods or services purchased by the government generally exceeds the order sizes of any other buyer. One governmental order for typewriters may exceed $500,000. In some cases, the government may be the sole buyer of the product offered by the seller. Generally, government is the only buyer of bridges, roads, and aircraft carriers.

However, sellers captive to the government must be aware that the government need for goods can disappear quickly. The effect on a business may

Table 3-8. *Government Purchases From Selected Firms (in Millions)*

Company	Amount
American Telephone and Telegraph Company	$635.6
General Tire and Rubber Company	364.4
International Business Machines Corporation	332.4
General Motors Corporation	255.8
Ford Motor Company	211.2

be very damaging. For example, cancellation of government support of the supersonic transport aircraft was a disastrous blow to the sales of the Boeing Corporation and the economy of Seattle, Washington.

Initiative by Buyers

Sellers to government do not have to depend solely on their own resources to find out how to sell to government. Most government purchasing agencies go to great lengths to find sellers and inform them on how to do business with them. Examples of helpful government publications are "Selling to the Military," published by Department of Defense, and "Selling to NASA," published by National Aeronautics and Space Administration.

Methods of Purchase

The government purchases goods and services in two ways:
1. Bidding.
2. Negotiation.

Bidding Procedures

A bidding procedure is required by governmental buyers for many types of purchases. In a bidding procedure, several businesses are invited to offer a price, or a *bid*, for the required goods or service. When all bids are received, the bid offering the lowest price to the government is accepted unless the government does not feel the bidder can deliver the required goods. Although the bidding process insures sellers equal opportunities to deal with the government, it also can prove detrimental. Information about a business and its technology, disclosed to meet bid requirements, may be leaked to competitors.

Negotiation

Bids are not used for all governmental purchases. It may be necessary for the government to work with a seller to decide what the government actually needs. This process of defining specifications and arriving at an acceptable price is called *negotiation*. This method is frequently used when one-of-a-kind products, such as moon rockets, are purchased.

Number of People

The government purchasing decision involves many people because forces involved in the political process influence what is bought. It would be impossible to detail all the influences behind the decision to build a new city hall. Some of the influences may even be kept hidden. However, it is essential that businesses try to understand these influences so that changes in government demand can be expected.

Legal Requirements

Legal restrictions on sellers to government include (1) requirement of forms needed to be completed by the seller and (2) requirements that the seller pay his workers minimum wages. A seller also has to try to use small business to supply his needs, or use only American-made goods. These and other requirements are summarized in Table 3-9. Despite these challenges and potential problems, more businesses try to sell to the government each year. It can be a worthwhile market.

Table 3-9. *Selected Federal Requirements for Government Contractors*

REQUIREMENT	AUTHORITY
Pay prevailing minimum wages.	Davis–Bacon, Walsh–Healey, and Service Contract Acts
Report job openings to state employment agencies to aid job-hunting veterans.	Executive Order 11598
Refrain from discrimination in hiring because of race, religion, sex, national origin, or age.	Executive Orders 11246, 11375, and 11141
Provide performance bonds for payment of wages in certain circumstances.	Miller Act
Provide "safe and sanitary" working conditions.	Service Contract, Contract Work Hours and Safety Standards, and Occupational Safety and Health Acts
Refrain from contracting with companies convicted of criminal violations of the Clean Air Act.	Clean Air Act
Refrain from buying from certain communist-controlled areas.	Armed Forces Procurement Regulations
Certify they comply with wage and price controls.	Economic Stabilization Act

Source: *Business Week*, February 5, 1972, p. 46.

THE DISPENSER OF FUNDS, GOODS, AND SERVICES ROLE

Government provides a multitude of funds, goods, and services to its public. The provision of these goods and services helps businesses in many ways.

The cost of acquiring funds and producing goods of American business has been reduced by subsidy programs of government. Subsidies, generally the giving of money, goods, or services to businesses, have greatly helped certain types of businesses. These subsidies have taken the form of free land (over 180 million acres to railroads), funds to build facilities ($59 million to build airports and runways in 1968), and available money (guaranteed home mortgages or investment in ship companies). Moreover, the government has purchased unneeded goods (stockpiles of zinc and lead) or higher-priced American-produced goods or services (move government mail in American-built and -operated ships) in order to help business sell those goods and services for which there is no market.

Funds

Governmental activities directly related to the availability of funds include (1) the Rural Electrification Administration, which makes loans to finance the construction and operation of electric lines by rural electrification cooperatives, and (2) the Small Business Administration, which lends money or guarantees loans to meet the capital needs of small businesses. Without the backing of the Small Business Administration, the initiation and continued operation of small businesses would be seriously hampered.

Goods and Services

The buying activity of business is made easier because the government provides many things that are needed by business. Government-provided police, fire protection, garbage service, and hospitals relieve business from involved purchasing procedures for these services, even though they are paying for them through taxes and other payments to government. Information collected and analyzed by the government is provided by many agencies, such as the Department of Commerce. This information includes age and education characteristics of the population, most valuable to businesses.

Government-dispensed goods and services may also help businesses in their buying activity by providing a better quality of goods and services than would otherwise exist. The provision of education for children and the training of certain types of workers has provided more and better human power than would otherwise exist. Extensive federal aid has been legislated for technical and scientific education (for example, National Defense Education Act of 1958), occupational training for the unemployed (for example, Manpower and Development and Training Act of 1962), and greater utilization of vocational programs in public schools (for example, Vocational Education Acts of 1962 and 1963). Moreover, security programs provided for workers by government helps make workers more productive and relieves business from bearing the total cost of such programs.

Other government-provided services such as electricity from government-owned power plants, as found in the Tennessee Valley, would probably have not been provided without government intervention due to the high costs and risks attendant on such projects. Many transportation facilities depend on governmental support for their present availability and price. The Alaska Railroad, the Panama Canal, and interstate highway systems have been built and are maintained by the government. For example, the Port of New York Authority, a government agency, owns and operates six bridges and tunnels, six ship terminals, two truck terminals, two bus terminals, and a $270 million world trade center in lower Manhattan.

Business has been helped in its buying activities by government sale of goods for less than they are worth. Provision of goods at a low price helps a business keep its costs low and enables it to compete with other businesses, especially those operating in foreign countries. Examples of government sales include the sale of $15 billion of government property for $4 billion after World War II, the sale of planes for less than the cost of gas in their tanks, and the disposal of machinery at the price of junk.

Producing activities of business are made easier by the various government supported services and goods. Water systems owned and operated by local governments are definitely a plus for producing activities that require clean water. Agriculture in many areas is dependent on the irrigation waters provided by government-owned river development projects such as those along the Columbia and Missouri Rivers.

Government dispensing of goods and services sometimes affects selling activities of businesses by competing with them. However, very few of the services or goods provided by the government are also provided by private businesses in the same markets. For example, the U.S. government is the only seller of postal services, energy in the Tennessee Valley, and electricity in rural areas. In fact, government has entered into many of these areas only after private business interest in such projects was found to be wanting. In other cases, when the same goods and services are produced by government and business, they may be sold in separate markets. For example, public housing is restricted to tenants who cannot afford to pay commercial rentals, and public loans are provided only to borrowers who cannot obtain credit from private lenders.

THE SETTER OF POLICY ROLE

Government influences American business in many ways other than through its regulator, buyer, and dispenser roles. It also affects business ability to operate in the American economy. It sets policies that affect the amount of money available to all people and the general level of prices in the economy.

Recent expansion of credit buying would have been much slower without the existence of the **Federal Reserve Banking System**, established in 1913. This system has the power to increase or decrease the supply of money and credit in the economy. Through its actions (called monetary policy), banks are told how much of their deposits they can lend, how many government securities they can buy or sell, and what interest rate member banks must pay for borrowed money. An example of how the Federal Reserve may act to reduce the supply of money is presented in Figure 3-4.

Another governmental agency that helps business by improving the ability of banks to lend money is the Federal Deposit Insurance Corporation (FDIC). The FDIC protects bank depositors for up to $40,000 from loss of their money if the bank fails.

Because of these government acts backing the monetary system, cash and credit flows more freely than if such safeguards were not available. Fewer buyers would be present, funds for business use would be more restricted, and

Figure 3-4. *Federal Reserve Action to Decrease Money Supply*

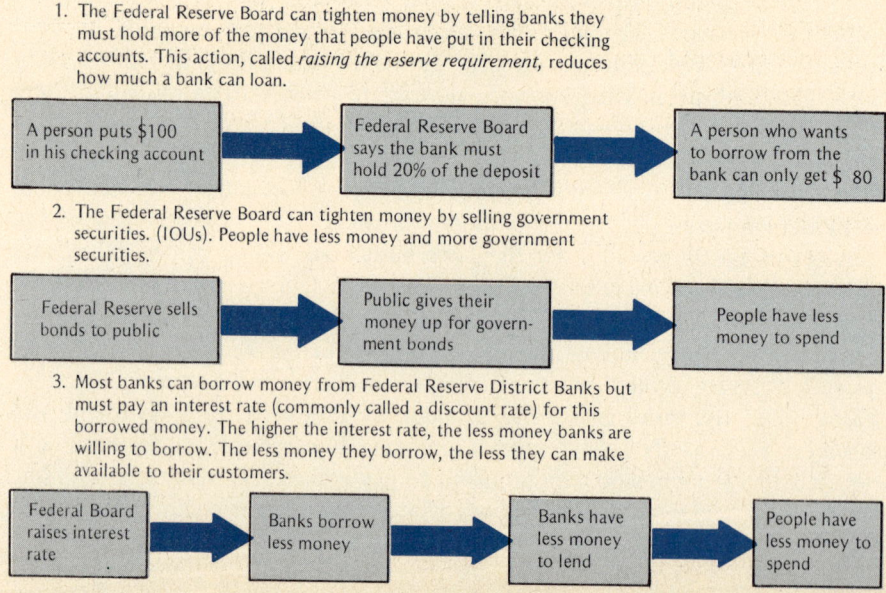

fewer potential suppliers would be in business, if there were no governmental support of monetary policy.

Another policy-setting influence on business has been felt through the actions of the President of the United States in the form of executive orders to carry out his decisions.

In matters related to economic matters and employment in the United States, another governmental body, the Council of Economic Advisors, may influence business. The Council was created by the Employment Act of 1946 and consists of three members appointed by the president with the approval of the U.S. Senate. This Council advises the president. Action by former President Nixon to freeze wages and prices in the United States is partially an outcome of such advice. These **wage and price controls** started with a 90-day freeze on all wages and prices in November 1971. This initial action and the subsequent wage and price controls instituted during 1972 and 1973 have not appeared to eliminate the inflationary trend in the United States. However, they have firmly established the right of government to control wages and prices directly during peace time if other governmental action which affects the supply of money in the economy does not stop inflation. These other actions include governmental taxation and expenditure activities (commonly called *fiscal policies*) and the activities of the Federal Reserve Board (*monetary policies*).

GOVERNMENT CAREERS

One of every six persons employed in the United States in 1970 worked for some governmental unit. Although college students may consider federal government employment more desirable than state or local, over three-fourths of the 12.6 million government workers work for state and local governments. Moreover, state and local government employment is expected to increase by more than 60% in the decade ahead, while the projected federal employment rate of increase is less than 20%.

Regardless of which level is considered, government is definitely an alternative to be considered when planning your future career. The federal government alone annually hires about 25,000 recent college graduates.

Nature of Jobs

Governmental employment opportunities are in the same areas as those in private business. The government needs managers, marketers, accountants, economists, and many other types of professionals, including lawyers and engineers. Overall, the government workforce is more professionally oriented

Figure 3-5. *Major Areas of Government Employment*

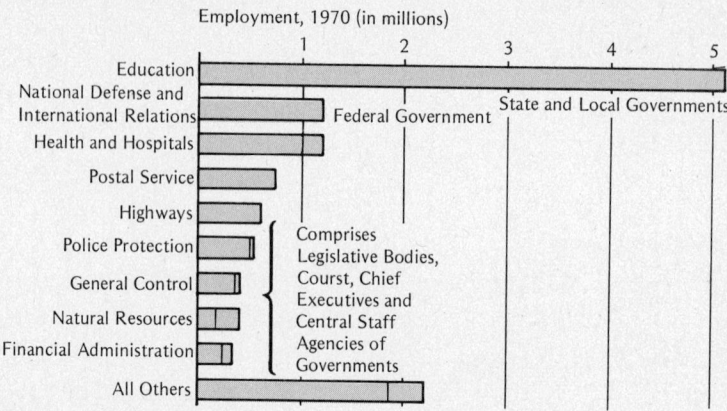

Source: Bureau of the Census

than private industry. Two-thirds is "white-collar," while less than one-half of the nongovernment workforce consists of "white-collar" occupations.

The major area of government employment, especially at the state and local level, is education; two-fifths of all government workers were so employed in 1970. Although this area clearly surpasses the others shown in Figure 3-5, its future growth rate does not appear so promising as the health, welfare, and related services areas. Government jobs are similar in many respects to jobs in business. However, they tend to differ in that the titles are different and jobs are with departments or agencies.

Governmental jobs in which a college graduate may be interested are many, and their discussion is beyond the scope of this text. However, job titles requiring a college degree in business administration are listed in Table 3-10. Further information can be found in the *Federal Career Directory, 1973: A Guide for College Students*, published by the United States Civil Service Commission, or by contacting appropriate state or local governmental units.

Required Background

Until recently, government has not emphasized college preparation in its recruitment of administrative personnel. Increased recognition of the benefits of hiring professionally-trained people has brought strong efforts to recruit college graduates. Many governmental units are visiting college campuses as well as advertising their jobs.

Government jobs in administrative and managerial positions usually do not require knowledge of a specialized field. However, applicants must indicate by graduation from college or by responsible job experience that they have

Table 3-10. *Titles of Federal Government Jobs Most Appropriate to the Business Student*

Administrative Assistant	Quality Assurance Specialist
Agricultural Commodities Inspector	Realty Specialist
Agricultural Marketing Specialist	Revenue Officer
Alcohol and Tobacco Tax Inspector	Statistician
Budget Analyst	Supply Management Specialist
Contract Negotiator	Tax Law Specialist
Financial Institution Examiner	Traffic Manager and
Industrial Relations Specialist	Traffic Management Specialist
Industrial Specialist	
Investigator (General)	
Loan Specialist	
Personnel Management Specialist	
Printing and Publications Officer	
Public Health Program Specialist	

potential for future development. For these general types of jobs, college courses in economics, political science, and statistics should be included in the curriculum. Government also needs specialists majoring in accounting, finance, marketing, industrial relations, and personnel administration.

Another requirement of most government jobs is successful completion of an examination. These examinations are given by the U.S. Civil Service Commission or state and local agencies. Regional Civil Service Offices are located throughout the United States. They provide information about requirements of federal jobs and conduct the appropriate examinations. Scores in such examinations, as well as training and experience, are used to make a list of those eligible for federal government jobs.

Reward System

Upgrading of pay scales by government has improved starting salaries offered by government to college graduates. The monthly salaries offered in 1973 to college graduates averaged $752 and $709 for federal and state (or local) governments, respectively. However, these rates are still not comparable to the $830 average monthly salary offered by business and industry.

When evaluating governmental positions, job features other than salary must also be considered. The civil service system has generally ensured government workers chances of promotion and new job opportunities as well as job security. Many government workers have found the pace less hectic and the working conditions more congenial than in private industry. These added benefits can make a government job quite attractive. Finally, the personal fulfillment of contributing to effective government proves important to many who are disconcerted with the present situation of government.

CHAPTER SUMMARY

Government influences the business activities of acquiring money, buying, producing, and selling. This is done by regulating, buying, dispensing, and setting national policy.

Government regulation, consisting of taxes and laws, influences the amount of money available to business and the conditions under which business can borrow money and sell stock. Taxes and laws also influence from whom business can buy and whether facilities will be bought or leased. Government regulation also influences business location of production facilities, dealings with labor, and production discharges that pollute the environment. The selling activity of business is affected by government taxes resulting in less consumer buying power or by laws requiring truthful advertisements.

Government buying provides a substantial market for business. However, because federal requirements are often very specific, businesses should investigate this market thoroughly before they try to enter it.

Government has dispensed many funds, goods and services to businesses through loans, subsidies, reduced-price sales, and operation of utilities and training programs. Frequently, business cost and necessary operations have been reduced by government dispensing.

Policy-setting activities of the government include setting the level of interest rates and prices of goods and services. These activities affect all businesses because the interest rate and general level of prices dictate the cost of goods bought by a firm. They also determine the amount of money consumers have to spend for the goods and services of business.

The government offers many employment opportunities in business-related areas. A college degree is valuable for the potential government employee. The rewards of government employment are job security, congenial working conditions, and personal contribution to effective government.

PROVOCATIVE STATEMENT

The Government Regulates Too Many Business Activities

1 "Although in America we have what is described as a free-enterprise economy, our government today regulates more business practices than most other democracies. Listen to the roll call: the utilities which produce heat, light, and power; railroads . . . , trucking companies, airlines, broadcasters, drug firms, dry cleaners, auto manufacturers, meat packers, film makers, farmers, brokers, banks, and a host of other enterprises. Most of these industries are highly competitive, but government has decided that they must serve a variety of objectives other than selling their products at the lowest price.

"... Whether it is whale oil, baby chicks, or energy, control by a bureaucracy is no match for the free market in the allocation of human and material resources for the good of everybody."

Chairman, Citicorp.
Walter B. Wriston
speech delivered before
the Economic Club of Detroit,
February 25, 1974.

PROVOCATIVE STATEMENT

*Business Executives Can Break Laws
as Long as They Do Not Get Caught*

2 "I was talking to an American businessman shortly after the electric industry antitrust suit. He told me that his industry and all other industries fixed prices just as the electrical manufacturing companies did but that, 'we are smarter than they; they were stupid to let themselves get caught. There's nothing wrong in that; it's only laws and regulations.' "

Japanese Executive
Raymond Baumhart,
An Honest Profit,
New York: Holt, Rinehart, and Winston, 1968,
p. 149.

REVIEW QUESTIONS

1. How do federal taxes affect each of the four major business activities?
2. How do state and local taxes differ from federal taxes?
3. What is the major purpose of each of the following types of legislation?
   a. Labor laws.
   b. Environmental protection laws.
   c. Antitrust laws.
   d. Consumer protection laws.
4. What special problems does business face in dealing in the government market?
5. How does government help business by dispensing funds, goods, and services?
6. What can the federal government do to regulate the expansion and contraction of business activity?
7. What are the advantages of working for the government?

Chapter Outline

Public Demands from Business
    Stockholders
    Creditors
    Employees
    Unions
    Government
    Competitors
    Suppliers and Distributors
    Consumers
    General Public

Perspective on Business Responsibilities in the United States
    Late 1800s
    Early 1900s
    1930s to 1950s
    1960s to 1970s

Problems with Social Response
    Profitable Public Demands
        Measurements of Benefits
        Costs of Social Responsibility
    Selection of Most Crucial Societal Problems
    Choice of Action

Resolution of Problems
    Unprofitable Demands
    Hard-to-Measure Benefits
        Society
        Business
    Competitive Disadvantage
    How to Act

Impact of New Responsibilities on Careers
    Changed Nature of Jobs
    Creation of New Jobs
    The Job of Coordinating Business Efforts

Chapter Summary

Provocative Statement 1:
    Social Responsibility Is Only Good if It Pays

Provocative Statement 2:
    Business Should Be Taxed for Pollution

Key Terms

Public forces
Stockholders
Creditors
Employees
Unions
Government
Suppliers
Distributors
Consumers
General public
Puritan ethic
Social responsibility
Cost of business social responsibility
Social indicators
Department of Social Affairs
Social audit

Business and Society

"To conduct a business is not enough; it must also be a business which does not pollute, which is compassionate as well as competitive, which not only performs but explains and justifies its performance, which is doing things for people, involves people."
—Chairman, CPC International

Every day business is faced with demands of society. Stockholders want more profits, employees demand higher wages, unions strike for longer paid vacations, and governmental agencies demand less sulfur emissions from factories. Other groups of society, such as competitors, suppliers, and consumers, are also asking business for action on various matters. This chapter considers the demands of nine different groups—business's *publics*.

A perspective is given on how these demands have changed over the life of businesses in the United States. Major problems, such as conflicts of interest and high costs encountered when business tries to satisfy its responsibilities to its publics, are discussed. The methods used by firms to resolve these problems of serving the demands of the public are reviewed. Discussion of the effect of the recent expansion in demands of society on business careers concludes the chapter.

PUBLIC DEMANDS FROM BUSINESS

The nine major public forces that face the modern business executive are shown in Figure 4-1. They are:

Creditors	Government	Stockholders or owners
Employees	Competitors	Suppliers and distributors
Unions	General public	Customers or consumers

78　The Environment of Business

Figure 4-1. Public Demands on Business

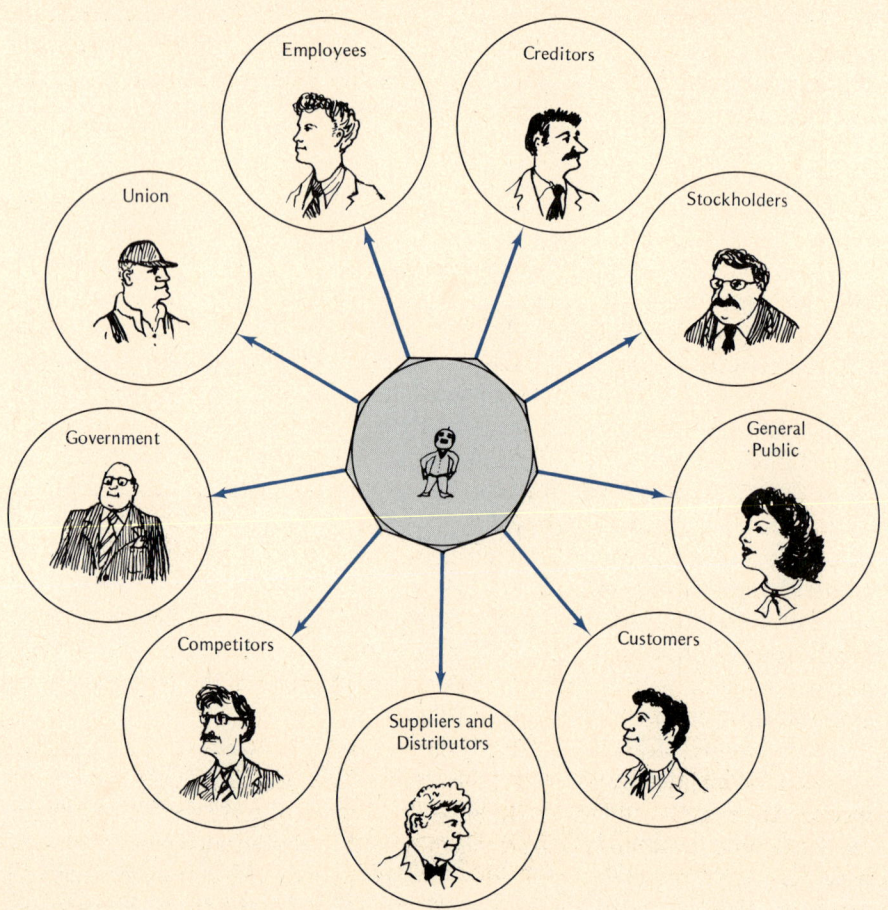

Stockholders

Stockholders or owners have been the first public that businesses have listened to in the past. It is easy to understand why this public has such a strong influence on business. Business would die a very quick death if owners withdrew their money. Few businesses, if any, can continue to exist without external funds.

Generally, stockholders charge business with wise use of their invested funds. This responsibility can be best served if the business makes maximum profits and distributes some of the profits to the owners in the form of dividends. The histories of businesses in the United States show many cases of stockholders forcing changes in the management of the business to help improve the profits of the business.

Creditors

Creditors are those who lend money to business. Banks and other creditors expect businesses to pay their debts when due. In addition, interest payments are required of businesses. Creditors can demand prompt payment. They can force the business to sell its assets if necessary.

Employees

Recent developments in employee demands have placed more responsibility on business. Today, employees are demanding more than just higher wages—a demand initiated by the first labor unions. Employee concern has also centered on the creation of more jobs or, at least, no cutbacks in the existing number of jobs. Employees see the failure of business to keep employment high in today's economy as a violation of its obligation to them. More and more businesses are being informed that they must provide employment or some type of readjustment provision for workers who are laid off because of changes in technology or demand, or because of the shutdown of an entire plant. Most of the decisions that affect employment now require consultation with and approval of employees.

Employees are also demanding meaningful jobs to perform instead of highly specialized, insignificant jobs on an assembly line. This demand and others related to rules of work caused a recent strike at a General Motors assembly plant located in Lordstown, Ohio.

However, as suggested in Chapter Two, the actions of employees on their own behalf have not been successful in forcing business to make pay raises, to increase the number of jobs, to improve working conditions, to give employees fair treatment, or to make jobs more meaningful. Since individual employees have very little power to cause harm to business if it does not honor their demands, business traditionally has not heeded these demands. If a worker threatened to quit because business ignored specific demands, business considered itself lucky to be losing a potential troublemaker. Employee replacements were easily acquired as long as many workers were unemployed.

Unions

Another public of business, one which developed out of the failure of individual employees to accomplish their demands, is the labor union. This public demands and gets business to negotiate in good faith over the terms of the employment of workers. It also wants business to hold to the terms of the labor contract. Business refusal to bargain with unions is forbidden by law and discouraged by the use of strikes and other displays of worker power which harm business.

Government

The impact of the fourth public, government, has been discussed at length in Chapter Three. Government expects business to obey laws, to pay taxes, to withhold employee personal income and social security taxes, and to provide willingly information of many kinds.

Government rules and regulations frequently reflect the desires of other publics. The degree to which government presses the demands of any one public depends on the power of the group and its ability to lobby in Congress. Generally, most public interest groups have become increasingly aware of the importance of joining together to voice their wishes to government. The minor impact of the so-called "silent majority" substantiates the need to voice demands to governmental bodies.

Despite increased government legislation and funding of law enforcement agencies, many people feel that government should be even more active in ensuring that business satisfy all its publics. Slowness of government action and insufficient dollar support are sources of irritation to these critics. They feel that business practices that are potentially harmful to society should be stopped by government force, even if these practices have not been proven harmful beyond a reasonable doubt. They object to waiting until somebody has been injured or killed before action is taken.

Current expectations of government seem to extend beyond a simple adherence to laws. Government, increasingly, is looking to business for help in solving societal problems facing humanity. However, business may be unwilling to give this help because of previous government attacks on business. In addition, recent court decisions suggest that cooperative efforts of business and government may be subject to the antitrust laws.

Competitors

The competitors of a business also have expectations of how they think the business should act. These expectations basically follow a "live-and-let-live" philosophy. They expect the business to use fair trade practices and to refrain from acquiring market power through secret agreements with others, cutthroat pricing, or other unfair practices.

Suppliers and Distributors

Basically, suppliers of goods to businesses as well as firms that distribute goods produced by businesses expect fair dealings from the business. Suppliers expect businesses to pay for products on time and to be truthful about damage claims or similar requests for adjustments in products or price. They also expect businesses to give fair consideration to their offers of goods for sale and to select the goods of the supplier with the best offer. They do not expect free gifts and past favors to affect choice of the supplier.

Distributors expect to be told the truth about a product and its sales potential, to be charged a fair price, and to be given any relevant market information the business is aware of. They do not expect to be stuck with unsalable goods.

The expectations of suppliers and distributors, like other publics, may or may not be honored by business. Distributors and suppliers have varying degrees of success in obtaining the fair treatment they expect. If a supplier or distributor is the only one who can give a business the type of supplies needed or the contact with a desired market, then business will be obliged to live up to his expectations. Relatively small suppliers or distributors may have little or no success in getting fair treatment. However, small suppliers or distributors may deal with businesses dependent on them. They may restrict their dealings to small businesses, or they may merge with competitors to gain more power over business.

Consumers

Ultimately, a business must sell its goods to cover its costs and accomplish its goals. This fact will bring business into contact with a most important public—the **consumer**. Consumers desiring a product for the satisfaction of certain needs or wants expect business to satisfy their expectations. They demand that the goods satisfy their needs and are consistent with what the business promised in its advertising. Consumers do not expect dishonest weights and packages, unfulfilled promises, hidden charges, and worthless guarantees or warranties.

The consumer is also concerned about the safety of the products purchased. Laws, such as the Food and Drug Act and the Automobile Safety Act, have been enacted to ensure consumers that they may eat food products without becoming ill or may drive a car without having an accident caused by manufacturing defects.

Consumer expectations, expanding rapidly in modern society, have not always been met. Businesses have not always been concerned with giving consumers what they need and what they feel they have paid for—a safe product, at the desired time, in the desired quantity. Witness, for example, the inconvenience recently experienced by consumers of gasoline, electricity, meat, paper towels, and plastic products, because of apparent insufficient supplies of these products.

One major reason for the failure of consumers to get what they expect has been their attempt to address business individually. Business has generally been in the driver's seat because of its relatively large resources. In addition, it has the support of many consumers for a variety of reasons. They may be satisfied with business performance, or they may see no alternative source of supply of the goods they desire. Too, they may fear that attempts to change the business will result in a business that retaliates by providing fewer consumer services or poorer quality goods for higher prices.

There are also many cases where consumers receive less than they expect because they are unwilling to pay the costs necessary to meet these expectations. Frequently, consumers do not realize how expensive it is for business to supply desired goods and services.

Another cause of disparity between consumer expectations and satisfaction is that advertisements have created too high a level of expectation. Advertising designed by businesses to differentiate their product from that of competitors may lead consumers to believe that business can produce a perfectly safe, indestructible, eye-appealing product at a "next-to-nothing" cost. Consumer expectations may also be high because of technological advancements that make the impossible of yesterday the possible and commonplace of today. The byline of a recent commercial—"If they can put a man on the moon, why can't they make a decaffeinated, freeze-dried coffee"—suggests the impact of technological advancements in one type of product on consumer expectations for all products.

General Public

The **general public** includes all other forces in the society other than the first eight groups discussed. The general public of a business consists of an ever-changing conglomerate of interests and people. A summary of modern demands of the general public presented in Table 4-1 shows the wide range of topics and actions covered.

"Sir, here are a few thoughts that have bubbled up from the people."
Drawing by D. Fradon; © 1975 The New Yorker Magazine, Inc.

Table 4-1. *Specific Demands of the Modern Public*

1. Government should own the largest corporations.
2. The size of huge corporations should be cut.
3. The federal government should charter corporations.
4. A proportion of the directors of a corporation should be elected publicly.
5. Directors should represent specific groups—labor, consumers, environmentalists, and ethnic or racial groups.
6. Business employees who divulge information about corporate activities harmful to society should be protected.
7. The president and other officers of business should be personally accountable for public offenses, such as pollution.
8. Companies should be prohibited from advertising if they are convicted of fraudulent advertising.
9. Businesses should be required to establish a complaint-handling procedure.
10. A business should be declared bankrupt if the costs of its activities to society exceed its benefits.
11. Tax returns of businesses should be open to the public.
12. Businesses should be required to clean up the environment.
13. Businesses should be required to recruit, hire, train, and promote the hard-core unemployed and members of minority groups.
14. Businesses should be required to participate in solving urban problems of unemployment, race relations, education, and housing.
15. Minority groups should be helped to develop their own firms.
16. Business contributions of money and manpower to community improvement efforts, hospitals, charity drives, and education should be increased.

Source: Council on Trends and Perspective, *The Corporation in Transition—Redefining Its Social Charter*, Chamber of Commerce of the United States, Washington, D.C., 1973, pp. 18–20.

People move into and out of the general public as they also participate as members of other publics. Moreover, a person may be the member of several or all publics of a business simultaneously. It is not unusual for an employee of a company to consume the product produced by the firm. Too, a government employee may use government and business services or goods and also own some interest in a business. Moreover, the publics really overlap when different businesses are considered. A stockholder in one business may buy from another, supply another, and work for yet another. As a result of this overlap of publics, the expectations of the publics become confused. It is nearly impossible to decide who is being represented when a person or group voices demands on business. If a union president says, "Business must produce better products," is this an expectation of consumers, unions, employees, government, stockholders, or the general public?

It is important for business to determine which public is being represented because different publics are accorded different priorities by business. Unions, stockholders, customers, and governments have been shown willing and able to press their demands in the past. Business must determine the implications of failure to meet the expectations of any public. Otherwise, publics that are most able to stop business from operating in society may be ignored by business and motivated to retaliate.

Today, the general public expects business to make both a societal and an economic contribution. It expects business not to pollute the environment —the water with discharges of sewage, oil, phosphates, and other chemicals; the air with sulfur dioxide, nitrogen oxides, carbon monoxide and exhausts from fumes of production processes and gasoline powered engines; the air waves with high levels of noise from factories, motor vehicles, aircrafts, construction equipment, or entertainment.

Business is also being held accountable for the creation of solid wastes through the use of packages that will not decompose, through the production of defective products that must be junked, or through the sale of products that are not easily recyclable into new products.

Business must share with consumers the responsibility for discarding beer cans along highways, abandoning broken-down automobiles on city streets, and throwing empty cellophane packages in waterways. Society expects business to produce decomposable packages, and to educate consumers on proper disposal or recycling of packages or junked products. Business must help to develop solutions for the problems of disposal of solid wastes without creating eyesores or stenches, causing death to wildlife, or endangering the environment.

Business is also expected to make efficient use of resources and not to deplete these resources without replacement. The wanton stripping of trees, minerals, and animals from the land is no longer tolerated by society.

The general public expects business to employ racial minorities by seeking out these people and training them, if necessary. This implies that business must go beyond simple lack of discrimination in hiring. Not only should the person with the best ability and skills be selected for the job. Indeed, those who are turned down must be helped to find employment so society does not have these unemployed persons destroying life, liberty, or property or requiring huge expenditures for policing efforts. Moreover, the general public expects the economically blighted areas of cities to be restored to clean, safe, healthful, pleasant places to live. This restoration entails business commitment of human power and money to these areas.

PERSPECTIVE ON BUSINESS RESPONSIBILITIES IN THE UNITED STATES

Public expectations have not always been so great. Before World War II, these expectations were few or, at least, the concern of business with these expectations centered on only a few issues. Furthermore, most publics had no power to press business into action.

Late 1800s

During the late 1800s, business was expected to hire workers, to produce a low-priced quantity of goods, to pay taxes, and, most importantly, to earn the maximum profit for the owner of the business. Based on the puritan ethic of the time, hard-working business managers were entitled to the profits they could earn. It was considered unethical for any with the abilities to earn profits not to use these abilities to their fullest. This philosophy dictated that workers receive no more than a fair day's pay for a fair day's work. Generally, the problems of society, which were unrelated to the economics of the business, were considered to be the burden of those people who were "too lazy" to do anything about their lack of education, their unemployment, or their poor housing. It was felt that the Good Lord helped those who helped themselves.

People assumed that the desire of business to make profits would lead to the most efficient provision of the types of goods wanted by consumers. The "invisible hand" of the marketplace was expected to keep businesses in check by making it unprofitable to charge consumers excessive prices or to offer goods they did not want. Presumably, consumers would refuse to buy overpriced, undesired, or worthless goods. As long as all the competition was workable, the marketplace operated reasonably well to satisfy consumers and to use resources efficiently.

However, the early trusts and other types of monopolies in railroads, steel, and other vital products soon jammed the market mechanism. These businesses acquired power by being the only source of a product. Thus, they could charge customers any price because the customers had no other source of supply. Early railroad companies bled the farmers of the Midwest with high freight rates for movement of agricultural commodities and livestock because they were the only reasonable source of transportation. These powerful businesses, under the direction of a group of men called "robber barons," pursued their objective of maximum profits without any checks from competitors or any other publics. People who tried to restrain them were overwhelmed by their power. Their ability to withstand public pressure was epitomized by one of the robber barons, William Vanderbilt, when he said, "Let the public be damned."

Early 1900s

The Sherman Act (1890) challenged businesses that completely ignored any social responsibility and that embraced the philosophy that "what is good for business is good for the public." This and later antitrust legislation showed public commitment to making businesses competitive. Government and society were starting to question the effect of some of the practices of the business giants of the times.

Business responsibility in the early 1900s soon included obedience to government laws regulating competition. However, business quickly set about finding loopholes to the laws and other ways to earn more and more profits through use of any legal means. Business responsibility to workers was only to employ workers and to pay them fairly for their output. Any methods that could be found to make each worker more productive were pursued by business and generally approved by society as a larger quantity of goods was made available. It was not considered within the province of business responsibility to worry about or to care for any unemployed workers nor to eliminate all safety hazards of the job. Furthermore, public policy did not demand that business take an active interest in community affairs or concern itself with pollution or other social questions.

1930s to 1950s

The rise of unions and government support of them during the 1930s brought new pressures on business. It could no longer ignore the needs and desires of its employees. Failure to satisfy their expectations was greeted with government suits or worker strikes.

Nevertheless, during this period business continued to have a limited view of responsibility to its public. Government expectations merely concerned obeying laws; unions were mainly concerned with improved economic benefits; consumers were concerned primarily with low-priced goods; competitors, distributors, and suppliers expected only the type of treatment required by law.

Although some business managers started recognizing the need to satisfy all publics, and especially the general public, before the 1950s, most felt that the responsibility to help with societal problems was of secondary importance. Profit maximization was still the primary concern. The total importance of profits and of production of a large quantity of goods and services is reflected in a statement by the president of United States Steel to a governmental committee in 1950:

> Only by making a profit can we provide work and security for our employees, protect our investors, and do our part in producing the steel upon which 150 million Americans depend in one way or another throughout their entire life.[1]

1960s to 1970s

A drastic turn of events in the sixties brought new demands on business and has resulted in the modern-day concept of business responsibility to its

---

[1] *Business . . . Big and Small Built America: Statements by Officials of United States Steel Corporation,* U.S. Steel Corp., New York, 1950, p. 7.

publics. The violent eruption of racial problems in this period brought public recognition that action was needed to cope with the causes of these problems. Furthermore, as students demonstrated against businesses contributing to the war effort and consumers boycotted and picketed retail stores, it became clear that business pursuit of profits had not resulted in all conditions desired by society.

Finally, the public became alarmed about ecology. Shortages of natural resources were resulting from previous misuse of resources by business. Oil spills were killing wildlife. Lakes and streams were too polluted to swim or fish in. Air pollution caused by automobiles and industry was endangering health and the existence of life itself. The public was jolted into realizing that many enduring problems had been created by business concern with the reaping of the maximum profit in the short run.

Many members of the public started to push government and business for action. It seemed only natural that business, which had proved able to meet previous demands of its public, would be the logical party to save the public and all of society. In addition, the recognized power of business made it appear able to cope with the problems at hand.

The major addition to business responsibility has been in three areas—the training and employment of minorities, the solution of pollution problems, and protection of consumers from unsafe products and fraudulent claims.

The rising standard of living in the sixties and seventies has resulted in satisfaction of basic economic needs. Now, many Americans have begun to focus their attention on societal needs. Societal problems that business created in an effort to produce a quantity of low-priced goods are coming back to haunt it.

PROBLEMS WITH SOCIAL RESPONSE

Business executives have become increasingly aware of the demands being voiced by all factions of society. Their reactions to these demands cover a wide range.

Some business executives now see business management "as trustees for all who have an interest in the enterprise... the stockholders, employees, suppliers, consumers and the public."[2] Others continue to think that the business of business "is making money, not making sweet music" and that government should be the sole resolver of societal problems.[3] Others profess concern with

---

[2] Donald S. McNaughton, Chairman, Prudential Insurance Company, in an address on October 10, 1971, before the Conference on Corporate Social Responsibility of the Life Insurance Industry.

[3] Theodore Levitt, "The Dangers of Social Responsibility," *Harvard Business Review*, September–October 1958, p. 13.

societal problems and state in annual reports to stockholders that responsible efforts are being made by their firm, while simultaneously acting in a way that ignores government-required safety precautions. Still others see that current public anger over social problems must be placated but that the business of making profits will be pursued as soon as concern over these issues disappears.

The lack of agreement among businesses as to their role in solving social problems is highlighted by the results of a recent survey of 500 firms.

To the question of the role of business in solving social problems:

1. 50% said business should do more, although their firms were inactive.
2. 20% cited social-related projects their businesses were involved in.
3. 30% said business should not become involved in social problems.[4]

Why are businesses divided and confused on their responsibility to society? They do not seem to know if their responsibility to society is:

1. To satisfy laws.
2. To satisfy laws and well-recognized public expectations.
3. To satisfy laws, meet well-recognized public expectations, and prepare in advance for new social demands.
4. To serve as a leader in setting new performance standards in addition to satisfaction of present public expectations.[5]

The basic problems with public responsibility of business entail deciding what demands of the public should be satisfied and how the selected demands will be satisfied. The demands must be ranked in order of priority, as no firm has sufficient resources to satisfy them all. However, firms are not aware of all the demands of society because in the past information about societal wishes has been gathered in a haphazard manner. Only those who draw the attention of business by threatening private property have been recognized. Other members of society have been ignored or dismissed as "harmless cranks."

Profitable Public Demands

The most common basis employed by business in deciding whether or not to satisfy public demands is the expected profitability of serving the different demands. Several ventures, such as those carried out in providing low-cost public housing by International Basic Economic Corporation, have proven profitable. Unfortunately, not all social demands can be profitably satisfied if short-run returns to the company itself are considered.

---

[4] R. Joseph Monsen, "Social Responsibility and the Corporation," *Journal of Economic Issues*, March 1972, pp. 125–126.
[5] Council on Trends and Perspective, *The Corporation in Transition—Redefining Its Social Charter*, Chamber of Commerce of the United States, Washington, D.C., 1973, p. 14.

Frequently, programs to hire hard-core unemployed, to clean up the environment, or to provide safe products benefit society over a long period of time (beyond the normal 10-year planning span of most businesses), but do not help consumers in the short run. Consumers may not actually be willing to pay for this extra cost, although they say they are (see Table 4-2). In fact, consumer behavior is often motivated by self-interest rather than by societal interest. Examples of rejection of social values by consumers include the smuggling of phosphate detergents into counties (e.g., Dade County, Florida) where they are prohibited by law, the use of prohibited pesticides (DDT), and the disconnection of pollution control devices on automobiles. Thus, since all members of the public do not agree on what is important, determining business reaction is difficult.

Measurements of Benefits

Not only is socially responsible behavior more likely to benefit future members of society rather than present customers, but benefits are also hard to measure. We can measure quantity much better than we can an improvement

Table 4-2. *Will Consumers Pay?*

ARE YOU WILLING TO PAY 10 PERCENT MORE FOR:	WILLING TO PAY	PROBLEM NOT SERIOUS	UNDECIDED
Detergents if it turns out to be the only way to eliminate their pollution of water supplies?	69%	17%	13%
Gasoline if it turns out to be the only way to eliminate the pollution caused by automobile exhausts?	68	16	15
An automobile if it turns out to be the only way to eliminate the pollution caused by the exhausts?	67	17	17
Electricity if it turns out to be the only way to eliminate the pollution caused by power plants?	64	22	14
Magazines and newspapers if it turns out to be the only way to eliminate pollution caused by paper mills?	60	20	20
Airplane tickets if it turns out to be the only way to eliminate pollution caused by their exhausts?	59	18	22

Source: *The Roper Report* (October 1971), published by The Roper Organization, Inc., New York, N.Y. Reprinted by permission of The Roper Organization, Inc.

in quality of life. This fact becomes especially crucial when resources must be taken from producing more goods in order to accomplish less pollution or to provide training to hard-core unemployed. Without measurement of the improvement of worker satisfaction, worker development, or societal values, it is impossible to determine if such a trade-off between economic and social goods is indeed worthwhile.

Another problem with the benefit from socially responsible actions of a business is that competitors who do not expend any money may profit. The public may identify the improvement in society with all members of the industry and upgrade the image of all without regard to amount of expenditure of each. Similarly, preservation of resources is good for all businesses, not just those who spend money fulfilling their responsibilities.

Costs of Social Responsibility

It is generally easier to estimate the costs, rather than the benefits, of programs to satisfy societal demands because they are incurred in the short run. One survey showed the average cost per business of such programs exceeded $40,000 annually, with a range of $25,000 to $250,000. However, some costs of business's involvement in solving social problems may be hidden. Business involvement in training the hard-core unemployed may decrease the satisfaction of the workers who presently work for the business. Another hidden cost is that which society pays because business enforces its wishes on society through its socially responsible actions. For example, Michigan Bell Telephone Company recently adopted Northern High School in Detroit. The company placed its own instructors and equipment in the school in order to improve the quality of teaching. This program could cost society dearly; the students may be taught business trades only, with no humanities or arts. Some critics of business action that attempts to solve societal problems advise against the spread of business influence any further into the lives of Americans.

Selection of societal problems based on their potential for profit can definitely keep business out of many areas, such as crime prevention and control, drug abuse, education, environmental quality, housing, humanpower development, and minority enterprise.

Selection of Most Crucial Societal Problems

If the most pressing areas of society are considered—"the 20% that cause 80% of the problems"—then business may be directly on a collision course with the demands of owners because there may be no profit in satisfying the problems.

A decision by business to select the issues most crucial to society brings us back to the difficulty of measuring benefits to society and the lack of information about the demands of all members of the public. The problems become vast when a business decides to take on all of society's problems. Such an approach may reduce or nullify the efforts of business. Therefore, it must choose among them.

Choice of Action

Even after choosing the issues to be resolved, it is difficult for business to decide what action to take. Different members of the public demand different actions. Frequently, the specific action desired by the public may not be possible within the resources of the firm. Thus, a firm may take action and be as vehemently criticized for taking the wrong action as for no action at all. A recently published study on the DuPont Company by a Nader Study Group criticizes the company for giving a charitable contribution of $60,000 to an urban renewal organization run by DuPont executives. Company reaction to the criticism was one of confusion and frustration with a company spokesman commenting: "You're damned if you do and damned if you don't." [6]

Many types of actions necessary to solve societal problems are not possible, given the capabilities of the personnel or other resources of the firm. It may not have the technological know-how or sociological skills to solve pollution problems or to remedy the causes of hard-core unemployment. A given business may be capable of actions that deal only with symptoms but not the causes of the problems. For instance, a business may be able to offer jobs to unemployed minorities but not to train them in all skills necessary for them to keep their jobs. As a result, these efforts may result in few net additions to the workforce in the long run. Those who do not make it may become embittered and convinced that business is not sincere in its efforts. Public skepticism about business and, for that matter, all societal institutions is at an all-time high. Therefore, business efforts to resolve societal problems, which are motivated solely by business self-interest, will probably be seen for what they are and may cause more harm than good. Some established businesses still feel that if they do anything to solve societal problems, no matter what its cost or impact, the public should be in their debt. They simply do not realize that many people expect business to solve these problems. If they fail to do so, they have fallen short of public expectations.

RESOLUTION OF PROBLEMS

As indicated earlier, recent demands of the general public have left businesses confused because many of these demands may:

[6] *The Wall Street Journal*, January 20, 1972, p. 17.

1. Appear unprofitable.
2. Provide hard-to-quantify benefits.
3. Place a business at a competitive disadvantage.
4. Not state clearly what business action is necessary.

Despite these uncertainties, many actions have been taken by business to try to satisfy these new public demands:[7]

1. Some businesses have lent top executives to minority businesses and governments to help them attack social problems. The salaries of those executives continue to be paid by the companies that employ the executives.

2. Quaker Oats, Inc., has required a city to pass a fair housing ordinance before it would locate a pet food plant there. It has also spearheaded drives for voter registration of youth.

3. Other firms, especially insurance companies, have placed their money in minority-owned financial institutions.

4. The president of American Airlines has formed a volunteer group of executives to clean up around corporate headquarters (located in New York City) and has assigned a company executive the job of use of company resources to improve the quality of life where American operates.

5. Wells Fargo Bank donates $0.25 of each $2 check order to an environmental group of the customer's choosing and prints all of its checks on a by-product of sugar cane stalks to save paper.

6. Standard Oil Company of Indiana has assigned a manager the title of Urban Affairs Director, has substantially increased its purchases from minority-owned businesses, and has recruited blacks to operate service stations.

Unprofitable Demands

Many suggestions have been offered as to how to solve the company dilemma of choosing which social needs to satisfy. Some people recommend that the goals of a business in today's society must be broadened beyond short-run profit maximization. Business must realize that failure to clean up the environment, to hire and train minorities, or to meet all demands of consumers will result in less profits in the future. This hard lesson has been learned in recent years by many businesses who have seen their factories deliberately burned down or their product, such as lettuce and grapes, boycotted.

Many people cite the need for business to adopt other goals in addition to profit. These goals include improvement of company image among the public, attraction of top notch personnel, and better worker morale. Recent efforts by Xerox Corporation, the United Bank of Denver, and others suggest that

---

[7] These examples of social action were taken from "Still Some More Examples of Corporate Leadership in a Changing Society," *Marketing and the Social Environment*, Leonard L. Berry and James S. Hensel, eds. New York: Mason and Lipscomb Publishers, 1973, pp. 353–364.

sponsorship of public service programs can provide beneficial results for the public image of the company. Top college graduates who have been disillusioned by the image of business must be attracted to management ranks. The loss of this talent is definitely a long-run cost that few businesses can afford. Improvement in worker morale is not only a plus for productivity; it can also avoid costly work stoppages.

Most businesses have become increasingly aware of the need to put goals of serving social needs at least on a par with profitability. Some of this awareness is evident as major investors in such corporations as First Pennsylvania Bank and Trust Company, the Dreyfus Fund, and the trustees of Harvard University state their intention to invest only in socially responsible firms. Moreover, a broader definition of the interests of all stockholders can justify socially responsible acts. Stockholders are not only owners of a business; they are also members of the public, consumers, and owners of other companies. Broadly defined, their interests are also best served by a healthy society.

Social responsibility is also justified by many as a necessity for continued freedom of action by business. The need to act before government exerts more pressure is highlighted by questions from Eastman Kodak's president:

> "Is it better to wage a tactical retreat, not conceding any new or improved benefit until the pressure for it becomes irresistible? Or is it better to exercise one's freedom of choice and planning, and treat responsibility more as an opportunity to be taken at the appropriate time, in the forward conduct of the business?" [8]

Many worry about the threat of government dictating the solutions to societal problems. Others feel that business should work with government to solve these problems. Business is expected to attack the problems of society which allow them a satisfactory, but not necessarily a maximum, level of profit. Government has the responsibility to act as the purchasing agent for society and its needs and to offer business profitable opportunities by subsidizing any projects that are unprofitable or pose a high risk to business.

Hard-to-Measure Benefits

Generally, the difficulties in measuring the benefits of societal improvements have been approached from the view of both society and the individual business.

Society

In order to provide a statistical measure of government's success in meeting the nation's social goals, social indicators have been devised. These

---

[8] Joseph C. Wilson, "Social Responsibility of the Businessman," *Personnel*, January/February, 1966, 4010C09-3.

94 The Environment of Business

Figure 4-2. *The Social Affairs Department and the Organization*

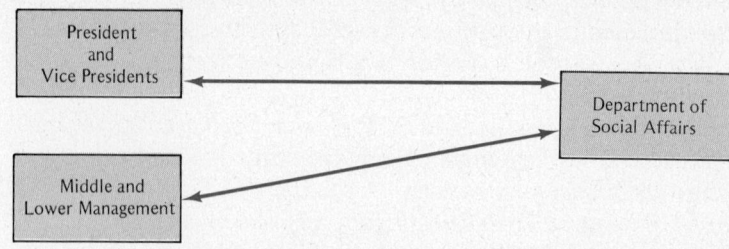

Department of Social Affairs helps the top executive committee (President and Vice Presidents) by:

1. Recommending social objectives and goals
2. Evaluating social consequences of corporate actions
3. Reporting on the firm's social performance

Department of Social Affairs helps line groups (middle and lower management) by:

1. Informing them about social affairs
2. Assisting them in programs to meet social goals
3. Helping them to monitor the social aspects of operations

Source: Michael Mazis and Robert Green, "Implementing Social Responsibility," *MSU Business Topics*, Vol. 19, No. 1, Winter, 1971. Reprinted by permission of the publisher, Division of Research, Graduate School of Business Administration, Michigan State University.

indicators go beyond description of physical events or quantities into the realm of people's perceptions and emotions. Measurement of behavioral aspects of society has been undertaken by the Institute for Social Research of the University of Michigan. It has focused on attitudes of the public toward inflation, taxation, crime, drug use, and environmental pollution.

Not only do business managers need social indicators, but also they need an annual social report of the priorities and progress toward an improved quality of life. Business has a responsibility to help develop and collect this information as well as to use it when it becomes available.

Business

Business evaluation of the benefits of social action to a firm should be looked at within each individual situation. Each business must define the needs of its publics, set its own social goals and priorities, establish programs to accomplish these goals, and evaluate accomplishment of the programs.

It is important that resolution of public demands be carried out in a logical manner instead of in one that encourages no planning but only reaction to the most immediately pressing demands. In order to make sure that social considerations are incorporated into all business decisions and that a written statement of social goals and priorities is established, some entity in the business must be assigned the responsibility of making recommendations to the managers of the regular business operations. The responsible party should be charged with developing a system to generate and process information concerning societal demands that might influence corporate activity. It should also help the firm plan realistic responses that balance long-term profits and benefits to society.

Until now, businesses have assigned responsibility to individuals charged with other responsibilities, to temporary task forces of top executives set up to deal with a currently crucial issue, or to a permanent committee of senior officers supported by a full time staff. However, a permanent **Department of Social Affairs** composed of representatives from all business activities as well as experts in ecology, urban affairs, and consumerism, which reports directly to top management, seems to hold the most promise.

Such a department, shown in Figure 4-2, could develop an expert, planned, integrated approach to handling social issues. Also, the establishment of such a department would show commitment on the part of top management to consider the societal impact of all decisions. The department would listen to all the publics, including those members who feel that large corporations should have direction from society. Experts would be in a position to measure the societal benefits from each avenue of action. This department could be crucial in evaluating the effectiveness of jointly planned programs. The evaluation of social programs is generally a part of the process of conducting a social audit. The **social audit**, which involves tracking the social performance of a business, is being informally carried out by many businesses. About 60% of the top 500 American corporations report the results in their 1972 annual reports.

Aspects that might be included in a social audit are detailed in Table 4-3. Just as firms must decide which social goals they should satisfy, they will have to experiment with different methods of satisfying these goals to find which produce the desired outputs. A department of social affairs should prove helpful in assessing the value of the various programs.

Competitive Disadvantage

Recent government legislation on pollution control, consumer protection, and worker safety suggests that government is ready to set minimum standards of performance for all businesses in an industry. Such governmental action will keep the socially responsible business from becoming noncompetitive because of higher costs.

One problem the government still has not solved is how to keep socially responsible American firms competitive in world markets. Attempts to reach an international accord on societal responsibility of business have not proven effective. Underdeveloped nations frequently oppose moves to make them more socially responsible at the cost of a lowered economic well-being.

Some people have suggested that government go beyond simple establish-

Table 4-3. *Aspects of a Social Audit*

I. Employee Relations
    Relative to competitors and company goals, how is the company doing with:
        Hiring and promoting minorities or females?
        Improving working conditions?
        Involving employees in decision making?
        Counseling employees?

II. Minority Enterprise Development
    How is the company doing in helping minority-owned businesses by:
        Buying from them?
        Depositing some company funds with minority-owned banks?
        Helping fund minority businesses?

III. Environmental Protection
    How good are company policies concerning:
        Use of nonpolluting processes and antipollution equipment?
        Use of recycled and biodegradable materials?
        Waste and its recycling?

IV. Consumer Affairs
    Does the company have a well-developed consumer affairs program with full-time specialists in charge?

V. Community Involvement
    Is the company involved in the community by:
        Having a community relations program?
        Contributing time of employees for community activities?
        Contributing its facilities for community activities?

VI. Corporation's Organizational Structure
    Has the organization been properly set up for socially responsible efforts by:
        Giving top management support to the corporation's social policy?
        Assigning responsibility for social policy to a single top executive?
        Establishing social objectives and a statement of the priorities of social problems?
        Holding managers accountable for social policies and objectives?

Source: Council on Trends and Perspective, *The Corporation in Transition—Redefining Its Social Charter*, Chamber of Commerce of the United States, Washington, D.C., 1973, pp. 32–35.

ment of minimum standards. They recommend revoking the charter of any business corporations that pose a threat to society. This would mean that corporate charters would be given and controlled by federal rather than state government, as at present.

Most business managers favor increased effort at the industry level to solve societal problems. The establishment of industrywide codes of ethics and a social investment corporation funded by all business are proposed as solutions to the problem of how to make all who benefit from such action share the cost.

Obviously, these proposals present problems of allocation of costs and measurement of benefits. They may lessen, but not eliminate, the inequality of cost and benefit.

How to Act

The final problem of deciding how to act must include a consideration of the objectives and resources of the firm. A department of social affairs, proposed earlier, provides the basis for business to consider all objectives and constraints before deciding how to act. Information about the needs of these publics and past progress in satisfying them is necessary. Government may also have to decide what actions are needed and to contract business to carry them out. However, business should not oppose government doing the jobs that business cannot handle economically.

IMPACT OF NEW RESPONSIBILITIES ON CAREERS

The rising demands of society have two major impacts on jobs in business. They change the nature of the jobs of many business executives, and they create new jobs in many businesses, especially large corporations. Business students should be aware of the new fields open to them.

Changed Nature of Jobs

The modern business executive needs to communicate effectively with all members of the public and with specialists such as sociologists, ecologists, and urban planners. The failure of many business executives to recognize the importance and nature of problems of the hard-core unemployed, of pollution, and of the consumer has brought about many of their problems. To learn about these problems and the people involved, students planning for a business career should include sociology, psychology, and urban economics courses in their curricula.

Another way in which the jobs in business are changing is that the rules governing job performance and everyday behavior are being changed. These rules have generally been made less rigid in order to accommodate hard-core unemployed who are not used to all of the rules. Moreover, young employees are less willing to follow unreasonable rules. They have demanded more comfortable dress codes and fewer restrictions on talking and other aspects of job conduct.

Creation of New Jobs

Many new jobs have been created as businesses have tried to decide how to react to demands from the general public. These jobs include many areas, such as the life sciences, urban planning, and research. In addition, new businesses have been created to sell products or services necessary for business to satisfy its publics.

The Job of Coordinating Business Efforts

The major job examined in this section is the job of coordinating business efforts to meet these new demands. This job, given many different titles, will be discussed with regard to its responsibilities, background requirements, and rewards.

RESPONSIBILITIES The specific responsibilities of the job differ from business to business and title to title. The Director of Consumer Affairs is assigned chief responsibility for consumer relations, while the Director of Employment may be assigned primary responsibility for hiring and training of the hard-core unemployed. Another common title, Manager of Urban Affairs or Social Affairs, is attached to a job that is concerned with all problems of the business as it operates in society.

Regardless of title, the responsibilities of the job include:

1. Gathering information about the demands of the public in question.
2. Assisting managers to set objectives and goals that consider demands of all publics.
3. Assisting managers to develop programs to meet social goals.
4. Telling managers how the public has reacted or may react to their programs.
5. Evaluating public consequences of corporate action.

The extent to which the manager carries out each of these responsibilities depends on the amount of resources he is given by the company. Frequently, he is only given an advisory role with no power to force his views on other managers in the business.

BACKGROUND REQUIREMENTS A college degree is usually required. Most current holders of these jobs majored in business in college and held other jobs before becoming Directors of Social Affairs. In general, companies have emphasized hiring persons in their late thirties, who are enthusiastic about solving business problems with publics, although they may lack specific experience with analyzing and solving them. For example, Union Carbide appointed a company lawyer as Director of Urban Affairs, Michigan Bell Telephone chose a general marketing manager, and Bank of America hired a governmental relations expert. Others have hired Peace Corps veterans, congressional aides, city planners, and college professors for the job.

As the commitment of top management of business to satisfying social needs and wants strengthens in the future, requirements for the job of Director of Social Affairs will place more emphasis on previous relevant experience and ability to do the job. This is especially true as more qualified people become available due to increased business use of social affairs departments and the expansion of university programs designed to train people in business relations with society. If you are interested in this field, you should consider courses offered in urban planning, consumerism, and other areas of public affairs as part of your college curriculum.

REWARDS The chief reward of working as a Director of Social Affairs is personal satisfaction from contributing to the well-being of society and business. Through this job you will be given a chance to solve some of society's problems or, at least, to develop a better understanding of these problems. You will also contribute to the well-being of business; its existence depends on its ability to satisfy its publics.

This job is also rewarding in terms of personal advancement. Persons who hold such jobs experience a great deal of exposure to the top managers of the business. Many who have taken such a job in the past have considered it only temporary; they see it as a good investment in their career in business management.[9]

Although salaries for this job vary greatly between businesses, the pay tends to be comparable to that of other managers with similar experience. In many companies, the Director of Social Affairs fares even better than other management counterparts.

CHAPTER SUMMARY

The expectations of nine publics are discussed in this chapter. They are:

1. Stockholders or owners.
2. Creditors.
3. Employees.
4. Unions.
5. Government.
6. Competitors.
7. Suppliers and distributors.
8. Customers.
9. General public.

[9] Jules Cohn, *The Conscience of the Corporations: Business and Urban Affairs, 1967–1970*, Baltimore: Johns Hopkins Press, 1971, p. 80.

Public expectations of business are shown to have broadened from profits and jobs to minority training, pollution control, and consumer protection. Business must try to meet the expectations of the public. However, business finds many of these expectations costly to satisfy. The benefits of satisfying these expectations have proven difficult to measure.

The dilemma of choosing which societal needs to satisfy is best handled by broadening business goals beyond short-run profit maximization. The development of social indicators will help business measure the benefits of societal improvements. The addition of a department of social affairs is also considered a method for business to meet the expectations of its publics.

Two major job impacts of changing expectations of business publics are discussed in the chapter. Jobs of business managers have changed to include the tasks of meeting these expectations and meeting the demands of new workers. In addition, the job of coordinating business efforts to meet public expectations has been created by many businesses.

PROVOCATIVE STATEMENT

Social Responsibility Is Only Good if It Pays

1 "I am not arguing that management should ignore its critics. Some of them have made a good case from time to time against business's social delinquencies and against its shortsightedness in fighting practically all of Washington's efforts to provide security. (Indeed, if business had not always fought federal welfare measures, perhaps the unions would not have demanded them from business itself.)

Nor am I arguing that management has no welfare obligations at all to society. Quite to the contrary. Corporate welfare makes good sense *if* it makes good economic sense—and not infrequently it does. But if something does not make economic sense, sentiment or idealism ought not let it in the door. Sentiment is a corrupting and debilitating influence in business. It fosters leniency, inefficiency, sluggishness, extravagance, and hardens the innovationary arteries. It can confuse the role of the businessman just as much as the profit motive could confuse the role of the government official. The governing rule in industry should be that something is good only if it pays. Otherwise, it is alien and impermissible. This is the rule of capitalism."

Theodore Levitt,
"The Dangers of Social Responsibility,"
Howard Business Review,
September–October 1958,
p. 17.

PROVOCATIVE STATEMENT

Business Should Be Taxed for Pollution

"Industry will not end or significantly reduce its emission until air pollution contaminates corporate income statements as well as human beings. All of us, including businessmen, treat air and water as free goods ... If we could somehow provide businessmen with an incentive to use the environment with as much care as they exercise in the use of other factors of production, then we would be well on our way toward solving the pollution problem. Various economists have proposed a plan designed to do this ... the effluent fee ... Pollution is taxed. If we demand less pollution, then we must accept that this will entail higher costs of production and consequently higher prices. There are disturbing signs that consumers are not yet willing to pay for pollution control."

R. Joseph Monson,
Business and the Changing Environment,
New York: McGraw-Hill Book Company, 1973,
pp. 37-38.

REVIEW QUESTIONS

1. How do the demands of different publics differ?
2. What does the general public want business to do?
3. Business executives are more socially responsible today because they are richer than their predecessors. Comment.
4. Why may business executives refuse to satisfy the demands of society?
5. It is easy for business to measure the cost and benefits of responding to the demands of society. Comment.
6. Give three examples of businesses that have taken socially responsible action. Why did they act?
7. All businesses should have a department of social affairs. Comment.
8. What is the job of a manager of social affairs?

Chapter Outline

The American Economic System
    Capitalism
    Concentration of Economic Power in American Business
    Competition and Concentration
    Competition and Monopoly

Comparison with Other Economic Systems
    Socialism
    Communism

Evaluation of the American Economic System
    Analysis of Economic Output
    A Philosophical Evaluation

International Trade and Investment
    The Motives for International Trade and Investment
    The Economic Importance of International Trade and Investment

A Perspective on Economic Problems
    Causes of Inflation
        Cost–push Inflation
        Demand–pull Inflation
    Effects of Inflation
        Penalties to Annuitants
        Scarcities
        Controls
    Is Inflation Curable?

Careers and Jobs in Economics

Chapter Summary

Provocative Statement 1:
    The Evils of Uncontrolled Economic Growth

Provocative Statement 2:
    The Failings of Capitalism

Key Terms

Capitalism
Market economy
Competitive system
Price system
Mixed economy
Pure competition
Monopolistic competition
Oligopoly
Pure monopoly
Countervailing power
Socialism
Communism
Gross national product (GNP)
Final goods
Intermediate goods
Double-counting
Inequality in income distribution
Equal opportunity employers
Direct investment
Inflation
Cost–push inflation
Demand–pull inflation
Consumer price index (CPI)
Annuitants

The Economic Framework for Business

"Economic growth is not good in itself. Economic growth, at too fast a rate, is a cancer, and the evils that are associated with it far outweigh any good that comes out of it."
—Executive Vice President, Major U.S. Multinational Firm

The American people enjoy one of the highest standards of living in the world. A major reason for this prosperity is the American economic system. In this chapter, we shall:

1. Examine the nature of the American economic system.
2. Compare it to other basic economic systems throughout the world.
3. Discuss current problems on the world economic scene and indicate areas of possible change.

THE AMERICAN ECONOMIC SYSTEM

Human beings are by nature consumers of goods and services. These goods and services are not without limit, however. The production of goods and services requires labor, money, raw materials, and machinery. The supply of each of these factors of production is limited. Economics studies the various ways in which these resources can be used so as to best satisfy people's wants and needs.

The three basic questions of economics are WHAT, HOW, and FOR WHOM. WHAT shall be produced? HOW shall it be produced? FOR WHOM shall it be produced? Answers to these questions indicate the nature of the economic system being analyzed.

Capitalism

Capitalism is a name given to the American economic system of free enterprise. Other terms often used to describe our economic system are the market economy, the competitive system, or the price system. Capitalism is a system of classical economics constructed in the latter part of the eighteenth and early nineteenth centuries, primarily in England. The basic principles of capitalism are:

1. Private property.
2. Freedom of enterprise and choice.
3. Self-interest as the dominant motive.
4. Competition.
5. Reliance upon the price system.
6. A limited role for government.

In a pure capitalist economic system, the natural resources and capital goods, that is, goods used to help manufacture other items, are owned by private citizens. People have the right to use these goods and resources any way they want. Furthermore, individuals have the right to select their own line of employment. They can work for themselves or sell their services to someone else. The profit motive encourages individuals to employ their talents where they are most in demand.

The price system supplies answers to the three basic economic questions. It does this by working through supply and demand in competitive markets. WHAT shall be produced is determined by the demand for goods from potential buyers. As people increase their demand for certain products, the profit opportunity on those products increases as prices rise. Producers are thus encouraged via the profit motive to manufacture more of those goods. HOW goods will be produced is determined by the relative costs of different production processes. Manufacturers will try to produce their products in the most efficient, least costly way. FOR WHOM shall products be made? People who are able and willing to pay the highest price for a given product will get that product.

Competitive markets are a keystone of the classical system. They require a considerable number of sellers in any trade or industry. The buyers and sellers must be in informed communication with each other. No buyer or seller should be large enough to control the common price. Thus, it is the *collective* demand for goods from buyers and supply from sellers that determines WHAT, HOW, and FOR WHOM goods will be produced.

The capitalist system is very efficient. All incentives encourage the use of people, money, and natural resources to produce most efficiently what people most want. Power is spread out enough to prevent the misuse of private economic influence. Thus, there is no role for government in the pure capitalistic economic system.

Concentration of Economic Power in American Business

As noted previously, competition is vital to a capitalistic system. The classical economists stated that the presence of many buyers and sellers was necessary for competition. No individual or group should be able to control the actions of all others. But the present day American scene is marked by concentration of economic power in a number of American industries. As John Kenneth Galbraith, a noted American economist, has said, "the large corporation can have significant power over the prices it charges, over the prices it pays, even over the mind of the consumer whose wants and tastes it partly synthesizes."[1]

How concentrated is power in the American economy? The following charts give a partial answer to this question. As shown in Figure 5-1, the hundred largest industrial corporations in the United States account for 62.4% of the sales, 63.9% of the assets, 57.9% of the employees, and 67.9% of the profits of the 500 largest industrial corporations in the United States.

Figure 5-2 shows the variation in concentration by industry. Some industries, such as motor vehicles and telephone equipment, are dominated by only a handful of firms. Other industries, such as plastic products and soft drinks, have no dominant firms.

The point is that competition in terms of having numerous sellers in the marketplace is absent from a large part of American industry. Thus, the American economy does not conform to the classical economists' model of

[1] John Kenneth Galbraith, *American Capitalism*, Boston: Houghton Mifflin Company, 1956, p. 7.

Figure 5-1. Statistics for the Largest U.S. Industrial Corporations

Percent Distribution

500 Largest	Sales	Assets	Employees	Net Income
Highest Hundred	62.4	63.9	57.9	67.6
Fourth Hundred	17.5	16.8	18.8	16.0
Third Hundred	9.6	9.5	10.6	8.0
Second Hundred	6.1	5.6	7.5	5.3
Lowest Hundred	4.4	4.2	5.2	3.1

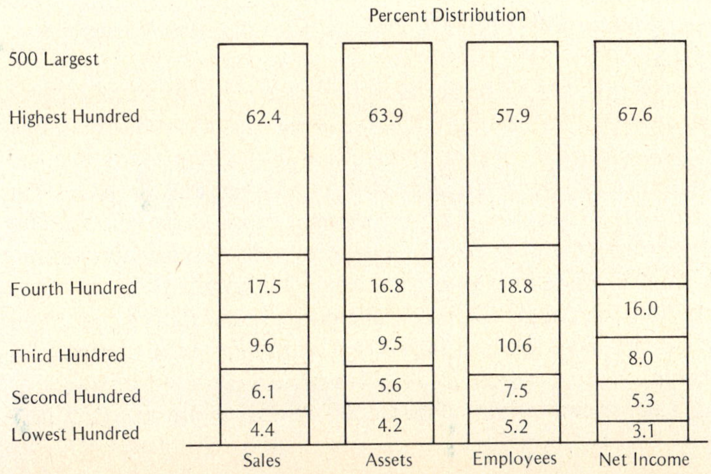

The Environment of Business

Figure 5-2. Concentration in American Industry—1970

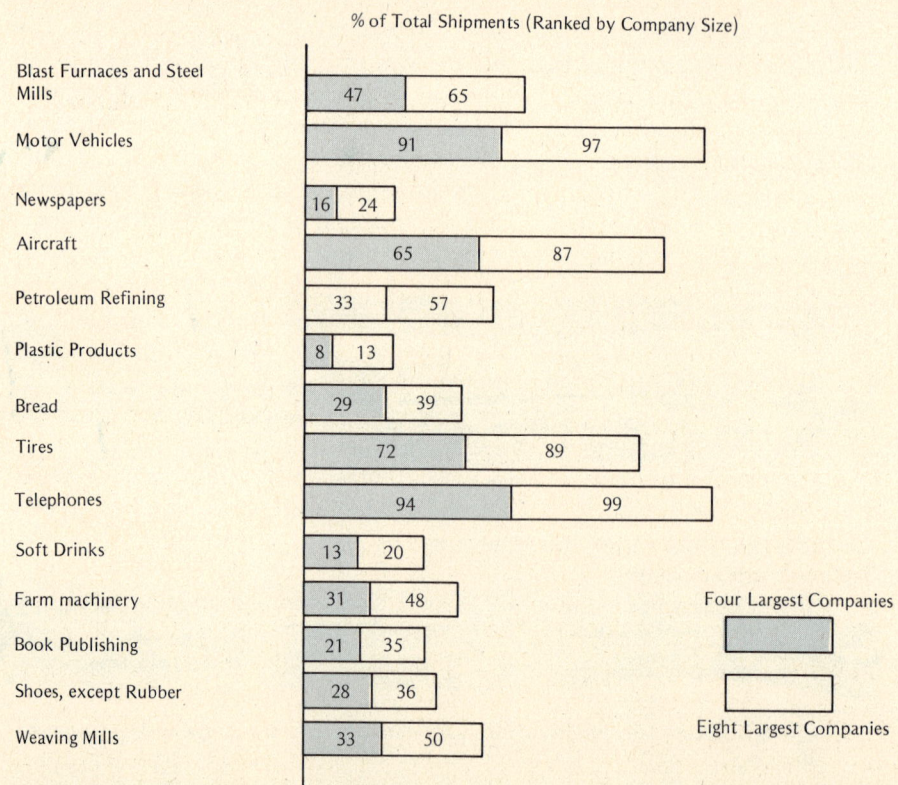

capitalism. How then can we characterize the American economy? The American economy is a *mixed economy*. It has areas characterized as *pure competition*, *monopolistic competition*, *oligopoly*, and *pure monopoly*.

A *purely competitive* system has a large number of firms selling a standardized product. No one seller or buyer has any control over price. All competition is based on price. Furthermore, the system is very easy to enter. The purely competitive system is thus the same as the classic capitalist system. One of the few remaining examples of such a model is agriculture.

There are many sellers in a *monopolistic competitive* market. Each seller, however, tries to make a product slightly different from those of the competitors. It is easy to become a member of such an industry. The monopolistic competitor has some control over price. Considerable emphasis is placed on nonprice competition, such as advertising, trademarks, brand names, and so on. An example of an industry that conforms to the monopolistic competition model is retail trade.

An *oligopoly* is characterized by only a few firms selling either a standardized or a differentiated product. Sellers often charge the same price for their products. A "price leader" is often found in the industry. When the price leader changes the product's price, all other firms in the industry follow suit. The huge scale of production and enormous investment in plant and equipment make entry into the industry rather difficult. There is usually a great deal of nonprice competition in an oligopoly, particularly with product differentiation. There are many examples of oligopoly in American business, including the steel and automobile industries.

A *pure monopoly* is a one-company industry with a unique product with no close substitutes. The monopolist has considerable control over product price. Entry into the industry by other firms is blocked. The monopolist engages actively in public relations advertising. Local utilities are the prime examples of pure monopolies, as is the American Telephone & Telegraph Co. on a wider geographic scale.

Competition and Concentration

There is clearly a considerable degree of concentration regarding economic resources in the American economy. But does this mean that there is no competition? Are the American consumers at the mercy of big business? The "typical" American industry is an oligopoly with a fringe of small survivors. But there can be competition with oligopoly. Competition need not come from other sellers. It can come from the other side of the market—the consumer. Private economic power is held in check by the **countervailing power** of those who are subject to it.[2] Workers form unions to protect their rights against big business. They can strike if they feel unfairly treated. Individuals can refuse to purchase products they feel are priced too high or are poorly constructed. For example, beef prices rose to record highs in the early 1970s. Consumers reacted by cutting down their eating of meat. They increased their consumption of other high-protein foods. Thus, both concentration and competition can exist in an oligopoly.

Competition and Monopoly

Competition cannot exist when a company has a monopoly. The American people have long realized the potential for abuse that monopoly power implies. The government in a mixed economy is given the responsibility of seeing that monopolists do not take unfair advantage of their economic power. For example, public utility companies are closely regulated by state government agencies. These agencies regulate the prices utilities may charge for their services. Thus, while there may be no competition in a monopoly, the potential for abuse of power is closely checked.

[2] The concept of countervailing power was originally developed by Galbraith and is discussed in more detail in his *American Capitalism*.

COMPARISON WITH OTHER ECONOMIC SYSTEMS

The American mixed economy is but one type of major economic system. The three major forms of pure economic systems are *capitalism, socialism,* and *communism.* We have already examined capitalism. To review, in a capitalistic system each economic unit decides what choices and policies are best for it. There is private ownership of the factors of production. Consumers, resource suppliers, and investors have freedom of choice. A system of competitive markets is counted on to ensure the efficient allocation of scarce resources. These markets are free of government planning and control.

Socialism

The basic philosophy of socialism is that some governmental intervention is needed to improve upon the choices and policies of individual economic units. Action by the government should foster a fairer distribution of wealth among the country's citizens. In a liberal or democratic socialist system, there is a mixture of public and private ownership of the factors of production. There is public and private decision making as to WHAT, HOW, and FOR WHOM goods will be produced.

In a socialist system—in practice—the government owns the large industrial firms. Free enterprise is allowed to exist in other areas of the economy. The profit motive as an incentive for work and production is lessened. High taxes on income and inheritances redistribute the wealth.

The British economic system is probably the best example of a socialist system. The government owns the steel and coal industries and the railroads. Wages are low and taxes are high compared to the United States. The British government provides basic social services—such as health care—at very low cost to the people. As should be apparent, the American mixed economy stands at some intermediate point between liberal socialism and pure capitalism.

Communism

The underlying assumption of communism is that the state is in the best position to know what choices and policies are beneficial for the economy as a whole and for its component parts. There is governmental ownership and control of the bulk of industry and agriculture. Severe restrictions are put on individual choices should they be in conflict with state-determined objectives. Government plans are established for solving economic problems by a central planning authority. The profit motive is eliminated in favor of the common good in a communist system. All prices are set by government authorities. The government periodically reviews the performance of the various productive facilities and almost totally controls business decisions.

The economy of the Soviet Union is often cited as a prime example of a communist system. In the Soviet Union, the state owns almost all factors of production. Soviet citizens earn a salary and have considerable choice of occupation. They do not, however, have unlimited right to seek employment in any region or industry that they wish.

How does the Soviet Union provide answers to the three basic economic questions? WHAT shall be produced is a political decision made by governmental planners. Soviet leaders have decided that defense spending and capital formation are to have top economic priority. The remainder of resources then go to consumer goods. HOW are goods produced in the Soviet Union? As we have already noted, private enterprise is minimal. The typical Soviet industry is state owned. The Soviet Union has historically had a physical quota system to gauge the efficiency and growth of its economy. Managers of business are evaluated on the number of units of output their firms produce relative to a budgeted objective. FOR WHOM shall goods be produced? Observation of actual practice suggests that the Soviet people are producing first for the security of the state. Only then is production used to satisfy the growing wants of the Soviet people.

EVALUATION OF THE AMERICAN ECONOMIC SYSTEM

We shall attempt to evaluate the American system of business in two ways. First, we shall examine the value of the output of the American system relative to that of other countries. The value of economic output and growth is a measure of an economy's strength. Secondly, we shall examine the philosophic arguments for and against a free enterprise economy.

Analysis of Economic Output

The people of the United States have long prided themselves on the tremendous productive capacity of their economy and the resulting high standard of living. Table 5-1 provides an indication of the production capabilities of the American economy versus those of other nations. Gross national product (GNP) measures the money value of all final goods produced by an economy. It is important to differentiate final goods from intermediate goods to avoid double-counting. For example, suppose we determined the money value of an automobile engine and the total price for an automobile with the engine included. If we included the sum of these two values in the GNP, we

Table 5-1. International GNP Figures

Country	1972 Amount (Billions of Dollars)	Growth Rate, Annual % Change, 1967–1972
Austria	20.1	5.7
Belgium	34.9	5.1
Denmark	20.3	4.8
Finland	12.8	5.5
France	197.0	5.7
Germany, Fed. Rep. of	257.0	5.4
Greece	12.2	8.1
Iceland	.7	3.4
Ireland	5.9	4.3
Italy	118.2	4.3
Luxembourg	1.2	4.1
Netherlands	44.0	5.4
Norway	14.9	4.4
Portugal	8.2	6.5
Spain	45.6	6.1
Sweden	41.4	3.2
Switzerland	30.0	4.7
Turkey	16.0	7.1
United Kingdom	162.0	2.8
Canada	102.5	5.0
United States	1151.8	3.2
Australia	43.3	5.0
Japan	292.0	10.4

Source: *Statistical Abstract of the United States 1973*, p. 812.

would be double-counting, since the value of the engine—an intermediate good—is included in the price of the automobile—a final good.

As shown in Table 5-1, GNP for the United States far exceeds that for any other nation listed. In fact, GNP for the United States is almost four times as large as that for Japan. However, the picture is not quite as rosy as it appears. The five-year average annual rate of growth in GNP for the United States lags behind that for most of the other countries. We should note, of course, that there is no reason to expect these historical rates of growth to continue into the future.

The GNP of the United States is so large for reasons other than the fact that its population exceeds that of the other countries listed. The United States also leads the way with the highest per capita or per person GNP, as shown in Table 5-2. But the differences shown between countries in per capita GNP are not nearly as striking as those in total GNP. Again, the growth rate for the United States per capita GNP trails that for most other industrial nations.

Table 5-2. *International GNP Per Capita*

Country	1972 Amount (in Dollars)	Annual % Change 1967–1972
Austria	2,709	5.5
Belgium	3,593	4.8
Denmark	3,978	4.0
Finland	2,723	5.3
France	3,810	4.8
West Germany	4,101	4.4
Greece	1,382	7.8
Iceland	3,493	2.4
Ireland	1,903	3.7
Italy	2,170	3.4
Luxembourg	3,509	3.7
Netherlands	3,298	4.2
Norway	3,779	3.6
Portugal	843	5.6
Spain	1,321	5.0
Sweden	5,061	2.4
Switzerland	4,702	3.6
Turkey	430	4.5
United Kingdom	2,877	2.3
Canada	4,704	3.6
United States	5,515	2.2
Australia	3,370	3.1
Japan	2,757	9.1

Source: *Statistical Abstract of the United States 1973*, p. 812.

A Philosophical Evaluation

One might conclude that the American economic system must be good because it has worked well in the past. After all, the United States has the world's largest economy and one of the highest standards of living. While other economies may be growing faster, some would argue, faster growth at the expense of individual freedom is just too high a price for Americans to pay.

Has the American economic system really provided its people with the "good life"? In purely quantitative terms, the answer to this question must be yes. Consider these points. The United States:

1. Has one of the lowest infant mortality rates in the world.
2. Is second only to India in the Free World in the number of occupied dwellings.
3. Has far more hospital beds than any other country.
4. Has more physicians than any country but the Soviet Union.
5. Has more dentists than any other country.

6. Spends more than twice as much as any other country in terms of public expenditure for education.
7. Has a high degree of individual freedom.

But the American economic system has its critics as well as its defenders. Valentin A. Nazarevsky, a leading Soviet economist, has noted that the growth of research and developmental complexes in the United States would have been impossible without substantial help from the government.[3] He has also noted that the absence of national economic planning can lead to results which no one can predict. He cites the case of the projected production of a plastic pipe, which had very favorable prospects. However, the companies that introduced this product suffered heavy losses as a result of overproduction. Lastly, he cites America's pollution problem. The country's industries are unable to solve this problem voluntarily. He argues that only through the intervention of the state will the pollution war be effectively fought and won.

A different group of critics has attacked the American economic system on the grounds that it has fostered and continues to maintain inequality in income distribution. These critics, often seen as major supporters of liberal socialism, advocate:

1. Equality of income and wealth.
2. Availability of a widening range of goods and services, completely free of charge.

[3] Valentin A. Nazarevsky, "A Soviet Economist Looks At U.S. Business," *Harvard Business Review*, May–June 1974, p. 52.

Figure 5-3. Income Distribution in the United States

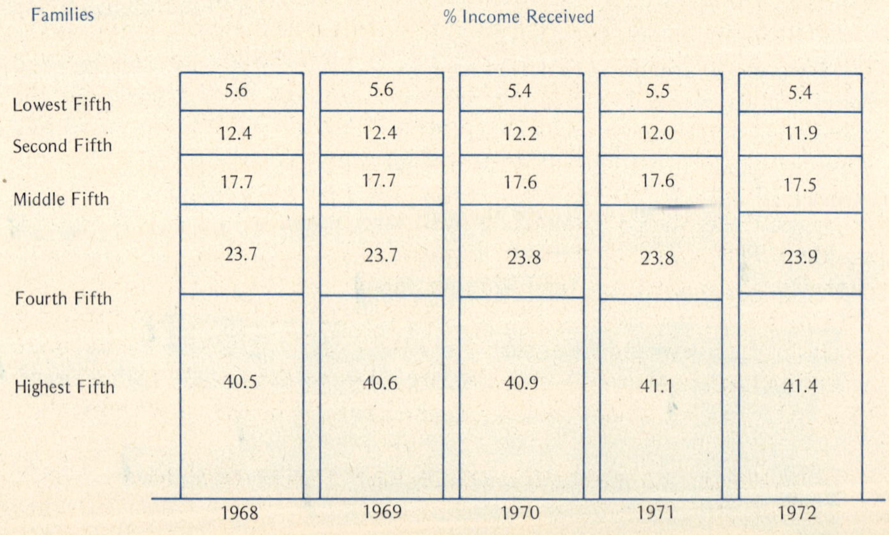

Families	% Income Received				
	1968	1969	1970	1971	1972
Lowest Fifth	5.6	5.6	5.4	5.5	5.4
Second Fifth	12.4	12.4	12.2	12.0	11.9
Middle Fifth	17.7	17.7	17.6	17.6	17.5
Fourth Fifth	23.7	23.7	23.8	23.8	23.9
Highest Fifth	40.5	40.6	40.9	41.1	41.4

Table 5-3. *Family Incomes in the United States*

	1968	1969	1970	1971
Family average	$8,632	$9,433	$9,867	$10,285
Upper limit of each fifth				
Lowest fifth	4,581	5,005	5,148	5,275
Second fifth	7,368	8,059	8,389	8,681
Middle fifth	9,972	10,826	11,363	11,863
Fourth fifth	13,491	14,799	16,298	17,483

Source: *Statistical Abstract of the United States 1973*, p. 330.

3. Replacement of "material incentives" by "moral incentives."
4. Release for all from the depressing aspects of modern industrial society.

We shall not argue the fundamental soundness of these propositions, but rather examine the extent of the inequality of income distribution in the U.S.

Figure 5-3 presents the percentage distribution of total income in the United States by families for the years 1968–1972. These figures reveal a glaring inequality in the distribution of income in the United States. In 1972 the poorest 20% of the families in the United States earned only 5.4% of total family income. On the other hand, the 20% highest-paid families accounted for about 41% of total family income. Furthermore, this inequality in income distribution has persisted over the entire time period shown. That is, the families in the lower end of the income scale have not been able to increase their share of the nation's total income. Table 5-3 presents the absolute levels of family income. In 1971 the average family income in America was $10,285. However, the highest earning family in the lowest fifth received only $5,275, while the highest earning family in the fourth highest fifth earned $17,483.

What should be done about this inequality in income distribution? Believers in socialism argue that the state must intervene to force income redistribution. Advocates of the American system argue that, in a free society, a man may earn according to his abilities. It is the responsibility of government, these people state, only to insure equal opportunity to all people. The U.S. government has passed and enforces laws requiring companies to be **equal opportunity employers**. Companies must hire people based on their abilities, not their religion, sex, or ethnic background. The American system of rewards encourages people to excel and improve themselves. Anthony O'Reilly, president of the H. J. Heinz Company, was asked if he could have become a successful executive under a communist system where people (in theory) work according to their abilities and receive according to their needs. He answered, "I would have died. There's no reward, and I'm a big believer in rewards."[4]

---

[4] David Boldt, "What Makes Tony O'Reilly Run?" *The Philadelphia Inquirer*, May 26, 1974, p. 13.

INTERNATIONAL TRADE AND INVESTMENT

In Chapter One, the growth of international business and the emergence of the multinational firm were noted. We are being faced with a worldwide economy with a character all its own. Economic trouble in any major developed country will produce tremors felt throughout the world.

The Motives for International Trade and Investment

Often, one country has a product or service that another country does not have but wants and/or needs. This provides a major motive for international trade. For example, the United States is highly dependent on other countries for many raw materials, as highlighted in Figure 5-4. Table 5-4 gives another picture of the allocation of the earth's natural resources. Uneven distribution of huge mineral deposits among different countries of the world thus encourages international trade.

Why should other countries trade their natural resources with the United States? The reason is really quite simple. Major industrial countries, such as

Figure 5-4. *United States Import Dependency*

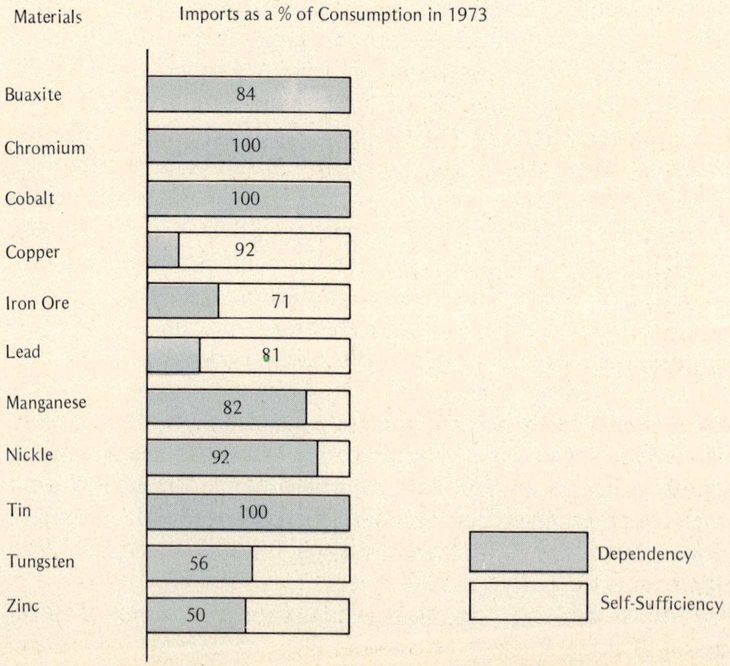

Materials — Imports as a % of Consumption in 1973

Material	%
Buaxite	84
Chromium	100
Cobalt	100
Copper	92
Iron Ore	71
Lead	81
Manganese	82
Nickle	92
Tin	100
Tungsten	56
Zinc	50

■ Dependency □ Self-Sufficiency

Table 5-4. *Who's Got the Major Mineral Reserves?*

	% OF WORLD RESERVES
Bauxite	
Australia	30.3
Guinea	22.6
United States	.3
Other Free World Countries	43.0
Communist Countries	3.8
Copper	
United States	22.4
Chile	15.7
Canada	8.9
Other Free World Countries	41.6
Communist Countries	11.4
Iron Ore	
Canada	14.5
Brazil	10.8
United States	3.6
Other Free World Countries	24.5
Communist Countries	46.6
Lead	
United States	38.9
Canada	13.2
Australia	8.3
Other Free World Countries	22.2
Communist Countries	17.4
Nickel	
New Caledonia	33.3
Canada	13.6
Cuba	9.1
United States	.4
Other Free World Countries	21.9
Communist Countries	21.6
Tungsten	
United States	6.4
Other Free World Countries	16.1
Communist Countries	77.5

Source: *The Morgan Guaranty Survey,* March 1974, p. 11.

the United States, Japan, and Great Britain, have well-developed markets and technological know-how. They can help the natural resource rich but technically poor countries make possible their own economic development. And with economic development comes rising standards of living.

There are many reasons why companies engage in international trade and invest in foreign countries. A special skill or strong public identification with its products can help a company surmount the added costs in communication and transportation of doing business in another country. Because this advantage is not shared by local competitors, the foreign company is capable of earning a higher profit than the average local firm in the same industry. It, therefore, can afford to pay more to acquire a local business than can local investors.

Of course, a company sometimes goes abroad not because it can make more than local companies, but because it is willing to earn less—at least in the short run—in order to safeguard markets. Suppose a company has been a major exporter of a particular product to a foreign country. In a burst of patriotism, the government of the foreign country threatens to stop the importing of the company's product. What can be done? One possibility is to build a plant in the foreign country. The Michelin Tire Corporation is one of many firms that became so concerned about being locked out of the American market that it decided to manufacture locally.

Finally, by locating in a foreign country, a company can shorten its pipelines to its buyers. Often the pipeline becomes so long when the product is manufactured overseas that companies are incapable of adapting rapidly enough to a changing market. For example, one likely reason for Volkswagen's interest in assembling its automobiles in America is a desire to be right on top of the rapidly changing economy car market. Similarly, Siemens Corporation, a German corporation, will use the facilities of Computest Corporation, a New Jersey firm it acquired, to quickly adapt its instruments and components for American use.

The Economic Importance of International Trade and Investment

How important is international trade to the American economy? As revealed in Figure 5-5, international trade constitutes a vital part of our

Figure 5-5. *United States Exports and Imports*

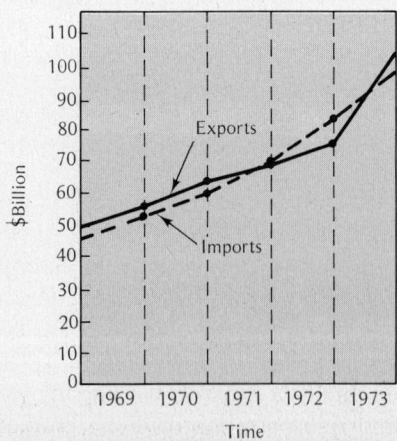

Table 5-5. *United States Employment Attributable to Exports*

Year	Total (Thousands)	% of Civilian Labor Force
1965	2,960	3.98
1969	3,334	4.13
1970	3,665	4.43
1971	3,542	4.21

economy. Exports of goods and services amount to over seven out of every hundred dollars of American GNP. Furthermore, export industries create jobs for American workers. As shown in Table 5-5, over 4% of the American labor force have jobs due to exports.

Another indication of the size of the international economic picture is presented in data on American direct investments abroad and direct foreign investments in the United States. **Direct investments** are purchases of plant and equipment. The value of American direct foreign investments has grown from $65 billion in 1968 to $107.3 billion in 1973. In 1973, these funds were allocated as shown in Figure 5-6 (see p. 118).

We should not be so naive as to believe that there is only one side to the coin; foreign direct investment in the United States is large and growing. Table 5-6 gives an indication of the magnitude of direct foreign investments in the United States, while Figure 5-7 shows the relative importance of foreign investment in the United States by country (see p. 119). American firms controlled by foreign companies produce a wide range of goods and services. A sampling of the many products is shown in Figure 5-8 (see p. 120).

An impressive indication of foreign direct investment in the United States is presented in Figure 5-9 on page 121.

Table 5-6. *Direct Foreign Investments in the United States*

	Millions of Dollars					
	1968	1969	1970	1971	1972	1973
All Areas	10,815	11,818	13,270	13,655	14,263	17,748
Canada	2,659	2,834	3,117	3,339	3,422	4,003
Europe	7,750	8,510	9,554	10,086	10,516	12,159
United Kingdom	3,409	3,496	4,127	4,438	4,621	5,437
Netherlands	1,750	1,966	2,151	2,225	2,357	2,550
Switzerland	1,238	1,395	1,545	1,537	1,567	1,825
Other European	1,353	1,653	1,731	1,886	1,971	2,347
Other Areas	406	474	599	231	326	1,585

Source: U.S. Dept. of Commerce, *Survey of Current Business*.

118   *The Environment of Business*

Figure 5-6. *Where American Direct Foreign Investment Goes*

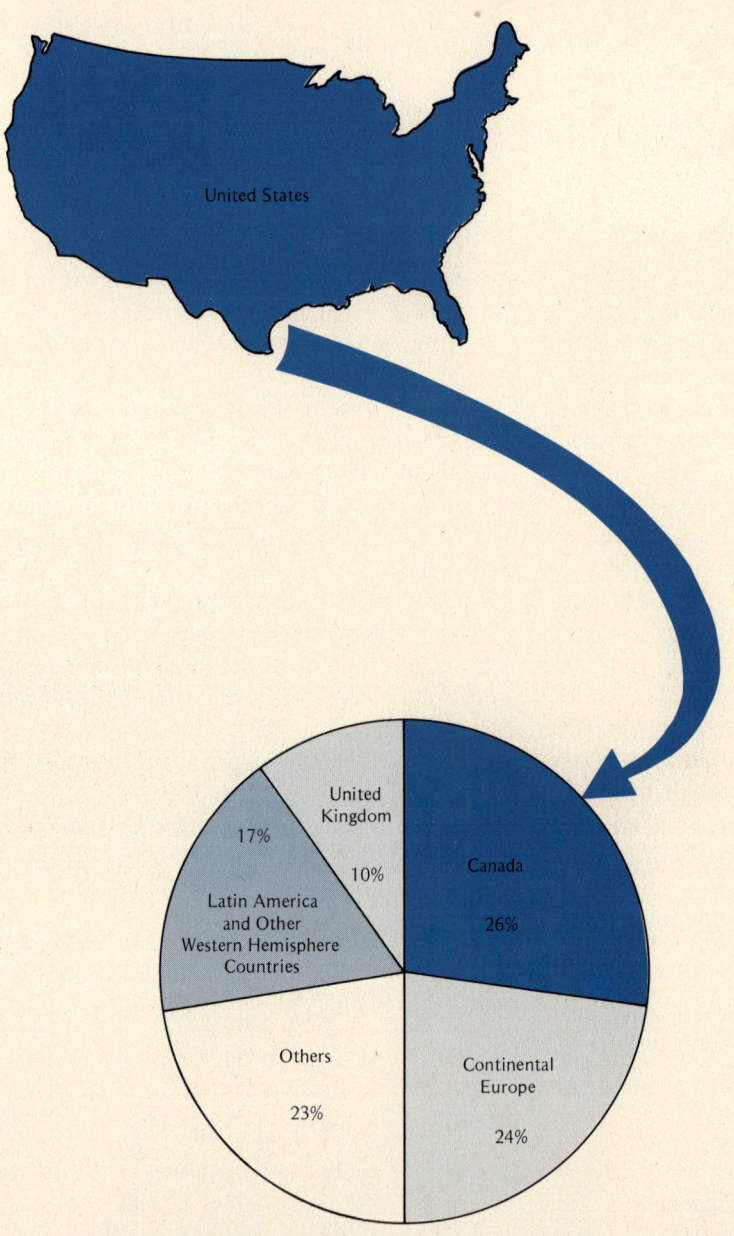

As shown in Figure 5-9 on p. 121, with the exception of 1971, the growth rate of European direct investment in the United States has exceeded that of the United States in Europe. International trade and investment are becoming a more important part of the lives of people not only in the United States, but

Figure 5-7. *Where Direct Foreign Investment Comes From*

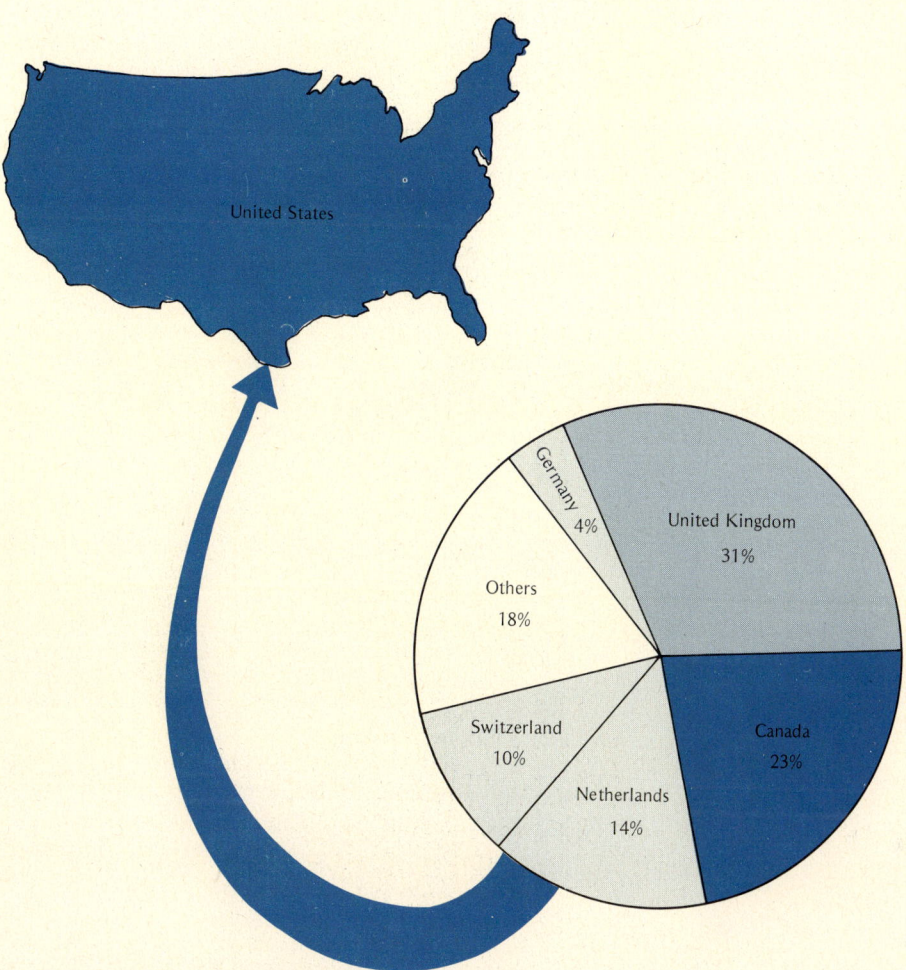

throughout the world. Economic interdependency and international economic cooperation have become facts of life.

A PERSPECTIVE ON ECONOMIC PROBLEMS

Worldwide economic growth has by no means been either uniform or stable. Even the American economy has had its share of shortcomings: politically unacceptable levels of unemployment and inflation, shortages, and inequality in income distribution. We have already discussed the income distribution

Figure 5-8. *Goods Made in America by Foreign Firms*

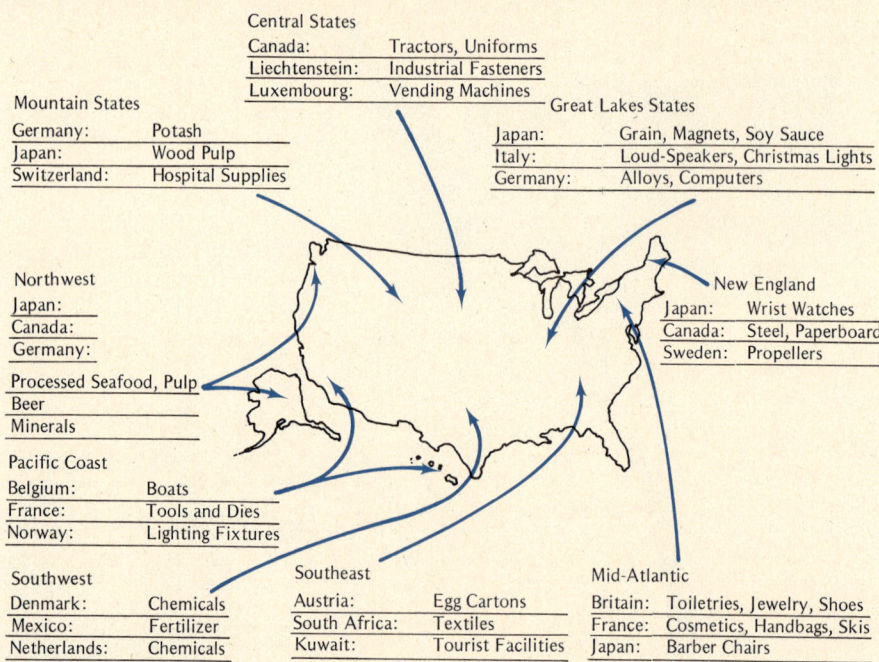

Source: Reprinted from *U.S. News and World Report*, July 8, 1974. Copyright 1974, U.S. News and World Report, Inc.

problem. In this section, we shall turn our attention to what some observers consider our most vexing economic problem—inflation.

Causes of Inflation

Inflation is defined as a general rise in the prices for goods and services. For example, suppose a family of four can specify its typical or average weekly purchase of groceries, rent, clothing, etc. For a given period in time, we can determine the cost of this bundle of goods and services. Let us say the cost is $100. We now let a year go by and then recalculate the cost of that bundle of goods and services. Assume that cost is now $110. Prices for the bundle or "market basket," as it is sometimes called, have risen by 10%, that is, the $10 rise in price divided by our "base" price of $100. This 10% figure would be our measure of inflation.

What causes the rising level of price? Economists cite two major types of inflation—cost–push inflation and demand–pull inflation—each with its own particular style.

Figure 5-9. *Growth Rate of Direct Investments*

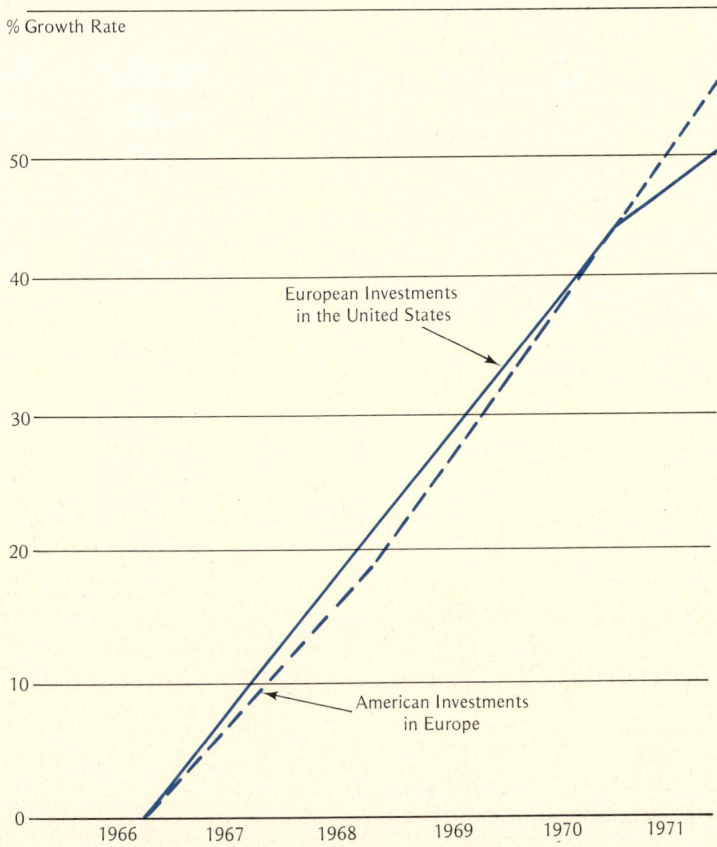

Reprinted through permission of the *Harvard Business Review*.

Cost–push Inflation

It is often argued that the major cause of inflation is political. Following World War II, peoples of the chief democracies of the world began to believe that their governments would provide an ever-increasing standard of living and, at the same time, minimize unemployment. Indeed, in the United States, Congress enacted the Employment Act of 1946. This Act set up a Council of Economic Advisors and a Joint Economic Committee in Congress to help ensure full employment and a healthy economic growth. Unfortunately, people began to demand more from the economy than they were willing to pay for. The spirit of moderation or self-denial to achieve a national objective waned. Workers wanted higher salaries. In order to raise wages and, at the same time, have a growth in profits, companies raised the prices of goods and services. Thus, rising costs "pushed" prices higher, resulting in cost–push inflation.

© Washington Star Syndicate, permission granted by King Features Syndicate, Inc.

A leading American economist blames cost–push inflation on an "escalation of expectations."[5] The growing attitude among the working population, so this argument goes, is that they are entitled to an increase in wages and salaries every year whether or not the improvement in their productivity justifies an increase. The result will be inflation. For example, suppose each worker earns 10% more in dollars, on the average, while not increasing the per hour output. No more goods or services have been produced for the increased salary paid. If business firms are to maintain the same percentage of profit on their sales, however, there must be something like a 10% increase in the cost of everything that one purchases. The worldwide extent of this phenomenon is seen in Table 5-7. The **consumer price index (CPI)** measures the "market basket" value discussed in our earlier example. In each country listed, wage gains have outstripped productivity gains, sometimes by a ratio of almost three to one.

Demand–pull Inflation

When the demand for goods and services is greater than the ability of the economy to generate them we have a case of demand–pull inflation. When an economy's plant and equipment are being operated at capacity, any increase in demand will result in price increases. People have money to spend but there is only a limited supply of goods and services available to purchase. People bid up the price of the existing goods and services until the supply satisfies demand. Again, rising prices are inflation.

Effects of Inflation

What is so bad about inflation? Why can't we learn to live with it rather than try to eliminate it? One thoughtful economist has listed the following on p. 123 as the dangers of inflation:[6]

---

[5] Tilford Gaines, "Is Inflation Curable?" *Manufacturers Hanover Trust Economic Report,* March 1974.
[6] Sidney Homer, "Inflation and Interest Rates in the 1970s," speech given to the Canadian Institute for International Affairs, Toronto, Canada, March 13, 1974.

Table 5-7. *The International Problem of Inflation: 1965–1972**

	(1) Change in CPI	(2) Change in Output	(3) Change in Compensation	(4) Ratio (3)/(2)
United States	4.1	2.5	5.9	2.36
Canada	3.8	4.3	8.0	1.86
Japan	6.8	11.1	17.6	1.58
Belgium	3.9	6.9	10.8	1.56
France	4.7	5.9	10.8	1.83
West Germany	3.5	4.8	10.2	2.13
Italy	3.6	4.3	12.3	2.86
Netherlands	5.7	7.9	14.0	1.77
Switzerland	4.4	6.1	9.0	1.47
United Kingdom	5.6	4.2	10.1	2.40

* Figures presented in Columns (1) through (3) are average annual percentage changes; changes in output and compensation are for manufacturing industries.
Source: *Statistical Abstract of the United States, 1973.*

1. Penalty to all annuitants and holders of dollar assets.
2. Sky-high interest rates.
3. Scarcities.
4. Controls and, then, rationing.
5. Hoarding.
6. Withholding of goods and services by producing groups who, because of inflation, have the whip hand.
7. Acute scarcities and large price increases.
8. Excessive speculation as a substitute for useful production.
9. Serious widespread liquidity problems leading to important bankruptcies.
10. Declines in productivity and production.
11. Efforts at self-sufficiency both internationally and nationally, at great cost.
12. Unemployment.
13. Sharply declining living standards.
14. Internal unrest, strikes against the public interest, power showdowns, and defiance of government.
15. The rise of economic nationalism and destructive government-financed competition for exports and imports.
16. Successful attacks on democracy.

We shall not examine all of these points at this time, but we shall briefly discuss a few of the major dangers of inflation, including penalties to annuitants, scarcities, and controls.

The Environment of Business

Penalties to Annuitants

Annuitants are people who live on fixed incomes, that is, incomes that are not geared to rise with inflation. Retirees form the major group of annuitants. A retiree's pension benefits are usually determined on the basis of the salary in the last few years of work. As living costs rise with inflation and the retiree's income fails to grow, the annuitant suffers a growing economic penalty.

Scarcities

Material shortages in the world in the decade of the 1970s have been caused not by a reduction in supplies, or even by a failure of supplies to grow normally. Rather, they have been caused by a worldwide increase in demand far larger than expected by most forecasts. As one economist has noted, our worldwide prosperity is based on the division of labor and a large area of free trade. As shortages develop, countries start to protect their resources and are less eager to trade. Valuable resources can be used for international economic blackmail, as was the case with the Arab oil situation in the early 1970s. This, in turn, encourages a worldwide rush to self-sufficiency. For example, Americans were in an uproar when oil and gas prices skyrocketed as a result of the Arab oil embargo in 1973. On November 7, 1973, former President Nixon responded to the Arab oil embargo and the "trillion-dollar ripoff" by a call for American self-sufficiency. He said, "Let us pledge that by 1980, under Project Independence, we shall be able to meet America's energy needs from America's own energy resources." But such a response destroys the benefits of specialization and the division of labor, and generates a decline in living standards.

"Twins!"

Reprinted through permission of the Minneapolis Star

Controls

As the president of a large American bank said, "Whenever our system appears to falter by not providing our accustomed relative abundance at a low price, the people who distrust freedom always stand ready with a simplistic solution: The government should intervene." [7] These people argue that the mixed-economy pricing system has failed and the time has come for a managed economy. Because of the worsening of inflation in the United States during the late 1960s and early 1970s, an attempt was made at replacing the function of the free market system by government control. The American control system went through four "phases":

1. A complete pay–price freeze.
2. A rigid surveillance, reporting, and approval system for wage and price increases.
3. A more flexible control system within which the regulation of price and pay changes would be possible in order to adapt to the emerging pressure of shortages of raw materials.
4. Another freeze and rigid surveillance.

After a two-and-one-half year period, the control system was dropped.

Were controls effective? Reflecting on the more than two years of controls, a member of the President's Council of Economic Advisors was quoted as saying, ". . . there is no clear evidence that inflation is lower today than it would have been without controls." [8]

In fact, some economists have argued that the controls worsened the inflation situation by discouraging the construction of new plants and equipment at a time when it was badly needed. That is, price controls diminished the profit that investors could expect on new plants and equipment and, thus, caused the delay of investment. Furthermore, price controls in the United States encouraged firms to export their goods and services to higher-priced foreign markets. This further aggravated the demand–pull inflation in this country. Clearly a key factor undermining the success of the controls program was the international nature of economic enterprise.

Is Inflation Curable?

If a system of temporary controls cannot curb the rise of inflation, are there any other solutions available? A number of economists have offered alternate strategies for combatting inflation and shortages.

Many economists believe that the pricing system of free markets can

---

[7] Walter B. Wriston, "The Whale Oil, Chicken and Energy Syndrome," address given before The Economic Club of Detroit, February 25, 1974.
[8] "Did Controls Flunk Their First Peacetime Test?," *Business Week*, April 27, 1974, p. 107.

eliminate scarcities and inflation without any need for government intervention. Rising prices will motivate the consumer to consume less and the producer to produce more and encourage someone to develop a better and cheaper product. These economists feel that politicians and economists do not have the ability to replace the wisdom of the marketplace.

Other economists see a role for government in the fight against inflation. Henry Kaufman, an internationally respected economist, sees the government solution to the problem as "a program of national austerity including, among other things, increasing incentives to save, taxing inflationary profits and wages, removing the wage and price rigidities, encouraging capital formation in essential sectors, and placing considerable emphasis on the quality and not just the quantity of economic growth." [9]

Of course, efforts must continue to uncover new sources of raw materials in order to take some of the pressure off the economies of the world. The problem of resource development—and the ultimate defeat of inflation—requires intelligent national policies and realistic international negotiations on trade relationships.

CAREERS AND JOBS IN ECONOMICS

You will find numerous and increasing opportunities as an economist in either government or business. As an economist for the state or federal government, you would be responsible for preparing reports that could influence national economic policy. Government economists also collect, tabulate, and present statistics on economic activity, such as GNP and employment levels.

As a business economist, you would provide top management with the information needed to make important policy decisions. You might be asked to determine the price for your company's new product. Or you may have to estimate the effect of government legislation on your company's opportunities for international trade.

The minimum background for becoming an economist is an undergraduate college degree with a major in economics. It is also becoming more important for you to obtain graduate school training if you desire a more responsible research position as an economist.

As an economist, you need to be accurate, like details, and be prepared to spend much time doing research. You could expect to take part in a number of team assignments and, therefore, should enjoy working with others.

[9] Henry Kaufman, "Economic Disarray and Disillusionment," talk delivered before the conference on "Wall Street and the Economy '74," The New School, New York, January 26, 1974.

You can expect to be well rewarded for your efforts. In 1970, the average annual salary for economists in business, industry, and nonprofit organizations was $20,000, while experienced economists working for the federal government earned between $14,000 and $23,000 a year.

CHAPTER SUMMARY

The growing complexities and international nature of industry require the student of business to be knowledgeable about the worldwide state of economic affairs. In this chapter, we presented a brief review of some of the basic terms and concepts of economics and examined a few of the problems that economists are trying to find answers to.

Capitalism is the label often given to the American economic system. It is based on the principles of the private ownership of property, freedom of enterprise and choice, self-interest as the dominant motive, competition, the price system, and a limited role for government. As time has passed, the nature of the American economic system has changed, and it is now best characterized as a mixed economy. It is a combination of pure competition, monopolistic competition, oligopoly, and pure monopoly. Furthermore, the government has taken an active role in influencing the state of the economy.

We contrasted the American economic system with socialism and communism. We saw how the government in a socialist country owns the basic industries while free enterprise exists in other areas. In a communist country the government exercises complete control over the economy, striving to eliminate free enterprise.

Economic growth was shown to be a worldwide phenomenon, not limited to any one country or part of the world. Specialization and the division of labor have made countries dependent on one another, and international trade and investment are becoming increasingly important. But economic growth and international trade have fostered problems as well as opportunities for human advancement. The problems of inflation, shortages, and inequality in income distribution threaten the stability of national and international peace. International cooperation will be needed for economic growth and prosperity to continue in order to improve the worldwide quality of life.

Career opportunities for economists exist in both the government and private enterprise areas. Business and government leaders will be calling upon economists for advice more and more in the years ahead as economic problems intensify and become more complex. As an economist, you could share in the excitement of finding solutions to these problems. Given the dynamic nature of the field, a career in economics promises to be both challenging and rewarding.

PROVOCATIVE STATEMENT

The Evils of Uncontrolled Economic Growth

1 "Economic growth is not good in itself. Economic growth, at too fast a rate, is a cancer, and the evils that are associated with it may far outweigh any good that comes out of it. As Americans, we tend to believe that economic growth must be good, that increasing gross national product must be good, and we have tended to turn a blind eye to some of the evils associated with economic growth. We have to talk about such things as a distribution of income. We have to talk about pollution. We have to help our host countries recognize how they can achieve balanced and positive economic growth.

I think our opportunity rests in helping to create stable and equitable economic and social systems and not creating an unstable situation merely for our own advantage. We're living in an age in which we begin to realize that the end to all ends is not how much the gross national product increased last year. We must be concerned about other things that are more difficult to measure.

For example, what is the gross national product and how does its composition really meet the needs of the American People? If it doesn't, why doesn't it? We have to ask the same questions in other countries. Do the underdeveloped nations in the world today really need diesel engines right now? Should they be spending their capital some place else? We have to be willing to face the questions and to talk about them openly.

We have to be willing to help those nations recognize the important issues."

John T. Hackett,
Executive Vice President,
Cummins Engine Company, Inc.

PROVOCATIVE STATEMENT

The Failings of Capitalism

2 "Capitalism is on trial. Young people are challenging the rights of private property in most countries in the West. These societies, including our own, are pseudo-democracies ruled by "liberal" authoritarians and dominated by social conditions of inequality and injustice. In the poverty-stricken lands of Asia, Africa, and Latin America, socialist movements flourish. It is only a matter of time until revolution occurs in these deprived nations.

Karl Marx believed that the precondition to a meaningful spiritual life was freedom from the necessity to perform coerced labor. Technology would allow humankind to triumph over nature. Capitalism, in Marx's view, stood in the way of true freedom because it fettered the development of production and technology. Marx was only partly right; technological development is a necessary but not sufficient condition to effect human liberation. The barriers to human development created by capitalism are not primarily material but rather psychological. We are induced to buy goods we do not need and things that bring us no spiritual joy, and, in so doing, we perpetuate our enslavement."

> David Mermelstein,
> "Toward a Socialist Alternative,"
> in *Economics: Mainstream Readings and Radical Critiques,* New York: Random House, 1973,
> pp. 401–05.

REVIEW QUESTIONS

1. What are the six basic principles that underlie the American capitalist economy?
2. How does the price system, through supply and demand, determine WHAT, HOW, and FOR WHOM goods and services shall be produced?
3. What are the differences between pure competition, monopolistic competition, oligopoly, and monopoly?
4. How do socialist and communist systems differ from the American system in solving economic problems?
5. Why do countries engage in international trade, and why is international trade and investment growing more and more important?
6. Define inflation and state how demand–pull inflation differs from cost–push inflation.
7. What alternate solutions have been suggested as possible cures for inflation?

Parts of a Typical Business

PART THREE

Chapter Outline

The Three Groups of Management Principles

Part 1: Management Fundamentals
    The Process of Making Decisions
        Tools for Decision Making
    The Functions of Managing
    Company Goals, Policies, and Strategies
        Policies
        Strategies

Part 2: Organization and Leadership
    Variables in Organizing Companies
        Fundamental Components
        Committees
    Leadership and Motivation
        Skills of the Manager
        Needs of Employees
        Theory X and Theory Y
        Motivation

Careers and Jobs

Chapter Summary

Provocative Statement 1:
    People Tactics in Management

Provocative Statement 2:
    Innovative Strategy

Key Terms

Quantifiable
Screening
Entities
Computer programs
Terminals
Reporting relationships
Implementing
Return on invested capital
Volume maximization
Internal policies
External policies
Dividends
Consumerism
Innovative
Counterstrategy
Market share
Tactics
Program
Strategic plan
Strategic variables
Contingency plans
Operating necessities
Operating variables
Synergy
Decision by consensus
Expediter
Feedback

Introduction to Management

"The ruling assumption of an innovative strategy is that whatever exists is aging. The assumption must be that existing product lines and services, existing markets and distribution channels, existing technologies and processes will sooner or later—and usually sooner—go down rather than up."

—Peter F. Drucker
MANAGEMENT—*Tasks, Responsibilities, Practices*

6

This chapter is concerned with the principles that are applied in managing large organizations. Three groups of management principles have evolved from theories and experience over the years. All three are used in most organizations.

1. *Classical.* An accumulation of *do's* and *don'ts*, resulting from decades of trial and error, provides the framework for running a business.
2. *Behavioral.* Concepts are developing, based on the human being as the focal point of the company and as the means of achieving company goals.
3. *Scientific.* Methods dependent on numbers as the bases of solutions have improved a manager's ability to forecast future performance, allocate resources, identify problem areas, and handle other quantifiable decision making.

This chapter is divided into two parts: one on fundamentals, covering principles in the classical school, and another on organization and leadership, which includes portions of the behavioral school. Elements of the scientific school are given in Chapter Seventeen.

PART 1: MANAGEMENT FUNDAMENTALS

This part includes the decision-making process, the functions of management, and the role of goals, policies, plans, and strategies.

133

Drawing by Lorenz; © 1975 The New Yorker Magazine, Inc.

"Have you gentlemen concluded the decision-making process?"

The Process of Making Decisions

Managers make decisions. They could take actions that have varying effects on the business. Their main objective is to select the best thing to do or not do, after considering the possibilities. If the manager's position in the company is high, the decisions are likely to have more impact on performance and will be harder to correct if they are wrong. Even people in lower levels of the organization are expected to make important decisions occasionally. Therefore, it is essential to know how to make them in the most efficient way. The process involved is summarized here.

1. *Definition.* What specifically is the purpose of the decision? What are the apparent courses of action? Later, other alternatives might surface, but it is advisable to identify those which are obvious at an early stage.

2. *Information.* Develop what needs to be known about each alternative. Having enough facts and opinions increases the chances that all the alternatives are evident and that the best choice will be made.

3. *Analysis.* Analyze the information by separating the appropriate facts and opinions according to the alternative actions that could be taken. Sometimes a new alternative, often a combination of actions, is uncovered at this stage, and it could be the best alternative to follow.

Introduction to Management

4. *Selection.* Decide which is the best alternative for solving the purpose of the decision. It could be a compromise because the best solution might be too costly or jeopardize more important situations.

5. *Evaluation.* Follow what happens after the decision is made. Perhaps a small change will improve the results. Certainly, people improve their decision-making ability by learning from mistakes.

Sometimes the process is a simple sequence that leads to an obvious conclusion. Sometimes, however, it becomes more complex because in business, decisions make or break a company. Figure 6-1 shows that important decisions are made by people who have progressed to middle management and above. However, these executives do not suddenly start the decision-making process when promoted to this level in the organization. They demonstrate their ability by a series of good decisions on less important items. Confidence builds in their ability. This confidence has the best chance of developing if the process just described is used on a regular basis from small personal matters to major decisions in business.

Tools for Decision Making

If an employee has inaccurate or insufficient information, there is a good chance he or she will make a poor decision. On the other hand, obtaining everything there is to know about most business decisions would take too long and be too costly. As a result, managers run businesses without knowing all that is required to be certain about their actions. This has led to decision making that utilizes the computer and other equipment for screening sources of information and providing enough to improve the chances of good decisions. People taking jobs in business must be aware of the information system provided by their company.

Figure 6-1. *Frequency of Decision Making in Management*

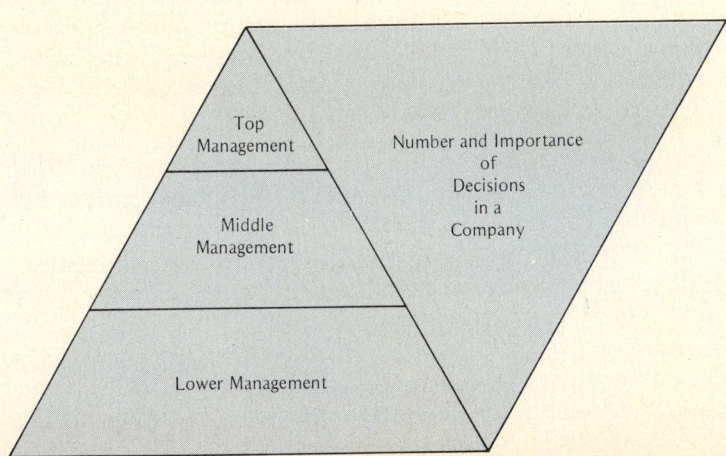

The facts and opinions gathered for a decision can be divided into three categories: (1) internal, (2) competitive, and (3) environmental. Internal information relates to details within a company such as operating details, interest paid on loans, and so on. Competitive information concerns the marketplace and information relating to the firm's ability to sell goods and services profitably. Environmental information involves community, government, and other entities potentially affecting the business. Often only one or two categories are involved, but all three would probably be considered for a major company decision.

Quantitative methods of problem solving have significantly improved in recent years. At the same time, these complex methods have been made more accessible and usable to employees who do not have training in mathematics and computers. Computer programs are designed for terminals located in offices far removed from the computer center. They permit engineers, market researchers, production managers, and others to obtain answers to problems in seconds instead of days or weeks. All levels of workers will be applying this tool to business problems in the years ahead.

The Functions of Managing

Some workers perform specific skills on a regular basis and rarely make decisions. As an employee is promoted in a company, the number of decisions he or she makes increases. The framework for managing, described as follows, has evolved from decades of business experience. It gives direction to individual decisions and makes the firm more efficient.

1. *Planning.* This consists of looking ahead. Forecasts are made for all parts of the business and are compiled into a plan that guides employees in their day-to-day work. The plan assures management that, for example, products being sold by the marketing department are being made in sufficient quantity by production. The entire organization has a means of coordinating its actions.

Forecasting operations for three months ahead is easier than for three years. Accuracy lessens as predictions are made for periods farther and farther into the future. As a result, plans must be revised regularly. Also, most companies have two types of plans: (1) detailed guides for operations during the coming 12 months and (2) less detailed estimates of the future for the company in three to five years.

2. *Organizing.* This step involves assembling the resources needed to carry out a company plan. These include people, money, equipment, materials, and property in the correct quantities at the proper places at the correct times. It also means tons of decisions to assure needed quality within costs specified in the plan. Finally, special attention must be given to organizing employees so that available talent is used most efficiently and so that reporting relationships improve performance.

Figure 6-2. *Frequency of Planning in Management*

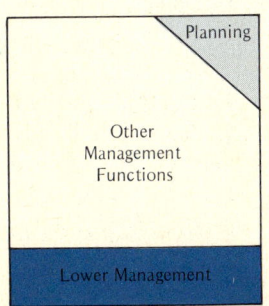
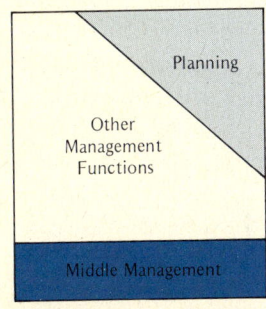
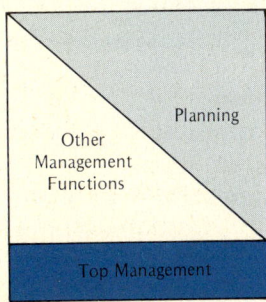

3. *Implementing.* Plans are put into action with the resources that have been organized. Employees begin the process of making and selling goods in the amounts stated in the plan. The flow of cash adjusts to the proper levels. Information is passed to appropriate parts of the firm. At this stage, leadership by management has a great impact on success. The attitude of employees will reflect this critical factor, and they will respond with the quality of work resulting from the leadership provided.

4. *Controlling.* Rarely do plans work perfectly. Adjustments must be made. When managers control their areas of responsibility, they use the details in the plan as a basis for detecting a change in actual conditions as compared to those that were expected. They will make the necessary adjustments and communicate what they have done to others. The computer has played an important part in expediting the process of keeping people informed. New systems of transmitting information quickly have greatly improved coordination between departments and divisions of companies.

If there is a major difference between plan and reality, planning, organizing, and implementing might begin again. For example, a competitor could enter the market with a wholly new product that, in time, could totally replace a company's product line. Quick, coordinated action would be needed, and a new plan would provide the basis of reacting to the competitor.

This approach to managing puts order in day-to-day activities. It provides priorities and a means of evaluating decisions. The process can be very elaborate in big companies or simply on a pad in the vest pocket of a small business manager. Figure 6-2 shows that planning becomes an increasing portion of a manager's activities as he or she climbs higher in the organization. Organizing, implementing, and control can be delegated to other employees.

Company Goals, Policies, and Strategies

Company plans reflect the goals of shareholders and management. This means that the heads of departments, divisions, and the overall company must set goals for their areas of responsibilities as guides for planning.

The primary goal of a company is after-tax profits to obtain the highest possible return on invested capital. This goal, however, must be achieved without jeopardizing other company goals, such as selling a high-quality product, creating a superior working environment for employees, and so on.

Profit goals can be stated in dollar totals, percentages on sales and invested capital, and/or earnings per share. Management of some companies can be satisfied with performance similar to previous year's profits, while others are quite aggressive, hoping for earnings to grow at 8 to 10% each year. Secondary goals that contribute to profit performance are:

1. *Cost minimization.* Through example and supervision, management attempts to control the flow of money out of the company by improving efficiency and eliminating unnecessary expenses. Good judgment is needed because spending is frequently necessary to grow and remain competitive.

2. *Volume maximization.* Volume maximization means that the company attempts to achieve production at full capacity. It results in a reduction of the cost per unit because more units are being divided into fixed costs. Lowering prices, better credit and customer service, discounts on large orders, and so on are means of achieving the needed volume. Price wars and other reactions by competitors can offset the advantages of this goal.

3. *Cash consciousness.* Controls serve to reduce the time between invoicing a customer and receipt of payment. The cash-conscious company also avoids early payment of its own bills. This goal reduces the working capital necessary to operate the business. It is especially important in times of inflation and when money is expensive to borrow. Also, the real value of money may decrease substantially during a short period of time.

Many other goals can be stated by a company. These include attaining superior technology, social progress through application of company resources, the best working conditions for employees, and scores of other possibilities commonly cited by the management of companies.

Policies

Management must establish policies for the company in addition to setting goals. Policies provide personnel throughout the organization with rules and guidelines on what to do in specific situations. Often the policies are verbal because written policies become outdated rapidly. Only a few companies allocate the time and money to keep written policies current.

Most policies are based on common sense. For example, the receptionist would not have to refer to a policy manual to call the controller when an auditor from the Internal Revenue Service arrives for a surprise visit. However, there are two reasons for maintaining updated written policies: (1) the rules and guidelines reflect the decisions of the manager in charge because of logical reasons that may not be apparent to the individual employee; (2) written policies gathered in a single manual assure integration. Various departments and divisions that have no rules or guidelines could work against each other.

A common way of classifying policies is by the people and organizations they affect. Those relating to matters inside the company are called **internal policies**, and those involving matters outside the company organization are called **external policies**.

EXAMPLES OF INTERNAL POLICIES These policies relate directly to company operations and involve the rules and guidelines for the board, management, and other employees.

An important example is the way **dividends** are distributed. If 100% of after-tax earnings is paid to the shareholders, they receive an attractive income. However, the company has little capital for expansion and research. On the other hand, keeping all the cash for growth may not be acceptable to most shareholders. The board of directors, which represents the owners, sets policy on dividends.

Other examples are the guidelines needed for pricing, customer credit, purchasing, inventories, and many other aspects of running the business. They give order to the job of managing and allow personnel to make many decisions without waiting for approval. When combined with company goals, such policies can give direction to the management functions of planning, organizing, implementing, and controlling.

EXAMPLES OF EXTERNAL POLICIES These policies cover situations involving organizations and individuals who are not shareholders, board members, or employees.

Companies are finding government involved in more and more aspects of their businesses. Pollution control, energy distribution, **consumerism**, treatment of minority workers, and so on combine to increase the necessity for policies to deal with authorities in these areas. In addition, communities are now expecting industry to participate in solving its problems.

Competition is becoming more intense because of the rise of giant firms outside the United States in the 1960s. In addition, materials and energy are getting scarce, and adequate supplies are no longer certain. New policies are needed to cope with these changes in conditions.

Labor unions can be an asset for a company and a source of strength in this period of global competition, or they can cause serious unrest. Updated rules and guidelines are necessary to retain cooperation of the workforce and improve the company's capability to respond to changes in the market.

Strategies

The creating of opportunities and **innovative** problem solving through company strategies is as fundamental to successful performance as application of decision making in the functions of management and the establishment of goals and policies.

A strategy has a specific overall objective and contains many components to achieve the objective. Each component also has a specific goal that contributes directly to achieving the overall objective. A strategy can involve all the major departments or only a single department, such as marketing or manufacturing. Usually strategies have most of their components included in the budgets and activities of short-range plans for existing operations. However, some of the components and most of the beneficial results are usually part of long-range plans for business in the future.

An example will clarify the business use of strategies. Imagine the situation in which a competitor has introduced a new product. The company is surprised by the move and is on the defense. It must create a counterstrategy. Components to retain market share in the immediate future could include: (1) a change in price; (2) advertising; (3) new packaging; (4) product modifications that are minor but change the appearance; (5) changes in credit policy; and (6) a legal search for infringement by the competitor on company patents and trademarks.

Management considers the result of these strategy components to be short range. More fundamental steps must be taken to secure the long-range future of the company. Therefore, parallel to the six steps just mentioned, the following could be initiated: (7) research and development would be authorized funds to discover a wholly different approach to meeting customer needs; (8) the acquisitions department would search for a firm which would be able to produce the product that R and D develops; (9) the finance department would seek the lowest cost funds to support the strategy components to seek both a short- and long-range solution.

TACTICS   This business term is commonly defined as a maneuver or deception within one of the components of a strategy to assist in accomplishing a narrowly defined objective. Military experts distinguish between tactics used to win a battle, and strategies employed to win the war. Tactics are short term in nature and are not normally very complex.

PROGRAMS   A program is a term for organizing several activities in such a way that the objective is achieved. Programs can be part of a specific strategy, or they can be the means of achieving broader goals. An example would be the R and D program in the counterstrategy just mentioned, involving many people, budgets, technical equipment, computers, and special requirements, such as a controlled environment. Success is dependent on the timing in putting these elements together.

Another example would be an acquisition program to replace R and D as the basis of growth in future years. Instead of depending on products flowing from the laboratory, the company decides to buy proven ideas that are already earning profits.

STRATEGIC PLANNING   This term is used two ways in business. First, a strategic plan can be the basis of controlling the many components of a strategy. This control is especially needed in strategies that last longer than a year; it specifies change as conditions change.

Second, the term is also used for plans that involve: (1) forecasts of probable decisions by governments, competitors, suppliers, labor unions, and

Figure 6-3. Summary of the Classical School of Management

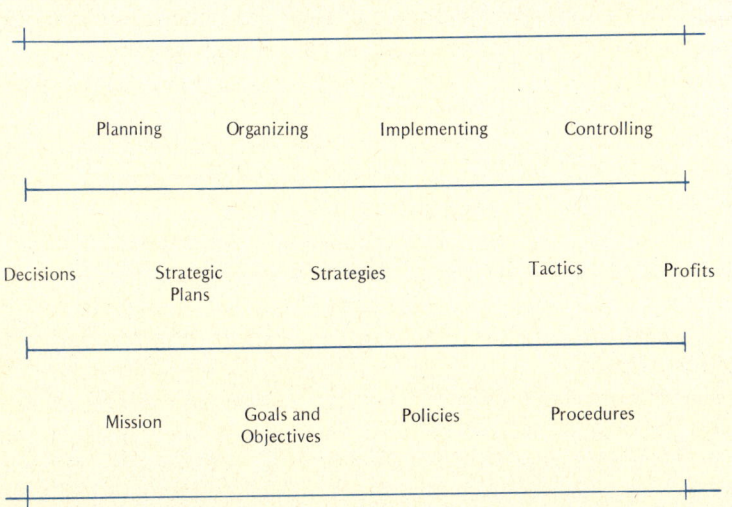

the communities in which the company does business, and (2) broad directions for products and services required to achieve goals in the predicted environment. The actions of outside organizations are commonly called **strategic variables**. The results of these forecasts are reflected mostly in the less detailed long-range plan.

Predicting strategic variables is very difficult but crucial to the success of many companies. To avoid being surprised by changes in conditions that nullify the forecasts, management often devises **contingency plans**. These are ready when a new situation suddenly occurs.

Figure 6-3 summarizes the topics discussed in the first part of this chapter.

PART 2: ORGANIZATION AND LEADERSHIP

Significant principles of the behavioral aspects of management are summarized in this part of the chapter. The personal characteristics of people in management positions and their style of leadership have a great impact on the organization of a company. These factors can affect the amount of authority that is actually given to middle and lower management from the top.

For example, an executive with one type of personality might create an organization similar to the classical pyramid shown in Figure 6-4, with many layers of authority, formal reporting relationships, and strict channels of communication. A comparable company could be headed by an executive who wants fewer levels and freer flow of facts and opinions from one department to another. This type is shown as a bell shape in Figure 6-4. A third firm might

Parts of a Typical Business

Figure 6-4. Two Extremes in Company Organization

have an organizational chart that appears normal, but in reality the chief executive delegates no authority to anyone. He becomes the supreme source for all major decisions, and his employees are afraid to take even the smallest initiative.

Businesses are usually organized according to **operating necessities** and past reporting relationships, in addition to personalities at the top. Operating necessities involve putting together departments that are most efficient because of location, type of job, relationships with outsiders such as customers, banks, and so on, and similar reasons. Tradition also plays a role because people usually resist changes and prefer existing situations regardless of problems caused by the arrangement.

Variables in Organizing Companies

Some of the basic factors to be considered in the design of an organization are line and staff personnel, span of control, departmentation, and centralization versus decentralization.

LINE AND STAFF The people involved in making and selling products, and handling the cash from customers and paying suppliers, are line personnel. The people who supply information and advice for operating decisions are called staff personnel.

These two divisions, however, are often interdependent. For example, the vice president of marketing is line because he is in charge of sales. Nevertheless, he also needs the support of staff personnel in advertising, sales administration, market development, and market research to perform most efficiently.

SPAN OF CONTROL This business term refers to the number of people reporting to a single manager. A low number—a narrow span of control—is good in that a supervisor knows his subordinates better and has the opportunity to work closely with each individual more often. On the other hand, this situation creates difficulties with vertical communications because there are more layers in the organization, and this slows or stops the flow of facts and opinions upward. Top management is sometimes forced to make decisions on

Drawing by Mulligan; © 1975 The New Yorker Magazine, Inc.

"Why, thank you, sir, and I had it in mind to tell you what a bang-up job I think you're doing."

inadequate information or, occasionally, misinformation. In addition, the many layers tend to create a formal organization, such as the pyramid in Figure 6-4, with "militaristic" *do's* and *don'ts*.

At the other end of the scale is a very wide span of control. Comparatively few layers result from many people reporting to one person, and this encourages upward flow in communications. Control can be a problem, however, because each manager does not know his subordinates as well and cannot supervise them as closely. Sometimes personnel at the same level duplicate each other's work or do not get needed information because it is not known that they need it. A broad span of control tends to create an informal structure and is often used by professional firms in accounting, engineering, technical research, and similar businesses.

The typical large company has both narrow and wide spans of control within its structure, and several departments between the two extremes. The variations reflect the type of work, the preferences of management, and the influence of "that's the way we've always done it."

DEPARTMENTATION   This factor involves dividing a company into departments, groups, or sections and assigning them specific kinds of jobs. The number of departments depends, however, on the span of control that is best for each situation. Highly motivated personnel who can work independently, supervised by a strong manager, might be consolidated into a single department instead of two or three departments. The same principle could be applied to divisions in a company, thereby consolidating two or three different product lines under one general manager.

In each situation the executive making the decision has to judge operating variables, the specific employees involved, and the potential supervisor. Since the same conditions will rarely be interpreted the same way by two different people, a change in management will frequently result in a change in departmentation.

CENTRALIZATION VS. DECENTRALIZATION The responsibility for company performance is at the top of every organization. If the authority to make major decisions is retained at this level, the power is centralized. On the other hand, if authority is given to divisions, and then to departments and individuals, decentralization is taking place.

Executives must know themselves and the degree to which they can feel comfortable about delegating authority. They must also size up managers to determine whether they can handle the authority and perform more successfully if they can make decisions without approval from a higher level. A trial-and-error approach to decentralization can be painful at times. Major mistakes have been made before the cause of the problem is detected. For this reason, some general managers are very slow to delegate authority.

Fundamental Components

Five different approaches to organizing a company are possible. These are summarized in Figure 6-5.

Usually a large company finds some combination of the five necessary to run efficiently rather than using only one. The most common combination involves a geographic or functional structure at the level next to the top and the reverse in middle management, with customer, product, or process breakdowns as required at lower levels.

The design selected will depend mostly on: (1) the nature of the business (retailing, industrial machinery, and so on); (2) the basic variables being utilized by management (span of control, centralization, and so on); and (3) the scope and diversity of operations in a company (many lines, national, international, and so on).

Committees

One form of organization used in nearly all businesses is a committee. The most important advantage of a committee is that more information will be gathered and better analysis is likely to result. This leads to determination of the best alternatives for the company. A committee decision is often superior to one resulting from individuals working by themselves. Another reason for committees is the transferring of responsibility for major decisions to a group

Figure 6-5. Types of Organizational Breakdowns

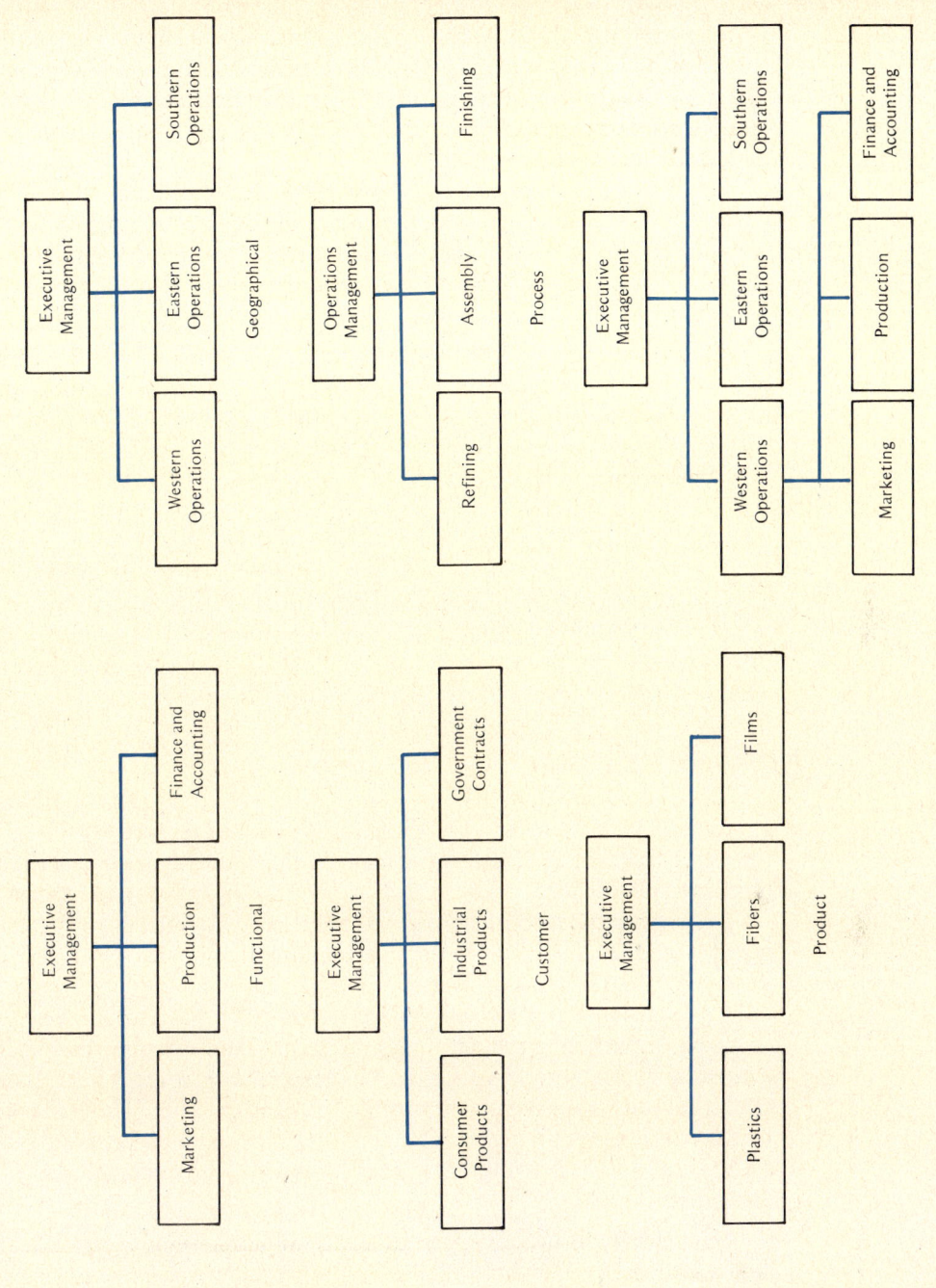

rather than placing the load on one or two people. Committees also allow management to have several people and departments or divisions to participate in a decision. Finally, broad participation in this decision makes it more difficult for the opposition in a company to obstruct a decision, since they were part of the conclusions.

However, many executives do not care for the committee approach to decision making. Sometimes one person can dominate a meeting and influence the group toward a decision that is good for one department or division but not necessarily good for the entire company. In addition, it usually takes longer for a committee to reach a conclusion. Some managers use the committee as a tactic to keep a decision from being made, as detail after detail is studied.

It is possible to achieve synergy with a committee. This means gaining more than the sum of the parts, or simply, more than expectations. Dynamic management teams can gain the advantages of formal groups without the disadvantages. Committees can be an obstacle to the speed needed to cope with today's global competition, inflation, and problems with supply. However, decision by consensus of a group is gaining support in the United States. In fact, some of the newest company information systems are designed to feed data, reports, and so on to a "Strategic Decision Center," where several executives can participate in making decisions. Figure 6-6 shows an example of this type of room.

Leadership and Motivation

The style of leadership greatly affects both the organizational design and the effectiveness of management. There are three basic types of approaches to directing subordinates.

Autocratic managers tend to make decisions without the participation of others. Some simply announce their conclusion. Many try to sell their decision. A few go to the effort of presenting ideas and opinions in a way which influences subordinates to come to the same position as the manager.

The *democratic* approach involves letting subordinates participate in the analysis and selection stages of the decision-making process. Such managers establish limits for the group's contributions and actually permit the workers to reach a decision by consensus. They act as expediters, stimulators, controllers, and so on in the meeting, but do not bias the conclusions with their own preferences.

The *laissez-faire* style requires "bottom up" management. The manager who uses this type considers the person closest to the problem as the one best able to solve it. The concept is an extreme of decentralization and involves complete delegation of authority to subordinates. Common sense suggests caution when the laissez-faire style is used, because the manager must be very confident that subordinates are competent in their jobs.

Figure 6-6. *One Approach to Strategic Decision Centers*

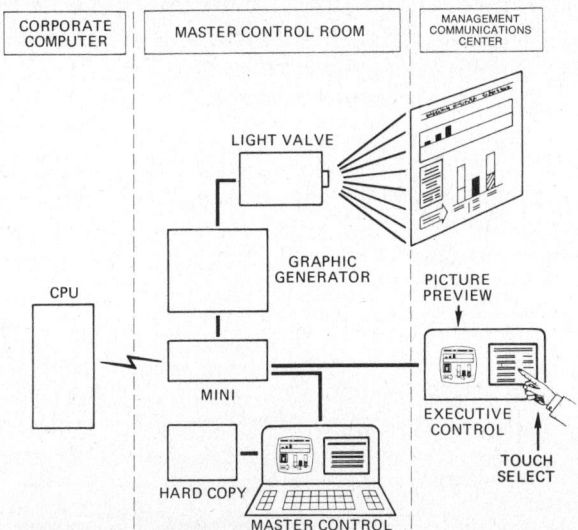

Courtesy of Information Management International Corporation, 425 Park Avenue, New York, N.Y. All rights reserved.

147

Skills of the Manager

Managerial competence is the result of three skills: technical, "people," and optimizing.

Technical skill involves more, for example, than knowing the fundamentals of the job. It also requires administrative talents. For example, sales managers must be more than good sales representatives. They must know the procedures for processing orders, deploying personnel, controlling shipments, and so on. In summary, they must be able to be effective in all four functions of managing—planning, organizing, implementing, and controlling.

"People" skill in managing means being able to influence employees to complete their work successfully, to respect the manager, and to enjoy their jobs. Obviously, no one can make people like their work if they are basically discontent. However, the person who has the greatest capacity in people skills will lead subordinates to the highest level of job satisfaction.

Optimizing skill involves putting technical competence and people skills in the best combination to accomplish objectives. Judgment is important in knowing the correct thing to do and in taking the steps needed to influence others to accept decisions.

Few people are born with the full potential of the three skills. However, each can be developed by the person who wants to be successful in business. Progress depends on self-knowledge and conscientious efforts to know others in the organization. Awareness of one's own weaknesses and strengths, and those of others, reduces the possibility of making bad decisions or being exploited.

Needs of Employees

People spend seven or more hours per day working, and they want the most satisfying jobs they can find. If a company is insensitive to the needs of its employees, dissatisfaction increases, and an undesirable cycle begins. The best of the skilled workers and managers can find positions in another firm, and they start to leave. Some of the replacements are frequently not as competent, and inefficiency increases. The pressures grow, and more of the better talent leaves.

It is difficult to reverse this cycle. Management often attempts to cure the symptoms of the problem instead of the cause. While the trouble is not always the organizational design and the job environment created by the structure, these are good places to start looking for the cause. In business there are three levels of needs. These are taken from A. H. Maslow's[1] five levels for life in general:

1. *Basic.* Enough after-tax income to meet an individual's goals for living standards; safe working conditions to protect him physically and preserve his

---

[1] Abraham H. Maslow, *Motivation and Personality*, New York: Harper and Row Publishers, 1954.

earning power; and job security to avoid periods when he is not earning because of an employer decision rather than his own.

2. *Social.* A reasonable job environment and opportunities for interaction with other employees both on company time and off the job.

3. *Personal.* Ego fulfillment through rewards on the job which are made known to others, such as compliments, citations, and promotions; personal satisfaction from performance on the work assigned.

More and more companies are recognizing that the individual is a better worker and a more loyal supporter of management decisions when these basic needs are satisfied. The attitude that people are "units of production" has gradually changed in the past two decades. Part of this improvement is general upgrading in the type of jobs people have (more skills and a higher level of technology) and the resulting respect due to the work. The other part has its origins in the increased social consciousness that has been induced by advocates for minorities, feminists, and other groups of workers.

Theory X and Theory Y

Table 6-1 summarizes the two extremes of attitude a manager can take in formulating a style of leadership.

Table 6-1. *Theories of Management*

Theory X	Theory Y
1. Work is distasteful. It has to be done to survive, but the smallest amount for the greatest income is the normal worker attitude.	1. Work is a normal activity like eating and recreation.
2. Most people must be coerced, controlled, directed, or threatened with punishment to get them to work toward company objectives.	2. People will exercise self-control and self-direction in working towards an objective. Commitment toward objectives depends more upon rewards associated with accomplishment than on coercion.
3. The average person prefers to be directed, wishes to avoid responsibility, has relatively little ambition, and wants security above all else.	3. The average person under proper conditions learns not only to accept responsibility but to seek it.
4. Workers are incapable of applying imagination and creativity to company problems.	4. The capacity to use a high degree of imagination and creativity in solving company problems is widely distributed in the population. In fact, the intellectual potential of the average worker is being only partially utilized.

It is possible to think of several jobs that would motivate a worker to behave according to either Theory X or Theory Y. For example, many people on the assembly lines in this country are bored with their work and become resentful of management. Supervisors react according to Theory X and begin to "run a tight ship" in order to get things done.

The opposite is true of research scientists who will spend long hours pursuing a solution to business problems with very little urging. Their job is challenging, and they respond without threats.

Managers, therefore, have three major factors to weigh in addition to their own characteristics and skills in selecting their approach to leadership: (1) the nature of the work; (2) the people working for them; and (3) the background of management/employee relations. If common sense tells them that the jobs are repetitive and uninteresting, more controls and direction are going to be needed. If they are challenging and stimulating, more of Theory Y applies.

Motivation

Another dimension of managing is the ability to influence individuals to feel their work is interesting and that their contributions are needed for success. More than money is involved. The benefits of motivated workers cannot be "bought" by increases in wages and benefits for long periods. They must like their jobs and respect their superiors. Motivation achieves this result.

The fulfillment of basic, social, and personal needs is critical in achieving good morale in business. Each company situation is different. Consequently, there is no formula for success in motivating employees. A fundamental step tried by many managers is to use a more democratic style of leadership and to exercise authority only when other courses of action have failed.

Productivity is the most measurable benefit from good morale. Happy workers can exert the extra effort needed to meet obligations, cut costs, build customer good will, and generally improve profit performance. Before the 1950s it was thought that employees would interpret concessions by management in meeting worker needs and improving working conditions as signs of weakness and that a decrease in productivity would occur. Studies in the 1960s and 70s have proved, however, that the good morale produced by such concessions usually leads to greater output because employees tend to pay more attention to their work and to standards for quantity and quality.

Communications also improve with good morale. People are less secretive, and company politics are minimal. This means that the cycle of communication and feedback shown in Figure 6-7 can take place without being blocked or distorted. Effective management depends on this cycle.

It also depends on the three-way flow shown in the other diagram in Figure 6-7. A bell-shaped structure is used because three-way flow occurs more freely in this type of organization than in a pyramid structure where relationships are more formal.

Figure 6-7. *Three-way Flow of Communications*

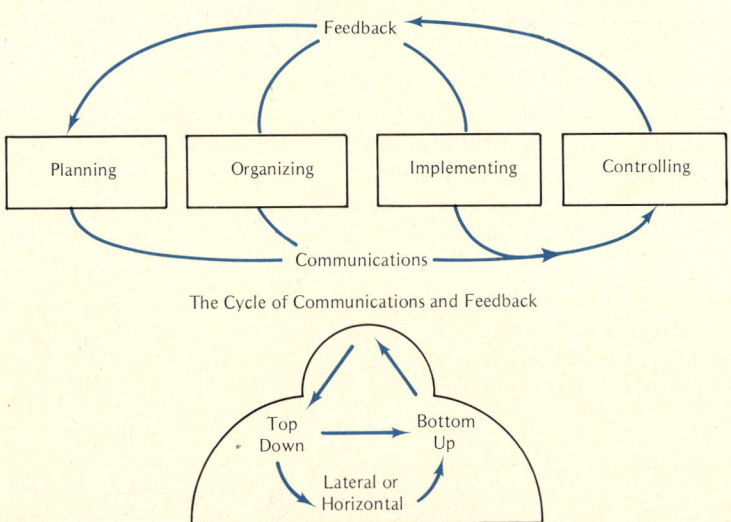

CAREERS AND JOBS

It is difficult to be a successful manager because there are so many variables involved. In fact, some people have been fired and their careers severely damaged because they handled an important assignment poorly. The most encouraging aspect is that most of the requirements for success can be learned. You do not need to be born with special qualities. Through education, self-analysis, and a well-planned approach to gaining experience in the early years after graduation, people have a chance to reach the top in business. Average managers tend to let things happen to them in business instead of carefully planning the way they will spend a major portion of their lives. Therefore, the competition for promotions is usually less in quality than in quantity.

Education is important for two reasons: (1) it provides the required technical skills, knowledge of the variables in managing, and the principles that lower the chance of making poor decisions, and (2) general information acquired by taking courses in political science, psychology, sociology, and so on makes an individual more interesting, and contributes to refinement of "people" skills. Rarely in the 1970s and in the future will people get to the top of organizations without a college education. Many will have advanced degrees that either give them special skills in a narrow field or broad knowledge in both business administration and a science.

Self-analysis is an important step in the earliest stage of considering a career, and the process is detailed in Chapter Twenty.

Gaining experience is also an important step toward success in business. Some people take the job that pays best or is closest to the home town where old friends are going to live. Others want to gain the most experience they can and will take training programs that move them frequently to strange places in the first five to seven years of their careers. It is a sacrifice in many ways to opt for experience. However, the odds are that young managers with the best training behind them will make better decisions. If they have gained experience in their field and developed themselves through education and a self-improvement program, the combination is hard to beat.

The jobs in management include the ones described in other chapters of this book, and many more. One way to get an idea about organizations, and where you might fit, is to compare the designs in Figure 6-5 with the published organizational charts for companies in your area. Collection and comparison could be an interesting project that will help your career directly.

CHAPTER SUMMARY

Part 1 discusses fundamentals of the classical school of management.

In order to increase the probability of making the correct decision, managers go through a process that assures that they have adequate information and that all the alternatives have been uncovered. This process involves: (1) defining the specific purpose of the decision; (2) gathering all the relevant information; (3) analyzing the facts and opinions for definition of alternatives according to advantages and disadvantages; (4) selecting the best alternative from the decision maker's point of view; and (5) evaluating the decision after it is made to see if corrections are necessary and to learn from what actually happened as compared with what was predicted.

The functions of managing provide a framework for the tens of business decisions that must be made each day. *Planning* involves looking ahead and forecasting the performance of every part of the company. *Organizing* involves having personnel, materials, facilities, and money available in the correct quantity, at the right location, and at the proper time to carry out plans. *Implementing* requires managers to put into action the resources that have been organized according to plan; directing and motivating employees to perform efficiently are fundamental for success. *Controlling*, the fourth function, involves adjusting plans for "real world" developments.

Management has an obligation to give guidance to employees by setting goals and establishing policies. The primary goal in business is profits, yet it must be balanced with other goals of the company. Secondary goals, such as cost minimization and superior work environment, contribute to achieving the desired level of profits. Other goals include social responsibility by business and special objectives such as maximum quality of product regardless of profits.

Policies establish rules and guidelines for employees. They range from very important matters such as dividends to less critical policies involving lower levels of the organization. In addition, management normally devises formal strategies. These are special plans that often span short- and long-range plans to solve a major problem or to reach a specific goal. Since many components are involved in a strategy, participation by many departments in the company is often necessary.

Part 2 discusses organization and leadership and covers some of the principles in the behavioral school of management.

Companies are usually organized according to operating necessities, personalities at the top, and the tradition of past reporting relationships. Variables in designing organizations include line and staff positions, span of control, departmentation, centralization, and decentralization. Actual components involve alignments according to job function, geographic location, type of customer and product, and the production process. Committees have advantages and disadvantages, but there is a growing trend toward major decisions being made by groups of key executives rather than one or two individuals.

Three extreme styles of leadership are possible. *Autocratic* managers tend to make decisions without the participation of others. *Democratic* executives permit subordinates to contribute directly to the analysis and selection stages of the decision making process. The *laissez-faire* style involves "bottom up" management and the principle that the person closest to the problem is best able to solve it.

Skills needed by a manager are: (1) technical skill, including administrative capabilities; (2) "people" skill, which involves influencing peers and those higher in the organization, as well as allowing a subordinate to be directed toward completing the work efficiently without losing respect for the manager; and (3) optimizing skill. These capabilities can be developed if the person recognizes strengths and weaknesses and consciously works at self-improvement.

Motivating workers to do their best will depend on recognizing the three needs in business: basic, social, and personal. The attitude of a manager will also affect leadership and motivation. Theory X holds that work is distasteful, and that people have to be forced into doing their jobs; it states that no average person readily accepts responsibility. Theory Y contends that work is a normal activity such as eating or recreation; it assumes that people can be trusted and that they have a tendency to seek responsibility and interesting problems to solve. The nature of the work and the type of people working for a specific manager will have a major bearing on the theory more likely to be applicable.

Motivation seeks to achieve good morale and loyalty to management. This leads to greater productivity and better communications. The most successful businesses usually have these elements.

Careers will develop best if they have the foundation of education, self-improvement programs, and early job selection that emphasizes training and experience rather than proximity to home, a company car, or other factors with less long-range assistance.

PROVOCATIVE STATEMENT

People Tactics in Management

1. "To have a successful career in business management, you have to manipulate people. You cannot just be smart and honest. It takes plotting your way around, through and over other managers. Let me give you an example of how executives in my company work their way toward getting something approved. From what I hear, this is typical of other companies, too.

   Bill Cromwell is manager of Product Development. He has become identified with a new product line in plastic fasteners because his department initiated the proposal to bring the line from concept to production. The process is coordinated by the proposer and involves supervising a market study to confirm the potential of the idea and the specifications of the product, carrying out technical research to uncover the best materials and designs, production planning to determine the plant layout, equipment and personnel required, and building pilot operations along with some market testing before going full scale.

   The plastic fasteners got to the pilot stage, and even the market testing went well with good response by customers. Going all the way with full scale operations depended on approval by two levels of management committees and the board of directors. If all three approved, Bill Cromwell would be general manager of the profit center and, if the plastic fasteners "took off," he could be a corporate vice president before the age of 40.

   One complication occurred. Another proposal for industrial coatings to increase the life of plant and equipment had been approved and was going for development through a similar process. According to tests, the coatings last for years and would be highly profitable, but sales volume would level off after the first three years. Return of money invested would be better and faster than Bill Cromwell's product for five years, but over ten years the plastic fasteners were a better investment. The company did not have the funds, nor did they think it was a good idea, to start two new things at one time.

   Bill started the political game by setting up a source of intelligence in the project. His secretary became very friendly with a girl who did filing for industrial coatings, and knew as much about progress and problems as the manager in charge. With intelligence flowing, the Cromwell team began selling plastic fasteners by keeping members of both management committees "informed." Without ever directly downgrading the other product, Bill Cromwell sold the advantages, especially the long term profit growth potential of plastic fasteners and the reliablity of his estimates: 'Our company needs the strength of a product that will double and double again five years.' He carefully avoided the fact that industrial coating products would level off from a very high base established by a high level of market acceptance in the early years.

   You would have thought it was a presidential election year with the meetings at breakfast, lunch and dinner. Even Mrs. Cromwell was part of the "people" plan. She lost ten pounds for the campaign, was fully briefed on the pros and cons of both coatings and fasteners, and never missed a cocktail party or dinner to do her part.

The other manager, Dick Greenwood, never really understood that there was a campaign going on. He knew that Bill Cromwell would take advantage of every opportunity to sell his project, but he did not know that Cromwell had a chart noting his progress with each committee member and the characteristics that made him susceptible to getting his vote. If the member had a strong-willed wife, Mrs. Cromwell would work on it. If he liked a weekend of golf, one of the staff members with a low handicap would help him with his game, and so on. Greenwood got suspicious about the intelligence leak, but never knew about the systematic "sell fastener" campaign. 'The projects will be judged on their own merit' was his position.

You can imagine what happened. The first committee gave plastic fasteners priority, and the second voted to delay introduction of industrial coatings for two or three years, 'if the product is a viable possibility at that time.' The board approved the investment, and now, three years later, Cromwell is campaigning for an expansion program, and Greenwood is still at his old job.

For myself, I could not manipulate people like Cromwell does. If it takes conniving and deception to succeed, maybe I better think about having my own business. I would rather be a big fish in a little pond, than have to play corporate politics."

Alan B. Cotich
Corporate Name Withheld

PROVOCATIVE STATEMENT

Innovative Strategy

2 "Like all business strategies, an innovative strategy starts out with the question 'What is our business and what should it be?' But its assumptions regarding the future are different from the assumptions made with respect to the ongoing business. There the assumption is that present product lines and services, present markets and present distribution channels, present technologies and processes will continue. The first objective of a strategy for the ongoing business is to optimize what already exists or is being established.

The ruling assumption of an innovative strategy is that whatever exists is aging. The assumption must be that existing product lines and services, existing markets and distribution channels, existing technologies and processes will sooner or later—and usually sooner—go down rather than up.

The governing device of a strategy for the ongoing business might therefore be said to be: "Better and More." For the innovative strategy the device has to be: "New and Different."

The foundation of innovative strategy is planned and systematic sloughing off of the old, the dying, the obsolete. Innovating organizations spend neither time nor resources on defending yesterday. Systematic abandonment of yesterday alone can free the resources, and especially the scarcest resource of them all, capable people, for work on the new.

Unwillingness to do this may be the greatest obstacle to innovation in the existing large business. . . .

The new and especially the as-yet unborn, that is the future innovation, always looks insignificant compared to the large volume, the large revenue, and the manifold problems of the ongoing business. It is all the more important, therefore, for an existing business to commit itself to the systematic abandonment of yesterday if it wants to be able to create tomorrow.

Second in a strategy of innovation is the clear recognition that innovation efforts must aim high. It is just as difficult, as a rule, to make a minor modification to an existing product as it is to innovate a new one. . . .

The majority of innovative efforts will not succeed. Nine out of every ten "brilliant ideas" turn out to be nonsense. And nine out of every ten ideas which, after thorough analysis, seem to be worthwhile and feasible turn out to be failures or, at best, puny weaklings. The mortality rate of innovations is—and should be—high.

Innovative strategy therefore aims at creating a new business rather than a new product within an already established line. It aims at creating new performance capacity rather than improvement. It aims at creating new concepts of what is value rather than satisfying existing value expectations a little better. The aim of innovating efforts is to make a significant difference. What is significantly different is not a technical decision. It is not the quality of science that makes the difference. It is not how expensive an undertaking it is or how hard it is to bring it about. The significant difference lies in the impact on the environment.

"Success" in innovating effort is a batting average of one out of ten. This is, of course, the reason for aiming high in innovative efforts. The one winner has to make up for the nine losers and has to produce its own results. . . .

An innovation does not proceed in a nice linear progression. For a good long time, sometimes for years, there is only effort and no results. The first results are then usually meager. Indeed, the first products are rarely what the customer will eventually buy. The first markets are rarely the major markets. The first applications are rarely the applications that, in the end, will turn out to be the really important ones . . . .

Social impacts of new technology are very difficult, and sometimes impossible, to predict. But even more difficult to predict than the eventual success of the genuinely new is the speed with which it will establish itself. "Timing is of the essence"—above all in innovation. Yet timing is totally incapable of being predicted. There are the computer, the antibiotics, the Xerox machine—all innovations that swept the market. But for every successful innovation that has results faster than anyone anticipates, there are five or six others—in the end perhaps, equally successful ones—which for long years seem to make only frustratingly slow headway. The outstanding example may be the steam-driven ship. By 1835 its superiority was clearly established; but it did not replace the sailing ship until fifty years later. Indeed, the "golden age of sail" in which the great clippers reached perfection began only after the steamship had been fully developed. For almost half a century, in other words, the steamship continued to be "tomorrow" and never seemed to become "today."

But then, after a long, frustrating period of gestation, the successful innovation rises meteorically. It becomes within a few short years a new major industry or a new major product line and market. But until it has reached that point it cannot be predicted when it will take off, nor indeed whether it ever will."

Peter F. Drucker
MANAGEMENT—
Tasks, Responsibilities, Practices.
Harper and Row, 1973, pp. 791–93.

REVIEW QUESTIONS

1. Distinguish between information gathering and analysis in the decision-making process. What contribution does evaluation make in this process?
2. Relate decision making to each function of managing.
3. Explain the difference between a policy and a strategy. Is strategic planning always related to a strategy?
4. How does a top executive's personality affect the organization and atmosphere in a company?
5. Identify the impact of span of control on departmentation in the design of an organization.
6. Is the *laissez-faire* approach to managing a a practical means of running an organization?
7. Could the objective of satisfying the needs of employees interfere with the goal of earning profits under any conditions? Name them.

Chapter Outline

The Proprietorship

The Partnership
   Types of Partners
   Forming a Partnership
   Dissolving the Partnership
   The Limited Partnership—A Special Case

The Corporation
   Nature of the Corporate Form
   Forming a Corporation
   Corporate Shareholders
   The Board of Directors
      Director Responsibilities
      Inside and Outside Directors
      Directors under Attack

Other Forms of Business Organization
   Joint Venture
   Joint Stock Company
   Business Trust

Choosing a Specific Form of
Business Organization
   Proprietorship
   Partnership
   Corporation

Chapter Summary

Provocative Statement 1:
   The Importance of Outside Directors

Provocative Statement 2:
   The Proprietor in the World of Big Business

Key Terms

Proprietorship
Income
Partnership
General partner
Limited partner
Limited liability
Silent partner
Secret partner
Dormant partner
Articles of partnership
Capital contribution
Partnership capital
Corporation
Charter

Articles of incorporation
Shareholders
Stock certificate
Pre-emptive right
Proxy
Dividend
Liquidation
Inside directors
Outside directors
Joint venture
Joint stock company
Business trust
Massachusetts trust

Forms of Business Organization

"The demise of the traditional American proprietorship has been exaggerated and the much advertised triumph of the organization is far from total."
—American Business Observer and Author

A problem common to all business executives is the selection of a particular form of business organization. By *form*, we mean the particular legal structure of the business enterprise. While there are many variations, there are essentially three fundamental forms: the *proprietorship*, the *partnership*, and the *corporation*. In this chapter we shall discuss the characteristics and importance of the different forms of enterprise. We shall also examine the reasons why a business executive might want to select one form over the others.

THE PROPRIETORSHIP

A *proprietorship*, or *sole proprietorship* as it is sometimes called, is a one-owner firm. Often the owner is the only worker in the company. For example, the local one-man barbershop is a proprietorship. The owner may, however, employ a number of people. In a large shop, the barber–owner may have several other barbers working for him or her.

The proprietorship is the easiest form of business to establish. It may cost nothing more than a fee for registration of the company name or a license fee. It is also free of government restrictions, except those that apply to the individual. For example, the proprietor may not engage in a business that violates the law, such as a gambling parlor.

This ease of organization and the desire of people to be their own boss have made the proprietorship the most common form of business organization

Table 7-1. *Enterprise Statistics in the United States*

	PROPRIETORSHIPS		PARTNERSHIPS		CORPORATIONS	
	NUMBER (THOUS.)	% OF ALL FIRMS	NUMBER (THOUS.)	% OF ALL FIRMS	NUMBER (THOUS.)	% OF ALL FIRMS
1960	9,090	81	941	8	1,141	11
1965	9,078	79	914	8	1,424	13
1967	9,126	79	906	8	1,534	13
1968	9,212	79	918	8	1,542	13
1969	9,430	79	921	8	1,659	13
1970	9,400	78	936	8	1,665	14

Source: *Statistical Abstract of the United States 1973*, p. 471.

in the United States. As shown in Table 7-1, proprietorships exceed corporations in number by a ratio of almost six to one.

Persons who form proprietorships have maximum incentive to succeed. They have control over the operation of their companies and the right to receive all of the profits earned by their ventures.

As a further incentive to succeed, proprietors are personally responsible for any debts of their businesses. In fact, the law views proprietors and their businesses as one and the same. Proprietors have unlimited liability. That is, they are personally responsible for any acts taken in the course of their businesses. Suppose, for example, a business owes money to another firm and cannot pay from the profits of its operations. The other firm can sue the proprietor individually in a court of law to collect what is due. The court can order the proprietor to sell investments, automobiles, jewelry, or anything else of value in order to repay business debts. Proprietors and their businesses are also considered legally one and the same for tax purposes.

Consider taxation of the firm's income, or profit. Income, or profit, is simply the difference between the money the proprietor takes in from the sale of the product(s) or services and the money paid out to make or promote the product or service. The inflow of money is *revenue*, and the outflow is *expenses*. Thus, profit is revenue less expenses. If revenue exceeds expenses, the proprietor must pay federal, and perhaps even state and city, taxes on this income. When computing taxes, the proprietor includes business income with any personal income and deductions to calculate the amount of tax owed to the government.

The proprietorship is as easy to end as it is to start. If the proprietor wants to stop the business, he or she simply closes up the shop (after, of course, repaying all the debts of the firm). Should the proprietor die or become too sick to work, the business would also come to an end.

One major drawback of the proprietorship form of business enterprise is lack of ability to grow. Proprietors may find it difficult to hire competent employees for their businesses. Furthermore, they may have difficulties in acquiring money to expand their businesses. Lenders prefer not to provide money to a firm that relies on only one person for its success. Should the key person die or become incapacitated, the proprietorship would fail. Lenders would then have a difficult time getting their money back. Thus, a proprietorship may be suitable for a small business, but it creates roadblocks to future growth.

THE PARTNERSHIP

A *partnership* can be defined as the association of two or more persons as co-owners for the purpose of carrying on a business for a profit. Its major advantage over a proprietorship is that the partners may pool their financial resources and professional specializations to enable the firm to grow. While a proprietor must be a jack-of-all-trades, a partnership may have persons who are experts in different areas of running the business. Partnerships are most often found in service industries, such as medicine and law, and in the finance, insurance, and real estate industries. It is quite common to find public accounting and law firms with partners numbering in the hundreds.

A partnership presents a situation requiring a tremendous degree of trust and confidence among the partners. Under the law, each partner has the right to be a manager as well as an owner of the business. Any one partner can commit the entire partnership to a *legal contract*, that is, a binding relationship to another party, in the course of the partnership business. This last point is very important. Let us consider an example.

Suppose, in the course of usual business, one partner unwisely borrows a huge sum of money from the bank in order to increase the company's production. However, the demand for the company's product falls off sharply, and the company cannot repay its bank loan. What happens? The bank sues *each one* of the partners in order to seek repayment of the loan. Obviously, each person should choose the partner or partners very carefully. The importance of this is recognized in Section 18(g) of the Uniform Partnership Act: "No person can become a member of a partnership without the consent of all the partners."

Types of Partners

Before we discuss how a partnership is formed, it may be useful to discuss the variety of types of partners. As we shall see, while a proprietor is always a proprietor, there is considerable leeway in defining a partner.

A *general partner* has unlimited liability for the debts of the firm. The general partner usually takes an active role in managing the firm's activities.

A **limited partner** has **limited liability** for the firm's debts. This person cannot be held responsible for more than the amount of money contributed to the partnership. Suppose the partnership is sued for a large amount of money and loses its case. Limited partners can lose no more money than they have already invested in the partnership. The courts cannot seek other sources of wealth that the limited partner might have in order to satisfy the claims of the suit. A limited partner takes no active role in the management of the firm.

A **silent partner** is a co-owner of the business. However, the individual has no say and takes no part in the management of the firm. The silent partner views any involvement in the partnership solely as an investment. This person wants to partake in the profits, but not the management, of the partnership.

A **secret partner** is a co-owner of the business, but does not want his or her identity revealed to the public. A secret partner can be an active manager in the firm.

A **dormant partner** is both silent and secret.

Forming a Partnership

Creating a partnership is very easy. It can be done by either oral or written agreement. To avoid confusion and perhaps bitter confrontation at a later date, the partnership agreement should be in writing. The written agreement is called the **articles of partnership**. It should include, as a minimum, the following items:

1. The name of the partnership and the names and addresses of the partners.
2. The nature and scope of the partnership business.
3. The intended duration of the partnership.
4. How much money and/or property each partner is contributing to the firm; this is called the partner's **capital contribution**.
5. How the profits or losses of the partnership will be shared by the partners.
6. The amount of time that each partner will devote to the business and the managerial responsibilities of each partner.
7. How much salary each partner will receive.
8. Restrictions on the authority of particular partners to obligate the partnership.
9. Provisions for the dissolution of the partnership.

The total money and property contributed by the partners for permanent use within the firm is called the **partnership capital**. Except upon termination of the partnership, no partner may withdraw any part of this capital without the consent of all the partners. It should also be noted that a person can become a partner without contributing any capital. The individual may contribute a service or the use of certain property rather than the property itself.

In the absence of any agreement to the contrary, the partners share the profits and losses of the partnership equally. The partnership *per se* is not required to pay federal income taxes. The business must, however, file an informational return each year, listing the income realized by each of the partners. Each partner is individually required to include partnership income with the personal income tax return.

Dissolving the Partnership

A partnership is dissolved with the death or withdrawal of any of the partners. It is also dissolved if a partner is declared insane or if the firm files for bankruptcy. The ease with which a partnership can be dissolved, when combined with the potential difficulties of transferring one's interests in the firm, places limits on the permanence and potential growth of the company in partnership form. Even in a firm with hundreds of partners, a new partnership must be formed each time there is a withdrawal or addition of a partner.

The Limited Partnership—A Special Case

A limited partnership differs in a number of significant ways from our discussion in the previous two sections. A *limited partnership* is formed by the union of one or more general partners and one or more limited partners. It must have at least one general partner who has unlimited liability for the debts of the firm.

The limited partnership agreement must be in writing. It can be formed only by authority of the government. The contribution of the limited partner may be cash or other property, but not services. This person is primarily an investor and can take no part in the management of the business. In this case, the withdrawal or death of a limited partner does not end the partnership.

THE CORPORATION

While the proprietorship is the most common form of business organization, the corporation is the major economic force in American society. The economic power of the corporation is revealed in the figures presented in Tables 7-2 and 7-3. The economic importance of the corporate form has increased in more than absolute terms. It has also increased in relative terms; the corporation accounts for an increasing share of total American business revenues. It is this domination of the corporation on the American economic scene that warrants all the attention it receives in this text.

Table 7-2. *Revenues of Proprietorships, Partnerships, and Corporations*

	PROPRIETORSHIPS		PARTNERSHIPS		CORPORATIONS	
	MILLION	% OF TOTAL	MILLION	% OF TOTAL	MILLION	% OF TOTAL
1960	171	16	74	7	849	77
1965	199	14	75	5	1,195	81
1967	211	13	80	5	1,375	82
1968	222	12	83	5	1,508	83
1969	234	12	87	4	1,680	84
1970	238	11	93	5	1,751	84

Source: *Statistical Abstract of the United States 1973*, p. 471.

Table 7-3. *Net Profit of Proprietorships, Partnerships, and Corporations*

	PROPRIETORSHIPS		PARTNERSHIPS		CORPORATIONS	
	MILLION	% OF TOTAL	MILLION	% OF TOTAL	MILLION	% OF TOTAL
1960	21	29	8	11	44	60
1965	28	25	10	9	74	66
1967	30	25	11	9	78	66
1968	32	25	11	8	86	67
1969	34	27	10	8	80	65
1970	33	30	10	9	66	61

Source: *Statistical Abstract of the United States 1973*, p. 471.

Nature of the Corporate Form

The classic definition of the corporation was made by Chief Justice Marshall of the U.S. Supreme Court in the 1819 *Dartmouth College* v. *Woodward* case:

> A corporation is an artificial being, invisible, intangible, and existing only in contemplation of law. Being the mere creature of law, it possesses only those properties which the charter of its creation confers upon it, either expressly or as incidental to its very existence. These are such as are supposed best calculated to effect the object for which it was created. Among the most important are immortality, and, if the expression may be allowed, individuality; properties by which a perpetual succession of many persons are considered as the same, so that they may act as a single individual. A corporation manages its own affairs, and holds property without the hazardous and endless

necessity of perpetual conveyances for the purpose of transmitting it from hand to hand. It is chiefly for the purpose of clothing bodies of men, in succession, with these qualities and capacities, that corporations were invented, and are in use. By these means, a perpetual succession of individuals is capable of acting for the promotion of the particular object, like one immortal being.

Chief Justice Marshall's definition deserves some comment. A corporation is a legal entity that must have a charter from a legislative body. The legislative body may be either federal or, as is usually the case, state. The powers of the corporation are limited to those the state has given it. The objects or purposes for which the corporation is formed must be expressly stated in its articles of incorporation. The business activities of the corporation are limited to those purposes. Fortunately, these purposes are stated in such general terms to allow the corporation wide leeway in its activities.

Many people are dismayed that the corporation is talked about in such life-like terms. As far as the courts are concerned, the corporation is a person and has a life of its own, distinct from its owners. In fact, the corporation can live forever. The owners may transfer or sell their ownership rights to other persons without disrupting the operation of the enterprise. The corporation can be sued and is liable for its own debts. The owners of the corporation are liable for the debts of the firm only up to the amount of money they originally contributed to form the corporation. Lastly, the corporation pays an income tax on whatever profit it may earn from its operations. This tax is independent of any taxes its owners may have to pay on their personal incomes.

The benefits of the corporate form have enabled the American economy to be transformed from one dependent primarily on agriculture to the most industrialized and important economy in the world. As the noted economist Paul Samuelson has written, "Without limited liability and the corporation, society simply could not reap the benefit that comes when large supplies of capital can be attracted to competing corporations that produce a variety of complementary goods, that pool risks, and that best utilize the economies of sizeable research units and managerial know-how." [1]

Forming a Corporation

The creation of a corporation is an extremely legalistic and detailed exercise. We shall not go through all of that detail here. Rather, we shall present a generalized approach to starting a corporation.

The first step in starting a corporation is to select a state for incorporation. Companies do not necessarily incorporate in the state where they do most of their business. As shown in Figure 7-1, a disproportionate number of major

---

[1] Paul A. Samuelson, *Economics*, New York: McGraw-Hill Book Company, 1973, p. 109.

Parts of a Typical Business

Figure 7-1. *Distribution of State Charters*

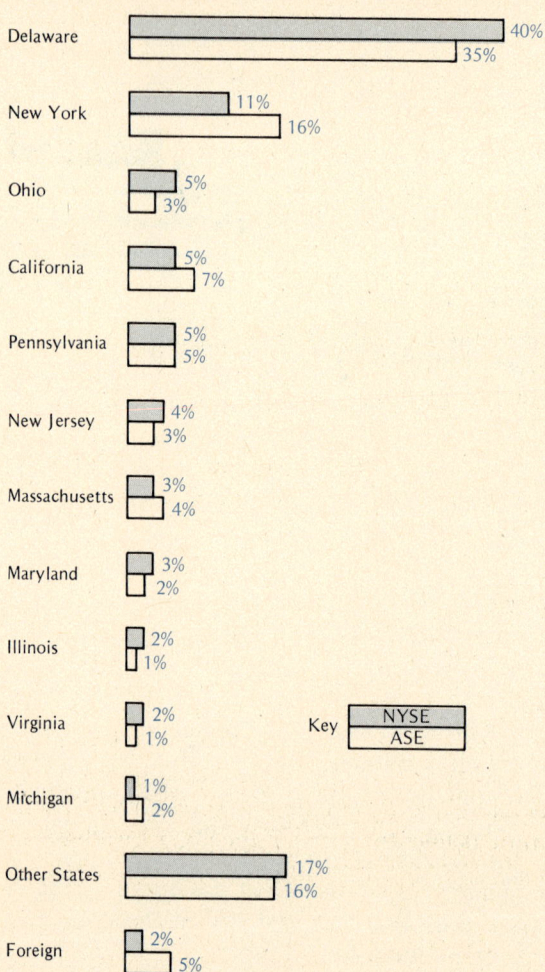

companies are incorporated in Delaware, one of the smallest—in terms of industry output—states in the union.

What factors encourage a company to incorporate in a given state? There are two basic factors: taxes and legal restrictions. Companies seek to minimize the taxes they pay. Delaware, for example, has very favorable corporate tax laws. It imposes no income taxes on companies incorporated in Delaware but not doing business in the state. Furthermore, it has a very low franchise tax—the tax charged for the privilege of being incorporated in Delaware.

A company likes a clear understanding of how a state's laws will affect its operations. Delaware, for example, has a well-established body of case law. As one large company put it: "Delaware law has been and no doubt will continue to be interpreted and tested in a large number of significant cases, thus assuring a sufficient measure of predictability to provide a sound basis for planning with respect to the legal aspects of the company's affairs." And, of course, companies would like to have the laws in their favor as much as possible. As one author noted, "Delaware is picked for its lack of legal strictures. For example, a Delaware chartered company can get away without having any annual meeting at all." [2]

After selecting the state in which to incorporate, the following steps are required to start the corporation:

1. Preparation of the articles of incorporation.
2. Signing of the articles by the required number of qualified incorporators.
3. Delivery of the articles to the secretary of state and payment of the required organization fees.
4. Filing of the articles by the secretary of state and issuance by him of the corporate charter.
5. Recording of the charter and articles of incorporation with the recorder of deeds, county clerk, or other county officials of the county in which the principal office of the corporation is located.
6. Holding of the directors' first meeting to adopt the by-laws, elect officers, and transact other business.
7. Issuance of stock and receipt of payment therefor.
8. Start of business.

Incorporators are the persons desiring to start the corporation. They are responsible for preparing the *articles of incorporation*. The articles are, in effect, an application to the state asking for permission to start the corporation. The articles are important, since they will determine the scope of the corporation's *charter*. The charter, in turn, defines the scope of the firm's legal business activities. The articles of incorporation typically include the following items:

1. Name and address of the corporation.
2. Intended life of the corporation, which may be either perpetual or for some limited amount of time.
3. Names and addresses of the incorporators.
4. Purpose(s) for which the corporation is being formed, expressed in general terms.
5. Number of authorized shares of stock, including rights of different classes of stock.
6. Number of shares to be issued to investors.
7. Number of directors constituting the first board of directors, and the names and addresses of those who are to serve as directors until the first meeting of the shareholders.

[2] Robert C. Townsend, "America, Inc.: A Review," *The New York Times*, May 30, 1971.

Figure 7-2. *Company Organization*

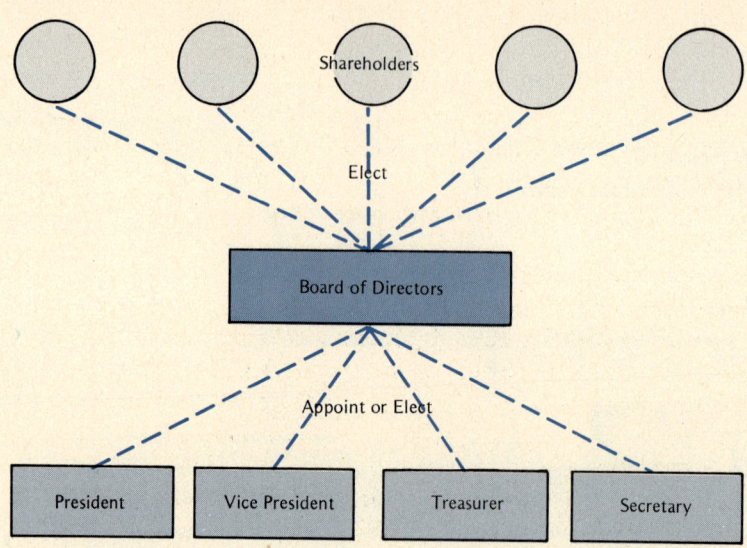

The articles of incorporation also indicate the general organizational structure of corporations, as shown in Figure 7-2 and discussed in detail in the following sections.

Corporate Shareholders

The owners of the corporation are called *shareholders* or *stockholders*. They get their name from the owning of shares of stock as evidence of their ownership in the firm. There are different kinds of shares of stock, the discussion of which will be deferred until Chapter Fourteen. For the present, we shall assume only one class of stock is outstanding, which we shall call *common stock*.

Shareholders are endowed with certain rights, which generally include the following:

1. The right to have their ownership of shares evidenced by a tangible stock certificate.
2. The pre-emptive right that permits shareholders to maintain their proportionate ownership in the firm, should new shares be issued.
3. The right to vote.
4. The right to inspect the books of the corporation.
5. The right to receive a dividend.
6. The right to participate in the assets of the corporation upon dissolution.

Forms of Business Organization

A typical stock certificate is shown in Figure 7-3. The stock certificate indicates how many shares the holder owns in the corporation. The certificate enables a person to transfer ownership in the firm easily.

The pre-emptive right is very important to those people who want to exercise their control of the corporation. For example, assume the corporation has 1,000 shares outstanding, and you own 40%, or 400 shares. In order to raise more money, the corporation decides to issue 1,000 more shares. Under the pre-emptive right, you are guaranteed the opportunity to buy 400 of these new shares. Without this right, it is possible that your interest in the firm would be diluted to 20% (400/2,000).

In most states today, a shareholder is entitled to one vote for each share of stock owned. A person who does not want to personally vote shares may transfer this right to a proxy. A proxy is a person or organization that pools shares from many investors and votes them as a block. The proxy can be a powerful force for change within the corporation, for a key shareholder right is the right to elect the firm's board of directors, a subject we shall turn to shortly.

Figure 7-3. Sample Stock Certificate

The right to inspect the books of the corporation enables the shareholder to determine the financial status of the firm. It also allows the shareholder to learn the names and addresses of other shareholders. This is an important point in a proxy fight in which a shareholder tries to get all the votes possible to further a cause.

A *dividend* is a distribution of the profits of the corporation to its shareholders. A shareholder will receive a sum equivalent to proportionate ownership in the firm out of the total amount of dividends paid. Individuals are allowed to omit from their taxable income the first $100 in dividends received each year. They pay taxes on any excess over $100 as they would on income earned from a job.

In the event of *liquidation*, or dissolution, of the corporation, creditors of the firm have first claim to the proceeds from the sale of the firm's assets. If there is any money left over after the creditors' claims have been satisfied, the shareholder is entitled to a proportionate interest in any such money. In practice, for firms that have gone bankrupt, shareholders have received none of the proceeds of the liquidation.

The Board of Directors

One of the striking features in the development of the American economy has been the separation of the owners of the firm from those who manage the firm. Specialization and the division of labor have bred a class of professional managers. Owners of the firm have generally lost interest in controlling the company's destiny. Shareholders who are displeased with what is going on within a corporation would, in most cases, rather sell their shares and invest their money in a company more to their liking than try to effect change in the corporation through the right to vote. Indeed, the shareholders only indirectly select the firm's managers. The shareholder's major opportunity to make an opinion be heard is through the right to vote for the corporation's *board of directors*.

Director Responsibilities

Directors are elected by shareholders at the firm's annual shareholder meeting. They hold office for a stated period of time. The board of directors acts independently of the shareholders. The shareholders generally cannot discharge directors during their term in office.

Directors hold a position of high responsibility in the corporation. However, they cannot act as individuals, but only as a board. A major duty of the board is to either appoint or elect the top officers of the corporation. The officers, in turn, are responsible for staffing the rest of the organization and handling the corporation's daily operating affairs. Thus, the board has broad authority to give power to the corporation's officers.

Forms of Business Organization 171

Drawing by D. Reilly; © 1973 The New Yorker Magazine, Inc.

In addition to designating the corporation's officers, the board of directors is typically empowered to:

1. Manage the business and affairs of the corporation, a power usually delegated to the company's officers.
2. Declare dividends.
3. Remove any officer of the corporation at any time.
4. Initiate proceedings to amend the articles of incorporation.
5. Sell, lease, or mortgage assets of the corporation in the usual course of business.
6. Initiate proceedings for the sale, lease, exchange, or mortgage of assets of the corporation.
7. Initiate proceedings to dissolve the corporation.

Directors of a corporation are not expected to guarantee the success of the business. They are required only to be honest, loyal, and reasonably careful. In performing their duties, directors must exercise ordinary care and prudence—what the courts have defined as "the same degree of care and prudence that men prompted by self-interest generally exercise in their own affairs." Directors are expected to delegate considerable authority to others. If the employees have been selected with care, directors are not liable for the negligent acts of such employees.

Inside and Outside Directors

There are two types of corporate directors—inside and outside. Inside directors are officers or employees of the corporation. Outside directors are those who do not hold executive posts or other employee positions in the company. The outside director should lend a needed degree of unbiased input to the board. This is important since inside directors may be so involved with the goings-on of the corporation that they may not be entirely objective in their appraisal of the company's financial position and future opportunities. But, as one leading business consultant has said, "Most [of the outside directors] still think of themselves in some honorary position. There is a considerable lack of awareness of how much a director can do and what his liabilities are if he does not." [3]

Directors under Attack

Why are many outside directors failing to do their job of promoting the best interests of the shareholders against the possibly divergent interests of a professional management? One expert observer has suggested that management is reluctant to make pertinent information available to outside directors. In 1972, Arthur Goldberg, formerly a U.S. Supreme Court Justice, resigned a directorship with a major international airline because he felt he could not get the data he needed to perform his duties. With the government prosecuting outside directors for failing to exercise their responsibilities with "care and prudence," we can either expect more directors to resign or the problem of information availability to improve. Hopefully, for the sake of the American free enterprise economy and for renewed credibility in our corporate system, outside directors will remain on-board and continue to press forward to protect the rights of the shareholders.

OTHER FORMS OF BUSINESS ORGANIZATION

As we mentioned earlier, proprietorships, partnerships, and corporations are the three major forms of business organization. There are, however, other mixed forms of organization, three of which we shall discuss briefly in the following sections.

[3] "Questioning the Role of Outside Directors," *Business Week*, May 11, 1974, p. 34.

Joint Venture

A **joint venture** is a form of temporary partnership organized to carry out a single business undertaking for profit. Unlike a more typical partnership, the joint venture is predetermined to be short-lived. Furthermore, a joint venturer, unlike a general partner, does not have the authority to bind a fellow venturer legally. Lastly, the organization is not dissolved by the death of a joint venturer.

Joint ventures are quite common in the investment securities business. When a corporation needs to raise a large amount of money, a number of investment firms form a *syndicate*, another name for joint venture. The syndicate members pool their resources to effect the transaction. By pooling resources, each joint venturer is able to reduce the amount of money put at risk. Once the transaction is completed, the joint venture is dissolved.

Major oil companies also combine efforts in joint ventures. Since oil exploration is so risky and requires a great deal of capital, the joint venture allows each firm to reduce its individual risk.

Joint Stock Company

A **joint stock company** has characteristics of both the partnership and the corporation. It has capital divided into transferable shares and has directors and managers elected by shareholders. However, a joint stock company is formed by contract, not by legislative authority. Furthermore, each member of the joint stock company has unlimited liability for debts incurred by it during the period of membership.

Business Trust

The **business trust**, often called a **Massachusetts trust**, was originally designed to avoid certain limitations of the corporate form, particularly the widespread ban on corporate dealing in real estate. A *trust* involves the legal transfer of title to a specific property to one person for the use and benefit of another. For example, in a real estate investment trust, title to real estate may be held in a trust. Income derived from the real estate is passed along to the *beneficiaries* of the trust, that is, the people for whose benefit the trust was created. The people who manage the trust are called the *trustees*.

The business trust may be created by a voluntary agreement without any authorization or consent of the state. The business trust has the following three characteristics:

1. A trust estate is formed for the purpose of carrying on a specific business.

2. Each beneficiary of the trust is entitled to a certificate evidencing ownership of a proportional interest in the trust; these certificates are freely salable or transferable.
3. Trustees have sole right to manage and control the business, free from the control of the beneficiary.

CHOOSING A SPECIFIC FORM OF BUSINESS ORGANIZATION

Presented here is a summary of the key features of the three basic organization types.

Proprietorship

Advantages

1. Owner and manager are one; the individual has maximum control of business and maximum incentive to succeed.
2. Owner receives all profits.
3. Creation is easy.
4. Legal restrictions are minimum.
5. Termination is easy.
6. Business income and owner's income are taxed together.

Disadvantages

1. Financial resources available for firm are limited.
2. There is a lack of permanence; firm ends with death, incapacity, or decision of owner to dissolve.
3. Growth is limited due to lack of available capital and managerial expertise.
4. Owner has unlimited liability for business debts.

Partnership

Advantages

1. Pooling of partners' financial resources creates larger capital base.
2. More managerial talent is available, as partners may specialize.
3. Legal restrictions are few.
4. Business income is distributed to partners and taxed with personal income.
5. High degree of personal incentive to succeed exists.

Disadvantages

1. Death, incapacity, or withdrawal of any partner dissolves partnership.
2. Transfer of ownership is restricted.
3. Partners have unlimited liability for business debts.

Corporation

Advantages

1. Large accumulation of capital is possible.
2. Life is long or perpetual.
3. Ownership transfer is easy.
4. Legal entity is distinct from owners.
5. Stockholders have limited liability.

Disadvantages

1. Creation of corporation is subject to state or federal law.
2. Legal regulations and restrictions are extensive.
3. There is possible divergence of objectives of owners and managers.
4. Income is taxed twice; double taxation of income occurs because corporations pay tax on income and shareholders pay tax on dividends received.

Our summary indicates the questions concerning organization form that a business executive should ask. "How much control do I want over the operation of the business?" "How much capital do I need for the business?" "What are the tax consequences of a particular form for me?" "How much risk am I willing to assume with respect to liability for the firm's debts?" "Is ease of ownership transfer of any consequence to me?" "Do I want to create a business that will be able to continue after I am no longer interested or able to run it?" Most likely, answers to these and other questions will not result in a clear-cut vote of approval for any one form. Perhaps the business executive wants maximum control—proprietorship—and limited liability—corporation. In the final analysis, personal trade-offs on goals and desires will determine the business form decided upon.

CHAPTER SUMMARY

The selection of a particular form of organization has important consequences for the owners of the firm. Organization form determines:

1. The control the owner has in the management of the firm's affairs.

2. The permanence of life of the firm.
3. The type of taxation of company income.
4. The ease of transference of ownership interest.
5. The ease of access to financing sources.
6. The amount of difficulty in starting the company.
7. The extent of government regulation and compliance.
8. The amount of liability of owners for company debts.

Business executives must weigh personal trade-offs in considering what organizational form is best for their particular circumstances—proprietorship, partnership, or corporation. In this chapter, we have discussed the different forms of organization and the advantages and disadvantages of each form. Hopefully, this material will enable you to make a more intelligent decision when you put textbook learning into actual practice.

PROVOCATIVE STATEMENT

The Importance of Outside Directors

1 "But the fact remains that the outside directors are the only real safeguards the stockholders have against incompetent management. And I honestly think that nearly all those decent guys serving on boards would very much like to be more effective than they have been. The main trouble is that there has been no procedure for them to follow in monitoring the top man so that they would have solid facts and fair evidence that he is—or is not—doing his job."

Edward McSweeney,
Management Consultant
and Veteran Outside Director

PROVOCATIVE STATEMENT

The Proprietor in the World of Big Business

2 "Who owns the 500 largest industrial corporations in the U.S., and—more to the point—who controls them? After more than two generations during which ownership has been increasingly divorced from control, it is frequently assumed that all large U.S. corporations are owned by everybody and nobody, and are run and ruled by bland organization men. The individual entrepreneur or family that holds onto the controlling interest and actively manages the affairs of a big company is regarded as a rare exception, as something of an anachronism. But a close look at the 500 largest industrial corporations does not substantiate such sweeping generalizations.

In approximately 150 companies on the current FORTUNE 500 list, controlling ownership rests in the hands of an individual or of the members of a single family. Significantly, these owners are not just the remnants of the nineteenth-century dynasties that once ruled American business. Many of them are relatively fresh faces. In any event, the evidence that 30 percent of the 500 largest industrials are clearly controlled by identifiable individuals, or by family groups, is something to ponder. It suggests that the demise of the traditional American proprietor has been slightly exaggerated and that the much-advertised triumph of the organization is far from total."

Robert Sheehan,
"Proprietors in the World of Big Business,"
Fortune, June 15, 1967.

REVIEW QUESTIONS

1. Briefly define the three fundamental forms of business.
2. What are the differences between a general partnership and a limited partnership?
3. What are the steps involved in forming a corporation?
4. List the rights commonly held by shareholders in a corporation, and state how shareholders are able to exercise their control over the corporation.
5. What are the responsibilities of the board of directors of a corporation?
6. Why is the proprietorship an unsuitable form for a large business firm?

Chapter Outline

The Four Basic Goals of a Production Manager

Materials and Components for Production
    Purchasing Items for Production
        The Place of Purchasing in the Organization
        Responsibility for the Goods
        Purchasing Policies
    Inventory Systems
        Inventory Control
        Factors in Maintaining an Inventory

Plant and Equipment for Production
    Mechanization
        Impact of Automation on Workers
    Design of Production Facilities
        Plant Location
        Plant Layout
        Materials Handling

Management of the Production Process
    Scope of Responsibilities
    Production Standards and Work Measurement
        Data Development
        Methods of Measurement
        Applications of Work Standards

Production Planning and Control
    Flow from Basic Inventory
    Scheduling
    Quality Control
    Traffic
    Maintenance

Career Opportunities in Industrial Management

Chapter Summary

Provocative Statement 1:
    A New Viewpoint on Productivity

Provocative Statement 2:
    Standards as the Language of Production

Provocative Statement 3:
    Zero Inventory Purchasing (ZIP)

Key Terms

Sales forecast
Goods
Services
Purchase requisition
Bids
Centralized purchasing
Decentralized purchasing
Purchasing task force
F.O.B.
C.I.F.
Direct cost
Overhead
Cost of capital
Safety stocks
Inventory
Idle capital
Stock out

Usage rate
Load time
Reciprocity
Deterioration
Obsolete
Mechanization
Automation
Closed loop automation
Numerical control
Flow charts
"Gozinto" charts
Quality control
Flow process chart
Net scrap generation
Tolerances
CRAFT
Functional layout

Product or line layout
Statistical techniques
Work standard
Work sampling
Continuous production
Intermittent production
Bill of materials
Scheduling
Bottlenecks
Production cycle smoothing
Quantitative methods
Routing
Cumulative
Master schedule
Schedule performance reports
Acceptance sampling
Downtime

Producing Goods and Services

"The old output-per-man-hour concept of productivity completely misses the boat for what has become of increasing importance to our society—the quality of economic performance."
—C. Jackson Grayson, Jr.
Counselor to Chairman, Cost of Living Council

"Don't buy anything you don't need or before you need it."
—Purchasing Manager
Solar Division of International Harvester

8

This chapter discusses the principles of producing goods and services. It includes systems for the smooth flow of materials and components, design of plants and equipment, and the fundamentals of managing the production processes. Those who run this portion of the business have four basic goals:

1. *Lowest cost.* Assuming the operation is fulfilling the other three goals, the primary objective is achieving the lowest possible cost per unit. Some expenses are not the responsibility of production managers, such as executive overhead or the advertising budget. Managers are evaluated, therefore, on items under their authority.

2. *Quantity required.* Output should equal customer demand plus the replenishing of the inventory of finished goods. If less is produced than is required, sales are lost and the company has spent money uselessly. If more is produced than required, the goods deteriorate while waiting for a buyer.

3. *Proper timing.* Customers want to buy products at specific times because they want to avoid paying for something they cannot use or will resell shortly after purchase. Production managers must, therefore, establish schedules for each item. They must avoid complications such as equipment failure, a strike at the plant of a supplier, and similar causes of delay that result in inability to ship on time.

4. *Expected quality.* Customers almost always buy a product with clearly stated specifications. When something is shipped, which was not according to these specifications, the company making the product is responsible for the expenses of recovering or destroying it. Sometimes companies maintain the goodwill of customers by absorbing this expense even when there is doubt about the cause of a defect.

The foundation for achieving these four goals is the sales forecast. It is a prediction by the sales department for a future period of the number of units by type to be shipped to customers. The future period ranges in duration from a week to a year. The breakdown of detail and time intervals depends on the type of business involved. The sales forecast is the basis on which most decisions are made in production management (often called operations or industrial management).

A distinction should be made between concern about customer requirements related to the four goals, which is the responsibility of production management, and the price, terms of payment, and efforts to get money owed by the customer, which is the responsibility of other departments. Occasionally, a cut in the price being paid by the buyer will force the production manager to reduce production costs by reducing quality, making the goods at a less convenient time for the customer, and/or spending capital to increase efficiency.

Another distinction to bear in mind is the difference between goods and services. This chapter primarily deals with production of goods. Services involve either the sale of something made by others or the offering of professional expertise, ranging from television repair to process engineering. Many of the principles discussed in this chapter will apply to businesses that provide services.

MATERIALS AND COMPONENTS FOR PRODUCTION

Companies that manufacture products require primary materials such as limestone, iron ore, and timber in a processed form. Cement, steel, and lumber are advanced products of these raw materials, while a third stage would be a concrete block, a car body, and a wooden roof frame. Figure 8-1 illustrates that only a few companies handle all phases of their products from the primary material to customer outlet sales. A tire company would be an example if it produced the basic chemicals that go into a synthetic tire and sold the finished tire through its own retail outlets. However, most companies depend on suppliers. Each level of processing adds value to the product. Thus, a profit can be earned at any stage if a company specializes in a product line and makes it in large numbers. Purchasing, therefore, has become a function important to company performance.

Purchasing Items for Production

The process of purchasing involves, first, the issue of a purchase requisition that specifies what is needed, the quantity, and the timing required. Then, there is an investigation of possible sources for the items and determination of

Figure 8-1. Simplified Stages for Complete Integration

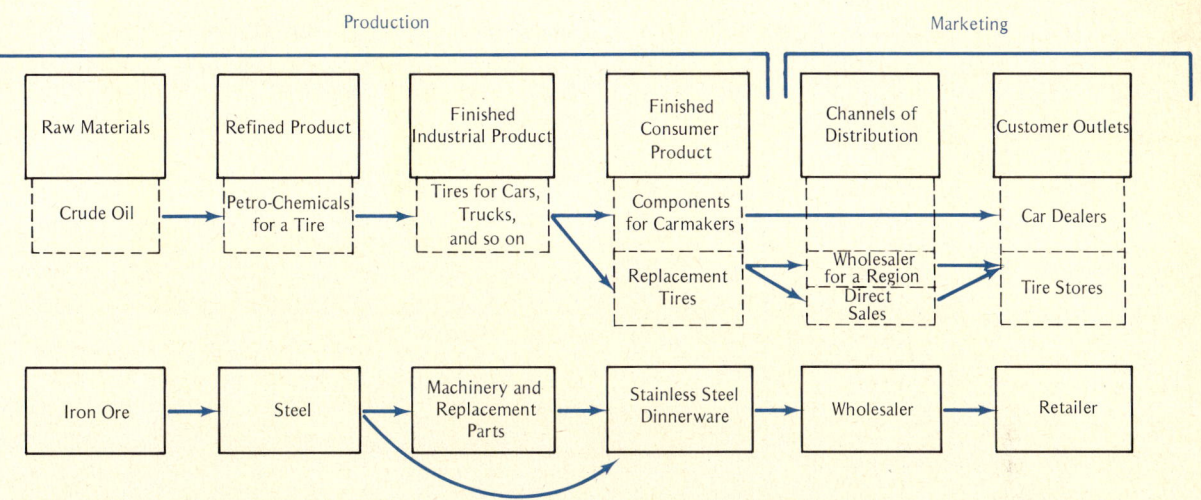

prices or receipt of bids. Often negotiations on price occur, especially for discounts based on volume of items ordered, but also on transportation costs and necessary timing for delivery. The order is placed with the supplier offering the best combination of delivered price, quality, and timing. Finally, the purchasing department expedites the order to assure that all obligations of the purchase agreement are met.

The Place of Purchasing in the Organization

Figure 8-2 gives various possibilities for the reporting relationship of purchasing within the company. The minicharts indicate that each firm has several alternatives, and that the appropriate placement of purchasing in the organization is based on its industrial and geographic needs as well as the variables discussed as follows.

A fundamental decision about the organization of purchasing is whether its function should be centralized or decentralized.

Centralized purchasing involves a single, separate department for the whole company. In this case, orders are larger than if individual departments obtained what they wanted independently. This results in volume discounts. Cost control is more effective because management has assigned this responsibility to one person instead of several people. The disadvantage is that paperwork typically multiplies. This "red tape" can delay receipt of items or cause large inventories.

Decentralized purchasing is very efficient about receiving the needed items on time, but cost control is poor. The volume of individual orders is less, so discounts are smaller. Also, investigation and negotiation of price are not usually carried out as thoroughly in small sections or departments.

Figure 8-2. Alternatives for Placing Purchasing

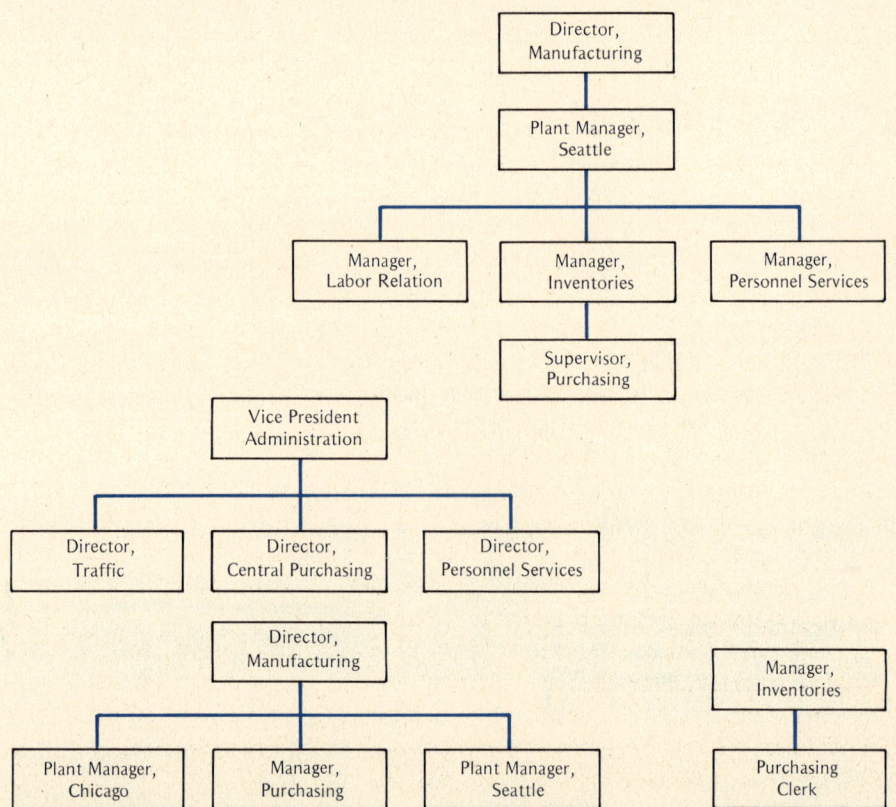

However, decentralized purchasing may be essential for some businesses to be certain that orders are placed promptly and that items arrive on time.

The importance and status of the person in charge of purchasing concerning job rating, title, and benefits will vary from company to company. However, an important change has occurred in some organizations during the 1970s. Not all the items needed are readily available at a reasonable price. Scarcity has resulted in more responsibility and status for purchasing. Placing an order is not always a routine procedure, and higher levels of management become involved to obtain supplies. Expansion of the purchasing department is often necessary to involve cost analysts and to coordinate research for substitute supplies.

The real power of purchasing managers may not always be apparent on the organizational chart. In a buyer's market, when there are abundant supplies, these managers are very important to the seller. Gifts, vacations, and even bribes have been offered to managers making the "buy" decision. On the other hand, in a seller's market, when there are supply shortages, managers' contacts become extremely important to their companies. For example, they might be able to obtain more than their quotas or be alerted to price increases in advance so that items can be purchased at a lower cost.

Purchasing task forces are now being used by industry. Department personnel are supplemented by technical experts and others experienced in production so that no opportunity to obtain a required item or an acceptable substitute is lost. Usually, this step is taken only when there is a serious problem because of the cost of high salaried employees normally on the purchasing task force who are not performing their regular job.

Responsibility for the Goods

A critical point to determine is the time and place at which responsibility for the items being purchased is transferred to the buyer from the seller. Defective goods are returnable under most circumstances regardless of the point of transfer, and the seller usually pays the expenses involved. However, if the goods are damaged after transfer of responsibility, insurance can cover losses on items that cannot be used.

The designation f.o.b. means "free on board" and indicates that a buyer has purchased an item at the seller's plant or warehouse. When the goods leave the premises, their condition after transportation is the buyer's responsibility. Often prices are quoted on an f.o.b. basis to avoid inflation of the price caused by transportation expense to the market.

The designation c.i.f. means "cost, insurance, and freight" and indicates that the price includes delivery to a place named by the buyer, such as a port of entry into a foreign country or a plant in this country. In addition, the damage en route is the responsibility of the seller. A c.i.f. price quote is usually higher than an f.o.b. quote by the added direct cost of insurance and freight plus an allowance for breakage en route.

Purchasing Policies

Companies establish rules and guidelines for placing orders. Experience is the basis of each rule or guideline, and a change from normal conditions would be necessary to justify varying from the usual policy. Important policy areas are discussed here.

MAKE OR BUY The "buy" decision is guided by the production manager's four goals of lowest cost, required quantity, proper timing, and expected quality. If the company has facilities and personnel to make the needed item more cheaply than a supplier, it could eliminate one stage shown in Figure 8-1. The company would still have to buy the materials that the former supplier purchased. However, a cost savings often occurs when a company can bypass a supplier (because of the supplier's profits).

Determining the company's cost requires, in addition to obvious direct expenses, consideration of overhead and the cost of capital involved. Allowances must also be made for alternative uses for equipment and personnel in some cases. In summary, the "make or buy" decision is not as simple as it appears, and companies sometimes shift from one policy to the other.

SAFETY STOCKS The details of a policy for having extras of an item (safety stocks) in case of emergencies result from trial and error. Large inventories mean idle capital not earning profits. Yet it is rarely practical to maintain low reserves of materials, parts, and components because of uncertainty about the flow of supplies. If a company were absolutely sure of receiving what was needed for production each day, inventories could be nearly eliminated. Also, if profit performance were not badly hurt by shutting down a plant affected temporarily by a stock out, inventory levels could be very low. Usually, very low inventories are not practical, and businesses buy what is needed for several days.

Figure 8-3 shows the elements of an inventory cycle. The basis of determining the point of reordering is the usage rate of the item involved. The time between placing an order and receiving the goods is called lead time.

The computer has helped greatly to reduce safety stocks. The lengthy calculations to determine the status of hundreds of items can be completed in a few seconds. Given a system that informs the computer of usage, those responsible for inventories will know when to make out a purchase requisition. In fact, the computer will do so automatically if programmed to handle this

Figure 8-3. *Elements of an Inventory Cycle*

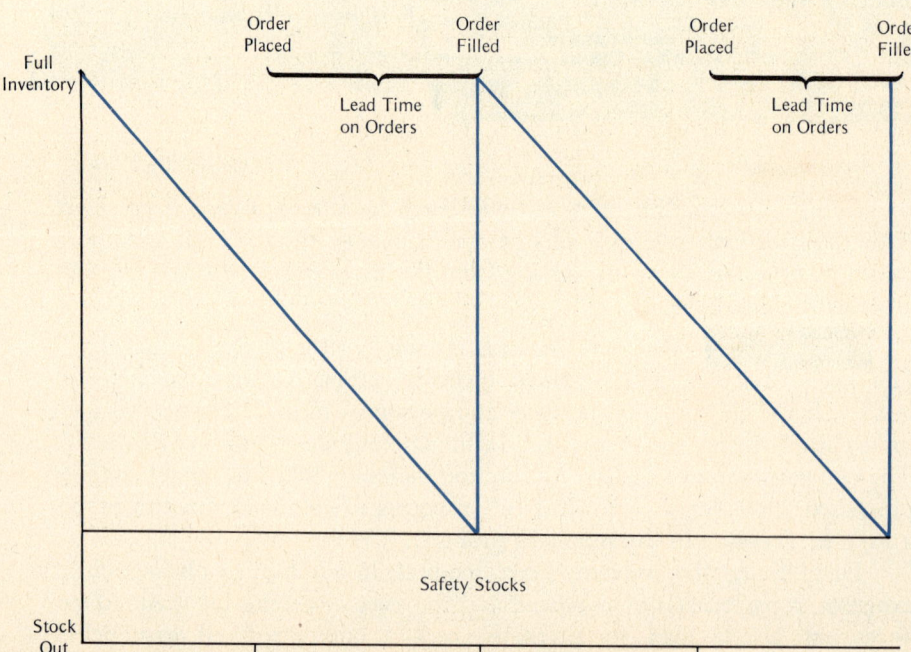

assignment. This means that the extras ordered in the past "to be sure we have enough" often can be eliminated.

RECIPROCITY This policy concerns a firm buying from companies to which it sells. The government has passed laws to protect the public from situations in which a seller is forced to buy from a company or else lose sales to this company, despite higher prices or lower quality or both. Common sense is necessary in applying the laws, however. Some companies are so big that one division may buy from a supplier and another division may sell to this supplier, without either knowing about the other's relationship.

In the past, firms with strong positions in their respective markets have made buy/sell agreements that lowered costs and increased profits. In most instances, the consumer did not benefit from the economies. Competition was hurt by the special arrangements, and eventually the public suffered.

Reciprocity is practiced every day on a level that is not illegal. Orders are frequently placed with customers when other purchasing criteria are equal. Actually, this is often the basis of a written or unwritten policy at a company.

ETHICS The potential influence of a purchasing manager in a company has been discussed. A company establishes policies and procedures for each step in the purchasing process to prevent this power from being misused. Acceptance of bribes and expensive gifts is normally specified as grounds for dismissal. Some firms also frown upon the "gray" areas: (1) vacations and weekends with suppliers at places that might otherwise be beyond the means of the purchasing manager; (2) gifts to spouses and similar attempts to influence the "buy" decision.

Management expects that the purchasing department will place orders with the supplier that best meets the four goals of production. Any gifts from the suppliers are discouraged, even minor items such as liquor and food. No breach of an ethics policy is permitted at most companies.

PURCHASING PROCEDURES Companies have a policy of updating buying procedures on a regular basis. The purpose is to eliminate past practices that have become inefficient or simply unnecessary. As the nature of each company's product lines changes, requirements change. In a period of shortages the need to update procedures could be critical to obtaining adequate supplies.

Revision of procedures is also necessary to reflect new methods of processing paperwork. Computers have been mentioned, but other types of information systems and eliminate portions of the purchasing process and greatly expedite order placement. An example is shown in Figure 8-4.

Inventory Systems

Three types of inventory are used in accounting, which also identify transfers of responsibility from one department to another.

Figure 8-4. *An Information System Used by Purchasing*

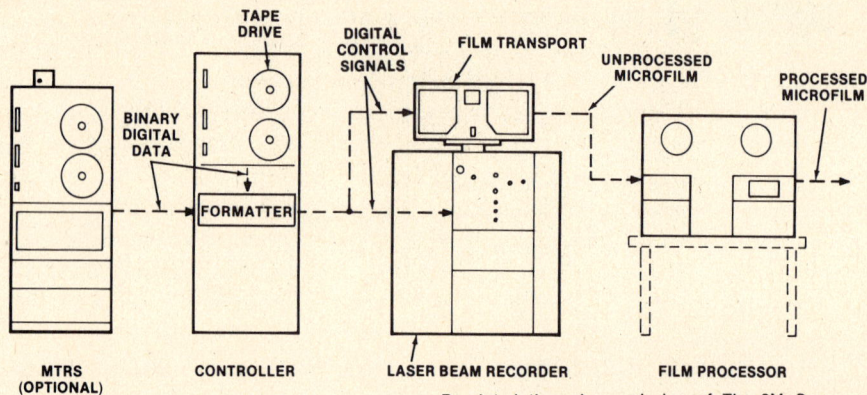

Reprinted through permission of The 3M Company.

The diagram shows how information is routed in a system using 3M's new Laser Beam Recorder (LBR). A mini-computer (left) is optional—if not used, a computer tape may be mounted on the tape drive of a controller. A controller's other function is to format information before feeding it to the LBR. In the LBR, information is written directly by a laser beam on Dry-Silver microfilm or microfuche—the film transport is top-mounted. The latent image is heat-processed in the final dry "paperless" step.

1. *Stocks or basic inventory.* This term refers to materials, parts, and components from the time a firm takes ownership until transfer to the production line. Changes in value during this stage include charges for space used (costs of heat, light, refrigeration, supervision, and security), return on capital tied up in the goods, insurance, taxes, deterioration, and depreciation. Therefore, the longer items are held in inventory, the more costly the end product becomes.

2. *Inventory in process.* It is necessary to account for goods that are being used to form a finished product but have not reached the end of the production line. Depending on the length of time between transfer from stocks to becoming a finished product, a substantial amount of capital may be involved, particularly because value has been added to the cost of the items.

3. *Finished goods inventory.* After production, the finished item is either shipped to a warehouse or a customer. A transfer of responsibility to the marketing department occurs at some stage in this movement. This type of inventory is discussed in Chapter Eleven.

The physical facilities for storing materials, parts, and components range from an open field to highly sophisticated, temperature-controlled environments. The amount of capital spent on structures and equipment depends on: (1) requirements for protection from weather, from theft, and from observation by anyone who should not see what is going on; (2) the size of inventories resulting from usage, lead time on orders, and the policy on safety stocks

Figure 8-4 continued

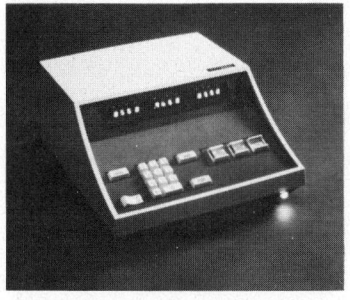 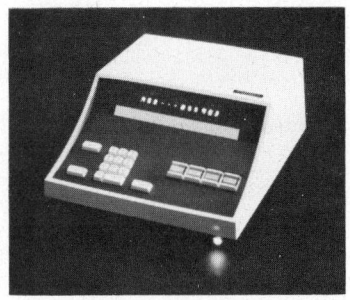

1. *Kodak Miracode II Encoder. The input unit is a compact tabletop electronic device which controls the code and document functions of the microfilmer.*

2. *Kodak Miracode II Controller, Mod 12. The Mod 12 is a small tabletop electronic control unit designed primarily for those applications in which the document coding requires standard search logic and a retrieval handle up to 12 digits.*

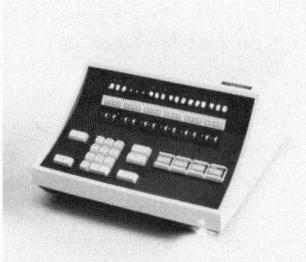 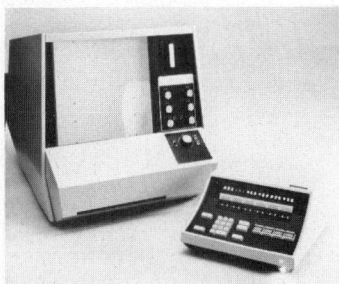

Courtesy of Eastman Kodak Company.

3. *Kodak Miracode II Controller, Mod 18. For more complex applications, the Mod 18 is used where greater depth of retrieval search and expanded logic capabilities are needed.*

4. *Kodak Miracode II Retrieval Terminal. Linked to either the Mod 12 or Mod 18, the retrieval terminal allows the operator to locate and display any coded document, regardless of its position on the film or the order of arrangement.*

reflecting reliability of supply; and (3) production line requirements for flow from basic inventory.

    Each addition to facilities has a cost in capital, but it should also have a benefit in efficiency and quality gained. The production manager must judge whether a proposed facility is a good use of the company's money. Usually there is a fixed standard for comparison. For example, many companies want the benefits to repay the capital within four years. This would be a 25% rate of return on the investment (100%/4 years) after allowing for taxes on the benefits. The standard will depend on the industry and the likelihood that the product line involved will continue to be profitable in future years. It will

Parts of a Typical Business

also depend on general expectations for after-tax earnings on the company's capital. More details about return on capital are given in Chapter Fourteen.

Inventory Control

A company must know what it has in each of the three stages of inventory. The materials, parts, and components are counted upon *entry into storage* in even the smallest of businesses, such as the corner retailer. In addition, there should be a system to identify the *withdrawal from inventory* and the transfer of responsibility to either another department or the customer. To obtain a balance it is also necessary to have *allowances* for theft, damage in handling and stacking, and deterioration.

MANUAL SYSTEMS Many companies maintain a handwritten log or card file on flow of items in and out of inventory. A form is completed by employees making the transfer. This accounting of changes is the basis of the manual system. Periodically an actual count is made, particularly at times when taxes on inventories are due, to check the totals in the file. Any differences are noted. Over the years a firm knows approximately how much it loses in allowances, and this is taken into consideration when deciding on a purchase requisition.

If a firm has thousands of items in inventory, maintaining count becomes either inaccurate or costly. Small armies of clerks are needed, and considerable space for keeping records is required.

AUTOMATIC SYSTEMS There are some automatic systems available to a company, which do not involve computers, but reduce the number of employees and the space required for inventory control. They also increase accuracy in knowing the actual items in storage. Entry and withdrawal systems have been mechanized. Minor investments are involved, and the concepts are usually designed to minimize theft by employees.

COMPUTERIZED SYSTEMS It is now possible for a company to know its position for all three stages of inventory at any plant or warehouse at any time of the day. The information can be printed on typewriter-like terminals or shown on a screen. At the end of the day, the computer calculates sales, shipments, production, and inventories and then prints a complete financial statement.

The same type of system will automatically print a purchase requisition and send the form to the purchasing department's terminal. Human error is minimized and paperwork is handled more rapidly.

Factors in Maintaining an Inventory

The points listed here are primarily directed at stocks of materials, parts, and components.

1. *Seasonal industry.* Customer demand or availability of materials, such as agricultural commodities, come only at certain times of the year in some

industries. Considerable sums of money may be saved through advance planning, such as purchasing when demand is light and prices are lower.

2. *Model changeovers.* When the model changes, as in the case of cars, appliances, and so on, many items become obsolete. It is necessary to order carefully as a model year ends in order to minimize the portion of inventory that cannot be used in the future and must be written off as a loss.

3. *Standardization.* A company can save on inventory investment by keeping changes in its product to a minimum. This may be contrary to the needs of marketing, but if it is possible, the purchasing department can plan the placement of orders more carefully and at the lowest possible price.

4. *Interchangeability.* Companies increase the volume of an order, lower costs, and reduce inventories by using the same item in several products. An example would be car bodies at General Motors; most of the divisions use the same silhouette for a specific size of car.

5. *Customer expectations on delivery.* If a company can quote a delivery time based on purchase of needed items after receipt of a confirmed order, no inventories are needed. At the other extreme is the customer who demands delivery the same day and will switch to another supplier if the company does not perform.

6. *Rate of perishability and obsolescence.* Flowers, vegetables, and items that have zero salvage value after one or two days force those holding the inventory to be extremely careful about the daily relationship between sales and purchases from a supplier. Some industrial products also require special handling or they lose value rapidly. Cement, for example, must be kept dry.

7. *Product life.* The finished product may be designed only for a short period of salability, for example, a political campaign button. If the product could be used for another campaign, such as having only the party name on the button, stocks need not be affected. Other products, like the shell of a telephone, may not change for years.

PLANT AND EQUIPMENT FOR PRODUCTION

Production involves transformation of materials and components into finished products. Three broad types of processes are involved: (1) chemical, (2) change of shape or form, and (3) assembly. Some examples will clarify the physical facilities used in each process and the transformation involved.

Chemical processes actually change the molecular structure of materials. For example, in an oil refinery crude oil is converted to several petroleum products, from heavy lubricants to gases such as propane used in heating. A blast furnace in the steel industry transforms ore into iron, and the by-products of gases and slag are the results of a new chemical composition. Other examples include extracting aluminum from bauxite, generating energy in nuclear power plants, and manufacturing some foods. Usually the plant and equipment necessary for chemical processes require millions of dollars.

These facilities are often the focal point of community campaigns against pollution. Only in recent years has industry attempted to control emissions into the air and water. Chapter Three mentioned government regulations to accelerate spending on devices that filter and convert harmful chemicals. Companies have been reluctant to use their capital in this way because little, if any, profit results from the investment.

Processes to change shape or form include casting, forging, stamping, milling, grinding, drilling, sanding, buffing, weaving, boring, planing, and other manufacturing methods. Such methods are used in the smallest of businesses as well as in large corporations doing similar jobs on an immense scale. The common characteristic of these processes is that operations use many pieces of relatively inexpensive equipment in comparison to those of chemical processes.

This type of processes would also be used by businesses that separate materials to create a product. Taking salt from the sea is an example. Mining diamonds is another example, but in this case very sophisticated equipment is used to identify the small objects as tons of earth are processed.

Assembly involves putting together components by bolting, screw and nail fastening, welding, riveting, stapling, adhesive joining, and soldering. Most of the things a consumer buys are assembled, such as a house, car, appliances, and furniture. The plant and equipment vary widely in scope. A table and manual assembly through use of mechanical fasteners by workers sitting at a bench is common in the toy industry. On the other hand, computer assembly requires heavy expenditures in plant and equipment for control of atmosphere and sophisticated machinery.

Mechanization

Mechanization is a major consideration in all three processes. It means providing a machine to enable a worker to produce more in the same time and/or with better quality. It might also add to safety. Mechanization does not mean a worker will directly lose his or her job to a machine. Often the factor behind the decision to mechanize is that human beings cannot pay attention to what they are doing for long periods of time. Items produced while workers are daydreaming are likely to be defective.

Automation involves new ideas and equipment that permit machines to replace people. The term is different from mechanization because equipment actually takes the place of labor in the job. Capital is needed to buy this equipment and to pay for maintenance and the expense of parts, but gains are made in paying no wages and benefits for the automated work.

One motivation to automate is to change the entire nature of a job. For example, a normal automotive assembly line might make 50 cars an hour. A fully automated line that turns out 60 cars an hour could increase production by 20%, reduce the workforce by 20%, and upgrade the job rating of remaining employees. As a result, to equal output of normal assembly lines in a previous period, the company requires 20% fewer automated lines. Thus, while automated lines might be more expensive per line, increased production could make them less costly overall.

A *plantwide system*, rather than randomly changing individual work stations, involves automating to the maximum degree possible and interrelating the output of all work stations. Closed loop automation is a term used within such a system to indicate that there is a means of the equipment adjusting itself or signaling that it needs adjustment in order to meet needs for volume and quality.

Other approaches utilize the computer to monitor what is going on at each work station and automatically to make the adjustments necessary to achieve programmed production within given quality requirements. The computer can receive information from many locations through sensors that tell dimensions, rate of flow, and so on. Experts can program it not only to identify the problems through a series of calculations but also to send out signals that activate means of correcting the situation. Thousands of calculations are made in seconds, and losses that could occur are prevented. This approach is often called numerical control.

Impact of Automation on Workers

Three things can occur when work stations are automated:

1. **Many jobs are eliminated.** For some workers this means termination. The objective is to substitute machines for people, and, in order to make the investment pay out, workers have to find other jobs.

2. **A few jobs are upgraded.** This means a promotion and an increase in pay for those with some combination of seniority, demonstrated skills, and a good record of reliability.

3. **Transfers are arranged for some workers.** In an expanding company the personnel department will attempt to find another job for the employee. It might be similar to the previous assignment or might require training to stay at the same level. In some cases, the worker accepts a cut in pay rather than be laid off.

Labor unions play a role in protecting the worker when the company is automating. To avoid a strike or slow down, companies usually discuss the proposed changes with union leaders and reach an agreement on the net impact. Occasionally, automation would result in the loss of too many jobs from the union's viewpoint. The union would resist installation of the new equipment. Management then has a major decision. Sometimes they go ahead and find that the union is bluffing. In other instances, automation never achieves its potential because of resistance by the workers.

Overall, automation is necessary for American business to remain competitive. It also permits people to retain a high standard of living because it increases output per employee. Sometimes workers are going to have to develop new skills; rarely will they be able to go through a lifetime, as their

Figure 8-5. Gozinto Chart

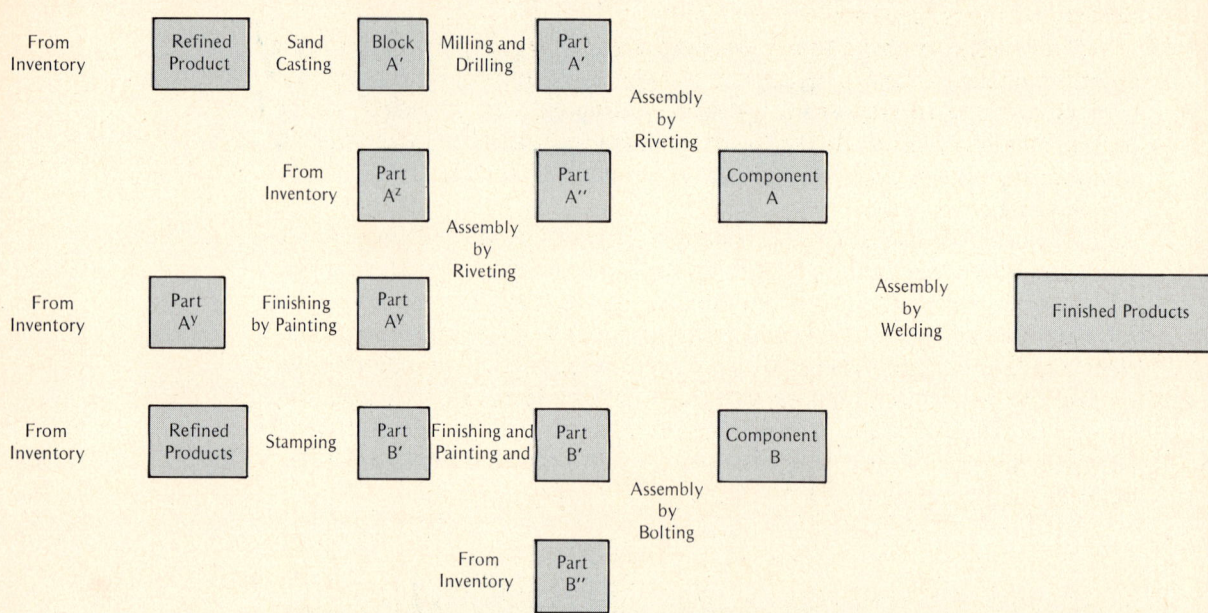

parents did, using a single skill to earn a livelihood, such as welding or operating a lathe. Training for capabilities not even dreamed of now will be needed in the future.

Design of Production Facilities

The design begins with the finished product to be produced on the facilities. **Flow charts** called **"Gozinto" charts** (for the words "goes into") trace each step of production backwards. Figure 8-5 gives a simplified example showing the content in the branches of a tree-like structure. When the flow chart is completed, the design team has a better picture of:

1. Materials and components involved, and their physical characteristics.
2. Processes required, whether chemical, of changing shape or form, or assembly.
3. Interrelationships and timing, so that the design can minimize the waiting time at each work station.
4. Preliminary layout ideas, given a new plant or the constraints of an existing facility.

Another input is the type and frequency of inspection for **quality control**. The design will allow space and capital for equipment to achieve quality objectives, based on feedback from marketing and unit cost limitations from production planning. In addition, a decision must be made about the dependency on multiple shifts. For example, two shifts would double production capacity if maintenance could be handled as a third shift.

After analysis of this information, the designers may decide to subcontract a portion of the process to an outside company with proven expertise in the work or with special facilities that might be too expensive to include in the design. This decision will enable the designers to prepare a **flow process chart**, shown in Figure 8-6, using symbols for each stage of the work.

Sometimes this chart can be quite complicated. The same equipment might be needed for two different jobs or for two or more stages of one job that requires work at another location between each stage.

Every design for production facilities has the primary objective of accomplishing the four goals of the production manager. Management usually allocates a specific amount of capital to production facilities based on estimates prepared by consultants, company experts, or a combination of both. This amount acts as a restraint on the designer. Compromises almost always have to be made between the best design and the one that is acceptable within the limits of the capital budget.

Plant Location

The designers of the production facility must weigh the impact of four categories of information in the final decision about plant location: (1) unit costs of the finished product; (2) capital cost of the facilities; (3) indirect factors that could have a bearing on long-run effectiveness; and (4) social costs and benefits.

Unit and capital costs are affected by the expense of land, local construction, taxes, rates for utilities and municipal services, and transportation of items in and out when operations begin. These are the classical factors considered in plant location. The answers to the economic aspects can be determined by computing the expected unit and capital costs at each possible location and making comparisons.

Social costs and benefits are also critically important in designing a production facility. Pollution controls, noise, community reaction to appearance, and access for workers can affect operations. An example of the impact of these factors would be the paper plant planned to be located near an expanding Cincinnati suburb on a tributary of the Ohio River. Fear of air and stream pollution and the desire to keep the community residential started a campaign that forced the plant to an alternative location requiring long commuting times for employees.

Noneconomic factors are the ones most likely to be overlooked in preliminary estimates and studies. A local of a labor union that is particularly militant about automation, or a pending change in local taxation could affect the choice. A list developed during the investigation period leading to a final

Figure 8-6. *Simplified Flow Process Chart and Explanations*

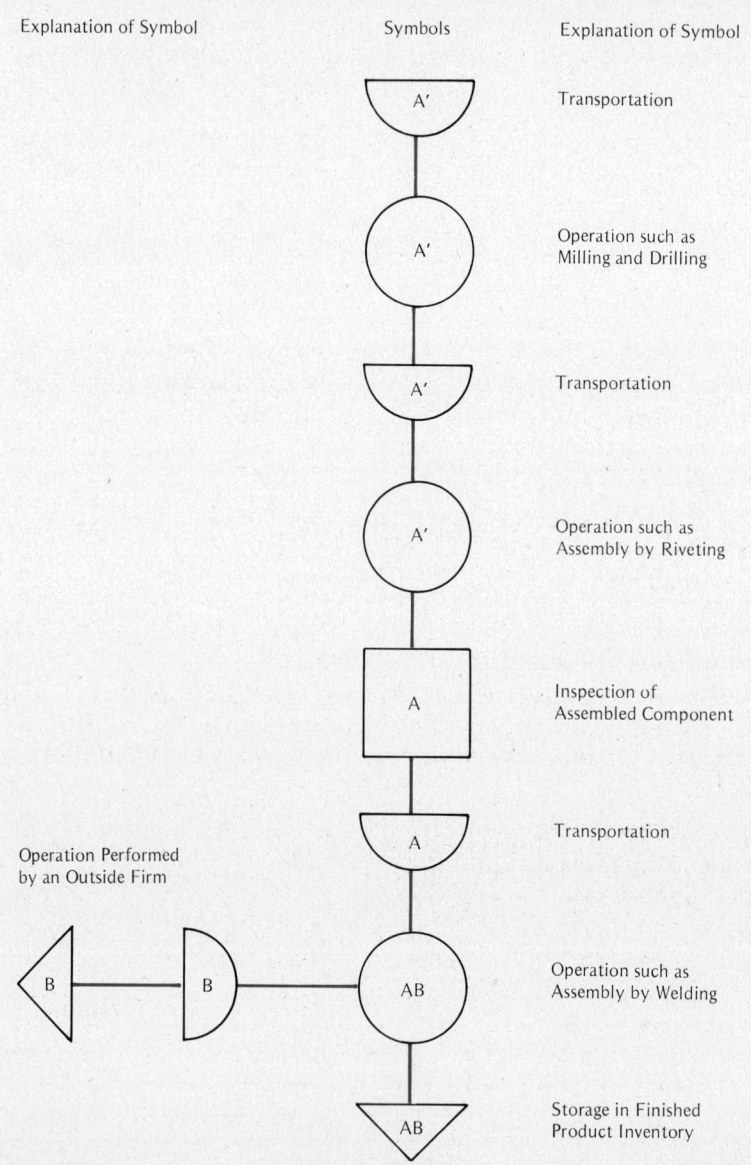

decision might also include termination of rail service, zoning approval for access to a main road, pressure from minorities to gain training programs for their members, and political turmoil that could affect government commitments.

Plant Layout

Several combinations of equipment are often possible for a major facility. It is true that the flow process chart for many products allows little choice, but even in these cases the designer of production facilities should use the following approach to selecting a plant layout:

1. *Alternative combinations of equipment and their priorities.* Identify the acceptable combinations of machinery and personnel, and rank them by efficiency (unit cost per finished product) and capital cost. "Acceptable" is defined as achieving minimum standards for cost, quantity, quality, and timing. The priorities could also be affected by factors such as energy consumption, social impact (pollution, noise, and so on), and recycling materials in short supply (net scrap generation).

2. *Alternative layout possibilities and their priorities.* The designer has the basic options shown in Figure 8-7, and any physical limitations from existing buildings and/or size of property, to guide individual preferences. The product or line layout requires reasonably stable finished product demand, product standardization, and continuous flow of supplies.

3. *Experimentation with alternatives.* This step develops the information needed to make an intelligent decision. Although estimates are involved, and these could prove wrong in actual operations, the designer has enough details to know the basis of any compromises that must be made. These compromises might include changes in the sequence of some operations in the tolerances, or in the specifications on materials and components.

4. *Selection of optimum layout.* Within specified limitations the designer makes a choice, and detailed blueprints are prepared. Purchase requisitions are completed for the equipment, and contractors are asked to bid on the work.

Until recently, the four steps in this approach were the result of human graphics, lists, and calculations. Now the experimentation can be conducted on the computer through the Computerized Relative Allocation of Facilities Technique (CRAFT). This program has saved many months in the search for the best layout. It probes five categories of data for the solution: (1) material, component, and product flow paths; (2) material handling systems by designer priority; (3) floor area requirements of work stations; (4) allowances for fixed work stations; and (5) material handling and total cost results.

CRAFT can also be used to modify existing operations to achieve greater efficiency. It accepts data such as breakage allowances when moving from one work station to another and works toward a layout that has the lowest possible waiting times in the flow.

Materials Handling

A distinction is usually made between the equipment needed for functional layouts and that needed for product or line layouts.

Figure 8-7. Two Fundamental Types of Layouts

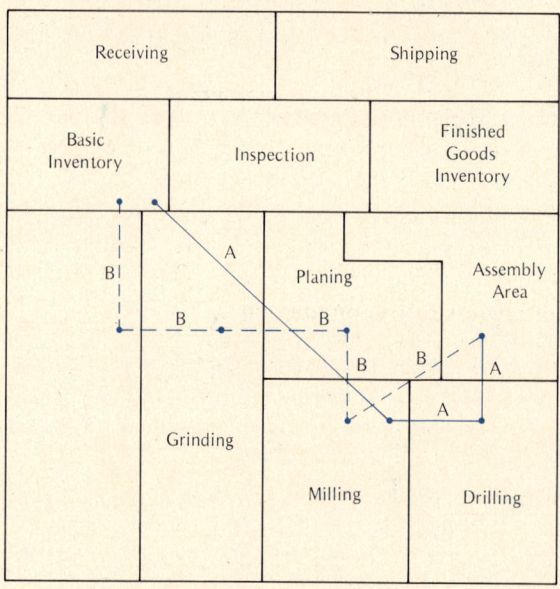

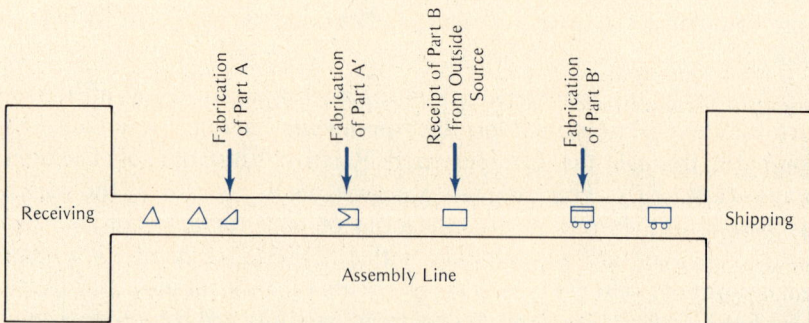

In a **functional layout**, the product must move to where a specific type of work is concentrated. Materials and components in the early stages, and the product in later stages, move from work station to work station in bins or on skids and pallets. A machine or an operator moves the unit in place, performs the assignment, and returns the unit to the bin, skid, or pallet. The movement between each station is usually by a lift-jack, fork-lift truck, or mobile and overhead cranes.

Overhead conveyor systems are also possible with some product lines. Carrousel variations permit production sequences in which a product can return to a station for additional work with minimum loss of time and no cross-flow of containers on ground level.

In a product or line layout the work is arranged in a sequence enabling the product to flow at a regulated rate. Jobs may be aligned in such a way that, when a worker has performed an assignment, the unit is placed within the grasp of the next worker, and so on. In this case, no equipment is needed. The most common situation, however, is the use of conveyors to move the unit to the next work station. Car assembly lines, bottling plants, and food processing operations are examples. Standardized conveyors are available for small lines, but manufacturers of this equipment usually design the details for specific customer requirements. Assembly lines require cranes and the use of containers, such as bins, to handle the finished product. Many plants use combinations of both types of layouts in the production of products.

MANAGEMENT OF THE PRODUCTION PROCESS

At this stage materials, parts, and components have been purchased, and sufficient inventory has been accumulated to begin production. In addition, the plant has been designed to permit the most efficient production. It is now possible to examine the production function and its place in the organization.

Scope of Responsibilities

Figure 8-8 gives some examples of reporting relationships between production and other parts of the organization, with titles common in American business.

Typically, the production manager is responsible for the following departments. They are arranged according to line and staff positions (see Chapter Six for definitions). The titles of these departments vary by industry and company, and some are consolidated. Other important functions such as quality control, which would normally be part of production line operations,

Line Departments	Staff Departments
1. Production Line Operations	1. Production Planning
2. Purchasing	2. Labor Relations and Personnel
3. Basic Inventories	3. Engineering
4. Traffic	4. Facility Planning
	5. Computer Operations
	6. Maintenance

Figure 8-8. *Typical Reporting Relationships for Production*

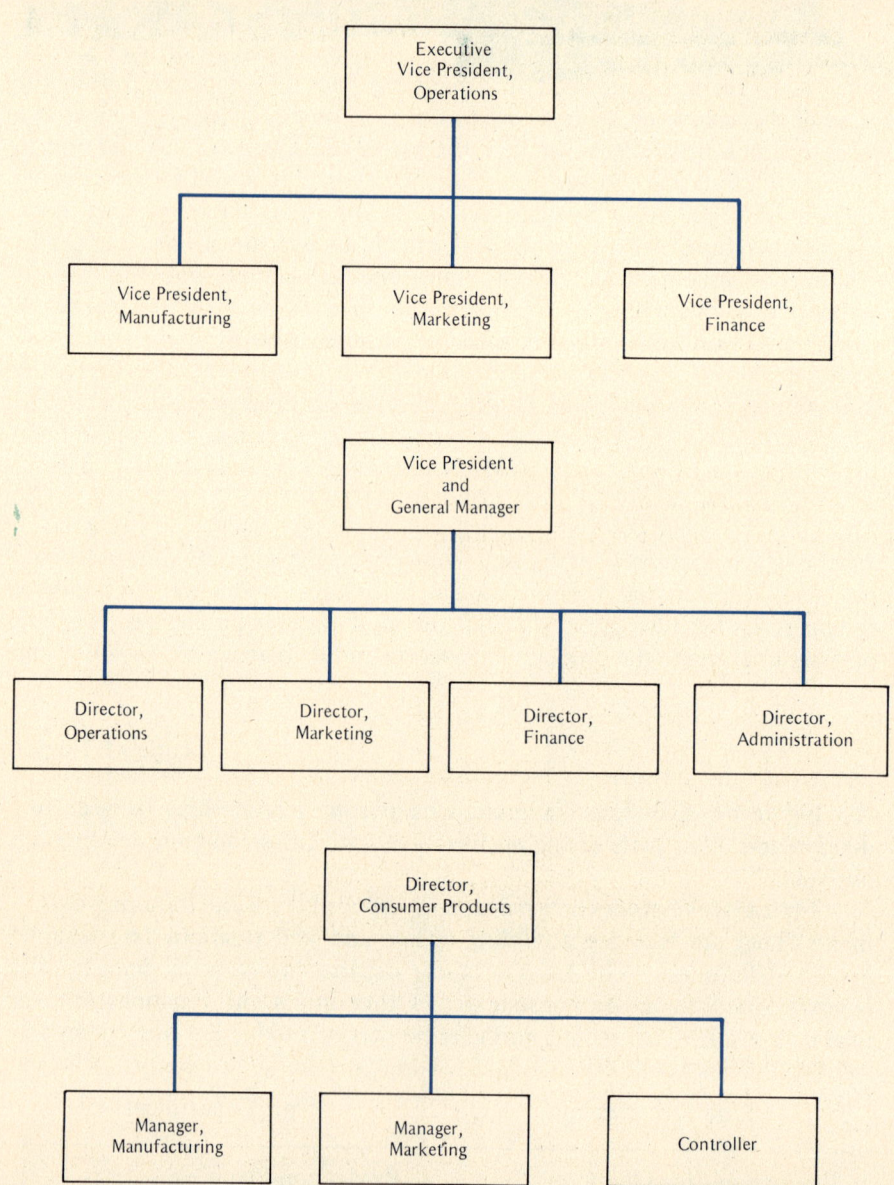

may require a separate department. Usually the analysis of sales forecasts and scheduling is done by production planning, and it acts as the focal point for coordination with marketing. Occasionally, Research and Development reports to the production manager. This is the case when R and D's objective is research directly applicable to manufacturing techniques.

Production Standards and Work Measurement

Answering the question "What is a fair day's work?" affects unit cost directly because of the impact on output per worker. It indirectly affects costs through worker morale and labor union relations. While the quality of management is involved in limiting these costs, work design is the foundation on which to build.

Data Development

Work measurement depends on statistical techniques to be reasonably certain that the time it takes for a certain level of output at a given minimum quality is typical of all workers with the required skills. When the average performance is calculated, it becomes the work standard for a specific job. If the assignment changes, it is necessary to take new measurements.

The expert using the statistical techniques determines: (1) normal job time; (2) an allowance for personal time (which can be an area of dispute between management and the worker and/or union); (3) an allowance for delays normal to the job, such as waiting for a pallet from the preceding work station; and (4) a fatigue and span of concentration allowance. The four time periods are measured frequently using many workers as the basis for determining an average. This data is compared with output, quality of product, and number of rejects or defectives.

Methods of Measurement

A common approach to determining a standard is to take times by using a *stopwatch*. These times are recorded at different periods of the day and with different workers. This information is compared with product samples for quantity and quality.

Work sampling eliminates some statistics. It is based on a large number of observations that simply record whether workers are working or idle. The idle category is usually separated into "delay" and "personal time." This method helps to establish a job standard, but it does not provide enough details for improving efficiency at a work station. As a result, work sampling is sometimes combined with the stopwatch method to achieve both a standard and the most efficient work sequence.

Applications of Work Standards

The most prevalent use of a work standard is simply to determine whether the work of each employee is adequate. Changes can be made with less trouble between management and workers or the labor union. Work standards also permit corrections on the production line.

The standards are also used for incentive systems. Workers who turn out more than the standard receive extra pay. Piece work is another application.

Based on the standard, the employee receives compensation in the form of dollars per unit. The company's objective in using incentive systems is increased output of workers performing a job and improved productivity.

Production Planning and Control

The sales forecast is the basis for scheduling output. It may be modified to allow for seasonal factors such as energy shortages, shipping times to warehouses, and other company or industry situations.

Flow from Basic Inventory

Production can be classified as *continuous* or *intermittent*. Continuous means that production regularly uses the same materials and components and that they regularly flow from basic inventory to the line for extended runs of the same product. Adjustments can be made in the rate of flow to reflect changes in demand. An example is any assembly line operation.

Intermittent means a product is produced in short runs. Examples are an item made occasionally by the company for its own basic inventory or one made under contract with a customer. Materials and components may be ordered specially or taken from inventory if the order is expected on a regular basis.

A bill of materials is issued for each product under either classification. This form authorizes the supervisor of basic inventories to release the items to the production line. The requirements for each product are identified, and the volume of each item is specified, usually in amounts per day (depending on the capacity of storage in the area just before production begins). In the case of a continuous process, the most important detail on the bill of materials is the volume required, since the inventory department knows what is needed to make the product. In intermittent production, this form is critically important because the requirements are not standardized, and any potential stock outs must be corrected quickly.

Another aspect of flow from basic inventory is parts requisitions to keep the production line operating. In order to control usage and minimize losses from employee theft, this could be a separate department in some companies. Figure 8-9 summarizes the link between inventories of materials, parts, and components and the production process.

Scheduling

Scheduling is the assignment of times and places to planned operations. The objective of scheduling is to make the most efficient use of the company's productive resources. Variables to be considered are: (1) equipment, buildings, and other facilities; (2) employees within the limits of union contracts and other obligations; (3) use of shifts and overtime in all or in portions

Figure 8-9. Link Between Basic Inventory and Production

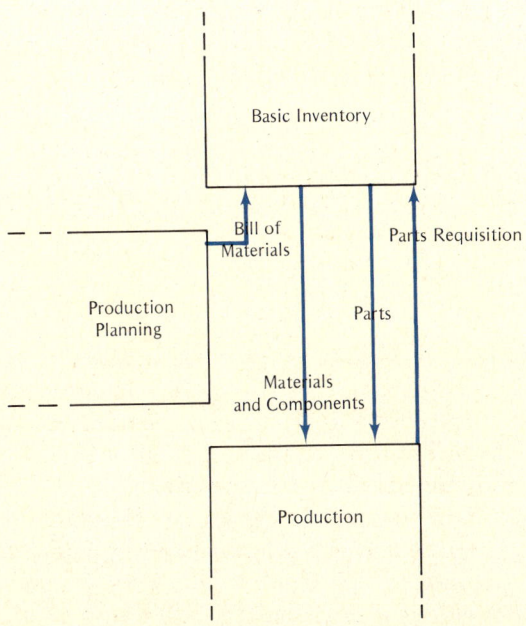

of the operation; (4) subcontractors for special requirements, peak loads, and bottlenecks; and (5) building or depletion of inventories to meet demand.

Scheduling managers have an important job because the decisions on use of the five variables can have a major affect on costs. If they are talented, unit costs will go down with a minimum of problems in the areas of customer satisfaction, labor relations, and outside contractors.

Figure 8-10 illustrates a typical problem confronting a scheduling manager in a seasonal business. There is a limited amount of normal production days in the peak demand period. Even when pay-premium days (Saturdays, Sundays, and holidays), three shifts, and minimum maintenance are added, the company cannot supply all its customers. On the other hand, scheduling has idle capacity for eight months of the year, and management has determined that it is impractical to expand for only a four-month heavy demand peak period. The ideal solution is to avoid all pay-premium days, overtime, and stress on facilities caused by round-the-clock shifts. This is accomplished by keeping a steady workforce all year and building inventories during low demand periods. The technique is called **production cycle smoothing**.

Smoothing is not always possible. The product may be costly to store, or supplies of materials and components may be seasonal as in the food business. In these situations, the scheduling manager must experiment to find the solution with the lowest cost. Several **quantitative methods** are used for this purpose. Linear programming and network models are two examples of these techniques explained in advanced courses.

Figure 8-10. Production Planning

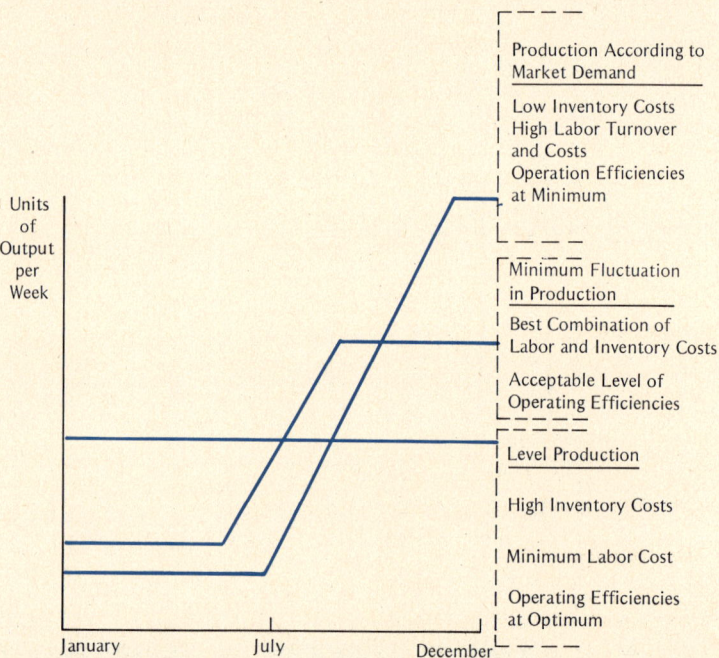

The computer has greatly increased the efficiency of production planning. Complex mathematical models have been constructed to simulate the company's productive facilities. These models permit scheduling managers to experiment to seek the best solution. The basic data on predicted sales, production days, and inventories are fed into the computer. Then, by changing the five variables, the lowest cost schedules are found within the limits of demand and obligations to labor unions, suppliers, and outside contractors.

THE SCHEDULING DECISIONS   When the schedule is determined, the bill of materials is prepared. A *routing* is also completed to clarify the exact route that materials, parts, components, and finished products will take through the plant. Even in plants with assembly lines, this route can vary, and production line personnel need guidance on flow.

Each section and department will receive a schedule to be met for specific days, including the *cumulative* requirements for each week of the month. These section and department schedules are part of a *master schedule* that is the means of controlling operations. Charts are often used to compare actual performance with the schedule, to identify problem areas, and to make adjustments.

Schedule performance reports provide feedback. The reports are essential because adjustments in the rate of production are made regularly to reflect changes in demand, inventory shortages, and problems in the plant. Figure

Figure 8-11. *Flow Schedule Performance Reports*

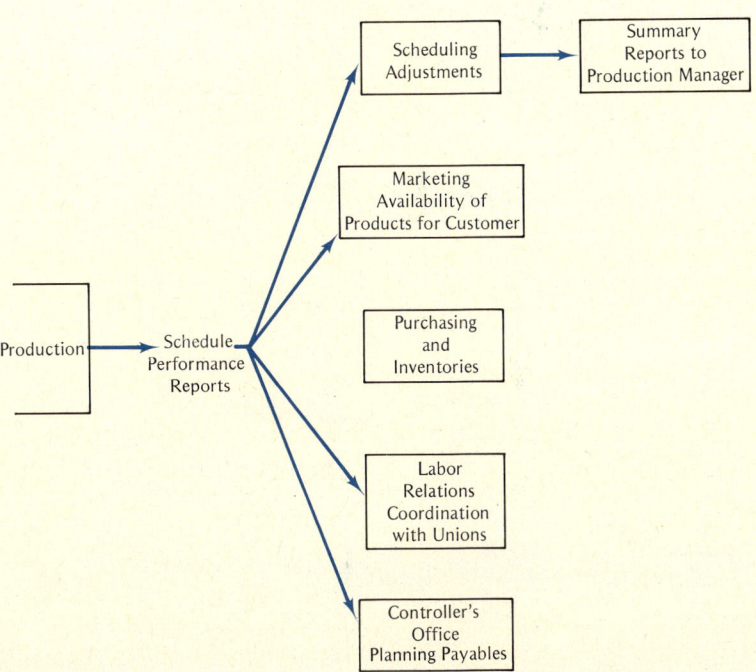

8-11 shows the departments that receive these reports and the reason they need the information.

Quality Control

Attaining specified quality requires good product and production process design. It also requires quality conscious workers, with management taking steps to obtain their cooperation.

Once these fundamental steps have been accomplished, the product must be inspected periodically while in process and also at the end of the line. These inspections are costly because they slow output, involve the expense of personnel to do the work, and take space. Therefore, companies try to minimize the number of inspections. On the other hand, it is expensive to permit a defective product to go through any part of the production process or reach the customer. As a result, companies are continuously trying to achieve a balance between economizing on the direct cost of quality control and avoiding expenses caused by inadequate inspection.

The following points summarize the basic factors involved in quality control.

1. *Determination of tolerances.* This defines quality at each stage in the production process. The worker knows the degree of accuracy, neatness, and

so on required, and the inspector has specifics on which to gauge whether the product should be passed.

2. *Data on performance.* A reporting system is needed to identify where rejects, defectives that were corrected, and extra scrappage took place. Paperwork needs to be minimized, but information on performance at certain stages of production is necessary to identify problems and make corrections in equipment and operators.

3. *Number of inspection stations.* A decision must be made on the number of times a product is inspected for quality in the production process. This establishes the points at which data is collected. Judgment is involved. In addition to direct expense, the manager responsible for quality control must coordinate with the production planning department to be certain that schedules are not upset by the number of inspection stations selected.

4. *Method of inspection.* Mechanical and electronic scanners can monitor many production processes without personnel being involved and with very little slowing of output. This requires investment of capital and is not always feasible. Observation by inspectors introduces judgment and human error, and opens the possibility that workers whose output is rejected may become discontented with management.

5. *Frequency of inspection at a station.* Rarely do companies inspect every product. If 100% inspection does not take place, it is essential that products observed be representative of the production process at each stage. Statistical techniques are involved. The term used to describe this method is **acceptance sampling**.

Most companies maintain quality control charts to assist in achieving the necessary tolerance levels at a minimum cost. The data flowing from the system set up for performance evaluation supplies the details to identify the cause for high rates of rejects.

Traffic

At the end of the production line the traffic department is responsible for getting the finished product to its destination (warehouse or customer). This department arranges transportation and tries for the fastest, lowest cost shipping with the minimum amount of damage en route. Traffic also handles the flow of materials and components into the plant. In addition, it provides information for decisions on purchasing f.o.b. or c.i.f.

Maintenance

Many plant managers regard this unglamorous department as the key to successful operations. The reason is that breakdowns upset the entire flow of the production process, and all of the departments are forced to modify schedules. The impact on cost can be tremendous. Maintenance has two basic functions: (1) prevention and (2) repair.

Preventive maintenance attempts to preserve the productive capacity of equipment and to avoid breakdowns before they occur. If nothing goes wrong, it is not always easy to defend budgets for prevention. However, computer programs have been devised to assist in these decisions.

The efficiency of *repair crews* is vital to operations. Each minute of down-time—time during which an operation is shut down during normal working hours—can represent thousands of dollars to companies. Management of these employees is often an important position in the plant.

CAREER OPPORTUNITIES IN INDUSTRIAL MANAGEMENT

The chapter describes many aspects of jobs in industrial management. In the past, the person in charge of manufacturing or operations has gone on to become head of the division or company less frequently than other positions, but this situation is changing.

Cost control, the obtaining of materials and energy sources during inflation or periods of scarcity, and the skill of using computers to best advantage have become increasingly important to industry. Since the vice president of operations is skilled in these areas, the board of directors and top management are now more likely to choose this person as general manager than in the past.

People attracted to industrial management are interested in machinery, how things work, and problem solving. They do not have to be mathematical geniuses, but they should be comfortable with statistics and quantitative methods. They might have a less out-going personality than a sales representative, but considering the spectrum of personnel working in a factory, they must be able to get along with people.

You must have a college degree to have a chance of reaching the top in the operations portion of the organization. Most companies recommend a combination of a technical undergraduate degree in engineering, chemistry, and so on and a masters degree in business administration. The undergraduate degree in industrial administration is also a good approach to this career path because this degree is usually offered by universities which can find an attractive first job for their graduates.

Courses taken at the undergraduate level should include mathematics, statistics, computer programming, and introductory engineering, as well as industrial management material. In addition, advanced cost accounting is essential for the professional. By the time you are in your senior year, you should be able to use the computer to solve problems. Capabilities could be limited to using programs designed by other such as CRAFT (see page 195) or linear programming solutions, but you should be comfortable using a computer terminal or processing cards at the computer center.

It is possible to have a career in operations without this preparation. However, your problem-solving capacity is limited, and the absence of a good foundation increases the possibility of making the wrong decisions. Industrial management is not a career in which a good personality and an attractive physical appearance will compensate for other shortcomings. Performance is measured by numbers coming from the computer every day.

CHAPTER SUMMARY

The four goals of production are: (1) cost minimization; (2) quantity according to schedule; (3) quality to specifications; and (4) proper timing. The sales forecast, modified to allow for shipping and handling, is the foundation for production management.

Purchasing has become increasingly important because of shortages of many items at a cost within budgets. An order is placed after receipt of a purchase requisition, investigation of sources, and receipt of bids or negotiations on details. Expediting orders is essential to maintain flow into company inventories. A critical factor in this process is the point at which responsibility is transferred to the buyer.

Companies establish purchasing policies that provide guidelines for such things as: (1) make-or-buy decisions; (2) safety stocks; (3) reciprocity; (4) ethics; and (5) purchasing procedures.

Inventories are classified into three groups: (1) stocks, or basic inventory; (2) inventory in process; and (3) finished goods inventory. Control of inventories is shifting from manual systems to automated and even computerized systems. Seven factors influence the amount of any item held in inventory.

Three processes are involved in production: (1) chemical; (2) changing shape or form; and (3) assembly. Automation means investing in equipment instead of paying an employee. The reason for the change is very often to eliminate human error in addition to cost savings.

Designing production facilities begins with the specifications on the finished product. From these it is possible to determine the materials and components involved, the processes required, the interrelationship of work stations, and preliminary layout ideas. A process flow chart assists in identifying alternative combinations of equipment and layout possibilities. CRAFT is an important computer program that assists in experimenting with designs in order to select the best possibility. A functional layout moves the product to a specific type of work whereas the product or line layout arranges the work so that the product can flow at a regular rate.

An important aspect of production management is determining a fair day's work for each assignment. Data is accumulated through many measurements of time and motion in each job with a stopwatch. Another method, called work sampling, involves taking hundreds of observations on whether an employee is working or idle at a specific job.

A bill of materials initiates the flow of items from inventory to operations. Scheduling also prepares a routing for a product to specify each step in the production process. Each section or department receives a schedule for expected volume. A master schedule is maintained to coordinate the output from various operations. Schedule performance reports supply feedback so that necessary adjustments can be made.

Quality control is best achieved if the product and process designs are adequate and if personnel are quality conscious. There must be a definition of quality for each job so that a worker knows what the company wants. Thereafter, decisions must be made on the number of inspection stations, method of inspection, and the sample of products inspected.

The traffic department guides flow of materials, parts, and components into the plant and flow of finished products to the customer.

Maintenance is important to prevent breakdowns and stoppages before they occur. When they do happen, management must be sure repair crews are able to correct the situation as rapidly as possible. The cost of stoppages can involve thousands of dollars.

Careers in industrial management are becoming more important than in the past. People who succeed in the field are usually interested in machinery, how things work, and problem solving. A college education is needed, with emphasis on mathematics, statistics, computer programming, and cost accounting as well as courses in industrial management. A technical undergraduate degree with a masters degree in business administration is highly recommended.

PROVOCATIVE STATEMENT

A New Viewpoint on Productivity

1 "When the final box score is written on the accomplishments of the Price Commission, it may well be that our most durable achievement will have been the fact that American businesses are more conscious of productivity—not simply as an abstract idea but as a very important yardstick of their own accomplishment.

A great many companies were simply unaware of the importance of productivity in their own operations and to their bottom-line results. A great many others had no idea of how to go about measuring it. Most businessmen have conceded that the Commission's control regulations have actually forced them to learn more about their own businesses.

The lesson has come none too soon. For at this stage in our knowledge of how things work. . . . we have already outgrown the old, simplistic output-per-man-hour concept of productivity. That definition, in widespread and common use today, attempts to measure quantities of goods and services produced. . . . But it completely misses the boat for what has become of increasing importance to our society—the quality of economic performance.

First is the quality of goods produced; it is sometimes said that this can be measured by price. In seeking to determine contributions to productivity, this measurement is a little like defining a thing in terms of itself. Try to use the price standard in comparing the value of any 1910 automobile with the air-conditioned, tinted-glass, radio-equipped, and self-starting cars of today. . . . And for example, do you value "permanent press," which is often worth more in maintenance savings than its original cost?

Second is the matter of services. According to The Conference Board, the service sector of our economy in 1972 contributed 38 percent of our country's gross national product, but employed 60 percent or more of our work force. The service industries are capable of producing some remarkably innovative practices, some of which result in greater output, as in the data processing field. . . . But it is not secret that the service sector, as important as it is, is an area of low productivity and as such it is a drag on the national averages.

Third is the quality of work itself, and that includes the satisfaction involved in working. This can range from the new mining laws to the almost intangible improvements being sought by many production-line workers, like those in the General Motors plant at Lordstown, Ohio. . . . There is an illusion that only the younger workers have been spoiled and coddled and complain about quality of work. Many people feel we should stop spoiling them. The reality is that they can become better and more productive workers than we have ever had before if we really understand what they are asking.

Fourth are the unintended effects of production—the many affronts to our environment and the effects that any business, particularly a large business, has on the economy and the social structure of its community. . . .

Fifth, and perhaps most often overlooked as a measure of quality, is the importance of choice to a free people, or what British economist Walter Bagehot describes as a disposition to variety throughout the animal kingdom. An inevitable consequence of the breadth of choice is change. Thus, change itself—change in tastes and habits and life styles—becomes a positive economic factor contributing to productivity. . . .

Getting a productivity measurement that will reflect all these values is immensely difficult, and perhaps impossible. But it is not only worth a good fighting try, it is imperative that we succeed."

C. Jackson Grayson, Jr.
Counselor to Chairman,
Cost of Living Council

PROVOCATIVE STATEMENT

Standards as the Language of Production

2 "Standardization is the language of production. Without it, modern manufacturing would be all but impossible.

Specifically, we're speaking of technical standards—those that provide physical descriptions of items and materials, specify performance criteria, etc.

This is not to say that companies don't develop standards in non-production areas. Policies—a synonym for standards in these spheres—exist for administrative responsibilities, intradepartmental procedures, personnel relationships, and so on.

But it is still the technical standards that characterize today's production methods. Without them, economies of space and money would be lost through vastly expanded inventories; production equipment would be almost impossible to design or use; and production itself would slow to a crawl.

If standards are truly production's language, then purchasing is the master spokesman, and design engineering keeps the vocabulary.

The relationship goes something like this:

* Production is responsible for manufacturing the products of the company. These must be—within practical limits—identical to each other in structure and performance. And production must find ways of accomplishing this in the most economical and efficient manner possible.

* Design engineering builds the first unit to show what it looks like and how it works. But it is not enough for design to just build a working model. It must be producible within the framework of production's guidelines and capabilities.

* Purchasing stands alongside both of these functions, on the one hand advising design about matters such as production inventories and equipment, and on the other helping production to prepare for new designs coming onto the line.

And now we come to the heart of the matter—in order to assure that the language is a common one, standards are devised by all three working together."

Purchasing Magazine
September 19, 1972

PROVOCATIVE STATEMENT

Zero Inventory Purchasing (ZIP)

3 "The question that plagues purchasing managers isn't how to function without inventory. It's "How much inventory is enough, and how much is too much?"

Systems contracting, consignment buying, all kinds of purchasing systems have come about to keep inventory levels as low as possible. Some companies are trying to combine the best of all the techniques.

International Harvester's Solar Division gives this objective a special title. Solar's program is called ZIP (Zero Inventory Purchasing). According to a purchasing manager, its philosophy is: "Don't buy anything you don't need or before you need it. . . .

"About a year ago, we studied our entire inventory. We found that we were holding all sorts of sheet metal and bar stock that was becoming obsolete.

"The reason was that new incoming shipments were being unloaded right on top of safety stocks. The same sheets remained on the bottom. As they deteriorated, we found ourselves with a lot of 'safety' stock that was virtually useless. . . .

"We called in the supplier, and together we went through our entire inventory. We sorted it out to see what was still good, what could be sold for scrap. Once we had thoroughly cleaned house, we made purchase arrangements with the supplier to ensure that excess inventory situations didn't crop up again, and the seed that became Zip was planted."

Now, the purchasing manager and his buyers have started concentrating on requirements contracts with suppliers participating in ZIP. Purchasing gets estimated usage requirements from production and other using departments. On the basis of these figures, purchasing negotiates a contract that in effect says, "We will give you a certain portion of our total requirements for this item, estimated at so-and-so many per year, if you agree to keep a specified amount on hand for us at all times." In other words, Solar has switched its safety stock to the supplier's location to eliminate the problems of obsolescence and tied-up capital. . . .

Non-purchasing people, generally heads of using departments, keep track of their own needs. Whenever they need a shipment, they simply call up the supplier, identify themselves, and initiate a new order, which goes directly to the using location. There's no more need for requisitions and purchase orders. . . .

"The supplier keeps similar records of what he's shipped. He tallies these up at prearranged intervals, and sends an invoice to accounting. It's a simple matter for them to check quantity against their packing slip records and price against their copy of the original contract, and mail him a check. We don't get involved at all."

Purchasing Magazine
March 20, 1973

REVIEW QUESTIONS

1. Name the four basic goals of production managers and explain how they are related.
2. What is used as the foundation for achieving the four basic goals? Give factors that could affect production planning in addition to the needs of the marketing department.
3. Identify the advantages and disadvantages of centralized and decentralized purchasing.
4. Distinguish between types of inventory. Who is responsible for the condition and movement of inventory in each type? (Give both his title and whom he reports to.)
5. Distinguish between mechanization and automation by how each affects a worker. What are the advantages to an employer?
6. Give the variables involved in production scheduling. How does the computer play a role in scheduling?

Chapter Outline

What Does Marketing Do?
   Determining the Target Market
   Planning the Product
      Business View
      Consumer View
   Pricing the Product
      Business View
      Customer View
      New Products
      Covering the Cost
      Fixed and Variable Costs
      Balancing Consumer View and Costs
   Satisfying the Government
   Promoting the Product
      Convincing the Buyer
      Pleasing the Buyer
   Distributing the Product
      Planning Distribution

The Impact of Marketing on the Firm
   Marketing and Production
   Marketing and Personnel
   Marketing and Finance/Accounting

Historical Change in Importance of Marketing
   Production Activities Emphasized (1900–1930)
   Selling Activities Emphasized (1930–1950)
   Recent Past

The Consumerism Movement
   Consumer Demand
   Business Reaction
   Government Reaction

Marketing as a Job
   Two Types of Marketing Jobs
   The Marketing Manager's Job
      Required Background
      Reward System

Chapter Summary

Provocative Statement 1:
   Prices Must Be High Enough to Produce Profits

Provocative Statement 2:
   One-way Mirrors May Be Used to Find Out about Consumer Behavior

Key Terms

Marketing activity
Target market
Product
Price
Survey of buyers' intentions
Fixed costs
Variable costs
Price discrimination
Robinson–Patman Act
Predatory pricing
Price fixing
Federal Trade Commission
Word-of-mouth communication

Buying guides
Promotion
Channel of distribution
Consumerism movement
Class action suits
Federal Cigarette Labeling and Advertising Act
Fair Packaging and Labeling Act
National Traffic and Motor Vehicle Safety Act
Consumer Credit Protection Act
Corrective advertising
Marketing manager

Marketing Concepts

"You can't do consumers a favor by trying to sell to them as cheaply as possible."
—President and Owner of Food Products Firm

The marketing activity can be defined as *that part of a firm's activity concerned with providing consumers with want-satisfying goods or services at a price they are willing to pay, at the place they want to buy them, and at the time they wish to buy or use them.* The purpose of this chapter is to explain the marketing activity.

Any business spends much of its money and hires many of its employees to carry out the marketing activity. It has been estimated that one-half of all money spent for goods and services is to cover the costs of marketing. Moreover, this same group of activities, marketing, accounts for one-fourth to one-third of all jobs in the United States. Finally, marketing has been one of the fields of study most frequently chosen by college students majoring in business administration.

WHAT DOES MARKETING DO?

Poor marketing is generally the major reason why products fail to provide firms with satisfying profits. Consider such recent events as rising food prices, recall of defective automobiles, energy and pollution crises. All of these events, which affect both business and society, are related to marketing activities. It is difficult to appreciate the true impact of marketing without knowing more about it and its components.

Good marketing leads to more sales and, thus, higher profits for a business. The marketing activity is composed of five major areas:

1. Determining the target market.
2. Planning the product.
3. Pricing the product.
4. Promoting the product.
5. Distributing the product.

The correct solutions in each area will benefit the company by producing the desired results. These answers are shown in question-and-answer form in Table 9-1 and are discussed more fully in the following sections.

Determining the Target Market

It is the job of marketing activity to tell those in charge of production activities of a business what customers want (see Table 9-1). In examining customer needs and wants, marketing must be sure to define the customers in the market who will be the target of the firm's marketing efforts. The target market must be determined so that buying behavior can be carefully watched before the product is planned and produced. For example, a sandwich shop is located in a college community. Its management must first pinpoint its market. Will it be composed mainly of college students, local construction workers,

Table 9-1. *Questions Which Must Be Answered Satisfactorily for Sales to Occur*

Question	Answer
1. Who is the target market?	1. It is the group of people whose needs and wants can be profitably satisfied.
2. What products should we produce?	2. We should produce the products we have planned because these are what consumers want.
3. What price should we charge the consumer?	3. We should charge those prices which meet customer value expectations and the costs of producing the product.
4. What do we have available for the customer's needs and wants?	4. We have available the products the customer wants, at a price he can afford and is willing to pay, when and where he wants them.
5. Where and when should the product be made available?	5. We should make the product available when and where the customer wants to buy.

Drawing by W. Miller; © 1974. The New Yorker Magazine, Inc.

"Come to think of it, we have a woman here in Perkins. How do you think the ladies might react to this marketing approach, Perkins?"

college faculty, or some other group of people? If the manager of the shop decides to try to satisfy the food needs of college students, he would be wasting time and money asking construction workers what kinds of sandwiches they would prefer. Similarly, determining the times when faculty members eat would not be of use in planning shop hours.

Firms frequently fail to specify their target market explicitly. They merely assume that they know all about their market. The marketing activity must first determine what group of people will be the target for its products and what the needs and wants of the group will be.

Planning the Product

Marketing is also concerned with setting the characteristics of the product that will be produced. In order to give guidance to production activities, marketing must determine what customers want or need and relay this vital information to production personnel. This aspect of marketing focuses upon determining the physical nature of the product, its colors, available sizes, brand names, and packages. The marketing activity in an automobile company will provide information about what kinds of cars people need, what colors and styles they prefer, and so on.

Reprinted through permission of *Advertising Age.*

"You carry the flavor you like, and I'll carry the flavor I like."

Business View

Determining the characteristics of the product is a concern of all firms and organizations that sell products or services to a target market. College fraternities become involved with product planning when they try to decide what services to offer members or prospective members. Universities must decide what courses to offer students. Thus, planning the characteristics of products, an important marketing activity, is the concern of every business. Planning must be done after the needs and wants of present or potential customers are considered.

When planning the product, the business generally emphasizes the activities that lead to its production. For example, the business view of a bicycle may be the steel, tires, and other parts assembled by the workers. A producer of a dental service may consider his or her product to be a combination of many years of training and the use of tools to drill and fill teeth.

Consumer View

The purchase of a product by a consumer represents an exchange. Buyers exchange their money for the product planned by marketing and produced by the production department. Although the production function provides a product with set physical characteristics, potential customers do not evaluate these characteristics on an objective basis. They generally make a subjective evaluation of these physical attributes. One aspect of this subjective evaluation is that prospective customers may consider only some of the physical dimensions of the product.

For instance, a prospective customer of a bicycle may observe that a bicycle is a certain color, has curved handlebars, and has 10 gears. For some reason, the individual may forget to inspect the size of the wheels, the height of the seat from the ground, or the metal used to make the gears. Many reasons may exist for this selective evaluation of the physical characteristics of a product. It may be that some characteristics are easier to evaluate, while other factors are not considered important by the customer. A person may assume that the metal used to produce the gears will not influence how well the bike will fit specific needs. Moreover, the customer may not feel capable of judging the various metals that might be used.

When the product is designed, it is important to understand the selective process the prospective customer uses. The marketer should realize that a customer's attitudes and past buying experience affect the evaluation of products and services.

Pricing the Product

Prospective customers consider other things besides physical characteristics of the products. Frequently, one of the first questions asked by a prospective customer is: "How much does it cost?" The answer is the selling or asking price of the seller. The selling price must be set for the final consumer—for instance, the student who buys a bike for personal enjoyment—as well as for any other customers who are buying the product for resale, such as the bike retailer who buys from the Schwinn Company. Prices are also set for products sold to manufacturers who use them to make a product sold to someone else, such as the Schwinn Company, which buys fabricated parts or raw materials for use in the manufacture of bicycles.

Business View

The planning of prices is another aspect of the marketing activity. Price planning includes setting the suggested list price to the consumer, determining how much *discount* (a reduction in price) will be allowed to different buyers and for what purposes, and changing prices over a period of time.

Price setting must be done in conjunction with the needs and wants of the target market. Failure to consider the value assigned to products by consumers may result in prices set too high or too low. If the price is higher than consumers are willing to pay, then no units of the product will be sold. The Mustang car would have been less successful if its price had been higher, because the number of consumers willing to pay the higher price would have been fewer. On the other hand, if the price is lower than the consumer is willing to pay, the seller is losing an opportunity to increase the return on an investment. A company offering a car equal in quality to the Cadillac for a price of $3,000 would find actual profits lower than potential profits because of the relatively low price.

Consumer View

The sales of the $3,000 car just mentioned may also be relatively low because of the buyer's reaction to the low price. Since buyers may use price as an indicator of the product's quality, they may feel that a relatively low-priced product is of low quality and only purchased by people with low incomes.

Although customers' willingness to buy a product at different prices must be considered before setting prices, it is often difficult to measure consumer demand before the customer actually makes a purchase. As a product is sold over a time, the seller may discover better prices by observing the quantity sold when different prices are charged. Unfortunately, this method of projecting past sales at different prices for the future is dependent upon the assumption no customers will change their buying behavior in the future.

The dynamic nature of customers frequently results in different responses to a price. For instance, a retailer may reduce the price on paint from $9.99 a gallon to $6.99 a gallon and increase sales by 100%. However, if the retailer leaves the paint on sale at the $6.99 price for one week and then raises the selling price to the original price of $9.99 the next week, sales may not return to the original level. The amount of time the paint is sold for $9.99 a gallon will influence customers' response to a lowering of price. If the two prices are alternated each week, the sales increase experienced for the $6.99 price will probably become less over a time. Generally, people are less likely to consider a price reduction as a bargain if it is made regularly or frequently.

New Products

Not only is it difficult to estimate demand at different prices for old or established products, such as paint and bicycles, but it is also difficult to estimate demand for new products. Since there has been no previous experience, there is little information to be used when trying to estimate demand for a new product. For example, a firm considering pricing its new product, which automatically serves ping-pong balls to a player, may find no past prices and related sales for a comparable product. However, it may be possible to use another method to determine customers' willingness to pay different prices. There may be existing products that the new product will replace. The automatic ping-pong server may replace ping-pong tables and other types of ping-pong equipment. If substitute products can be defined, the quantity of them sold at different prices may provide a base for setting prices. The success of this method is dependent upon the degree of substitutability between the new and old products. If the new product possesses distinctive advantages over the products it replaces, the price should reflect these differences.

Consumers' willingness to pay may also be determined by asking consumers how many units of a product they will buy at different prices. This method (commonly called **survey of buyers' intentions**) may be one of the few avenues available to the seller of a new product, but may result in the setting of erroneous prices. Consumers may not know or be unwilling to tell how much they are willing to pay for a product. Moreover, consumers may not consider a statement of intended purchases to mean they must actually act that way. It is only when consumers are giving something of value to the seller, such as a down payment or a legal agreement to buy, that their actions can be interpreted with any degree of certainty. Even then, a buyer can cancel a contract for purchase of goods.

Covering the Cost

Price setting must also reflect the costs of producing and marketing the product. Just as a firm will not be successful if its products are not priced with regard to consumers' willingness to pay, pricing below the costs of producing and marketing the product will be financial suicide for the firm.

Therefore, costs are more likely to be used as the basis of prices than consumer demand. Costs are generally known since they can be determined by examination of the accounting records of the firm. Moreover, cost figures are less likely to change in an unpredictable manner over time. The demand, on the other hand, is dependent upon consumer purchase behavior. This behavior is, in turn, dependent upon many factors beyond the control of the firm, such as the prices of competitive products, income of consumers, and their tastes.

Fixed and Variable Costs

One of the major difficulties that results when a seller tries to determine costs before setting a price is that the cost of producing and selling one unit depends upon the total quantity produced and sold. For example, a producer of pleasure boats may determine the costs of producing and selling boats is $10,000 each, assuming that 20 boats are produced and sold. Using this estimate of cost ($10,000 per boat) and desired profit ($5,000 per boat), a price of $15,000 per boat may be set. At the price of $15,000 (he doesn't produce more than can be sold), 10 boats are sold. The producer may not be making a desired profit or even covering all the costs because the per boat costs of producing and selling 10 boats may be higher than for 20 boats.

The problem is caused by fixed costs. **Fixed costs** are those that stay the same, regardless of the number of units produced or sold. The cost of lighting a bicycle factory or of salaries for its managers will not vary for different sized production. If the total fixed costs of the boat producer are $150,000, the individual will have to sell 10 boats at $15,000 to cover these costs.

However, not all costs of producing and distributing goods are fixed. Some costs, such as those for raw materials, labor, or sales commissions, change as the number of units produced changes. These costs are called **variable costs**.

The difficulty of using costs to determine selling price is that costs, selling price, and the number of units produced are interrelated. The cost of producing and selling one unit cannot be determined until the business knows how many units it wants to produce and sell. Any business will want to produce no more units than it can sell. The demand for a product cannot be determined until the selling price is set. Consequently, selling price must be set to determine how many units will be sold. At the same time, the number of units that will be produced and sold must be determined before total and unit costs can be known. Although this seems to be an insoluble problem, common sense and experience allow manufacturers to find an acceptable range of prices that will provide an adequate profit. In addition, *break-even analysis*, a planning tool discussed in Chapter Thirteen, is frequently used by business executives to see the interrelationships between costs, selling price, and expected demand.

Balancing Consumer View and Costs

Costs can only be considered part of the basis for setting prices, however. A price that covers all costs will not be in the long-run interests of the firm if no consumers are willing to pay the price. A manufacturer of a new type of mousetrap learned this the hard way. The product was priced at $28 per unit, but it did not sell because this price was considered too high by consumers. Furthermore, a price may be considered too high by the sales representatives or retailers who are hired to sell the product. As a result, their sales efforts may be less than enthusiastic.

Satisfying the Government

Prices must also satisfy the regulations of government. There are government regulations on pricing products lower, higher, or the same as competitors. In addition, selling a product (of like grade and quality) to different customers for different prices, called **price discrimination**, may be in violation of the **Robinson–Patman Act**.

Predatory pricing, pricing a product for less than cost in hopes of driving a competitor out of business, is regulated at the national level by antitrust laws (Sherman and Clayton Acts). Several states have passed acts, called *unfair practices acts*, requiring businesses to sell their products for more than cost. Generally, predatory prices are prohibited by society because of the fear of big businesses. Everyone expects that big businesses will take advantage of consumers after they have driven small competitors out.

Price increases draw government attention, especially in times of fast rising prices. Price controls, as imposed by former President Nixon in 1971, affect pricing practices.

Agreements among competitors to charge an identical price, called **price fixing**, are generally in violation of the Sherman and Clayton Acts. However,

Marketing Concepts

dealers can all agree to charge the price suggested by manufacturers, provided their state has passed a law (called *fair trade law*) permitting this. Prices identical to those of competitors are not illegal if no agreement has been made between competitors. Identical prices may result because businesses are very competitive or because the prices are set equal to those of the leader, such as General Motors or United States Steel.

Price discrimination may mean trouble for a business. The **Federal Trade Commission**, for example, ruled against Thompson Products, Inc., for selling certain automobile parts to the Big Three automobile makers at prices lower than Thompson's own distributors were being charged. Discriminatory prices are illegal (in violation of the Robinson–Patman Act) if they "substantially lessen competition or may tend to create a monopoly in any line of commerce." However, lower prices to a buyer are legal if based on lower costs of producing and selling the goods to the buyer or on a good faith attempt to meet a competitor's equally low price.

Promoting the Product

A customer's evaluation of a product is dependent upon factors other than physical characteristics and price. When consumers consider buying a product, such as a camera, they start to remember what they have heard about it. The marketing department influences their choice of product through its promoting activity.

There are many sources of information for customers considering the purchase of a product. Since the focus of this text is the business firm, all the

"By George! I think you've done it!"

Drawing by D. Frawley; © 1975 The New Yorker Magazine, Inc.

sources of buyer information can be divided into two categories: *business controlled* and *nonbusiness controlled communications*. Business controlled communications include informative and persuasive messages provided to customers by sales representatives, television commercials, store displays, or mail coupons. A major source of nonbusiness controlled communications is customers who tell their buying experience to others. This verbal communication between customers is generally termed word-of-mouth communication. Reports of product experiences have been formalized in the form of buying guides. Individuals and groups, such as Consumers' Research, Inc., and Consumers Union of U.S., Inc., have sprung up to provide consumers with information about products they are considering buying. Their testing activities and publications, *Consumers' Research Bulletin* or *Consumer Reports*, are generally paid for by consumers. However, some product evaluations, such as the seals shown in Figure 9-1, may be made by businesses or by those paid by businesses who produce the products.

Because of the vital importance of business controlled communication to the sale of the firm's products, the marketing activity includes the planning of this communication. Generally, this area of marketing activity is called promotion since the purpose of this communication is to stir up interest for, or *promote*, the product of the firm.

Promotion is defined as *any method of business controlled communication designed to inform or remind customers about a firm's products and/or to persuade them to buy*. Generally, promotion is divided into these categories:

1. Personal selling activities that use a sales representative to provide informing, reminding, or persuading information.
2. Mass selling or advertising activities that use nonpersonal carriers or mass media to take the message to the target market.

Figure 9-1. *Seals May Provide Consumer Information*

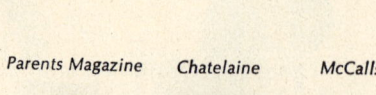

Source: Money Management Finance Corporation, Chicago.

3. Sales promotion activities that use message carriers other than personal or mass media. Trade fairs or displays in stores are examples.

Convincing the Buyer

Promotion is another important influence on the willingness of customers to make an exchange for the product or service offered by the seller. If consumers have never heard of a particular brand of camera and its benefits, they will probably be reluctant to buy the product even though it may be low priced. However, if a sales representative or an advertisement has informed consumers about the benefits of owning this brand of camera and has convinced them that these benefits fit their needs or wants, then they may be willing to part with their hard-earned money. In addition, a money-back guarantee, if they are not completely satisfied, can help overcome resistance to buy this product.

Planning promotion concerns not only the choice of what type of carrier to use for the message—sales representatives, television, or radio—but also the designing of the messages to be carried. Planners of promotion must decide not only how but also what potential consumers will be told. This includes deciding what appeals to use and whether to use pictures or not.

Pleasing the Buyer

Since potential customers in a capitalistic economy generally have the freedom to choose which information they believe, a firm finds that its communication must be carefully planned and watched so that potential customers are favorably influenced. However, the firm's management must also be aware that word-of-mouth communication is often more effective than business controlled communication.

Even though word-of-mouth communication is not business controlled, it can be influenced by a firm. Frequently, the basis of word-of-mouth communication is a consumer's past experience with the product. If consumers get what they expect in a product, they will encourage their friends to buy that product. A firm definitely has influence over the kind of product experience consumers have. The firm should consider the reactions and expectations of consumers when planning the product, pricing it, and promoting it.

Distributing the Product

Desired services and goods must be provided according to the rules established by consumers and their buying habits. The available goods must, first, be available at prices the consumers are willing and able to pay. In addition, through promotion, the consumers must be convinced that the available goods fit their needs and wants. One other aspect of satisfying consumer demands concerns distributing the product—where, when, and how.

Planning Distribution

Goods or services must be available where and when consumers want to buy the products. If a college student wants to buy a ballpoint pen on the college campus during lunch hour, he or she will not consider buying a pen that is not available on campus during this time. Thus, marketing includes the planning of the places where and the times when goods and services will be available.

This activity generally requires the establishment and management of the channels of distribution. A **channel of distribution** includes all the firms and activities necessary to move the *title*, or legal ownership, of the goods from the seller to the buyer. The channel may include retailers who take title to the goods they sell to consumers. Moreover, wholesalers who sell to retailers may be part of the channel if they are needed to perform activities necessary to get the goods to consumers.

Ultimately, the channels used will depend upon the wants and needs of customers. Marketing must decide where the product should be available. If a customer wants to buy toothpaste in supermarkets, then the manufacturer of toothpaste will try to sell toothpaste in supermarkets. Similarly, if customers express the desire to buy at home, a marketing decision to use mail-order catalogs or door-to-door sales representatives may be appropriate.

Channel decisions also include the issue of *when* goods should be available for customer purchase. If customers wish to purchase a product between 8:00 p.m. and 11:00 p.m., a retail outlet that is open during these hours should be provided. If customers wish to purchase a product primarily during one month, such as December, then those retail stores willing to carry a large number of units in stock during this period should be used. It may be necessary, such as in the case of tire manufacturers, for a firm to set up its own retail stores and warehouses to ensure customer delivery at the right time.

THE IMPACT OF MARKETING ON THE FIRM

Marketing does not exist alone. It must have a product to market, as well as personnel and money to carry out its activities. Thus, marketing has important interrelationships with the other departments of the firm.

Marketing and Production

If a product is not correctly marketed, the product will not be sold successfully. Even though the production activity has produced what the company considers a good product, sales will not occur if the customer does not like it.

Consequently, the marketing activity must provide the managers of production with a description of products desired by consumers. Product planning activities, a part of marketing, involve developing ideas into new products consumers will buy. In addition, old products are eliminated from production if their profit potential is inadequate.

Just as production activities must depend upon marketing activities, the relationship works in reverse. If the marketing activity has convinced customers to take delivery of products at a certain time or price, it must be sure that the company's production facilities and workers can produce the products in time to make the delivery or at a cost less than the price.

A business may find that initial demand for a new product exceeds its ability to produce that product. Recently, Volkswagen was very successful in marketing its new car, the Rabbit; it set a record for imported cars by selling 12,000 cars during the first month it was on the market. However, the demand for the Rabbit, which has resulted from the company's marketing program (see Figure 9-2), has exceeded the company's ability to supply the product. VW dealers in the United States are not able to get the cars from Germany, where they are produced, as fast as customers demand them.

Marketing and Personnel

The marketing activity also has important interactions with business activities other than production. The nature of marketing activities will influence the personnel needs of the organization. Moreover, if marketing personnel available to the company are few in number or are unqualified for their jobs, the company's marketing activities may have to be cut back. Instead, the services of independent organizations, which perform marketing activities such as selling to consumers, warehousing, or transporting products, may be substituted for the firm's own activities. This substitution requires a decision on the part of the marketing managers of the company.

Marketing and Finance/Accounting

Marketing influences the financial activities of a firm. The marketing effort affects the amount of sales dollars received by the firm as well as the timing of the receipt of these revenues. Hence, financial planning is dependent upon marketing-generated sales and costs.

Accounting and marketing interact, since planning future marketing efforts requires knowledge of past marketing efforts and resultant sales. This type of information is available in the records compiled by the accountants in the firm.

Figure 9-2. A Typical Advertisement

Reprinted by permission of Volkswagen Corporation of America.

HISTORICAL CHANGE IN IMPORTANCE OF MARKETING

It would seem that firms could not be successful without devoting as much attention, if not more, to marketing as they do to other parts of the business. However, a wide variety of relative emphasis on the marketing function has been noted for various firms over time. The variation in emphasis on marketing over time can be traced to changes in the environment of business in the United States.

Production Activities Emphasized (1900–1930)

During the early part of the twentieth century, the full effect of the mass production capabilities of the Industrial Revolution were being realized. Through specialization, more goods than ever were being produced. *The primary emphasis during this time was the production function.* Firms were concerned with making production more efficient so that the supply of available goods would be increased. This production emphasis ruled the day, for the demand for goods exceeded the available supply. A firm could safely assume that if goods could be produced, they would be purchased and consumed by members of the society.

Another reason for little emphasis on marketing was that producers were mainly local in nature and supplied markets located close to their production plants and homes. Furthermore, the United States had primarily an agricultural economy and was not at a stage where many different products could be purchased by the majority of the population. Consequently, firms were not too far removed from their markets, and these markets consisted of relatively simple demands.

Selling Activities Emphasized (1930–1950)

As the age of mass production came to the United States, firms experienced two things that had a lasting impact upon the emphasis placed on marketing.

First, firms were serving larger markets and trying to serve many different needs and wants of consumers. Firms quickly became out of touch with markets with complex needs and wants.

Second, competitive structure was becoming flooded with firms producing relatively similar goods. Hence, consumer demand was being exceeded by supply, and consumers had the opportunity to choose between products offered by different sellers.

The result of this relative tightening of markets during the two decades following 1920 was that firms placed increased emphasis upon pushing the product onto the consumer. This increased sales emphasis produced many types of selling practices that were designed to persuade the consumer to buy. Although such a selling orientation may work relatively well with an unexpecting consumer who has very little nonbusiness controlled information, the approach was destined for hard times after World War II.

Recent Past

Since the early 1950s businesses have increased their efforts to satisfy their consumers so they can maximize long-run profits. Their efforts, resulting from adoption of the marketing concept, bring more emphasis to all marketing activities in the conduct of the business. The major force pushing for increased emphasis on marketing has been consumer refusal to deal with firms that are not satisfying their needs. This force has sprung mainly from the *consumerism movement*.

THE CONSUMERISM MOVEMENT

As mentioned in Chapter Four, the consumerism movement, which started in the late 1960s, placed a host of new demands on business. These demands, emanating from the consuming public, established *consumerism* as "a demand that marketers give greater attention to consumer wants and desires in making their decisions."[1]

Consumer Demand

The consumerism movement, which appears—like the labor movement—to be here to stay, received its initial push from John F. Kennedy and Ralph Nader. In 1962, President Kennedy in his message to Congress maintained that the government has a responsibility to help consumers exercise their rights to be safe, to be informed, to choose, and to be heard.[2] More specifically, the demands of the consumerism movement are:

1. Products that do not threaten health or life.
2. Advertising, labeling, or other information that is not fraudulent, deceitful, or misleading but is complete so that the consumer can make an informed choice.
3. Access to a variety of products and services at competitive prices that result from efficient production and marketing activities.
4. Products and services that perform satisfactorily together with the ability to get any problems that result during use resolved immediately, at no cost to the buyer.

Ralph Nader, through his writings and speeches about the "unsafe" Corvair automobile, demonstrated that consumer desires were important to government and that the traditionally more powerful lobbies representing business interests could be overcome. Congress reacted to the findings from congres-

---

[1] Louis E. Boone and David L. Kurtz, *Contemporary Marketing*, Hinsdale, Illinois: The Dryden Press, 1974, p. 392.
[2] "Message from the President, Relative to Consumers' Protection," Document No. 364, House of Representatives. 87th Congress, 2nd Session, March 15, 1962.

sional hearings about consumer experiences with the Corvair and to the attempts by General Motors to stop Nader by passing the Highway Safety Act.[3]

Basically, the consumerism movement has occurred because:

1. Consumers have become increasingly discontented with a market that provides goods below their (rising) expectations, provides less information than desired by highly-educated consumers, or overcharges low-income segments that recently have become highly visible.
2. Consumers have found more effective ways than before to express their demands by using consumer representatives or by boycotting or looting businesses.
3. The government has accepted responsibility for consumer protection and created new federal agencies, legislation, regulations, and legal devices.

The movement has gained momentum, with over 500 active consumer organizations presently speaking for the movement and its members.

Business Reaction

Marketers must realize that the needs and wants of consumers must be considered and served to the best of their ability. Although the action most appropriate for any business must be determined by its marketing manager, consumer expectations are best understood if some major actions instituted by business in response to the movement are presented.

One action has been to provide more consumer information through unit pricing of food products, distributing a guide on how to buy automobiles, marking phosphate content of soaps on supermarket shelves, and distributing tips on how to repair products. Moreover, many companies are designing programs to inform buyers of all sides of issues pertaining to consumer problems.

Another action, instituted by Avis, Whirlpool, and Travelers Insurance, has involved making available top management people for consultation on consumer complaints. Generally, these people must be easily accessible to consumers and must have the ability to act quickly.

Other actions being taken include attempts to make advertising more factual and less deceptive. Industrywide efforts, under the direction of industry trade groups and the Better Business Bureau (BBB), are being stepped up to establish and enforce standards for truthful advertising. For example, the advertising standards established by the BBB state that:

> An advertiser should not use general claims that state or imply that his prices are always the lowest, as low as, or less than prices charged by others.[4]

[3] James J. Bishop and Henry W. Hubbard, *Let the Seller Beware*, Washington, D.C.; Washington National Press, 1969, Chapter 5.
[4] "Retail Advertising Copy Standards," Better Business Bureau of Delaware, Inc., November 1, 1966.

Consumer problems can also be lessened by listening more closely to consumers—for instance, a recent advertising program of Philadelphia Electric Company. Consumers can be helped by designing products that are easier to repair, such as Motorola's Quasar television with its "works in a drawer," and by establishing a separate corporate department for consumer issues. Pan American Airways has set up a Department of Consumer Affairs with a vice president in charge.

Government Reaction

Failure of business actions to satisfy consumerism demands has resulted in government passing new legislation, creating or pushing for new consumer protection agencies, allowing class action suits, requiring corrective advertising, or requiring business to provide desired information.

Consumer protection laws have been passed by all levels of government. Initial consumer protection was provided by the Pure Food and Drug Act (1906) and the Meat Inspection Act (1907). The acts were broad attempts to prevent practices of the day that were dangerous to the health of consumers of foods and drugs. The Food and Drug Administration, which administers the Act, has acted to stop the sale of filthy candy, decayed fruit, worm-eaten nuts, and raisins infested with insects.

Subsequent experience with the food and drug bill showed the need to broaden the coverage of the term "adulterated" and to include cosmetics and therapeutic devices. The Food, Drug, and Cosmetic Act of 1938 gives this coverage. In addition, it provides the government with the power to inspect factories producing foods, drugs, and cosmetics. Intentional violation of either law may result in a penalty of $10,000 and/or 3 years in jail.

Until the 1930s, protection offered to consumers was restricted to practices likely to be harmful to health. Moreover, the FTC was not given the power to protect consumers. This situation was remedied when the FTC Act was amended in 1938. The amendment, the Wheeler–Lea Act, prohibits all "unfair or deceptive acts or practices," regardless of their impact on competition. This act has been used to stop Charles of the Ritz from advertising its Rejuvenescence Cream as a restorer of youth; General Motors from using deceptive camera techniques to show more optical distortions in automobile safety sheet glass than in automobile plate glass; and Mary Carter Paint company from claiming "Every Second Can (of paint) Free of Extra Cost" when the first can, which had to be purchased to get the second can free, was twice the normal price of one can of paint. In general, business has been stopped from misrepresenting its products, especially in television advertising.

The authority of the Federal Trade Commission has been extended to cover labeling and truthful disclosure on labels of packages. Included are the Wool Products Labeling Act (1939), the Fur Products Labeling Act (1951), the Flammable Fabrics Act (1954), and the Textile Fiber Products Identification Act (1960). According to these laws, manufacturers and sellers of clothing must disclose on labels the type of wool in garments, use FTC accepted names for furs, show percentage by weight of each fiber contained, and refrain from selling articles of wearing apparel that are "so highly flammable as to be dangerous when worn." Another example of labeling requirements is set forth by the Federal Cigarette Labeling and Advertising Act (1965). Through this act and the Public Health Cigarette Smoking Act (1971), which also bans TV advertising of cigarettes, cigarette advertisements and packages must disclose a health warning, as shown in Figure 9-3.

Figure 9-3. *Advertisement of Cigarettes with Surgeon General Warning*

Permission granted by Liggett & Myers Incorporated to use the above advertisement. All rights reserved.

Further federal regulation of packaging resulted from the **Fair Packaging and Labeling Act** of 1966. Although its sponsors were anxious to stop the multitude of sizes of food and drug products, the practice of half-filled boxes, and the use of terms like "super dooper," and "king size," the act, as revised and passed, places more restrictions on labeling than it does on packaging. The law permits the FTC to regulate "cents off" claims. It also requires that ingredients of packaged products be listed by their common names in the order of quantities contained. However, it is important to note that package standards established by the FTC are not necessarily restrictive since business compliance is voluntary.

Another area that has received intense legal scrutiny in recent years is the manufacture and sale of automobiles. The **National Traffic and Motor Vehicle Safety Act** placed the automobile industry under new regulation requiring adherence to safety standards prescribed by the National Highway Safety Bureau. These standards, designed to reduce the likelihood of crashes and severe injury, are enforceable through a fine of $1,000 per car or requirement of recall of cars from buyers.

Many buyers frequently do not have the cash to buy needed goods. To protect these buyers from being deceived about the costs of borrowed money, the **Consumer Credit Protection Act** has recently been passed. Those businesses making loans to consumers are required to disclose the actual cost of credit both in dollars and cents and as a percentage of the unpaid balance. It is no longer legal for a lender to simply tell the borrower he has to pay "$10 down and $10 per month" without specifically disclosing the actual cost of the borrowed money.

Federal, state, and city governments have also established government agencies to protect consumers. These agencies, such as the FTC and New York City's Department of Consumer Affairs, represent a threat to business if it fails to foresee future demands of consumers. In addition, creation of a Department of Consumer Affairs at the federal level is a strong possibility.

Class action suits are claims placed in a court by private citizens for damages caused to themselves and any other consumers by unfair business practices. Although the conditions under which courts will award such suits in favor of the consumers are unclear, recognition of the right of consumers to bring such suits has definite implications for business.

Corrective advertising, ordered by the Federal Trade Commission, consists of telling consumers, deceived by previous advertising, that they have been told a lie. The FTC has required the producers of Profile Bread to spend 25% of their annual advertising budget to inform consumers that previous claims that their product was a diet-control item were untrue. The bread had fewer calories only because it was more thinly sliced.

The FTC has also required businesses to provide information to substantiate its advertising claims. This information, available to the public, may be used to accuse business of deceptive advertising practices in violation of the Wheeler–Lea Amendment to the FTC Act.

MARKETING AS A JOB

Marketing is important to the student as a source of possible employment. There are many different types of marketing jobs that can provide future careers and job satisfaction for students. The organizational chart of a marketing department of a manufacturing firm shown in Figure 9-4 should help the student understand possible marketing jobs.

Two Types of Marketing Jobs

Generally, marketing employment opportunities are either in the management or the actual performance of the marketing activities.

Figure 9-4. *A Basic Organization for Marketing Management*

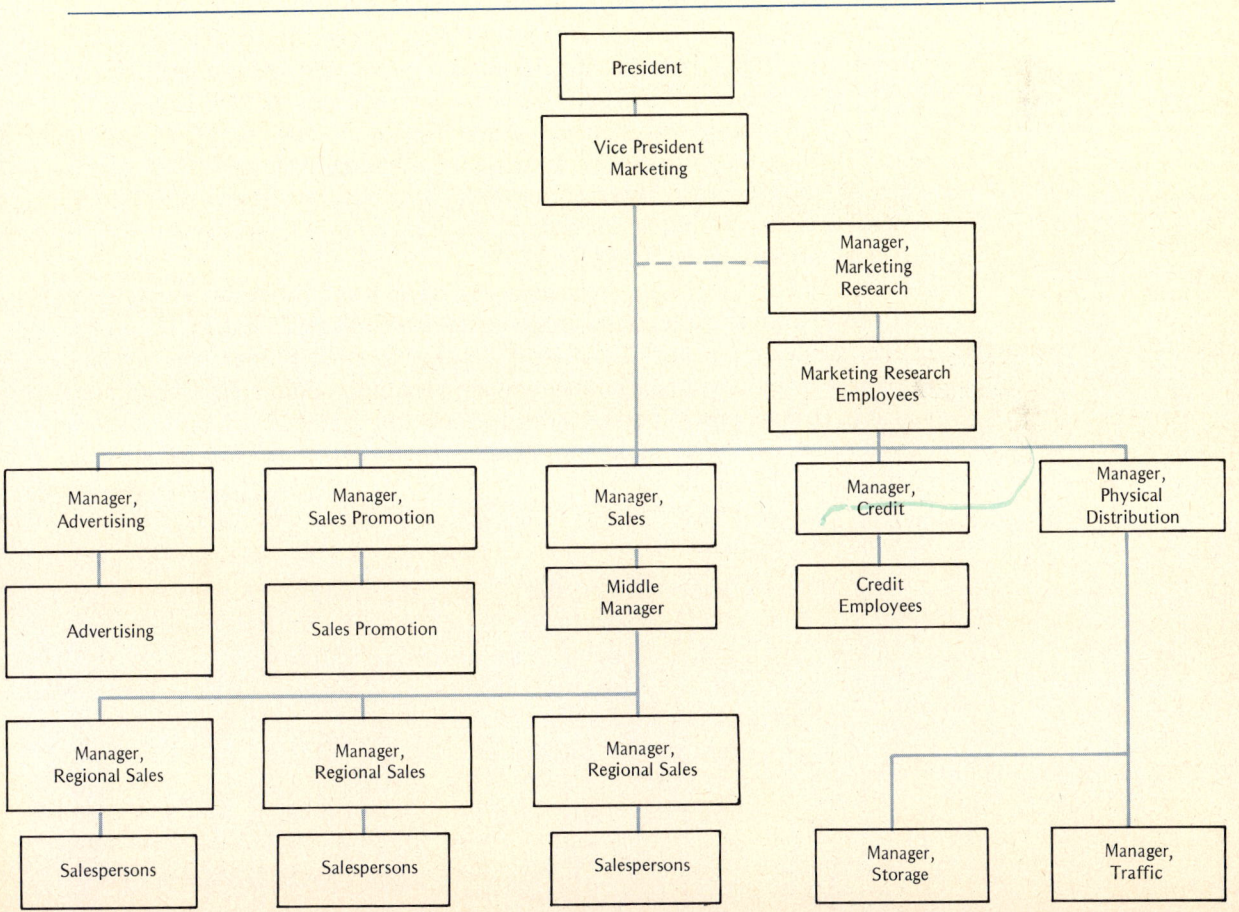

A top position in marketing management is held by the **marketing manager**, to whom the line managers in advertising, sales promotion, sales, credit, and physical distribution report. Accordingly, management jobs are available in advertising, sales promotion, sales, credit, physical distribution, and marketing research. Too, a marketing job may entail selling products, preparing advertisements, or gathering marketing research information.

Further discussion of employment opportunities in the specialized areas of marketing such as promotion, physical distribution, or marketing research is deferred until Chapters Ten and Eleven. The job of the chief marketing manager of a firm will be explored in the next part of this chapter. In addition to a definition of the job, a discussion of the required background for the job and financial opportunities offered by this position will be presented.

The Marketing Manager's Job

The chief marketing manager may have different titles in different organizations; "marketing manager," "director of marketing," or "vice president of marketing" are the most common. Regardless of the title, the responsibility of marketing managers is to see that those products they are assigned are sold, at a profit, to the customers who make up the firm's target market. They are responsible for any failure of marketing activities to accomplish the desired goals and objectives of the firm. However, the exact areas they are responsible for are dependent upon the specific companies involved.

The responsibilities for different marketing executives in companies that are not organized on a divisional basis are summarized in Figure 9-5. In general, marketing managers in nondivisionalized companies are responsible for market planning, merchandising, and marketing research. In more than 60% of the companies, their responsibilities include sales promotion, product planning, and sales management. Marketing managers in these companies are least concerned with foreign marketing operations, export sales, and physical distribution.

Required Background

More than in any other field, the educational requirements in business and commerce have become increasingly demanding. Today it is virtually impossible to be hired for a training position leading to jobs at the junior- and middle-management levels without a bachelor's degree. The top-echelon managerial positions in marketing are increasingly held by holders of a first professional degree—for example, the master's degree of business administration.

Now and in the future, the top-level management of most companies will be made up of persons who have come up through the marketing area.[5] To

---

[5] S. L. Johnson and J. J. Tenge, Jr., "The Man Behind the Marketing Concept," *Sales/Marketing Today*, June 1967, pp. 14–17.

Marketing Concepts 235

Figure 9-5. *Areas of Responsibility for Marketing Managers*

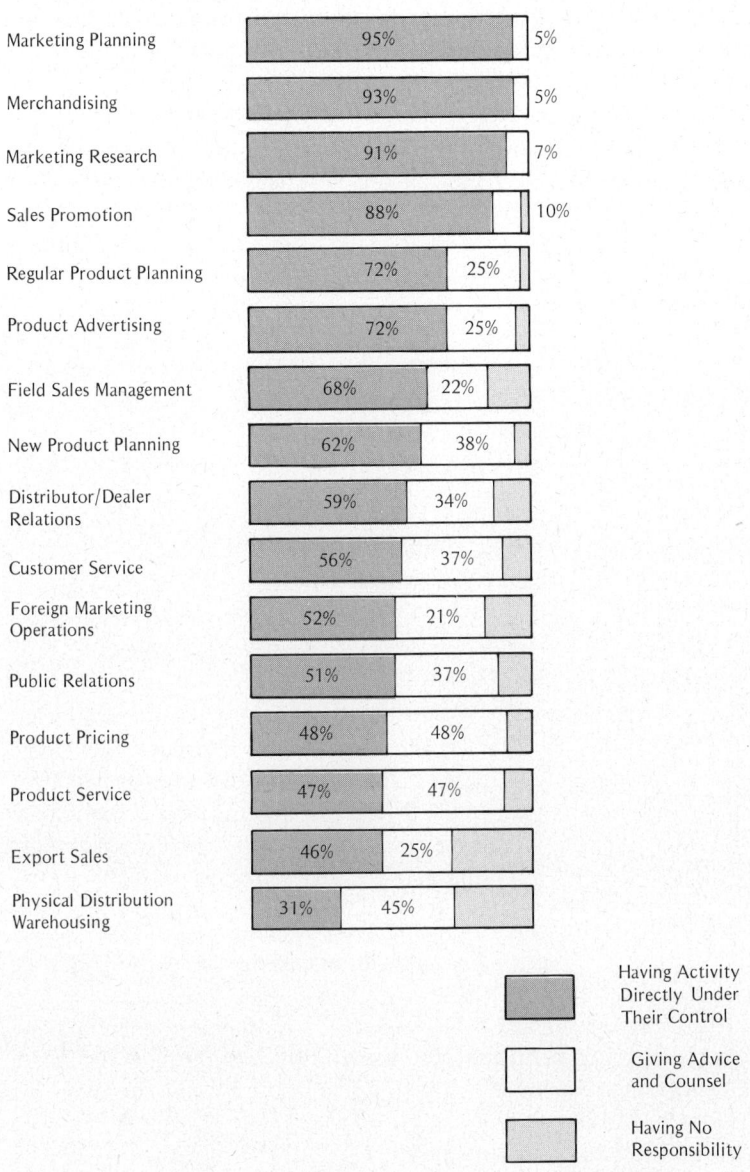

Reprinted by permission of the Conference Board, Inc.

advance in management, people in marketing must not be too narrowly trained. A broad range of capabilities in the many business and marketing areas is desirable. They need a knowledge of economics to understand changes and shifts in the economy as they affect the firm. Markets are composed of people, so chief marketing managers must have a solid background in humanities and social sciences. Depending upon the nature of the products the company produces and markets, they may need knowledge of the physical sciences and engineering areas.

In addition to an understanding of the company's markets, workers, and products, the chief marketing manager must have the ability to make decisions and to analyze the results of those decisions. This decision-making and evaluation skill is not easily learned. In fact, the lack of this skill accounts for the failure of many marketing managers.

Students who desire to become chief marketing managers must work to develop their decision-making and analytical skills as they move toward that position over the next 20–25 years (the average age of the chief marketing manager is over forty). Students will want to learn and understand the basic scientific problem-solving process. In addition, the learning of analytical tools, such as break-even analysis and statistical analysis, should prove helpful in the execution of such responsibilities.

Reward System

Although it may take several years for a college graduate to reach the position of chief marketing manager, the rewards are worthwhile. It is to the advantage of the company to assure that the manager understands the company, its workers, its policies, and its customers before the individual is assigned to the role of chief marketing manager. A mistake by a marketing manager could be very costly to the company. Therefore, companies require chief marketing managers to demonstrate their capabilities in company positions where an error will be less likely to hurt the company before taking on the responsibilities of this very important position.

Not only could an error by the chief marketing manager seriously affect company performance, but it could also mean that the company is wasting the salary paid. The annual salary of the marketing manager generally exceeds $20,000, although this figure varies a great deal. A 1972 survey of 86 marketing executives by the staff of *Sales Management* magazine showed an average annual salary of $73,022 for these executives.[6] As shown by the selected figures in Table 9-2, the salary of the marketing manager will depend upon the company involved, the personal characteristics and abilities of the marketing manager, and the environment in which he or she operates. Generally, the larger the company's sales are, the higher the marketing manager's salary will be. The salary will also be influenced by experience, educational background, and by any change in company sales while the individual is in the position of chief marketing manager.

[6] "What Top Sales and Marketing Executives Earn," *Sales Management*, October 26, 1972, pp. 26–30.

Table 9-2. *What Top Sales and Marketing Executives Earn*

Company	Individual and Title	Gross Total Remuneration	Shares Common Stock Owned
Farah Mfg. Co., Inc.	James P. Viola V. P., Marketing	$ 35,000	4,408
Quaker State Oil Refining Corp.	Lewis R. Freeman V. P., Marketing	50,475	22,980
Standard Register Co.	W. B. Rodemann V. P., Marketing	65,065	
Milton Bradley Co.	Millens W. Taft Senior V. P., Production Marketing	80,000	9,305
Cheesebrough-Pond's, Inc.	William W. Jackson Group V. P., Domestic Marketing	90,553	16,350
Jos. Schlitz Brewing Company	Fred R. Haviland Executive V. P., Marketing and Corporate Planning	133,100	
Merril, Lynch, Pierce, Fenner & Smith, Inc.	John A. Orb Executive V. P., Marketing	150,800	
Sears, Roebuck & Co.	James W. Button Senior V. P., Merchandising	215,000	29,901

Reprinted by permission from *Sales Management, The Marketing Magazine.* Copyright 1972.

CHAPTER SUMMARY

Marketing is defined as *that part of a firm's activity concerned with providing consumers with want-satisfying goods or services at a price they are willing to pay, at the place they want to buy them, and at the time they wish to buy or use them.* From the business view, marketing management is concerned with determining who is the target market, designing products needed by the target market, setting the prices for the goods, planning their promotion, and distributing them to fit consumer needs and wants. The business activities of producing goods, providing workers, and finding money and information are very important to marketing.

The emphasis in business has been traced from the emphasis on producing to selling and finally, to marketing. Modern businesses are turning their attention to the satisfaction of consumer needs and wants, especially since the consumerism movement initiated in the 1960s. This movement has resulted in more consumer demands, governmental legislation, and business action.

Marketing activities provide two types of opportunities. The position of the marketing manager is discussed here. It demands many talents, much determination, and the ability to make decisions in an environment of ever-changing demands from all publics.

PROVOCATIVE STATEMENT

Prices Must Be High Enough to Produce Profits

1 "You can't do consumers a favor by trying to sell them as cheaply as possible. And you don't do yourself any good, because no company can possibly grow and flourish without the revenue to support advertising, not to mention a profit. Set then, a price high enough to produce revenues for quality and advertising. And, if consumers won't pay it, don't try to economize. Drop the item."

> Jeno F. Paulicci with Les Rich,
> *How It Was to Make $100,000,000 in a Hurry*,
> New York: Grosset and Dunlap, Inc., 1969,
> p. 25.

PROVOCATIVE STATEMENT

One-way Mirrors May Be Used to Find Out About Consumer Behavior

2 "One product of the X company is brassieres and the firm has recently been having difficulty making some decisions on a new line. Information was critically needed concerning the manner in which women put on their brassieres. So the new marketing manager planned a study in which two local stores cooperated in putting one-way mirrors in their foundations dressing rooms. Observers behind these mirrors successfully gathered the necessary information."

> C. Merle Crawford,
> "Attitudes of Marketing Executives
> Toward Ethics in Marketing Research,
> *Journal of Marketing*, Vol. 34, No. 2, April 1970,
> pp. 47–49.

REVIEW QUESTIONS

1. Name and discuss briefly the five major marketing activities, from the business point of view.
2. Discuss the compromises that take place when a firm prices a product.
3. Give several examples of business controlled and nonbusiness controlled communications. Which do you feel are most effective? Why?
4. Why is it important to coordinate marketing with the other three areas of management?
5. How has the emphasis of business on marketing changed? Why?
6. In what major ways has the consumerism movement affected marketing?
7. Discuss the role of the marketing manager in an organization.

Chapter Outline

Promotion Objectives
   Defining the Audience
      Size
      Geographic Scope
      Type of Customer
      Buying Habits
   Setting Objectives
      Goals
      Be Accurate

Promotion Budget
   Sales
   Competitive Expenditures
   Available Funds
   Objectives and Tasks
   Combination of Methods

Promotional Balance
   Customer Characteristics
   Firm Considerations
   Environmental Considerations

Promotion Activities
   Personal Selling
      Hiring
      Training
      Organizing
      Compensating
   Advertising Activities
      Selection of Media
      Choice of Advertising Agency

Promotional Effectiveness
   Sales Representative Performance
   Advertising Message

Promotion Jobs
   Selling
      Nature of Jobs
      Qualifications
      Rewards
   Advertising
      Nature of Jobs
      Qualifications
      Rewards

Chapter Summary

Provocative Statement 1:
   Marketers Must Deliver
   What They Promise Consumers

Provocative Statement 2:
   A Transamerica Corporation
   Executive Talks Selling

Key Terms

Promotion objectives
Audience
Industrial users
Middlemen
Household consumers
Installations
Accessory equipment
Fabricated parts and materials
Raw materials
Operating supplies
Convenience goods
Shopping goods
Specialty goods
Promotion budget

Promotional balance
False advertising
Deception
Bait and switch advertising
Promotional allowances and services
Personal selling
Order getting
Order receiving
Sales supporting
Sales process
Advertising media
Advertising agency
Promotional effectiveness
Sales results tests

Promotion

"A president of an advertising agency was asked: 'What does your agency really do?' He replied that a client walks into his office and puts two identical half-dollar pieces on his desk. He says 'Mine is the one on the right—go out and convince people that mine is better.' This is what a salesman really does."
—Regional Sales Manager for Computer Services Firm

10

Business executives consider promotion one of the most important marketing tools. Successful promotion is based on carefully thought out promotion programs. Promotion programs involve several key decision areas. These areas, discussed in this chapter, are:

1. Promotion objectives.
2. Promotion budget.
3. Promotion balance.
4. Promotion activities.
5. Promotion effectiveness.

Each of the areas is discussed more fully than in Chapter Nine. The discussions focus on specific dimensions of each decision area and recommended actions, and are followed by a discussion of jobs in promotion.

PROMOTION OBJECTIVES

Promotion is business controlled communication. It, like any other communication, is most effective if the promotion objectives of the communication are specifically defined. A firm cannot successfully present its message if it is unsure of what it wants to accomplish. The objective of "increased sales" is not specific enough for guidance of promotional planning. Too, promotional planning requires knowledge of the characteristics of the intended audience.

Reprinted by permission of Jeff Keate, Cartoonist and The American Legion Magazine.

"Look Herb, can't you and Fenton stop this lemonade war and let the boys do the best each can!"

Defining the Audience

The promotion process aims a message at a group of people, the audience. The audience must be defined in terms of:

1. Size.
2. Geographic scope.
3. Type of customer.
4. Buying habits.

Size

The number of people in a target audience affects the cost of alternative methods of communication. Generally, the larger the audience, the more a business will rely on mass selling. For example, a seller of soap purchased by a very large number of consumers would probably find it too expensive to hire personal sales representatives to call on each consumer. Instead, the seller would probably rely on national television or magazine advertisements. On the other hand, a seller of encyclopedias may find the audience small enough to employ door-to-door sales techniques.

Larger audiences mean more costly communications. Sellers of goods or services purchased by a large audience may enlist others in their communication effort. They may give middlemen—wholesalers and retailers—promotional allowances. These allowances, which must be matched by middlemen, help decrease the burden on manufacturers. Moreover, middlemen may be able to advertise in local newspapers at a lower rate than the national manufacturer.

Geographic Scope

Promotional costs of reaching an audience depend on the geographic dispersion of audience members. A large audience located solely in New York City will be easier to reach than an audience spread out over the United States. Personal selling is more feasible for the concentrated audience. The widely dispersed audience will probably require more mass selling. Furthermore, it will be more difficult and costly to measure the effectiveness of promotion to a widely dispersed audience.

A related dimension of the geographic scope of the audience is its precise location. The exact place of residence of audience members should be known. Newspapers, radios, and other media may not reach people in the areas where a firm's audience is located. In addition, some media hit too many people, resulting in wasted communication.

Type of Customer

The promotion plan is influenced by whether the business is aiming its communications at industrial users, middlemen, or household consumers.

Industrial users purchase goods to be used in the production of other goods for resale. Generally, they are most favorably influenced by communications delivered in person by sales representatives. Their needs may be unique and require a tailor-made communication. Industrial users frequently hire purchasing experts who are well aware of what other sellers have to offer. They are not easily persuaded to buy. The promotional effort must convince industrial users of the cost-saving and revenue-producing benefits of the company's product.

Middlemen are members of the channel of distribution. They include retailers, wholesalers, and brokers. They handle products that are on their way to the consumer, but they do not change the physical form of the product. Their concern is acquiring goods that will sell to household consumers. They, like industrial users, are not concerned with the sex appeal or other emotional appeals of the product. Communications aimed at middlemen will have to highlight consumer acceptance of the product. Middlemen will also be receptive to messages about cost savings.

Household consumers are people who buy products that can be used without further processing. These customers are concerned with personal benefits to be gained from product use. Communications appealing to the emotions are more effective with this type of customer. Ultra-Brite toothpaste's "How's your love life?" commercial is an example of this type of communication.

Buying Habits

It is not enough merely to identify the audience. The manner in which the audience buys the product must be known. Buying habits vary for the three types of customers.

Successful promotion is based on knowledge of customer buying habits. Information about the different members of the market should be gathered prior to design of the promotional program.

INDUSTRIAL USERS   The buying habits of industrial users may differ for:

1. *Installations.* **Installations** are the long-lived, expensive, major equipment of industrial users. They include heavy machinery, land, and buildings. Industrial users buy installations only after careful consideration of competitive offerings and evaluation of long-range costs and benefits of each. Buying considerations include after-sale service, technical assistance provided by the seller, and product performance over its useful life. Because of the relative importance of installations to a firm, buying firms generally assign responsibility for their purchase to top management.

Since a long period of negotiation is generally involved, sellers of installations must provide continuous promotional communications. These communications must be designed for the individual buyers. Consequently, personal sales representatives with technical expertise are hired to carry the message. Little reliance is placed on advertising for the promotion of installations.

2. *Accessory equipment.* **Accessory equipment** is less expensive than installations. It generally lasts a shorter time than installations, but longer than a year. Examples of accessory equipment include typewriters, small power tools, and fork-lift trucks. Buying considerations include quality, service, and price. The promotional message to buyers of accessory equipment may be less individualized than to buyers of installations. Greater reliance can be placed on advertising in promoting accessory equipment.

3. *Fabricated parts and materials.* **Fabricated parts and materials** are industrial goods that become part of the finished good. These goods, which may need to be processed more before they are reused in production, include spark plugs, tires, cloth, and flour. Buyers of these goods are concerned that they have an adequate supply of goods of uniform quality. Consequently, they may want sellers to guarantee delivery through a contractual arrangement. The promotional effort will depend on personal selling in order to negotiate these contracts. However, only a few contacts are necessary to sell these goods. Therefore, the cost of personal selling is not prohibitive.

4. *Raw materials.* **Raw materials** are industrial goods that become part of the finished products but have not been processed any more than necessary to facilitate physical handling. They include goods found in their natural state, such as coal and copper, as well as farm products.

Buyers of raw materials also are concerned with quantity and quality of goods available. They generally want to negotiate a contract with sellers. Direct communication through personal sales representatives is also likely. However, some sellers, such as small farmers, may not be able to afford sales representatives.

5. *Operating supplies.* **Operating supplies** are frequently purchased, low-priced industrial goods. Examples include floor wax, heating fuel, and stationery. Buyers want to buy these with a minimum of effort, although prices

are a key consideration. Promotional effort is on a mass basis, as there are many buyers of small quantities of operating supplies. Personal sales calls on buyers of operating supplies prove too costly.

MIDDLEMEN   The buying habits of middlemen depend on those of their customers—industrial users or household consumers. They want enough goods to satisfy these customers. Generally, middlemen will not buy goods that are not demanded by customers. Variations in types of middlemen frequently lead to different buying habits. The different types of middlemen are discussed in Chapter Eleven.

HOUSEHOLD CONSUMERS   Buying habits of consumers differ for:

1. *Convenience goods.* **Convenience goods** are products consumers buy frequently with minimal effort. These items generally include groceries, inexpensive candy, toothpaste, and staple hardware items, such as nails, screws, and so on. Most consumers feel that they will not gain enough from shopping around when buying these goods. Instead, they buy them at the most accessible place. Consumers will not go out of their way for a particular brand. Therefore, the manufacturer must make sure that these goods are available in many places.

Promotion of convenience goods may center on developing consumer loyalty to certain brands. An example is the "all aspirin are not alike" advertisement. However, emphasis on telling consumers where the products are available seems most effective with convenience goods. Moreover, the unit value of convenience goods will not support the cost of personal selling.

Point-of-purchase displays may also be effective in promoting convenience goods. Some convenience goods are bought because they are seen by consumers in a store display. These purchases, resulting from impulse buying, may include a *TV Guide* or a candy bar. Sellers must effectively promote these products in stores through attractively designed displays. Moreover, manufacturers must convince retailers to place the displays in high traffic areas of their stores.

2. *Shopping goods.* Consumers buy some products only after consideration of different brands or styles of products. These products, which consumers compare on such bases as quality, price, and style, are called **shopping goods**. The consumer prefers to shop around for higher-priced items such as jewelry, clothing, and furniture.

Frequently, buyers of shopping goods base their comparisons on what they see in stores. The promotional communication provided by retail sales personnel helps buyers in the evaluation. In addition, the character of the store and its services may be part of the buyer's evaluation of goods.

Manufacturers of shopping goods must recognize the importance of retailers in their promotional effort. They must encourage retailers to promote their product effectively to consumers when they shop and compare. Manufacturers will also want to select retailers who carry a good selection of shopping goods.

3. *Specialty goods.* Previous communication efforts may result in consumer insistence on a particular brand. If consumers are not willing to accept

any other brand, the good is called a **specialty good**. Examples of specialty goods may include automobiles, home appliances, and stereophonic equipment.

Promotion of specialty goods requires effort by both manufacturers and retailers. Both must work to keep consumers loyal to a particular brand, so that buyers continue to believe a certain brand is the best. These high-priced items also require a persuasive sales pitch at the retail store. The promotional effort is designed to try to get more consumers to view the product as a specialty good. Success in keeping consumers loyal to a company's brand means effective promotion.

Consumer buying behavior determines whether a good is a convenience, shopping, or specialty good. Frequently, the buyers of a product buy it in different ways. Some buyers treat the product as a convenience good, while others want to shop around or buy only one brand. For example, some consumers may buy a new car at the closest automobile dealer. Others trek around to different dealers to see which has the nicest looking, lowest-priced model. Finally, some car buyers insist on buying a particular brand or model, regardless of the effort or cost involved.

Setting Objectives

The objectives of promotion emphasize sharing an idea, an attitude, or some other kind of information with the defined audience.

Goals

Promotion may be designed to:

1. Inform.
2. Persuade.
3. Remind.

INFORM The objective of promotion may be to inform the audience about a product or the company selling it. Informative promotion is successful if audience members are made aware of attitudes, ideas, or other information. Specifically, a firm may want to make all members of the target audience aware of their new product. Other informational objectives of promotion include telling current customers that stores have new locations or that they are now open for business 24 hours a day.

PERSUADE Promotional programs all desire favorable buyer actions whether it be immediate or long run. Businesses use promotion to persuade consumers to act in some way or to accept a particular idea. They may want buyers to believe that their product is superior to that of competitors. Persuasive promotion may also be designed to convince buyers that they must buy immediately or lose the opportunity to buy at the current price.

Promotion designed to persuade requires more effort than that which is to inform. Buyers will remember received information more readily than they will use it to alter currently held beliefs. It is easier to make potential buyers aware of the latest type of Polaroid than it is to convince them that it is the best camera in existence or that it is the only one that fits their needs.

Persuasive communications must be frequent and personalized. Repetition is necessary to get the audience to give the message serious consideration. Personalized messages are necessary to show the audience what they stand to gain from being persuaded. Personal selling has proven to be most effective in accomplishing persuasion objectives. It provides intense, frequent, and flexible communications to buyers. Contrary to common belief, mass selling is relatively ineffective for persuading buyers. It is generally best for information or reminder purposes.

REMIND   Objectives of promotion may be concerned with reminding buyers about a company and its products. Reminder objectives are adopted for established products that are experiencing stabilized or declining sales. Previous purchasers of the product may be reminded of the brand name and the satisfaction of product use. Reminder promotion entails a "softer sell" than a persuasion promotion. Mass advertising may be the lowest-cost way to accomplish reminder objectives.

Be Accurate

The objective of any promotional effort must be defined in terms that are as specific as possible. Examples of specific objectives are:

1. The company wants to persuade 75 people to buy their product in the next 6 months.
2. The company wants to convince 50% of the licensed drivers in the United States that car pooling is necessary to conserve energy supplies.
3. The company wants to convince 100 new dealers that they will profit if they carry the company's line.

Clearly and specifically stated promotional objectives will guide planning and evaluation of promotion. They may also guide establishment of the promotion budget.

PROMOTION BUDGET

A firm's success in accomplishing promotion objectives depends on how much it is willing to spend for promotion. Ideally, a business should maximize the profits received from promotion expenditures. The promotion budget should be set at a level where increased promotion expenditures result in less benefits than costs. Although most firms recognize the existence of diminishing returns from increased expenditure of promotional dollars, few have been able to measure these benefits exactly.

The methods frequently used by companies to set **promotional budgets** are based on experience and improvement in performance. The point where profits are maximized is difficult to find. Promotional budgets may be set by relating promotional expenditures to:

1. Sales.
2. Competitive expenditures.
3. Available funds.
4. Objectives and tasks.

Sales

Promotional expenditures are set as a percentage of sales by many businesses. The simplicity of this method is appealing. A firm need only set sales and the desired percentage. Determination of the budget is then simple multiplication. If 5% of sales, for example, is allocated for promotion, a company with $100,000 sales will budget $5,000 for promotion.

The shortcomings of this method include the lack of bases for choosing the sales and percentage figures. It is difficult to determine whether past, current, or future sales should be used. Choice of a percentage is also arbitrary. The method does not ensure that promotional expenditures will be based on expected benefits. In fact, sales seem to be considered the cause of promotion, not vice versa.

The sales method may be especially bad if promotional expenditures are linked to forecasted future sales. A decline in sales will mean a decline in promotional expenditures. Such behavior seems dangerous if promotion is considered to be a sales-creating tool.

Competitive Expenditures

Recognition of the importance of promotion with regard to competitive success may result in competitive-based promotional budgets. A firm may match the promotional expenditures of a successful competitor or set its budget proportional to sales.

This method assumes that the competitor knows its best level of promotional expenditures. Unfortunately, competitors may also be unsure of their promotional budget. Moreover, their success may be due to something other than promotion. Their product or related services may be superior. Finally, the objectives of competitors probably are not the same.

Reprinted through permission of *Advertising Age*.

Available Funds

Many businesses recognize promotion as an expense with hard-to-measure benefits. They realize that promotional expenditures can reduce company profits. Promotional expenditures may be based on how much the company feels it can afford for promotion. This view may be adopted by retailers who receive minimal benefits from promotional expenditures. The introduction of new products may also require allocating as much as possible for promotion.

This method helps ensure that a firm does not go bankrupt because of excessive promotional expenditures. However, it suffers from the same shortcoming experienced by the sales and competitive expenditures methods: promotional expenditures are not related to promotional objectives. There may not be enough funds available to accomplish the desired objectives. In this case, expected revenues from the promotional effort may justify diversion of company resources from other uses. Also, short-term loans may be worthwhile to supplement available promotional funds.

Objectives and Tasks

Another method used to determine the amount of promotional expenditures is to spend an amount that is required to accomplish the firm's promotional objectives. This method consists of:

1. Knowing promotional objectives and determining tasks necessary to accomplish these objectives.
2. Estimating costs of tasks and adding all costs.

The specific definition of promotional objectives is necessary so that promotional tasks can be determined. If, for example, the objective is to make 200 people aware of a company's product, the task may be preparation and delivery of a direct-mail advertisement. Other promotional tasks might include personal sales calls, newspaper advertisements, or television advertisements. The appropriate tasks are derived from the objectives.

Promotional activities are not free. Costs are incurred for resources used in preparation and delivery of promotional messages. The costs of carrying out promotional tasks are generally easy to estimate. Previous company experiences with promotional programs as well as information available from advertising agencies, media, and media-rate reporting services (Standard Rate and Data) are used to estimate the cost of task performance. The promotional budget set by the objectives and tasks method is the total cost of carrying out tasks necessary to accomplish promotional objectives.

This method is more logical than the first three because it builds on objectives. It assures that a firm spends enough to get the job done. However, this method is more complex. It requires the determination of certain facts generally difficult to ascertain. It is difficult to set objectives specifically and to decide which promotional activities will result in the accomplishment of objectives. Considerably more effort and, therefore, more expense will be needed to implement this method. Morover, this method assumes that all promotional objectives are worth accomplishing. In addition, the total appropriation needed may be larger that the company can afford.

Combination of Methods

A combination of the four methods discussed may be used by a firm to set promotional expenditures. Companies may initially set promotional expenditures they can afford and subsequently use experience to specify clearly promotional objectives and tasks.

PROMOTIONAL BALANCE

Firms must decide the relative share of the budget to be spent on personal selling, advertising, and sales promotion. Since sales promotion is only a secondary promotional tool, the major issue is the balance between personal selling and advertising. Wide variations in the mix between personal sales and advertising are found. Variations in promotional balance result from:

1. Customer characteristics.
2. Firm considerations.
3. Environmental considerations.

Customer Characteristics

Personal selling is more likely to dominate if customers are relatively few, are geographically concentrated, buy in large lots, and buy only after a period of negotiation. Sellers to industrial buyers often experience such conditions, making the flexibility and persuasiveness of personal selling a necessity. The cost of personal selling is not prohibitive if buyers are few and easy to reach.

Operating supplies are the only type of industrial goods that place a major emphasis on mass selling. However, sellers of most consumer goods emphasize mass selling in their promotional mix. Sellers of shopping and speciality goods emphasize personal selling, especially in the retail store, more than sellers of convenience goods.

Firm Considerations

Firms may find they have insufficient resources to hire a sales force. Moreover, their managerial capabilities may not be adequate to manage a sales force. Thus, independent sales organizations may be more effective in accomplishing objectives than a predominantly mass selling promotional program within the firm.

A related consideration is the unit value of the product. The higher the value of the product, the greater the chance that personal selling costs can be covered by sales revenues. In addition, the higher-valued items make personal selling worthwhile.

Environmental Considerations

Legal considerations may discourage use of advertising. The many effects of laws on advertising are summarized in Table 10-1. The FTC has recently increased its control on advertising by forcing firms to substantiate their advertising claims. Thus, many firms now feel it is necessary to ask the Federal Trade Commission for clearance before launching advertisements.

Personal selling is not free of legal regulation either. Door-to-door selling has received increasing public criticism. Cooling-off laws have been passed in many states to give consumers the power to cancel sales contracts entered into at their place of residence. Although the contents of the laws vary among states, cancellation is generally allowed during a three-day period after the contract is signed. Limitations on value and nature of purchase also vary among states.

The suspicious attitude of the public toward sales representatives has also influenced the balance of the promotional mix. Many qualified persons stay away from sales jobs because of the low public regard for such jobs. A shortage of qualified personnel may reduce a firm's reliance on personal selling in its promotional mix.

Table 10-1. *Impact of Laws on Advertising*

1. *Advertising content.* The Federal Trade Commission Act of 1914 and the Wheeler–Lea amendment of 1938 are the principal vehicles by which public policy regulates advertising content. There are three major categories of such regulation.

    (a) **False advertising.** The FTC has become much more vigorous in its prosecution of false advertising claims in the 1960s and 1970s. Gone are the shaving cream commercials that used plexiglass instead of sandpaper, the ice cream commercials featuring mashed potatoes, and the marbles in vegetable soup to cause the vegetables to rise to the top.

    (b) **Deception.** Advertising that is not necessarily untrue, but which may tend to deceive the consumer, is more difficult to regulate. Here, too, enforcement in the 1960s and 1970s has become more vigorous. The FTC has, for example, ruled that "diet bread" cannot be advertised as having fewer calories simply because the loaf is sliced thinner, or that "Six-month floor wax" is not appropriate unless the wax does last for six months under typical conditions.

    (c) **Bait and switch advertising.** This is the tactic of advertising an unusually good buy ("three full rooms of furniture for $199"), and then switching the consumer attracted to the store by this advertisement to a more expensive product. This type of advertising is illegal in some states, but the practice is widespread. Recently, the FTC has taken action against advertisers who misrepresent the true nature of their offer, and has issued guidelines designed to curb the use of bait advertising.

2. **Promotional allowances and services.** Under Sections 2(d) and 2(e) of the Robinson–Patman Act, sellers must make promotional allowances and services available to all customers on proportionately equal terms. It is exceedingly complex and difficult to interpret these provisions. Specifically, public policy has not established the meaning of "proportionately equal terms," particularly where large and small customers are involved. Again, the FTC has issued guidelines, and subsequent litigation may clarify the meaning of these sections of the Robinson–Patman Act.

Source: Ben M. Enis, *Marketing Principles: The Management Process*, Pacific Palisades, California: Goodyear Publishing Company, Inc., 1974, p. 441.

In addition, competitive promotional balance may influence a business setting the relative importance of personal selling and advertising. Personal selling may be relied on because competitors are also emphasizing personal selling in their mix. However, competitive use of a particular type of promotion may result in clogging message channels. A firm's promotion may be more effective if it emphasizes advertising instead of personal selling like the competitor.

PROMOTION ACTIVITIES

The two major types of promotion are personal selling and advertising. Both types of promotion require several activities related to various personnel in order to be successful.

Personal Selling

Personal selling activities include:

1. Hiring sales representatives.
2. Training sales representatives.
3. Organizing sales representatives.
4. Compensating sales representatives.

Hiring

Companies need to hire the sales personnel who will be the most effective in accomplishing the objectives of the sales effort. Although many buyers see all sales representatives charged with getting people to buy, sales personnel may be given one or some of three basic sales tasks: order getting, order receiving, or sales supporting. **Order getting** is the sales task of persuading customers to feel a need and to see that a firm's product can satisfy that need. **Order receiving** generally is required when current customers are ready to reorder. The sales task is filling the order the customer is ready to give. This selling task is common at the wholesale and retail level. **Sales supporting** is the task of providing pre- or postsale service to customers without having them order anything. This indirect method of selling emphasizes building customer loyalty for future orders.

The desired qualifications of candidates for sales jobs should be based on the type of tasks expected. Moreover, qualifications of currently successful sales representatives and failures may help a firm decide who should be hired. A frequently cited cause of sales personnel failure is lack of initiative.[1] Generally, sales representatives also must be able to plan their sales activities and be thoroughly familiar with them, and be thoroughly familiar with their product and that of competitors. Another factor linked to sales success is the degree to which sales personnel characteristics (height, name, politics, and religion) match those of customers.[2]

---

[1] Charles A. Kirkpatrick, *Salesmanship*, 5th ed., Cincinnati: South Western Publishing Company, 1971, p. 131.
[2] Franklin B. Evans, "Selling as a Dyadic Relationship—A New Approach," *The American Behavioral Scientist*, May 1963, p. 70.

Training

Newly hired sales personnel cannot be 100% effective immediately. They need to be trained to gain the necessary knowledge and experience. Sales training may take many forms depending on the goals of the program. In general, sales training programs are designed to provide trainees with knowledge about the organization they work for and about how to sell the product.

Introduction of sales representatives to the sales process is an integral part of many training programs. The sales process as shown in Table 10-2 consists of: (1) prospecting; (2) preparation; (3) presentation; and (4) postsale activities. Sales trainees will probably be given hints on how to effectively carry out each stage. The experience of successful sales representatives may form an important part of training.

Organizing

Sales representatives must be assigned customers to avoid an inefficient sales effort. Without assignment of accounts, sales representatives will fight for the best accounts and ignore other customers. Thus, organizing is important.

Table 10-2. *Content of Selling Process*

1.	Prospecting	The sales representative searches for potential customers who have needs and ability to buy the product.
2.	Preparation	Information gathered about prospective customers is used to prepare the sales call and its contents. The sales representative tries to ensure that his or her message will be on target and will convince qualified prospects to act.
3.	Presentation	The carrying out of the plans set for the sales call is the presentation. The sales representative must be sure to gain the customer's *attention*, to arouse *interest* in the product, and to make the customer *desire* the product enough so he or she will *act*. The sales representative should be prepared to demonstrate the benefits of the product as well as meet objections raised by the customers. Eventually, the representative will try to close the sale by seeing if customers are ready to buy.
4.	Postsale activities	Repeat purchases may result if a sales representative makes sure customers receive what they thought they ordered. If a customer is dissatisfied, he or she will probably blame the sales representative. Postsale activities also include representative evaluation of success or failure. The individual should try to determine why he or she failed or only received a partial order.

Organization may be based on geographic location of customers, types of products, or type of customer. Geographical sales regions may be assigned to minimize travel costs. However, sales personnel may need to specialize in selling only certain company products or in selling to only certain types of buyers in these geographical regions. The knowledge required to sell all products to all customers may be too great for any one sales representative to remember.

Regardless of the method used for sales representative assignment, the firm should be aware of the effect of the sales potential of customers on sales personnel performance. A sales representative, for example, cannot be expected to sell as much as other representatives if the person has fewer potential sales in a specific territory or a wider geographical area to travel.

Compensating

The rewards received by sales representatives determine the quality of their performance. High-quality performance generally requires both financial and nonfinancial rewards. The financial rewards should provide representatives with a steady income as well as a monetary incentive based on performance. Many companies have accomplished this by paying their representatives a salary sufficient for living plus a commission on sales. However, some companies consider their sales representatives as order getters and pay them only if they sell. On the other hand, order receivers, and support representatives are frequently paid only a salary because they are not expected to generate orders.

Financial benefits also include reimbursement for traveling or selling expenses and fringe benefits such as paid vacations, pensions, and insurance plans. These elements may not be motivators of good performance. The representative expects them in any kind of employment. Moreover, they are generally not linked to sales personnel performance.

Nonfinancial benefits should include opportunities for advancement, recognition of the sales representative's contribution to organizational success, and display of understanding of individual problems. Sales representatives may be rewarded by being given more customers or a sales management job. Many representatives may desire recognition instead of a promotion to manager. They consider themselves professionals and will work hard for the designation of "Sales Representative of the Year." Sales representatives also expect sales managers to listen to their problems and advise them. Sales managers with selling experiences often are the best listeners and advisers.

Advertising Activities

Advertising requires management to make decisions similar to those required for personal selling. The message to be presented to the audience must be prepared for both types of promotion. Appeals and possible objections must

Parts of a Typical Business

also be considered by both. However, advertising requires two unique decisions: (1) selection of media; and (2) choice of advertising agency.

Selection of Media

Users of advertising must decide what media will carry their message. Advertising media are of three types: print, broadcast, or direct. As shown in Figure 10-1, the two print media of newspapers and magazines have been a frequent choice of advertisers. Newspapers, despite a decreasing share of advertising expenditures, still receive the largest share (30%) of total advertising revenues.

The broadcast media of television and radio provide verbal contact with the audience. Television, with its added visual contact, has been receiving an increasingly large share of advertising expenditures.

Direct-mail advertising provides the opportunity to hit a select audience excluding the mass audience covered by print or broadcast media. Billboards are another type of direct media.

Media selection is based on matching advertising objectives with media characteristics. Advertising objectives include statement of target audience

Figure 10-1. *Media Share of Advertising Expenditures*

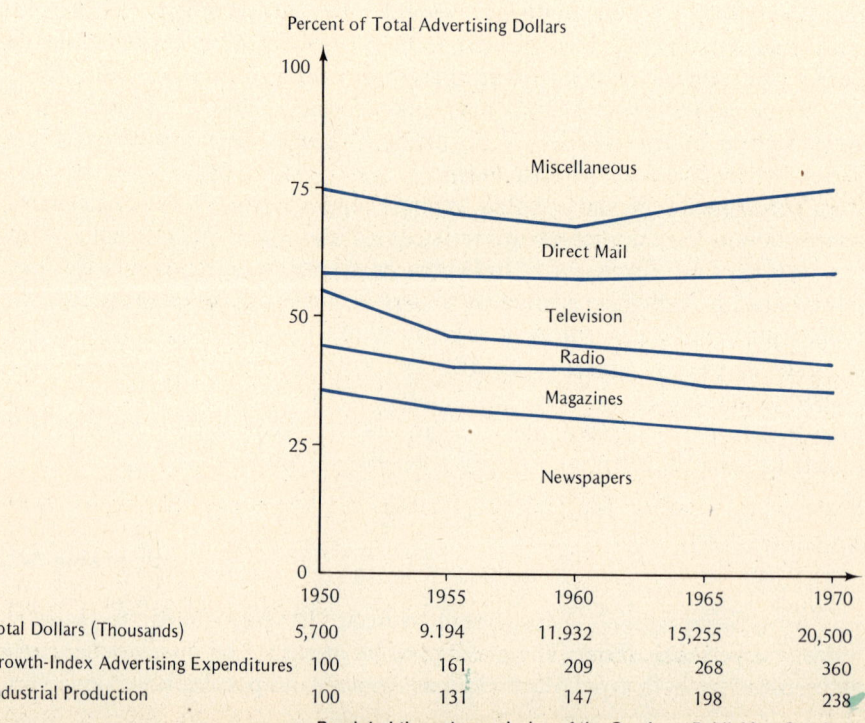

Reprinted through permission of the Goodyear Publishing Co., Inc.

characteristics, type of effect desired in audience, and budget constraints. Media characteristics to be considered include: (1) cost; (2) characteristics of the media audience; and (3) length of message possible.

COSTS Certain media may be eliminated from consideration because their cost exceeds the amount allocated for advertising. For example, television commercials that cost over $200,000 for a 60-second advertisement during movies (*The Godfather*) and the Super Bowl may be too expensive for a small business.

Evaluation of media cost may be misleading if benefits from use of the media are not considered; cost per exposure must be computed. The total cost of an advertisement in a medium is divided by the number of people exposed to it.

All costs of preparing an advertisement and placing it in a media should be included. Television advertisements, for example, require a longer and more expensive production process than those in other media.

The number exposed to a medium is hard to determine, although most media do measure the size of their audiences. However, their figures may exceed the actual audience size because they realize the promotional value of these estimates. Furthermore, all those exposed to a medium may not be qualified customers.

CHARACTERISTICS OF MEDIA AUDIENCE The geographical location of media audience members must be compared to that of the target audience. A retailer trying to hit an audience living in a town may find audiences of magazines, television, and even radio to be too broad. Firms should select the media that hit their audience with the least amount of wasted exposure.

Firms should also know the interests, needs, and other buying behavior characteristics of the audiences of the media. Certain media, such as magazines and direct mail, allow a firm to deliver its message to a special interest group. For example, sellers of skiing equipment may find skiing magazines an effective way to communicate with their potential customers. On the other hand, advertisements on a television program featuring skiing contests may have exposure among many who cannot ski or are not interested in going skiing.

LENGTH OF MESSAGE POSSIBLE Print media generally permit longer messages than do broadcast media. Receivers of broadcast messages generally can retain less than through leisure reading of print media. Moreover, print media can be read when the receiver is in a proper frame of mind.

Long messages may also be possible with direct mail. However, the tendency of respondents to ignore junk mail increases as the length of the advertisement increases.

Choice of Advertising Agency

An **advertising agency** is an independent organization that provides promotional activities for client firms. These agencies, numbering less than 10,000 in the United States, may research media audiences, create messages, or select media for a client. The 10 largest agencies (J. Walter Thompson; McCann-Erickson; Young and Rubicam; Ted Bates; Leo Burnett; Batton, Barton, Durstine, and Osborne; Ogilvy and Mather; Doyle Dane Bernbach; Grey Advertising; and Foote, Cone and Belding) are the most popular. Their clients in 1971 spent almost $3 billion for advertising. The other agencies handled $6 billion of advertising.

Advertising agencies are not used for approximately one-half of all advertising expenditures. They may not be used because companies have formed their own in-house agencies. However, advertising agencies may be able to provide the services for less cost. Their fixed costs may be spread over several clients. Moreover, the traditional method of compensation of advertising agencies may result in no extra cost to users of the agencies.

Advertising agencies originally acted as sellers of media space. Therefore, they have traditionally been paid by media. Broadcast and print media give advertising agencies 15% off of the price normally charged users. Consequently, a firm pays the same for its media whether it uses an agency or not. An exception is the use of a medium not privately owned—direct mail.

The traditional method has been criticized because it encourages agency uses of the most expensive media and provision of few services. There is a definite trend toward the use of a fee method to pay advertising agencies. Agencies are being paid for services to their clients, not for the sale of media space.

Advertising agencies may also be used by firms because they provide creativity and objectivity. Their experience with similar problems may give a company use of more knowledgeable personnel than can be maintained in a company advertising department.

PROMOTIONAL EFFECTIVENESS

Promotion may not always accomplish its objectives. Promotional communications may fail to get to the intended audience. Moreover, the audience may ignore or misunderstand the message.

In order to evaluate the **effectiveness of promotion**, information about the audience must be fed back to the originator of the promotion. Information about audience reaction may be supplied by sales representatives or by marketing research. It is important to note that personal selling has the ability to provide feedback information without undertaking an effort separate from the promotional effort. Mass selling, on the other hand, does not include a feedback capability. Audience reaction must be measured by a separate effort.

The kind of feedback needed by advertisers for evaluating promotional effectiveness depends on promotional objectives. Informational objectives will be accomplished if there is evidence that the audience is aware of the message.

Persuasive promotion requires information about attitudes or behavior of audience members.

Determination of the effectiveness of personal selling generally involves evaluating sales representative performance. The effect of the message on the audience is commonly used to measure advertising effectiveness.

Sales Representative Performance

Sales representatives charged with getting orders will be evaluated on the basis of sales volume generated compared to expected sales volume. Other personnel, concerned with taking orders or creating goodwill, may be evaluated on the basis of their amount of effort. Their number of calls per day, selling expenses, and number of advertising displays set up indicate the quality of their performance.

Not all factors that contribute to sales representative success are easy to measure. Knowledge, personal appearance, and personality are vital to successful communications. Evaluation of these factors must be done in as objective and impartial a manner as possible.

Advertising Message

The effectiveness of an advertising message may be measured before it is launched to the general public. Many companies have consumer groups or panels that react to advertisements. These panels must be as representative of the population as possible, although certain types of people are reluctant to participate on panels. Moreover, the responses of panel members to advertisements may be different from those of other consumers because they want to please the firm paying them or because they are not asked to make a financial commitment to buy.

It is impossible to replace the realism of the actual purchase situation. **Sales results tests** attempt to measure the sales volume created by a particular advertisement. However, the difficulties involved with separating the sales effects of other factors from that of advertising have discouraged the use of sales results tests.

A more common method is to measure audience awareness of the advertisement. Many firms buy information provided by Daniel Starch, Inc. This company sells the results of surveys it conducts. These surveys consist of asking a sample of consumers if they remember seeing certain advertisements. The proportion of respondents who remember seeing the advertisement is called the *noted score*. A noted score of 70 means that 70% of those sampled indicated they had seen the advertisement. Audience awareness may be a good indicator of the effectiveness of advertisements. However, advertising that results in high buyer awareness may not lead to sales.

Efforts to measure promotional effectiveness must also include information about causes of the audience behavior. Firms must uncover the reasons for failure of sales representatives and of advertising messages. Without information about why promotion failed, corrective action cannot be taken. Frequently, firms assume they know what caused promotional problems because of past experience. It is common to blame sales representatives for poor sales performance and advertising copywriters for poor advertising results. The true causes may instead be unrealistic promotional goals, substandard product quality, or competitive actions.

PROMOTION JOBS

Over 10% of the Amercian labor force is employed in promotion. Approximately 90%, or 6 million, of those in promotion are involved in selling. The remainder are involved in advertising.

Selling

Moderate increases in the number of sales jobs are expected in the next decade. Selling has been and will continue to be a good source of employment for college graduates. Moreover, changes taking place in the sales job will make it a more challenging profession. Increased emphasis is being placed on sales representatives' use of modern business tools and techniques to solve problems of their customers.

Nature of Jobs

Sales jobs are varied, depending on whether the required sales tasks are order getting, order taking, or supporting.

The Bureau of Labor Statistics classifies sales jobs by type of employer. Their seven categories are:

1. Retail salesworkers.
2. Wholesale salesworkers.
3. Manufacturer's sales representatives.
4. Insurance agents and brokers.
5. Real estate agents.
6. Securities sales representatives.
7. Others.

The most important category, as shown in Figure 10-2, is retail. Over one-half of all salesworkers are in retail sales jobs. The other categories are of less

Figure 10-2. *Composition of Sales Force*

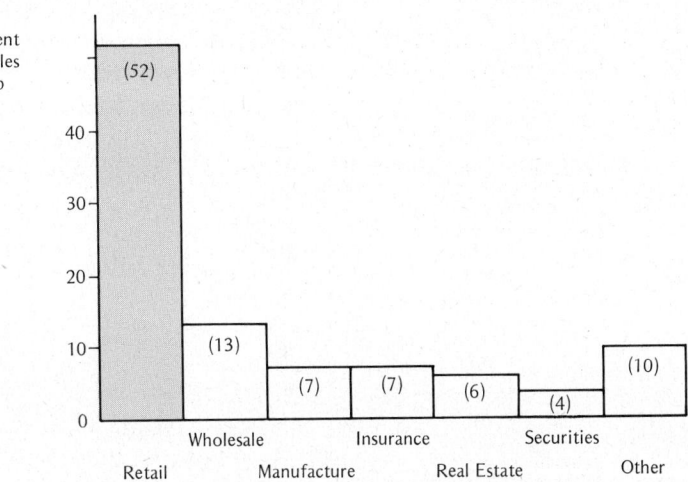

significance in terms of total number of jobs. The 10% of salesworkers in the "other" category are in a variety of jobs: automotive salesworkers, models, routemen, and gasoline service station attendants.

Few people understand all of the different sales jobs. Frequently, people stereotype sales jobs based on their experience. You may have had contact with retail salesworkers and door-to-door sales representatives. Thus, your image of the sales jobs may be the same as found in an attitude survey of almost 1000 students in 123 colleges and universities. Their image is:

1. Selling is a job—not a profession or a career.
2. Sales representatives must lie and be deceitful in order to succeed.
3. Salesmanship brings out the worst in people.
4. To be a good sales representative, you have to be psychologically maladjusted.
5. One must be arrogant and overbearing to succeed in selling.
6. Sales representatives lead a degrading and disgusting life because they must be pretending all the time.
7. The personal relations involved in selling are repulsive.
8. Selling benefits only the seller.
9. Sales representatives are prostitutes because they sell all their values for money.
10. Selling is no job for a person with talent and brains.[3]

[3] Donald L. Thompson, "Stereotype of the Salesman," *Harvard Business Review*, January/February 1972, p. 21.

In order to provide a different perspective, the discussion on sales jobs will center on industrial selling. Industrial selling does not fit the stereotype just given. Moreover, it requires college training, while many selling jobs dealing with consumers do not require more than a high school diploma.

As an industrial sales representative you would most likely work for manufacturers, although you may be employed by middlemen. Many industrial sales jobs are in the food, printing, and chemical industries. Industrial sales jobs require creative selling effort. Sales representatives must use their knowledge of the customer and of the products to develop a sales program. These representatives would also be charged with servicing customers, maintaining records, planning work programs, and training customer employees. The sales job expectations of Scott Paper Company are presented in Table 10-3.

Qualifications

The requirements for success in a selling job depend on the nature of the job. Businesses that hire industrial sales representatives for nontechnical products generally require a college degree in business administration or related fields. Engineering or chemistry majors are preferred by firms selling technical products—electrical equipment, heavy machinery, or chemicals.

Companies generally supplement college training with their own training. The training program includes information about the company's policies and its products. Most companies consider actual sales experience a vital part of the training program.

Personality characteristics are emphasized by many sales people as the most important qualifications for sales jobs. Personal selling requires:

1. Enthusiasm about selling.
2. Confidence in oneself.
3. Optimism about sales success.
4. Sincere interest in the problems of others.
5. Determination to succeed.
6. Initiative.
7. Imagination for preparation of sales presentations.
8. Mental agility.
9. Control of one's feelings and affairs.
10. Courage to be persistent and forceful.
11. Social maturity and poise.
12. Ability to get along with many types of people.

Rewards

In 1972 the average starting salary for beginning sales representatives was $9,000 annually. Industrial sales representatives of technical products generally receive more than those selling products requiring less technical knowledge. Their average beginning salary may be $2,000 a year higher than other sales

Table 10-3. *Analysis of Scott Retail Sales Representative's Job*

I. Making the sale on Scott products.
   A. Sells new orders to retail outlets.
   B. Sells repeat orders to retail outlets.

II. Service on Scott products.
   A. Renders merchandising advice and assistance to retail outlets.
      1. Builds displays.
      2. Plans and conducts demonstrations.
      3. Distributes dealer helps related to Scott products (including visual aids such as special display stands, price cards, and folders).
      4. Delivers merchandise where required.
   B. Secures newspaper and handbill advertising and other tie-in promotions from indirect customers (coordinates trade features with company advertising campaigns).
   C. Counsels with retail customers on most advantageous Scott resale prices, that is, those that produce profits yet largest possible volume of repeat business.

III. Routine duties.
   A. Records daily calls and results, and mails this report to divisional office daily.
   B. Maintains selective selling records on our products and on leading competitive brands, and summarizes these periodically, upon completion of each route coverage.
   C. Sends orders to divisional office daily.

IV. Executive.
   A. Plans daily and long-range work programs.
   B. Helps in training of younger retail sales representatives.
   C. Observes facts in his territory that have a bearing on the sale of the products.
   D. Works out new ideas and mails suggestions to superiors.
   E. Studies and keeps abreast of merchandising and marketing in other fields. Discusses some of these problems with other sales representatives and superiors.

V. Creating goodwill toward himself and the company.
   A. Sells Scott Paper Co., its concepts and policies to retail dealers.
   B. Offers retail dealers constructive merchandising ideas not related to Scott products.
   C. Distributes dealer helps not specifically related to Scott products.
   D. Continually strives to maintain and improve friendly relationship with retail customers.

Source: D. M. Phelps, *Sales Management Policies and Procedures*, Homewood, Ill.: Richard D. Irwin, Inc., 1953, pp. 545–46.

representatives. Most sales representatives are paid a salary and a commission. The opportunity to earn above average earnings are great for those representatives who receive a commission on their sales.

Successful experienced sales representatives earn incomes as high as

$40,000 per year. Their earning potential has been the greatest in the paper, textiles, petroleum, and chemical industries.[4]

Personal selling is also rewarding because of:

1. Opportunities for advancement.
2. Challenging, competitive work.
3. Opportunity to personally grow and develop.
4. Variety of work.
5. Importance of job to company.
6. Independence.

Successful sales representatives are given better territories or the chance to advance in management to such jobs as sales supervisor, district manager, sales manager, or even vice president of sales. The rewards of such advancements are both financially and personally satisfying.

Personal satisfaction can result from selling products creatively. Customer objections and competitive sales effort make sales a most challenging job. Satisfaction can also result from having to get along satisfactorily and pleasantly with all types of people. Sales jobs are not boring. The variety in customers and their specific needs offer sales representatives stimulating differences in their jobs.

Sales jobs frequently provide a good measure of security. Good sales representatives are considered to be a necessity to their employers. Moreover, established relations with customers can result in customer attachment to representatives. If sales representatives are fired, their customers will often go with them to new companies.

Sales jobs provide independence. Sales representatives are free to plan their calls on customers. They draft their own work schedules, including their sales routes. Subject to their supervisors' approval, they are basically their own boss.

Advertising

You can find advertising jobs with companies that advertise their products, media that sell their space, and advertising agencies that work for advertisers. The future for advertising, like personal selling, suggests a moderate increase in the number of jobs.

Nature of Job

The approximately one-half million advertising workers are employed in seven types of jobs. Advertising work includes:

1. Advertising copywriter.
2. Artist and layout worker.

---

[4] Allan L. Reid, *Modern Applied Salesmanship,* Pacific Palisades, California: Goodyear Publishing Company, Inc., 1970, p. 75.

3. Production manager.
4. Advertising researcher.
5. Media director.
6. Advertising agency account executive.
7. Advertising manager.

The first three jobs require technical expertise in production of advertisements. Copywriters need creativity and psychological abilities to create headlines, slogans, and the text of the advertisement. Visual effects are created by artists and layout workers. Production managers need a thorough knowledge of printing and photography so they can transform copy and art work into a finished product.

Advertising researchers assemble and analyze information used to plan advertising programs. They may need to be adept at conducting buyer surveys and statistical analysis of data.

Media directors, account executives, and advertising managers are decision makers. Media directors, who work for advertisers or advertising agencies, decide which media to use. Account executives decide what advertisements are needed by the clients of the agency they work for. Advertising managers make decisions about the advertiser's budget, type of advertising, and agency.

Deadlines and last minute changes make this job interesting and challenging. Competition affects the success of advertising as well as personal selling. Personal satisfaction can result from seeing one's idea in print.

Qualifications

Producers of ads are generally best prepared if they have a journalism or technically related degree. Researchers should have a background in behavioral research and statistical methods. College graduates are preferred for many advertising jobs. The decision-making jobs are best filled by students with degrees in marketing, management, and related fields.

College training is supplemented by on-the-job training. Those who choose a career in advertising should have communication skills. There is also a need to be able to sell one's ideas to superiors, advertisers, and the public. Problem-solving ability is also an asset for advertising workers. Every project generally requires special handling.

Rewards

Variations in advertising jobs also result in a wide range for starting salaries: $6,500 to $10,000 in 1972. Moreover, wide variations are found in different firms.

Experienced advertising workers also receive varying levels of compensation. For example, account executives' salaries average between $18,000 and $22,000 a year, media directors between $10,000 and $16,000. Advertising jobs offer many rewards similar to personal selling. Opportunities for advancement into management are good.

CHAPTER SUMMARY

The objectives of promotion must be specifically defined. Companies must decide where their audience is located and what their degree of concentration should be. In addition, different types of promotion are needed for industrial users, middlemen, and household consumers.

Promotion objectives and programs will also depend on the buying habits of these three groups. Industrial users have different buying habits for installations, accessory equipment, fabricated parts and materials, raw materials, and operating supplies. The buying habits of middlemen depend on their customers. Buying habits of household consumers differ for convenience goods, shopping goods, and specialty goods.

Basically, promotion is intended to inform, persuade, or remind members of the defined audience of the advantages of the product.

Promotion budgets may be set using a simple method, such as allocating a percentage of sales for promotion, or a realistic, but complex, method of allocating the amount necessary to accomplish promotional objectives. Firms will probably use different methods as they gain experience in measuring effectiveness of promotional expenditures.

Each firm must decide on its relative emphasis on the two major promotional tools. Customer characteristics, firm considerations, and environmental considerations help each firm decide whether it will emphasize personal selling or advertising in its promotion mix.

The relative balance between personal selling and advertising serves as an indicator of activities necessary to plan and implement the promotion program. Personal sales activities require hiring, training, organizing, and compensating sales representatives. Selection of media and advertising agencies are specialized tasks involved in planning advertising.

The promotional job is not complete until the success of the promotion is considered. The effectiveness of promotion is difficult to determine because the audience is subjected to communications of other businesses, institutions, and people. It is almost impossible to isolate the effect of one communication. Furthermore, the cause of the failure of promotion to accomplish its objectives is hard to pinpoint. Without information about causes of promotion failures, improvements in effectiveness of future promotional efforts seem unlikely.

Personal selling and advertising jobs are discussed. Both types of jobs provide considerable choice of jobs. Sales representatives may work for manufacturers, wholesalers, or retailers. Opportunities for high salaries and career advancement are good for sales representatives with the right qualifications. College training and a personal desire to sell help ensure success in the highest-paid sales jobs.

Advertising jobs are available for managers as well as creative artists. Communication and problem-solving skills are assets to advertising workers.

PROVOCATIVE STATEMENT

Marketers Must Deliver What They Promise Consumers

1 "This past year, retailers all over the nation got themselves into trouble by ignoring the basic rules of selling: (1) Deliver what you promise. (2) Live up to your sales pitch. (3) Treat your buyers with respect.

My agency works for a retailer, the Pathmark supermarket chain. Last year, Pathmark had all the problems everyone else had and a few more all its own. The difference is that we turned our problems into advantages while most of our competitors went on talking the way they had always talked. We were talking the truth. They had their heads in the sand, operating on the theory that if they didn't mention problems, their customers wouldn't notice there were any.

When the government's price freeze was called off, Pathmark created our own 60-day price freeze. Not only was it good consumer advertising, but we made every darned newspaper and TV and radio station in our trading area. . . .

In our TV ads we talked about everything our customers wanted to hear: good ways to get protein and vitamins on the table, cheaper cuts of beef, pasta prices rising next week, price reductions when they happened. What produce was in season. What precautions to take on Halloween. . . .

When we became a target in the energy crisis because of our policy of keeping stores open 24 hours a day, we turned the opportunity into a major asset. Pathmark began televising a commercial showing the Newark Boys Chorus unscrewing the bulbs in a Pathmark electric sign.

Goodwill at Pathmark has never been higher. And goodwill means good sales. We're proud of Pathmark's story, but it wouldn't have been possible if we didn't deliver on promises."

Zal Venet,
"The Truth Pays Off,"
Sales Management, July 22, 1974,
p. 28.

PROVOCATIVE STATEMENT

Herbert Eagle
Photo by Richard Hewett

A Transamerica Corporation Executive Talks Selling

2   **On the changing role:** "As today's salesman becomes part of a larger marketing team, some people claim that his individual role begins to diminish. This is not true. In 1950, for instance, there were 3,000 items in the average supermarket. Today, there are 8,000. The salesman thus helps position and differentiate that product for the chain."

On corporate backup: "The salesman needs plenty of management and marketing support. He does not always get it. Take insurance. One of the problems of that business is that the industry spends 30 times as much for advertising to tell people what and when to buy as it spends on market research. This is not an indictment of advertising but an indictment of how much we have been telling and how little we've been listening."

On upward mobility: "Today's salesman is moving higher faster. One out of every three publicly-owned U.S. corporations is now headed by a man whose background is primarily marketing or sales. And this ratio is bound to grow as companies become more sensitive to consumerism."

On resilience: "The salesman gets paid for the number of times he hears 'no.' The well-adjusted salesman knows in advance that he may close one sale out of 25 calls. He is mentally prepared to suffer those 24 turndowns. Still, it takes its toll. So he gets paid for hearing 'no.'"

On picking a sales career: "Nothing really happens until somebody sells something. Or, as Robert Louis Stevenson once put it, 'Everyone lives by selling something'."

"The New Salesman: Wired for Success,"
Business Week, January 6, 1973,
p. 47.

REVIEW QUESTIONS

1. Promotion depends on the audience. Explain.
2. How do buying habits of industrial users differ from those of household consumers?
3. What are the objectives of promotion?
4. How might a company decide how much to spend for promotion? What is the best way? Explain.
5. Personal selling is better than advertising. Comment.
6. How does the sales representative's job differ in different companies?
7. Explain the sales process.
8. How should a business decide which advertising media to use?
9. All companies should use an advertising agency. Comment.
10. How can a business decide if its promotion is effective?
11. How do personal selling jobs differ from advertising jobs?

Chapter Outline

Planning Title Transfer
   Title Changes
      Use of Middlemen
      Elimination of Middlemen
   Number of Title Changes
      Customer Characteristics
      Manufacturer Characteristics
      Product Characteristics
      Trend to Shorter Channels
   Types of Wholesalers and Retailers
      Wholesalers
      Retailers
   How Many Middlemen?
      Intensive Coverage
      Selective Coverage
      Exclusive Coverage
   Which Middlemen?
   Performance of Effective Middlemen
      Characteristics Desired in Middlemen
      Motivating Middlemen
      Evaluating Performance of Middlemen
      Improving Performance of Middlemen

Planning Physical Movement
   Transporting
      Modes
      Type of Carriers
      Who Pays?
   Storing
      Warehouse Decisions
      Inventory Decisions

Jobs in Distribution Channels
   Industrial Traffic Manager
      Nature of Job
      Qualifications
      Rewards

Chapter Summary

Provocative Statement 1:
   A Beer Sales Representative
   Must Understand Tavern Owners

Provocative Statement 2:
   The Quality of Service Provided
   by a Trucking Company
   Depends on Its Personnel

Key Terms

Title
Direct channel
Loss leader
Agent
Retailer
Wholesaler
Sales offices
Sales branches
Merchant wholesalers
Agent wholesalers
Selling agent
Manufacturer's agent
Broker
Commission person
In-store retailing
Wheel of retailing
Independent retailers
Chain stores
Wholesaler-sponsored voluntary groups
Retailer cooperative groups
Franchise organizations
Consumer cooperative
Scrambled merchandising
Intensive coverage
Selective coverage
Exclusive coverage
Trade discounts
Facilitating agencies
Modes of transportation
Railroads
Trucks
Water carriers
Pipelines
Airlines
Common carriers
Contract carriers
Private carriers
F.O.B. origin
Uniform delivered pricing
Zone pricing
Phantom freight
Public warehouse
Private warehouse
Industrial traffic manager

Channels of Distribution

"Without any question Lou (a beer salesman) talked a language that the tavern owner understood. He never mentioned profit; he always talked about 'making money.'"
—Retailing Consultant

Channels of distribution are necessary to provide customers with desired goods. Distribution generally involves the transfer of ownership (legal title) and movement of physical goods. Several activities necessary to plan title and physical movements are discussed in this chapter. A discussion of job opportunities in the distribution channels concludes the chapter.

PLANNING TITLE TRANSFER

Several decisions are required of a firm planning the transfer of *title* of goods. It must decide:

1. If any other firms will take title to goods before consumers take title.
2. How many times title will change hands.
3. What types of wholesalers and retailers should be used.
4. How many middlemen are needed.
5. Which individual middlemen should be used.
6. What should be done to ensure that middlemen are effective.

Title Changes

Many businesses perform services that help manufacturers transfer the title of goods to consumers. These firms, called *middlemen,* are either whole-

Figure 11-1. Direct Channel Distribution

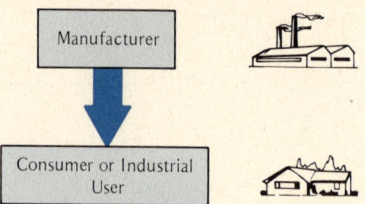

salers or retailers. In return for their services they receive either a discount from the selling price to consumers or a percentage commission on the selling price.

A business may elect to use no middlemen to distribute its product. This decision would result in a **direct channel** depicted in Figure 11-1.

Few firms selling to consumers use the direct channel. Avon Products' use of door-to-door sales persons is an example of direct channels. Direct channels are also popular for the sale of installations, accessory equipment, fabricated parts, and raw materials to industrial users.

Use of Middlemen

Middlemen are a necessity for many firms. The middlemen provide many services required for distribution. Their fees for these services are often lower than if manufacturers provide the services themselves.

Middlemen may provide:

1. Promotion.
2. Information.
3. Financial assistance.
4. Physical movement.

PROMOTION Middlemen help in promotion by contacting customers personally. They may hire sales representatives to call on industrial users, other middlemen, or consumers. Advertisements and store displays arranged by middlemen also help promote a manufacturer's product. Finally, retail clerks aid many manufacturers by delivering sales presentations and providing customer service.

INFORMATION Manufacturers find middlemen to be good sources of information about their customers. Middlemen can provide information about how customers react to current or proposed marketing programs. They can also alert manufacturers to competitive plans.

FINANCIAL ASSISTANCE Manufacturers prefer to be paid for their sales soon after the sales are made. Industrial users, middlemen, or consumers favor extended time to pay their bills. Middlemen help satisfy both manufacturers and customers. They pay manufacturers before they collect from their customers. Consequently, manufacturers using middlemen will have less money tied up in accounts receivable. Middlemen bear the risk of uncollectable accounts.

PHYSICAL MOVEMENT Middlemen may transport, store, or divide goods for manufacturers. Wholesalers and retailers deliver goods to customers. They may be able to do it more frequently and at less cost than manufacturers. Their delivery cost to customers is divided among all the manufacturers whose products they sell.

Customers consider available products worth more than those that must be ordered. However, it is costly for manufacturers to keep warehouses full of goods near customers. Middlemen can help by storing goods at locations convenient to customers.

Many costs are reduced if manufacturers can produce and transport goods in large lots. A manufacturer of cleaning products, for example, will experience more efficient production if he produces a large lot of each product, for instance, cleansers, dish detergents, and soap powders. Moreover, per-unit transportation costs are substantially less if the railroad car or truck is filled and contains only one type of product. However, few customers want to buy a carload of cleansers or dish detergents. Middlemen help the manufacturer provide goods in the quantities and assortments desired by customers. They divide carload or truckload lots into smaller lots desired by customers.

Retailers are the major middlemen involved in distributing goods produced by different manufacturers to provide customer assortment. A supermarket accumulates an assortment of household cleaning products and groceries that customers like to purchase at the same place. Sporting goods stores may offer Wilson tennis equipment, Head snow skis, Remington hunting equipment, and Shakespeare fishing rods and reels.

Elimination of Middlemen

The services of middlemen may not be economical for all manufacturers. Some companies may be able to distribute goods more cheaply and effectively than available middlemen.

Frequently, manufacturers of industrial goods find that their customers have less need of middlemen services. Consequently, middlemen who provide a full line of services may be more costly than if the manufacturer provides only the necessary services. Manufacturers may produce all the products that customers want to buy together. They will also find less need for middlemen if customers buy in large lots. Moreover, customers may need neither credit nor a lot of promotion.

Middlemen can provide low-cost services because they represent several manufacturers at the same time. However, they generally do not emphasize the product of any one manufacturer. Their promotion to customers encourages customers to buy from them. They do not necessarily push a particular brand. Manufacturers of high-value products may need the promotion push only possible from use of their own sales representatives. In addition, middlemen may not provide customer service. Middlemen may not have enough technical expertise or equipment to repair computers, bulldozers, or typewriters.

Manufacturers may also avoid middlemen in order to control the price or freshness of goods offered to customers. Retailers may use a manufacturer's product as a **loss leader**: they sell it at a low price to build store traffic. However, the manufacturers may be trying to build a high-quality image for their products. Elimination of middlemen gives manufacturers the power to control prices and their price image.

Perishable items may require direct channels. Middlemen may be unwilling or unable to provide fast transportation. Therefore, manufacturers may ship goods directly to customers to ensure delivery of fresh goods.

Manufacturers may want direct feedback from customers. They may feel they cannot afford to wait until middlemen relay information. This need for direct and immediate feedback is important for sellers of perishable or custom-made products. Manufacturers must know if customers have received spoiled goods. Sellers of custom-made products need to know specifically what the customer demands before production.

Middlemen are not always eager to perform their services. Manufacturers selling new products unknown to customers may present middlemen with a risky situation. Products for which no demand has been established may not sell. Direct channels may have to be used if middlemen refuse to handle the product.

Number of Title Changes

If channels are not direct, it is likely that a middleman will take title to the goods from the manufacturer. Traditionally, title to consumer goods has passed through two levels of channel members, as shown in Figure 11-2.

Figure 11-2. *Passage through Two Levels of Channel Members*

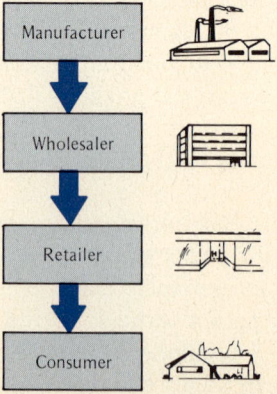

The number of title changes usually depends on characteristics of the customer, of the manufacturer, and of the product. There is a growing trend toward shorter channels.

Customer Characteristics

Many customers require the two-level channels. Such a channel is needed if many services are demanded by the customer. Also, if customers are geographically dispersed, both wholesalers and retailers will be needed to provide proper distribution. The market for convenience goods, for example, is big and widely dispersed, with each customer buying frequently and in small quantities. Consequently, convenience goods are often sold through two levels of middlemen.

Manufacturer Characteristics

Characteristics of the manufacturer also may encourage the movement of title through wholesalers and retailers. Small manufacturers with limited financial resources and managerial abilities need the services offered by wholesalers and retailers. These small companies may only have the capabilities to produce goods. Therefore, they may hire another type of wholesaler to find potential wholesalers to buy their products. This type of middleman, called an agent, does not take title to the goods. The agent's function in the canning industry, where this middleman has received frequent use, is to find wholesalers who want to take title to products of canning factories. The channel that results is shown in Figure 11-3.

Figure 11-3. *A Channel Distribution*

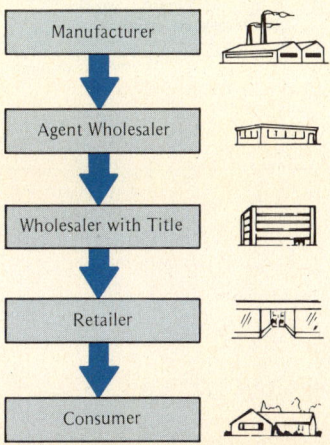

Parts of a Typical Business

Product Characteristics

In addition to customer and firm characteristics, long channels may result because of the characteristics of the product. Products that are low cost, nontechnical in nature, and nonperishable will generally be distributed through long channels. Low-cost products such as convenience goods and industrial supplies will not provide sufficient revenue to cover costs of direct channels. This is especially true if the manufacturer sells a narrow line of products. Nontechnical products permit the use of more middlemen because no technical knowledge is needed. Nonperishable items are not affected by the delays in movement caused by several levels of channels.

Trend to Shorter Channels

A trend among retailers has been growth in the size of their operations. Many retailers have increased the size of their operations by opening branch stores. Since the 1930s, the growth of chain stores, such as A&P, Grants, and Sears, has produced large retail giants. Moreover, the increase in cooperative organizations of independent retailers has left few small retailers who buy in small quantities.

Manufacturers have found it beneficial in these cases to deal directly with retailers. These retailers are large enough to provide services originally carried out by wholesalers. This intermediate length channel, shown in Figure 11-4, is used for the sale of convenience goods to large retailers.

Shopping and specialty goods are frequently sold through the channels of manufacturer to retailer to consumer. The higher-valued, less frequently purchased shopping and specialty goods do not need wholesalers.

The channel with one title exchange between manufacturer and customer is also used for sale of small accessory equipment and operating supplies. This channel is shown in Figure 11-5.

The middleman in this channel is called a wholesaler. **Retailers** are defined as middlemen who sell only to household consumers. **Wholesalers** are middlemen who sell to those who are buying for purposes of resale or production.

Figure 11-4. *An Intermediate Length Channel*

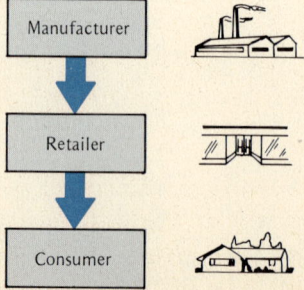

Figure 11-5. *A Channel with One Title Exchange*

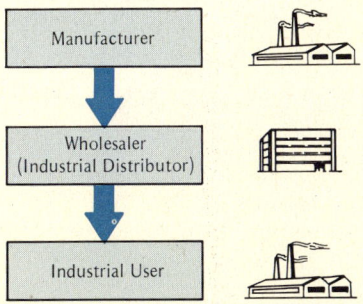

This channel is used because accessory equipment and operating supplies are of lower value than other types of industrial goods. Furthermore, the high degree of regional concentration of industrial users makes channels with more than one title change unnecessary. Finally, large-quantity purchases of operating supplies make relatively short channels feasible.

Types of Wholesalers and Retailers

The decision to include wholesalers and retailers in a channel of distribution leads to other decisions. Manufacturers must decide which type of wholesalers and retailers they want to use.

Wholesalers

Three major types of wholesalers are possible. These categories, as defined by the U.S. Bureau of Census, are:

1. Sales offices and branches.
2. Merchant wholesalers.
3. Agent wholesalers.

SALES OFFICES AND BRANCHES The Bureau of Census reports that approximately one-third of all wholesale transactions move through sales offices and branches. This share, which has increased in recent years, is shown in Figure 11-6. Sales offices and sales branches are facilities owned and operated by manufacturers who do their own wholesaling. These facilities, physically separated from the manufacturing plant, allow manufacturers' sales representatives to have offices near their retail or industrial customers. Sales branches also provide storage facilities near customers.

Manufacturer owned wholesale facilities are preferred when large volume is possible. This helps explain why manufacturers' sales branches and sales offices account for 34% of wholesale sales but only 10% of wholesale establishments.

Figure 11-6. *Types of Wholesalers and Their Importance*

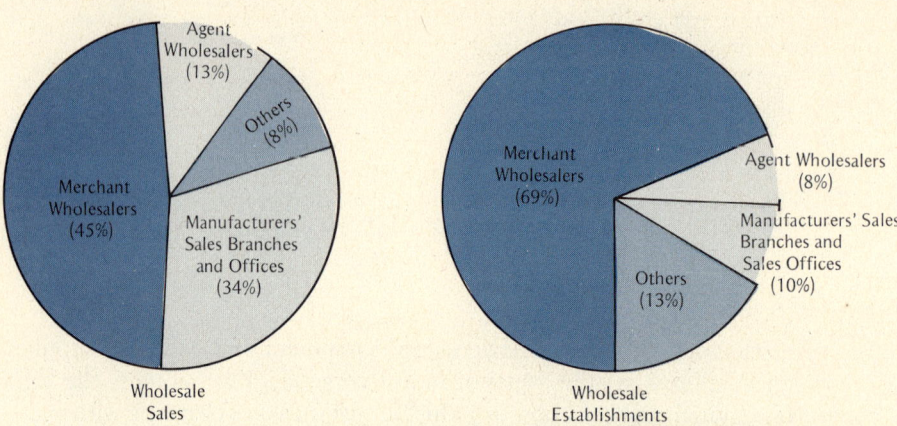

MERCHANT WHOLESALERS Wholesalers who are independent of manufacturers and take title to the goods they sell account for almost one-half of all wholesale sales (see Figure 11-6). These wholesalers, called **merchant wholesalers**, increased their share from 42% of sales in 1948 to 45% in 1967.

Merchant wholesalers may offer either full or limited service. Full-service, merchant wholesalers provide retailers or industrial purchasers with all the services identified with middlemen. They promote, inform, extend credit, store, transport, and divide goods. The demand for this type of merchant wholesaler has decreased as manufacturers, retailers, and industrial purchasers have become larger. These wholesalers with their high costs due to provision of many services have been cut out of many channels.

Many merchant wholesalers have started to offer fewer services. The three most common limited-service wholesalers are described in Table 11-1. In general, their operating costs are less than those of full-service, merchant wholesalers.

AGENT WHOLESALERS **Agent wholesalers**, unlike merchant wholesalers, do not take title to the goods they buy or sell. In addition, agents have lower costs and perform fewer services. The major services provided by most agents are promotion and information. They try to sell for their client and give them information about objections and behavior of customers.

As shown in Figure 11-6, agent wholesalers are the least important type of wholesaler, accounting for less than 15% of sales and establishments in 1967. Moreover, their share of sales has fallen by more than 20% in the past 20 years because manufacturers have replaced agents with sales branches and sales offices.

The four major types of agent wholesalers are described in Table 11-2. Each type has characteristics that attract sellers and buyers. **Selling agents** are beneficial to small, poorly financed, production-oriented manufacturers.

Table 11-1. *Characteristics of Limited Service Merchant Wholesaler*

Type	Characteristics
Cash-and-carry wholesaler	This wholesaler does not grant credit or deliver goods to retailers.
Truck jobber	This wholesaler carries a limited line of goods to retailers. He sells and delivers his merchandise on the same call. His operating costs are high because of his delivery of small orders. Retailers are willing to pay this high cost for perishable food items or fast-moving supplies.
Drop shipper	The drop shipper does not take possession of the goods he sells. He gets orders from industrial users and instructs the manufacturer to ship the goods directly to the users. However, the manufacturer gives the drop shipper the title and the bill for goods shipped. Manufacturers of bulky and low-value items such as coal and lumber use drop shippers because they provide promotional and financial assistance without increasing the physical movement costs.

Manufacturer's agents are best fit for developing new sales territories. Brokers are suitable for occasional sellers or buyers who need market information quickly. Commission persons are used most frequently by businesses that sell goods in central marketplaces. The businesses need someone to be responsible for goods and price negotiations while the goods are at the marketplace.

Retailers

Retailers are harder to classify than wholesalers. Three classifications of retailers are made according to

1. Method of operation.
2. Form of ownership.
3. Type of goods handled.

METHOD OF OPERATION Manufacturers may choose retailers who have buildings or stores where the goods can be displayed for customers. This method of operation, in-store retailing, accounts for over 95% of all retail sales. It is advantageous because the retailer can use the store to display all products. Moreover, the physical characteristics of the store can be used to create an image for products handled.

In-store retailers may operate as full-service retailers or limited-service retailers. *Full-service retailers* traditionally offer many services to consumers such as delivery, credit, unlimited returns, and check cashing. Department

Table 11-2. Characteristics of Agent Wholesalers

Selling agent	"An agent who operates on an extended contractual basis sells all of a specified line of merchandise or the entire output of his principal, and usually has full authority with regard to prices, terms, and other conditions of sale." His average operating expenses average about 4% of sales. Selling agents are common in the coal, textiles, and food industries, although their use has been declining since World War II.
Manufacturer's agent	"An agent who generally operates on an extended contractual basis often sells within an exclusive territory; handles noncompeting but related lines of goods; and possesses limited authority with regard to prices and terms of sales." His operating expenses average about 6% of sales. The use of manufacturing agents is increasing in most industries.
Broker	"An agent who does not have direct physical control of the goods in which he deals but represents either buyer or seller in negotiating purchases or sales for his principal. He has no authority to set prices or terms of sales. A broker provides fewer services than other types of agents and has lower operating costs: 2-3% of sales. Brokers are most prevalent in the food industry but are also found in real estate and used machinery.
Commission person	An agent who is located at the central market place and takes possession of goods owned by principal and negotiates prices, methods, and terms of sale with buyers. His authority is constrained by the wishes of the principal. He may arrange delivery and extend credit. He does not take title. Sellers of fresh fruit, grains, and livestock find commission men useful. Operating costs of commission men vary widely but are generally higher than other agents because of provision of storage and credit.

Excerpted from *Marketing Definitions: A Glossary of Marketing Terms*, compiled by the Committee on Definitions of the American Marketing Assoc., Ralph Alexander, in *Marketing Principles: The Management Process*, Ben M. Enis, pp. 92–93.

stores and general stores are examples of full-service retailers. Their operating costs, relatively high, equal about one-third of sales.

Discount stores and supermarkets are examples of *limited-service retailers*. They generally offer fewer services and lower prices. Their operating philosophy is to sell a large volume of fast-moving goods at a low profit per unit. Their operating costs are about one-seventh of sales.

These limited-service retailers may not continue to operate in the same manner in the future. They may get involved in a pattern of retail change called the **wheel of retailing**. In the wheel of retailing, new types of retailers will offer limited services but will increase services as they continue in business.

However, once they become fat with services and costs, new low-cost, minimal-service retailers will undermine their market. Department stores, supermarkets, and discount stores have all seemed to follow the wheel. Notable exceptions to the wheel include suburban shopping centers and automatic vending machines.

Nonstore retailing includes door-to-door selling, mail-order selling, and automatic vending. Door-to-door retailing consists of calling on consumers at their place of residence. Samples of merchandise may be taken on door-to-door calls. Encyclopedias, vacuum cleaners, cosmetics, brushes, and pots and pans are commonly sold door-to-door. This method may be advantageous to both the seller and the consumer. Sellers generally benefit from the ability to control the sales pitch and to offer an aggressive sale. Consumers may benefit because of the ease and convenience of buying at home. Retailing scholars suggest that door-to-door selling will become more popular in the future because of consumer convenience.

Mail-order retailing involves delivery of goods to consumers by mail. Sometimes the orders are sent by mail. This type of retailing has a lower cost than in-store retailing. Less money is spent for facilities. However, the costs of catalog preparation and delivery as well as adjustments for returned goods may eliminate any cost advantages. Its major advantage may be the convenience it offers to consumers. The large mail-order retailers (Sears, Montgomery Ward, and Penney's) have instituted telephone order systems and customer pickup to increase the speed of product delivery.

Automatic vending has about the same volume as other nonstore retailers: 1% of retail sales. This type of retailing involves the sale of goods through coin-operated machines. Automatic vending is a favorite method for sellers of convenience goods because machines can be made widely available. They are accessible when stores are closed. However, the high operating, maintenance, and repair costs, the inability of consumers to inspect goods before purchase, and the lack of opportunity to return unwanted goods restrict the use of machine vending to fast-moving, well-known, low-value items.

FORMS OF OWNERSHIP   If manufacturers decide to use retailers, they may be independent, corporate chains, contractual retailers, or consumer cooperatives. **Independent retailers** are single retail units owned by a company. They offer the advantage of being flexible to meet the demands of their customers. Frequently, independent retailers have the advantage of a management strongly committed to the business and its success, especially if the manager is the owner.

Chain stores are two or more stores centrally owned and managed. They may offer the most sales potential. For example, chains account for over one-half of retail sales in the food, shoe, and variety store industries. Generally, fewer contacts are needed to sell to chain stores. One purchasing agent may buy for the 4,000 A&P stores. Chain retailers may also be chosen because they can make more effective use of promotion dollars. They promote for all stores with the same advertisements. Furthermore, they can hire specialists in each major function: buying, promoting, layout, and accounting.

Independent retailers have adopted new methods of operation to meet the competition of chains. The predominant method used has been to enter into formal agreements with other retailers or wholesalers. These *contractual relations* are designed to ensure retailer competitiveness and independence. Their success, accounting for 40% of retail sales, has helped keep independent retailers and wholesalers in business.

The three major types of contractual arrangements, summarized in Table 11-3, are:

1. Wholesaler-sponsored voluntary groups.
2. Retailer cooperative groups.
3. Franchise organizations.

Wholesaler-sponsored and **retailer cooperative groups** have been most common in the grocery field. They were generally formed to combat the supermarkets. However, these two types of contractual agreements have also been used by retailers in auto supplies, drugs, and hardware.

Franchise organizations have been used for years by manufacturers of automobiles and petroleum products. They have experienced substantial increased use in retailing of services since 1950. Franchise organizations have sprung up in the fast-food, lodging, and recreational industries.

Manufacturers have had mixed success with franchising. The successes of

Table 11-3. *Three Types of Contractual Retailers*

Wholesaler-sponsored voluntary group	A group of retailers associated with a wholesaler to carry on joint promotional activities including use of a common name and standardized facilities. The wholesaler also offers retailers management help, lower prices, and their own brands. Retailers agree to buy most or all of their goods from the wholesaler. IGA Food Stores is an example.
Retailer cooperative group	A group of retailers who pool their purchasing power to get lower prices. Each member owns stock in a warehouse owned and operated by the cooperative. In effect, the retailers perform their own wholesale activities. An example is Associated Grocers.
Franchise organization	A group of retailers contractually bound to manufacturers. The retailers get the use of the manufacturer's common theme and other promotion. They also receive managerial and financial assistance. Lower costs of supplies may result from purchasing power. In return, the manufacturer receives payment for use of his name and the power to ensure that his product is marketed as he desires. The capital supplied by retailers eases the financial burden on manufacturers. McDonald's, Howard Johnson, and Hertz Rent-a-Car all operate as franchise organizations.

Table 11-4. *Retail Trade by Type of Operation*

TYPE OF OPERATION	NUMBER OF ESTABLISHMENTS	SALES (billions)	PERCENTAGE OF TOTAL SALES
Lumber, building materials, hardware, farm equipment	86,373	$ 17.2	5.5
General merchandise	67,307	43.5	14.0
Department stores	5,792	32.3	10.4
Variety stores	21,046	5.4	1.7
Food stores	294,243	70.3	22.6
Eating and drinking places	347,870	23.8	7.6
Automobile dealers	105,500	55.6	17.9
Gasoline service stations	216,059	22.7	7.3
Apparel and accessory stores	110,164	16.7	5.3
Furniture and home furnishings stores	98.826	14.5	4.6
Drugstores	53,722	10.9	3.5
Other retailers*	288,772	27.3	8.7
Nonstore retailers	94,468	7.6	2.4
Total retail trade	1,670,600	$310.1	100.0

*Includes liquor stores, jewelry, sporting goods, florists, etc.
Source: Bureau of the Census, *Census of Business. Retail Trade,* Washington, D.C.: Government Printing Office, 1967.

McDonald's, Colonel Sanders, Howard Johnson, and Kampgrounds of America are known by most. However, the problems of others, such as Burger Chief (a General Foods franchise), Broadway Joe's, and Minnie Pearl's, should be considered before choosing this method of retailing. Successful franchisers need more than a well-known name. They must have a base of sound marketing knowledge.

A **consumer cooperative** is a retail business owned and operated by household consumers. Cooperatives such as GEM (Government Exchange Mart) purchase and distribute goods primarily to the membership.

This method of retailing has never accounted for more than 1% of all retail sales in the United States. Generally, the price competitiveness of other forms of American retailing has made consumer cooperatives of minor benefit. However, the benefits of lower prices offered by consumer cooperatives have proven worthwhile to foreign consumers.

TYPE OF GOODS HANDLED Manufacturers want to pick retailers who handle the type of products they are selling. Food is retailed in food stores, clothing in apparel and accessory stores, and furniture in furniture and home furnishing stores. The different types of retailers, as classified by the Bureau of Census, are shown in Table 11-4.

The number of establishments available for the different manufacturers varies from less than 6,000 department stores to over 300,000 eating and drinking places. Sales potentials also differ greatly—approximately $5 billion for variety stores and $70 billion for food stores.

Bureau of Census categories help manufacturers decide what types of retailers are available. However, the product line of retailers varies within each category. Some food stores, for example, may carry a limited line of food items, while supermarkets and others carry a wide line of food items as well as hardware, health and beauty aids, drugs, clothes, and automobile accessories.

The increased use of scrambled merchandising by retailers has resulted in confusion between different retailers. **Scrambled merchandising** is the practice of adding unrelated products to a retailer's assortment. It is no longer true that drugs are only available in drugstores, hardware only in hardware stores, and food only in food stores. Many stores simply do not fit into only one Bureau of Census category.

Manufacturers generally favor scrambled merchandising because it provides more retail possibilities. However, manufacturers must be careful in dealing with new new types of retailers. These retailers will probably expect services different from what manufacturers currently provide.

How Many Middlemen?

Manufacturers must decide how many of each type of middleman are needed. The number chosen may range from one wholesaler or retailer to all American wholesalers (311,000 in 1967) or retailers (1,763,000 in 1967). The choice of intensity of market coverage (setting the number of each type of middleman) falls into three general categories:

1. Intensive.
2. Selective.
3. Exclusive.

These categories are discussed in the context of retailers, since the intensity of wholesale coverage is generally dependent on that chosen for retailing. If, for example, many retailers are used, many wholesalers will be needed to distribute goods to them.

Intensive Coverage

Manufacturers are employing **intensive coverage** if they have their product sold in every retail outlet where customers might look for it. This broad exposure is common for convenience goods. Such goods must be easy to buy. Cigarettes, candy bars, and chewing gum are generally made available in as many places as possible: drugstores, hardware stores, theaters, laundromats, factories, and professional buildings. Automatic vending is a key retailing method for those desiring intensive coverage.

Selective Coverage

Consumers may buy from those retailers who provide the best service or the nicest displays. Manufacturers may want to choose only certain retailers, rather than all those possible. **Selective coverage** results when manufacturers choose only a few retailers for each geographical part of their market. A manufacturer of men's clothing may choose only those men's clothing stores in a town, which are known for carrying a broad assortment of quality goods. Automobiles are also generally sold through the use of selective coverage.

Selective coverage is preferred if the products sold are shopping goods. Consumers are willing to search for the product. In addition, they will consider the retailer when making their decision. The use of fewer outlets enables manufacturers to do a better job of controlling retailers. Retailers are generally more likely to help promote a manufacturer's product if consumers cannot buy the product from all competitors.

Exclusive Coverage

A manufacturer may use **exclusive coverage**: only one retailer in each market area. This method may be necessary when retailers need to carry a large inventory of goods. Furthermore, the large promotional effort expected of retailers selling specialty goods may require giving a retailer an exclusive territory. The manufacturers may also use this method of coverage to ensure that their retailers do not sell any competitive brands.

Exclusive coverage can be profitable for both retailers and manufacturers. However, both parties should consider what will happen if the other party fails to perform. Manufacturers may be seriously hurt if their exclusive retailers drop them. Retailers stocking only one brand may be in for hard times if the manufacturer withdraws a product.

Legal difficulties may also plague exclusive coverage agreements. According to the Clayton Antitrust Act (described in Chapter Three), exclusive coverage agreements that substantially lessen competition are illegal. Two examples of illegal practices are:

1. Standard Oil of California prohibiting Chevron dealers from handling competing products (commonly called *exclusive dealing contracts*).
2. General Motors automobile dealers preventing the sale of cars to discount dealers.

Which Middlemen?

Manufacturers with well-known products frequently find most middlemen want to handle their products. Even the producers of less well-known goods may wish to use only some of the middlemen willing to handle their products.

The middlemen chosen must give sellers access to desired customers. It is important that the customers of middlemen are those the firm considers to be its market. The middlemen's method of operation should also be considered. The services they offer to customers should be consistent with the desires of the manufacturer. The product line and promotion policies of middlemen will also serve as a basis for middleman selection.

Middlemen may be rejected because the quality of their product line is too low or because they do not provide adequate personal selling or advertising. Middlemen with a record of slow payment of bills may not fit channel needs. Moreover, the resources of middlemen can be used as indicators of quality of performance. The abilities of management should be given careful consideration before a manufacturer selects a particular middleman.

Selection of middlemen must be based on established criteria and information. The established criteria consist of characteristics desired in middlemen. Information is gathered about available middlemen. This information, which must be carefully gathered, should be collected from suppliers, competitors, and customers of middlemen.

Performance of Effective Middlemen

The management of channels does not end upon selection of middlemen. The middlemen must be motivated to do a good job. Their performance will need to be evaluated. Changes in channels may be necessary to ensure effective channels.

Characteristics Desired in Middlemen

Middlemen cannot be expected to perform effectively if manufacturers do not tell them what they expect. Manufacturers must tell middlemen:

1. What other products to carry.
2. What they should know about their products.
3. What prices to charge.
4. What type of promotional push they expect for the product.
5. How much inventory to carry.
6. What information to provide.

Middlemen may not accept manufacturers' expectations passively. The viewpoint of middlemen is that they are independent businesses trying to satisfy customers. They are interested in selling any product their customers want to buy, regardless of the manufacturer. Middlemen are interested in selling an assortment of items to their customers so they can spread their costs. The added cost involved in selling several items at once is minimal. Thus, their profit is greater.

In order to understand middlemen, it is necessary to realize they expect certain things from their suppliers (manufacturers). They expect:

1. A wide variety of quality products.
2. Low-priced goods they can sell at a high price.
3. Extensive advertising to customers by suppliers.
4. Fast delivery of small quantities.
5. Liberal return policies.

Manufacturers and middlemen have often conflicted because of misunderstandings about expectations. These conflicts may also come from differences in goals and language. Manufacturers generally have a goal of growth in sales. Middlemen are more concerned with keeping sales at a satisfactory level. Language differences occur because of differences in educational background and experiences. Middlemen, for example, may use the term "merchandising" instead of "marketing." Communications between middlemen and manufacturers may be ineffective because of these goal and language differences.

Motivating Middlemen

Middlemen need to be motivated to perform according to the manufacturer's expectations. The best way to motivate middlemen is to create a strong consumer demand. Middlemen will market a manufacturer's product as desired if there is a payoff. The payoff results when consumers buy the product. The monetary rewards of middlemen can be increased by increasing the margin between the cost of goods to middlemen and the selling price. The size of this margin is set by the discount offered to middlemen. This discount, expressed as a percentage on price to the consumer, is called a **trade discount**.

Motivation may also be accomplished by extending better credit terms to middlemen, sponsoring sales contests for middlemen, or threatening to cut off ineffective middlemen. However, the success or failure of all these tactics depends on the actual strength of consumer demand for the manufacturer's product.

Evaluating Performance of Middlemen

Manufacturers must check to see how successful they have been in motivating middlemen. They need to evaluate middleman performance regularly.

The standards (expectations) used to evaluate performance should be agreed upon at the beginning of relations between the manufacturer and middlemen. Manufacturers may want to evaluate the level of sales, average inventory levels, customer delivery time, cooperation in company promotional programs, and promptness in paying bills.

Middleman ability to achieve the standards over a period of time should be considered. It may be necessary to change expectations if middlemen cannot meet them.

Parts of a Typical Business

Improving Performance of Middlemen

Evaluation of channel performance must include determination of why standards are not met. Channel expectations may be set too high. Channel members may be making more from the sale of competitive products.

After the causes of performance failure are identified, alternatives must be devised. Alternatives may include changes in standards, in discounts to middlemen, in promotion to consumers, in specified middlemen, or in types of middlemen. The expected cost and revenues from each alternative should be estimated, and the one that promises the greatest long-run profit should be selected.

PLANNING PHYSICAL MOVEMENT

Marketing scholars have emphasized movement of title in channels of distribution. Channel members with title generally have the power to choose the methods of movement of goods. Businesses that help move goods but not title are not considered channel members. They are called **facilitating agencies**.

The two major physical movement activities are transporting and storing.

Transporting

Transporting occurs when goods are moved from one place to another. Goods produced in one city must be transported to consumers living in other cities. These goods will be worth more to consumers in their own cities than at the place of manufacture. Manufacturers must decide how to transport their goods. They must also decide who pays for the transportation.

Modes

There are five ways (**modes**) **of transporting** products: railroads, trucks, water carriers, pipelines, and airlines. Each mode has advantages and disadvantages.

RAILROADS **Railroads** carry more goods than any other carrier. They are preferred by businesses because of their versatility. In comparison to other modes, they are average in speed of delivery, number of scheduled shipments per day, dependability in meeting schedules, capability to handle various products, availability to different geographic points, and total transportation costs.

TRUCKS **Trucks** have become increasingly popular as a way to move goods. Their share has more than doubled in the past 30 years. They now account for over one-fifth of all tons moved. The ability of trucks to offer faster and more consistent service to more geographic points has led to substantial gains in truck businesses. Most of the gain has come from business previously handled by railroads.

WATER CARRIERS About one-sixth of American freight traffic moves on inland waterways and the ocean. **Water carriers** are preferred for movement of bulky, low-value products. These products require the lowest total cost mode of transportation. Other products may not use water carriers because of their slowness, infrequent movements, undependability, and limited availability.

PIPELINES Continuous, on-schedule movements make **pipelines** a popular mode of transportation. However, their use is restricted to liquids (gas and oil products) and to products (coal) that can be transported in a powder form, mixed with water.

AIRLINES **Airlines** carry less than 1% of all American freight. Although they can move goods faster than other modes, their high cost has limited their use to highly perishable products (fresh-cut flowers, fresh seafood, and high-fashion clothing) or high-value, urgently needed products (electronics equipment).

Types of Carriers

Transportation carriers are regulated by laws. These laws, including the Interstate Commerce Commission Act, have resulted in three different types of carriers:

1. Common.
2. Contract.
3. Private.

COMMON CARRIER **Common carriers** are licensed by regulatory agencies to provide service between set geographical points. This service must be offered to all who wish to use it. Moreover, the rates charged must be approved by regulatory agencies. There are firms in each mode which have been legally declared common carriers.

CONTRACT CARRIER **Contract carriers** can be hired to carry goods, but they are not licensed to operate between set points. They make specific contracts each time they agree to haul any firm's goods. More personalized service is offered to users of contract carriers. Most contract carriers are trucking firms.

PRIVATE CARRIERS **Private carriers** are businesses transporting their own goods in their own transportation vehicles. They are not subject to regulation, but they cannot haul goods owned by others. Businesses using this method have total control over movement. However, costs may be high if businesses do not have goods to back-haul from places of delivery.

Who Pays?

The seller of goods must decide whether the buyer pays:

1. All the costs of transporting goods.
2. Less than the total transportation costs.
3. More than these costs.

ALL THE COSTS The seller may quote the price as **f.o.b.** (*Free on Board*) **origin**. This means that the seller will pay to load the merchandise on the carrier. The buyer is responsible for selection of carrier, carrier costs, and losses while goods move from the seller to the buyer.

This method ensures that each buyer gets the transportation service paid for. The further the goods are moved, the higher the buyer's transportation costs will be. Although this seems to be fair to all buyers, sellers of heavy, bulky, low-unit-value products find it limits their geographical selling area. Potential buyers, located closer to competitors, will be lost with this method.

LESS THAN ALL COSTS Some buyers pay less than all transportation costs if a uniform delivered or zone pricing system is used. A **uniform delivered price** means that all buyers pay the same total price regardless of where they are located. Since the uniform delivered price is based on average transportation costs, those buyers furthest away from the seller will pay less than it costs to ship the goods. For these buyers, the seller is partially absorbing freight costs.

Zone pricing is a modification of delivered pricing. All buyers in the same zone pay the same price. The difference between the price paid by the buyer furthest away from the seller and the actual transportation costs will be less than if a uniform delivered price is used.

MORE THAN ALL COSTS Uniform delivered and zone pricing mean that some buyers pay **phantom freight**: their transportation charge exceeds the cost of shipment. For example, a buyer located in the same city as the seller who charges the same price to all American buyers will pay phantom freight. Phantom freight may be necessary to cover the losses on sales to distant buyers. However, local buyers will not continue to pay it if they have a lower-cost alternative.

Storing

Storing requires decisions about warehouses and inventories.

Warehouse Decisions

Warehouse decisions involve the type of warehouse and its location.

TYPE OF WAREHOUSE A firm may operate its own warehouse or use the services of a public warehouse. The **public warehouse** is owned by an independent business. It provides a range of services to a number of different firms on a fee basis.

Public warehouses may be preferred because goods require costly, specialized services or because the owner of the goods has only a small lot of goods to store. It may be cheaper to rent facilities than to make large investments in building warehouses.

Private warehouses are preferred if they can be continuously used at peak capacity. A half-full warehouse means high storage costs per unit. However, available public warehouses may not provide the type of facilities desired.

LOCATION OF WAREHOUSE   Warehouses should be located to achieve the highest profits. The costs and revenues affected by warehouse location should be considered for several alternative locations.

The costs include costs of warehousing and of transporting goods. Revenues are influenced because warehouse location affects time for delivery to customers. Generally, these costs and revenues move in opposing directions. A location closer to consumers, for example, will produce higher warehouse costs if less volume is moved through each warehouse. There may be higher transportation costs from point of production to warehouse, but lower transportation costs from the warehouse to the consumer and higher revenue because of faster delivery to consumers.

Some costs of warehouse operation may be dependent on community conditions. Different communities may have different taxes, labor costs, and access to transportation carriers. Community services and attitudes can be a key determinant of warehouse location.

Inventory Decisions

The key inventory decision is determination of inventory size. The average number of units in stock depends on how often goods are ordered, how much is ordered each time, and what the rate of customer demand will be. Business has control over the number of orders and the order size. Accurate forecasting of sales is necessary for estimation of customer demand. Further discussion of inventory decisions is presented in Chapter Seventeen.

JOBS IN DISTRIBUTION CHANNELS

Over 18 million Americans work in distributing products. Approximately 16 million work for wholesalers and retailers, and more than 2 million work for transportation companies. A wide variety of jobs is available in distribution channels: managers, clerical workers, vehicle drivers, and sales workers.

Over one-half of the jobs are blue-collar and generally do not require college training. Many of the white-collar distributing jobs are managerial or sales jobs. Since the discussions presented in Chapters Six, Ten, and Twenty adequately cover most managerial and sales jobs in distribution, attention in this section is focused on one specific job: **industrial traffic manager**.

Industrial Traffic Manager

Most traffic managers work for manufacturing firms. However, some of the more than 20,000 traffic managers work for large retail chains. The future for traffic managers looks good. More and more firms are recognizing the need for effective management of movement activities.

Nature of Job

Industrial traffic managers arrange the movement of goods and services for industrial firms. They must select the best transportation carrier and route for goods being shipped into and away from the firm. Traffic managers must be familiar with the rates, schedules, dependability, and loss rates of all available carriers.

Frequently, traffic managers must check to make sure carriers have charged their companies correctly and have delivered the goods as promised. Many companies expand the manager's responsibility to storing and packaging activities. They may have to manage warehouse facilities and supervise packaging of goods for shipment.

A traffic manager often finds it necessary to consult with other company managers about their transportation needs. The manager needs, for example, to work with the purchasing and production departments to plan shipping schedules.

Familiarity with federal, state, and local government regulations relating to transportation is important to traffic managers. They may have to represent their companies before the Interstate Commerce Commission and other regulatory bodies.

Qualifications

Experience in a traffic department is often an important qualification for traffic managers. In addition, a college education is becoming increasingly important to those who desire to be traffic managers. Some companies prefer college graduates who have a degree in traffic management. More than 100 colleges, universities, and junior colleges offer such a degree. Other companies hire graduates with majors in transportation, marketing, management, or business administration.

Courses in statistics will generally be helpful to traffic managers. They use statistics when calculating freight charges and analyzing transportation data.

Rewards

The average starting salary for traffic managers is about $9,000 a year. Experienced traffic managers make from $16,000 to $40,000 or more a year. Generally, the highest salaries are given to those managers with the most experience who work for companies with relatively large transportation costs.

Successful traffic managers can expect to be promoted to supervisory jobs. The top job a traffic manager may achieve in the field is general traffic manager.

Company fringe benefits for traffic managers are comparable to those given other supervisory personnel. Job security depends on a manager's success in minimizing movement costs.

CHAPTER SUMMARY

The decisions involved in planning the movement of title to goods are discussed. Middlemen may be included in channels because of the services they offer: promotion, information, financial assistance, and physical movement. However, available middlemen may charge too much, or their services may be inadequate.

The number of levels needed in channels depends on characteristics of customers, manufacturers, and products. The general trend in these has made shorter channels—with no wholesalers—profitable.

Manufacturers have many choices among different types of wholesalers and retailers. They may choose sales offices and branches, merchant, or agent wholesalers. Retailers vary in method of operation, form of operation, and type of goods handled. They may have stores or sell through door-to-door, mail, or vending machines. Retailers may be part of a corporate chain, wholesaler-sponsored voluntary group, retailer cooperative group, or franchise organization. Retailers carry different types of goods; the practice of scrambled merchandising has made many unrelated products available in the same store.

The number of retailers and wholesalers is a choice of the manufacturers. They will prefer intensive coverage for convenience goods, selective coverage for shopping goods, and exclusive coverage for specialty goods.

The middlemen selected should be those best able to do the job—sell the product. Middlemen who do not have good sales representatives, adequate promotion budgets, or sufficient display areas may be eliminated from consideration.

Manufacturers must motivate middlemen to do a good job—tell them what is expected and pay them adequately. A check on middlemen performance is needed periodically. Changes may be necessary.

Physical movement—transporting and storing—must be planned. Modes of carriers—railroads, trucks, water carriers, pipelines, or airlines—must be chosen. In addition, it must be decided if a common, contract, or private carrier will be used.

Sellers have three options for charging buyers transportation costs. They can charge them all, less than, or more than what it actually costs.

Decisions must be made about storing goods. Private or public warehouses may be used. Location of warehouse is also an important decision. Costs of transporting goods and operating the warehouse and the speed of delivery of goods to customers differ for different locations.

The job of industrial traffic manager involves planning and controlling movement of goods. This job frequently offers a good salary and a chance for promotion to those qualified. A college degree in traffic management is preferred.

PROVOCATIVE STATEMENT

A Beer Sales Representative Must Understand Tavern Owners

1   "It quickly became apparent that Lou personified the most essential characteristic of success as a beer salesman—namely, the ability to operate comfortably on the same level as the tavern owner. The latter is often a rough, uncouth, uneducated man who is in business "to make a buck," and whose attitude is essentially "what's in it for me?"

Without any question Lou talked a language that the tavern owner understood. He never mentioned profit; he always talked about "making money." He never mentioned merchandising or display; he simply talked about getting the product out where the customer could see it. If the tavern owner shouted at him, he shouted back. If the tavern owner called him a "no-good s.o.b.," he called the tavern owner a "no-good cheap b - - - -."

His basic approach to the tavern owner in trying to sell him on the idea of take-out beer was: "Look, you gotta stand behind this bar all day long. You can't go anyplace so you might as well make some money when you're here. If a guy comes into your place for a shot and a beer and he's got extra money in his pocket, he's going to spend that money someplace else if he doesn't spend it here. So you gotta figure out a way to get him to spend that money here. Remember, if you don't get that money, somebody else will . . ."

Warren J. Wittreich,
"Misunderstanding the Retailer,"
Harvard Business Review,
Volume 40, May–June 1962, p. 150.

PROVOCATIVE STATEMENT

The Quality of Service Provided by a Trucking Company Depends on Its Personnel

2   "Any trucking company can buy a given make of tractor, trailer, or city pickup and delivery truck . . . They can build the same type of terminal, and install the same type of electronic data processing system. So what . . . makes the difference in the type of service the shipper receives from one carrier as compared with another? People . . . It's how people are trained for the job they do, and what each individual is able to do with the physical equipment provided by his company that determines whether that service is good or bad. . . .

The company [McLean Trucking Co. of Winston-Salem, N.C.] is one of the few in the industry that operates its own driver training school. Another program is designed to train college graduates for management careers in the industry, and successful completion of this year-long program leads to assignment somewhere in the McLean system of 95 terminals as a sales representative, terminal manager, or maintenance supervisor."

"The Trucking Industry: Working Behind the Scenes,"
Transportation and Distribution Management,
April 1972, pp. 21–22.

REVIEW QUESTIONS

1. What major functions or services do middlemen provide?
2. What is meant by marketing channels? Give examples of short and long channels.
3. Why might a company prefer long channels over short channels?
4. What are the differences between retailers, merchant wholesalers, and agent wholesalers?
5. Discuss the three different methods of classifying retailers, giving examples of each.
6. What type of market coverage is preferred by sellers of convenience goods? Why?
7. Contrast the expectations manufacturers and middlemen have of each other.
8. What advantages are offered by each mode of transportation?
9. Name the decisions to be made by a traffic manager.

Chapter Outline

The Personnel Function in the Organization

The Employment Process
    Job Analysis
    Sources for Candidates
    The Employment Sequence

Training and Development
    Training
    Development
    Evaluation of Training and Development
    Making Adjustments
    Requirements for Successful Programs

Labor Relations
    Union Organization within the Company
    Collective Bargaining
    Grievances
    Employee Discipline
    Discharging a Worker

Personnel Administration
    Wage and Salary Administration
        General Factors Affecting Salaries and Wages
        Systems for Ranking Jobs
        Incentive Systems
    Benefits Package
    Evaluation of the Personnel Function

Careers and Jobs

Chapter Summary

Provocative Statement 1:
    Fire the Whole Personnel Department

Key Terms

Overhead
Job description
Résumé
Interview
Transfer
Promotion
Demotion
Layoff
Sponsor system
Job rotation
Understudy program
Coaching
Management by objectives
Three-way flow

District representative
Steward
Collective bargaining
Bargaining unit
Contract
Grievance
Grievance procedure
Arbitrator
Salary
Wages
Blue-collar workers
Base pay
Profit sharing
Paternalism

Employing, Developing, and Administering Personnel

"The policy of labor unions is more."
—Samuel Gompers, 1st President, AFL
(before the merger with the CIO)

"Fire the whole personnel department."
—Robert Townsend, *Up the Organization*

THE PERSONNEL FUNCTION IN THE ORGANIZATION

12

The personnel function is handled differently by each individual firm. Sometimes departments within a firm have specific operating reasons for having separate personnel sections. At other times the position of the personnel function is a result of neglect or of changes in company emphasis over the years. The reasons behind such a wide range of treatment within a company's organization provide some insights on the personnel function.

1. Managers often take a personal role in hiring, training, developing, and firing workers and do not call on the services offered by a personnel department. They retain a mini-department within their part of the organization and depend on the payroll section and others for administrative support.

2. Consultants and employment agencies provide some personnel services on an "as required" basis. This influences a few firms not to pay the **overhead** of a full-time department. Employee selection and training by outside specialists is expensive, but often less than the overhead cost of the company handling these services.

3. The benefits of a well-managed personnel department usually become less apparent over time because the company's "people" problems become fewer and fewer. A cycle that reaches a point where management decides it does not need a personnel department eventually leads to a rising number of complications with its employees. After a period of time, executives again see a need for a separate full-time function.

4. Areas of specialization in a firm can necessitate separate personnel

298 *Parts of a Typical Business*

sections in three or four departments. Coordination is frequently accomplished through a personnel committee instead of an overall manager. Such a committee might be used in a company with a production process involving unskilled labor with a high rate of turnover, sales performed by technical specialists, and a research department handling many government contracts.

There are important reasons for companies to centralize the personnel functions rather than to disperse them throughout the firm.

1. Employee training and development are likely to take place in a more thorough and practical manner, utilizing the most effective techniques. Consultants are helpful in introducing the latest methods. However, greater knowledge of the company and the worker by the personnel department leads, in most cases, to better results than do either dispersion and consultants or a less professional approach by small departmental sections.

2. Laws and regulations affecting employment of minority races, women,

Figure 12-1. *Organization of the Personnel Functions*

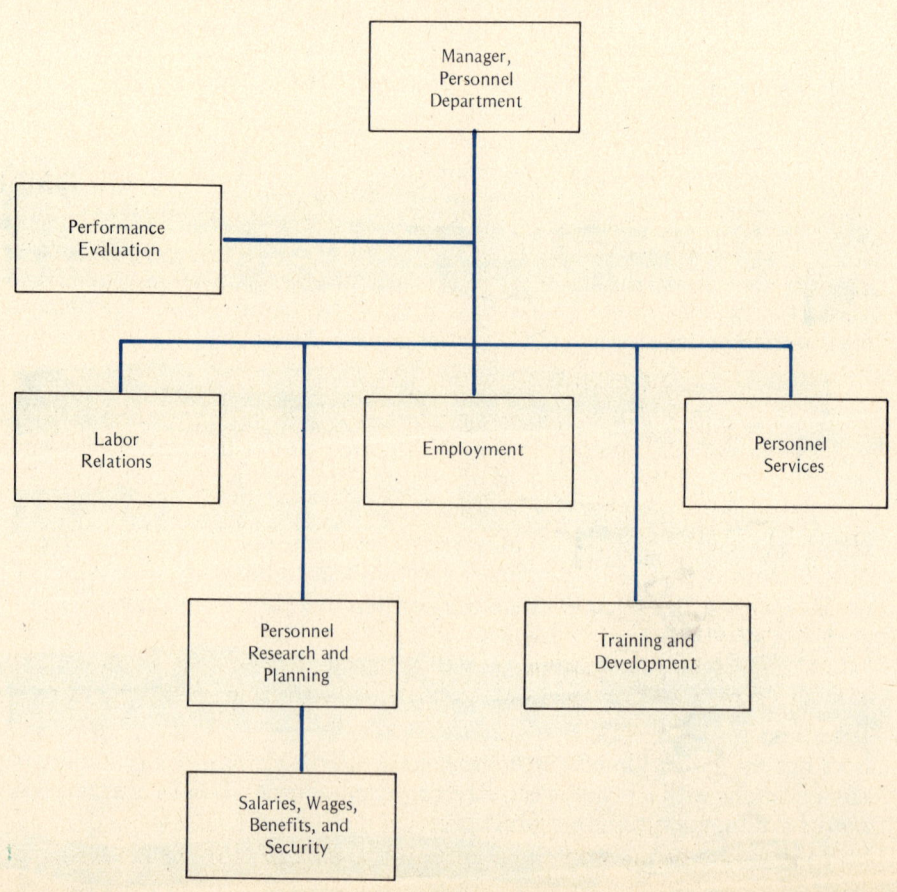

certain age groups, and members of some religions, along with those on safety, health, working hours, payment of withholding and social security taxes, and unemployment and other benefits are complex. These laws and regulations need on-the-spot experts to guide company practices. Penalties for violations can be very costly. Therefore, keeping track of regulations affecting the company can be important.

3. Professionals can help a manager design new positions and recreate jobs if there are problems with the existing organization. Personnel can also act as a link between departments and divisions. Qualified employees can be upgraded by promotions to better jobs by transferring to another department. If outside sources are needed to find candidates, personnel can develop continuing relationships with the most effective firms in the appropriate fields.

4. Terminations are sensitive situations. They can involve labor union and legal implications. Even resignations or layoffs under guidelines established in a contract with a union require processing and changes in records. A centralized personnel department permits control of the number and type of job openings in the firm.

Figure 12-1 shows a typical organizational chart for a large personnel department. It identifies the kinds of work involved and serves as the order in which personnel work is described in the chapter.

THE EMPLOYMENT PROCESS

The employment process involves analysis to define a job, finding qualified candidates, and selecting the best available person.

Job Analysis

A carefully defined job starts the employment process. An employee will have duties and responsibilities under a supervisor who will give specific assignments. The skills required and the importance of the work will classify the job in a certain pay scale with appropriate benefits.

The details of the work and departmental relationships are spelled out in the job description. Figure 12-2 illustrates what is involved. A logical structure of relationships results from a well-designed organization that assigns individuals to a section, sections to a department, and departments to a division.

Assume that departments expand as a firm grows. Rarely does the workload increase uniformly. In addition, a new product may require completely new duties in the same kind of work. Too, advanced production methods could alter the nature of the work. The net result is change that needs analysis to

Figure 12-2. *Sample Job Description*

Position Description for
MARKETING MANAGER, CONSTRUCTO PRODUCTS DIVISION

Title: Marketing Manager, Constructo Products Division

Reports to: General Manager, Constructo Products Division

Responsibilities: *Primary* — Sales performance equaling or exceeding that which is expected for the Constructo line of products.

Facilitating — Employ competent personnel to carry-out the work of the Marketing Department. Optimize use of funds, equipment, and other assets.

Forecast marketing operations in the approaching twelve months and an average year 3-5 years in the future, including Department budgets. Conceive programs and projects which achieve profit growth, selecting the best alternatives for inclusion in Department plans.

Duties: Communicate progress toward objectives to the General Manager regularly, both through routine formal reports and informal verbal and written contacts.

Establish policies and procedures for the orderly management of the Marketing Department.

Develop personnel to carry out their regular assignments more effectively and to replace those who are promoted or who leave.

Institute an information system which helps management to make good decisions.

Design an organizational structure, and update this structure, in order to allow personnel to carry out their assignments in the most efficient manner.

Attend the weekly Division Management Committee meeting to communicate the division's current position, coordinate business activities with other Committee members, and receive information on the company.

Location: Chicago headquarters.

Compensation: Salary — Range of $24,000 to $30,000 per year. Benefits Package 2A. Company car of any make up to $5,000 in cost to be replaced every other year; full company-paid maintenance and insurance.

---

define the new jobs and to outline proper specifications for each job before the employment process is started.

A personnel expert outside the department is usually best at analyzing a job situation. The manager of the department might not be as impartial in the rearrangement of work assignments and the methods used to complete reorganization. The manager might also have less experience with new developments in organizational design.

On the other hand, know-how concerning the technical aspects of the job is important in making new definitions, and this cannot be expected from the personnel department. Therefore, the best results come from a "give-and-take" between the manager and the personnel expert. This exchange can generate new positions or redefinitions of existing positions most efficiently.

It is possible that, in either the new or the redefined jobs, present employees may not have the required skills or the overall potential to handle the responsibilities. Transfers into the openings and/or terminations could result. Sometimes, valued employees might be specially trained to take over the new assignment. After all the possibilities have been considered, the company may still have to look outside the firm for people to fill the new jobs.

Sources for Candidates

The following list identifies the usual means of finding suitable candidates.

1. *Advertisements* in local and regional papers, trade journals, union releases, and other publications.
2. *Employment agencies.* These firms are a source for middle and lower management, salaried nonmanagement, and certain kinds of skills, from bookkeeping to welding.
3. *Executive recruiting firms.* Management consultants often make contributions to job analysis and then fill the positions resulting from their work through a recruiting division. They identify, screen, and test candidates in order to minimize executive time taken in the search. These firms increase the probability of getting highly qualified managers.
4. *Recommendations* resulting from informing friends, competitors, and others about the opening(s). Professional firms in accounting, engineering, law, market research, and similar specialties are good sources for executives and do not involve the payment of fees to recruiters.
5. *Relatives and personal friends of managers. Nepotism* is the practice of hiring solely on the basis of family relationships and often leads to employing people who are not the best qualified candidates for the position.
6. *Miscellaneous sources.* These include the posting of openings where passers-by can see the sign, advertisements on radio and television, and announcements and recruiting at trade conventions and professional society meetings.

The primary objective is to match the position with the best available candidate. Usually, the more who are aware of an opening, the greater the chance of finding the best candidate. Frequently, qualified people are not aware, and some simply will not change companies. Others, whose backgrounds seem to fit the position, are not impressive in interviews and testing. It is essential to have an adequate number of candidates from whom to choose.

The Employment Sequence

To achieve the objective of hiring the best available candidate, most companies have a strict procedure through which everyone goes before being hired.

First, a statement of interest by a candidate is followed by completion of an *application form*, which gives the firm details about the individual in a specific sequence. Many candidates may have provided a résumé, but comparisons are difficult with only this information since details are not uniform. Screening takes place upon receipt of the application form, and letters of rejection are mailed promptly to those who can be eliminated immediately.

Second, those who survive are invited to an interview. This session is usually conducted by a professional from the personnel department. This person attempts to identify the candidate's "people" skills and to clarify the individual's reasons and objectives for applying. Added details about the person's background may be learned in the interview. Various techniques are used, from the very friendly approach to a pressure interview that places the candidate under the stress of intensive questioning.

Third, the skill needed in many jobs often requires *testing* before a candidate can be considered seriously. Potential managers might be examined for their general knowledge, quantitative capability, and other areas of specialty that may be needed. Shorthand and typing tests are given to secretaries. The objective is to be certain that a person has the necessary competence to be a prime candidate.

Fourth, those remaining after the first three steps, perhaps three to five candidates, are *investigated*. References are contacted, and some information is developed about performance in the individual's previous and current jobs. This rarely eliminates anyone, but occasionally a candidate exaggerates work experience. Some terminations listed as resignations turn out to be dismissals.

Fifth, interviews are conducted with the people who are working with, or managing, the departments involved. The objective is to find candidates with skills directly applicable to the job and to get the best personality match. If there is a team relationship involved in managing or handling a lengthy assignment, existing members of the team will also participate in the interviewing.

Sixth, the selection is made by management, followed by a telephone call, making the offer and receiving the candidate's reply. A letter of confirmation follows an acceptance. Also, many firms require a medical examination before a final commitment is made. The process is completed with the first work day, which includes an introduction to the job and the people with whom the new employee will be working.

In the mid-1960s two laws were passed by the federal government that affect the employment process. The *Equal Pay Act of 1963* requires equal pay for equal work and is aimed at providing women and minority races with improved compensation. The free-market concept of supply and demand for workers had created serious salary and seniority discrepancies, and this law was enacted to eliminate such problems. In addition, the *Civil Rights Act of 1964* requires employers to consider all candidates regardless of sex, race, religion, or national origin. In combination, the two laws force companies to be very careful in carrying out each of the six steps to avoid being taken to court by pressure groups on behalf of individuals who claim to have been mistreated.

Affirmative action programs, programs to eliminate any form of discrimination and to ensure compliance with the law, have been initiated by nearly all types of employers. This development has created opportunities for people, which would not have occurred in the past.

TRAINING AND DEVELOPMENT

An important responsibility of management is to train and develop its employees. These two aspects of improving performance are explained briefly in separate sections of the chapter. First, however, some terms on the movement of employees within a firm are defined in the following paragraphs.

A transfer is a change in position with no major change in responsibilities or level of skills. For example, an engineer may be shifted from one project to another. This change would involve little more than working under a new supervisor. The decision to make the move may be a part of a development program or a need to strengthen a part of the organization.

A promotion involves an increase in responsibilities and/or level of skills. The job description signifies progress for an employee. It is important for company morale to consider qualified candidates within the organization before looking elsewhere.

A demotion is a decrease in responsibilities and expected level of skills. Something unfavorable has occurred. An individual may have committed a serious mistake or performed poorly. Also, a downturn in business could force a worker to take a lesser job instead of being laid off. Occasionally, a demotion is used to encourage a manager to resign.

A layoff is defined as a period of time during which a worker does not report for work at the request of tre company. The person has not been fired and continues as an employee. The worker is frequently paid part of the normal wage or salary under present labor union contracts.

Training

Two examples will assist us in defining training. Assume that a new computer is purchased by a firm. Analysts, programmers, technicians, and administrative personnel attend instruction classes at the computer center to learn about the new equipment. In another situation, the manager of the acquisitions and mergers department participates in a seminar on the latest techniques for buying other companies. Training, as indicated in the examples, concentrates on the "how-to" aspects of jobs as they change in a dynamic business environment.

Some facts must be mentioned about training. Not all companies need or want to invest in improving the skills of employees. Many managers will mechanize, if possible, rather than train. In most cases, the absence of training programs means the existence of jobs that are basic and require only standard skills. However, some managers feel that, because of worker indifference about the firm and high turnover rate, the company is training people for its competitors.

At any rate, assume that an employee training program has been established. There are three sources from which to obtain the knowledge and skills needed to teach others: (1) workers presently performing the job; (2) company personnel who are professional instructors; and (3) outside consultants and organizations selling a service.

On-the-job training usually means that workers, presently performing the job satisfactorily, teach those who are upgrading their own skills by working with them day-to-day. This occurs through the **sponsor system**. An example would be a sales representative who brings a new employee on actual calls so the new representative may see how to put the "how-to" reading material into action. The **apprentice system**, unskilled workers learning from skilled workers over a lengthy period, is still used for some jobs in which years of experience are needed to develop a skill fully.

Training of supervisors is generally handled differently. Courses are offered to people who are being promoted or could be promoted upon successful completion of the studies. These courses are usually run by company personnel, but consultants often supplement course content with ideas and practices learned from other firms. Potential supervisors are particularly in need of knowledge about leadership, motivation, grievance procedures, laws and regulations, and workgroup behavior. In addition to preparation for a new job, supervisors are also offered courses to broaden their skills and to learn about new developments in their fields.

Several approaches are used to increase the capabilities of personnel with potential. Formal *management training programs* are given to college graduates and selected employees to provide them with exposure to many departments in the firm. After completion of the program, sometimes two years, they are assigned a position, and their progress is monitored. When opportunities for advancement occur, they are prime candidates.

Executive training is almost always conducted by outsiders through seminars. The seminars could take one day, a weekend, or several other time combinations. Frequently, candidates for top positions are given the opportunity to attend programs at a major university for several weeks. The correction of apparent shortcomings in one of the three management skills (Chapter Six) could be a specific objective. In a few companies, special training programs are given by the personnel department and by upper level employees in their area of specialty. They instruct those wishing to be promoted in an area and managers who want to know how to work better in another type of job. The cost of executive training can be high, and care is taken about objectives for the programs to justify the expense.

Table 12-1 summarizes the broad spectrum of employee training at all levels of the organization and the degree to which the principles of learning are utilized.

Development

Development involves transfers and promotions of talented employees to make maximum use of their training, experience, and general competence during a long period of service with the company.

Job rotation is a commonly used method. For example, it might involve assigning a sales representative with the potential to be director of marketing to successive jobs as analyst in market research, assistant manager in sales administration, regional sales manager, and assitant director of marketing. The purpose of these rotations is to give the individual knowledge of potential contributions by departments that could be under his or her direction, of how they function, and of the personnel working staff as well as line positions. In

Table 12-1. *Training Techniques and Primary Learning Principles Involved*

	ACTIVE PARTICIPATION OF TRAINEE	FEEDBACK OF KNOWLEDGE GAINED	PRACTICE AND REPETITION
On-the-Job Techniques			
Apprentice Training	X	X	X
Job Instruction Training	X	X	X
Off-the-Job Techniques			
Case Study	X	X	
Conference or Discussion	X	X	
Films			
Laboratory Training	X	X	X
Lecture			
Programmed Group Exercises	X	X	X
Programmed Instruction	X	X	X
Role Playing	X	X	
Special Study	X		
Simulation	X	X	X
Television			

addition to development of this executive, the company also determines whether the person has the capacity to direct marketing operations. Perhaps the person is only a super sales representative and not an administrator or problem solver, despite company attempts to develop higher management skills.

Another approach is an **understudy program**. Promising personnel are assigned to senior managers for varying periods of time. The program is created for development and gives the fortunate person selected valuable insight on a particular function such as production manager or general manager.

Coaching is another means of developing personnel. While working in an assigned position, the employee receives instructions, criticisms, advice, and suggestions from specified managers who have proven their competence in various fields. This can include psychological guidance as well as the development of abilities directly related to the job to gain perspective on functions of other parts of the company. While making contributions in their own areas of competence, developing employees learn about the work of others and how it relates to profit performance.

Miscellaneous approaches to development include periodic *invitations to staff meetings* and *observation trips and tours*. Employees have no specific responsibilities. They are taken from the routine of their jobs and given a chance to see others at work.

Evaluation of Training and Development

The job description specifies duties and responsibilities. Qualifications for the individual filling the job are also defined. This gives a basis for identifying the strengths and weaknesses of employees and the areas in which individuals need improvement. Training seeks to provide the knowledge and skills for eliminating weaknesses and to update knowledge and skills as the work content changes. Figure 12-3 illustrates the need for a standard in each job specification, an appraisal of where employees stand relative to the standard, and the training needed to achieve the standard.

Assessing the actual performance of specific employees is a necessary part of program evaluation. It is possible, for example, to have a noncollege graduate doing better work than someone with a degree. The former might have less than the minimum education for the position (perhaps education was set aside because of performance in a previous job), but the nongraduate is using personal resources, expanded by company training, to an extent that permits success in the company.

How does management know whether one employee is doing better than another? Standards must be set for each job in a company. For example, a machine worker may have to produce eight units per hour. An assembly line

Figure 12-3. Standards, Performance Rating, and Areas Needing Training

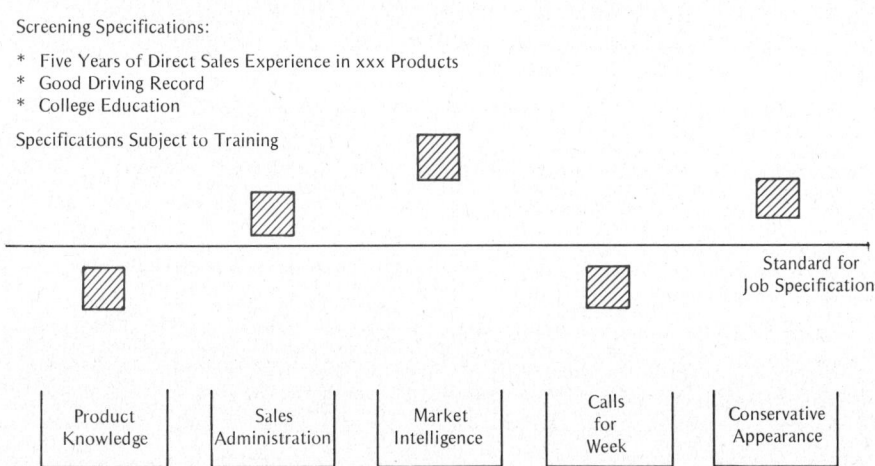

Screening Specifications:
* Five Years of Direct Sales Experience in xxx Products
* Good Driving Record
* College Education

may be permitted only five rejects per hour. These numerical standards are easy to establish and adjust with experience. However, it is much more difficult to set standards for the many positions that do not have definite quotas but involve intangibles, such as leadership and motivation.

Accordingly, **management by objectives** sets goals for managers and measures performance against the goals rather than the means used to achieve them. A goal might be the completion of a thorough report in a crash period of 30 days. The timing can be measured precisely, but a rating of the quality of the report will be based on the judgment of the receiver. Another example might be the goal of trouble-free operations at a plant. Productivity or an event such as a strike or a breakdown in supply lines can be identified, but evaluation of morale based on good leadership and methods of motivating employees involves judgment by an individual.

Table 12-2 (see p. 308) shows a method commonly used by individual managers to rate the performance of their workers. It includes job specifications to identify problem areas that may be corrected by training. The primary objective of rating methods is to gauge actual performance. The categories selected will vary by job and manager. The personnel department can play an important role in initially setting up the system.

Usually, evaluation is much more informal, and rating methods are ignored. People are rated on the basis of impressions gained over varying periods of time, plus a few memos in their personal files about being on a project study team or completing a course. This approach is less costly and may be adequate in small firms. As the size of a company increases, however, it is much more efficient and fairer to all parties to use a formal system of evaluation.

Parts of a Typical Business

Table 12-2. *Simplified Performance Rating System*

RATING PERFORMANCE

POTENTIAL	ACTUAL
1. Training compared to job specifications.	Supervision required to achieve goals.
2. Experience in similar work.	Mistakes or errors in judgment.
3. Results of testing nad interviews.	Creative contributions and problem solving.
4. Maturity, bearing, appearance, and personality.	Willingness to work, attitude, and reaction to others.
5. Capacity to replace the supervisor.	Rating by supervisor.

Ratings: 0–Deficient   2–Average
               1–Below Average   3–Above Average
                          4–Superior

Sample:	1	2	3	4	5	Total
Potential	2	3	2	3	2	12
Actual	2	2	2	1.5	1.5	9

Making Adjustments

If the company knows what it wants, and the employee knows and agrees with what is expected from training and development, the program gets off to a good start. However, most programs are for groups of employees, and effectiveness could vary widely within a group. Therefore, check points are needed at various intervals to determine if changes should be made to help individuals. Even in programs tailored to an individual, often adjustments are necessary to achieve a goal. For example, a computer programming course for an accountant may be accelerated because of a high-priority project assignment.

Communication is critically important to success. The **three-way flow** of communication is illustrated by the simplicity of Figure 12-4. The individual(s), the trainer/developer, and the manager for whom the trainee works must be able to discuss problems. This takes some prodding by the personnel department because often individuals are reluctant to admit they are not absorbing the material being taught.

Requirements for Successful Programs

Top management support is essential. If key executives are only tolerant or even openly critical of training and development programs and evaluation

Figure 12-4. *Three-way Flow of Communication*

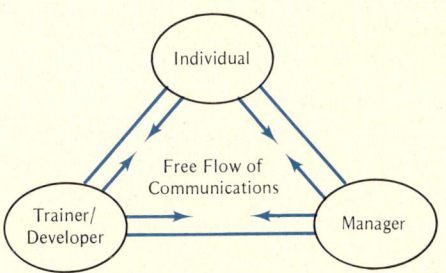

methods, effectiveness will soon decrease. The attitude that the company is training employees for competitors or is spending money on programs that have no tangible benefits will have the same result. It is interesting that in many companies managers see training and development as constructive for subordinates, but not for themselves.

Program direction is needed for success, as it is in any other job. A demanding level of "people," technical, and optimizing skills is required. The personnel department manager must assemble not only the best programs, but also the best means of program acceptance and implementation. The manager might choose, for example, a committee approach, in order to have participation of other departments in the design. This approach might be necessary to gain and maintain departmental support. Regardless of the techniques used part of the manager's responsibilities will be to measure programs against standards and communicate progress to top management.

Balance in the programs prevents the accusation that their purpose is for only a selected group within the company. Sometimes the personnel department manager has difficult decisions about the best use of the budget and limited resources. Each program must be successfully completed, yet there must be a sufficient number of programs to involve all of the employees for whom training and development was intended.

LABOR RELATIONS

Most companies have a section or department that deals with the unions recognized and certified as the bargaining agents for employees. The primary responsibilities of this department are: (1) concluding contract negotiations with the unions; (2) administering details of the contracts; and (3) handling grievances initiated by the unions. In small companies the responsibility for labor relations is often assumed by the chief executive because of the need not to have excessive contract concessions, unnecessary problems from grievances, and similar difficulties. Control of labor relations is particularly desirable if the firm does not yet have a union and wants to remain unorganized.

The company can make decisions about unionized employees without consulting the union in only a few areas. Union influence on decision making has broadened in many instances to plant location, subcontracting of work, introduction of new equipment and methods, and scheduling of operations. Areas of potential conflict motivate management to avoid having labor unions whenever possible and, if company employees are organized, to be cautious about information released to the unions.

On the other hand, a good manager of labor relations, supported by other executives of a company, can establish very satisfactory working relations with a union. By minimizing the effects of personality conflicts and building trust through good communications, serious problems can be lessened or eliminated. Misunderstandings may occur in nearly all instances. Their degree of impact on the company will depend on the individual's ability to discuss, persuade, and compromise.

Union Organization at the Company Level

Local unions have officers and committees similar to those given in Figure 2-9 for the national union but with less elaborate staff support. The union also has full-time employees who are responsible for several firms, usually grouped by related industry or activity. These union employees are called **district representatives** and usually negotiate contracts, handle major grievances, deal with company decisions affecting membership, and act as the focal point for all communications with the union. In important negotiations, the representative's union boss at national headquarters might participate in the bargaining, or even act as the chief negotiator.

District representatives have administrative responsibilities to keep their portions of the union local functional and efficient. These may include operating an office separate from the local's headquarters, maintaining a staff, collecting dues, conducting membership drives, arranging social activities, and holding meetings of members. In addition, they must inform headquarters of developments and draw on its services and experience when appropriate.

Stewards represent union members within the firm in which they work. Sometimes they are elected and are not paid for their efforts. Usually companies allow them "release time" to receive, submit, and discuss grievances on behalf of union members. Occasionally, the scope of this position is sufficient to justify a salary by the local. The steward's attitude and behavior will significantly affect the relations between the company and union in a plant.

Another point about unions is their value to many employees for its opportunities to participate in the activities of an organization. The satisfaction is similar to volunteering for jobs in a social or sport club.

Collective Bargaining

Collective bargaining is the process by which the employer and the union negotiate conditions under which the members of the bargaining unit are to be employed. The **bargaining unit** is the group of employees acknowledged by the employer as the employee organization for the purpose of bargaining. The resulting **contract** covers an agreed period, such as two or three years.

Each side prepares for the negotiations by developing information on salaries, wages, and benefits actually paid to each job, comparable details for competitors and neighboring firms, and increases in the regional cost of living. Careful analysis is made of gains in average output of each worker.

This research is followed by deciding on a strategy. Management wishes to minimize the gains of the union. The union desires to improve significantly the package received by the worker. Each side identifies points that are less important and can be conceded for more crucial issues.

Written proposals, counterproposals, verbal concessions, refusals, and a gradual narrowing of differences are all part of the bargaining process. Usually, sufficient concessions can be obtained from both sides to reach an agreement. Sometimes an arbitrator is needed to avoid a strike. In some cases, however, negotiators cannot reach agreement within minimum terms. This leads to strikes, picket lines, boycotts (calls for all union members to stop buying the company's product and to influence others to stop buying), and bargaining under pressure.

The union tries to prepare for financial pressure on its members by creating a strike fund to provide some income for strikers. The company tries to build inventories in advance of bargaining so that sales may continue for a limited period. It also arranges its financial position in the best possible way to strengthen its bargaining position. Eventually, the issues are resolved, and a contract is signed.

Table 12-3 gives standard sections in a contract and identifies points that are part of the contract discussions (see p. 312).

Grievances

When employees become dissatisfied with working conditions, regardless of the validity of the complaints, the complaint is termed a **grievance.** The basis of dissatisfaction can be either a contract with omissions or loosely worded provisions, or job-related problems usually caused by changes in conditions after the contract was signed. In addition, personal problems, such as alcoholism, can be the basis of a grievance.

Parts of a Typical Business

Table 12-3. *Sections of a Typical Labor Agreement*

1. Purpose, intent, scope, and period covered
2. Responsibilities of the parties
3. Union membership
4. Grievances and arbitration
5. Suspensions and discharge cases
6. Savings, vacation, pension, and other plans
7. Rates of pay and hours of work
8. Overtime, holidays, and vacations
9. Seniority
10. Safety and health
11. Severance procedures and allowances
12. Prior agreements

The **grievance procedure** is outlined in the contract with the union. It usually contains the following requirements:

1. No reprisal is threatened or implemented.
2. Employees understand each possible stage of the system.
3. All parties wish to solve the problem.
4. Employees have adequate assistance in preparing their case.

In many situations, employees will bring the problem to the steward to be certain there is a valid complaint. The business representative might even be consulted when there is doubt about coverage under the contract or when the matter is serious.

Usually, employees will take grievances to their supervisor, expressed either orally or in writing. This stage is important in keeping small issues from becoming serious ones. Supervisors must be aware of the importance of handling a grievance tactfully. Many times, the complaint can be solved immediately. Perhaps it was only a misunderstanding of instructions. However, sometimes the supervisor does not have the authority to make necessary changes.

When a grievance is not easily resolvable, it goes through the following stages:

1. A written statement of the problem is submitted to the supervisor, and this is forwarded to the foreman.
2. The steward and employee meet with the foreman. About 60% of grievances not resolved at the supervisor level are settled at this second step.
3. To handle grievances still unsettled, a group composed of stewards meets with representatives of the labor relations section to reach an agreement. Roughly 90% of grievances are resolved at the conclusion of the third step.

4. The remaining grievances are negotiated in a meeting between local union officers and the plant manager or head of operations. In some situations an international officer of the union will meet a senior officer of the company before going to Step 5.
5. Finally, an arbitrator who is officially independent of both management and the union is asked to resolve the matter. This is a binding judgment under most contracts.

The accumulation of unresolved grievances has become a serious issue in some industries. It takes time to handle each complaint not solved at the supervisor level, and the business must continue. This means that employees may spend weeks working under conditions causing dissatisfaction—an unhealthy situation. Such problems have forced the grievance procedure to be accelerated by means of approaches ranging from bypassing steps to round-the-clock meetings that must reach a compromise.

Employee Discipline

Company supervisors of the workforce must find a balance between loss of control through ignoring employee infractions and complete domination by applying disciplinary measures for each problem. "Fair treatment" is the guideline taught in training, and good judgment is developed through case situations where the supervisor is required to make quick decisions on what to do. Training emphasizes the need for facts and documented evidence for each case. Observations unsupported by written proof or witnesses have caused problems for the company when the union has objected to penalties given to a union member.

The union sees protecting its members from disciplinary action as one of its most important responsibilities. Unless management builds a good working relationship with the union, many decisions to discipline a worker will lead to grievances.

Rules for the job, the factory, and the office should be posted and clearly stated. Besides being reasonable, they should not infringe on the employee's private life. When a rule is broken, the objective of action taken should be the prevention of reoccurrence of the situation rather than the punishment of the individual. Also, there should be uniformity in the discipline for a given problem.

Discharging a Worker

A serious offense could cause management to discharge an employee. Because of protection by labor union contracts, it is easier to fire a manager than a union member. This has removed the authority to dismiss a worker from the direct supervisor in unionized firms and has placed it in the hands of specialists in labor relations. The supervisor can take other kinds of action, but he can only recommend firing an employee.

One source of problems is the worker who agitates on behalf of some specific cause. It may or may not be a union cause. Under the Taft–Hartley Act of 1947, it is illegal to discharge an employee because of union activities. Some troublemakers with political and other motivations, such as social issues, have used this law to advance their causes.

Another restriction on dismissals is the Civil Rights Act of 1964. Workers who can prove discrimination on the basis of race, religion, color, and/or sex have a right to reinstatement with damages. Because this potentially includes many employees, supervisors have to be particularly careful about documenting the basis for firing someone who could counter with a claim of discrimination. The trend toward greater restrictions on an employer's right to discharge a worker adds to job security and can be constructive for the economy. However, concern about this security being abused, leading to a decline in productivity, has encouraged management to automate wherever possible. Another approach has been to include unions in aspects of planning so that they may better understand problems facing the company before bargaining for a contract or bringing a grievance.

PERSONNEL ADMINISTRATION

Records must be kept on: (1) each employee; (2) vacations, holidays, and other factors affecting employee availability for scheduled work; (3) training and development programs; (4) labor relations matters; (5) insurance, education, and other company-paid benefits; and (6) miscellaneous personnel matters, such as layoffs, cases of terminated employees, and transfers.

In addition to maintaining these records, alerting management about matters in each category that might affect the business, and carrying out activities previously discussed in this chapter, the personnel department handles other responsibilities that are important to the business:

1. Wage and salary administration.
2. Systems for ranking jobs.
3. Incentive systems.
4. Benefits package.

Wage and Salary Administration

The objective is to pay employees an amount that is proper in relation to amounts received by other employees, considering level of responsibilities, skills required, and any special factors such as remote work locations, danger, or unusual hours. When the amount is calculated on a weekly, biweekly, or monthly basis, it is called a **salary**. This is the usual method of paying management and administrative employees.

The amount is called **wages** when it is calculated on an hourly or daily basis or on units produced. The work is referred to as *daywork*. **Blue-collar workers** usually receive this type of income.

General Factors Affecting Salaries and Wages

Worth of the job is the principal factor in establishing the **base pay** for employees. A manager responsible for many employees will receive much more than a worker with a skill but no supervisory duties. The ranking of jobs from top to bottom makes use of several techniques discussed in the next section such as the point system, factor comparison system, and job grade and ranking system.

The *cost of living* has become the prime factor in adjusting wages. Recently, inflation has forced increases so that people can maintain their standard of living. However, cost of living has always been a major factor for management. A transfer to New York City from a medium-sized city requires a 35 to 50% increase in pay to stay even. Taxes, commuting, schools, and other expenses make this type of adjustment necessary in lesser amounts for other transfers.

The *condition of the marketplace* for specific skills, education, and experience will affect the salaries and wages. For example, 7 doctoral and 82 master's degree holders in engineering were among the nearly 800 people who applied for 3 gas meter reading jobs in Los Angeles in 1970. This situation resulted from cutbacks in defense and aerospace spending by the federal government. Oversupply often affects workers in the bargaining process with management. On the other hand, when demand exceeds supply, salaries and wages increase more rapidly at this level than in other types of jobs.

Prevailing salaries and wages influence the amount paid by an employer. Banks are known for paying less than other businesses. The southeastern part of the country pays less, job for job. Employment in some communities pays more than do comparable jobs in other communities, and there is a real gain in standard of living.

Ability to pay has been a major factor in bargaining for some labor union contracts. Industries facing foreign competition have demonstrated that certain wage demands by the union would hurt the business and result in layoffs. The opposite situation occurs when a firm has been declaring large profits.

Collective bargaining can lead to unionized firms paying more than non-union companies. Also, even within unionized firms, negotiating expertise can have a major effect on what a company pays.

Productivity is an important factor. Mechanization increases output per worker. It depends on investment of capital for new equipment and does not relate to worker effort. Some employees have, however, demonstrated consistent capability of producing or selling more than competitors or other company divisions. Such performance is rewarded with increases in both base pay and incentive income.

Systems for Ranking Jobs

In Figure 2-1, an organizational chart was given with an indication of job ranking from the chief executive officer to a shop worker. In Chapter Six, fundamentals for organizing a company were discussed. Here, the details on how to rank jobs in the organization are summarized. In many companies, management arbitrarily establishes rank with no system. However, unions have played a role in forcing companies to adopt a formal approach to setting wage scales by job type.

THE POINT SYSTEM This system was conceived initially by Western Electric and has been applied successfully by several major corporations as well as smaller companies. First, ranking factors applicable to all jobs are selected by the personnel department, in cooperation with other departments. An example is given in Table 12-4. Then, a *manual* is set up, with a form for each job to be ranked. In some cases, the manual includes executive management.

Every job is studied, and a degree is established for nine factors (there could be more or less factors in a given industry and company). Points are established for each degree, and this gives the total. The totals per degree are

Table 12-4. *Typical Factors and Degrees for a Point System*

	1ST DEGREE	2ND DEGREE	3RD DEGREE	4TH DEGREE
Skill Required 1. Education and Training 2. Experience 3. Initiative and Creativity				
Type of Effort 4. Mental 5. Physical Labor or Visual Readings				
Responsibility 6. Employees Supervised: Number, Skills and Safety 7. Equipment, Process, Materials and Product				
Job Conditions 8. Conditions of Job 9. Hazards and Hardships				

Progressively higher points are assigned from 1st degree to 4th degree—the higher the number, the more important the job.

compared for ranking, and the rating for salaries, wages, benefits, and career paths through a firm.

FACTOR COMPARISON SYSTEM   Ranking factors are selected in a manner similar to the point system. However, instead of assigning points to the factors and rating each job independently, the factors for jobs to be rated are compared with the specifications of key jobs such as auditor, sales representative, or foreman. The number of key jobs depends on the business, and careful attention must be given to the ranking of these standards for other jobs. Once a salary or wage is set for the standard, other jobs in the company can be scaled accordingly.

JOB GRADE AND RANKING SYSTEM   Salary and wage classes are predetermined and are assigned a designation such as S-1 for lowest ranking jobs in the shop or A-4 for a medium ranking job in office administration. When the specifications are established for each grade, individual jobs are studied and given a rating. This also defines the salary or wage to be paid. The Federal Civil Service is an example of this system.

All of the systems allow for a range in a given classification. For example, a job with xxx points, a rating under the factor comparison system, or a x-4 rating under the job grade system will have a starting amount such as $100 per week and an allowance for increases within the rank to a ceiling of $140.

Incentive Systems

The objective of a company in giving more pay for greater output per person is a lower average cost for each product sold and more products to sell. Quality becomes a control factor because the increased expense of rejects, scrappage, and other types of costs under an incentive system offset the reason for having the system.

Other problems related to incentives include: (1) selection of the standard above which the incentive is paid; (2) voluminous record keeping; and (3) breakdowns or other stoppages in the flow of materials, components, parts, and products, beyond the control of the employee striving for incentive pay.

Some examples of incentive systems are given here:

1. *Group bonuses.* Work in many departments cannot be measured directly by specifics such as number of sales or unit cost, nor can it be identified with an individual. Therefore, an incentive can be created for a group of employees based on a goal set at the beginning of the year. Sometimes the previous year acts as a standard. Performance that exceeds the standard results in a bonus shared with the group. Almost every company that has such a system calculates the amount and distribution in a different way. Often the same percentage is used for everyone in the system, for example, 10% of each salary in the group as a bonus.

2. *Piecework.* A standard based on average performance is established for jobs that can be measured in output per time period. This serves as the basis for calculating a pay rate per unit, and everyone is paid this amount. Manage-

ment has to be very careful about fixing the rate per unit produced because a miscalculation can be very costly for the company and the worker will regard a change as unfair.

3. *Production bonus systems.* Instead of using the standard as a basis for a rate per unit, it is used to establish expected output for a given time period. If a worker or group of workers exceeds the standard, a bonus is paid. Sometimes the expected output is higher than average performance but possible to attain. Labor unions play a role in setting the terms of the incentive.

4. *Sales incentives.* Salespersons have worked on a "commission only" basis for centuries. This means the more that is sold, the greater the individual's income. However, this concept is not always the best approach because, from the company's viewpoint, customer service is sometimes neglected or, from the sales representatives' viewpoint, factors beyond their control limit capacity to sell. The trend is to pay a salary plus an incentive designed for a specific firm. Variations on increased income include gifts for the spouse, trips, "sales representative-of-the-year" awards, and similar rewards.

5. *Executive programs.* The Tax Reform Act of 1969 limits the possibilities for top management incentives that are not taxed to the point of losing their purpose. A high tax bracket lessens the benefit from bonuses, stock options, and stock purchase plans. Benefits, such as company-paid insurance, have supplemented the pay package in recent years, but they are not based on performance. Numerous plans have been designed in the 1970s which are tailored to the needs of individual executives and involve tax-paid incentives.

The idea that incentives are a basis to increase profits for shareholders is also changing. **Profit sharing** with workers in the lowest classifications occurs in some companies to reward their contributions. This has been combined with stock purchase plans that involve matching funds from the company, deferred payment by the employee, and payroll deductions. The concept is that performance will improve beyond what is paid in bonuses if all employees feel they are sharing in the profits.

Benefits Package

Most employees expect a benefits package in addition to their income. The principal components are described here.

UNEMPLOYMENT BENEFITS Under the Social Security program, the federal government provides funds for people who have lost their jobs. States also have programs that usually require the individual to make weekly contact with the state unemployment office to locate suitable employment. In addition to taxes paid by companies to support these programs, some firms are offering *supplemental benefits* during a layoff (not in cases of dismissal). This increases a person's income to the point where the individual can avoid debt and hardships from most work stoppages.

DISABILITY BENEFITS   Workmen's compensation is generally financed by employers and administered by the state. This aspect of protection for an employee is so common that only in rare situations are these benefits not provided.

RETIREMENT BENEFITS   Companies have greatly improved the pension benefits for their employees. The fund is administered by professionals, and the employer often matches the contribution by the employee. It is sometimes used as a means of reducing turnover by withholding the company's portion until the employee has been with the company for a certain period, such as three or five years. After each time segment, the company's contribution becomes part of the employee's equity.

HEALTH INSURANCE   A group plan reduces the rate an individual pays for medical insurance, and the benefits at the lower rate are generally greater. Many companies pay for some or all of the insurance.

LIFE AND ACCIDENT INSURANCE   Term and accident insurance are frequently paid by the employer. The amount of coverage usually depends on a base salary or estimated annual income per job multiplied by a factor such as two. For example, a person earning $15,000 per year would have $30,000 life insurance, with other provisions for accidents.

LOANS   Credit unions are set up by companies to provide employees with a source of funds that is less costly or might not be available from commercial banks. In addition, a few companies lend moderate sums directly to employees. Others provide mortgage assistance through either guarantees to lenders or cash to the employee. Usually, the latter situation occurs only in special situations such as when the company has established operations in unusual locations. Many companies guarantee a sales price for homes of employees being transferred. This improves attitudes towards moving.

COUNSELING SERVICES   Companies are providing everything from marriage counseling to legal advice. Programs for alcoholism are common. Assistance to employees is being provided with conscious attempts not to create an image of **paternalism** (gifts to gain the goodwill of employees or their dependence on the company as compared to earned benefits and services).

RECREATIONAL SERVICES   Several firms have organized athletic programs, including instruction as well as leagues, in a variety of sports. Social programs in dancing, family picnics, and parties, such as banquets and cocktail hours, are common. Some corporations employ specialists to build a feeling of loyalty for the firm through this approach.

MISCELLANEOUS SERVICES   Purchasing, transportation, and child care facilities are offered by many large companies. A few provide housing, although these are usually in remote locations, such as foreign countries. Food service is also provided in such locations and in a few areas of the United States.

Evaluation of the Personnel Function

This chapter began with the fact that many companies have dispersed the personnel function to several departments with no central coordinator. Others have established a formal department that handles all of the activities described in this chapter. A careful analysis is needed to assure management that the objectives of the personnel function are being achieved under any approach to organization.

A checklist for principal activities of the personnel function is given in Table 12-5. By determining the present status and estimated future outlook in each category, a company can appraise performance.

CAREERS AND JOBS

Some job positions in personnel functions are given in Table 12-6. The titles may change with the size of a company. For example, a college graduate with no experience might head a one-man department in a small business and be called manager of personnel. In a larger corporation with an established department, a person with the same background might start as job analyst or employment interviewer. Usually, the importance of labor relations requires special training in college, and perhaps within the company, for a career in personnel.

Advancement opportunities in personnel work are favorable because of the trends toward social responsibility and greater concern about the overall welfare of employees. In addition, government legislation is increasing the administrative burden of the personnel department. The Occupational Safety and Health Act (OSHA) of 1973 is an example of constructive regulations that require continuous attention with provisions for fines and shutdowns.

Table 12-5. *Checklist for Evaluation of the Personnel Function*

1. Absenteeism	9. Payroll Comparisons
2. Accidents	10. Personnel Record Status
3. Arbitration Awards	11. Productivity Performance
4. Employee Turnover Rate	12. Recruitment Costs
5. Employee Transfer Frequency	13. Scrap Loss Record*
6. Employee Use of Services Offered	14. Suggestion Program
7. Grievance Record	15. Training Costs
8. Health Record	16. Tests Before and After Training

* Records are kept on losses of materials and components. Improvement should result from an effective employment process and development and training programs.

Table 12-6. *Jobs in the Personnel Function*

Manager / Director / Vice President } PERSONNEL	
Manager / Director / Vice President } **Labor Relations** Negotiator Grievance Analyst Contract Administrator Research Analyst	Supervisor / Manager / Director } **Employment** Job Analyst Interviewer References Analyst Organization Planner
Supervisor / Manager / Director } **Training and Development** Supervisor of Executive Development Programs Testing Analyst Supervisor of Training Design	Supervisor / Manager / Director } **Employee Benefits or Personnel Services** Employee Counselor Insurance Administrator Pension Program Administrator Recreational Programs Administrator
Supervisor / Manager / Director } **Safety and Health** Plant Safety Supervisor Nurse OSHA* Administrator	Supervisor / Manager / Director } **Employee Records** Personal Files Administrator System and Procedures Analyst Wage and Salary Administrator

* OSHA is the abbreviated name for the safety and health programs resulting from the Occupational Safety and Health Act of 1973.

Specialization will help you to find a better job and to rise quickly within the department. A generalist in business administration will find initial advancement more difficult because of competition with people who have had better training. Even those who specialize in fields such as labor relations or wage and salary administration should study psychology and sociology.

Because of the competition for some personnel jobs that do not require special education, you might have to consider taking other assignments with a company and waiting for an opportunity to transfer. This approach establishes your reputation and facilitates getting the position you want.

CHAPTER SUMMARY

The many functions of personnel are often centralized in one department, but occasionally they are dispersed throughout the organization. This dispersion has occurred because many managers take personal charge of employees reporting to them, and they can hire outside personnel services for special help. Also, there is a real need for some operating departments to have specialists to deal with problems reoccurring daily.

Employment is a critically important function because it is the means through which a company obtains needed talent. The objective is to employ the best skilled workers, specialists, and managers available. This requires an efficient approach to: job design, search for candidates, screening through interviews, testing, and reference checks, and selection of the employee. If management hires personnel without the assistance of available professionals, there is a high probability of employing less than the best available candidate.

Training concentrates on the "how-to" aspects of a job. Some companies do not offer training beyond the basics of a job. Other companies feel that efficiency is increased and the number of serious grievances decreased by more comprehensive training programs. Development involves transfers and promotions of talented employees in a planned manner to make maximum use of their training, experience, and general competence.

Labor relations deals with concluding a contract with labor unions, administering the details of the contract, and handling grievances initiated by employees covered by the contract. The unions have a full-time district representative, who coordinates union affairs with company officials. Within the company, an employee acts as steward for groups of jobs. As steward, the individual becomes involved with settlement of grievances. Collective bargaining is the way in which agreement on a union contract is reached. It involves considerable preparation and strategies on both sides. The building of good relations between management and the union depends on the flow of communications, but this is often prevented by policy and personality conflicts.

Personnel administration covers a broad field of activities from record keeping to the highly sensitive issue of wages and salaries. Several factors affect employee pay, and systems have been devised to establish orderly and fair scales for wages and salaries. Incentive systems are also designed to increase output per worker and to give employees a share in the results. The benefits package has become an important means of attracting and retaining employees.

A checklist for performance of the personnel functions is given in Table 12-5. It is important for management to review the current status of each item on the list and to make comparisons with the past performances of their own company, of industry averages, and of the competition, if available, in order to assess the progress toward objectives.

The opportunities in personnel are expanding because of increasing consciousness about the welfare of workers and the passage of government legislation intended to accelerate social progress. Specialization in fields such as labor relations or wage and salary administration is often a better approach to personnel jobs than a general degree in business administration.

PROVOCATIVE STATEMENT

Fire the Whole Personnel Department

1 "Unless your company is too large (in which case break it up into autonomous parts), have a one-girl people department (not a personnel department). Records can be kept in the payroll section of the accounting department and your one-girl people department (she answers her own phone and does her own typing) acts as personnel (sorry—people) assistant to anybody who is recruiting[1]. She lines up applicants, checks references, and keeps your pay ranges competitive by checking other companies.

On the subject of pay ranges, I've long held the conviction that it's much less expensive to recruit from the top of the barrel by paying top wages. Yet many big personnel departments in insurance companies, banks, and the like, consciously recruit from the lower half of the barrel to "save money." If they only realized what they were doing to themselves.

The trouble with personnel experts is that they use gimmicks borrowed from manufacturing: inventories, replacement charts, recruiting, selecting, indoctrinating, and training machinery, job rotation, and appraisal programs. And this manufacturing of men is about as effective as Dr. Frankenstein was. As McGregor points out, the sounder approach is agricultural. Provide the climate and proper nourishment and let the people grow themselves. They'll amaze you."

Robert Townsend,
Up the Organization,
New York: Alfred A. Knopf, Inc., 1970,
pp. 126-127.

[1] The important thing about hiring is the chemistry or the vibrations between boss and candidate: good, bad, or not there at all.

REVIEW QUESTIONS

1. Explain why there are several approaches to handling the personnel function in an organization. If you became a manager, how would you handle it?
2. What can a firm do to improve the chances that it is hiring the best possible person for a job opening?
3. Discuss how federal legislation in the 1960s changed the employment process.
4. Explain the difference between training and development.
5. Outline the general method used to settle disputes between a union member and the company. Contrast this procedure with one that might be used at a company with no unions.
6. What factors affect the amount of salaries and wages paid to employees?
7. Do you think job rotation is a good method for development? Identify the pros and cons.
8. Explain the role of the steward in union/company affairs. How does the steward relate to the business representative?

Chapter Outline

The Purpose and Need for Accounting
  What Is Accounting?
  Who Uses Accounting?
    Internal Users
    External Users

Accounting Fundamentals
  The Accounting Equation
  The Accounts
    Assets
    Liabilities
    Equity

Financial Accounting
  Generally Accepted Accounting Principles
  Financial Statements
    The Balance Sheet
    The Income Statement
  Analyzing the Financial Statements
    Some Important Financial Ratios
    Other Analyses
  The Role of the CPA

Management Accounting
  Forecasting Financial Performance
    Budgeting
    Break-even Analysis

Cost Accounting and Control Systems
  Cost Accounting
  The Need for Evaluation

The Controller and Staff
  General Accounting
  Management Accounting
  Taxes
  Internal Auditing
  Data Processing

Career Opportunities in Accounting
  Public Accounting
  Industrial Accounting
  Government Accounting
  Rewards

Chapter Summary

Provocative Statement 1:
  Financial Reporting: The Executive's Liability

Provocative Statement 2:
  The Credibility Gap in Financial Reports

Key Terms

Accounting
Transaction
Bookkeeping
Current assets
Fixed assets
Current liabilities
Long-term liabilities
Stockholders' equity
Balance sheet
Income statement

Depreciation
Ratio analysis
Pro forma statements
Auditing
Budget
Break-even analysis
General accounting
Internal auditing
Data processing

Accounting and Control Systems

"The conduct of the American corporation is being challenged by its adversaries, and at least questioned by its friends. One might then expect the implementation of procedures for assuring the corporation and its management the highest degree of visibility and accountability—so that all who are entitled to know will know, and thereby be able to make rational decisions. This expectation notwithstanding, the situation is very much otherwise."
—Certified Public Accountant and University Professor

13

Any person interested in pursuing a career in business should have a strong background in accounting. The need is evident whether one is interested primarily in marketing, production, personnel, finance, or any other aspect of business. Accounting is often called the language of business, and how can one expect to excel at a job if one does not have the required vocabulary for it? This chapter explores the many areas of accounting, including the purpose and need for accounting, accounting fundamentals, financial accounting, management accounting, the controller and staff, and career opportunities in accounting.

THE PURPOSE AND NEED FOR ACCOUNTING

Defining accounting as simply the language of business is much too vague to be of much use to us. In this section, a more detailed definition of accounting will be developed. In addition, the many uses and users of accounting information will be discussed.

What Is Accounting?

One accounting expert defines accounting as "the body of knowledge and functions concerning the systematic originating, authenticating, recording, classifying, processing, summarizing, analyzing, interpreting, and supplying of dependable and significant information covering transactions and events which are, in part at least, of a financial character, required for the management and operation of an entity and for the reports that have to be submitted thereon to meet fiduciary and other responsibilities." [1] This definition can be summarized to state that the purpose of accounting is to provide information that is useful to decision makers. But since it provides a useful point for departure, we shall spend a little more time examining this definition.

Working mostly from historical information, decision makers weigh alternative courses of action that will affect the future of their firms. The accountant is responsible for knowing what information the decision maker needs, gathering that information, putting it into understandable form, and communicating it to the proper people. This accounting/decision-making process is shown in Figure 13-1. An economic event occurs. Suppose it is the sale of one unit of a company's product. The accountant must decide if this event is important enough to be recorded.

If the event is important, the accountant must measure the extent of the economic change. In this example, it would be the revenue brought in from the sale of one unit of product. Executives in the company are concerned with how many units of product are being sold and at what price. Thus, at periodic intervals, perhaps weekly or monthly, the accountant summarizes how many units of product have been sold and prepares a report for management. What does management do with this report? Perhaps sales are less than expected. A price reduction may be in order to encourage consumers to purchase more of the product. On the other hand, sales may be more than expected. Management must then schedule overtime on the production line to meet this increased demand. In any event, the reports prepared by the accountant help management to motivate, plan, and control. That is, based on the information in the report, management makes decisions that will produce future economic change.

How does the accounting/decision-making process fit in with the definition of accounting given earlier? The attachment of the word "systematic" to the accounting functions and the words "dependable" and "significant" to the information emphasizes the need for planning and control and the use of accounting on the *exception-basis*; that is, only relevant events are noted and acted upon. The phrases "required for the management and operation" and "reports . . . to meet fiduciary and other responsibilities" indicate that accounting presents information to decision makers, both internal and external.

Who Uses Accounting?

Two main groups are interested in the reports prepared by accountants—those inside the company and those outside the company.

[1] Paul Grady, *Inventory of Generally Accepted Accounting Principles for Business Enterprises*, New York: American Institute of Certified Public Accountants, Inc., 1965, p. 4.

Figure 13-1. *The Accounting/Decision-Making Process*

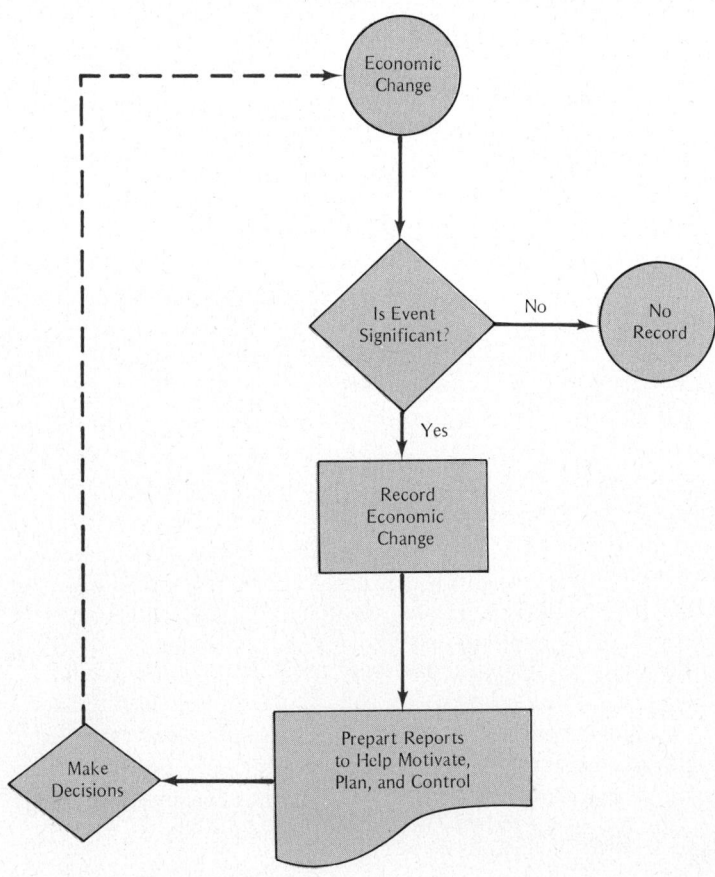

Internal Users

Internal users include the management and directors of the firm. Management uses accounting information in such diverse areas as (1) determining the minimal sales price for a product so that each unit sold will at least cover its costs of production and (2) deciding whether to expand operations by renovating existing plant and equipment or by building an entirely new plant. Management can also use accounting information to determine in which state the company should incorporate so as to minimize money to be paid for taxes. Furthermore, management and the board of directors use accounting reports to evaluate the performance of the firm.

External Users

Creditors of the company—both current and prospective—use accounting information to determine whether they should lend money or other items to the firm. A creditor may feel that a company already has too much debt outstanding and that it would be too risky to extend it any more. That is, if a company has too much debt, it may not be able to generate enough cash to pay off its bills as they become due.

Investors have a choice of many companies in which to put their money. Current and prospective shareholders in a corporation use accounting information to evaluate the investment merits of the firm relative to other investment possibilities. If a company's financial performance is not up to investor expectations, investors will place their money elsewhere.

The government is also highly dependent on accounting data to determine such things as the amount of taxes a company owes and the rates a utility should be allowed to charge its customers for electricity. Accounting helps determine the amount of income to be taxed and the applicable tax rate for that income. Regulatory authorities, such as the Interstate Commerce Commission, rely on accounting data to determine whether customers are being overcharged for rail and truck services or whether the industries under regulation deserve higher usage rates.

ACCOUNTING FUNDAMENTALS

Before reports can be prepared for the ultimate users of accounting information, a framework must be developed for the recording and classifying of economic events. In accounting vocabulary, an economic event is called a **transaction**. The sale of a unit of a company's product for cash is a transaction. The purchase of new plant and equipment with money borrowed from the bank is a transaction.

The Accounting Equation

The *accounting equation* is a convenient means for understanding the recording and classifying of all transactions. It can be stated as follows:

$$ASSETS = LIABILITIES + EQUITY$$

ASSETS are things that the business owns, such as cash in the bank, the furniture in its office, and the machinery used to produce its products. LIABILITIES are debts. They can be money borrowed from the bank or from other lenders or credit extended by a seller for goods purchased. For example, if a business buys some furniture for the office and promises to pay the seller of the furniture at some future date, it has created a liability. EQUITY is the owners' claim to the resources of the firm. Equity can be either (1) the initial money or services the owner has contributed to the firm, (2) any additional money or services contributed since the firm was started, or (3) profits of the firm that the owner has left for reinvestment in the company.

The accounting equation must always be in balance. That is, assets must always equal liabilities plus equity. The reason for this should be apparent. Everything the firm owns must be accounted for. Consider an example.

Suppose a firm is a used car dealership. Its assets consist solely of some cash in the bank, a fleet of used cars, and a car lot. The assets can be valued at $10,000. Who has supplied the resources that have created these assets? Assume that the owner—from personal savings—has contributed $5,000 for the purchase of the firm's assets and that the other $5,000 was borrowed from the bank. Then, in terms of the accounting equation:

ASSETS = LIABILITIES + EQUITY

Cars
Cash   = Bank loan   + Owner's contribution
Lot
$10,000   = $5,000   + $5,000

Now suppose that the dealer sells for $2,000 one car that cost $1,000. Sale of a good or service is called *revenue*. What happens to the accounting equation? Assets first fall by $1,000 since the dealer no longer has the car. However, assets also rise by $2,000, the cash the dealer received from selling the car. Liabilities have not changed, but equity has increased by $1,000, the profit from the sale of the car. That is, the car cost $1,000, the dealer sold it for $2,000, and thus the dealer has a profit of $1,000 on the sale of the car. Let us see if the accounting equation is still in balance.

ASSETS = LIABLITIES + EQUITY

$10,000   = $5,000   + $5,000
+ 2,000 Cash   + 1,000 profit on
   from   sale of car
   car
   sale
− 1,000 In
   value
   of car
   sold
─────   ─────   ─────
$11,000   = $5,000   + $6,000

As should always be the case, the equation balances.

The Accounts

The accounting equation presents an interesting method of understanding how economic events can be recorded in the form of transactions. **Bookkeeping** is the branch of accounting concerned primarily with the recording of transactions. Fortunately, bookkeepers have been able to change the accounting equation into a more workable framework for recording transactions. It is not unusual for a company to have thousands of transactions per month. The accounting equation as presented here would be hard-pressed to record all such transactions. Bookkeepers must make a record of every transaction. Therefore, a system of accounts is used to help make the recording of transactions easier to handle. Rather than record the verbal details of a transaction, the bookkeeper need only record the changes in the affected accounts. In recording, the three major areas to be considered are assets, liabilities, and equity.

Assets

The *major categories of assets* are: (1) current assets; (2) fixed assets; (3) prepaid expenses; and (4) intangibles.

CURRENT ASSETS Assets which in the normal course of business will be turned into cash in the near future are called **current assets**. These usually include: (1) cash; (2) marketable securities; (3) accounts receivable; and (4) inventories.

1. *Cash* is just what you would expect it to be—dollar bills and coin in the cash register and money that is in the checking account at the bank.

2. *Marketable securities* are temporary investments of the company's temporarily idle cash. Suppose the company just received payment of a big contract and does not have to make use of this cash for 90 days. It would be foolish to let this money sit idle when it can be invested at some positive return for the 90-day period. Such an investment would be in marketable securities, a topic which shall be discussed in more detail in the next chapter.

3. Most companies sell their products or services on credit as well as for cash. Sales on credit create *accounts receivable*.

4. If a company could produce and sell its products at the exact same time, there would be no need for *inventories*. However, there are usually delays between when a company receives materials it needs to make its products, the production of its products, and the ultimate sale of its finished product. There are three types of inventories—raw materials, work-in-process, and finished goods. *Raw materials* are used to produce the company's goods. For example, steel, rubber, and glass are some of the raw materials used in the manufacture of automobiles. *Work-in-process* represents goods that are partially completed. An unassembled or unpainted car would be work-in-process for an automobile manufacturer. *Finished goods* are inventory that is ready for sale to the firm's customers. A finished automobile off the assembly line and ready for shipment to a dealer is a finished good for the automobile manufacturer.

FIXED ASSETS **Fixed assets** are items that are not expected to be consumed in the normal course of the firm's business. Fixed assets are often referred to as *property, plant,* and *equipment*. These assets are not intended for sale to the firm's customers but are used over and over again to manufacture, display, store, and transport the firm's product.

PREPAID EXPENSES   A company may pay in advance for a service it wants to receive. For example, it may pay in advance for two years' worth of property insurance. Since the insurance has been paid for but the protection for the insurance is not yet received, the company would record the insurance payments as a prepaid expense. As the insurance coverage is used—that is, as the two years go by—the company would reduce the amount of prepaid expense shown on its records.

INTANGIBLES   Intangibles are assets that have no physical existence, but have substantial value to a company. For example, "Coke" is a trademark of the Coca-Cola Bottling Company. This label is known worldwide. While it is not a tangible item, it is of considerable value to its owners.

Liabilities

As previously noted, liabilities are debts of the firm. They include (1) current liabilities and (2) long-term liabilities.

CURRENT LIABILITIES   **Current liabilities** are debts that are expected to be paid in the normal course of the firm's operating cycle, usually one year. Furthermore, it is often expected that current liabilities will be paid from current assets. The major classes of current liabilities are: (1) accounts payable, (2) notes payable, (3) accrued expenses payable, and (4) federal income taxes payable.

1. *Accounts payable* represent the money the company owes to its regular business creditors from whom it has bought goods. Thus, if a company buys some raw materials and promises to pay for them at a later date, it has created an account payable.

2. A *note payable* arises when a company signs a written note promising to repay a given amount of money at a specified future date. The note is a legally binding obligation.

3. Periodically, the company accountant determines the amount of assets, liabilities, and equities the company has at a specified date. On that date, the company may owe salaries to its employees, fees to attorneys, insurance premiums, and other money, which it has not yet paid. These are *accrued expenses payable*. For example, suppose a company has a monthly payroll of $20,000 and the salaries are paid at the middle of the month. If the accountant determines the amount of liabilities a company has at the end of the month, the company will owe its employees $10,000—salary for the third and fourth week of the month—which it has not yet paid. This expense for salaries is called an *accrual*. Thus, in the example, the company would have had accrued expenses payable of $10,000.

4. The amount of taxes owed by the company to the federal government is called *federal income tax payable*. Since this figure often can be quite substantial, it deserves a separate account in our expanded accounting equation instead of being included under accrued expenses payable.

LONG-TERM LIABILITIES   Long-term liabilities are debts that will not become due in the firm's normal operating cycle, usually one year. Bonds are one example of a long-term debt. A bond may not have to be repaid for ten to thirty years from the date the money was originally borrowed. A more detailed discussion of bonds is found in Chapter Fourteen.

Equity

The types of equity that a firm will have depend to a certain extent on the firm's type of organization—proprietorship, partnership, or corporation.

PROPRIETORSHIP   In a proprietorship, the equity is simply the owner's interest in the business, that is, the amount of money personally invested in the enterprise.

PARTNERSHIP   In a partnership, the equity is called the *partners' capital accounts*. The interest of each partner in the capital accounts is specified in the partnership agreement.

CORPORATION   In the corporation, the equity accounts become very complex. The equity account in the corporation is often called **stockholders' equity**. This account is usually broken down into three categories: (1) capital stock, (2) capital surplus, and (3) retained earnings.

1. *Capital stock* represents shares in the ownership of the firm. These shares, as noted in Chapter Seven, are represented by stock certificates issued by the corporation to its shareholders. A corporation may have more than one type of capital stock.

Preferred stock owners have some preference or *prior right* over other shares as regards dividends or distribution of assets in the case of the firm's liquidation or both. The specific provisions, with respect to any issues of preferred stock, can be obtained from the corporation's charter. For example, suppose a company has a $5 cumulative preferred stock outstanding. Each year, the preferred stockholder is entitled to receive $5 cash in dividends on each share, provided the board of directors decides to declare that a dividend should be paid. The preferred stockholder must receive the dividend before the board can pay any dividend whatsoever to other stockholders; however, the preferred stockholder cannot receive more than the prespecified $5 in dividends from the company. *Cumulative* means that if in any year the dividend is not paid, it accumulates in favor of the preferred stockholders and must be paid to them when available and declared before any dividends are paid to the common stockholders.

Common stockholders are the ultimate owners of the corporation. Common stock has no limits on the amounts of dividends to be paid to it in any one year.

The capital stock account of the corporation is valued by the accountant at the number of shares outstanding multiplied by the *par* or *legal* value per share. For example, if a company sells 100,000 shares of common stock, each share with a par value of $1, for $10 per share, the common stock account would be valued at $100,000.

2. The excess of the amount paid by the shareholders over the par value of each share is called *capital surplus*. Thus, the capital surplus account would be valued at $900,000.

3. *Retained earnings* are profits of the firm that have not been paid out in dividends to the shareholders. These earnings have been retained for reinvestment within the firm. Retained earnings are the major source of money for the future growth of the corporation. Discussion of profits, which are simply the revenues of the firm less its expenses, brings up a whole new set of accounts and further expansion of the accounting equation, a topic we shall defer until later in this chapter.

FINANCIAL ACCOUNTING

The preceding section dealt with the recording of transactions in the context of the accounting equation. Furthermore, there was a discussion of the accounts that provided the detail for the generality of the accounting equation items of assets, liabilities, and equity. We noted in our definition of accounting, however, that summarizing and reporting of information to decision makers was a prime responsibility of the accountant. The preparation of reports of overall company operations is called *financial accounting*. More specifically, financial accounting is concerned with the preparation of reports to users external to the management of the firm, such as stockholders and creditors. The financial accounting framework is presented in Figure 13-2 (see p. 334).

Generally Accepted Accounting Principles

The key product of financial accounting is financial statements. In the preparation of financial statements, the accountant follows six basic standards and assumptions. These standards and assumptions are referred to as *generally accepted accounting principles (GAAP)*.

The first basic tenet of GAAP is that the firm must be viewed as a *separate business entity*. The entity must be clearly defined before the reports are prepared. Only the activities for that entity are reported.

Second, the firm is viewed as a *going concern*. It is assumed that a business will continue to operate for an indefinite period of time into the future sufficient for it to carry out its commitments. Thus, assets of the firm are valued on a going concern basis, not on a value that might be derived should the firm be forced into liquidation.

Third, GAAP assumes that the unit of measurement of asset, liability, and equity values is a *dollar of stable value*. Sales are not reported in units but rather in dollar value. Similarly, the number of bolts or pounds of rubber in inventory

Figure 13-2. *The Financial Accounting Framework*

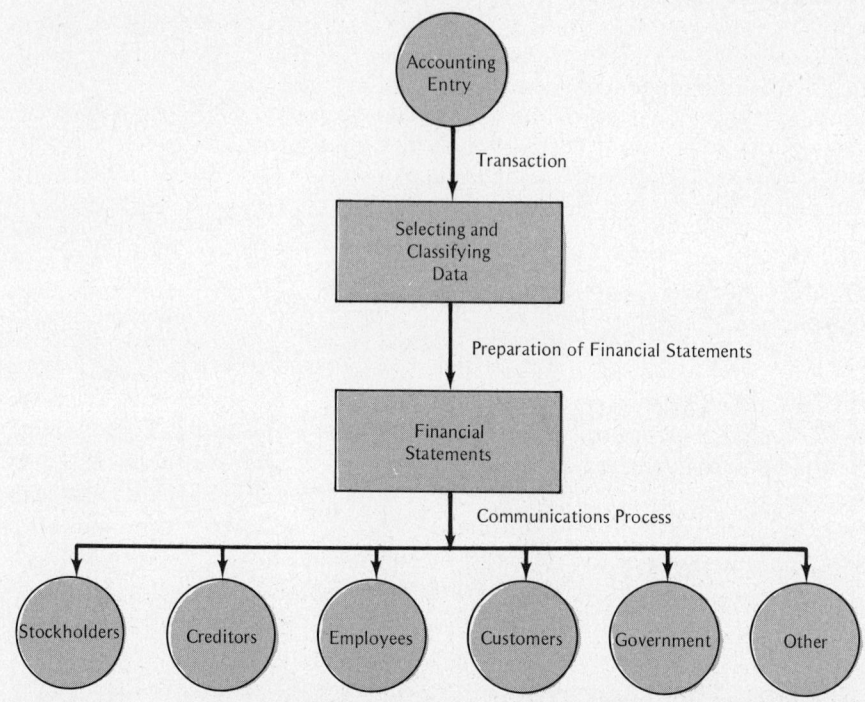

is not reported, but rather the dollar value of these items. No adjustment is made for declines or increases in the purchasing value of the dollar.

Fourth, there are four quality considerations in the preparation of financial statements:

1. *Objectivity.* The valuation of assets and liabilities should be based on objective evidence. An objective value is one that is free from bias and can be verified by an independent party.
2. *Conservatism.* When estimates are made, the accountant should favor understatement of asset values and profits rather than an overstatement.
3. *Consistency.* Once an accounting method is selected, it should be used constantly and not changed from period to period. Thus, an external user of accounting statements should be able to compare the firm's progress over time, believing that changes reported are due to economic events rather than to a change in the accounting method employed.
4. *Uniformity among firms.* All firms within a given industry should use the same accounting method for reporting. Thus, an investor should be able to compare the performance of firms within an industry as reported in the financial statements and believe that the only reason for differences is economic change and not accounting artificiality.

Fifth, the life of the firm is broken up into *accounting periods*. External users need timely and accurate accounting information. To facilitate the transfer of financial information from the firm to the external users, the accounting period is specified as a given interval, often a quarter of a year or, at a miminum, a whole year. Thus, an investor should expect to receive at least annual financial statements from the firm.

Lastly, the principle of *materiality* requires that all significant and relevant facts concerning the financial position and operating results of the company be communicated to the users of the financial statements. This disclosure may either be in the body of the financial statements or in the footnotes to the statements.

Financial Statements

Given that we have a framework for preparing financial statements, what are the commonly reported financial statements? While there may be variations, for our purposes there are only two basic financial statements: the balance sheet and the income statement.

The Balance Sheet

The **balance sheet** or the *statement of financial position*, as it is sometimes called, reports the financial condition of the firm at a point in time. The balance sheet can be viewed as a snapshot picture of the firm: at periodic intervals, the accountant pretends that the firm suddenly stands still and records the accounting values of the firm's assets, liabilities, and equities. As shown in Figure 13-3 on p. 336, the balance sheet is nothing but an extension of the basic accounting equation:

$$\text{ASSETS} = \text{LIABILITIES} + \text{EQUITY}$$

There are a few differences between the earlier discussion of accounts and the information presented in the balance sheet in Figure 13-3. In accord with objectivity, the asset values in the balance sheet are recorded at their original cost to the firm. Thus, the balance sheet figure of $1,000,000 for marketable securities was the cost of those securities. The amount reported in parentheses ($1,001,000) is the *market value*—the price at which the securities could be sold on December 31, 19xx—of the securities.

The company expects a certain percentage of its customers to fail to repay their debts to the firm. This percentage is determined from the company's past collection experience. To allow for these uncollectables, the company establishes an *allowance for doubtful accounts*, in order to show the accounts at their probable collectible value.

Fixed assets are shown at cost less depreciation. Plant and equipment have limited lives. Through the normal wear-and-tear of the manufacturing

Figure 13-3. *Balance Sheet of the HKP Corporation*

HKP Corporation
Balance Sheet as of December 31, 19xx

ASSETS

Current Assets
Cash		$ 1,000,000
Marketable securities at cost (market value $1,001,000)		1,000,000
Accounts Receivable	$ 4,200,000	
Less: allowance for doubtful accounts	200,000	
		4,000,000
Inventories		4,000,000
Total Current Assets		$10,000,000

Fixed Assets
Land	$ 5,000,000	
Buildings	7,000,000	
Equipment	20,000,000	
Total	$32,000,000	
Less: accumulated depreciation	5,000,000	
Net Fixed Assets		27,000,000

Prepaid Expenses		1,000,000
Intangibles		2,000,000
Total Assets		$40,000,000

LIABILITIES

Current Liabilities
Accounts payable	$ 2,500,000
Notes payable	1,000,000
Accrued expenses payable	1,000,000
Federal income tax payable	500,000
Total Current Liabilities	$5,000,000

Long-Term Liabilities
6% bonds, due 1990	10,000,000
Total Liabilities	$15,000,000

STOCKHOLDERS' EQUITY

Capital Stock
Preferred stock, 8% cumulative $50 par value; 10,000 shares outstanding		$ 500,000
Common stock, $1 par value; 500,000 shares outstanding		500,000
Total		$ 1,000,000
Capital surplus		12,000,000

Retained Earnings
Balance, 1/1/19xx	$11,000,000	
Net profit for year	2,000,000	
Total	$13,000,000	
Less: dividends on preferred stock	40,000	
Common stock	960,000	
Retained Earnings, 12/31/19xx		12,000,000
Total Stockholders' Equity		$25,000,000
Total Liabilities and Stockholders' Equity		$40,000,000

process, equipment runs down and/or becomes obsolete. To take note of the declining usefulness and ultimate need for replacement of the equipment, the accountant periodically reduces—or depreciates—part of the value of the fixed assets as shown in the balance sheet. Depreciation is an expense of running the business and must be offset against revenue when calculating the company's income.

The *net fixed assets* figure reported in the balance sheet is not intended to reflect the market value of the assets or their replacement cost in the future. Market values fluctuate continuously and may be difficult to obtain, while replacement costs may also be extremely subjective estimates. Because of the principle of objectivity, the accountant records asset values at cost less accumulated depreciation.

The company's only long-term liability is $10,000,000 of 6% bonds maturing in 1990. This means that the company must pay annually $600,000 (0.06 times $10,000,000) interest to the owners of the bonds and repay the entire $10,000,000 principal of the bonds in the year 1990.

The balance sheet shows that the company began the year with a balance of $11,000,000 in retained earnings. The company's net profit of $2,000,000 for the year should have increased the retained earnings balance to $13,000,000. However, the company paid cash dividends of $40,000 to its preferred stockholders and $960,000 to its common stockholders. These distributions of earnings resulted in the retained earnings account having a balance of $12,000,000 at the end of the year.

The rest of the accounts on the balance sheet were defined in the discussion of the accounting equation. While balance sheets for specific companies may differ in form from the example given here, the basic purpose and information presented are essentially the same.

Reprinted through permission of Forbes, Inc. and Henry R. Martin

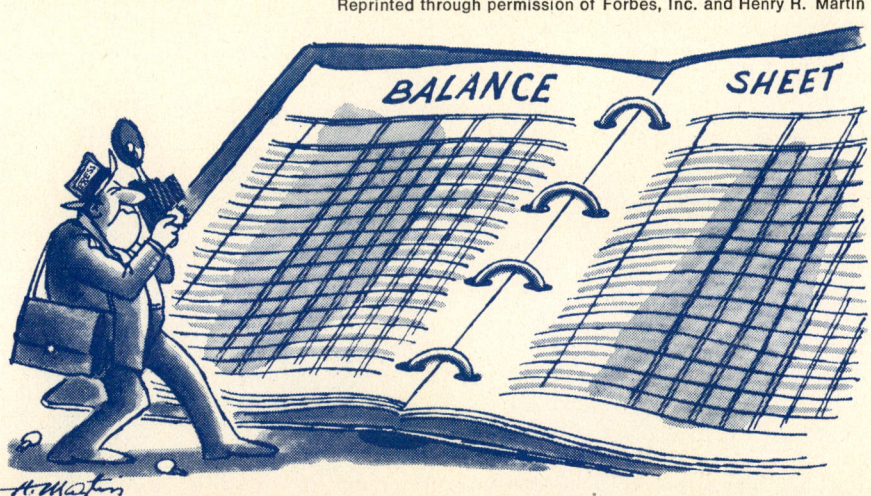

The Income Statement

Figure 13-4 presents the income statement for the HKP Corporation. The **income statement** is also referred to as the *earnings statement* and the *statement of profit and loss*. While the balance sheet presents a snapshot of the firm's operations, the income statement is a motion picture, reporting the firm's operations for a given period of time.

The basic equation for the income statement is:

INCOME (or profit or earnings) = REVENUES − EXPENSES

Net sales are the major source of revenues for industrial corporations. Net sales are calculated by subtracting from total sales any discounts given to customers or any allowances for returned merchandise.

Following the net sales, the major expenses are grouped under cost of sales and operating expenses, which includes all costs involved in making and selling of the company's products. *Costs of goods sold* represents the amount of inventory, direct labor, and factory overhead consumed in the manufacturing process during the accounting period. Direct labor costs are wages paid to employees who work *directly* on the company's products, such as machine operators but *not* supervisors. Factory overhead costs include indirect labor (such as supervisors' salaries), occupancy costs (such as heat and taxes), and machinery and equipment costs (such as repairs of machinery). Since it can be a substantial dollar amount, **depreciation** is shown as a separate item on the

Figure 13-4. *Income Statement of the HKP Corporation*

HKP Corporation
Income Statement for the year ended December 31, 19xx

Net Sales		$50,000,000
Cost of Sales and Operating Expenses		
Cost of Goods Sold	$35,000,000	
Depreciation	1,000,000	
Selling Expenses	5,500,000	
Administrative Expenses	4,000,000	
Total		45,500,000
Operating Profit		$ 4,500,000
Other Income		100,000
Total Income		$ 4,600,000
Other Expenses		600,000
Earnings Before Taxes		$ 4,000,000
Taxes on Income		2,000,000
Net Earnings After Taxes		$ 2,000,000
Less Dividends on Preferred Stock		40,000
Net Earnings Available to Common Stockholders		$ 1,960,000
Net Earnings Per Share of Common Stock		$ 3.92

income statement. *Selling* and *administrative expenses* are listed separately so that the reader of the financial statements will have as much detail as possible in the information available for analysis. Selling expenses include outlays for advertising, sales representatives' salaries and commissions, entertainment expenses, and travel. Administrative expenses include executives' salaries, office payroll, office expenses, and the like.

Other income is revenue not related to the firm's main line of business. For example, suppose an automobile manufacturer has a considerable sum of money invested in marketable securities. Income on the marketable securities should be included as other income and not income from operations. *Other expenses* are treated the same way. The major class of other expenses is interest paid on the corporation's debt or bonds.

Taxes are also an expense of doing business. Payroll taxes—such as the employer's contributions to Old Age and Survivors' Insurance (Social Security)—are included in the cost of sales and operating expenses. Income taxes on the corporate income are shown as a separate item on the income statement. The federal income tax on corporate income is 22% on all taxable income plus additional tax of 26% on all taxable income over $25,000.

Note that dividends paid on preferred stock are shown as a deduction from net income *after* taxes. Preferred stock dividends are not considered an expense of doing business but rather are a distribution of the firm's income to its owners. Similarly, dividends on common stock also paid out of after-tax income.

Earnings per share of common stock are computed by dividing the amount of earnings available to common stockholders by the number of outstanding shares of common stock. For HKP Corporation, the earnings per share are $3.92 ($1,960,000 divided by 500,000 shares outstanding). This figure is very important since current and prospective investors are vitally concerned with their proportionate interest in the profits of the firm. The earnings per share determine, in part, what investors will be willing to pay for each share of the company's stock.

Analyzing the Financial Statements

What does the external user of financial statements do with the data given to him? *Financial analysis* involves putting the data in the financial statements into a more meaningful form.

One major area of financial analysis is **ratio analysis**. A ratio involves relating one piece of financial data to another. Ratios computed from information presented in the financial statements can be compared either on an *historical* or *interfirm* basis. Historical analysis involves computing the same ratio for each year over a number of years and examining the trend of the ratios. For example, suppose we were interested in the relationship of the firm's net profits to sales, one measure of the relative profitability of a company. By examining the trend of this ratio over time, we can tell if management has followed a course of action that has led to increased or decreased profitability of the company.

The analyst may also be interested in the company's performance relative to other companies in the same industry or in a similar line of business. Financial ratios for various industries are published by Robert Morris Associates, Dun and Bradstreet, and various other credit agencies and trade associations. Robert Morris Associates, which is an association of bank credit and loan officers, publishes industry averages based upon financial statements supplied to banks by borrowers. Eleven ratios are computed annually for 156 lines of business. Dun and Bradstreet annually publishes key business ratios for 125 lines of business in the retailing, wholesaling, and manufacturing and construction industries.

Some Important Financial Ratios

Since a ratio simply relates one piece of financial information to another, there are literally hundreds of ratios that can be computed. The specific ratio to be calculated depends on the information desired. In this section, we shall examine some of the more important and frequently calculated ratios.

1. The *current ratio* is computed by dividing the current assets of the firm by the total current liabilities. This ratio gives an indication of the ability of the firm to repay its current debts. The current ratio for the HKP Corporation, whose financial statements are presented in Figure 13-3 and 13-4 is 2.00 ($10,000,000 in current assets divided by $5,000,000 in current liabilities).

2. The *acid test ratio* divides quick assets by current liabilities. *Quick assets* are current assets less inventories. This ratio is another measure of the liquidity of the firm. Inventories are excluded from quick assets since they are the least liquid of assets—the last to turn into cash The acid test ratio for HKP is 1.2 times ($6 million in quick assets divided by $5 million in current liabilities).

3. Annual net sales are divided by 365 to obtain *average daily credit sales*, and then the average daily credit sales are divided into notes and accounts receivable to provide the *collection period*. This ratio is helpful in analyzing the collectibility or quality of the receivables. The average daily credit sales of HPK are approximately $137,000 ($50,000,000 sales divided by 365 days in a year). The collection period is 31.41 days ($4.2 million in accounts receivable divided by $137,000 average daily credit sales).

4. *Asset turnover* is computed by dividing net sales by tangible assets. Tangible assets are total assets less intangibles. This ratio measures the degree to which management efficiently uses the assets of the firm. HKP Corporation has tangible assets of $38,000,000 ($40 million total assets less $2 million in intangibles). Asset turnover is thus 1.3 times ($50 million in net sales divided by $38 million of tangible assets).

5. *Inventory turnover* measures the ability of management to control the firm's production costs and produce its products efficiently. It is calculated by dividing costs of goods sold by inventories. The inventory turnover for HKP

Corporation is 8.75 times ($35 million cost of goods sold divided by $4 million in inventories).

6. The *debt-equity ratio* is calculated by dividing the firm's total debt by its total equity. It is an indication of how the firm's assets are financed. When this ratio exceeds 1.00, the creditors have more money invested in the assets of the firm than do the company's owners. HKP Corporation has a debt-equity ratio of 0.60 times ($15,000,000 of liabilities divided by $25,000,000 stockholders' equity).

7. The *coverage ratio* indicates the extent to which the firm is earning the interest charges on its long-term debts. This ratio is computed by dividing net earnings before taxes *plus* interest payments on its long-term liabilities by the interest payments on the long-term liabilities. The coverage ratio for HKP is 7.67 times.

8. *Gross profit margin* is computed by dividing operating profit by net sales. This is a measure of the relative profitability of the firm. The gross profit margin for HKP Corporation is 9% ($4.5 million in operating profit divided by $50 million in net sales).

9. The *net profit margin* is calculated by dividing net earnings after taxes by net sales. It is an important measure of the firm's profitability. The net profit margin for the HKP Corporation is 4% ($2,000,000 in net earnings after taxes divided by $50,000,000 in sales).

10. *Return on tangible net worth* is computed by dividing net earnings after taxes by the tangible net worth of the firm. *Tangible net worth* equals the stockholders' equity less any intangible assets the firm may have. There is a tendency among financial analysts to look at this ratio as a final criterion of profitability. The tangible net worth of HKP Corporation is $23,000,000 ($25,000,000 in stockholders' equity less $2,000,000 of intangibles). The return on tangible net worth is 8.7% ($2,000,000 net earnings after taxes divided by $24,000,000 tangible net worth).

Other Analyses

Ratio analysis tells only part of the story that external users of financial information may be interested in. Other analyses that provide specialized information are *aging of accounts, quality of the inventory,* and *pro forma statements*.

A banker may be interested in knowing more about the quality of the firm's accounts receivable. An *aging of accounts* separates the amount of receivables due by 30-day periods. The purpose of the aging is to determine how many accounts are sufficiently past due to expect them to be uncollectable. This is of major importance to a banker extending short-term credit that is expected to be repaid from the collection of receivables.

The external user may also be interested in the *quality of the inventory*. He may want to know how much of the inventory is obsolete or damaged. This information, like the aging of accounts, is not found in the financial statements of the corporation. The corporate accountant may be asked to prepare special reports to provide the necessary information to interested parties.

Lastly, the external user must be aware that ratios and other types of analysis mentioned represent only past experience. The external user of financial statements is interested primarily in how the firm will perform in the *future*. A major lender, such as a bank or a very important customer, may ask the corporation to provide it-with pro forma statements. Pro forma statements are projections of what the financial statements are expected to look like at some time period in the future. These statements involve many assumptions and "guess-timates" on the part of the corporate accountant, but they are nonetheless important sources of information to certain external users.

The Role of the CPA

A potential drawback to any type of analysis that might be performed on the financial statements of the company is the possible lack of quality of the figures presented. To help ensure the quality of the information presented, the external user relies to a great extent on the opinion of the *certified public accountant*, the CPA. The CPA is granted a license to practice by the state and performs professional accounting services for clients for a fee. An individual is required to pass a rather stringent examination before he is awarded the coveted title of Certified Public Accountant. In addition, many states require the individual to either have a college degree in accounting, or be a practicing accountant for a minimum number of years, or both, before being made a certified public accountant.

The most important service performed by the CPA, as far as the external user of financial statements is concerned, is auditing. An *audit* is an investigation of a company's accounting system to determine whether the financial statements present fairly the company's financial position and operating results. All large corporations and many small companies are audited at least annually by a CPA firm.

An example of the CPA's opinion is presented in Figure 13-5. As noted, the CPA examines the financial statements of the corporation according to generally accepted auditing standards to determine if the information presented in the financial statements conforms to generally accepted accounting principles. The American Institute of Certified Public Accountants, the national association of CPA's, is responsible for adopting auditing procedures and broad policy concerning generally accepted accounting principles (GAAP). The Securities and Exchange Commission, a branch of the federal government, also influences changes in what are generally accepted auditing standards and accounting principles.

The CPA does not guarantee the accuracy of the financial statements. Moreover, the CPA does not pass judgment on the firm as an attractive investment opportunity or a credit worthy borrower. The management of the firm prepares the financial statements. The CPA only examines them to ensure that they conform to GAAP.

Figure 13-5. CPA Letter
___

To the Board of Directors and Stockholders,
MNP Corporation:

We have examined the balance sheet of MNP Corporation as of December 31, 19X2 and 19X1 and the related statements of earnings and changes in financial position for the respective years then ended. Our examination was made in accordance with generally accepted auditing standards, and accordingly included such tests of the accounting records and such other auditing procedures as we considered necessary in the circumstances.

In our opinion, the above-mentioned financial statements present fairly the financial position of MNP Corporation at December 31, 19X2 and 19X1 and the results of their operations and changes in financial position for the respective years then ended, in conformity with generally accepted accounting principles applied on a consistent basis.

Nichols and Michaels, Certified Public Accountants
January 16, 19X3

The CPA may give one of three opinions on the financial statements of the firm. An *unqualified opinion* gives the financial statements a clean bill of health. The statement presented in Figure 13-5 is an unqualified opinion. A *qualified opinion* is given when the CPA feels that the firm has violated some GAAP. When the CPA feels that the financial statements do not fairly present the financial position and operating performance of the company, he issues a *disclaimer*. The users of financial reports should be extremely careful when dealing with companies whose reports are qualified. They should have little or no confidence in reports that are disclaimed by a CPA. The CPA is the external users' main line of defense against unethical accounting practices by a company. Considerable faith should be put in the accountant's opinion when it is qualified or is a disclaimer.

MANAGEMENT ACCOUNTING

While financial accounting is concerned with the preparation of financial information for external users, *management accounting* pertains to the preparation of financial information to be used *internally* by a company's decision makers. Management accounting deals with the planning and controlling of

Parts of a Typical Business

the daily activities of the firm. The information required by a company's decision makers is much more detailed than that presented to the external users. The accuracy and timeliness of this information can determine the ultimate profitability of the firm.

Forecasting Financial Performance

Financial accounting deals almost entirely with the recording, summarizing, and analyzing of *historical* economic events. The generally accepted accounting principle of *objectivity* requires that the financial accountant base reports on historical fact. The management accountant is not bound by accounting principles. In fact, there are no generally accepted accounting principles for management accounting. The accountant prepares information requested by management according to the form best suited to management's needs. The management accountant spends a good deal of working time deal-

"I have a confession to make. We won't know if our company is financially sound until after the fifth race."

Reprinted through permission of Management Accounting, National Association of Accountants 919 Third Avenue, New York, N.Y. 10022

ing with economic events expected to happen in the future. Estimating these future economic events is the accountant's *planning function*.

Budgeting

A **budget** is a statement of forecasted financial performance. The general policies and objectives of a company's management must be turned into operational profit goals for decision makers at all levels of the firm. Through budgets, the management accountant translates the company's overall goals into departmental targets which will direct activities toward the attainment of the final goal.

At the company level, the accountant prepares a *master budget* that forecasts companywide performance for a specified period of time. A master budget is, in effect, a detailed set of *pro forma* financial statements. It is a summary of the budgets provided to decision makers at lower levels in the organization.

The accountant develops budgets based on historical experience and in-depth interaction with the affected decision maker or manager. The key to effective budgeting is the preparation of budgets by *areas of responsibility* with clear specification of what is expected of the person in charge of each area. The accountant bears a large part of the burden of defining the manager's area of responsibility. Failure to clearly specify this can lead to an inability of higher levels of management to hold the proper person responsible for individual areas of performance or to hold a person accountable for something over which there was no control.

Break-even Analysis

In addition to the preparation of budgets, the management accountant develops other planning tools. **Break-even analysis** is one of the most common planning devices put together by the accountant. The purpose of this type of analysis is to permit the decision maker to see the interrelationships between a product's costs, selling price, and expected sales volume.

The accountant begins the break-even analysis by defining the costs of production as either *fixed* or *variable*. Variable costs vary directly with the volume of output produced. For example, the costs of materials and direct labor are fairly constant per unit produced and, in total, will vary directly with the number of units manufactured. Fixed costs, such as a supervisor's salary, stay at the same level and must be paid regardless of the number of units produced. A supervisor receives his salary if the plant runs at full capacity or if the company is on strike.

The basic equation for break-even analysis is

$$SX = VX + F$$

where S is the selling price per unit, V is variable costs per unit, F is fixed costs, and X is the number of units sold. *Break-even sales volume* is the number of units that must be sold for the firm just to recover its costs of manufacturing—to result in zero profit. For example, suppose there is a company that manufactures widgets. The variable costs for each widget are $3, expected selling price per unit is $5, and fixed costs per year are $1 million. What is the firm's break-even sales volume?

The equation becomes

$$\$5X = \$3X + \$1,000,000$$
$$\$5X - \$3X = \$1,000,000$$
$$\$2X = \$1,000,000$$
$$X = 500,000$$

Thus, the company must sell 500,000 widgets per year to just recover its costs of manufacturing. Only after selling 500,000 widgets will the company begin to make a profit.

How is break-even analysis a useful planning tool for management? Manipulation of the basic break-even equation can provide management with much interesting information. For example, an estimate from the sales manager as to how many widgets can be sold per year at $5 per widget will provide an initial estimate of the expected profitability of the production of widgets for that period. If the sales manager estimates that the company can sell 750,000 widgets at $5 each, the estimated profit for the year is

```
Revenue         = 750,000 × $5 = $3,750,000
Variable costs  = 750,000 × $3 =  2,250,000
Fixed costs                    =  1,000,000
Expected profits               = $  500,000
```

The manager might be interested in seeing what happens if the company raises the price of widgets to $7 per unit. Consultation with the sales manager and the company economist reveals that at a price of $7, customers will buy only 600,000 widgets per year. The profit then becomes

```
Revenue         = 600,000 × $7 = $4,200,000
Variable costs  = 600,000 × $3 =  1,800,000
Fixed costs                    =  1,000,000
Expected profits               = $1,400,000
```

Thus, the decision to raise product price could result in more profit. But what if raising the price to $7 reduced expected sales to 300,000 units? Profit would then be

```
Revenue         = 300,000 × $7 = $2,100,000
Variable costs  = 300,000 × $3 =    900,000
Fixed costs                    =  1,000,000
Expected profits               = $  200,000
```

Now the company would actually lose profits by increasing selling price to $7 per unit. The accountant—in communication with professionals in other areas of specialization within the firm—can vary each of the factors in the basic break-even equation to present to management the possible results of alternative courses of action.

Cost Accounting and Control Systems

Management is vitally concerned with how closely the firm is performing to its predetermined game plan. Cost accounting and control systems are designed to provide management with the necessary information for comparing actual results with predetermined objectives.

Cost Accounting

Cost accounting provides management with a record of costs of products, operations, or functions and compares actual costs and expenditures with predetermined standards. The standards are an output of the planning process. In the case of a product, the accountant must estimate the cost per unit produced. The accountant works closely with production people to determine the engineering specifications of a unit of product. This includes the amount of materials and labor that are required to produce one unit. Information from the purchasing and personnel departments enables the accountant to trans late the physical characteristics of the production process into dollar dimensions.

Standards are also developed for areas of the business that are not directly tied into the manufacturing process. For example, the accounting department would have its own budget. Standards of performance are developed for different functions within the accounting department. It is estimated that a certain amount of work can be accomplished by a given work force being paid a prespecified salary. Cost accounting measures the extent to which actual costs were either over- or underanticipated.

The Need for Evaluation

The continuous comparison of the budget plan with actual results not only provides a measure of the amount of deviation but also reflects the reasons for the variances or differences. Management needs to know how closely the game is going according to plan. Material deviations call for remedial action. Actual events must be reflected in an updating of the budgets so that the budgeting process is a continuously on-going cycle.

A *control system* is simply a framework for monitoring variances. It should alert management when a variance becomes material. The control system acts on an *exceptions-basis*: only *significant* differences of actual from standard are

Figure 13-6. *The Controller and Staff*

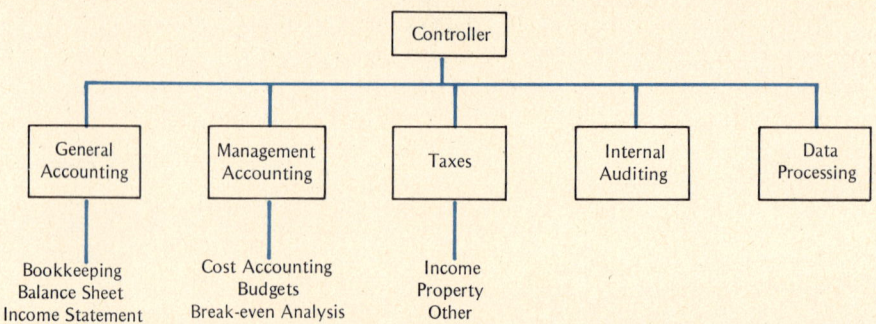

called to management's attention. As always, benefit must be weighed against cost. A manager's time is very valuable and expensive. The benefit attained from a manager's examination of a difference of actual from standard must be compared to its cost. The smaller the variance, the less likely that the benefit will exceed the cost. Thus, *management by exception* is practiced.

THE CONTROLLER AND STAFF

The individual responsible for the accounting function within the firm is the *controller*. A typical organization chart of the accounting function within a company is presented in Figure 13-6. The controller has a number of department heads reporting directly to him. These departments include general accounting, management accounting, taxes, internal auditing, and data processing. In essence, it is the controller's responsibility to coordinate the actions of these departments.

General Accounting

The person in charge of general accounting is responsible for maintaining the company's bookkeeping system. Every significant economic event that can be expressed as an accounting transaction for the firm must be recorded. Periodically, the *books*, or records of transactions, must be summarized or *closed* in order to prepare the financial statements. Thus, general accounting is also concerned with the preparation of the firm's balance sheet and income statement.

Management Accounting

The person in charge of the *management accounting department* must see that records are kept on the manufacturing process of the firm. The staff prepares the budgets and standard costs, collects the financial information on actual results, and prepares reports on the variances of actual costs from standard. Special reports, such as break-even analyses, also come from this department.

Taxes

The director of *taxes* has the responsibility to determine periodically the firm's federal, state, and local income taxes. The staff also calculates payroll taxes and property taxes and sees that the firm complies with all government tax statutes. In addition to record keeping, the tax department staff does *tax planning*, which involves studying the tax laws and finding accounting methods to use that will help minimize the firm's tax burden. *Tax avoidance* is the process of finding accounting strategies that will *legally* minimize the company's tax liability. Tax avoidance is perfectly legal and actually encouraged by the government. *Tax evasion* is illegal avoidance of tax and is punishable in courts of law. Since the corporation can pay as much as 48 cents out of every dollar of profit in federal income taxes, tax planning is a very important function in the firm. The accountant helps to minimize the firm's tax liability through tax avoidance methods.

Internal Auditing

Internal auditing differs from the audit done by the certified public accountant. The CPA periodically evaluates the firm's financial position and operating results and passes judgment on the fairness of their presentation to external users. The internal auditor performs a more on-going role of inspection of the control system of the firm. This person acts like a consultant to different decision makers within the firm. In addition, this individual audits managerial performance as well as accounting data.

Data Processing

Data processing may or may not be under the province of the controller. Since a large part of the data processing of the firm is accounting in nature, the controller often has control over this department. Data processing can be either manual or electronic. Manual data processing involves maintaining the ac-

350   **Parts of a Typical Business**

"That's not what I meant when I said to get ready for the auditors, Kleaton!"

counting system by handwritten entry. Electronic data processing involves either the computer or sophisticated accounting machines. These devices are intended to produce, more quickly with less chance of error, accounting reports which were formerly done by bookkeepers. In addition to preparation of basic accounting statements, electronic data processing equipment helps in the control of cost variances by management by exception. The computer can be programmed to alert management when a variance reaches an unacceptable level.

CAREER OPPORTUNITIES IN ACCOUNTING

Accounting is one of the major opportunity areas for jobs in the 1970s. You can find a promising and challenging career in three major fields: public accounting, industrial accounting, and government accounting.

Public Accounting

Earlier in this chapter, we discussed the requirements for the designation of Certified Public Accountant. To repeat, each state sets the requirements for licensing as a CPA. The individual must pass a rigorous, nationally standardized test in addition to meeting education and/or practice requirements peculiar to the state.

While auditing is the most common aspect of a CPA firm, CPA's also do tax and management services work. A CPA who specializes in taxes helps both corporate and individual clients compute their taxes and develops strategies to help minimize tax liability. The function of management services is consulting and covers topics both close to and rather distant from accounting. Management services can range all the way from the design and implementation of cost-control systems to executive search; that is, helping a company to find a person for a key managerial opening.

CPA firms range from one-man shops to international firms with hundreds of partners and thousands of employees. All CPA firms are either partnerships or proprietorships. You would enter the firm as a junior accountant and spend one or two years as an auditor. Depending on the geographical boundaries of your firm's operations, you might be expected to do considerable traveling. From junior, you would rise to senior accountant with responsibility for a number of juniors working under you. A manager is one step higher in the organizational structure than senior. At the top of the firm are the partners.

The large international and regional accounting firms are known for open access to top management. In most firms, age has little to do with how quickly you will advance—talent is the key. For those who find that a lifelong career in a CPA firm is not for them, there is excellent opportunity to move from a highly regarded CPA firm to a corporation. Training in a CPA firm is an excellent start on any career path in business.

Industrial Accounting

Industrial accounting involves working in the controller's area in a corporation or other firm. Assignments vary considerably from bookkeeping to control system design and analysis to tax planning to internal auditing. A bookkeeper records the day-to-day business transactions in journals, ledgers, and other accounting forms and helps in the preparation of periodic financial statements. In 1970, there were more than 1.34 million bookkeepers in the United States with 9 out of 10 being women. The necessary background for bookkeeping is a high school diploma, with courses in business arithmetic and bookkeeping.

Accounting positions in industrial accounting require anything from a high school diploma through a junior college degree to an advanced degree from a university. Cost accountants generally have some college education with courses in cost accounting and cost control systems. They prepare budgets and variance reports as well as do special studies on planning and control. In recent years, the National Association of Accountants, an organization of industrial accountants, has sought to increase the prestige of their profession. The Certificate in

Management Accounting recognizes professional competence in management accounting acceptable to both the profession and the business community. Candidates who pass a series of uniform examinations and meet special educational and professional standards qualify for the certificate.

A position as internal auditor in a corporation generally requires a college degree in accounting. Preference is often given to individuals who are CPA's and have worked for a CPA firm for a number of years. The Institute of Internal Auditors, a trade group of internal auditors, offers the Certified Internal Auditor (CIA) certificate as a means of upgrading the professional status of the internal auditor. Candidates for the CIA program must meet education and experience requirements and must pass a four-part written examination. To be eligible for certification, the candidate must have a baccalaureate degree from an accredited college-level institution, have a minimum of three years of experience in internal auditing, submit a character reference from either a CIA or a member of company management, and subscribe to a Code of Ethics.

Corporate tax accountants also usually have junior college or university level degrees in accounting with specialization in taxes. Since tax laws are constantly changing, it is expected that accountants will continue with their education to stay abreast of current developments in the field.

There are also opportunities in data processing for the industrial accountant or with the CPA firm. We will defer discussion of these opportunities until Chapter Sixteen, the chapter on computers, since these careers presuppose strong familiarity with computer science techniques.

Government Accounting

The government—local, state, and national—offers numerous career opportunities in accounting. Jobs for both the college and noncollege graduate abound in government accounting positions. Jobs range from bookkeeping through budgeting and auditing to the development of accounting principles. The General Accounting Office, for example, is the fiscal watchdog of Congress. Employees of the GAO are college graduates and perform audits on government owned enterprises as well as on firms that are under contract to the U.S. government. Professional tax-accounting opportunities are available with the Internal Revenue Service as an auditor of tax returns of both individuals and corporations. The accounting staff of the Securities and Exchange Commission formulates accounting principles for the many firms under its jurisdiction.

Rewards

In addition to the excellent career advancement opportunities, positions in accounting offer excellent financial rewards. In the early 1970s, accounting clerks with only a high school education averaged about $450 per month in salary for jobs in bookkeeping. Accountants with college degrees can expect to start at the $9,000-to-$13,000-per-year level with CPA firms, industrial firms, and government, the salary varying with the individual's qualifications and experience. Managers in large CPA firms earn in the $25,000 to $35,000 range, while partners in some of the major international CPA firms earn well in excess of $75,000. Industrial salaries are comparable to those for CPA firms at beginning levels. Furthermore, the industrial accountant is in a position for excellent advancement to the top managerial positions in the firm. More and more corporations are bringing up their top managerial talent from the accounting area of the firm.

Regardless of whether you start as an accountant for the government, industry, or a public accounting firm, a career in accounting will provide you with a wealth of opportunities for moves into other lines and areas of business.

CHAPTER SUMMARY

In this chapter, we have examined the many aspects of accounting. Accounting is the field concerned with providing timely and pertinent information about the firm to decision makers. The output of the accounting area is vital to the efficient allocation of resources within our economy.

Accountants have developed a fairly rigorous framework for recording economic events affecting the firm. This framework is designed to facilitate the collection and summarization of the information desired by decision makers.

Financial accounting deals with the preparation of financial information to be used by persons external to the firm. Investors, creditors, and government agencies rely on accounting statements as their major source of information about the firm's operations. The external users have a variety of techniques at their command to evaluate the performance of the firm. They rely on the independent auditor, the Certified Public Accountant, to examine the accounting system of the firm and determine if the accounting statements presented to the external users fairly present the results of operations and the financial position of the firm at a point in time. The CPA is the external user of financial information's main line of defense against misleading financial statements from a company.

Management accounting deals with the preparation of financial information to be used internally by a company's decision makers. The management accountant is responsible for planning and controlling the daily financial operations of the firm. This person plans by means of budgets and special reports, such as break-even analyses. The control system alerts management to variances of the actual results from the predetermined game plan. Management can then revise the game plan and at the same time act to bring about corrected behavior in areas where the variances are too large to be acceptable.

The controller has the responsibility of coordinating the various accounting functions within the firm. In addition to financial and management accounting, the controller and staff are concerned with taxes, internal auditing, and data processing.

There are numerous career opportunities available in accounting. These opportunities vary considerably in the education and experience backgrounds required for them and the exposure provided to upper management in the firm. In any event, accounting is one of the major career opportunity fields of the 1970s.

PROVOCATIVE STATEMENT

Financial Reporting: The Executive's Liability

1 "The obligations of the inside professional go deeper than those of the outside auditor for a simple reason: the inside professional knows more about the company that the auditor ever can. The auditors may spend many years poring over the books and records of an enterprise, but they weren't there when deals were discussed in the privacy of the executive suite, they weren't there when the impacts of transactions and corporate decisions were discussed in terms of earnings per share, they weren't there when the five-year forecasts were put together. They are not and cannot become privy to the plethora of detailed information that is the natural possession of the financial executive because of his submersion in the day-to-day business of the enterprise. The financial executive has the opportunity to know better than the auditor whether financial statements are presented fairly. It follows that the financial executive has a commensurately heavier obligation to be sure they are fair presentations.

Financial executives have a further obligation. They have, in my estimation, an obligation not only with respect to the integrity of the financial statements, but they must also make the full program of corporate financial reporting their responsibility. They must be alert lest the more meticulously prepared financial statements are not prostituted by misleading graphs, charts, or assertions in the textual portions of annual reports and other published documents."

A. A. Sommer, Jr., Commissioner,
Securities and Exchange Commission,
"Financial Reporting: Who's Liable?"
Financial Executive,
March 1974, p. 27.

PROVOCATIVE STATEMENT

The Credibility Gap in Financial Reports

2 "... an expanded and expanding environment demands of the corporations, and those who exercise the power and control over the corporations' resources, a full measure of visibility and accountability—qualities which, ostensibly, should be assured by the independent certifying or attesting auditors of these corporations. I believe these standards to be inadequately implemented by the accounting profession as presently structured; this book will consider in some depth a number of areas where financial statements deviated seriously from an objective standard of fairness, and where despite these most serious aberrations the statements were deemed by the auditors to be "fair in accordance with generally accepted accounting principles (GAAP)." We will see that this "fair" versus "GAAP-fair" is a most invidious distinction. . . .

This dichotomy of "fairness" and "GAAP-fair" has confronted the accounting profession (as well as the corporations for whose historical narratives the accounting profession is supposed to be responsible) with the challenges of "crisis in confidence," "credibility gap," and "creeping irrelevance." The conduct of the American corporation is being challenged by its adversaries, and at least questioned by its friends. One might then expect the implementation of procedures for assuring the corporations and its management the highest degree of visibility and accountability—so that all who are entitled to know will know, and thereby be able to make rational decisions. This expectation notwithstanding, the situation is very much otherwise."

Abraham J. Briloff,
CPA and University Professor,
Unaccountable Accounting,
New York: Harper & Row, Publishers, 1972,
pp. 4–6.

REVIEW QUESTIONS

1. What are the two types of users of the financial reports prepared by accountants? Give examples of each type.
2. Briefly explain the three components of the accounting equation. Why must the accounting equation always be equal?
3. What are the two most important reports prepared by financial accountants? What is the purpose of each report?
4. Why does the accountant record fixed assets at cost less accumulated depreciation?
5. Why are inventories the least liquid of the firm's current assets?
6. List and briefly discuss the major types of financial analysis.
7. What are the major differences between financial accounting and management accounting?

Chapter Outline

What Is Finance?

The Uses of Funds
   Profitability versus Liquidity
   Analysis of Working Capital
      Cash Management
      Management of the Marketable
         Securities Portfolio
      Accounts Receivable Management
      Inventory Management
   The Capital Budgeting Decision
   Summary

The Sources of Funds
   Debt and Equity
      Maturity
      Claim on Income
      Claim on Assets
      The Right to Voice in Management
   Selecting the Financing Source
      Permanence of Capital
      The Debt–Equity Mix
   Sources of Short-term Debt
   Sources of Intermediate-term Debt
   Sources of Long-term Debt
   Sources of Equity

The Dividend Decision

External Growth

Career Opportunities in Finance
   The Cash Manager
   The Credit Manager
   The Financial Analyst
   The Treasurer
   Qualifications for Careers in Finance

Chapter Summary

Provocative Statement 1:
   Poor Financial Management at Large
   Multinational Companies

Provocative Statement 2:
   The Coming Era of the Financial Executive

Key Terms

Funds
Liquidity
Treasury bills
Commercial paper
Certificates of deposit
Cost of capital
Liquidation
Leverage
Line of credit
Revolving credit agreement
Transaction loan
Collateral loan

Factoring
Trade credit
Term loan
Lease
Preferred stock
Common stock
Capital gain
Retained earnings
Merger
Consolidation
Holding company
Subsidiary

Finance and Capital for Business

"The ... fact is that the largest and best-known companies are missing so many opportunities for extra profits through better financial management."
— Business Observer and Author

14

Chapter Thirteen introduced a number of key business terms, such as assets, liabilities, and equity. But that chapter left unanswered a number of very important questions relating to these items. For example, should a company issue debt or equity to finance its growth? Who is responsible for determining how much cash the firm should keep on hand? Answers to these questions involve a look at the finance function of the firm. In this chapter, we shall first develop a definition of finance. We shall then examine the various responsibilities of the financial manager in the context of how the decision is made as to where the firm should invest its financial resources and where the firm should obtain those resources. A discussion of career opportunities in finance concludes the chapter.

WHAT IS FINANCE?

We could borrow some terminology from economics and define finance as the "efficient allocation of scarce resources within the firm." But this definition would be of little use to us since people working in the areas of production, personnel, marketing and accounting could give identical definitions to their specialties. Alternatively, then, we could state that finance involves planning, control, raising funds, and using funds. Again, however, our definition is too general, since the responsibilities of planning and control run through all the functional areas of the business. Perhaps the simplest, yet most effective, definition is that *finance is the area of business concerned with gathering and using funds*.

THE USES OF FUNDS

Funds are cash. The uses of funds fall within the area of decision making by the financial manager. The determination of the assets and the amounts in which the firm should invest its funds is the job of the financial manager. The use of funds is often called the *investment decision*. What are the identifying features of the decision-making process for investing funds? What are the available assets suitable for the investment of the firm's funds? As points of departure, we shall first look at the problem of risk versus return confronting the financial manager. We shall then turn our attention to the analysis of each of the major components of the firm's asset mix.

Profitability versus Liquidity

In performing the job, the financial manager must perform a balancing act between liquidity and profitability. **Liquidity** refers to the ease with which an asset can be turned into cash. The company can reduce the risk of not being able to repay its liabilities by keeping a large amount of cash on hand.

However, the profit earned on cash is very low. Cash that is idle is funds that could be invested in plant and equipment. These, in turn, would produce more goods and services and provide the company with more profits. On the other hand, investing too much cash in plant and equipment may not leave enough money for the company to pay its bills as they become due. Thus, the financial manager must see that enough funds are in cash so that the firm can repay its debts. There must, however, not be so much in cash such that funds are sitting idle and the company is missing possible profits due to a shortage of product resulting in an inability to meet demand.

As we discuss each of the components of the firm's asset mix, we shall present approaches to handling this trade-off between risk and return that will enable the financial manager to perform successfully in the firm.

Analysis of Working Capital

Working capital can be defined as either *net working capital* or *gross working capital*. Net working capital is simply the firm's current assets less its current liabilities. In this section, we shall be concerned with the concept of gross working capital—the firm's current assets.

Figure 14-1. *Investment in Working Capital as a Function of Time*

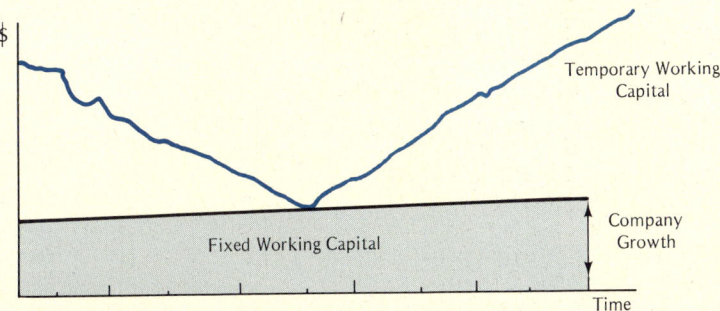

Working capital can be further classified either by its investment in the various components of the firm's current assets or by its degree of permanence over time. The time related classification of working capital is shown in Figure 14-1.

Fixed or permanent working capital never leaves the business process and increases as the firm grows. The permanent working capital can be viewed as a base amount. For example, firms usually have a minimum amount of sales in accounts receivable. As sales grow, this amount grows. Temporary working capital arises from seasonal sales patterns. For example, one would expect a buildup in inventories for department stores before the Christmas selling season and a sharp reduction in inventories following the first day of the new year.

As the firm goes through its operating cycle, the working capital changes from one asset to another. This flow of working capital is shown in Figure 14-2. Cash is used to purchase raw materials. The raw materials become finished goods. These goods can be sold for either cash or credit. If the sale is for cash, the working capital flows from finished goods to the cash account. If it is a credit sale, an account receivable is created. As the account is collected, the working capital flows back into cash.

The amount of working capital the firm should have on hand is a function of (1) production needs and (2) management's attitude toward risk. Thus, the amount of receivables and inventories will be related to the level of the firm's sales. Risk can be defined as the chance the firm will be unable to meet demands on its working capital. For example, a sales order and the repayment of a debt are both demands on a firm's working capital. The more management wants to avoid risk, the greater the amount of working capital needed on hand. For example, the greater the desire to avoid lost sales due to lack of finished goods in stock, the larger the amount of inventory that must be kept on hand.

As noted earlier, working capital can be classified as the funds invested in the various components of the firm's current assets. Since it is the responsibility of the financial manager to develop effective policies for each of the

Parts of a Typical Business

Figure 14-2. *Working Capital and the Firm's Operating Cycle*

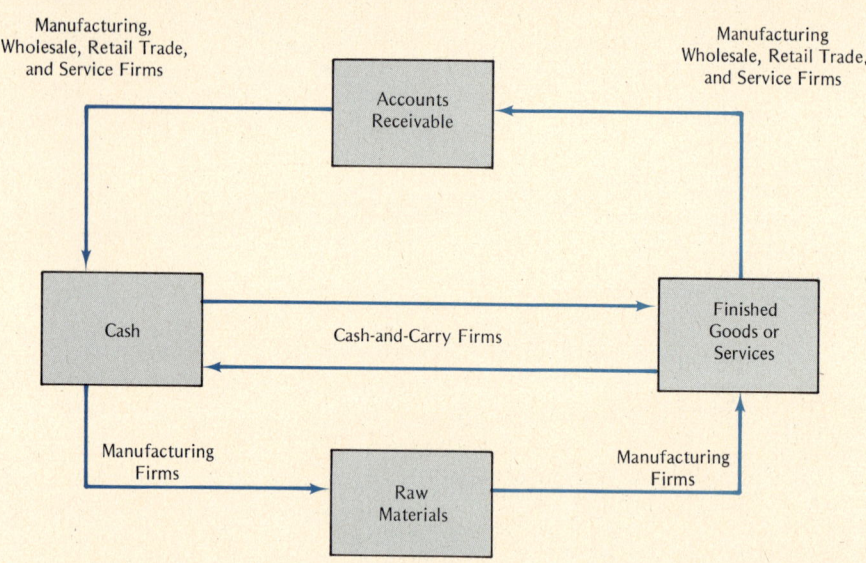

components of working capital, we shall now turn our attention to a discussion of each of the working capital classifications.

Cash Management

Cash is held for two main reasons—the transactions motive and the precautionary motive. The amount of cash held for the transactions motive is the stock absolutely necessary to conduct the day-to-day business of the firm under normal conditions. The amount of cash held for the precautionary motive is that level held to guard against unanticipated demands for cash.

Cash can also be held for speculative reasons to allow the firm to take advantage of anticipated price changes. For example, if the management of the firm believes that the price of its raw materials is going to increase due to inflation, cash balances may be reduced to allow additional investment in those raw materials. On the other hand, if the prices of the raw materials were expected to decline, the firm could allow cash balances to increase and postpone purchase of the materials until prices decline.

The major aspects of cash management are planning, control, and utilization of excess funds.

Cash planning involves both short-range and long-range cash projections. The financial manager must develop cash budgets. These budgets indicate when cash will be received by the firm and when it will be spent. When cash outflows are expected to exceed inflows, the budget will indicate how much cash must be raised. If funds from inflows are expected to exceed outflows, the budget indicates how much cash is available for other uses.

Cash control involves:

1. Speeding up collections of cash.
2. Reducing investment in inventories through better estimation of product demand and production capability.
3. Other areas such as reducing balances with banks, improving control over intercompany cash transfers, and strategic tax planning.

The company's credit manager has the responsibility of speeding up cash collections. This individual must keep control of the company's receivables and encourage late payers to pay their bills more promptly. Modern techniques for sales forecasting and determination of the proper inventory size must be employed to assure that the company does not have too much funds invested in inventories. Compensating balances are idle cash balances maintained with banks in exchange for bank services, such as free checking accounts. They are a negotiable quantity. The company should use its bargaining power to minimize these balances. Strategic tax planning allows the company to pay a minimum tax bill. As noted in Chapter Thirteen on Accounting and Control Systems, tax minimization through tax *avoidance*—not tax evasion—is a perfectly legal business practice.

Some choices involved in the *allocation of excess cash* are:

1. Reduction of outstanding loans payable.
2. Extension of loans to other parties.
3. Long-term investment in plant and equipment.
4. Purchasing of the company's stock in the market place.
5. Investment in marketable securities.

It is this last item to which we now turn.

Management of the Marketable Securities Portfolio

One must always remember when investing in marketable securities that the safety of the amount invested is of prime importance to the firm. Funds invested in marketable securities are only *temporarily* idle cash. The corporation has very specific uses for investment of these cash balances at a later date, sometimes as soon as the next day but usually within a year. Thus, it wants to earn as high a rate of return as possible on these assets without taking so much risk that the securities will later prove to be uncollectible.

The following are some examples of marketable securities which are suitable for investment by most firms:

1. U.S. government treasury bills: short-term debt guaranteed by the federal government.
2. Prime commercial paper: short-term debt issued by major corporations.
3. Certificates of deposit: short-term debt issued by commercial banks.

All three of these marketable securities have a number of important features that make them particularly attractive to corporations. First, their safety in terms of the ability of the issuer of the security to repay the debt when it matures is very high. Thus, there is little fear of loss of funds due to the failure of the issuer to repay his debts. Second, all three issues are highly marketable. For example, suppose a corporation buys a security which will be repaid by the issuer in one year. After two months, the company finds that it needs its money back. The corporation will have no trouble finding another corporation to buy its marketable security if that security is really marketable.

Which of these three investment instruments should the company purchase? The answer to this question depends on management's attitude toward risk, the amount of money available for investment, and the returns offered on the different instruments. Some key features of treasury bills, commercial paper, and certificates of deposit are shown in Table 14-1. Treasury bills are guaranteed as to repayment by the full taxing power of the federal government. Commercial paper and certificates of deposit are backed only by the strength of the issuing corporation or bank. Thus, a manager with a strong dislike for risk may buy only treasury bills, even though they return less profit than other investments. As little as $10,000 can be invested in treasury bills, while the minimum is $25,000 for commercial paper and $100,000 for certificates of deposit. Lastly, interest rates on these investments vary quite a bit over time. The investment manager must be aware of current developments so that the investment purchased has the greatest relative yield for the risk-taking level at a point in time.

Accounts Receivable Management

All firms are engaged in selling either goods or services for a profit. Some of these sales are on a cash basis, while others involve the use of credit. Dun and Bradstreet has estimated that over 95% of all interbusiness sales are credit sales. Furthermore, accounts receivable typically make up 15 to 20% of a firm's assets. There is really no profit on a sale until the account is collected. Thus,

Table 14-1. *Characteristics of Important Marketable Securities*

Investment	Quality	Minimum Size	Yield Range 1974
Treasury bills	Highest: guaranteed by U.S. government	$10,000	5.14%– 9.45%
Commercial paper	High-medium: depends on quality of issuing corporation	$25,000	6.25%–13.00%
Certificates of deposit	High-medium: depends on quality of issuing bank	$100,000	6.30%–12.70%

control of receivables is important because prompt collection will determine both the liquidity and profitability of the firm.

Increases in accounts receivable in the firm's asset structure are attributed largely to increases in sales. They can, however, also be due to more lenient credit policies. As managers are under pressure to increase sales, the firm is forced to increase its amount of accounts outstanding.

The credit manager is responsible for determining to whom and in what amounts credit should be granted. By examining the financial statements of the credit requester, questioning other suppliers and the customer's banker, and resorting to private credit investigating agencies, the credit manager decides on the credit worthiness of the customer.

In applying the information, the credit manager is concerned with the prospective customer's four C's: capital, character, capacity, and conditions. A check on capital is done to determine the applicant's stake in his business. The more personal money—equity—a person has in a business, the greater is the incentive to keep the firm from failing. Capacity determines the maximum amount of debt the applicant is financially capable of maintaining. Character refers to the applicant's willingness to repay debts on time. A company may have capacity but not the character. That is, some very large and profitable companies are very slow to repay their liabilities. Conditions relate to general business conditions. A company would be more willing to extend credit when the economy is booming than when a recession is predicted to occur and the chance of another company failing to repay its debts increases.

Some general factors influencing the degree of credit riskiness assumed by the credit granting corporation are:

1. Firms with higher profit can afford more risk.
2. A firm with a weak cash position will hesitate to accept a poor risk customer.
3. A firm with sound collection methods generally is able to accept poorer risk credit applicants than a firm without these facilities.

Inventory Management

The problem of inventory management was discussed in detail in Chapter Eight. However, the interrelation of the various functions within the business is worth noting here. While determination of the ideal inventory size is in part a production function, it is also a finance function since the size of the inventory will require a commitment of funds. The financial manager must decide if these funds are being invested wisely.

The Capital Budgeting Decision

Capital budgeting is the name given to the decision process for new investment in fixed assets. Capital budgeting projects are typically investments that require large cash expenditures and are relatively infrequent in nature. Examples of capital budgeting projects are:

1. An investment in a new machine to replace an existing piece of equipment.
2. An investment in a new plant facility to manufacture a new product line.
3. An investment in a new sales outlet to service a new market area.

Capital budgeting decisions are important for two reasons. First, they generally commit the firm to a course of action over a fairly long time. Second, they are costly to reverse if the decision proves wrong.

The capital budgeting program can be expressed as a series of steps:

1. Creative search for profitable opportunities.
2. Long-range capital plans.
3. Short-range capital plans.
4. Measurement of project worth.
5. Screening and selection.
6. Control over authorized outlays.
7. Retirement and disposal.

The creative search for new profitable opportunities is undoubtedly the most crucial, yet most difficult and least objective, part of the investing problem. Corporations spend millions of dollars each year attempting to discover and develop new products. Finding new opportunities is not only a finance function. It is clearly a responsibility of all the functional areas of the business. Marketing may propose a new way of packaging the company's products to increase sales. Production may suggest a new machine which could reduce the cost per unit of the product. Personnel may suggest that a new training program for employees could lead to more efficient use of employee time on the job. Accounting might suggest that purchase of a new computer would lead to better control over accounts receivable and reduce the time for collection on receivables.

Long- and short-range capital plans are needed to assure that funds are available for investment in the new capital projects. Furthermore, these plans indicate to management the direction of the firm toward achieving the company's goal.

While the final decision to accept or reject a project is a job of top management, measurement of project worth is the responsibility of the finance function. What are the steps for determining project worth? The particular techniques are quite involved and are left for a later "in-depth" course in financial management. For the present, however, we can simply state that the measurement of investment value includes:

1. Determination of the cost of the proposal.
2. Measurement of the net cash benefit anticipated from the project.

3. Comparison of numbers 1 and 2 in some logical manner to determine the rate of return expected from the project.
4. Adjustment for risk.
5. Ranking projects in descending order for expected rates of return.

The desirability of an investment is measured relative to a cutoff rate that the firm establishes. This cutoff rate is referred to as the firm's cost of capital. It represents the minimum return the firm must earn on the investment to justify raising the funds necessary to undertake the investment. The firm ranks the projects in descending order of their rates of return since it wants to invest in the most profitable project first. It continues investing in projects until either there are no more funds available for allocation or there are no more projects that have rates of return in excess of the cost of capital.

Control over authorized outlays is important since the rate of return depends on the actual cost of the project not exceeding what was anticipated. Retirement and disposal of assets involve the continual evaluation of existing assets to determine when they have become obsolete. How to best dispose of them once they are no longer of value to the firm must also be considered.

Summary

In this section, we have examined the various aspects of the uses of funds problem confronting the financial manager. We now turn our attention to the problem of where the financial manager should raise funds to finance investment decisions.

THE SOURCES OF FUNDS

Without cash the firm cannot pay its bills when they become due or invest in new plants and equipment to allow the firm to grow. Without cash the company cannot pay dividends to its owners. Where should the company raise its cash? Certainly from the profits of the corporation. But this may not be enough to satisfy all of the firm's needs for cash. The company must then seek sources outside the business for the rest of the needed cash. The selection of the source of these funds is one of the key functions of the financial manager.

Debt and Equity

What are the sources of funds available to the firm? The basic sources can be divided between debt, or liabilities, and equity. Debt and equity differ in four basic ways:

1. Maturity.
2. Claim on income.
3. Claim on assets.
4. The right to voice in management.

Maturity

Debt matures. That is, it must be repaid at some stated future date. Equity—such as preferred stock and common stock—has no maturity date. The corporation is under no legal obligation to repay equity holders the money they have invested in the firm. If the owner of common stock, for example, wants to sell an investment, the individual must find someone else to sell it to.

Claim on Income

Holders of debt must be paid their interest before any of the income of the firm can be paid in dividends to the equity holders. Payment of interest to debt holders is a legal obligation of the firm. Failure to pay interest or repay principal, that is, the amount lent to the firm, at maturity can result in the lender taking legal action against the firm. The firm may even be forced out of business. Equity holders can hopefully expect a larger return than the debt holders in return for their inferior claim on income. They might even receive a growing stream of dividends if the firm continues to prosper. However, equity holders receive dividends only at the discretion of the board of directors of the corporation. Dividends are not a legal obligation of the corporation.

Claim on Assets

If the company goes out of business, debt holders receive all funds from the sale of assets until their claims for repayment are met. The selling of the assets of a firm that has gone out of business is called **liquidation**. Only after debt holder claims are fully met will equity holders receive any of the proceeds from the sale of assets.

The Right to Voice in Management

Debt holders are creditors of the firm. They have no voice in the management of the affairs of the company except in cases of default of payment of interest or principal.

Equity holders are the owners of the corporation. They have the right to a voice in management through the power to elect the board of directors of the corporation.

Selecting the Financing Source

There are two factors that must be considered when the financial manager has to select between debt and equity as sources of funds. The first factor is the

Figure 14-3. *Need for Permanency for Capital*

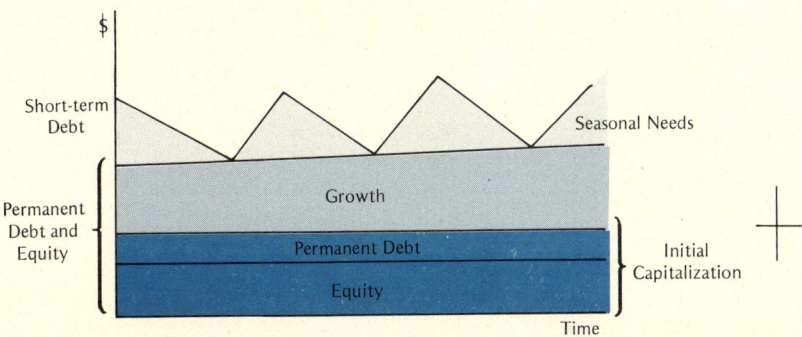

length of time the funds will be needed—their permanence. The second factor involves the mixture of debt and equity in the capital structure.

Permanence of Capital

In general, short-term debt should be used for short-term needs, and long-term debt or equity used for permanent expansion. Capital is another term for financing source. The relationship of capital to permanence of need is shown in Figure 14-3.

Initial capital consists of some mixture of common stock, preferred stock, and debt. The debt is usually considered to be permanent. As one debt issue matures, it will be replaced with new debt. If the firm is successful, it will grow and need new permanent capital. Some of this financing will be provided by earnings retained by the firm. Any financing in excess of retained earnings must come from new debt or new issues of stock. In our discussion of the composition of working capital, we noted the seasonal need factor. Financing here is usually very short term so that it can be retired when the need for the financing ends.

The Debt–Equity Mix

If the firm needs permanent capital, how does the financial manager choose between long-term debt and equity? Shareholders may prefer debt to equity financing because of the favorable effects of leverage. Leverage is the ratio of total debt to total assets of the firm. Debt financing, as noted before, incurs fixed interest charges. Any earnings on investment above interest charges accrue to the shareholders. Shareholders prefer this for two reasons:

1. Higher earnings may enable the firm to pay more dividends.
2. Higher earnings may result in higher prices for the shares of the company's stock.

Leverage is best understood by reference to an example. Consider two firms with the following simplified balance sheets.

Firm A

Total assets	200	Total debt	0
		Capital stock	200
	200		200

Firm B

Total assets	200	Total debt	100
		Capital stock	100
	200		200

Firm A has leverage of 0 while Firm B has leverage of 50%. Further assume that A has 20 shares of common stock at $10 per share and no interest charges while Firm B has 10 shares of stock at $10 per share and interest charges of $6. If each firm has an operating profit of $80, what are the earnings per share for each firm given an income tax rate of 50%? For Firm A we have:

Operating profit	$80
less interest	0
Earnings before taxes	$80
less taxes	40
Earnings after taxes	$40
Earnings per share	$40/20 = $2.00

For Firm B:

Operating profit	$80
less interest	6
Earnings before taxes	$74
less taxes	37
Earnings after taxes	$37
Earnings per share	$37/10 = $3.70

For the same operating results, the shareholders of Firm B have higher earnings per share. If the investors feel that this difference in earnings more than offsets the higher risk of Firm B, Firm B's stock will sell at a higher price than A's stock.

Why does Firm B have a higher risk? Leverage can also work in a negative fashion. Suppose neither firm had any operating profits. In this case, Firm A would have earnings per share of $0 while B would have earnings per share of negative $.60. (Students should calculate these answers themselves.) Firm B's shareholders are now in an inferior position. This potential for loss makes Firm B more risky than Firm A. Thus, if investors feel that the firm already has enough debt, any additional debt will make the firm too risky and the share price will fall. This would, therefore, cause a decrease in each shareholder's wealth. Responsible managers should not allow this to happen.

The financial manager must determine when the firm has just enough debt and when any more leverage would be to the disadvantage of the shareholders. There are no formulas to let the financial manager know when the firm has the ideal amount of debt. The manager must rely on experience and judgment in deciding on the mix of debt versus equity that best suits the firm.

Sources of Short-term Debt

There are a number of prime short-term sources of debt funds. In this section, we shall examine some of the more important ones.

A line of credit is an *informal* arrangement between a bank and a borrower. It specifies the maximum amount of *unsecured* credit the bank will permit the firm to owe at any one time. Unsecured means that the bank lends solely on the promise of the borrower to repay the loan when due. The bank does not ask the borrower to pledge any specific assets as collateral for the loan. The key aspects of the line of credit are (1) it is informal in that there is no contractual agreement between the parties, and (2) the firm only pays interest when it borrows money. A line of credit is usually established for about one year at a time.

A revolving credit agreement is a legal commitment by the bank to extend credit up to a maximum amount. A revolving credit agreement is set up for periods of a few months to a few years. A charge, usually amounting to one-quarter to one-half of 1%, is paid on the *unborrowed* amount.

A transaction loan is the traditional bank loan for a specific purpose. It is short-term and self-liquidating. For example, a transaction loan could be used to finance a seasonal buildup in inventories. The sale of these inventories would provide the cash for repayment of the loan.

As a short-term source of funds, the company could also take out a collateral loan. In a collateral loan, the company pledges specific types of assets as security for the extension of the loan. For example, the company could pledge its accounts receivable as collateral for a loan. The accounts receivable loans can involve (1) notification, in which the borrower's customers are notified to send payment of their accounts directly to the lender, or (2) non-notification, in which the borrower collects the receivables and then passes along the proper payment to the lender.

Another type of collateral loan involves the use of the firm's inventories as collateral. The lender will advance some percentage of the inventory value. If the borrower fails to make payment on the loan, the lender can take ownership of the inventory. Since the lenders want their money as quickly as possible, they will be willing to extend more cash on inventories that can be sold as easily as possible. Banks and commercial loan companies are prime sources of collateral loans.

An alternative to the accounts receivable collateral loan is factoring.

Factoring involves the outright sale of the company's receivables to a factor—a company specializing in the purchase of accounts receivable. The factor has no legal claim against the company should one of the accounts prove uncollectible. The factor also relieves the firm from collection expenses.

Trade credit is a very common short-term source of funds. Trade credit is different from other forms of short-term credit in that it is not associated with a financial institution. Trade credit is defined as credit extended by a supplier to a buyer in conjunction with the purchase of goods for resale. Small firms rely more heavily on trade credit than do larger firms. As a firm grows, trade credit becomes less important as a source of funds. Trade credit is used primarily to finance inventories. It is, therefore, more important to firms whose inventories are a large proportion of total assets.

Lastly, *commercial paper*, as noted in our discussion of marketable securities, is a form of short-term debt issued by major corporations. Commercial paper is issued by only the highest quality companies and is completely unsecured.

Sources of Intermediate-term Debt

Intermediate-length financial arrangements are generally referred to as term loans. They have maturities of between 1 and 10 years. A characteristic of term loans is that they are paid off in installments. Term loans are especially important to firms that are too small to issue either bonds or stock. A disadvantage of term loans is the requirement for correct cash flow forecasting since the payments on the loan must be made periodically. Banks, insurance companies, and pension funds are primary issuers of term loans.

Sources of Long-term Debt

There is a wide variety of long-term debt sources for the firm. These sources range from *debentures*—unsecured long-term debt—to *convertible securities*—those that have characteristics of debt but may be converted to equity at the holder's option—to *first-mortgage bonds*—those secured by first claim on the firm's assets in the event of liquidation. The objective of the financial manager is to choose that type of debt that will result in the least cost to the firm. However, we should interpret the term "cost" in a very broad sense. The interest payments on the debt are a clear dollar outlay but are not the only costs to the firm. For example, debt holders might specify the minimum amount of working capital the firm must keep at all times. This restriction should be considered a cost of issuing debt since it reduces the investment alternatives available to the firm. If a convertible bond is converted into common stock, the profits of the firm would be spread over more shares. This is also a cost to the firm's existing shareholders. The financial manager must consider these less visible factors when deciding on the source of debt to be issued.

A lease can also be considered a source of long-term debt funds. A lease is a contract that grants use of an asset for an extended period of time in return for periodic payments. The grantor of the lease retains ownership of the asset. Leases vary considerably in terms of length, cancellation provisions, and maintenance and insurance responsibilities. The advantage to the firm leasing the asset is the freeing of large sums of funds for investment elsewhere. Disadvantages, however, are (1) the firm has no claim on the leased asset once the lease expires, and (2) a lease usually involves higher "cash" costs. The latter occurs because the firm granting the lease runs the risk that the asset will become obsolete and demands cash compensation for bearing this risk.

Sources of Equity

The major sources of equity funds are preferred stock, common stock, and retained earnings. Preferred stocks generally carry fixed rates of dividends. Although preferred dividends must be paid before common stock dividends can be paid, dividends on preferred stock are paid at the discretion of the firm's board of directors. Most preferreds, however, are cumulative. This means that if a dividend is not paid in one period, it becomes an *arrearage*—back payment—that must be removed before common stock dividends can be paid. Preferred stockholders generally have no voting rights in the firm. But provisions are usually made so that the preferred stockholder gains some voting rights in the event of a period—usually a year or two—of passed preferred dividends. In the event of liquidation, the preferred stockholder must be paid in full before the common stockholder can receive anything.

Preferred stock has fallen out of favor with both investors and corporations in recent years. The investor in preferred stocks has a position inferior to debt holders with respect to both claim on income and claim on assets in the event of liquidation. The return, however, is limited to the amount of dividends paid on the preferred. Corporations do not like to issue preferred stock since preferred dividends are not deductible as an expense by the issuer. Interest payments on debt, on the other hand, are a tax-deductible expense.

Common stock holders are the real owners of the firm. They have the right to vote and to elect the corporation's board of directors. The claim of common stock holders to assets in the event of liquidation follows that of the holders of all other securities issued by the firm. Furthermore, dividends are paid on common stock only at the discretion of the board of directors. What, then, is the attraction of common stock to investors? As the residual owners, holders of common stock may participate in whatever earnings are left to the firm after interest on debt and dividends on preferred stock are paid. If the firm continues to grow, this stream of dividends could become quite sizable. Moreover, if the prospects for growth in the firm are recognized by other prospective investors, the value of the share price of the common stock will increase. In such a case, the investor can realize a **capital gain**, that is, sale of the stock at a price greater than that which was paid for it.

Retained earnings are funds left in the firm from the earning's stream of the corporation after dividends have been paid to the common stockholders. That is, earnings after taxes and preferred stock dividends can either be paid to common stockholders as cash dividends or be held for reinvestment in new assets. The typical American corporation retains between 40 and 60% of its earnings and pays the rest out in dividends.

THE DIVIDEND DECISION

Should a company pay a cash dividend to its shareholders or retain these funds for reinvestment in new assets? The dividend decision is both an investment decision—a use of funds—and a financing decision—a source of funds. Since earnings not paid out in dividends are retained for investment in the firm, the dividend policy, in effect, determines the availability of funds to reinvest through retained earnings. The market value of shares of common stock represents what investors think they will eventually get in dividends from the company. Therefore, the dividend decision is an investment decision because it influences the performance of the shares.

What should the dividend policy of the firm be? In theory, as long as the firm has attractive investment opportunities, dividend payments should be held to a minimum. As a result of increased retentions invested at good rates of return, future dividends will be greater because of growth. This will produce share price appreciation. In practice, however, firms tend to maintain a stable dividend policy related to some proportion of dividends to earnings over the long run.

Dividends also tend to lag behind profits. They are generally neither increased nor decreased unless management expects the new level of earnings to be permanent. Evidence on the stability and lag behind profits of actual dividend policy is shown in Figure 14-4.

How do we reconcile theory and practice? That is, why do firms maintain a stable dividend policy even when there are no profits or when acceptable investment opportunities are available? One answer is that some investors, such as pension funds and insurance companies, are prevented by state law from holding common stocks that have not paid a dividend for five consecutive years. A stable dividend policy prevents these investors from having to sell the firm's shares and depressing stock prices when the firm does not pay the dividend.

Furthermore, dividends transmit information to investors. A reduction in the regular dividend signals that management expects lower profits for a long time. Similarly, an increase in the regular dividend signals that profits are

Figure 14-4. *The Stability of Corporate Dividend Policy*

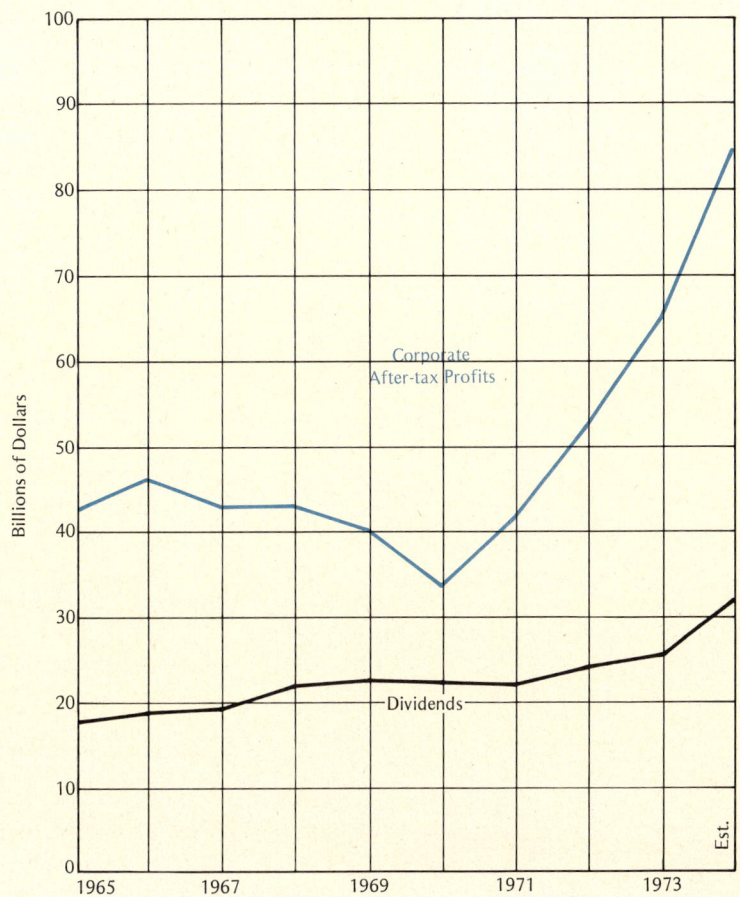

From *Fortune Magazine*, March 1975, p. 82. Courtesy of *Fortune Magazine*.

expected to be permanently higher. A stable dividend enables investors to form expectations more easily about future dividends. Since investors dislike risk, reduction in uncertainty to investors should result in a higher price for the firm's common stock.

We also find that dividend policy across firms suggests that the theory on dividends is correct. For example, firms with low dividend payout ratios are:

1. Fast growing companies with high return investment opportunities.
2. Firms that are not yet well enough established to have easy access to the capital markets.
3. Firms with unstable earnings streams.
4. Firms that are short of cash or underfinanced.
5. Firms that are closely held by persons in the high tax brackets.

EXTERNAL GROWTH

To this point in the chapter we have been concerned with how a company acquires and finances assets. This area of concern is called *internal* growth. The firm can also have *external* growth by acquiring other companies.

There are three major types of external growth.

1. A merger is a combination of two corporations wherein one loses its corporate identity, that is, $A + B = A$.

2. A consolidation is a combination of two firms whereby an entirely new corporation is formed, that is, $A + B = C$. The distinction between a merger and a consolidation is not very important and is generally ignored in discussion of this area.

3. Instead of purchasing the whole company, the firm may choose to purchase sufficient stock to gain control of an attractive acquisition. The purchaser is called a holding company, while the acquired firm is called a

"It appears that our many acquisitions have finally resulted in our buying ourselves out."

Reprinted with permission of *The Saturday Evening Post*, © 1974 The Curtis Publishing Company.

subsidiary. For example, Citicorp is a holding company that has a subsidiary the First National City Bank, the second largest bank in the world.

How should an acquisition opportunity be evaluated? In effect, the acquisition decision is another capital budgeting decision. There is an initial cost and an expected stream of uncertain benefits. The objective is simply to determine the returns from this investment and to compare them to the firm's cost of capital.

CAREER OPPORTUNITIES IN FINANCE

If you have a desire to rise to the top levels of management in a corporation, you should consider starting your career in the finance area. According to two recent surveys, chief executive officers (CEO's) with financial backgrounds accounted for 24% of all CEO's in 1971, an increase from 15% in 1967. Furthermore, of all CEO's appointed in 1971, about 33% had backgrounds in finance, exceeding all other areas by a wide margin. Of course, not everyone wants to or can become the CEO. The finance function has challenging jobs at all levels of the organization. In this section, we shall first examine some of those opportunities. Then we shall chart the route you might take by way of the finance function to rise in the world of business.

The Cash Manager

The responsibility for developing cash budgets and investing idle cash belongs to the cash manager. Since cash flow is so vital to the existence of firms, cash managers have an important job. They must see that enough cash is on hand to pay bills on time. Furthermore, they must make sure that cash does not sit idle in the bank. Any excess cash should promptly be invested in marketable securities. Cash managers are also in charge of company relations with banks. They help set up company checking accounts and negotiate the size of compensating balances.

The Credit Manager

The credit manager's job is to decide who gets credit and to control the collection of accounts receivable. Credit managers must collect data on credit applicants and determine the maximum amount of credit to be given. They must also keep tabs on all the accounts and see that prompt collections are made.

The Financial Analyst

Financial analysts are responsible for evaluating the attractiveness of competing capital projects. They determine costs and expected benefits and apply different techniques to measure project worth. The financial analyst has access to executives in all areas and at all levels of the firm in order to get the necessary data for the capital budgeting decision.

The Treasurer

Treasurers are the persons in charge of coordinating the various specialties that make up the finance function. As such, they must have a thorough background in all the areas of finance. Treasurers are considered members of the top management team. Their opinion carries great weight in deciding which projects the firm should undertake and how it should raise funds.

Qualifications for Careers in Finance

If you are interested in becoming a financial manager, you must plan your academic career to maximize your chance of getting a visible and mobile starting position with the firm. You must have a strong background in accounting, since the finance function is closely related to the accounting function. You should also obtain an overview of banking and capital markets, since these areas fall within the responsibilities of the finance function. And lastly, you are encouraged to seek depth in quantitative methods, since the application of mathematical models and procedures will enable you better to clarify the structure of the problems which you will eventually face.

You will enter the corporation as a financial management trainee and be exposed to service in a variety of functions in the finance area. The time period as a trainee can last up to a few years. After exposure to the various jobs, you will become an assistant to a department head responsible for a particular area in the finance function. If the corporation is a multinational business firm, you may be asked to spend a term with an overseas affiliate of the corporation. You will need time to get the necessary experience to be top man and to show management your capabilities. This may lead to further advancement to department head and, eventually, to the top financial position in the firm. You should always remember that the successful financial executive is the one who is able to learn from the past, perform in the present, and project into the future.

CHAPTER SUMMARY

The topic of this chapter has been finance—the function involved with the gathering and using of funds. We have seen that there is a vast variety of assets into which the firm can invest its cash. These assets differ in a number of respects, including their liquidity and permanence within the firm. We examined factors that should be considered in managing the firm's cash, accounts receivable, marketable securities, inventories, and capital expenditures.

We also looked at the alternate methods by which the firm can raise the money for investment. The major differences between debt and equity were noted as well as the effect each can have on the shareholders' wealth. The various forms of short-term, intermediate-term, and long-term debt as well as the different types of equity were discussed.

The dual characteristic of the dividend decision as both a source and use of funds was presented. And for firms that are not satisfied by the way in which they are growing from within, we discussed the three methods of external growth.

The chapter concluded with a discussion of career opportunities in finance. As was noted, for ambitious individuals who seek the highest levels of responsibility in the corporation, entry into the firm through the finance function is a proven route to success.

PROVOCATIVE STATEMENT

Poor Financial Management at Large Multinational Companies

1 "Of the 187 companies we studied, only about sixty could be described as financially aggressive. In general these are the middle-sized companies. The rest of the companies do not manage their money very effectively. One would expect this of the small enterprises, since most of them are newcomers to multinational business, and they lack the experience required for efficient global arbitrage. But the surprising fact is that the largest and best-known companies are missing so many opportunities for extra profits through better financial management.

Many of the big companies don't borrow as cheaply as they might. Most don't invest their cash effectively. The principal reason for the lack of financial aggressiveness in the large enterprises is the enormous scope and complexity of their global operations. Managements would like to maintain tight, centralized control over the financial affairs of these behemoths, but in practice they find that impossible."

Robert Stobaugh and Sidney M. Robbins,
Authors and researchers,
Money in the Multinational Enterprise:
A Study of Financial Policy
New York: Basic Books, 1973

PROVOCATIVE STATEMENT

The Coming Era of the Financial Executive

 "Corporations may well be on the threshold of a new era, the age of the financial executive. Important changes are under way which will have considerable impact on the task of the financial executive. His traditional task of determining the need for funds, procuring them, and investing temporarily available portions will have to be broadened to include actively managing all of the corporation's major balance sheet items. This will require a financial executive who is not only a financial specialist, but in addition, one who possesses general management know-how and experience, for he will increasingly become involved in strategic issues."

Hermann H. Pohl,
Senior Consultant, McKinsey and Co.,
Zurich, Switzerland

REVIEW QUESTIONS

1. What is meant by the "balancing act" between liquidity and profitability?
2. What is the purpose of the transaction motive and the precautionary motive in cash management?
3. List and briefly discuss the components of cash management.
4. What is the series of steps to be followed in a capital budgeting program? Why is the capital budgeting decision of such critical importance to the firm?
5. Define the four C's of credit evaluation.
6. Distinguish between a line of credit and a revolving credit agreement.
7. The two basic sources of funds to a firm are debt and equity. What are the major differences between these two sources?
8. What is the difference between internal and external growth?

Chapter Outline

The Nature of Risk and Insurance
    Types of Risk
    What to Do about Risk
        Reducing Hazards
        Self-insurance
        Professional Insurance

Kinds of Insurance Companies and Insurance
    Types of Insurance Companies
    Major Types of Insurance
        Life Insurance
        Property and Casualty Insurance
    Other Types of Insurance

Trends in the Impact of Insurance on Business
    Impact of Fire Insurance on Business
    Impact of Product Liability Insurance on Business
        Better Product Design and Quality Control
        Caution in Product Promotion and Distribution
        Insurance Implications
        Other Implications

Careers and Jobs in Insurance
    Sales
    Underwriting
    Claims Adjustment
    Actuary

Chapter Summary

Provocative Statement 1:
    Are Insurance Policies Unreadable?

Provocative Statement 2:
    Time for the Insurance Industry to Defend Itself

Key Terms

Risk
Speculative risk
Pure risk
Peril
Hazard
Self-insurance
Contingency fund
Term insurance
Whole life policy
Limited pay life policy
Endowment policy
Incontestability clause
Allied lines clause
Coinsurance clause
Disability insurance

Risk and Insurance for Business

"One reason for consumer confusion about insurance is the inability of the average person to read a policy."
—State Insurance Commissioner

15

Every day of your life, you are exposed to risk. If you should die, those dependent upon you for financial support would be subjected to possible financial hardship. If, while driving your car, you should fail to stop at a stop sign and crash into another car passing through the intersection, you could be sued for damage done to both the other car and its occupants. This suit could threaten to eliminate all your financial resources.

Like the individual, a business is subject to risk. Death of the president of a small firm could put the company in ruin. A fire could destroy all of a company's assets. The purpose of this chapter is to examine the risks to which a business is exposed and the means by which the firm can reduce its exposure to risk. The different types of insurance and insurance companies will be discussed and the impact of insurance on business will be noted. Lastly, career opportunities in the field of insurance will be examined.

THE NATURE OF RISK AND INSURANCE

Risk is an integral part of business. In this section the different types of risk, risk-reduction methods, and the principles of insurance will be discussed.

Types of Risk

Risk can be defined as a chance of loss. A **speculative risk** involves a chance for loss and a chance for profit. Anyone going into business is incurring a speculative risk. A person cannot be absolutely sure that the business will be a success. There is always the possibility that a firm will suffer a loss. Perhaps the marketing manager has overestimated the potential demand for the company's product. Perhaps a competitor introduces a better product at a lower price. These and similar circumstances can force a company to operate at a loss or can even result in ruin.

It is an axiom of business that the opportunity for profit is directly related to the amount of risk assumed, as shown in Figure 15-1. The business executive who wants to minimize possible risks must be willing to give up the opportunity for larger returns. On the other hand, this business executive reduces the chance that the firm will suffer a large loss. Alternatively, the business executive who takes greater risks in hopes of larger profits also incurs a higher chance of a sizable loss.

What are some of the speculative risks of business? The two major risks are *business risk* and *financial risk*. Business risk relates to the nature of a firm's operations. A company that specializes in wildcat oil drilling has a higher degree of business risk than does a public utility having a monopoly for its necessary product. Financial risk pertains to the financial structure of the firm. As noted in Chapter Fourteen, Finance and Capital for Business, a firm increases its opportunity for return—but also its risk of loss—as it increases the proportion of debt relative to equity in its capital structure.

A **pure risk**, unlike the speculative risk, provides no chance for profit. It allows only for the chance of loss. The chance of a fire at a company's production facility is a pure risk to the firm. Methods for controlling pure risks are the major topics of this chapter.

Figure 15-1. *The Risk-Return Trade-off*

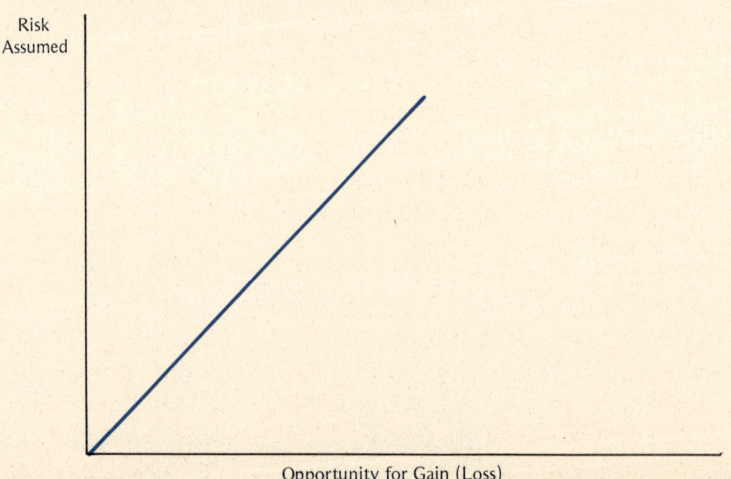

What to Do about Risk

Dealing with speculative risk has been the underlying thrust of the majority of this text. Good management practices are the key to handling speculative risk. Expertise in the various functional areas of business provides the basis for effectively controlling speculative risk within the firm.

There are three basic methods of managing pure risks. These methods are: (1) reducing hazards; (2) self-insurance; and (3) shifting the risk to professional insurers.

Reducing Hazards

The most obvious way of lessening exposure to pure risk is to reduce the potential hazards. For purposes of definition, a **peril** is a circumstance that may cause a loss, while a **hazard** is a condition that makes the occurrence of the peril more likely. For example, the death of a key executive is a peril, while the executive's high blood pressure is a hazard. A program of periodic medical examinations combined with a companywide physical fitness program is a means of reducing this hazard and peril.

Most hazard reduction programs involve little more than common sense. Keeping a plant modern and outfitted with the latest fire detection equipment obviously reduces the chance of a catastrophic fire. Industrial safety programs —often conducted under the auspices of the personnel department—reduce the chance of injuries on the job.

Self-insurance

A business that is willing to assume pure risk rather than shift it to others may **self-insure** by establishing a **contingency fund**. For example, a company may feel that the cost of insurance through professional insurers for a particular peril is just too expensive compared to the chance that the peril will occur. Rather than make payments to an outside insurer, the company establishes a fund to help provide compensation if the peril should actually occur. The company will periodically make cash contributions to the fund until it achieves a size sufficient to compensate for the damage done by the peril.

A self-insurance program is not a foolproof scheme, however. It can easily backfire to the loss of the firm. Contributions to the fund are not compulsory, and the company management may be tempted to omit a contribution if it feels money is more urgently needed in some other area of the business. Furthermore, the self-insurance fund provides the least protection against the effects of loss in the early years of its existence, as is shown in Figure 15-2. Suppose the firm is self-insuring against loss due to fire. If a fire occurs in the early years of the fund's life, the firm will suffer a major unprotected loss. Such a loss could mean the ruin of the firm. It is only in the later years of the fund's existence that the firm will have sufficient resources to make up for its

Figure 15-2. *Protection by Self-Insurance*

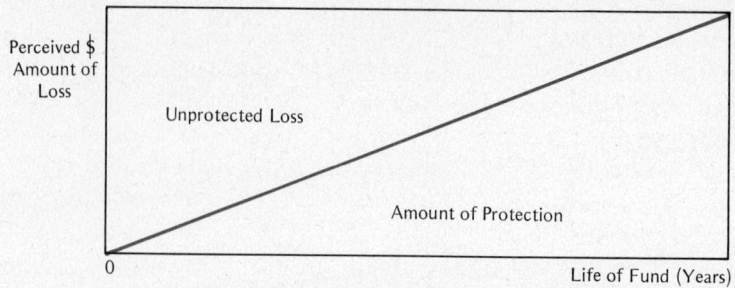

losses. Obviously the company is gambling that a sizable loss will not occur early in the life of the fund.

Professional Insurance

A firm unwilling or unable to self-insure must seek the aid of professional insurance companies to aid in reducing its pure risks. Insurance companies provide protection for a variety of perils, as will be seen in a later section of this chapter. For now, however, the focus of our discussion will turn to some of the fundamentals associated with shifting pure risk to professional insurers.

An *insurance policy* is a contract that binds the insurance company and the insured firm. Every policy includes:

1. The amount of insurance coverage.
2. A complete identification and definition of the risks assumed.
3. The cost of the coverage.
4. Procedures for the proof and settlement of loss.
5. Conditions for transference of the risks insured.
6. Identification of the hazards not covered by the policy.

A policy is not valid if the insured uses misrepresentation or fraud in obtaining it. All property and liability policies may be cancelled by either party on written notice. Life insurance policies, however, cannot be cancelled by the insurance company. Before a policy will be issued, certain principles of insurance must be adhered to. These include: (1) the principle of insurable interest; (2) the principle of insurable risk; and (3) the principle of indemnity.

THE PRINCIPLE OF INSURABLE INTEREST The principle of insurable interest states that payments will be made on a claim only when the policyholder can show a personal loss because of the occurrence of the insured peril. This principle is most vividly understood in the case of life insurance. Individuals can take an insurance policy only on persons within their families and on their business partners. The death of any of these people would result in financial hardship for the person purchasing the insurance. If it were not for this principle, a person could take out life insurance on some other individual and murder that person to collect the insurance proceeds.

THE PRINCIPLE OF INSURABLE RISK   Not all risks are insurable. In order to be insurable, a risk must conform to certain standards. First, to be covered by insurance, the loss from a risk must have been unintentional and accidental. If the loss were intentional and not accidental, chance would not be present. Insurance is designed only for cases in which uncertainty is involved.

Second, the extent of the risk must be measurable and determinable. If the loss is not measurable, the claim cannot be paid. The likelihood of the peril occurring must be determinable in order for the insurance company to ascertain a charge for its service. For example, a person's probability of death can be determined by reference to the proper occupation category, health record, and age in a mortality table. The probability of death determines the charge per $1000 of insurance.

Lastly, the risk must be similar for all persons or things in the group, and each group must have a large number of cases. Persons are grouped by age and occupation in determining life insurance costs. Insurance costs for fire protection differ from residential houses to apartment dwellings to commercial buildings because of the difference in hazards facing the different groups.

By requiring a large number of cases in each insurable group, insurers are appealing to the law of averages. In life insurance, an insurer does not know specifically who is going to die in a given year. But, from mortality tables developed from historical experience, the insurer knows approximately what percentage of members of a particular group will die. According to the law of averages or large numbers, as it is sometimes called, the larger the number of cases in the group, the closer the actual number of cases will approximate the estimated. Thus, the charges of an insurer for coverage seem surprisingly low compared to the amount of coverage obtained.

THE PRINCIPLE OF INDEMNITY   Regardless of the amount of insurance stipulated in the policy, the principle of indemnity states that a person cannot collect more than the actual cash loss in the event of damage or injury caused by an insured peril. Thus, if a $50,000 house is insured for $75,000 and the house burns to the ground, the insurance company will pay only $50,000 in settlement on the claim. In general, the principle of indemnity applies to property and liability insurance but not to life and most health insurance.

KINDS OF INSURANCE COMPANIES AND INSURANCE

Given that a business executive decides to seek the services of an insurance company rather than to self-insure, where does one turn? And what types of insurance should a business executive investigate? Answers will be provided in this section.

Types of Insurance Companies

Two types of insurance companies account for the bulk of all insurance sold each year in the United States. These are *stock companies* and *mutuals*.

A stock insurance company is a corporation. Like any other corporation, it receives its charter from a state and is owned by stockholders. The stock company is in business to make a profit for its owners. The stock company's main source of revenue is from *premiums*—the charges it levies for its coverage. Income equals premiums received plus profits on an investment portfolio minus expenses and payments on claims. The stock company invests in government securities, stocks, bonds, and mortgages in order to increase the income for its stockholders. Stock companies do about 75% of their business in fire insurance. They are also major issuers of other types of insurance, with the exception of life insurance.

A mutual insurance company is a nonprofit corporation owned by its policyholders. Like the stock company, the mutual is created according to state law. Policyholders elect a board of managers to run the affairs of the company.

Whereas the profits of the stock company are paid in dividends to its shareholders or held for reinvestment within the firm, the profits of the mutual are returned to the policyholders in the form of dividends. In effect, if the mutual invests wisely, its policyholders' premiums are reduced by the amount of dividends received.

There were 1,829 life insurance companies in business in mid-1972. Over 90% of these were stock companies. However, the 10% that were mutual life companies had about two-thirds of the assets of all life insurance companies in the United States and accounted for slightly in excess of half of all the life insurance outstanding.[1]

Major Types of Insurance

There are nearly as many different types of insurance policies as there are different perils. For purposes of discussion, we shall concentrate on life insurance, property and casualty insurance, and some other miscellaneous types of insurance.

Life Insurance

The Institute of Life Insurance reported that in 1969 at least one member of 86% of all families in the United States interviewed in a national survey owned life insurance. Furthermore, Americans purchased nearly $212.3 billion in life insurance in 1972. Why did Americans make such an enormous financial outlay? The institute suggests that people buy life insurance for a

---

[1] Institute of Life Insurance, *Life Insurance Factbook* 1973, p. 91.

variety of reasons, but the major one is to provide financial protection for their families in case they themselves should die prematurely.[2]

There is probably no product more often purchased and less understood than life insurance. Insurance companies bombard the public with magazine and television advertisements to push their products. What is essentially a single product is packaged in so many different ways and given so many different names that it is unintelligible to the layman. Perhaps this discussion will remove some of the mystery.

TYPES OF LIFE INSURANCE POLICIES There are basically four different types of life insurance: (1) term; (2) whole life; (3) limited pay life; and (4) endowment. Other types of life insurance that an agent may sell are simply combinations of the four basic types.

1. *Term insurance.* Term insurance is pure insurance. While whole life, limited pay life, and endowment insurance combine both insurance and savings components, term insurance has no savings component.

With term insurance, the insured pays premiums periodically for a pre-specified term, be it one year, five years, or any other length of time. In order to qualify for the insurance, the applicant must pass a physical examination. If the term policy is *guaranteed renewable*, the insured need only pass the physical the first time. Even if the person's health deteriorates, the insured is able to renew the policy when the stated term lapses. Without this feature, the applicant could not assure insurability.

The face amount of the term policy is paid to the insured's beneficiary—the person designated by the insured to collect on the policy—only upon the insured's death. If the insured does not die during the term of the policy, the policy expires, and the insured must renew it. Since the chance of death increases as a person gets older, the premiums charged for the term policies will increase each time the policy is renewed.

Term insurance is the most common type of business life insurance. It is usually used in *group* insurance policies, where a company provides its personnel with insurance at some multiple of their salaries. In many cases, the company pays all the premiums on these policies since they provide a rather low-cost fringe benefit to workers. Members of the group do not have to pass a physical examination; the premiums are computed on an average age basis for each job risk category. The group policy is usually a one-year guaranteed renewable plan.

Term insurance is also widely used as *"key-man"* insurance. The death of a key man in a company—a partner, important stockholder, or key employee—can wreak havoc in a company. The company pays the premiums and is the beneficiary of the policy. In a partnership, the surviving partners can use the proceeds of the life insurance policy to compensate the deceased's family for its inherited share. In a corporation, the policy proceeds can be used to protect against losses following the death of a key man. The proceeds can even be used to find and train a new key person.

[2] *Life Insurance Factbook* 1973, pp. 14–15.

Credit life insurance is another use of term insurance. Suppose an individual borrows a large sum of money from the bank. The bank requires the borrower to purchase a credit life policy in the amount of the loan with the bank made beneficiary of the policy. If the borrower dies, the bank is able to recover its lent money. In an age of widely expanding consumer credit, credit life insurance is becoming increasingly more important.

2. *Whole life insurance* Under a whole life policy, the insured pays premiums for a lifetime or until the person reaches the age of 100. The face amount of the policy is paid to the insured's beneficiary upon the insured's death or to the insured when reaching age 100, whichever comes first.

Although the chance of death increases as the insured gets older, the premiums on the whole life policy stay at a level amount. The insurance company uses the premiums to pay its expenses and death claims and to build up an investment fund. The part of the premium which exceeds the expense and mortality charges is, in effect, the savings aspect of the whole life plan. The amount of money in the savings plan is called the *cash value* of the policy. As shown in Figure 15-3, the cash value increases as the insured continues to live.

The cash value is also called the nonforfeiture value of the policy, since it legally belongs to the insured. The insured can take out a loan from the insurance company for this value, cash in the policy for this amount, or use the cash value to buy term insurance. Why may these be of interest to the insured? The interest rate on a policy loan is determined when the policy is first issued. If interest rates have risen since then, the insured may find it advantageous to borrow money from the insurance company rather than a bank or other lenders. Furthermore, the insured need never repay the loan. At the insured's death, the insured's beneficiary will receive the face amount of the policy less any loan outstanding.

If the insured cannot afford to continue paying the premiums on the policy, the latter two alternatives may be of interest. If the insured needs money, the individual can simply cash in the policy for its cash value. If the person still wants insurance, he or she can convert the whole life policy to a term policy, using the cash value to pay the premiums.

Figure 15-3. *The Whole Life Policy*

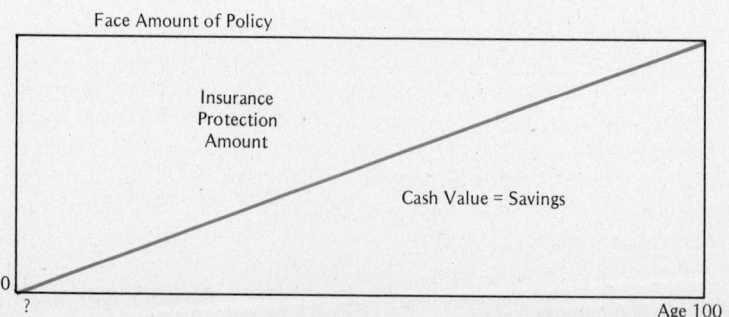

3. *Limited pay life.* A limited pay life policy is similar to the whole life policy with one difference. Premiums are paid for only a limited time period, say twenty or thirty years. Perhaps the insured does not want to be paying premiums after retirement. The person can buy a limited pay life policy in order to have payments cease when retiring. Since the individual pays premiums for a shorter time span, the insured will find the premiums to be higher on the limited pay life than on whole life policies.

4. *Endowment.* The endowment policy has the highest premium cost and is the extreme in savings plans for life insurance. Under an endowment plan, the policy face amount is paid to either the beneficiary of the policy at the insured's death or to the insured at the end of the endowment period, whichever comes earlier. The savings aspect of a 20-year, $10,000 endowment policy is shown in Figure 15-4.

SELECTING A LIFE INSURANCE POLICY There are a number of factors to consider in selecting a life insurance plan. The first is *cost*. Table 15-1, p. 390, shows the costs in terms of annual premiums for different types of policies.

The extremely low cost of term insurance—which would be even lower for group policies—makes it extremely attractive for business insurance. But what about for the individual?

Term insurance provides no savings aspect. A company is not concerned with the savings part of insurance, only with the pure protection amount relative to out-of-pocket cost. But the individual may find the savings aspect attractive. The rate of return earned on the savings component of an insurance policy is about 5% per year. Given this low rate of return, some experts and many others suggest that an individual purchase term insurance and invest the difference in premiums between the term policy and the savings type policies in higher yielding assets. Thus, the insured gets the best of both worlds: insurance protection and a higher return on savings. Will this work? It might. Then again it could easily fail if the individual could not keep up with a savings plan or invested unwisely. After all, a forced savings plan returning 5% is better than no savings plan at all.

Does it pay to shop for life insurance or are all policies alike? As noted

Figure 15-4. *A 20-Year, $10,000 Endowment Policy*

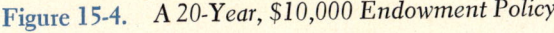

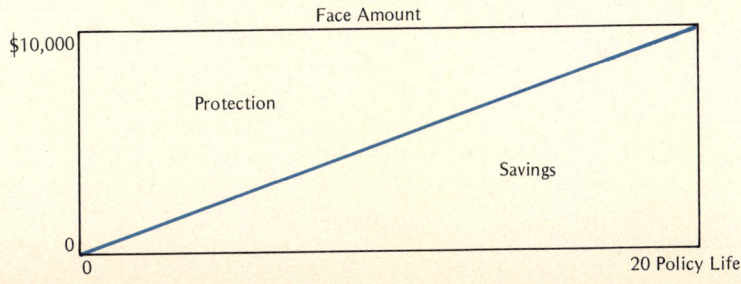

Table 15-1. *Cost of Life Insurance for a 22-year-old Male*

Policy	Annual Premium per $1,000 Insurance
1. 5-year renewable term	$ 4.30
2. Whole life	11.22
3. Life paid up at age 65	12.46
4. Endowment at age 65	15.73
5. 20-year limited pay life	19.69
6. 20-year endowment	41.60

Source: Institute of Life Insurance.

earlier, as much as insurance companies try to differentiate their products, insurance policies have far more in common than an insurance sales representative will ever tell you. But the cost of life insurance varies widely. A study conducted in 1972 by the Insurance Commissioner of the State of Pennsylvania found a difference of more than 170% from the lowest cost to the highest cost whole life policy sold by the 50 largest insurance companies selling in the state of Pennsylvania.[3] Although differences in term policies are not as great, they still vary widely.

How does one compare the cost of policies? Unfortunately, not by just comparing premium charges. One must consider premiums, the rate of build-up in cash value, dividends, and *when* dividends are received. The sooner a dividend is received, the better it is for the insured, since the person can reinvest it for a longer period of time. The true cost or interest-adjusted cost method, based on certain assumptions about when dividends will be received and the rate of growth in cash value, provides the best measure of insurance cost. These must be provided to you by an insurance agent—but only at your request. The Pennsylvania study—and others as well—have found that low cost *premium* policies are often very high true cost policies.[4] Also, failure to adjust for reinvestment possibilities—the so-called net cost method that simply averages what you pay less what you get back without adjusting for *when* you get cash value and dividends—will provide a misleading ranking of the cost of policies sold by different companies. In Table 15-2, the differences between measuring insurance cost by the premium versus true cost methods are highlighted.

THE FINE PRINT Like any other insurance policy the life insurance policy is a contract binding the insured and the insurer. There are a multitude of legalistic clauses in every policy, but four are of particular interest. These are:

---

[3] Pennsylvania Insurance Department, *A Shopper's Guide to Life Insurance*, April 1972.
[4] *A Shopper's Guide to Life Insurance*. An excellent book written on this topic especially for the layman is Joseph M. Belth's *Life Insurance: A Consumer's Handbook*, Bloomington, Ind.: Indiana University Press, 1973.

Table 15-2. *Costs of a $10,000 Whole Life Insurance Policy Sold by the Five Lowest and Five Highest True Cost Companies in Pennsylvania*

Company Ranking	Male Age 20 or Female Age 23	
	Annual Premium	Average Annual True Cost
1. Connecticut Mutual Life Insurance Company	$135.00	$22.40
2. Home Life Insurance Co. (New York)	150.70	23.10
3. Bankers Life Company (Iowa)	149.70	24.70
4. Phoenix Mutual Life Insurance Company	157.00	26.60
5. National Life Insurance Company (Vermont)	152.70	28.30
46. United Benefit Life Insurance Company of America	116.40	51.00
47. Business Men's Assurance Company of America	118.20	51.70
48. Northwestern National Life Insurance Company	177.80	51.90
49. Old Republic Life Insurance Company (Illinois)	122.00	52.30
50. The Travelers Insurance Company	118.00	53.10

(Listing limited to 50 largest companies selling insurance in Pennsylvania)

Source: Pennsylvania Insurance Department, *A Shopper's Guide to Life Insurance,* April 1972.

(1) incontestability; (2) suicide; (3) misstatement of age; and (4) alteration of policy.

1. *Incontestability.* The incontestability clause states that the insurer cannot contest—or challenge—the policy after it has been in effect for usually a two-year period. In the absence of this clause, a company could refuse to honor a death claim on the basis that the insured made a misstatement on the original application. As long as the insured lives through the two-year period without the company contesting the policy, the beneficiary is assured of receiving benefits at the death of the insured.

2. *Suicide.* Most policies include a clause that limits death benefits to the amount of premiums paid if the insured commits suicide in the first two years of a policy's life. Once the two-year period is up, the company must honor the face amount of the policy even if the insured commits suicide.

3. *Misstatement of age.* The amount of insurance that one dollar will buy is determined, in part, by the insured's age at time of application. When the insured dies, a difference is sometimes found between the age of the insured at death and the alleged age at date of issue. In this situation, the misstatement of age clause provides for the face amount to be adjusted to what the premium would have bought at the correct age.

4. *Alteration of policy.* A modification of a policy is not valid unless it is done in writing and signed by a company officer. Verbal and written commitments by an insurance agent do not bind the company unless a company officer supports those commitments in writing.

Property and Casualty Insurance

A fire at a company's main manufacturing facility can put the company out of business. If someone is injured while using a company's product, the company can be sued for enormous amounts of money. To protect themselves against these and other perils, companies buy property and casualty insurance. The major type of property insurance is fire insurance. A casualty is an unfortunate occurrence or an accident. The major types of casualty insurance are: (1) automobile insurance; (2) theft insurance; (3) accident and health insurance; (4) public liability insurance; and (5) workmen's compensation.

FIRE INSURANCE   The risk of loss of property due to fire or lightning can be insured by fire insurance. A fire insurance policy covers only losses directly related to fire. Damage done by other perils is not covered in the context of the fire insurance policy. Since there are many other perils, a company is wise to add an allied lines clause to the fire insurance policy. The allied lines coverage protects the business against damage due to hail, riot, explosion, tornado, hurricane, wind, aircraft, automobile, or other vehicle. Furthermore, the company may be covered by *business interruption insurance*, which covers the loss of income resulting from an interruption in business due to the occurrence of any of the perils stated in the policy. Business interruption insurance is commonly issued to cover one year's profits at a plant.

Most companies and individuals tend to underinsure their property against the peril of fire. Because of improved fire detection systems, better built structures, and modern firefighting equipment, the likelihood of a fire totally destroying a factory is fairly small. There is a much higher chance of a small fire. The business executive reasons that there is no need to pay premiums for unneeded insurance.

Most states permit fire insurance companies to include a coinsurance clause in their policies. A typical coinsurance clause reads as follows:

> It is a condition of this policy, that the insured shall at all times maintain insurance on all property covered by this policy of not less than _____ percent [usually 80%] of the actual cash value thereof, and that failing to do so, the insured shall be insurer to the extent of such deficit.

Thus, the business executive who underinsures must share the loss due to fire.

An example will best clarify the concept of coinsurance. Suppose a company carries a $6 million fire insurance policy on its $10 million building. Coinsurance requires the company to carry fire insurance at 80% of the property value. The building is totally destroyed by fire. How much will the businessman collect? The following formula applies:

$$\frac{\text{Amount of insurance carried}}{\text{Amount of insurance required}} \times \text{Amount of loss} = \text{Amount collectible}$$

Thus, in this example, the business executive would collect:

$$\frac{\$6 \text{ million}}{\$8 \text{ million}} \times \$6 \text{ million} = \$4.5 \text{ million}$$

The business executive would be out $5.5 million ($10 million less $4.5 million). Note that if the business executive carried $10 million in fire insurance, he would have met the 80% coinsurance obligation and received the full $10 million in settlement. Of course, relying on the principle of indemnity, the insurance company will never pay more in settlement than the value of the loss, regardless of the amount of the policy.

Why do fire insurance policies have a coinsurance clause? Essentially, the reason is to equalize the cost burden of fire insurance among property owners. Suppose two business executives have identical buildings worth $100,000. Executive A carries $50,000 in fire insurance, while B carries $80,000. An 80% coinsurance clause is in effect. If both executives file claims for $40,000 for loss from fire, A will collect $25,000 ($50,000 ÷ $80,000 × $40,000). B will collect the full $40,000.

AUTOMOBILE INSURANCE The continually growing use of the automobile in both business and pleasure has meant a rise in automobile insurance issued in this country. Thousands of people are killed and millions are injured each year because of automobile accidents. To lessen the risk of loss due to damages involved in an automobile accident, business executives and other individuals carry automobile insurance.

The six basic areas covered by an automobile insurance policy are: (1) collision; (2) bodily injury liability; (3) property damage liability; (4) medical payments for injury; (5) comprehensive damage; (6) protection against uninsured motorists.

1. *Collision coverage* pays back the insured for damage done to the person's own automobile through collision with another automobile or a stationary object. Since smaller accidents are more likely than total destruction of a vehicle, collision coverage generally includes a deductible in order to minimize the cost of coverage. Under a $50 deductible clause, the insured must pay the first $50 of damage to the car from a collision before collecting anything from the insurance company. This helps keep nuisance claims to a minimum.

2. *Bodily injury liability* provides coverage for injury, sickness, disease, or

death of persons for which the insured is legally liable because of an accident involving his car. Claims will be honored up to the limits of the policy, with the insured personally liable for judgments in excess of the policy limits. Given rising court settlements in bodily injury suits, it is becoming quite common for an individual to have protection of $100,000 for an accident involving one injured person and $300,000 for accidents having two or more persons injured.

3. *Property damage liability* covers the costs of damage done to the property of others for which the insured is liable. Most individuals carry between $10,000 and $25,000 in property damage liability insurance.

4. *Medical payments coverage* pays, up to the policy limits, medical expenses from accidental injury. It applies to anyone injured while riding in the insured's car.

5. *Comprehensive damage insurance* covers losses due to fire and theft. Items stolen from the car—as well as the car itself—are insured under this feature.

6. *Uninsured-motorist protection* guards the insured against losses caused by a hit-and-run driver or a person with no automobile insurance. With *uninsured-motorist protection*, the insurance company will pay damages to the insured to the same extent it would if it had carried insurance on the uninsured or unknown driver.

THEFT INSURANCE The law clearly distinguishes between burglary, robbery, and theft. A *burglary* is a crime against property, while a *robbery* is a crime against a person. A *theft* is a simple act of stealing. A burglary insurance policy requires signs of forced entry before payment will be made on a claim. Similarly, some sort of personal contact must be made in order for the insured to collect on a robbery insurance policy. Since a theft insurance policy does not require the evidence of the burglary or robbery policies, its premiums are considerably higher, while its coverage is much broader. Premiums can be reduced, of course, if a company employs a night guard or other crime prevention devices.

ACCIDENT AND HEALTH INSURANCE Accident and health insurance policies are designed to reimburse the insured for medical expenses due to accidents and losses of health not related to accidents, respectively. It is quite common for a business to provide group accident and health plans for its employees as a fringe benefit. The company pays all or part of the premiums for the plans.

The major accident and health plans are *first dollar coverage* and *major medical plans*. The first dollar coverage is designed to pay the initial cost of medical attention. The Blue Cross and Blue Shield policies are the most common of the first dollar coverage plans. Blue Cross and Blue Shield are nonprofit corporations. Blue Cross pays for hospital bills, while Blue Shield covers surgical costs and doctor fees. First dollar coverage policies generally have a limited amount of coverage on a per accident or payoff range basis. There is also a maximum on the amount paid for doctor bills. A common stipulation of surgical policies is that the insured will pay a given percentage—usually 20%—of the cost of physician's services.

Major medical insurance is designed as protection against catastrophic medical expenses. These plans usually have a deductible feature and coinsurance. The insured must bear the initial $100 or whatever deductible is stated in the policy and carry a minimum amount of first-dollar coverage before any major medical claims will be honored. Additionally, the insured must share the cost of medical expenses with the insurer. A major medical plan will typically pay 80% of all covered bills up to a stated maximum.

One other type of accident and health insurance plan is worthy of note. This is called **disability insurance**. While first-dollar coverage and major medical policies are designed to pay medical bills, disability insurance is intended to cover income loss from disability. A person out of work for an extended period of time due to disability will need a source of income to replace normal income source. Disability insurance is important since the chance of disability is much greater than that of death. For example, the probability of long-term disability—defined as "the inability of the insured, by reason of sickness or bodily injury, to engage for at least three months in any occupation for which he is reasonably fitted by education, training, or experience"—is 3.45 times greater than the chance of death for an individual age 32.

Disability insurance plans generally require a waiting period of up to six months before any benefits are paid. Since short-term disability is much more likely than long-term disability—although the economic hardship of long-term disability is especially devastating—the waiting period lowers the cost of the policy. There is no need to carry disability insurance in an amount equivalent to the insured's salary, since the insured does not pay income tax on these benefits.

PUBLIC LIABILITY INSURANCE   Public liability insurance is designed to protect the insured against claims caused by injuries to others on the insured's property or by the insured's products. A company can be successfully sued for enormous amounts of money if someone is injured using its products. And the company does not have to be guilty of negligence for it to be successfully sued. The simple fact that a product was defective is enough for a settlement against the firm. The amount of coverage needed depends on the loss potential. A $750,000 to $1 million per incidence product or public liability insurance policy is certainly reasonable for most firms. For companies susceptible to major suits, coverage of $100 million may prove inadequate. The key to effective public liability insurance is more care in manufacturing a company's products and maintenance of its production and administrative facilities.

WORKMEN'S COMPENSATION INSURANCE   The laws of most states require employers to compensate—at least in part—medical expenses and wages lost from job-related injury or disease. Most states require companies to purchase workmen's compensation insurance by either paying premiums to a state-administered fund or to an insurance company. The premiums paid are related to the risk classifications of the jobs performed by the company's employees. In addition, the premiums are related to the company's safety record. If a company has instituted an effective safety program and subsequent claims against it are low, the premiums paid to the insurance plan will be correspondingly reduced.

Other Types of Insurance

The variety of insurance policies that exist is limited only by the imagination of insurance companies in their marketing efforts. The major types of policies have, for the most part, already been touched upon. The remaining types of policies to be considered are fidelity and surety bonds, title insurance, and marine insurance.

FIDELITY AND SURETY BONDS Fidelity bonds are designed to protect a business against acts of theft by its employees. In the age old tale of the country bank president suddenly leaving town with all the money from the vault, the bank would recover all its losses from the insurance company which carries the bank's fidelity bond.

A surety bond protects the insured against the failure of the terms of a contract being fulfilled. Construction companies are often required to purchase a surety bond to guarantee that, if the contractor fails to complete the building on time or according to specification, the insurance company will assume the financial burden for completing the job.

TITLE INSURANCE An owner of property is protected by title insurance against any loss incurred because of defects in the title to the property. A *title* is simply a claim of ownership to the property. Suppose a company buys a warehouse from an unscrupulous builder who had used the warehouse as collateral for a loan. The builder leaves town with the company's money and without repaying the loan. The lender claims the warehouse since it was collateral for the loan. Legally, the lender has ownership of the warehouse. What happens to the company? Without the title insurance, it would be plainly out of luck. But with title insurance, the insurer will compensate the company for the loss of the building.

MARINE INSURANCE Surprisingly, marine insurance covers more than water-related perils. There are two types of marine insurance: ocean marine and inland marine.

Ocean marine insurance protects a ship and its cargo in port or on the high seas against a variety of perils. These perils include theft, collision, sinking, and capsizing.

Inland marine insurance provides protection for all forms of transportation, whether it be land, air, or water (but not the high seas). The perils include theft, collision, flood, fire, wind, and hail.

TRENDS IN THE IMPACT OF INSURANCE ON BUSINESS

Insurance and insurance companies have an enormous impact on business. In this section, two specific areas will be examined: fire insurance and product liability insurance.

Impact of Fire Insurance on Business

Industrial fires are becoming an ever-increasing risk. The settlement costs are rising at an astronomical rate. From 1965 through 1973, losses of $50,000 or more on industrial fires increased over sixfold. In order to compensate for rising claims, fire insurers have continued to increase the premiums they charge. At the rate fire insurance premiums are rising, many firms may find they can no longer afford coverage.

Why have settlement costs risen so dramatically? One major reason offered is the growing size of one-site facilities. Some factories are simply becoming too big to insure economically. The nation's largest fire insurer is reluctant to insure a plant for over $100 million. Yet some companies are building plants costing in excess of $200 million.[5]

What will be the trend in the impact of fire insurance on business? First, more and more companies will have to self-insure against the peril of fire. And secondly, business executives will have to give more thought to the wisdom of constructing huge factories. One fire insurance executive has suggested that, because of the danger of overconcentration, the government will have to step in and prohibit giant plants if business executives and their financial backers cannot be persuaded by insurance limitations to cut back themselves.

Impact of Product Liability Insurance on Business[6]

The frequency of product liability claims against business and the monetary settlements on these claims are both rapidly increasing. Insurance companies, which have suffered considerable losses in product liability claims, are raising their premiums and being more selective in risks that they are willing to insure. A consequence of this is that businesses are finding the cost of insurance to be at unacceptably high levels, while the degree of self-insurance the businesses must assume is rising to such a point that more firms may be forced out of business by a product liability suit.

---

[5] "The Rising Cost of Plant Fires," *Business Week*, July 20, 1974, 78.
[6] This section is based, in large part, on Herbert C. Cox's excellent article, "Product Liability—Can the Problems be Solved?" *Financial Executive*, August 1974, 36–43.

What are the implications of this situation for business? There are many, and in the following sections some of the more important ones are discussed.

Better Product Design and Quality Control

It may seem obvious, but a company that spends more time and effort in the safe design and manufacturing of its products is going a long way toward reducing its product liability risk. Safety engineers must work with designers, production and insurance personnel, and top management to make a firm's products as accidentproof as possible. Higher costs at this end of the line can prevent catastrophic losses from a product liability suit.

Caution in Product Promotion and Distribution

A product should be packaged so as to enhance its safety. Advertising people should not be permitted to make unwarranted promises about a product. All advertising should be checked by an attorney to see if the company is exposing itself to a possible product liability suit.

A company should be sure that retailers of its products are reliable. The retailer should not make unwarranted claims about a product's use and should make an extra effort to inform the consumer about a product's proper use. The manufacturer and retailer must maintain a dialogue so that the defects in any product are immediately noted at both ends. Proper record keeping by both manufacturer and retailer will facilitate a product recall, should that step be necessary.

Insurance Implications

To reduce the cost of insurance a company may have to have a high deductible clause in the policy. Furthermore, more insurers are going to require companies with poor product liability experience to participate in any losses in addition to the deductible. Thus, a company may have to self-insure the first so many dollars of a product liability loss *and* bear a certain percentage of the loss in excess of the deductible.

Other Implications

A company considering the acquisition of another firm should fully investigate the product liability loss experience of that firm. The acquiring company may find itself liable for the product liability of the other firm. This can be a rather large and unexpected loss exposure.

Lastly, a lender can be left with a worthless loan if one of its creditors fails because of a product liability suit. The lender should make sure that the creditor either has adequate product liability insurance coverage or has the capacity to self-insure against such loss.

CAREERS AND JOBS IN INSURANCE

The insurance industry employed over 1.5 million people in 1972. About half of these persons were employed in clerical positions, with an additional 35% in sales and 15% in other management positions. The outlook for employment in this industry is expected to continue favorably at least into the early 1980s.

You will find career opportunities in insurance—in addition to clerical posts—in the fields of sales, underwriting, claims adjustment, and actuary.

Sales

Insurance agents and brokers sell insurance policies to both individuals and business. They may specialize in the sale of one line of insurance or sell a variety of types. Agents usually work for only one company, but *independent agents* can act as representatives for more than one company. They place policies they sell where they feel their clients will be best served.

An insurance agent must be licensed in each state in which he wishes to sell insurance. Most states require applicants to pass a written examination on insurance fundamentals and state insurance laws. While there is no stated educational requirement for being an insurance agent or taking the state tests, most insurance companies seek their prospective agents from college campuses. If you are a student with a background in business or the liberal arts, you would be of interest to the insurance companies. The most important factor is your sales ability.

Underwriting

An *insurance underwriter* selects risks for the company to insure. The underwriter also outlines terms of policies and the amount of premiums to be charged the insured. Underwriters are usually college graduates with degrees in either liberal arts or business administration. An underwriter also specializes in a certain area of insurance: life, property and casualty, or health. The American College of Life Underwriters administers a rigorous series of examinations to persons desiring to become Chartered Life Underwriters (CLU's). Individuals wanting to attain the professional designation of Chartered Property and Casualty Underwriter (CPCU) must pass tests given by the American Institute for Property and Liability Underwriting. The Life Underwriter Training Council gives courses in life and health insurance for experienced agents. It awards a life insurance marketing diploma to graduates of its two-year program. The job market outlook for insurance underwriters is one of the brightest for all professions.

Claims Adjustment

Claim adjusters investigate, negotiate, and settle insurance claims. They must determine that a claim is legitimate and that a fair settlement is reached —for both the insured and the insurer. A claim adjuster can either specialize in a particular line of insurance or work in many areas. Although there is a trend toward hiring college graduates for claim adjusting, there are still many opportunities for individuals with only some college education.

Actuary

Actuaries have strong backgrounds in statistics and mathematics. It is the responsibility of the actuary to study rates of mortality (death), morbidity (sickness), injury, disability, fire, theft—in other words, all the perils that an insurance company insures—to determine the premiums to be charged for a given insurance policy. An actuary has, at a minimum, an undergraduate degree in statistics or mathematics or, preferably, graduate training in statistics. It is mandatory for an actuary to complete either the ten examinations given for life insurance by the Society of Actuaries or the nine examinations given for property and casualty insurance by the Casualty Actuary Society in order to attain true professional stature. Without successful completion of these tests, the actuary's career will be seriously hampered. The job outlook for actuaries is particularly attractive for those who have undergraduate degrees in statistics or mathematics and have successfully completed one or two actuarial examinations while still in college.

CHAPTER SUMMARY

Risk is a vital part of business. Speculative risks give a business executive the opportunity to reap profits as well as incur losses. Good business practices are the key to controlling speculative risks. Pure risk provides only for loss, not profit. The business executive tries to control this type of risk by hazard reduction, self-insurance, and professional insurance.

To be insurable, a risk must conform to certain principles. The insured must show that he or she has suffered an economic loss in order to collect on a claim. The loss from a risk must be unintentional and accidental, measurable and determinable. It must be the same for all items in a group and conform to the law of large numbers. Lastly, an insured can never collect more on a claim than the actual cash loss.

Insurance policies are available for virtually every kind of insurable peril.

Life insurance provides financial protection for a beneficiary in the event of the insured's death. Life policies can be term, whole life, limited pay life, endowment, or some combination of these four. The buyer of life insurance would be wise to shop carefully since policy costs vary widely among companies.

Property and casualty insurance protects the insured against losses to his property and accidents. The main type of property insurance is fire insurance. Casualty policies include automobile insurance, theft insurance, accident and health insurance, public liability insurance, and workmen's compensation insurance. Other types of coverage are fidelity and surety bonds, title insurance, and marine insurance. These are all vital kinds of protection for both the businessman and the individual.

Insurance is having an important impact on business. Fire insurance trends are requiring business to reexamine the construction of giant plants. Business firms are being exposed to enormous degrees of risk in the area of product liability. There are both business and insurance approaches to reducing this product liability risk exposure.

The insurance industry will continue to increase its importance in both domestic and international business affairs for decades to come. As the industry expands, exciting and rewarding career opportunities will await the interested candidate.

PROVOCATIVE STATEMENT

Are Insurance Policies Unreadable?

1   "One reason for consumer confusion about insurance is the inability of the average person to read a policy. So for the first time in insurance regulatory history, the Pennsylvania insurance department rejected an insurance policy because it was not readable. In fact, it was less readable than Einstein's Theory of Relativity, according to a well-accepted scale. The scale, running from 100 as a perfect score, puts *Time* magazine at 52, Einstein's theory at 18, the standard auto policy at 10 and the homeowners policy at close to zero."

> Herbert S. Dennenberg,
> Insurance Commissioner, Commonwealth of Pennsylvania,
> "Insurance 1973: A Commissioner's View,"
> *Best's Review* (Life/Health Insurance Edition),
> January 1974, 22–24.

PROVOCATIVE STATEMENT

Time for the Insurance Industry to Defend Itself

2 "Criticism of the insurance industry isn't necessarily accurate or even fair. But the fact that it exists, that it goes largely unchallenged, and that it is repeated often enough to take on the appearance of original truth, should be of concern to all of us.

On the one hand, we are accused of being a 19th-century industry that has yet to turn the corner into the 20th. Still raking money in and shoveling money out the same old way.

On the other hand, it's said we're playing poker with the consumer, with all the cards stacked in our favor:

—Rates and profits are too high.
—Claims payments are too small and too slow.
—Insurance policies are incomprehensible.
—. . . the whole insurance system—companies, regulators, and lawyers
. . . all of us—are seen as hopelessly inefficient and corrupt. In business not to serve the public interest, but to serve ourselves.

In the face of this mounting public disenchantment, I think that it's important that we remind ourselves of the strong positive role, the almost pivotal position, that the insurance industry plays in our society. For unless we are strong and articulate in our convictions, we will have little influence with others.

Insurance has been called the handmaiden of commerce. But it's really a good deal more. For business stands at the very crossroads of human concerns and human aspirations: the need for protection, and the desire for security and growth."

> Charles K. Cox,
> Executive Vice President, INA Corp.,
> "Insurance at the Crossroads:
> Consumerism, Inflation, Government Encroachment,"
> *Best's Review* (Property/Liability Edition),
> December 1973, p. 12–13.

REVIEW QUESTIONS

1. Distinguish between speculative risk and pure risk.
2. List and define the three principles of insurance.
3. What is a product liability claim? What is being done to reduce the number of these claims filed each year?
4. Why do so many homeowners take out title insurance on their claim to ownership of property?
5. Why is it unnecessary to carry disability income insurance in an amount equal to the employee's income?
6. Define the basic areas covered by automobile insurance.
7. Compare and contrast the features of the several types of life insurance policies.

Chapter Outline

Information
   Types of Information
      Customers
      Employees
      Channel Members
      Competitors
      Suppliers
      Government
      Other Information
   Uses of Information
      Planning
      Controlling
   Value of Information
      Benefits
      Costs

Systems to Provide Information
   Input
   Processor
      Control Element
      Arithmetic-Logic Element
   Storage
      Internal
      External
      Nature of Stored Data
   Procedures
   Output

Computers and People
   Users of Information
   Suppliers of Information
Successful Computer Use
   Do's of Computer Use
      Management Commitment
      Plan Development
      Feasibility Check
      Output Scanning
   Don'ts of Computer Use
      Canned Computer Operation
      Computer Spending
      Letting Suppliers Decide
      Computers without Management
      Love of Computers
      Underestimated Costs

Future Business Use of Computers
   Decision-making Aids
   Management Involvement

Jobs in the Computer Industry
   Systems Analyst
      Qualifications
      Rewards
   Computer Programmer
      Qualifications
      Rewards
   Computer Operator
      Qualifications
      Rewards

Chapter Summary

Provocative Statement 1:
   A Systems Analyst Comments on Jobs in the Computer Industry

Provocative Statement 2:
   Executives Do Not Trust Their Computers

Key Terms

Computers
Information
Benefits of information
Costs of information
Input
Processor
Control element
Arithmetic-logic element
Storage
Magnetic spots
Procedures
Output
Users of information
Suppliers of information
Compiler
Computer service bureau
Systems analyst
Computer programmer
Computer program
Console operator

The Computer in Business

"... all too many executives don't trust their computers. They regard them as electronic mistresses, devoted to raiding the corporate treasury while spewing out an endless flow of mostly useless paper."
—Editor for Computer Journal

16

Computers have been accepted by businesses as necessary management tools. Over $25 billion (2% of the Gross National Product) is spent annually on computers and operating staffs. The computer is described in this chapter as a method of providing business information. The components necessary to provide information and the responsibilities of managers and other employees concerning use of computers are discussed. In addition, future trends in business use of computers, including multinational computers, are highlighted. The job section of this chapter concerns those who provide business information: systems analysts, computer programmers, and operators.

INFORMATION

Any business needs information. **Information** is data (facts, figures, opinions, and so on) useful to business decision makers. Many different types of information are useful for planning and controlling business activities. However, the value of information must be considered before it is collected.

Types of Information

As mentioned in Chapter Four, business must know what its publics are thinking. Information about customers, employees, channel members, competitors, suppliers, government, and other publics is necessary for business decisions.

405

Customers

Customer information needed includes characteristics such as age, occupation, income level, or number of employees. Customer buying habits, attitudes, and purchasing intentions are also helpful business information.

This information can help managers to evaluate the effectiveness of company activities. The number of purchases and the customer's image of the business suggest whether or not promotional objectives have been accomplished. Similarly, customer complaints and returns of merchandise are indicators of the effectiveness of distribution channels.

Information about buyers' intentions to purchase as well as past sales help decision makers forecast sales. These sales forecasts are important for planning production activities, resource (humanpower, equipment, materials, and capital) needs, and marketing activities.

Employees

Plans to hire and train new personnel are set according to expected future humanpower needs and currently available humanpower. Information about employees leaving the company or changing jobs is needed to determine the number and type of employees available in the future.

Other information needed about employees may include their abilities to produce and their attitudes toward the organization. Information about employees can be used to pinpoint reasons for past performance.

Channel Members

Channel members may not be performing as expected. Information about purchases of middlemen, their operating characteristics, their attitudes toward the organization's product, and their future plans can prove helpful in deciding what is causing poor performance. Similar types of information about channel members will also be needed when channels are planned.

Competitors

Present actions and future plans of competitors will affect the success of a company's plans. Information about competitors help firms decide what caused previous performance. Moreover, new product introductions, price changes, or distribution channel changes will affect the success of future company actions. Therefore, the company must have information about these changes.

Suppliers

Suppliers may expect future shortages or price increases. Companies will want to know this so they can plan purchasing activities accordingly. Attitudes of suppliers toward a company can also be useful for understanding supplier performance. Suppliers may not like the buyers' slowness in paying bills or other aspects of their behavior.

Government

Government legislation has a broad impact on business. Decision makers need to know the effect of legislation on their activities. Court interpretations of laws and congressional intentions toward future legislation serve as important bases for managerial planning. Some company actions, such as price increases, may be altered because of expected governmental reaction.

Other Information

Information about the economy and the general public is valuable for decision making. Economic information may include forecasts of economic conditions: prosperity, recession, or depression. The modern business executive must be aware of public reaction to business activities. Demands for clean air, minority employment, and fair treatment of consumers must be considered.

Uses of Information

Information is useful because it helps business executives to be more certain about the outcome of planned future action. Business executives also need information to see if company activities are going as planned. This information, for control purposes, should also help them decide what action is necessary to get the activities back on track, according to plan.

Planning

Planning consists of deciding on a *future* course of action. Generally, information can prove helpful in each stage of the planning process. These stages are:

1. Problem or opportunity identification.
2. Identification of alternatives.
3. Alternative evaluation.
4. Alternative selection.
5. Implementation of plan.

PROBLEM OR OPPORTUNITY IDENTIFICATION Plans are frequently made to solve a problem or to take advantage of an opportunity. Decision makers must be kept informed of the problems and opportunities facing their businesses.

Problem-related information includes past sales and related indications of performance as well as statements of specific performance goals and objectives. Other problem-related information, which may not be available in company records, is needed to help determine the cause of the problem. Low sales performance, for example, may be explained by information collected about competitors or channel members.

Information can reveal opportunities for the company. Suggestions for cost-savings in operations, for new products, or for methods of improving sales of present products may be received from employees. Other sources of opportunities may include competitors, the U.S. Patent Office, or suppliers. Frequently, information about opportunities is inadequate because decision makers are overconcerned with solving present problems. However, opportunities that are neglected may turn into future problems.

IDENTIFICATION OF ALTERNATIVES Business executives must discover alternative ways to solve problems or to take advantage of opportunities. Information about company behavior in the past or about competitive solutions of similar problems will prove helpful in deciding what can be done. Information may help business executives decide, for example, that they can solve the problem of poor sales performance by increasing sales representatives' wages or hiring more salespeople.

ALTERNATIVE EVALUATION Different courses of action result in different outcomes. A course of action of increasing promotional expenditures by 10%, for example, will probably result in different sales, profits, and other outcomes from a course of action of a 15% decrease in prices.

Evaluation of alternatives requires two types of information: predictive and evaluative information.

1. *Predictive information* allows decision makers to decide the effect of the course of action on company sales, costs, profits, and other performance indicators. This information may include a statement of relationships between promotion and sales or price and sales.

2. *Evaluative information* relates to company objectives. The worth of the predicted outcomes is interpreted based on company objectives. This type of information can be used, for example, to resolve the question of whether an alternative giving a 10% increase in both profits and sales is of more value to a company than one resulting in a 15% increase in profits but a 5% decrease in sales.

ALTERNATIVE SELECTION Selection of the best alternative should be easy once the outcomes of each alternative are evaluated. However, business executives require information to help reduce the uncertainties underlying outcome evaluation.

Uncertainties are encountered by business executives trying to select a course of action because any course of action may result in one of several outcomes. The introduction of a new product may result in different levels of sales, depending on customer and competitive reaction. Information may be used to predict the chances of each outcome occurring. For example, available information may suggest that there is a one-out-of-ten chance that competitors will duplicate a company's new product.

IMPLEMENTATION OF PLAN Once decisions have been made, more detailed plans are needed to implement—or carry out—the decision. Information is needed to set the specific activities and the order in which they should be carried out. Those responsible for carrying out the activities may be asked how much time and how many resources will be required. Their estimates can be used to lay out the schedule of jobs and assign responsibility to company personnel.

Controlling

Once plans have been implemented, the management process shifts to the control phase. Information is needed for the three steps of control:

1. Setting standards.
2. Measuring actual performance.
3. Taking corrective action.

SETTING STANDARDS   Desired outcomes from plans need to be set. These outcomes serve as standards to compare against actual performance.

These standards may be developed in terms of effectiveness or efficiency. *Effectiveness*, concerning accomplishment of benefits, is frequently the objective of marketing executives. For instance, marketing may want to achieve maximum sales at any cost. *Efficiency* is the concern of production decision makers. They want to produce with least cost. Top management people need to be informed about both effectiveness and efficiency goals. They must coordinate them.

Standards set for plans are generally based on industry performance, past company performance, and managerial expectations. Trade magazines, annual reports, and observation of competitors provide information about industry sales, profits, prices, number of employees, and so on. The performance of competitors may be the standards for company performance. However, past company performance may provide more realistic expectations. Company resources and objectives may not make matching of competitor performance possible or desirable. Internal records of past company performance will come from the accounting, marketing, and personnel departments. This information should help those setting standards to decide if past behavior has relevance for the future. Managerial expectations—what the boss thinks—may include industry and past performances.

However, management usually sets standards based on estimates of future conditions. Uncertainty is generally greatest for these managerial expectations. In the future, customer buying habits may change, governmental units may change their positions, or competitors may change their marketing activities.

MEASURING ACTUAL PERFORMANCE   The performance of those responsible must be measured in terms of the performance standards. Information about costs and benefits generated through actions of company personnel is necessary for these measurements. Sales reports and expense vouchers are examples of actual performance information.

TAKING CORRECTIVE ACTION   Recognizing failure of performance to meet standards is easy. Determining what to do requires more information. Information is needed to isolate the causes of performance failure. Since any outcome, such as amount of sales, is influenced by multiple factors, the impact of specific company activities on outcomes is hard to determine. Moreover, information may provide limited insight into the future outcome of company action. Factors beyond company control will probably change. The situation may change before corrective action can be taken.

Difficulties in achieving satisfactory performance frequently occur because changes in the behavior of people are required. Information about people and their reactions to company action is difficult to collect accurately. Employees may not be able or willing to tell of their personal commitment to the present method of doing things or their change in feeling toward the company when computers are used to provide information.

Value of Information

Management often feels that decisions will improve if more information is made available. However, businesses have found that the benefits from using some information does not justify the cost of obtaining it.

Benefits

Many pieces of information are used to make a business decision, making it difficult to place a value on the benefits from any one piece. Moreover, the total value of all pieces of information is hard to determine, especially before decisions are made. Difficulties are encountered because the outcomes of a management decision made with and without information are not known. Since the decision is made only one time, under a given set of circumstances, what might have happened if the decision had been made under a different set of circumstances (more information) can only be guessed.

Costs

Despite the difficulties of estimating value of information, no business can afford to assume that all information is worthwhile. It must be sure that the expected benefits of information exceed its cost. Information has three types of cost:

1. Cost of providing information.
2. Cost of data errors.
3. Cost of decision delay.

COST OF PROVIDING INFORMATION Most businesses realize that it is an expense to gather data and convert it into useful information. These costs include time of company personnel and payments to other companies that provide the information, as well as equipment and supply costs. Remember, money tied up in provision of information cannot be used for other activities.

COST OF DATA ERRORS Data is sometimes not an accurate or true representation of the actual situation. Since data errors may lead to incorrect decisions, such errors can be costly.

Data may be in error because information was collected from only some people (commonly called a *sample*) rather than from all people. Information may also be inaccurate because those who collected it were biased. Biased data collectors may ignore any facts that disagree with their opinions. Chambers of Commerce, for example, provide information about the economic conditions in their cities. This information generally emphasizes the positive values of a city's economy because the members of the Chamber of Commerce want to convince businesses to locate in their city.

Information collected from people may be inaccurate because people lie to interviewers. Few people will answer questions in a truthful manner if they feel the answers will make them appear dumb or if they consider the questions too personal.

Data errors are hard to measure because the correct information is not known. The best approach to information inaccuracies is to plan collection of information carefully to avoid the potential problems. Accuracy of available data may be determined by evaluating the people who collected it.

DECISION DELAY Decisions may need to be delayed because the desired information is not available. This delay will result in cost because benefits from the decision will not be realized as soon as they would if the decision were made immediately. Moreover, environmental factors surrounding the decision may change while information is collected. A change such as entrance of new competitors may reduce the value of the outcome.

The cost of delaying revenues until information is gathered can be determined by calculating the present value of the two patterns of revenue. One results from immediate action, the other from a delayed decision.

Since great uncertainty surrounds changes in the environment of business, the cost incurred from environmental changes during a decision delay is hard to estimate. However, the most likely changes and their impact can be guessed.

SYSTEMS TO PROVIDE INFORMATION

Information is provided by the effective coordination of five components. These five components, forming an information system, are:

1. Input.
2. Processor.   *KNOW*
3. Storage.
4. Procedures.
5. Output.

Parts of a Typical Business

Input

Data gathered from external sources and company records is the **input**. It may be in the form of verbal or written reports (such as invoices, shipping documents, or annual reports) if no machines are used to process the data.

The inclusion of computers in the information system requires input to be in machine acceptable form. Normally, this input takes the form of punched cards, paper tape, magnetic tape, paper documents with magnetic ink, magnetic discs, and direct input from keyboards. The type of input required depends on the type of machine used to read the data. Examples of machine readers and corresponding forms of data required are shown in Figure 16-1. These machine readers, linked directly to the computer, use sensing

Figure 16-1. *Types of Input Devices*

Device/Card Reader

Input/Keypunch Card

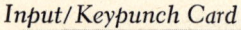

Input/Magnetic Tape

Device/Tape Drive

By permission of the University of Delaware Computer Center

mechanisms to change the input into electronic pulses. The electronic pulses are required for computer processing.

Processor

The processor is the part of the system which transforms input data into relevant business information. Regardless of whether a manual or machine based system is used, the processor has a control element and an arithmetic-logic element.

Control Element

The control element guides the operation of all input and output devices, the entry or removal of data from storage, and the movement of information between storage and the arithmetic-logic element. It decides the sequence and extent of processing among data contained in input, storage, and output. A human is the control element in a manual information system. The computer is the control element in a machine based system.

Arithmetic-Logic Element

The arithmetic-logic element performs four arithmetic tasks (addition, subtraction, multiplication, division) and the logic task of comparing two quantities to see if one quantity is equal to, greater than, or less than the other.

In a manual system, individuals use their brain to perform these five operations (addition, subtraction, multiplication, division, comparison). The central processing unit (CPU) of the computer carries out these tasks at fantastically increased speed and accuracy. An example of a CPU is shown in Figure 16-2 (see p. 414).

Storage

Data may need to be stored before it is processed or used. All data must be placed in storage before it is processed by the computer. Storage may be internal or external to the processor.

Internal

Internal storage is data stored in and directly accessible to the processor. People may remember facts for later use. Internal storage for computers, frequently called *memory*, consists of data from input devices as well as sets of instructions, called *programs*, which tell the computer what to do.

Computer storage is magnetic in form. Data is stored by recording a series of magnetically polarized spots on a metallic surface. The use of these magnetic spots to record numbers is explained in Figure 16-3 on page 415.

Figure 16-2. *Central Processing Unit*

Courtesy of IBM

External

External storage consists of data held outside the mind or memory of the processor. This data is stored until it is needed for future reference or processing. Files of paper documents may be the external storage for a manual system. For machine based systems it can generally be in the same form as input: punched cards, paper tape, magnetic tape, paper documents with magnetic ink, and magnetic discs.

Nature of Stored Data

Data that is stored frequently needs to be summarized and organized.

SUMMARIZATION Summarized data will be easier and less expensive to store than keeping all details available. Storage of average monthly sales for the past year requires less space than daily sales for 365 days. Moreover, summarized data is easier to find when needed. However, data may be too generally summarized. Management may need to know each day's sales.

ORGANIZATION It is necessary to decide the basis for organization of stored data: what data will be stored together or separately. Information about company workers may be organized by workers; all information about a particular worker is stored together. Operating costs may be stored by department of the company; costs of the marketing department are stored separately

Figure 16-3. Computer Storage of Numbers

Groups of magnetic spots are used to represent a number since each spot can be in only one of two electrical states -- 0 or 1 polarity. The position of a spot in a group determines the value of the spot. If, for example, there are 4 spots in a group, the first spot on the right takes on a value of 1 if it is charged with a polarity of 1. Otherwise it is zero. The values of all four spots are:

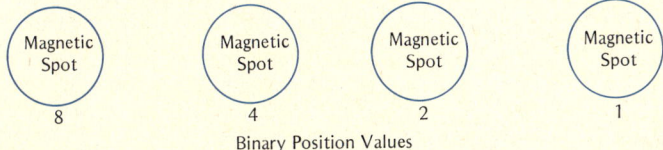

Binary Position Values

These spots will take on the values of their positions only if the spot is polarized with a 1.

The total value of a number stored in a group of spots is the sum of all the position values polarized with a 1. If, for example, each spot in a group of four was polarized with a 1, the number 15 (8 + 4 + 2 + 1) would be stored. If, however, only the first spot on the left of a group of 4 spots was polarized with a 1, the number 8 (8 + 0 + 0 + 0) would be stored in that group of spots.

from those of production. Name, size, or geographical location may be used for organization of stored customer information.

The type of data organization used will depend on the uses of the stored data. The organization should allow managers to get the information they need easily. If the sales manager, for example, wants to know sales for the different sales territories, the information should be stored so it can be retrieved in this manner.

Procedures

The processor must be told what to do with the input. The people or machines who do the processing are given precise instructions for each step of the process. Procedures consist of these instructions, telling which data is to be used, what arithmetic-logic tasks should be performed, and what should be done with the results.

The instructions given to human processors can be less specific than those for computers (programs). Inventory clerks know what the boss means when it is said to value inventory as if the first goods bought are the first sold.

On the other hand, computer programs must be as meticulous as one would be in leading a blind man over a difficult path unknown to the individual. Computers do not think for themselves. They slavishly follow instructions. Beginners at writing instructions for computer programs soon realize they cannot assume that computers know anything. If, for example, the computer is not told where to find the data it is to process, it will stop. A human processor, on the other hand, might know where the data is without being told.

Output

The desired output is information useful to business decision makers. Output may be records or reports. The records will be stored for future use. Reports must be in a form understandable by people. These reports may include written and visual information.

Output for decision makers from computers may be printed by a printer, such as that shown in Figure 16-4. Although printers print at very high speeds, varying from 10 to several thousand characters per second, they cannot keep up with the electronic speed of the central processor. Thus, the computer must store processed information until the printer can finish its job.

Increasingly, computer output is presented in visual displays. Cathode-ray tubes are used to display results on a terminal like that shown in Figure 16-5. Airlines, for example, use terminals at their ticket counters. Requests about available space on flights receive instant visual response.

COMPUTERS AND PEOPLE

Computers have been used for provision of many types of information. Successful use of computers depends on the people (managers, systems, analysts, and computer programmers) who select the computer and tell it

Figure 16-4. *Computer Output*

Figure 16-5. *Visual Display on Terminal*

what to do. **Users of information** and **suppliers of information** have different responsibilities, yet they must learn to work together.

Users of Information

Managers, as users of computer produced information, cannot assign responsibility for selection of company computers to those who run computers or sell them. The responsibility for choice of machines must be that of those who pay for it—the managers. Managers need to decide the objectives to be accomplished by information provided by a system. Once the objectives are set, the method of providing information can be selected—this may or may not include a computer.

The initial responsibility of managers is to work with information providers to determine information needs. Decision makers will need to answer questions about information needs like those shown in Table 16-1. These information needs will be set only after personal communication between managers and providers. Managers need to indicate how certain they are for each information need. An information system should be designed so it is easy to change that information for which uncertainty is high.

Managers do not find working with computer specialists easy. They have different backgrounds, use different words, and have different orientations. Information suppliers tend to be highly educated specialists in such fields as computer science or statistics. Users of information tend to have less formal education, but more experience in their jobs. Computer programmers and other information suppliers have a language of their own; they use scientific terminology. The manager, on the other hand, feels more comfortable with the jargon of business. Differences in orientation frequently do not motivate suppliers and users to resolve their differences in communication. Information suppliers are oriented toward the design of procedures and techniques that generate information. They are in favor of computers that process faster or

Table 16-1. *Information Needs Questionnaire*

1. What types of decisions are you regularly called upon to make?
2. What types of information do you need to make these decisions?
3. What types of information do you regularly get?
4. What types of information would you like to get which you are not getting now?
5. What types of special studies do you periodically request?
6. What information would you want daily? Weekly?
7. What magazines and trade reports would you like to see routed to you on a regular basis?
8. What specific topics would you like to be kept informed of?
9. What types of data analysis problems would you like to see made available?
10. What do you think would be the four most helpful improvements that could be made in the present information system?

Source: Philip Kotler, *Marketing Management: Analysis, Planning, and Control,* Englewood Cliffs, N.J.: Prentice Hall, 1972, p. 302.

provide more internal storage. Users are interested only in the output and its total cost. The results are what they want.

Decision makers must understand the process by which information inputs are changed into outputs. They must learn how computers are programmed and how they work so they can communicate with suppliers. Only decision makers really know their information needs. The working knowledge of computers that is provided in the computer course required of business students does not make the user capable of supplying information. More than one course is required to learn how to program computers efficiently.

Suppliers of Information

Information suppliers in computer based information systems are called *systems analysts* and *computer programmers*. System analysts work with managers to specify information needs and determine ways to provide needed information. They recommend machines and turn procedures into machine understandable language.

Programming is simplified because computers can be given capabilities to change a set of instructions into machine language. These capabilities are provided by a set of instructions called a **compiler**. A Cobol (Common Business Oriented Language) compiler, for example, can change the instruction "ADD RECEIPTS TO STOCK ON HAND" into computer language. The computer would be told to locate the data stored in the locations called RECEIPTS and STOCK ON HAND and to add them together. Many types of compilers are available. Besides Cobol, Algol and Fortran are two that are frequently used.

Suppliers are responsible for bringing technical competence to information problems. They must know alternative ways for business to gather and produce desired information. They should also be aware of costs and potential benefits of the different alternatives.

In addition, the responsibility of suppliers includes an understanding of the goals and activities of the business they work for. They must learn the jargon of the field and the constraints within which decision makers operate.

An understanding of users is another responsibility of suppliers. This understanding is necessary to ensure communication between suppliers and users of information needs and capabilities of the system. Suppliers must help ensure that the user is confident that the information provided is reliable. If the user does not trust the information, the individual will not use it.

Managers at General Mills have come to trust and use their information system because they know how to type requests for information to the computer and receive a quick response. For example, a product manager could retrieve the dollar sales for three products (Lift-Off, Orbit, and Blast), six markets (Boston, Buffalo, New York, Philadelphia, Baltimore, and Cleveland), and six time periods (7 through 12) by typing the following command on the teletype:

? Get FCT (sales); MKT (BOS; BUFF; N.Y.; PHI; BAL; & CLE); PER (7-12); PROD (LIFT-OFF; ORBIT; & BLAST)[1]

SUCCESSFUL COMPUTER USE

Some businesses that have adopted computer systems have been disappointed with the results. They have not received what they expected from computer use. The cost of using computers has been greater than the benefits. Moreover, the information that has been provided frequently is not adequate for managers.

Some examples of companies with computer-related problems are presented in Table 16-2. However, as is common practice, the companies are not identified. Most companies will not name their specific failures. They will only discuss general problems. Borden, Inc. is one of the few that has been willing to talk about its failures. The company experienced a costly failure when it computerized accounting activities. It found that the use of independent consultants was not adequate for development of computer systems.

[1] Lawrence D. Gibson, Charles S. Mayer, Christopher E. Nugent, and Thomas E. Vollmann, "An Evolutionary Approach to Marketing Information Systems," *Journal of Marketing*, April 1973, 53.

Table 16-2. *Computer-Related Problems*

> CASE A–A manufacturer changed from an inadequate and poorly controlled manual system to a computer operation. The company's management did not understand the problems that were to be solved by this installation nor the computer's role in overcoming the problems. As a result, after the computer was installed, the company was unable to ship orders to customers, and the level of customer complaints rose appreciably.
>
> CASE B–A bank experiencing considerable difficulties with its computerized applications had a consultant evaluate the mechanized procedures. The consultant reported that the applications were poorly designed and controlled. The bank officials refused to accept the facts and continue to live with the present set-up and its associated problems.
>
> CASE C–A manufacturer asked for a computer feasibility study, then refused to accept the consultant's recommendation that computers not be installed. The company went ahead and installed an expensive computer, but six months later quietly dropped it.
>
> CASE D–A hospital requested an evaluation of its existing computer installation. After the consulting firm began its study, the hospital's management called it off, but not before the consultants found that the hospital had 60% more computer equipment than was necessary.

Source: Jerome D. Baker, "Rational Computerization," *Business Horizons*, April 1972, p. 36.

Successful uses of computers receive much more public exposure than failures. American Airlines, for example, instituted use of computers so management could quickly receive desired stored information or perform extensive analysis on available information. Their computerized system, called AAIMS (An Analytical Information Management System), cost them $62,500 but returned $361,000 in cost saving and increased passenger revenues during the first 18 months of operation.[2] Motorists Insurance, Sterling Drug, United Stationers Supply, Pillsbury, Weyerhaeuser, Univac, and IBM are other companies that have reported success with computer use. However, most of these companies have not indicated the exact amount of benefits received from computers. Broad statements of benefits are common: "An efficient (computer-based) infosystem at Sterling Drug Company helps management produce needed goods at the right time, keeps the company's distributors supplied, and simultaneously avoids costly warehousing of products." [3]

[2] Janet M. Taplin, "AAIMS: American Airlines Answers the What Ifs," *Infosystems*, February 1973, 58.
[3] "COGS Overcomes Product Inventory Crises," *Infosystems*, November 1973, 50.

The rules for successful use of computers depend on the specific needs and resources of each business. However, there are certain do's and don'ts for prospective computer users.

Do's of Computer Use

Success of computer use is more likely if:

1. Management is committed and involved.
2. A plan is developed.
3. Feasibility is checked.
4. Output is scanned.

Management Commitment

Top management must be committed to the use of computers. Their commitment should be in the form of providing adequate resources for development. Support of computer use when problems arise should also be provided. Top management support will ensure that lower-level managers will cooperate during planning of computer use.

All levels of management should also be involved in development of plans for computer use. This involvement is necessary for management understanding. Otherwise, they are expected to use a tool—the computer—that they do not understand.

Plan Development

Successful use of computers requires careful planning. This planning includes setting objectives, determining necessary activities and their sequence, and identifying time restrictions and other constraints.

Planning helps computer users to ensure they are focusing on objectives. Provision of desired information helps get users to trust computers. In addition, costly future changes may be avoided by planning which activities computers will be used for first, second, and so on.

Feasibility Check

Computers were initially considered a status symbol by businesses. They felt being one of the first companies with their very own computers would be worth the cost. Other computer adopters have mistakenly assumed that computers are guaranteed to produce more benefits than costs. One company, for example, paid $2 million for a computer to provide inventory information. The result was $150,000 more in inventory costs than the replaced manual system.[4]

[4] R. L. Ackoff, "Management Misinformation Systems," *Management Science*, Vol. 14, No. 4, B-149.

The addition of computers should be preceded by questions of technical, economical, and operational feasibility. Available technology and resources must be sufficient so the computer can be used as planned. Company personnel may not have the expertise necessary to design computer-based information systems. Careful consideration must be given to all costs and benefits. Many companies have underestimated costs and overestimated benefits. Operational feasibility poses the issue of whether the computer will be used by decision makers. It may not fit into present management behavior. They may refuse to change for a "lousy" computer.

Output Scanning

Computers make errors because they cannot exercise judgment. A bank computer once credited all savings accounts with 31 days of interest for November. Typically, the computer may not be programmed correctly. A programmer at Cape Kennedy, for example, omitted a hyphen in the instructions causing a launched rocket to be diverted toward Rio de Janiero. The rocket, which cost $18,500,000, had to be destroyed.[5]

The output of the computer should be scanned before it is used. Companies have made trial runs of computers to produce output they examine. The computer is generally given data that has already been transformed by the manual system. Thus, the outputs of the two information systems can be compared. Costly errors may be avoided, and management will have more confidence in computers.

Don'ts of Computer Use

Many problems await the computer user. They should be avoided by:

1. *Not* buying a canned computer operation.
2. *Not* spending all money for computers and related equipment.
3. *Not* letting computer sales representatives or computer programmers make computer decisions.
4. *Not* trying to install a computer without having good management.
5. *Not* falling in love with computers.
6. *Not* underestimating time and costs of setting up and using a computer.

Canned Computer Operation

Computer manufacturers and consultants may recommend that the company use an information system developed for other companies. This standard, or *canned*, computer operation is most inviting to businesses. It only seems necessary to turn on the computer, and instant benefits will result.

[5] Bill Surface, "What Computers Do," *Systems Review*, July 13, 1968, 58.

These canned systems should be avoided because they assume that the information needs and constraints of all companies are the same. In reality, personnel differences alone result in variations in information needs. Moreover, adoption of such standardized packages neglects the importance of preparing the organization for use of the computer. Users of the information will not be involved in the development of the systems. Therefore, they will probably distrust it. Finally, company personnel will be unable to operate the computer correctly and efficiently, resulting in less user confidence.

Computer Spending

Dollars spent for information systems are mainly for purposes other than purchase of computers. On the average, thirty-five cents of each dollar spent for information systems is for computers and related equipment. Almost the same amount (thirty cents per dollar) is spent for staff to plan and operate currently used computers, while the other thirty-five cents is generally spent for planning future computer use.[6] The costs for planning are most important. Planning determines whether computers provide information needed and used by managers.

Letting Suppliers Decide

Managers must decide what computers they need. They need to understand computers so that obvious lies and promises by sales representatives can be recognized. The biases of sales representatives and computer programmers must be considered. Some managers have described computer specialists as "foxes who like to eat chickens."[7] They may not be concerned with providing management with the best information at the least cost.

Computers without Management

Computers are not substitutes for good planning, organizing, and controlling of company activities. They are only tools. Companies that have not planned for the future will not be able to plan computer use effectively. If you do not know where you are going, a high-speed method (the computer) of getting there will not help. Similarly, information provided by the computer is not useful to managers who are unsure of their responsibilities. Failure to control current activities will not allow a company to focus its efforts on evaluating and correcting the performance of computers.

Love of Computers

Some people treat computers as many treat cars; they even wonder how the computer feels. Their personal attachment to the computer leads to a

---

[6] Joel E. Ross, "Computers: Their Use and Misuse," *Business Horizons,* April 1972, 57.
[7] "The Perils of Data Systems," *Business Week,* June 5, 1971, 62.

belief that it can do no wrong. They may try to change management problems to fit the computer rather than changing the computer. This love for computers may carry over to the need to own one.

The advantage of having a machine readily available for use may not offset the high cost of the computer. Studies have shown companies use computers less than one-half of available time. Moreover, many companies do not keep accurate records of the use of computers.[8]

A company may find that more efficient use of computers is possible by joint ownership of a computer or use of a computer service bureau. By sharing a computer with other companies, a company can save from 30 to 60% of costs. Individual ownership of a medium-sized computer can cost from $24,000 to $72,000 a year. However, joint ownership does require scheduling of use so the computer is available to each user when needed.

A *computer service bureau* is an independent organization that sells computer time. Users need not buy a computer or hire people to run it. They are charged only for what computer time they use. However, the services available may not be what is needed by a company.

Underestimated Costs

Users of computers have generally underestimated the time and cost of planning and operating a computer-based information system by 50 to 90%. Weyerhaeuser Company, for instance, estimated it would take 10 people working for one year to install part of their computer system. It took 3 years and 50 people.[9]

Specific errors in estimating benefits, costs, and related effort include the following:

1. Initial computer program preparation and debugging time have been underestimated.
2. The difficulty of training programmers has been underestimated.
3. The degree of employee resistance to change has been underestimated.
4. Time to run computer programs has been underestimated.
5. The organizational impact has not been considered or has been underestimated.
6. Benefits have been overstated.
7. Costs of training management to use computers have been overlooked.[10]

The general failure to understand what is involved in getting computers working has led many companies to adopt the wrong approach—a crash program. They try to convert to computer use in less than a year. Successful changeovers require 15 to 30 months. Often, companies can get delivery of

---

[8] "Status of Computer Use," *Business Automation*, January 1971, 35.
[9] "The Perils of Data Systems," *Business Week*, June 5, 1972, 65.
[10] Donald H. Sanders, *Computers in Business: An Introduction*, New York: McGraw-Hill Company, 1973, p. 256.

Reprinted through permission of Tom Zib, *The Wall Street Journal*

"You mean it's going to take two of these things just to replace Hartwell?"

computers in six months. Therefore, they want the expected benefits from the computer immediately.

Crash programs generally fail. Many information needs may be ignored or incorrectly developed due to the rush. Resistance from company personnel may also be great. They may not have time to understand the computer that was forced upon them.

FUTURE BUSINESS USE OF COMPUTERS

Two major effects of computers on future operations of businesses can be expected. First, business will increasingly use computers as aids in decision making. Second, management involvement in computer-related decisions will increase.

Decision-Making Aids

The initial computer use in the late 1940s was for processing large batches of paper work. The 1950s and 1960s saw a major emphasis on the adoption of faster methods of communicating data processed by computers. Although smaller companies and those in traditionally noncomputerized industries such as health care are now in these initial stages, businesses are starting to use computers to help improve use of available information. Computers will be used more and more frequently to predict and evaluate outcomes for decision makers. Moreover, computers will be used to recommend action in some cases.

This capability of computers will be possible in the near future for several reasons. Improved access of users to computers helps tremendously. Remote terminals and new compilers will allow managers to use simple English commands to direct the computer. Users will no longer need to explain their decision-making process explicitly to computer specialists. They will develop their needs through direct interaction with the computer, further reducing possibility for error.

The improved sets of stored data also make computer aid in decision making likely in the future. Huge storehouses of data are being centralized so users can have access to available information in all parts of a company and the world. A Japanese-based firm, Mitsui, has a fully computerized, global communications network linking 115 branch offices in 69 countries. Independent computer service networks, such as University Computing Company, Limited, are making multinational data available.

These broad bases of data permit computers to analyze trends and relationship in company, industry, and society data. However, the question of privacy of owners of the data will probably become more complex as these storehouses of data are built. The rights of individuals as well as those of countries to use available data will have to be resolved so that benefits can be gained from such use.

Management Involvement

Increased management use of computers will result as new managers with computer exposure are hired to replace retiring managers. The new breed of managers will realize what computers can and cannot do. They will treat the computer as a powerful tool that requires careful planning. The current management attitudes of distrust toward computers should disappear in the future.

Future managers will need increased understanding of computers. Computer use will become more complex as many new types of equipment and techniques are offered as alternatives. Management understanding will also be necessary. Managers will need to translate needs into computer commands. Managers without computer knowledge will be at a disadvantage in almost all industries in the future; few firms will be able to remain competitive without the use of computers.

JOBS IN THE COMPUTER INDUSTRY

Over one million jobs are available because of computers. Many of these jobs, in the manufacturing and marketing of computers, are discussed in other chapters. You may be interested in one of three major types of computer-related jobs: systems analyst; computer programmer; or computer operator. Over 500,000 people hold these jobs, with great increases in demand for all three expected.

Systems Analyst

You may want to join the more than 100,000 people who are systems analysts. They generally work for business firms or the federal government. As a systems analyst you would be responsible for defining, analyzing, and structuring information problems of managers. By working with users, you would identify all of their information needs. The information systems you devise will need to show specifically how data will be collected and how it will be processed into needed information. All the detailed steps necessary in changing data to information are worked out by the systems analyst. If you decide to be a systems analyst, you will also have to recommend to management the equipment to be used and prepare detailed instructions for computer programmers.

Qualifications

In most cases, a college degree is a must for a systems analyst. The best type of college preparation depends on your future employer. Business administration majors are preferred by those with finance or other business information problems, while engineering backgrounds are preferred for engineering or scientifically oriented systems.

You should also try to get as much experience in computer programming as possible. Courses offered by colleges, employers, or computer manufacturers are possible ways to prepare for your first job as a systems analyst; your title will probably be "junior computer systems analyst." However, you may have to work for your employer as a computer programmer before promotion to systems analyst.

To be a successful systems analyst, you also need to be able to break problems into their components. If you cannot learn to analyze a variety of problems in a logical way, you will not be able to handle analysis of complex information systems. Frequently, this analytical ability is possessed by those who do well in mathematics; you should improve your mathematical skills to prepare for a career as a systems analyst.

Parts of a Typical Business

Rewards

Your beginning salary as a junior systems analyst will probably be between $10,000 and $14,000 a year, depending on the type and amount of experience you have. Growth in your salary should also be good. Annual average increases of 7 and 8% are common.[11]

Shortages of qualified personnel also make your chances of promotion good. You could move to higher-level analysts' positions; your responsibilities would include management of lower-level systems analysts. Senior or lead computer systems analyst are examples of higher-level job titles. Promotion to these jobs with more responsibility results in a 30% or more increase in salary. Experienced systems analysts with proven leadership capabilities may earn annual salaries of $19,000 or more as managers of all computer personnel.

Computer Programmer

You can find great challenge in the job of **computer programmer**. Many errors in computer processing are due to faulty programming. These machines must be told what to do in detailed, logical steps. Generally, programmers or systems analysts write out the necessary steps in English or in the form of boxes and arrows called *flow charts*.

The steps are translated into detailed, machine-understandable instructions, the **program**. The techniques necessary to write the program depend on the types of machines used and the nature of the problem. The programmer generally has to prepare an instruction sheet for the computer operator. This sheet tells the operator what to do when running other programs.

The final task of writing a program would be your responsibility. The program must be "debugged." *Debugging* is checking on whether the instructions have been correctly written and will produce the desired information. A sample of data that has been processed by hand is generally used to see if the computer processes as desired. Locating problems in computer programs may require a lot of creative thinking. One problem may be hidden by another problem. Moreover, the wrong changes in the program may create even more difficulties.

Qualifications

You should have an aptitude for logical thinking if you want to be a computer programmer. The work also calls for patience, persistence, and the ability to work with extreme accuracy. You should also be able to use ingenuity and imagination in solving programming problems.

College training in computer programming is helpful, although many employers promote qualified workers having previous experience in account-

---

[11] "Salary Survey: 1973," *Infosystems*, September 1973, 49.

ing, payroll, or machine tabulation. Some employers who use computers for science and engineering prefer college graduates with degrees in engineering, the physical sciences, mathematics, or computer science. However, other employers hire college graduates with accounting or other types of business administration majors and courses in computer programming, mathematics, or engineering.

Your college training will be supplemented by on-the-job training. Initially, you will probably have to attend company training sessions. Experience as a programmer will not prove sufficient for all future company needs. Additional training will be necessary to learn about new machines and new programming techniques.

Rewards

Your starting salary should be around $9,000 annually. Annual salary increases should be about 6%. However, your salary and annual increases will get better as you become experienced. Annual salaries for higher-level programmers average $14,000. These higher-level programmers—senior or lead programmers—have averaged 7% annual salary increases.

Promotional opportunities include the positions of manager of programming, systems analyst, or manager of all computer personnel. Jumps in annual salaries of 20% or more can result from such promotions.

You may find programming provides tremendous job satisfaction. Many people feel that making the computer work properly is a real challenge. Moreover, a programmer is of vital importance to an employer. Without this person the computer would be useless.

Computer Operator

A computer often requires many specialized operators. Someone must change the input into punched cards, magnetic tape, or whatever medium is required for the computer. These operators may be keypunch operators, data typists, or card-to-tape convertor operators. Other operators are involved in translating machine output to words and numbers. The type of operator emphasized here is the one who runs the computer: a **console operator**.

As a computer operator you will examine the programmer's instructions to decide what you must do for each run of the computer. You will make sure the computer is loaded with tapes, discs, or other types of input data. You will manipulate and watch lights as the computer runs. These lights may signal an error requiring you, as the operator, to locate the difficulty.

Qualifications

You will need at least a high school education to work as a computer operator for businesses, universities, or governmental agencies. Specialized training in machine operation is generally also required. This training can be acquired through colleges, technical schools, or on-the-job training. You may also be required to show your ability to reason logically before being hired.

Rewards

Computer operators make less than systems analysts or computer programmers. The average starting salary is $7,000 annually. However, experience will help you earn annual salaries of $10,000 or more. Generally, salaries are better for computer operators in large computer operations.

You will probably work in an air conditioned room. Computers must be housed where temperatures are carefully controlled. However, the high level of noise generated by the computers may prove a disadvantage to operators.

CHAPTER SUMMARY

Business executives need information about customers, employees, channel members, competitors, suppliers, government, and other publics. Information is used to plan business activities; information helps managers to identify problems, state alternative courses of action, evaluate alternatives, and select the best alternative. Successful control of implemented plans requires information so that standards can be set, actual performance measured, and corrective action selected. Only information which provides more benefits than costs—providing information, data errors, and decision delay—should be gathered by a company.

The five components of an information system—input, processor, storage, procedures, output—are discussed in this chapter. Input is data gathered from different sources, and it is prepared in a form acceptable by the information system. The processor—a human brain or a computer—guides the operation of the system as it changes input into useable management information. Data is placed in storage until it is needed by users. The processor is told what to do with the input by procedures. Output is the information provided by the processing of input and stored data according to procedures.

Users of information tell those who supply information what they need. Users find information suppliers have different backgrounds, use different terminology, and have different orientations. Suppliers have responsibilities to suggest methods to provide needed information and to understand the goals of the users of the information.

Businesses may unsuccessfully use computers because management is not involved, plans are not developed, feasibility is not considered, and output is not scanned. Computer pitfalls discussed include use of canned computer operations, overreliance on recommendations of computer sales representatives, and underestimation of costs of computer use.

Increased business use of computers for decision making is predicted in this chapter. Moreover, increased management involvement in computer decisions is expected.

Possible jobs in computers include that of systems analyst, computer programmer, and computer operator. All three jobs involve supplying information; generally these jobs require the ability to think logically. Moreover, there is a shortage of qualified personnel for these jobs.

PROVOCATIVE STATEMENT

A Systems Analyst Comments on Jobs in the Computer Industry

1 "It is trite but true to believe it's not *what* you know, but *whom* you know. I am still a systems analyst, not a dp (data processing) manager, because my technical abilities are not sufficient to offset my lack of political skills."

"Ballot on the Issues: Up the Manager, Down the Doer."
Infosystems, January 1973, p. 33.

PROVOCATIVE STATEMENT

Executives Do Not Trust Their Computers

2 "On the one hand, all too many executives don't trust their computers. They regard them as electronic mistresses, devoted to raiding the corporate treasury while spewing out an endless flow of mostly useless paper.

On the other hand, far too many . . . (computer) people create an air of mystery about what they do. They don't like to speak plain English, but talk to management in 'computerese' employing many exotic 'buzz words.' For example, the systems analyst may say, 'The program blew and I have to get a core dump.' The English translation is: 'The program failed and I have to find out whether bad data or a programming error caused the failure.'"

Patricia Garnett,
"Take Your Computer to Lunch This Week,"
Infosystems, January 1973, p. 55.

REVIEW QUESTIONS

1. What types of information are needed by management for making decisions? p. 406
2. What steps are involved in planning future courses of action? p. 407
3. Name and briefly explain the five components of an information system. p. 412
4. What are the key factors in determining the success of a computer installation? p. 421
5. How does the job of systems analyst differ from that of computer programmer? pp. 427, 28

Chapter Outline

The Quantitative Approach to Problem Solving
   Purpose of the Quantitative Approach
   Basis for the Quantitative Approach
     Problem Definition
     Consideration of Alternatives
     Analysis of Alternatives
     Selection of Course of Action
     Evaluation of Course of Action

Business Statistics
   The Framework for Business Statistics
   Descriptive Statistics
     Measures of Central Tendency
     Measures of Dispersion
     Measures of Association
   Statistical Inference

Techniques and Terminology in Quantitative Methods
   Forecasting Methods
     Trend Line Analysis
     The Delphi
   Resource Allocation and Other Planning Tools
     Mathematical Programming
     Inventory Models
     Queueing Models
     Competitive Models
     Simulation

Bridging the Management Gap
   The Pitfalls of Management Science
   Bringing Management Science Back to Management

Careers in Management Science
   Nature of Job
   Qualifications
   Career Rewards

Chapter Summary

Provocative Statement 1:
   The Management Scientist and the Manager: Partners or Opponents?

Key Terms

Quantitative methods
Distribution
Central tendency
Average
Mean
Median
Mode
Dispersion
Range
Variance
Standard deviation
Correlation
Statistical inference
Parameter
Controlled feedback
Consensus
Sensitivity analysis

Modern Quantitative Methods

"Managers and management scientists are operating as two separate cultures, each with its own goals, languages, and methods. Effective cooperation—and even communication—between the two is just about minimal."
—Educator and Consultant to Government and Industry

The modern-day business executive is caught in a pressure-packed and competitive environment. Companies are no longer satisfied to operate on a limited geographical scale. The international market provides the arena for intense competition among firms. The increasing scope of the domestic and international economies creates problems of enormous importance. Solutions to these problems will determine the destinies of individual companies and will affect the lives of people throughout the world.

Decision makers will have to make more far reaching and timely decisions in this environment. To aid business executives in their decision-making duties, a new field of inquiry has developed: the application of quantitative methods to the solution of economic-related problems. Quantitative methods are mathematical and statistical techniques that offer a systematic way of analyzing problems. In this chapter, the quantitative approach to problem solving will be examined. The discussion will focus on business statistics, forecasting, and some techniques and terminology of quantitative methods. The gap between the state of the quantitative art and actual practice by management will also be analyzed. Lastly, career opportunities in the area of quantitative methods will be reviewed.

THE QUANTITATIVE APPROACH TO PROBLEM SOLVING

The quantitative approach to solving business-related problems is referred to by many names. These include quantitative business analysis, decision sciences, management science, decision analysis, and operations research. One reason for the large number of labels is that the field is rather new, having its origins around the time of World War II. A number of independent groups of researchers in industry, government, and universities around the world have explored this approach to problem solving. So far, coordination of all the different efforts has been lacking. Also, as people develop vested interests, no common vocabulary has been developed. For the purpose of this chapter, the particular label to be used is the *quantitative approach*.

Purpose of the Quantitative Approach

To the average person, business executives appear to make their decisions in an aura of mystery. Decision makers combine some mixture of experience and intuition to arrive at solutions to complex problems. There is no doubt that many business executives still make their decisions this way. In fact, it is not the purpose of the quantitative approach to replace the executive's judgment, experience, or intuition. Rather, the quantitative approach is designed to help executives make more intelligent decisions by enabling them to reach decisions in a systematic manner and with as much accuracy as possible. By showing executives *how* they are making decisions, the quantitative approach hopes to allow them to improve the quality of their decisions.

Basis for the Quantitative Approach

The quantitative approach has as its basis five factors or steps:

1. Problem definition.
2. Consideration of alternatives.
3. Analysis of alternatives.
4. Selection of course of action.
5. Evaluation of course of action.

Problem Definition

The most common failure of decision makers is the inability to define correctly the problem they want to solve. Correct solutions to the wrong problems will do little to help the firm achieve its goals. Indeed, failure to correctly define a problem usually results in a terrible waste of the firm's resources.

Why are problems incorrectly defined? Most errors in this area are due to the analyst's inability to see the real problem through all the symptoms of the problem. Eliminating a symptom does not necessarily eliminate the problem itself. Thus, the analyst must take the time and effort to define clearly the problem that needs to be solved.

Consideration of Alternatives

Very seldom is there only one way to solve a problem. For example, suppose a company is faced with a loss in sales and wishes to increase sales. The company may lower its price, increase advertising, improve product quality, pay sales representatives higher commissions for each unit sold, or some combination of these and possibly other alternatives. The analyst should not present the decision maker with only one alternative and see whether or not the person likes it. Rather, the decision maker should be presented with all workable alternatives so that the merits and demerits of each may be taken into consideration.

Analysis of Alternatives

The effect of each alternative on the outcome of the problem should be specified. It is most likely that each alternative will have disadvantages as well as advantages. There are very few problems for which one alternative will provide the perfect solution. In most cases, the decision maker must "satisfice" —find an alternative that provides the most satisfactory solution to a problem, realizing that an "ideal" solution is unattainable. Furthermore, the expense of trying to find the best solution may exceed the possible benefit to be derived from it. The executive must make a decision in a given amount of time. One cannot continue to search for the perfect answer for unreasonable periods of time.

Selection of Course of Action

After weighing the pros and cons of the alternative courses of action, the decision maker must decide which alternative to implement. The individual should clearly specify the reasons for a particular selection.

Evaluation of Course of Action

Hindsight is a wonderful thing. Everybody likes to be a Monday-morning quarterback. In time, the decision maker will be able to see whether the particular alternative selected adequately satisfied the problem. It does no good to stew over problems that, with hindsight, should have been attacked in a different way. The executive deals with the future, and no one knows the future with any degree of certainty. The reason for evaluation of the chosen courses of action is to allow the decision maker to refine the analytical processes further, not to punish the individual for choosing the wrong alternative. This is why it is particularly important for the decision maker to clearly state why a particular course of action was selected in the first place. In retrospect, the person's reasoning may have been faulty. However, it is quite likely that at the time the decision had to be made, the decision maker chose the correct course of action given the information then available.

BUSINESS STATISTICS

The quantitative approach differs from a purely subjective or qualitative approach to problem solving by expressing as much as possible of the decision-making process in quantitative terms. It is deeply rooted in the fields of statistics and mathematics. Indeed, the quantitative approach can be viewed as applied statistics and mathematics. It would be impossible in the context of this chapter to provide you with the necessary statistical tools and mathematics to plunge in depth into the details of the quantitative approach. However, at least a quick examination of business statistics and mathematical methods is needed in order to grasp the importance of the quantitative approach. The purpose of this section is to give you a little background of business statistics. The next section will present a brief review of mathematics and some of the applications of the quantitative approach to solving business problems.

The business decision maker has a two-fold problem: (1) getting a grasp on what has happened and what is happening and (2) anticipating what is going to happen in the future. In other words, the intelligent decision maker tries to account for change and to go beyond the confines of the present situation. Business statistics are designed to aid the business executive in solving the two-fold problem.

The Framework for Business Statistics

The economic and business environment is very complex. Thousands upon thousands of interrelated events occur daily. The analyst assigned to aid business executives in their decision-making duties must determine from all these events or factors those that are pertinent to the problem. The analyst must not only find the relevant factors, but must also specify how they relate to the problem and what degree of confidence the person has in the specified relationship. In summary then, business statistics try to accomplish three things:

1. To abstract from many factors those that are related to the problem or outcome.
2. To define a relational structure among factors.
3. To specify conditions in which the relational structure will be adequately represented.

The basic framework of business statistics is presented in Figure 17-1. This framework is based on the principles of scientific procedure. These principles are:

1. *Observation.* Analysts must observe real world economic events. Their

Figure 17-1. *The Framework for Business Statistics*

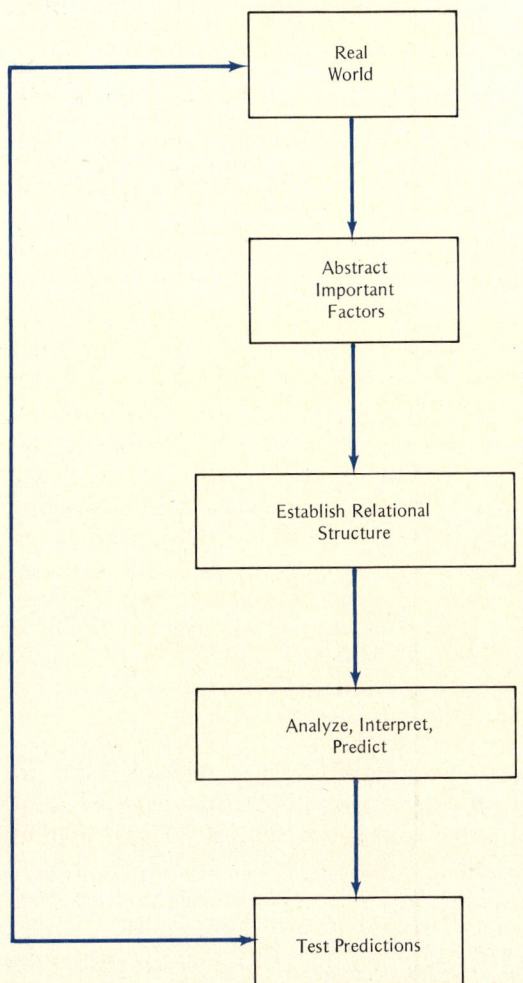

observations will be guided by the definition of their problems and experiences with causal relationships. For example, suppose an analyst is trying to forecast new car sales for a particular model in the upcoming year. Based on experience, the person knows that the number of cars sold depends on the number of potential buyers who as a group have certain characteristics. These characteristics may be age, income, education, marital status, and part of the country in which the person lives. Based on already collected data—from previous studies by the government, trade associations, or the firm—the analyst observes the number of occurrences of each of these characteristics in the population or in the sample.

2. *Classification.* Analysts must classify each event they see. Thus, to con-

tinue with the example, the analyst will classify every person in the population or sample by age, income, education, marital status, and geographical region. Many events are due to the same factor, and the analyst must sort out the events into a manageable number of factors. For example, it is doubtful that the number of cars sold varies directly with a person's exact age in years. Rather, they vary by age group. People can thus be classified by age bracket: 16–20 years, 21–30 years, 31–40 years, and so on. Since few if any people under 16 are purchasers of cars, the analyst will not waste time including those persons in the classification.

3. *Organization.* All the data collected by the analyst must be organized to facilitate analysis. If the analyst has access to a computer, the individual may prepare the data on data cards or magnetic tape. For example, it might be useful to have one card for each person observed. Each card would record the person's age, income, education, marital status, and geographical region. The computer can be used to manipulate the data in any way the analyst desires.

4. *Analysis.* The analyst examines the data and—based on relevant theory—tries to develop causal relationships. It is some *combination* of age, income, marital status, education, and geographic region that determines the likelihood that a person will buy a particular car. The analyst must examine the data to determine what this relationship is.

5. *Interpretation.* Analysts must interpret what the causal relationship means. Perhaps the analyst has found that the typical buyer of the company's car is between 21 and 30 years old, earns between $25,000 and $30,000, is divorced, has at least an undergraduate college degree, and lives in the northeastern United States. What the analyst now needs to know is the significance of this relationship. If this "typical buyer" accounts for a large portion of the company's sales, the relationship can help predict sales for the upcoming year. But if this typical buyer accounts for only a small portion of total sales, the relationship may be rather meaningless. For example, suppose this typical group accounts for only 10% of company sales and the second most typical buying group is in the over 60 age bracket, is married, lives in the southwest, has a grade school education, and earns between $8,000 and $10,000 per year. From the analysis, the analyst may conclude that the company does not have a well-defined target market for its product and that sales will be difficult to predict by this type of analysis.

6. *Prediction.* Based on the developed relationship, the analyst tries to predict the nature of the economic event in the future. The analyst in the example tries to predict sales for the next year. If the analyst developed the relationship on historical sample data—the most common approach—he next extends the relationship to the population as a whole. For example, the analyst will try to calculate how many typical buyers there are in the entire population and from this estimate what the sales will be in the upcoming year.

7. *Test prediction.* The most desirable way of testing a relationship is to run it on historical data. For example, how well would the typical car buyer relationship have predicted sales in the past two time periods? If, for some reason, this cannot be done, the analyst must make a prediction and wait till the next period is over to see how well the prediction worked. To reduce the

chance of economic disaster in this latter case, many firms test-market their new products. That is, a company tries out its new product on a limited geographical basis to see how well it will sell.

8. *Refinement of understanding to get better prediction.* After a relationship has been tested, the analyst is in a better position to refine it. Hopefully, a revised relationship will result in a better prediction. The analyst, however, must weigh the costs of refining understanding against the benefits to be derived. Refinement costs money and thus reduces the net benefit to the firm. If the cost is expected to exceed the benefit, it is time to stop refining the relationship. An analyst always likes to gather more information in order to get a better understanding of a relationship and to arrive at a more accurate prediction. But eventually the cost of obtaining the additional information will exceed its expected value.

The scientific principles apply to many other fields of study besides business statistics. In order to make this discussion more specific, it will be convenient to further refine the basic framework into descriptive statistics and statistical inference.

Descriptive Statistics

Descriptive statistics are designed to reduce the maze of available information to a workable size. Suppose the vice president of a company asks a statistical analyst to conduct a study on employee income within the firm. The analyst collects the data shown in Table 17-1. Presenting all of this data to the vice president would probably result in the analyst being shown a quick exit from the vice president's office. An executive's time is very valuable, and it can best be used if the data is summarized into a few meaningful numbers. This is the purpose of descriptive statistics.

Table 17-1. *Salary Levels within Hypothetical Firm*

Salary	Number of Persons Earning this Salary
$10,000	10
12,000	12
14,000	8
16,000	15
18,000	10
20,000	12
22,000	10
24,000	8
26,000	6
28,000	2

Parts of a Typical Business

Measures of Central Tendency

The manner in which the data is presented in Table 17-1 is called a *distribution*—it shows how income is distributed among workers in the firm. Measures of central tendency refer to the center of the distribution. These measures are called averages and can be of three types. (1) mean; (2) median; and (3) mode.

MEAN Suppose the analyst is interested in the average income earned by workers in his firm. To find the mean income, the analyst simply adds up the income earned by each worker and divides this sum by the number of workers. Alternatively, when data is already categorized, as in Table 17-1, the analyst follows the following steps:

1. Multiply each salary by the number of persons earning that salary—called the frequency.
2. Add up all the products from 1.
3. Divide the sum in 2 by the total number of frequencies.

To illustrate, using the data in Table 17-1 the mean salary would be $17,634.41, computed as follows:

SALARY	FREQUENCY	(1) SALARY × FREQUENCY
$10,000	10	$ 100,000
12,000	12	144,000
14,000	8	112,000
16,000	15	240,000
18,000	10	180,000
20,000	12	240,000
22,000	10	220,000
24,000	8	192,000
26,000	6	156,000
28,000	2	56,000
Total	93	(2) $1,640,000

$$(3) \quad \text{Mean} = \frac{\$1,640,000}{93} = \$17,634.41$$

The analyst could thus report to the vice president that the average salary in the firm—by "average" we really mean the mean—is $17,634.41.

MEDIAN A second measure of central tendency is the median or middle value in the distribution. It is the value that has 50% of the frequencies above it and 50% of the frequencies below it. Going down the list of salaries in Table 17-1, the median would correspond to the salary earned by the 47th person in the salary scale. This figure would be $18,000.

Mode A final measure of central tendency is the mode. In the example, it is the salary earned with the greatest frequency—earned by the most people. This would be $16,000, which is earned by 15 employees in the firm.

As seen in the example, three different averages can be calculated. It is, thus, important for the analyst to clearly specify what type of average is being talked about.

Measures of Dispersion

In addition to knowing an average value, the analyst may also wish to know how varied or dispersed these values are. Three widely used measures of dispersion are the range, standard deviation, and the semiquartile range.

The Range The range is the difference between the smallest and largest value observation. For example, suppose a firm is concerned about the length of time it takes its employees to become vice presidents. If this process takes too long, employee turnover may rise and morale may fall as employees become upset with the lack of promotion opportunities. An analyst determines how long it has taken each of the twelve current vice presidents to reach their status after entry in the firm. These lengths of time, in years, are: 8, 10, 11, 15, 17, 22, 25, 28, 29, 31, 32, and 36. The range of these values is 28 years (36 minus 8). The mean, incidentally, is 22 years. The analyst would report that it has taken the average vice president 22 years to reach the position with a range of 28 years.

Standard Deviation It might seem logical, at first glance, to consider as a measure of dispersion the average or mean difference of each observed value from the mean. However, this would be a futile exercise since this value will always be zero. To prove this point, consider the case of the number of years the vice presidents took to attain their current rank.

Number of Years	Minus Mean	=
8	22	−14
10	22	−12
11	22	−11
15	22	− 7
17	22	− 5
22	22	0
25	22	3
28	22	6
29	22	7
31	22	9
32	22	10
36	22	14
264		Sum = 0

Mean = 264/12 = 22

This problem can be solved by *squaring* each difference before adding them together. Thus,

DIFFERENCE	DIFFERENCE SQUARED
−14	196
−12	144
−11	121
− 7	49
− 5	25
0	0
3	9
6	36
7	49
9	81
10	100
14	196
	Sum = 1006

The **variance** is the mean of this sum of differences or deviations from the mean. The variance equals

$$1006 \div 12 = 83.83$$

The **standard deviation** is computed as the square root of the variance, or approximately nine years. This figure is called a *standard deviation* since it is expressed in the same units of measure as the original observations, years in this case. The standard deviation is a very important measure of dispersion since, if the analyst can make certain technical assumptions about the shape of the frequency distribution, it is a fact that 68% of the observations will be within one standard deviation of either side of the mean.

SEMIQUARTILE RANGE A problem with the range is that it can be distorted by extreme values at either end of the frequency distribution. For example, the range in the preceding case would fall to 19 years if the vice president who rose in the firm the fastest had achieved the present position in 17 years rather than 8. The semiquartile range overcomes this distortion by considering only those values that fall in the 50% range around the median. The semiquartile range in this case is 14 years (29 minus 15).

Measures of Association

An analyst is often interested in the nature of the relationship or association between economic events and factors. For example, the vice president for personnel would like to know if there is a relationship between employee salary and number of days per year an employee takes time off for illness. The statistical analyst collects the necessary data and plots it on a graph, the general character of which is shown in Figure 17-2.

Figure 17-2. *General Data Graph*

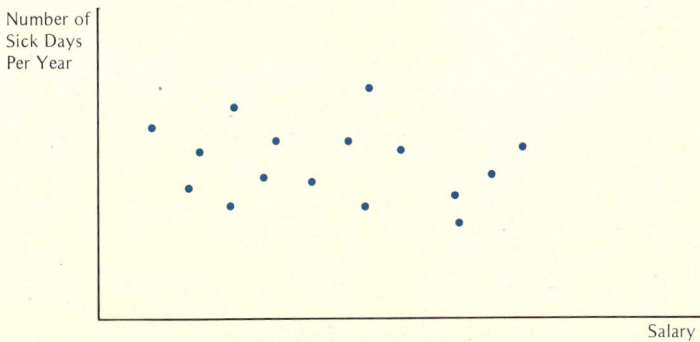

From this graph, the analyst concludes that there is no relationship or correlation between salary and number of sick days taken per year. Figure 17-3 summarizes the three types of correlation: (a) *negative*, (b) *positive*, and (c) *zero*. With *negative correlation*, the value of one factor falls, while the value of the second factor rises. For example, the proportion of income spent on food tends to fall, while the amount of income rises. The value of two factors will rise or fall together in *positive correlation*. To illustrate, the grade you get in this course is positively correlated with the amount of time you spend studying for it. With *zero correlation*, there is no necessary relationship between two factors. For example, the number of pounds of rice consumed in China each year has zero correlation with the annual number of gallons beer consumed by college freshmen in the United States. Correlation gives the decision maker further insight into the structure of relations.

Statistical Inference

The process of gathering relevant information on all members of a population can be very time-consuming and expensive. A company wanting to know how many people in the United States would purchase its product might conduct a massive nationwide survey. This survey would be very expensive to run and could take many months of valuable time. To overcome this problem, a company can resort to statistical inference: the process of making inferences or statements about a population on the basis of information contained in samples. A company can survey a sample of people around the country or in a limited geographical area and, from the results of the sample testing, estimate the demand for its product in the population as a whole.

In essence, an analyst tries to *estimate* the population value—called a parameter—from the information contained in the sample. As noted earlier, the analysts must state how much confidence they have in their estimates or predictions. The more confidence they have, the greater use decision makers can make of the information given to them. For example, if the analyst reports

Figure 17-3. Types of Correlation

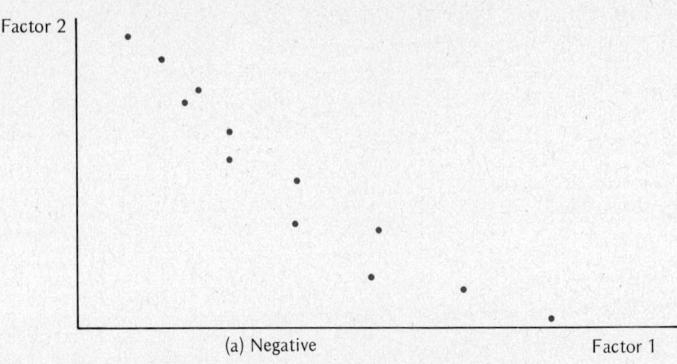

(a) Negative

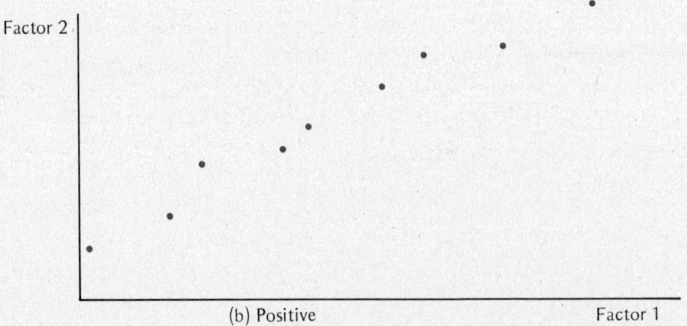

(b) Positive

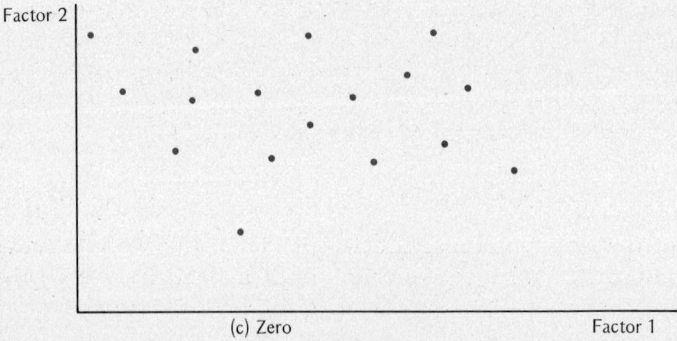

(c) Zero

that new car sales will fall between 900,000 and 1 million units next year with *near certainty,* the decision maker is in a much better planning position than if the person were told new car sales would range between 500,000 and 2 million. The term "near certainty" is important since the decision maker wants to know what the relative chances are that a particular event will occur. Fortunately, with the aid of descriptive statistics such as the mean as a measure of

Modern Quantitative Methods   445

central tendency and the standard deviation as a measure of dispersion, the analyst can quantify the chance of an event occurring. For example, the analyst can predict from a sample that the true car sales for next year will fall between 900,000 and 1 million units next year with 95% *confidence*. That is, he is confident that 95 times out of 100, true car sales will range between 900,000 and 1 million units based on the results of the sampling and the use of statistical inference. Unfortunately, the mechanics of statistical inference are quite involved and beyond the scope of this text. The purpose of this brief discussion is simply to let you know some of the power and usefulness of business statistics.

TECHNIQUES AND TERMINOLOGY IN QUANTITATIVE METHODS

"Quantitative methods" is a rather all-encompassing term. One could rightly argue that business statistics is a quantitative method. However, techniques and terminology in quantitative methods are presented as a separate section to highlight business statistics as an important field in its own right. In this section, attention shall be focused on forecasting methods and resource allocation and other planning tools.

Forecasting Methods

Business executives try to anticipate what is going to happen in the future. They need to estimate sales for the next period so they can assign production schedules to manufacturing departments. They need to know the long-term outlook for their company's products to determine if a major change in policy is called for. Two types of forecasting methods deserve special attention, one for its widespread use and the other for its imaginative approach. These methods are (1) trend line analysis and (2) the Delphi.

Trend Line Analysis

From descriptive statistics the analyst develops a familiarity with historical economic relationships. If these relationships form a definable trend, the analyst may extend the analysis into the future. Consider two examples.

THE NAIVE APPROACH Suppose an analyst charts the relationship between company sales and time, as shown in Figure 17-4. Each point on the graph relates the dollar amount to the year in which sales were made. The solid line depicts the trend of *actual* historical sales over time. The dashed line extends the historical trend line one more year into the future to get an estimate of the next period's sales. This approach is sometimes called *simple extrapolation*.

Figure 17-4. *Company Sales and Time*

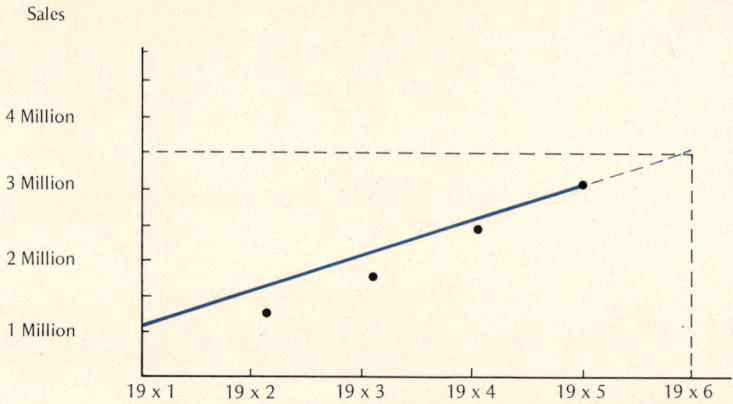

The analyst has most confidence in using the naive approach—so called since it relates the economic variable only to time and no other possible causal relationships—when the historical points fit tightly around the trend line, as in Figure 17-4. When the points are scattered all over the chart in random fashion, as in Figure 17-5, the analyst has little confidence in using trend line analysis as a valid forecasting tool.

THE SOPHISTICATED APPROACH   An analyst should make use of the data and economic relationships available. For example, suppose from a correlation analysis, an analyst finds that automobile sales and gross national produce (GNP) are highly correlated. Furthermore, the analyst refines understanding of this relationship to know that auto sales average around 5% of GNP with very high reliability. Based on this economic relationship, which can be developed by applying a trend line relating auto sales to GNP, the analyst need know only next period's GNP in order to estimate auto sales. Thus, based on economic relationships and trend line analysis, the analyst develops a much more sophisticated grasp of what is happening and what is going to happen than that provided by the naive approach.

The Delphi

The Delphi method of forecasting gets its name from ancient Greek history. Delphi was the home of a famous oracle or fortuneteller. Thus, the Delphi refers to seeing what is going to happen in the future. Fortunately, the Delphi method is much more scientific than the oracle's skills.

The Delphi is particularly well suited to problems where there is not a sufficient amount of historical data available to develop structural relationships or where the historical relationship cannot be expected to extend into the future. Trend line analysis is slow to find basic changes in relationships. Delphi tries to overcome this problem by use of a group decision-making technique.

Figure 17-5. *Invalid Use of Trend Line Analysis*

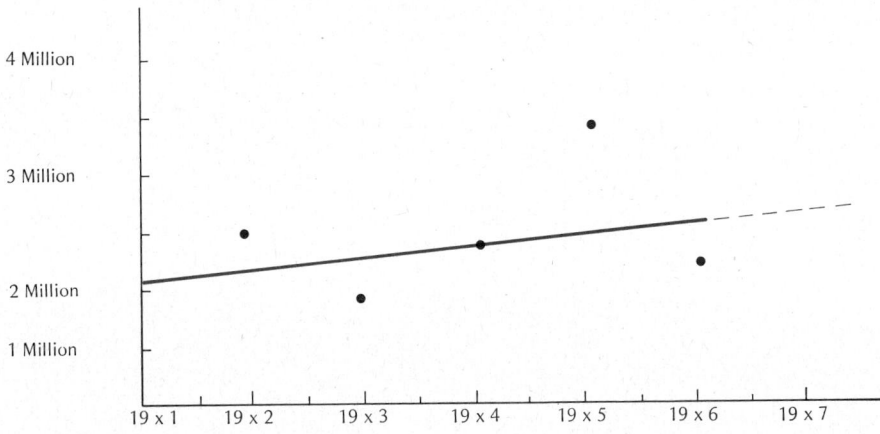

In Delphi, a panel of experts is formed to solve a problem. Each expert must remain anonymous to the rest so as not to bias the others' viewpoints. By use of questionnaires, an analyst obtains each expert's responses to the problem. For example, each expert might be asked to give an estimate of what interest rates will be one month, six months, and one year from now. This would be important to finance people trying to decide the best time to raise money through the issuance of debt. The analyst gathers all the responses, summarizes them, and returns them to each expert for a revised estimate. This procedure is called **controlled feedback**. After four or five rounds of responses, the group consensus should be attained. This **consensus** is the group's best estimate of interest rates at stated dates in the future. Study has shown that the group consensus method results in greater accuracy than that achieved by any individual member acting independently of the group. In effect, the group is more accurate than any of its members.

Delphi is finding many applications in business. It is also being used by social scientists concerned with the quality of life. These professionals use Delphi to project into the future what earth will be like for humans—and what humans will have done to the earth—at time periods in the future.

Resource Allocation and Other Planning Tools

In addition to descriptive statistics and forecasting techniques, there are a number of other quantitative tools that can aid an executive in decision-making responsibilities. To help you understand some of the techniques, descriptions of some common types of business problems and possible solution techniques will be presented.

Mathematical Programming

A company executive must time and time again make decisions on how the company should best allocate its resources. "Resources" is a very general term as seen in the following problems:

1. A company is considering 10 independent projects for funding. All 10 projects cannot be accepted since their total cost would exceed the amount of funds available for investment. How should the company allocate its capital among the 10 projects so as to maximize its return on investment?

2. A company has six factories and 20 warehouses around the country. The cost of shipping goods from each factory to each warehouse is known. Furthermore, each factory has a fixed capacity for output, and each warehouse has a minimum demand for goods. How should the company assign delivery of goods from factories to warehouses in order to minimize its shipment costs, subject to the requirement that the demand at each warehouse is satisfied?

3. A company manufactures 14 different products, but many of the products use the same components. There is a limit on the availability of components. How many units of each product should the company produce in order to maximize its profits?

Each of these problems can be solved by *mathematical programming* methods. The term "programming" as used here does not have the same meaning as in the case of computer programming. Mathematical programming methods are formal computational procedures for solving certain types of problems. Resource allocation problems are particularly suited for mathematical programming solution. They are usually very well structured or defined and fit the necessary assumptions for use of the programming techniques.

The programming techniques assume that the analyst can specify a relationship wanted to maximize or minimize. Perhaps the analyst wants to maximize profits from the sales of products or minimize costs of shipments from production facilities to warehouses. Furthermore, there must be a constraint on the availability of resources for satisfying the stated relationship. For example, the company may have a limit on its capital budget in a given time period. Lastly, certain mathematical relationships must not be violated. These relationships vary for the particular programming technique being used. While these relationships are beyond the thrust of this text, the student is encouraged to explore these conditions in depth before trying to fit a technique to a given problem. When the incorrect technique is applied, the results are generally not satisfactory.

Inventory Models

Both manufacturers and retailers are faced with the problem of how much inventory to keep on hand. If there is not sufficient inventory to meet demand, the result will be lost sales and perhaps costly overtime as the manufacturer tries to build up depleted inventory. On the other hand, having too much inventory on hand is also costly. Inventories must be financed, stored, and insured. Further, they can spoil or become obsolete. The analyst must minimize the total inventory cost—carrying costs (costs of keeping inventory on hand) plus ordering costs (costs of setting up the production line, for example). Inventory models are designed to compute the optimal amount of inventory the firm should keep on hand in order to minimize total inventory costs.

It should be noted that inventory models can be applied to any stock of assets the firm has on hand. An example, in addition to merchandise or goods inventories, is cash on hand. The company can weigh the cost of keeping cash on hand—not having it invested in higher yielding assets—against the cost of ordering or borrowing cash if the necessary balance gets too low.

Queueing Models

A queue is a line. Queueing models are often called waiting line models. For example, a supermarket has the problem of deciding how many checkout counters to have open at any given time of day. Not having sufficient checkout counters open when a lot of customers are in the store results in customer bad will and potentially lost sales. But having idle counters open is also an expense that management would like to avoid. What can be done? A queueing model can be constructed to determine the optimal number of check-out counters to keep open at different times of the day. An analyst can spend a week or two in the store seeing what customer traffic is like at different hours during the day and different days of the week. Next, the analyst can determine how long the average customer spends in the store before going to the check-out counter—that is, how frequent are the arrivals for checking out. Lastly, the person can calculate the average length of time it takes for a clerk to total up the customer's bill and bag the groceries. Given this information, plus the costs of maintaining the service facility and costs of keeping a customer waiting too long for service, the analyst computes the desired number of check-out stations to be kept open at different hours and days of the week.

Competitive Models

All of the techniques discussed thus far in this chapter have assumed the decision maker's actions were unaffected by the actions of competitors. In the real world, however, business executives find themselves in competitive—or gaming—situations. For example, an automobile manufacturer can forecast sales for next year based on a 10% price increase. Given sales estimates, the manufacturer can allocate financial and processing resources to produce cars to be sent to dealers throughout the country. Production runs are assigned according to sound inventory theory. But then a major competitor *reduces* car prices by 5%. The car manufacturer's plans were all for nothing because the possible actions of competitors were not taken into account.

As in all other areas of business, uncertainty pervades the development of

Figure 17-6. *Outcome Table for Alternate Strategies*

		UCAN Strategies	
WECAN Strategies	U_1	U_2	U_3
W_1	6	13	5
W_2	7	9	9
W_3	6	9	12

competitive strategy. A business executive does not know with absolute certainty—unless there is collusion—what a competitor will do to counter each aspect of the game plan. It is the purpose of competitive model building or game theory to help the decision maker come to grips with the problems involved.

Consider a simple example. Suppose there are two advertising companies in competition with one another. WECAN is making major inroads on the territory of the old established firm of UCAN. Both WECAN and UCAN management are plotting out their strategies for the upcoming campaign. No matter what else may happen, WECAN will increase its share of the market relative to UCAN. In other words, WECAN has to come out ahead and UCAN has to lose. But how much WECAN gains and UCAN loses will depend on the strategy each takes. The outcomes of the three WECAN and three UCAN strategies are shown in Figure 17-6. For example, if UCAN selects strategy U_1 and WECAN selects strategy W_2, UCAN will lose 7% of the market to WECAN. All the other entries in the table can be interpreted the same way.

Which strategies should WECAN and UCAN select? If WECAN selects W_1, and UCAN selects U_2, WECAN will gain 13% of the market. But if UCAN had selected U_3, WECAN would have gained only 5% of the market. If WECAN wishes to maximize its minimum increase in market share, it will select strategy W_2. Then, no matter what UCAN does, WECAN will increase its market share by 7%. Similarly, if UCAN desires to minimize its maximum loss, it will select strategy U_1. No matter what WECAN does, UCAN can lose no more than 7% of the market. Thus, if the two firms are run by rational decision makers, strategies W_2 and U_1 will prevail and WECAN will increase its share of the market by 7% at the expense of UCAN.

Unfortunately, not all game situations are as simple as the one just presented. However, the basic thought processes of considering how a competitor will counteract one's own strategies are the same, regardless of how complex the game may become.

Simulation

Not all problems are sufficiently structured to be adapted to mathematical programming techniques or inventory or queueing models. Furthermore, competitive models become hard to manage when the number of competitors and possible outcomes become excessive. A technique that is well suited for complex problems and those which are unstructured or do not conform to the requirements of the mathematical programming assumptions is simulation. In fact, it can be said that simulation is used when an analyst cannot do anything else.

Simulation can be defined as a technique that enables the user to represent the performance of a system over an extended period of time. The analyst tries to build a model that will duplicate the system. For example, an analyst may want to build a simulation model of the firm's cash management system. From historical accounting data, the analyst can follow the flow of cash throughout the firm. Inventories become sales for credit and for cash. Accounts receivable are collected. The firm must pay its debts. Occasionally, the firm must borrow money while at other times it has surplus cash. None of these economic events occur on a precise time schedule. Some accounts receivable are slow to be collected, especially at certain times of the year. Sales vary seasonally. A simulation is based on the structural relationships of these economic events and their frequency distributions. The analyst can vary the values assigned to each event—a process called sensitivity analysis—to see how the system will act under different conditions. Of course, the analyst could never do this experimentation with the real system. The simulation model is thus a convenient information generator for decision makers.

BRIDGING THE MANAGEMENT GAP

The tools of the quantitative approach are potentially very powerful. To be useful to decision makers, however, the quantitative analyst must communicate with the decision maker. So far, this communication process has been minimal. Some of the reasons for this quantitative analyst–management gap shall be explored in this section.

The Pitfalls of Management Science

The quantitative analyst, or management scientist as he is often called in practice, often does not have a true appreciation of the problems confronting the decision maker. *Management science*—the quantitative approach—has developed largely as an academic discipline. Researchers have developed models and techniques to solve hypothetical business problems. Whether these hypothetical problems bear a very close resemblance to any real life counterpart is a matter of debate.

One must always remember that the *output*—or information supplied by a particular quantitative method—can be of no more worth than the quality of the inputs to that method. That is, if the data available for analysis is faulty or hard to obtain, the output of a quantitative technique will be of questionable value to the decision maker. Data is expensive and sometimes impossible to gather. Very seldom will a real life problem fit all the necessary assumptions of a particular quantitative technique. Management scientists must take these factors into account in their work.

Since management scientists have staff positions within the firm, they often fail to see the urgency of solving a particular line-oriented problem. They do not realize that decision makers are working under a time constraint. Decision makers need immediate solutions to problems; they cannot wait days or weeks for analysts to develop a model and provide them with information. The information will have arrived after the decision has already been made.

Management scientists have developed their own peculiar vocabulary and have failed to communicate effectively to the responsible executive level personnel the essence of what they can do for the decision maker. Executives —bombarded with a new and strange language—have grown distrustful of management scientists. Instead of helpers, management scientists have come to be viewed by decision makers as feared opponents. Management scientists, in general, have done little to reduce this fear.

Bringing Management Science Back to Management

The gap between management and the management scientist must be bridged. Management scientists have much to offer decision makers. They have a bag of tools that can ultimately help executives make better decisions. They must communicate this potential contribution to the decision maker.

Decision makers need to be educated about the values of the quantitative approach. This does not mean that every decision maker must have the statistics and mathematics background of a management scientist. Rather, decision makers must be aware of the nature of the tools of management science and the types of problems they can help solve. They must not fear management scientists. Management scientists can aid decision makers by supplying them with relevant information to help solve their problems. However, the executives still make the decisions, not the management scientists or a particular quantitative technique.

Management scientists must become more aware of the types of problems confronting decision makers. All too often, management scientists have quantitative techniques in search of problems. The process should be reversed: the nature of a problem should indicate to the management scientists the type of technique that would be applicable. Management scientists must spend more time in the operating departments of the organization to find out what the real problems are. Developing more techniques for hypothetical problems is a waste of resources when these hypothetical problems are seldom even remotely encountered in practice.

Management scientists must familiarize themselves with the quantity and quality of data available for inputs into their models. They must be aware of the timeliness and cost of this data. Data that takes a long time to gather for a model is of little use to a decision maker who must come up with an immediate answer to a pressing problem. If the cost of supplying information to a decision maker exceeds the benefit in terms of a better solution to the problem, the management scientist has not served a useful purpose. Management scientists must be selective in terms of applying sophisticated quantitative techniques to relatively minor problems.

Management scientists have a difficult problem of their own. They should not be an extra frill in the organization. They must justify their existence to management.

CAREERS IN MANAGEMENT SCIENCE

Wherever decision makers feel that their decisions can be improved by the use of quantitative analysis, job opportunities for management scientists can be found. As the gap between management and the management scientists narrows, new career opportunities will appear.

Nature of Job

As a management scientist, you can find employment in industry, government, or with a consulting firm. Management scientists in industry do marketing research—provide decision makers with information about marketing new and existing goods and services—and other types of quantitative analysis. You might be called on to develop a new inventory system, choose a new plant location, or help select new investment opportunities for a company.

Management scientists in government develop information systems for government decision makers and aid in making policy decisions at both the local and national levels. You might be asked to develop a model of a water supply system, determine optimal deployment of nuclear war heads, or select locations for new health care facilities.

Management consulting firms employ many management scientists. Consulting firms complement the planning and control staff functions of both government and industry. Since management science is a staff function, it has a logical place in a consulting firm. You would visit with clients on a variety of assignments and help develop solution techniques for client problems. You would also have excellent mobility from the consulting firm to a career position with a client.

Qualifications

As a management scientist, you must have a strong background in the basic business disciplines, mathematics, statistics, and computers. It is not unusual for a management scientist to have an advanced college degree, even a doctorate in management science or mathematics. You must be able to adapt quickly to a new setting and define problems since there will be a great deal of variety in your assignments.

Career Rewards

Starting job salaries in management science vary with your experience and educational background. First time job market participants with undergraduate degrees will draw salaries in the $9,000 to $12,000 range while those with advanced degrees can command salaries in the $15,000 to $18,000 range. Since management science is a relatively new field, career advancement is dependent on your individual abilities and aspirations.

A possible drawback is that, as a staff function, the management scientist does not always see a problem all the way through to solution. Your job is to provide executives with information for making decisions, not to make the decisions for them. But the insight you will get into how a firm and how decision makers operate will prove extremely valuable should you eventually move into a line position.

CHAPTER SUMMARY

In an effort to make more accurate and timely decisions, decision makers have investigated the quantitative approach to problem solving. The quantitative approach provides a systematic framework coupled with the tools of statistics and mathematics to enable decision makers to make better decisions.

Business statistics can be used for description or inference. Descriptive statistics provide the executive with a better understanding of his economic environment by extracting and summarizing relevant factors and relationships from the total environment. Statistical inference permits the decision maker to make logical and calculated statements about the likelihood of occurrence of future economic events.

Quantitative methods can also be used for forecasting, resource allocation, and other planning purposes. A naive or simple extrapolation as well as a more sophisticated but complex approach to trend line analysis was examined in this chapter. The Delphi approach, which offers a group consensus method for forecasting, was seen to be particularly applicable in cases where historical experience is lacking.

The particular technique to be applied to resource allocation and planning problems depends on how well the problem is defined or structured. Mathematical programming techniques, inventory models, and queueing models are most useful when a problem is very well defined or structured. Competitive models have the advantage of explicitly recognizing the possible actions of a firm's opponents. They are limited, however, to rather simple situations. Simulation provides the quantitative analyst with a very useful escape mechanism: when all else fails, simulate.

While many decision makers have investigated the quantitative approach, few have implemented it to any great extent. The management scientist—a more professional sounding name than "quantitative analyst"—has done much to incur the executive's wrath. Management scientists have tended to live and work in a world of their own, developing their own vocabulary and being not fully aware of the real problems facing decision makers. The quantitative approach has much to offer management, however, and all effort should be made to fill this management gap.

Being a new profession, management science will offer exciting and important careers to those with the necessary skills and ambitions. As management becomes more aware of the benefits of the quantitative approach—and as the management–management science gap narrows—excellent mobility and advancement possibilities will be clear characteristics of a career in management science.

PROVOCATIVE STATEMENT

The Management Scientist and the Manager:
Partners or Opponents?

1 "Managers and management scientists are operating as two separate cultures, each with its own goals, languages, and methods. Effective cooperation—and even communication—between the two is just about minimal. And this is a shame.

Each has much to learn from the other, and much to teach the other. Yet, despite all kinds of efforts over the years, it seems to me that the cultural and operating gap which exists between the two is not being closed.

Let me quickly acknowledge that there are some management scientists who operate effectively in both cultures. But they are rare birds. Most management scientists are still thinking, writing, and operating in a world that is far removed from the real world in which most managers operate. They often describe and structure nonexistent management problems, tackle relatively minor problems with overkill tools, omit real variables from messy problems, and build elegant models comprehensible to only their colleagues. And when managers seem confused or dissatisfied with the results of their activities and reject them, these scientists seem almost to take satisfaction in this confirmation of the crudity and inelegance of the managerial world."

>C. Jackson Grayson, Jr.,
>Dean of the School of Business Administration
>at Southern Methodist University and
>Chairman of the Price Commission in Phase II of
>President Richard M. Nixon's Economic Stabilization Program,
>in "Management Science and Business Practice,"
>*Harvard Business Review,*
>July–August 1973,
>pp. 41–48.

REVIEW QUESTIONS

1. What is the "quantitative" method?
2. List and briefly define the five basic factors in the quantitative approach to problem solving.
3. a. What are the three types of averages?
   b. What are the three types of dispersion?
4. Define statistical inference.
5. What are the two basic types of forecasting? Briefly discuss each one.
6. What should be done to bridge the gap between decision makers and management scientists?

Pulling Together Business Functions: The Company

PART FOUR

Chapter Outline

The Three Functions of the General Manager

Responsibilities of General Management
    Softening the Profit Motive
    Secondary Responsibilities

The General Manager's Role in Planning and Strategy
    Methods of Planning
    Short-range Planning
    Long-range Planning
    Strategies

Sources of Growth
    Decisions on Internal Growth
    Decisions on Growth through Acquisitions
        Checklist for Company Acquisitions and Mergers
        The Price to Pay
        Types of Payment to the Seller
    The Framework for Growth
        Employees and Organization
        Capital Expenditures
        Timing

Plans, Strategies, and Reality
    Management Competence
    Other Factors Affecting Performance
    Strategic Variables

International Operations
    Reasons for International Business
    Establishing an International Operation
    The Multinational Corporation (MNC)

Careers and Jobs

Chapter Summary

Provocative Statement 1:
    Getting Enough Good People

Provocative Statement 2:
    The Chief Strategist of the Firm

Key Terms

Downside out analysis
Conflict of interest
Bottom-up planning
Top-down planning
Full-resource planning
MBO (Management by objectives)
Strategic variables
Operating variables
Strategy
Diversification
Spin-off

Divestiture
Applied research
Synergy
Go/no-go decision
Capital gain
ROI (Return on investment)
Contingency
Promissory note
Bonds
Nonvoting equity
Peter Principle

General Management: Direction, Coordination, and Growth

"It is quite clear that the chief executive is the chief strategist of his firm ... his mores, habits, and ways of doing things determine how he behaves and decides. His sense of obligation to his company will decide his devotion and choice of subject matter to think about. The rewards system which he is responsible for establishing and maintaining will be significant in how people respond to the strategic planning program."

—George A. Steiner
Top Management Planning

18

A company is divided according to its various functional responsibilities as described in previous chapters. This division of a company into highly specialized functions is intended to increase efficiency. However, to achieve consistently high profit performance, the general manager of the organization must do the following:

1. *Direct existing operations.* People usually reach the top because of superior performance in the three management skills: "people," technical, and optimizing. General managers have accumulated experience in company operations and have a better perspective on the overall operation than do managers of individual functions. This enables them to direct lower-level managers to perform more efficiently than if they carried out responsibilities without direction.

2. *Coordinate components of the organization.* It is essential that all functions meet the same overall goals and time schedules. Formal plans help maintain a balance of activity and avoid having too little or too much inventory, employees, cash, and so on. However, business conditions change more rapidly than plans can be revised. Management must coordinate the functions and other components of the organization to achieve the best profit performance.

3. *Plan the future.* The combination of capital, facilities, and employees currently earning profits for a company is planned, organized, and implemented well over a year in advance, sometimes as many as five years. Success depends on using the best techniques for predicting the future, good judgment, and some luck. Figure 18-1 shows that a portion of most large companies is "dying" at all times. New operations must be added to exceed the present level of profits in future years.

Figure 18-1. *Transition of Company Operations*

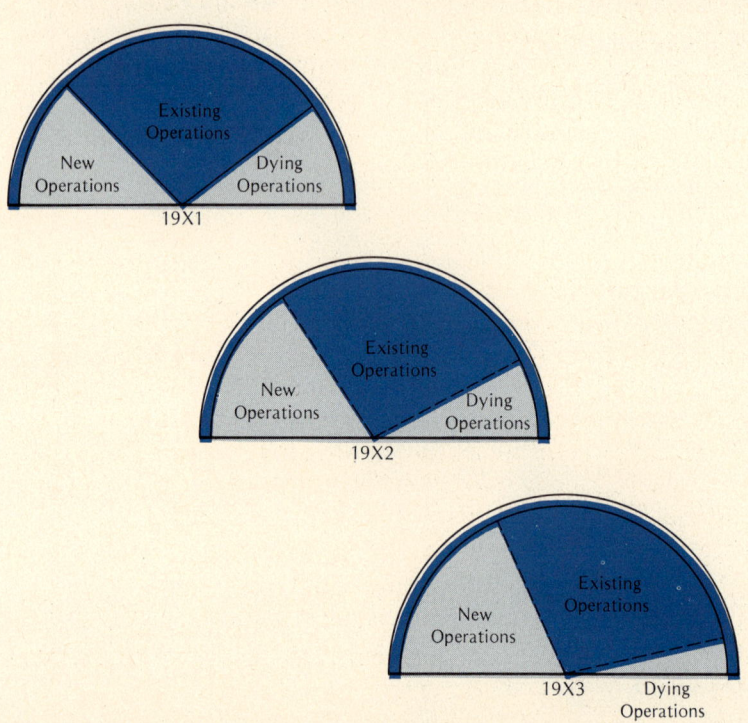

RESPONSIBILITIES OF GENERAL MANAGEMENT

Directing, coordinating, and planning are the methods used to achieve management's primary responsibility: satisfying the wishes of shareholders. These wishes can be summarized as earning the greatest possible return on investment within defined limits of risk. The amount and rate of profit growth are part of the goal setting discussed in Chapter Six. If performance is satisfactory, capital for future growth is easy to obtain from new investors or lenders. If after-tax profits are not satisfactory, a downward spiral can occur: money to overcome problems does not flow into the business, and a bad situation gets worse.

Communication between shareholders and management is infrequent unless large blocks of stock are owned by a family or by those investing for others, such as mutual or pension funds, bank trusts, and insurance companies. Without contact with shareholders, the trend is for executive management to receive counsel rather than specific direction from the board of directors. Therefore, management directly controls policy and decision making within the company. The reason for this trend is that the stock of large companies is traded on stock exchanges. Thus, the identity of shareholders keeps changing.

When a shareholder becomes dissatisfied with management, the individual sells to another person who perhaps thinks it is the right time to buy. Rarely does a shareholder take an issue to the floor of the annual shareholders' meeting. The real pressure on management to think about matters other than after-tax profits, such as social responsibility, began with the unrest of the 1960s and continued with well-organized pressure groups in the 1970s. "Nader's Raiders" is one example, but other organizations supporting various movements are also affecting decision making.

Softening the Profit Motive

A few business executives do not think that the primary responsibility of a company is after-tax profits. They view the company as part of the American business system, as described in Chapter One. The purpose of this system, in their opinion, is social progress to the point where the benefits of private enterprise are distributed more evenly throughout society. Accordingly, companies frequently choose socially responsible programs and projects over those concerned only with earning a high rate of profit.

This position has been influenced by:

1. *Public expectations.* Public authorities and citizens want more aid from companies in solving community problems. People are more highly educated and well informed. They realize companies have the capacity to help if their zeal for profits is lessened.

2. *Professional management.* Generally, most executives own a very small percentage of the company for which they work, if any. Profits are a measure of their performance, but executives are also members of the community. This fact makes them more willing to listen to public pressure and make decisions accordingly.

3. *Government intervention.* Free enterprise is a revocable privilege. Business recognizes that more laws and regulations will be passed to force allocation of resources for social progress unless it is done voluntarily. Therefore, business leaders are taking initiative to avoid mandatory limits on decision making.

Despite these facts, most business executives view their responsibilities from a personal standpoint. Their performance is measured by high profits, balanced budgets, increased sales quotas, and other goals that are rarely related to social responsibility. Their career success largely depends on performance, and social progress could stand between executives and promotions, raises, and additional fringe benefits.

Secondary Responsibilities

In addition to carrying out the wishes of the shareholders, general managers have other responsibilities that relate to this primary obligation.

PRUDENT RISK EXPOSURE   Risks taken to earn profits must never be excessive. General managers must take some chances to show above average performance, but they should never risk losing substantial portions of the business to creditors. To avoid this, they normally complete a **downside out analysis** before making a commitment. This analysis estimates the results of a venture should *everything* go wrong. It is one means of estimating whether a prudent risk is being taken in any new major situation.

OPTIMUM DECISION-MAKING ENVIRONMENT   Every company is plagued with some degree of politics. Power centers are created when an organization is formed, and it is fundamentally important to direct the energy of these power centers toward the goals of the company rather than those of individuals. General managers must consciously prevent political maneuvering simply because if it occurs to excess, much more time is spent in personal battles than in running the company.

PROPER ETHICS   Whether executives at the highest level in the organization have faultless or questionable standards of behavior, the other employees will accept their leadership and follow their example. If behavior is illegal, public exposure and legal prosecution are possible results. In any case, usually company loyalty, even speaking well of the firm, disappears. On the other hand, integrity and honesty lead to ethical conduct and generally a more effective company.

CONFLICT OF INTEREST   A **conflict of interest** may arise when external involvements of an executive become related to company responsibilities. The executive may then be placed in a situation in which decisions within the business appear to favor personal interests outside the company. A general manager must strive to prevent executives from using their positions to benefit themselves at the expense of the company. Specific do's and don'ts are often issued by top management to fulfill this responsibility.

IMPLEMENTATION OF FUNDAMENTAL MANAGEMENT PRACTICES   Top management must provide the framework for other members of the company to carry out their jobs. Such a framework includes the following:

1. A carefully designed organization with clear statements on what is expected from each employee.
2. The most advanced technology feasible, including modern information systems.
3. Goals, policies, and procedures to give the company direction and order.
4. Plans and strategies must be implemented as well as corrected when reality differs from the forecasts, to guide operations.

DEVELOPMENT OF EMPLOYEES   Top executives must develop their personnel and also overcome the reluctance of some lower-level managers to develop subordinates. Reluctance stems from fear of strong managers, ignorance of the importance of development, and lack of time. Regardless of the cause, formal steps toward development at all levels must be encouraged by top executives.

THE GENERAL MANAGER'S ROLE IN PLANNING AND STRATEGY

Heads of divisions or companies are directly responsible for performance. Therefore, they must make the major decisions on allocation of resources—capital, employees, and facilities. Often they will delegate portions of their authority to a department's functions, such as accounting or marketing, to improve the quality and efficiency in planning and managing the business. General managers cannot, however, transfer their responsibility for performance.

Plans and formal strategies guide top executives as to what the overall division or company should do in a future period and the role of each part of the organization in achieving the objectives. As "captain of the ship," an executive determines the final course the company will take during a specific time period and controls the factors involved in staying on that course.

Methods of Planning

There are three types of planning techniques depending on who is involved with the planning.

First, **bottom-up planning** seeks the contributions of all levels of the organization in both short- and long-range plans. Time is taken from operations, but the justification for this use of company time is that more practical plans come from people "on the firing line." Generally, considerable coordination and several revisions are necessary, since individual departments look after their own interests, which are not always in concert. Compromises are basic to bottom-up planning. This method requires a democratic style of leadership.

Second, **top-down planning** is an autocratic approach. The general manager and staff lay out a plan, which is forwarded to those who will be affected. Usually, there is provision for some input by departments so that any impractical aspects resulting from the manager not being aware of specific developments can be eliminated. Top management tends to adopt this approach when it feels that operating people tend to see the business from a very narrow perspective or are thought to have limited competence.

Third, **full-resource planning** utilizes the best elements of the first two approaches. Usually, this method of planning starts with the general manager's office as the focal point for all aspects of plans and strategies. The first version of a new short- or long-range plan is exactly what top management wants. However, departments are encouraged to make substantial revisions, or even submit completely new plans. Eventually, a compromise plan is reached based on overall contributions from all levels of the organization.

The general manager's attitude toward planning greatly affects who participates and the importance given outside opinions. If the individual is considered the day-to-day manager of the business and future problems and opportunities are secondary, short-range plans will receive the emphasis. If the reverse is true and the general manager delegates daily business to the departments in order to plot the future course of the company, long-range plans will dominate.

Short-range Planning

Chapter Six explained that a short-range plan usually covers a time period of up to twelve months. It is revised monthly or quarterly to adjust for changing conditions. The plan is usually limited to the scope of existing facilities, since there is not enough time to make major changes within a year. The general manager has special interest in the short-range plan in the following areas:

1. *Achieving long-range goals.* Future changes in the composition of company operations must be implemented in the present. Constructing new facilities, starting a program to buy other companies, beginning a reorganization, and so on must be initiated and controlled by a short-range plan.

2. *Improving the level of technology.* Equipment, systems, and personnel needed to upgrade a company's level of technology must be introduced in the company in the present. Coordination is necessary as plans change (for example, as product lines are dropped or portions of the organization are eliminated). A specific technology might not be needed, or a different type might be required.

3. *Guiding the direction of research and development.* The R and D department is the source of internally discovered ideas to increase profitability of the company. General managers must be certain that programs and projects concentrate on the primary goals of the business and properly reflect changes that have occurred in the business environment.

4. *Coordinating strategy.* Many strategies span the short- and long-range plans. Some components can be implemented immediately, while others wait for the results of the first stages. This places some components in a time period after the short-range plan but before the long-range plan. Control of strategies is needed to be sure that needed components of the strategy are taking place at the right time.

The four areas of interest have a common factor: each depends on the overview of a general manager. This person is making decisions for both the present and the future, and must choose the best thing to do in these important areas.

Management by objectives (MBO) is a technique used frequently in business and other types of organizations. Its emphasis is on the present, and it involves stated performance objectives. Employees know what is expected from their assignment, such as thoroughness of reports and types of communications. Some of the objectives can go beyond the short-range plan. However, the purpose of MBO is to improve performance by giving the entire organization guidelines not only on what general results should be but also on what is expected from individuals.

Long-range Planning

The future of a company is difficult to forecast. Accuracy of predictions starts to decrease after a few weeks. Some serious mistakes can be made when the business environment for a company is forecast three or five years in advance. Yet, very important decisions depend on this type of forecasting to adjust for changes in the marketplace, product processes, and other components of the company. The general manager must anticipate the problems, see opportunities, and plan appropriate courses of action. Figure 18-2 shows a situation involved in long-range planning.

Top executives have two primary roles in achieving quality in long-range plans. First, they must be certain that strategic variables, those variables outside company control such as federal government policy, are being predicted by reliable sources. If talent in the company is limited or biased, outside sources must be consulted on areas that are important to profit performance. Second, unless top-down planning is being used, the general manager must be

Figure 18-2. *Projection of a Company's Future*

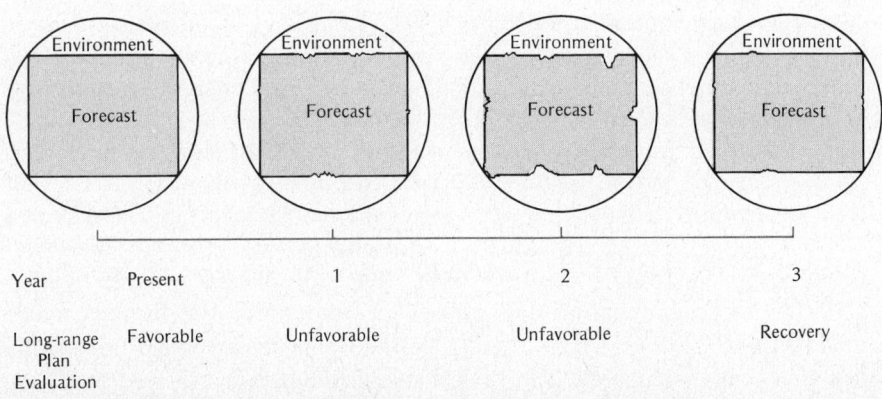

acquainted with early versions of departmental plans and use experience and insight on the company's future to obtain the best balance of proposed ideas, programs, and projects. This improves the quality of decisions on **operating variables**—those variables within company control.

Another quality dimension in long-range plans is increased use of computers. Complex calculations for forecasting can be made in seconds. Interrelationships among many factors can be identified and used by the general manager to speed up quality decision making. Those who know the computer's capacities and limitations and who can communicate practical ideas on its use to analysts and programmers have a higher probability of accurate plans and superior profit performance.

Strategies

A **strategy**, as defined in Chapter Six, involves an objective, multiple components, a time framework, and coordination between the components to achieve the objective. The term *master strategy* has been developed to describe large-scale business strategies since a department carrying out one of the components could have a strategy within a strategy. Some texts refer to these as *substrategies*. Another term used quite frequently in business is *counterstrategy*. It is a reaction to an action initiated by a competitor, the government, or other outside party. The purpose of a counterstrategy is to make the best of a problem situation.

As previously mentioned, strategies often have a time framework different from that of short- and long-range plans. The general manager initiates some strategies and participates in making others. However, in all circumstances, the manager must be sure there is a means to include components of a strategy in a plan at the appropriate time. This is usually accomplished by informing the general manager about strategies active in the firm and using updated versions of these strategies as the bases for adjusting plans.

Control of programs and projects in a master strategy, which extend beyond the short-range plan, but which are in the long-range plan only as a positive result of being successful, is essential. However, many programs and projects are independent of strategies. They are single efforts to improve some part of the organization. The head of planning must also keep track of these situations. Such programs must be included in current budgets, and their results must integrate with other efforts by various departments.

Good communications are extremely important in bringing strategies to a successful conclusion. Feedback facilitates changes necessary to "fine-tune" the objectives of strategy components so that they reflect new conditions. A general manager has considerable impact on communications through individual style of leadership, motivation of personnel, and general attitude toward formal strategies and modern management techniques.

SOURCES OF GROWTH

Some fundamental decisions must be made by a general manager to achieve goals for profit growth.

The *first* decision is the allocation of resources between the two primary sources of growth: (1) internal development of profitable new products through research sponsored by the company, and (2) acquisition of businesses already in operation with proven product lines. Many companies use both approaches to seize every profit opportunity. Figure 18-3 shows how a company's existing products gradually become less profitable and reach the breakeven stage. The reasons for this are increasing competition, better products for the price from competitors, and/or a disappearing consumer need. Accordingly, the general manager must find new ways not only to replace discontinued products, but also to achieve goals for profit growth.

The *second* decision is whether to expand the company's existing line of products or to develop new lines. The term for choosing new lines is **diversifica-**

Figure 18-3. *Declining Product Profitability*

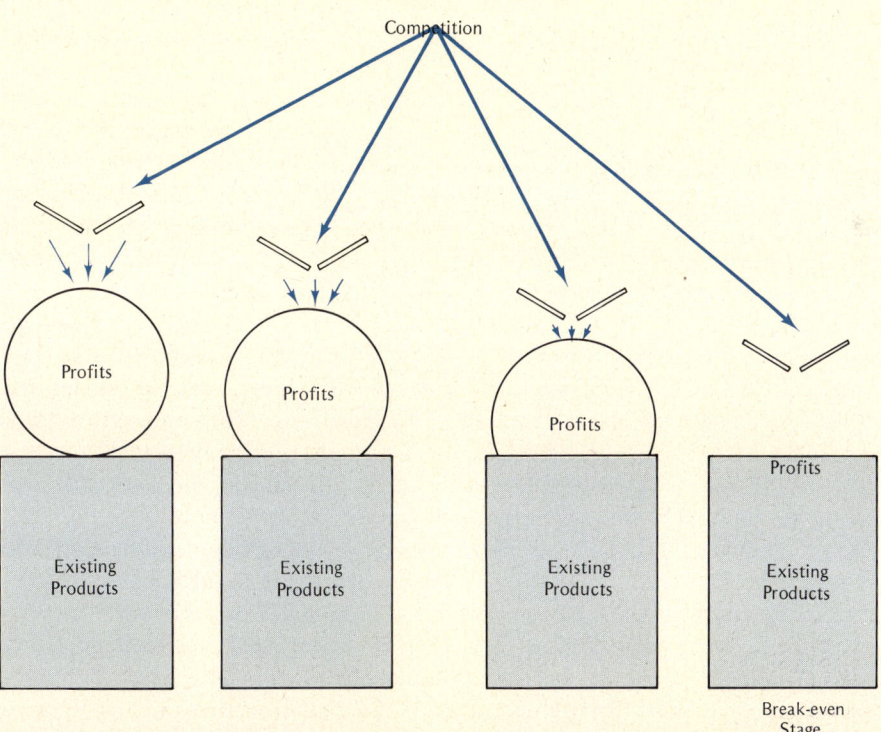

tion. The advantages of diversification are that the firm would not be totally dependent on its present customers and that it could select opportunities with superior profit margins and those that stabilize income. If diversification is successful, the company gains strength from the experience of managing new lines and is better able to grow in the future.

There have been failures in diversification, however. The primary reason is lack of knowledge about the new industry and the resulting poor decisions. Another reason for failure is faulty analysis leading to the decision to invest in diversification. This, too, can be partially blamed on inexperience with the new industry, but it also stems from using improper techniques in conducting research studies.

The *third* decision concerns sources of capital. Property or even a division of the company could be sold to convert fixed assets into cash. Sometimes a sale is the best means of raising funds to invest in other profit opportunities. A **spin-off** is the sale of a segment of the firm, which can function as a separate operation but which was originally part of a division or subsidiary. A **divestiture** is the sale of a whole division or subsidiary. This sometimes occurs as a result of government intervention to prevent overly large companies from destroying competition. However, the usual reasons for selling are:

1. A shift in company policy for product lines.
2. Better opportunities for the selling company.
3. Age of the owner/seller and no heirs for continuing family management.
4. Disappointing performance under existing management.
5. A need for cash to operate the remaining divisions of the business and/or to meet financial obligations.
6. Capital beyond the reach of the seller to develop the business being sold.

Many other reasons could exist in various situations, and the buyer must investigate the reasons carefully to avoid acquiring somebody else's problems.

The *fourth* decision concerns the choice between proposals for existing product lines and any type of new investment in these product lines. Frequently, the most attractive use of capital is expansion of the company's present business. Management has the know-how to make good judgments about the future. Therefore, the probability that profits will achieve the predicted level is higher than the estimates for profits from diversification.

The *fifth* decision entails merging with another firm. A merger involves two companies joining, not one being bought by another. The power of the original shareholders and management of each firm is diluted to gain economies from eliminating duplicated work and a variety of possible other benefits.

The results of these five decisions for an individual company form the avenue a general manager will take to achieve profit growth. The following discussion covers principles to be used in carrying out an expansion program.

Figure 18-4. *Research and Development Programs*

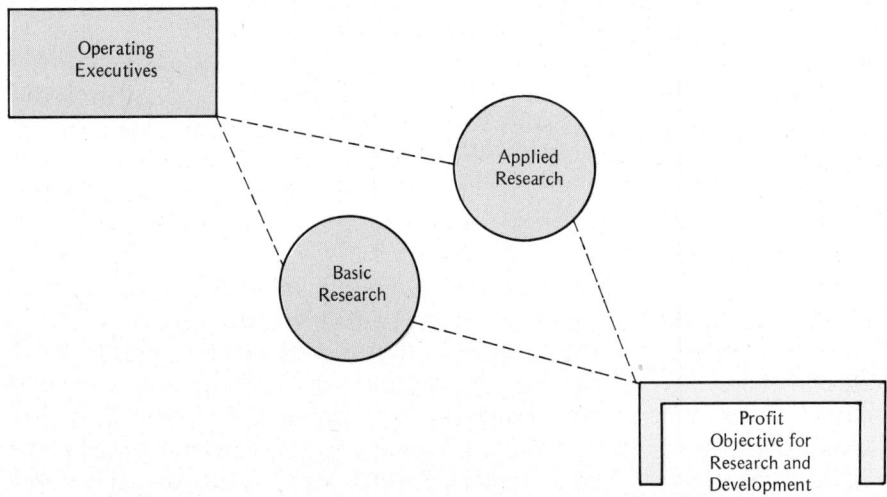

Decisions on Internal Growth

Most decisions on internal growth are based on research. Four areas of research are typical in companies with large-scale R and D: (1) improvements in existing products; (2) improvements in processes, packaging, handling, and transportation of existing products; (3) new related product lines; and (4) processes and product lines wholly new to the company.

Applied research works with the existing operations and attempts to improve it, as is the case of (1) and (2). Basic research begins with the assumption that something entirely new will result, as in (3) and (4).

An analysis of costs and potential benefits from applied and basic research is needed for the general manager to decide on the company's commitment to research. It can be expensive if nothing results. However, DuPont, Eastman Kodak, IBM, and others have made spectacular discoveries that have justified research budgets many times over. Operating executives dealing with one or both types of programs, applied and basic, being conducted by their organizations must relate these programs to profit objectives for research. This is illustrated in Figure 18-4.

A general manager cannot schedule discoveries. However, to encourage results basic principles of management can be applied to the programs and projects. These points are matters of common sense, but are often overlooked.

1. State the objective(s) of the research clearly. If they are modified to reflect market conditions or other environmental factors, restate the objective(s) so that there is no misunderstanding between management and the technical expert conducting the research.

2. Relate expenditures to potential benefits. Control budgets, and communicate to the technical expert the value of the discovery as compared to costs being incurred. The individual may have no concept of economics or the profit motive.

3. Establish target dates for degrees of progress, and formally review the status of the program at each date. The general manager should participate in those sessions that are important to achieving plans. Schedules for each part of a program help to control research because an executive can now ask for progress reports and obtain an accurate status report.

4. Obtain an outline of the order in which procedures and experiments will be conducted. Understand the objectives, not the technical aspects, as an independent means of measuring progress.

This approach to managing the research department can be handled by an administrator within the department, but all information should be available for review by the general manager. Technical experts often complain about this type of supervision, but efficiency improves significantly. Management of research may be the key to retaining the American standard of living. Some executives speculate that valuable discoveries could double in the years ahead without a corresponding increase in research budgets.

Decisions on Growth through Acquisitions

It is necessary to distinguish between acquiring: (1) ideas, patents, product rights, and similar potential opportunities that have neither been proven in the marketplace nor confirmed in the amount of capital required to construct facilities, and (2) on-going concerns with a history of operations and financial statements showing profits (or losses). The risk of losing money or of not earning predicted profits is much greater in (1) than in (2). Internal development of new products through research is more risky than either type of acquisition.

The general manager decides the amount of risk exposure to be taken by allocating funds for growth to R and D and the two types of acquisitions. The quality of these decisions is ultimately the basis on which the manager will be judged. Early criticism about extreme risk is not important to this executive if the investments succeed. If they fail, the individual will be quickly replaced.

Checklist for Company Acquisitions and Mergers

The decision to proceed with an acquisition or merger depends on the results of studies on the following:

1. *Audit of accounts.* Validation of earnings is fundamental. Confirmation of the quality of receivables, actual payables, and the amount of debt is also essential. A *business audit* is the minimum requirement; this is a comparatively superficial examination of the accounts. It is much less expensive

than a *detailed audit*, which balances every number and record in the company. If there is doubt about the present financial position of the company, either a detailed audit is necessary or the buyer can acquire the assets rather than the company. The latter approach leaves an empty firm behind, with any problems still the responsibility of the original owners.

2. *Survey of personnel.* If the acquisition is intended to strengthen an existing product line, acquiring management may not be critical to success. If, however, it is a diversification and the buyer is dependent on the personnel who have teamed to achieve acceptable performance, a survey of personnel is fundamental. In most situations the buyer will want to determine the talents needed to run the business profitably, to have an assessment of the existing personnel, and to know whether employees intend to resign as a result of the change in ownership. This study sometimes uncovers inaccurate rumors about massive firings, reorganizations, and so on.

3. *Market position.* The key questions are, "Will a change in ownership change the attitude of customers toward the company (positively or negatively)?" and, "Is there a fundamental shift occurring in the need for the seller's products (positively or negatively)?" If it is the buyer's industry, there is less insecurity about the possibility of surprises.

4. *Inventory of facilities and properties.* The condition and competitiveness of facilities are basic to investments expecting years of operation. Also, the general manager (or staff) must have accurate estimates of any capital needed for improvement to meet the buyer's standards. This could affect negotiations on price or eliminate the acquisition from consideration.

5. *Compatibility test.* A "before-and-after" analysis must be made to be certain that superficial assessments of the value of the acquisition are actually supported by a detailed examination. Often synergy is expected; this is obtaining results that are greater than the sum of the two parts separately. The compatibility test will help confirm or contradict this position.

The person responsible for each of the five studies will have another checklist, which is longer and more detailed, to assure thoroughness. Eventually, the general manager gets a summary report of the information and a suggested approach for making the acquisition. The manager then must make the go/no-go decision, which either eliminates the candidate or starts discussions on terms of purchase.

The Price to Pay

The principle that guides the modern buyer is profits, not the value of assets. If a company has overinvested and the rate of return based on after-tax profits is low, the owners must expect to take a loss and receive less than the capital invested in the business. On the other hand, some firms have earned very high rates of return through careful investment and good management. This type of seller can expect more from the sale than was invested. This yields a capital gain. The following examples will clarify the position of the normal buyer.

	Seller #1	Seller #2	Seller #3
Sales	$1.5 million	$1.5 million	$1.4 million
Assets Invested	1.3 million	1.0 million	0.7 million
After-tax Profits	0.1 million	0.1 million	0.1 million
Return on Investment	7.5%	10%	14%
Buyer's Offer	$0.8 million	$0.8 million	$0.8 million

The performance of Seller #3 is the best. The rate of return on investment (ROI) is above average at 14%, and the 7% profit margin on sales is acceptable. Seller #2's performance is average. It would only be regarded as superior if company expenses included substantial incomes and benefits for owner/managers that might be saved by the buyer. The company of Seller #1 has either been poorly managed, or unusual conditions have led to overinvestment. An example would be pollution control devices.

The general manager of the buyer always has a standard for return on investment. The rate usually ranges between 12 and 20%, depending on the industry, location, management, and other factors. Let us use 12½% per year or a payback of invested capital in 8 years (100% ÷ 12½% = 8), to explain the use of this standard in acquisition programs.

The standard acts as a guide for the amount that can be prudently paid to the seller. The buyer will not want to lower a company's performance as a result of the acquisition. Therefore, the maximum price, based on current financial information, to each of three sellers would be $800,000. However, the following four factors might influence the buyer to pay more:

1. Potential is not being achieved under present management. For example, Seller #1 could have sold $2 million per year and earned $200,000. This would justify a maximum price of $1.6 million, if all improvements could be made immediately. The price is the result of multiplying $200,000 (after-tax profits) times eight. Eight is the number of years it will take to return the $1.6 million under the company's standard.

2. The seller's company will make the buyer's present operations more profitable. For example, although Seller #2 is earning only $100,000 per year, the product lines and plant locations will enable the buyer to earn an extra $100,000 per year from his own facilities. This would permit the buyer to pay up to $1.6 million and meet the standard.

3. The seller controls valuable assets, such as property with mineral deposits. Under the control of the buyer, these assets would permit substantial expansion and improvement of earnings in future years. It would be necessary to discount much of the potential if it was not intended for use in the near future, but the immediate gains could permit an increase in the amount paid to the seller.

4. Special circumstances influence buyers to pay more than the standard would indicate. These include: (1) tax losses from previous years that would reduce taxes paid by the buyer; (2) accumulations of cash or other liquid assets that would reduce the actual amount paid by the transfer of these funds to the parent after purchase; and (3) technical and/or managerial expertise needed by the buyer.

The decision on how much to pay becomes clearer when these factors are considered. The general manager will almost always allow for a deviation from the estimates. This allowance is called a **contingency**. Instead of paying $1.6 million, the manager might establish the maximum at $1.3 million and allow for $300,000 of earnings potential that would not be realized due to problems not foreseen when studies were being conducted.

Types of Payment to the Seller

The general manager rarely pays cash from the company's funds. Usually, some of the money is borrowed from a bank or other type of lender, such as an insurance company. The standard used by most executives is that the expected rate of return from the investment, for example, 12½%, should be at least double the interest rate paid on the borrowed funds. This is not always possible. Also, lenders are cautious about how much they permit to be borrowed, in case things do not go as planned.

Often there is an exchange of shares, the buyer giving stock for the stock of the seller. In this case, the value of the buyer's company becomes important to the seller. Many of the studies conducted to determine the price will be repeated, even if the shares of the buyer are traded regularly on a stock exchange or over-the-counter. Once a value is established that satisfies the seller, the individual then becomes a shareholder in the buyer's firm. If a merger takes place instead of an acquisition, either a new company can be formed, or one of the two firms can act as a *survivor*, and an exchange of shares takes place. In either instance, each company has a contractually determined and substantial voice in day-to-day affairs.

The buyer may wish to prevent the seller from having too much voting stock. However, the buyer may not use either cash or borrowed funds to complete a stock transaction. Under these conditions, the following can be substituted:

1. *Promissory notes*. This is a loan from the seller to the buyer to make up the amount required. Sometimes **promissory notes** soften the tax impact on the shareholders of the selling company by spreading out payment over several years.

2. *Bonds*. This form of debt to a seller is a registered certificate that would be easier for a seller to convert to cash than a promissory note. In some cases, **bonds** are traded on bond exchanges or over-the-counter and are easy to sell.

3. *Forms of nonvoting equity*. Companies issue **nonvoting equity** in the form of common stock and preferred shares. Sometimes they have

a guaranteed rate of return to influence the seller to accept this type of paper instead of cash.

Many acquisitions fall through because the seller will not accept an offer that contains too much "funny money" and not enough cash. Lack of real money often results from buyers having insufficient capital or attempting to use too much of the seller's own future cash flow to repay debt obligations needed to complete the purchase.

The Framework for Growth

The decisions made in the early stages of setting up a new venture or taking over an existing business will greatly affect the resulting business. Potential profits are estimated in studies, and occasionally good management will cause profit performance to exceed expectations. However, mistakes in the beginning stages frequently have reduced the growth potential to a point below the company's standard. At the outset, the primary areas of concern are: (1) employees and the new organization; (2) capital expenditures; and (3) timing.

Employees and Organization

The quality and attitudes of the people in a business new to a company have a great influence on its success or failure.

In a new operation arising from *internal development*, the personnel process described in Chapter Twelve is critically important. Best results for design of the organization will come from participation by key members of newly hired management. By participating in these decisions at the start, these key people create the basis for profit performance instead of relying on someone else's ideas.

Taking over management of an acquired company creates sensitive issues for all parties. Rumors start, and people become insecure. Quick decisions, straightforward answers, and fairness are essential. The general manager knows that the best qualified people can find a job with another company quite easily. If an exodus begins, it is most often the employees with lesser talents who remain.

When reorganization is needed to realize full potential, the manner in which it is handled is extremely important. Acceptance of reorganization usually is best gained by allowing some participation by those affected. Terminations should not ruin careers. If people have to be fired, separation pay, time to look for another position, and a counseling program will generate loyalty and support from the remaining employees. The inevitable disappointment and bitterness involved are minimized. The buyer of a company can earn respect by carefully identifying the personnel who are responsible for good performance and promoting them.

Capital Expenditures

The number of completed investments that stay within the original budget is small, perhaps as low as 10%. Too, after-tax profits achieving or exceeding forecasts are equally rare. The result is actual performance that is far less than the projection on which the investment was approved.

To avoid this, the general manager must supervise major expenditures very carefully. An increasingly common approach is control of construction and *start-up* (a trial period of 30–60 days preceding full-scale operations) through computerized network models. Without calling meetings or harassing the project manager, the general manager can read a summary printout of the current status and know whether or not there is a problem. Part of a general manager's responsibility is to develop a cost consciousness among his employees. This is particularly true in new investments.

Timing

Delays cost money. Interest is being paid on money that is not producing. Products are not being sold, and cash is not flowing into the business. Expenses for employees and other items are still being paid. Furthermore, people get nervous when things go wrong, and morale is affected.

Poor timing can play the primary role in *overruns* (spending more money than was budgeted). However, the control on costs must also relate to schedules for initial shipments to customers, payments due to lenders, market entry by competitors affecting sales, promises to the community about employment, and operating factors, such as advertising campaigns. An analysis of the extra costs necessary to complete a job on time must be compared to the drawbacks of finishing behind schedule.

The general manager must stay informed about progress because the typical project manager will have many excuses for a poor investment in timing and/or cost trouble.

PLANS, STRATEGIES, AND REALITY

Operations never go exactly according to the forecasts. Therefore, *business reality* can be defined as plans and strategies that are:

1. On-target, or exceeding expectations.
2. Off-target, or with predicted performance unsatisfactory to management.

Some of the reasons for success and disappointments in business are given here.

Management Competence

The Peter Principle[1] states that employees rise to the level of their incompetency. It means that people attain positions of increased responsibility before a company finds out they are beyond their ability to be effective. Many observers feel that Laurence Peter's idea is valid, and that it is a primary reason for companies faltering and not reaching their potential.

The employee selection process becomes critical under this premise, because the firm must try to employ people with more potential than those working for competitors. Managers and the personnel department must be alert to situations in which an employee could be "over his head." While there are no precise means of measuring a person's potential, the systems given in Chapter Twelve will help.

Management by objectives (MBO) has been mentioned as a means of evaluating performance. This is very helpful in middle and lower management, but, at the top, power has been given to the person who can make a series of judgments which could sink the company, yet who can only be fired by the board of directors. These judgments could be made to appear the rational and the best thing to do under the circumstances, but they are not what a competent executive would do under identical conditions.

Other Factors Affecting Performance

It is possible that other factors are contributing to management performance. These may include:

1. *Organizational structure.* Competent people are reporting at the wrong level or to the wrong function. The relationship could have been proper in the past, but conditions may have changed. Also, it could be a remnant of a past management team.

2. *Hiring, training, and development practices.* People with the needed capabilities are being employed at lower and middle management levels, but there is not enough formal training and development to prepare them to be top executives. In other cases, managers are hired from outside the firm, and their style of leadership is not compatible with existing management.

3. *Information and communications.* Decision makers may not have adequate information. Perhaps it is worse; people in the channels through which information flows distort the actual situation. Modern systems may not have been installed or are not being used to their potential.

4. *Planning techniques.* The format of a plan must be tailored to an individual company. While too many revisions and excessive paperwork will

---

[1] Laurence J. Peter and Raymond Hull, *The Peter Principle: Why Things Always Go Wrong*, New York: William Morrow & Co., Inc., 1969.

General Management: Direction, Coordination, and Growth

discourage planning, not "fine tuning" the process and procedures to current conditions can lead to disastrous results. The general manager has to have the planning system that fits the business and the employees.

Strategic Variables

It is possible that the problems confronting a company are largely out of its control. One of the fundamental reasons for planning is to anticipate such a situation and to start as early as possible to correct and adjust. If a general manager is caught off guard, the individual must react quickly. Decisions are made from facts and opinions readily available, and this may not be enough. Figure 18-5 illustrates that the frequency of minor surprises is high, but their impact on company performance is rarely significant. In contrast, one major unexpected surprise such as a revolutionary new product introduced by a competitor, could wipe out a division of a company.

The scope of factors affecting business has greatly increased in recent years, even for small firms. A Nebraska farmer can affect the price of bread in Tokyo, and a plastic hanger manufacturer in Genoa can break the market in Dallas. Government regulations to correct one set of problems cause another set. The general manager acts as the coordinator of the functions and is the person knowledgeable about factors that could affect their performance. The

Figure 18-5. *Strategic Variables and Corporate Policies*

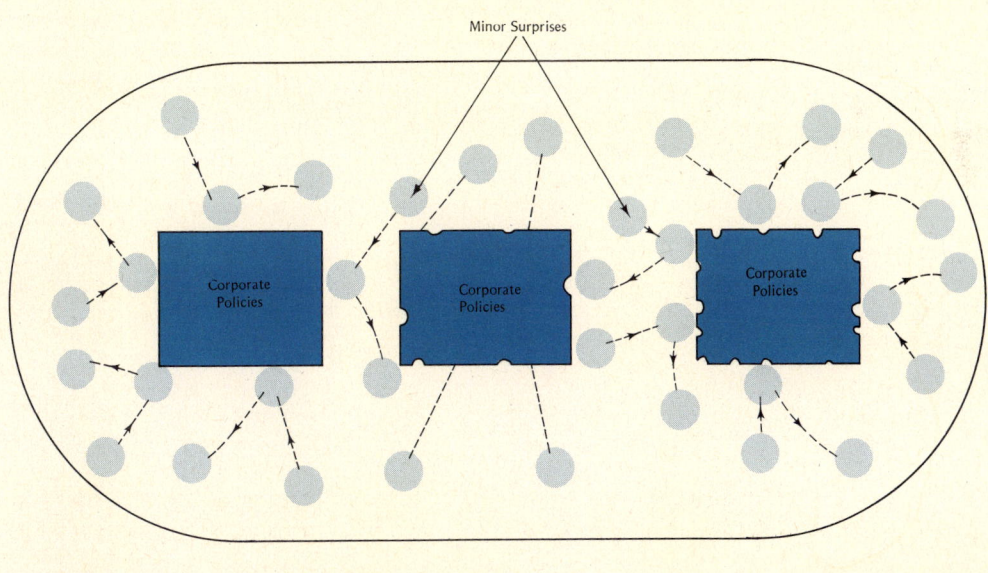

individual must develop a "sixth sense" to pick up seemingly unrelated pieces of information, sort them out, and foresee possible surprises that could affect the company.

It is this "sixth sense" that will have a major impact on success in the years ahead. Top executives must see their job in this perspective and balance their time in a way that permits efficient operations, yet stays one step ahead of major surprises.

INTERNATIONAL OPERATIONS

Top executives are motivated to see profits grow, and they will seek out opportunities wherever they can find them. Led by people who see the world as their potential, some companies have expanded in markets far from the United States. Managers who are less dynamic, or sometimes more prudent, (because of risks associated with different political and economic environments) go through the cycle shown in Figure 18-6.

Reasons for International Business

In addition to profitable markets, companies are drawn into foreign business dealings for the following reasons:

1. *Sources of basic materials.* Oil, copper, iron, bauxite, and so on, are not extracted in sufficient quantities in this country to support the economy. Suppliers of these materials have had to go where they can find an adequate supply.

2. *Cheap labor.* Although increasingly difficult to find, some areas in the Far East and other locations still provide labor for relatively low wages with high rates of output (productivity). Toys and electronics are examples of products that can be made and sold profitably despite increased transportation costs.

3. *Managerial and technical expertise.* Such services can be sold abroad because of the advanced state of many industries in the United States compared to those in other countries. Opportunities to sell concepts and systems have been a "foot-in-the-door" approach to international business. By gaining firsthand knowledge of a country through a low level of risk exposure, the general manager can judge whether it is prudent to expand.

4. *Miscellaneous.* Many companies have acquired firms with foreign operations, thereby inheriting international business. Opportunities to license their product abroad have alerted executives to other possibilities. (*Licensing* is giving the rights to a product or service to another company in a specific territory.) Too, financial management may have led to *blocked currency* and

Figure 18-6. *The Cycle of International Operations*

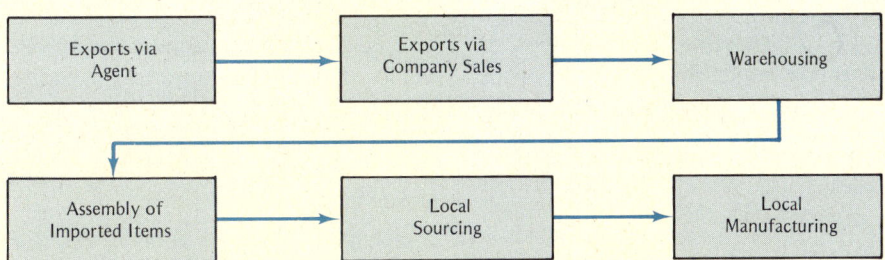

the need to use these funds abroad. (*Blocked currency* is money, that is restricted from being taken out of a country and/or converted to a free currency.)

American companies continue to explore abroad for profitable operations, even in cases where a company's first international business began tens of years ago. For newer companies looking for ways to expand, the process is just beginning. One reason for exploration is that the economies of many countries may be prosperous while the United States is in a recession.

Establishing an International Operation

An investigation for possible investment abroad is similar to research studies conducted in this country. However, the factors listed here make the process somewhat more complicated:

1. *Language.* To make investigations, establish the company, and conduct business, it is necessary to speak and think in the native language. English has become the second language of the world. However, fundamental factors influencing possible success may be expressed only in French, German, Spanish, a dialect of Chinese, and so on.

2. *Mentality.* This is the sum of a people's characteristics, standards of value, tastes, traditions, traits, religions, and many common attitudes shared by the group. Occasionally, it is so different from that of Americans that the business executive is totally confused by a foreign people's priorities.

3. *Nationalism.* In some parts of the world, being a foreigner, particularly an American, can lead to severe penalties and losses. Laws and regulations often assist nationals (citizens of the host country) at the expense of foreigners.

4. *Distances and communications.* Modern technology has greatly facilitated the input of American top management in a company's foreign operations. However, it is still far from the ease of, for instance, supervising business in Los Angeles from Chicago. Important information for decisions frequently is not communicated over distance.

5. *Management availability.* Local people are usually unable to run the firm's business initially. Some Americans dislike the idea of living in another

country and, in addition, of being out of the mainstream of promotions. At the same time, careful selection of quality management is necessary because of points 1 through 4.

(6) *Operating factors.* Some facilities needed to run business operations may not be available. For example, the red tape involved in getting a perishable product through customs could prevent its usage due to the time factor. Electrical power surges and failures could ruin equipment. Public facilities such as roads for trailer trucks or docking space in a harbor may not necessarily exist.

Each of the six factors exists to a minor degree in this country. It is the extreme situations in foreign countries that complicate the investigations.

After a company identifies a potential investment as worthwhile and conducts a feasibility study, a "go/no-go" decision is made. If it is "go," negotiations are undertaken with the local government, local partners (if any), banks, and other authorities. This stage can be extraordinarily quick if the foreign country wants the company's capital and technology. It can be a nightmare, however, if the firm will be competing with nationals in the local market. Negotiating techniques are frequently different abroad because of the different mentalities involved.

The Multinational Corporation (MNC)

Although the *multinational corporation* is a common reference in newspapers and on television, in fact there are very few true MNCs. The fully evolved MNC has no national loyalties. Management can be from any country. Ownership is dispersed throughout the world. The ease of converting profits to strong currencies takes precedence over obligations to any country in which the MNC has had headquarters and/or operations, and it protects itself by whatever means available.

Most so-called MNCs are very national in their orientation. They are American, German, Japanese, or another nationality in origin. They are strongly influenced and regulated by the country in which they have their headquarters. They depend on nationals—citizens of that country—to manage their business. A few shares of the company may be traded on foreign exchanges, but even 10% foreign ownership of large American corporations causes anxiety in Washington, D.C.

In summary, nearly all international business is conducted by companies with close ties to a particular country. Furthermore, the governments of these countries continually try to increase their influence over MNCs through strategies to secure sources of energy and materials, protect their money, and regulate foreign ownership of important operations.

CAREERS AND JOBS

Reaching the top of any organization is a major accomplishment for anyone. It means that the individuals have demonstrated a very high level of "people," technical, and optimizing skills. They also have developed their "sixth sense" and have anticipated problems and devised solutions to minimize the problems. This type of executive is rare. They demonstrate that they are superior to their competition for promotions by consistently high performance through the years.

It would be misleading to imply that things always go smoothly in the careers of top executives. But they must have the ability to absorb disappointments and criticisms without losing either their ambition or their confidence that they will make it to the top. Words such as "tenacious," "resilient," and "persistent" describe them, as well as "intelligent," "resourceful," and others pertaining to their business abilities. In short, very few "softies" get to the top.

Some cynics have commented that you must forfeit all your principles and values to climb up, around, and over the careers of others. The opposite is probably closer to the truth. The person who has integrity and honesty without naiveté, who has the capacity to be realistic and practical without losing a sense of fairness, and who has vision without always living in the future is the individual with the highest probability of succeeding.

The one thing that many executives sacrifice is time with their families. In most corporations, the scope of their responsibilities is awesome, requiring sixty-hour weeks and considerable traveling to carry them out. Also, executives usually grow to like their work and the ego satisfaction of being important. Their competitive drive is characteristically strong, and work is their outlet rather than homelife or sports. Some are able to adjust to the demands of both an office life and a homelife, but others have trouble.

Some talented people have decided that the price is too high. They opt to stay at a level in the organization where they can achieve a favorable balance between business and a private life. Others are attracted to small companies, in which responsibilities are less and travel is greatly reduced. In any case, there is recognition of the price and a conscious choice of the path to take.

CHAPTER SUMMARY

General managers must: (1) direct existing operations; (2) coordinate components of the organization; and (3) plan the future. Their primary responsibility is to fulfill the wishes of shareholders. This is interpreted as a high rate of return on investment through after-tax profits. However, companies are also accepting responsibility for social progress. General managers are under pressure to allocate resources to programs and projects that are beneficial to the community, but yield a low rate of return.

Secondary responsibilities of general managers include: (1) prudent risk exposure; (2) an optimum decision-making environment; (3) proper ethics; (4) the avoidance of conflicts of interest; (5) fundamental management practices; and (6) development of employees.

The three types of planning are: *bottom-up*—there is a broad level of participation throughout the organization in a plan that results from this input; *top-down*—only top management puts the plan together, and there is minimal input by the rest of the company; and *full-resource*—the framework of the plan is initiated by top management, but the remainder of the organization makes major contributions.

In short-range planning, general managers must be certain that steps needed to realize long-range goals are being initiated. They must work constantly to upgrade the level of technology that is included in the short-range plan and must implement R and D programs and projects under this plan to achieve internal growth and support existing operations. Because strategies have components in the short-range plan, and other components extending into the future, general managers must be certain that components being implemented are compatible with those in the future.

In long-range planning, general managers must minimize inaccuracy in forecasting future periods by using the most modern methods, including computerized models. Their greatest direct contribution will be predicting strategic variables and interpreting their effect on the company. Concern with operating variables increases as the firm shifts toward top-down planning.

Strategies are classified into master strategies, substrategies, and counterstrategies. Since they usually cover a period longer than the short-range plan, general managers must control major strategies directly, or indirectly through staff members, to assure that changes in conditions are reflected in adjustments of the strategies. Good communications and feedback are essential to successful strategies.

The two primary sources of growth are (1) internal development of new product lines through research and (2) acquisition of existing companies. General managers must choose the direction of growth by deciding on some combination of diversification, expansion in related lines, and growth of the existing products. Sometimes they can raise capital for growth programs by selling whole divisions or segments of the company that can operate independently. One option is to merge with another company. This means a joining together rather than a takeover. The objective is improved performance through synergy.

Applied research involves improvements in existing products, processes, packaging, handling, and transportation. Basic research seeks wholly new concepts leading to profitable lines. Fundamental principles of management can be applied to increasing the probability of worthwhile discoveries. Success in the management of R and D could make a substantial contribution to maintaining the American standard of living.

Acquisitions for growth can be divided into those involving risks because the product or service purchased has not been proven and those involving existing businesses with proven records. Investigation preceding acquisition includes five studies plus a summary report: (1) audit of accounts; (2) survey of personnel; (3) market position; (4) inventory of facilities and properties; and (5) compatibility test. The price paid is based on actual earnings and potential rather than on valuation of assets. At least four exceptions to acquiring a company with a profit performance less than the buyer's standard can be cited. Sellers sometimes will take "funny money" in addition to cash to complete a transaction.

The early stages of dealing with a new investment or a newly acquired company are extremely important. If dissatisfied about the new situation, the best employees can find other positions, and only the less effective personnel remain. Control of capital expenditures and timing is important because overruns and delays are very costly.

The Peter Principle states that employees rise to the level of their incompetence. Management by objectives (MBO) will assist in controlling this potential problem throughout most of the organization, but serious mistakes at the top can ruin a company before the incompetence is confirmed. In addition to poor organizational structure, inadequate personnel development, lack of communications and information systems, and faulty planning techniques, the company's profit performance can be adversely affected by strategic variables. General managers must develop a "sixth sense" about these variables and anticipate major problems before they occur if they are to be successful in management.

International business evolves as companies seek new markets for their products. It also occurs because of need for basic materials, sources of cheap labor, profits from managerial and technical expertise, and miscellaneous situations such as inheriting an operation from an acquisition. Six factors complicate investigations to decide on an investment abroad. The multinational corporation, one form of international business, is actually misnamed. Most companies involved with international business have close ties with the country in which they have headquarters. In fact, they are likely to be instruments in national strategies to secure basic raw materials and to counter runaway speculation in the dollar.

Reaching the top of an organization means the persons have a high degree of competence in the three necessary management skills and have developed the "sixth sense." They are also not discouraged easily and can take criticism. There is no need for people to lose their principles or ethics on their way to the top.

PROVOCATIVE STATEMENT

Getting Enough Good People

1 "Probably whenever Sitting Bull, Geronimo, and the other chiefs powwowed, the first topic of conversation was the shortage of Indians. Certainly today, no meeting of the high and the mighty is complete until someone polishes the conventional wisdom: 'Our big trouble today is getting enough good people.'

This is crystal clear nonsense. Your people aren't lazy and incompetent. They just look that way. They're beaten by all the overlapping and interlocking policies, rules, and systems encrusting your company.

Do you realize that your people can't make long-distance calls without filling out a report? Do you know what they have to go through to hire somebody—or buy something? Stop running down your people. It's your fault they're rusty from underwork. Start tearing down the system where it has defeated and imprisoned them. They'll come to life fast enough. Be the Simón Bolívar of your industry. Olé!"

> Robert Townsend,
> *Up the Organization,*
> Greenwich, Conn.: Fawcett Publications, Inc., p. 96.

PROVOCATIVE STATEMENT

The Chief Strategist of the Firm

2 "All that has been said previously makes it quite clear that the chief executive is the chief strategist of his firm. At this particular point it is useful to classify some of the major ways in which he exercises an impact on strategic planning.

His aspirations about his personal life, the life of his company as an institution, and the lives of those involved in his business, are major determinants of choice of strategy. His mores, habits, and ways of doing things determine how he behaves and decides. His sense of obligation to his company will decide his devotion and choice of subject matter to think about. The rewards system which he is responsible for establishing and maintaining will be significant in how people respond to the strategic planning program. The way the top executive level of the company is organized is his choice and, as noted previously, is vitally important to strategic planning. The time horizon which the chief executive has will obviously impact heavily on planning. These are but a few of the major personal characteristics of the chief executive which must be examined in considering his influence on strategic planning."

> George A. Steiner,
> *Top Management Planning,*
> New York: Collier-Macmillan Limited, 1969, p. 241.

REVIEW QUESTIONS

1. Name and explain the three tasks general managers must perform in order to achieve consistently good profit performance.
2. Express your view on the primary responsibility of the management of a company.
3. Define and distinguish between the three approaches to planning.
4. How does the chapter explain the difference between strategies used when a company is on the offensive and those used when the company is on the defensive?
5. What are the two primary sources of growth? Which would you choose as the source to emphasize, and why?
6. Do you think the Peter Principle is a real problem in business? Defend your position.
7. What are some different sources of capital a company could use?
8. What is the difference between a fully evolved multinational corporation and a typical American company doing international business?
9. Give an example of how each of the six factors affecting the establishing of an international operation could have impact on the success of the venture.

Chapter Outline

Definition of a Small Business

The Entrepreneur
   Advantages of Self-employment
   Disadvantages of Self-employment
   Motivations to Leave Big Business
   The Family as an Asset or Liability

Part 1: Establishing a Small Business
   The Capital Estimate and Ownership Structure
   Percentage Ownership
   Type of Partners
   Sources of Capital
   Estimates of Cash Inflow
   Estimates of Cash Outflow
   Nonfinancial Considerations
     Location
     Marketing Strategy
     Labor Unions
     Availability of Personnel
     Future Potential
   The Go/No-Go Decision

Part 2: Managing the Small Business
   Causes of Small Business Management Problems
   Types of Small Business Management
     Retailing
     Services
     Manufacturing
     Wholesalers
     Franchises

Careers and Jobs

Chapter Summary

Provocative Statement 1:
   Entrepreneurial Energy

Provocative Statement 2:
   Failure as a Part of Success

Key Terms

Entrepreneur
Leasing
Small Business Administration
Regional development organization
Venture capitalists
Cash inflow
Cash outflow
Cash flow statement
Cooperative
Voluntary
Franchise

Establishing and Managing a Small Business

"The essential ingredient for entrepreneurial success is energy. You may have all the ambition in the world, gobs of capital, a gambling man's soul, and business degrees covering an entire wall, but if you aren't virtually a human dynamo, forget it."

—Joseph Mancuso
Fun and Guts: The Entrepreneur's Philosophy

19

What is small business? The Small Business Administration of the U.S. government places an upper limit on the size of companies receiving loans and other assistance:

Retailing and Service	$1 million or less annual sales
Wholesaling	$5 million or less annual sales
Manufacturing	250 or fewer employees

(If employment is between 250 and 1,000 a standard for the specific industry is used.)

Probably the most realistic way of defining a small business resulted from the Committee for Economic Development of 1947:

1. Management is independent. Usually the managers are also the owners.
2. Capital is supplied and ownership is held by an individual or a small group.
3. The area of operations is mainly local. Workers and owners mostly live in one community. Markets need not be local.
4. The business is small when compared to the largest firms in its industry.

The successful small business with an ambitious owner will eventually test the upper limits of both sets of definitions through expansion. In such cases, the **entrepreneur**—a self-starting person who prefers meeting the challenges of business on an individual basis rather than working for someone else—uses a proven formula for profits in a specific area of interest. This person sometimes sells stock to the public to raise capital, and employs managers for new operations who probably live in different parts of the country. When the company gains sufficient scope to be regarded as influential within its industry, it is no longer considered small by any definition.

THE ENTREPRENEUR

It is a special person who wants to run a small business. The personality profile is quite consistent in success stories.

DRIVE The individual must have energy, and ambition, and be willing to accept responsibility. The entrepreneur's initiative, persistence, tenacity, and resilience are similar to the characteristics of the general manager described in Chapter Eighteen.

OPTIMISM Some analysts cite this word as a synonym for "entrepreneur." It takes considerable optimism to overcome the disappointments usually encountered in small business ventures.

HEALTH Most small businesses require specific contributions and regular supervision by the manager. Consequently, there is little time for being sick. The person should avoid any illness that would interfere with the job for a few days, because rarely is there anyone to replace this individual.

EGO An entrepreneur likes being the boss. It is satisfying for the individual to see things happen as a result of personal ideas. This desire is sufficiently strong to make the person leave a secure job with a large company to accept the risk and headaches of a small business.

PROBLEM-SOLVING ABILITY The entrepreneur is regularly confronted with new problems. The person must have an orderly mind that instinctively uses the five-step process for decision making given in Chapter Six. An important aspect of success in small business is not repeating mistakes and learning from experience.

The three managerial skills in Chapter Six—"people," technical, and optimizing—are ultimately responsible for the success of a small business owner, if the necessary personality traits are present. A minimum of "people" and technical skills is required in every business, and using these skills wisely is necessary for consistent performance. These requirements may be beyond the range of a single entrepreneur. Frequently, the individual must utilize supplementary talent either as part of the company or as regular professional assistance. Figure 19-1 is an excerpt from a Small Business Administration (SBA) pamphlet (Small Marketers Aid No. 71), which asks the key questions a person must consider seriously before launching a small business venture.

Figure 19-1. Worksheet No. 1

Under each question, check the answer that says what you feel or comes closest to it. Be honest with yourself.

Are you a self-starter?
- ☐ I do things on my own. Nobody has to tell me to get going.
- ☐ If someone gets me started, I keep going all right.
- ☐ Easy does it, man. I don't put myself out until I have to.

How do you feel about other people?
- ☐ I like people. I can get along with just about anybody.
- ☐ I have plenty of friends — I don't need anyone else.
- ☐ Most people bug me.

Can you lead others?
- ☐ I can get most people to go along when I start something.
- ☐ I can give the orders if someone tells me what we should do.
- ☐ I let someone else get things moving. Then I go along if I feel like it.

Can you take responsibility?
- ☐ I like to take charge of things and see them through.
- ☐ I'll take over if I have to, but I'd rather let someone else be responsible.
- ☐ There's always some eager beaver around wanting to show how smart he is. I say let him.

How good an organizer are you?
- ☐ I like to have a plan before I start. I'm usually the one to get things lined up when the gang wants to do something.
- ☐ I do all right unless things get too goofed up. Then I cop out.
- ☐ You get all set and then something comes along and blows the whole bag. So I just take things as they come.

How good a worker are you?
- ☐ I can keep going as long as I need to. I don't mind working hard for something I want.
- ☐ I'll work hard for a while, but when I've had enough, that's it, man!

- Do you know what financial statements you should prepare?
- Do you know how to use these financial statements?
- Do you know an accountant who will help you with your records and financial statements?

YOUR STORE AND THE LAW

- Do you know what licenses and permits you need?
- Do you know what business laws you have to obey?
- Do you know a lawyer you can go to for advice and for help with legal papers?

PROTECTING YOUR STORE

- Have you made plans for protecting your store against thefts of all kinds — shoplifting, robbery, burglary, employee stealing?
- Have you talked with an insurance agent about what kinds of insurance you need?

BUYING A BUSINESS SOMEONE ELSE HAS STARTED

- Have you made a list of what you like and don't like about buying a business someone else has started?
- Are you sure you know the real reason why the owner wants to sell his business?
- Have you compared the cost of buying the business with the cost of starting a new business?
- Is the stock up to date and in good condition?
- Is the building in good condition?
- Will the owner of the building transfer the lease to you?
- Have you talked with other business men in the area to see what they think of the business?
- Have you talked with the company's suppliers?

Reprinted through permission of the Small Business Administration.

Advantages of Self-Employment

Surveys of entrepreneurs consistently show that "being your own boss," the independence from the control of an employer over a person's working life, is more important than financial rewards. "Doing something you like" and "accomplishing something on your own" also rank above profits in most questionnaires. Rarely is security high on the list of factors motivating a small business person and most are willing to trade security for a chance to earn attractive profits.

Other advantages attract specific individuals to small business. For example, being an important part of a community and offering a valued service can be strong motivations for some people. The need to prove oneself, a drive for power, and a need to compete could lead others to start their own businesses.

For some people, it is a necessary way of life. Their personalities prevent them from being successful in large companies and they turn to small business as the best career option.

Disadvantages of Self-Employment

Failure rates of small businesses, discussed later in the chapter, indicate that there is a real possibility of the entrepreneur losing both money and valuable time which could have led to promotion in a large company. Bankruptcy can have a serious impact on a person beyond loss of capital. It can affect self-confidence and self-esteem. However, in some cases it is an important learning experience.

Another drawback is the time needed to run the small business properly. A company employee comes and goes at specific hours, with no worries about what happens after leaving work. However, the owner/manager is usually kept busy during business hours and uses mornings and evenings to catch up on bookkeeping, inventory control, and other tasks the individual cannot afford to hire someone to do. Vacations are hard to arrange. Freedom from an employer is often traded for slavery to one's own business and the needs of its customers.

Pressures can become enormous. Situations occur where customer payments are delayed, and the line of credit from the bank is totally extended. Suppliers are late. Employees are stealing. The wife or husband is fed up with the long hours. The bookkeeper is in the hospital. Some entrepreneurs, discouraged by such obstacles, are often convinced to sell out and take a steady job.

In addition to problems of financial risk, demands on time, and the pressure of sole responsibility, some of the hoped-for advantages might not materialize. The community may have no interest in the product or service being offered. Satisfaction of accomplishment is buried beneath the problems. The list of factors causing discontent can be long if the entrepreneur loses confidence and optimism.

Motivations to Leave Big Business

People with entrepreneurial characteristics often will see the balance of advantages and disadvantages in favor of entry into small business. Part of this judgment is based on the alternative of being an employee of big business. The complaints listed here are typical statements of entrepreneurs about large companies, from individuals who have had direct experience with big business.

1. *Mobility*. A person is transferred so often that the individual is not part of any community and is always an outsider.
2. *Politics*. Too much time is spent in maneuvering and "cutting up" other people. A "doer" gets frustrated. Careers are uselessly ruined.
3. *Insecurity*. Mechanization and the computer have eliminated many jobs. The need for technical skills fluctuates. Also, if a person has a personality conflict with one of the bosses, the individual can be affected.
4. *Lack of job satisfaction*. An employee is often blamed for something that he or she had nothing to do with and rarely is complimented for anything. More important, the company is so big, the employee never sees the conclusion of what he or she works on.

Most entrepreneurs admit that large companies have some advantages. These include a steady salary and fringe benefits, such as insurance and vacations, which are superior to that of most small businesses. No risk of personal capital is involved. There are opportunities to socialize with other employees. Working hours are limited unless the person is in top management. Of course then the incentives are sufficiently great to justify the time spent.

The Family as an Asset or Liability

A small company usually involves the entrepreneur's family members directly. Sometimes they work in the business and become underpaid employees. Their desire for material things is affected by the company's financial condition. Also, time for outside activities is not always available. These demands can result in either positive or negative attitudes from family members.

The family, particularly the wife or husband, can have a major impact on performance. Psychological support is important when things go wrong. There are times, such as when inventories must be taken, when willing help is needed. If there is a spirit of cooperation and understanding, the entrepreneur feels the small business is worth the effort. Complaints and grudging assistance have the opposite effect.

Lenders frequently require personal interviews with both the entrepreneur and the spouse. Signs of discontent about the venture can have a bearing on whether or not the loan is granted. Avoiding failure, especially in the early stages when disappointments are commonplace, can depend on a "second effort" inspired by the business person's family.

PART 1: ESTABLISHING A SMALL BUSINESS

Let us go ahead with establishing a small business. The principles used to start a new investment for a large company should be applied. The primary difference with a small business is that one or two people are doing all the work, not many experts from a number of large company departments. This means the probability of making a serious mistake is quite high.

There are two roads to small business. One is beginning from scratch. The other is buying a company already in operation. If the entrepreneur selects a going concern, many more facts are known. However, even in this case, a careful examination of the information is required.

The fundamentals discussed in the following paragraphs emphasize points for individuals or partners looking into establishing a business.

The Capital Estimate and Ownership Structure

The entrepreneur must first make decisions about capital and about the ownership structure of the business (see Chapter Five). It is important to know how much it will cost to go into the business selected by the entrepreneur. As the individual investigates each aspect of being an owner/manager, the capital estimate will be refined to a reasonably reliable total. However, at the beginning a small business person should have an idea of whether $50,000 or $500,000 is involved. The reasons for this preliminary estimate are:

1. The business could be beyond the means of the entrepreneur. Money and time spent on audits, market analysis, and other appropriate studies would be wasted.

2. Partners might be needed for equity capital. If no suitable partner can be found or their demands are unreasonable, another less expensive business should be looked for. Demands considered unreasonable might include control of key decisions by one person.

Very rarely does everything go smoothly when starting any new operation. In calculating the estimate and considering the ownership structure, the small business person must allow for financial reserves on which to draw if the investment runs into trouble. The entrepreneur could lose everything by not having these reserves. Overoptimism can be a serious mistake at this stage.

Percentage Ownership

Regardless of the form of company selected, the entrepreneur must choose the minimum percentage he or she will accept in the new venture.

Setting 100% as the goal will keep out outside parties. 51% allows control of the business while permitting one or more minority partners. The individual can agree to less than 51% if he or she has a greater percentage than any other investor. This usually involves a friendly investor who will vote regularly with the entrepreneur to achieve control. Finally, the person can take a minority position, with others having more, if he or she is the general manager of the business and the person making the day-to-day operating decisions. The choice made will help clarify how the entrepreneur sees a personal role in the business.

Settling the ownership structure will dispel any unrealistic visions of power. Identifying who is in charge of daily activities will determine the degree to which the entrepreneur will manage the business.

Type of Partners

Some entrepreneurs do not want investors involved in management. This minimizes the interference in decision making. Others see a need to supplement their talents in areas such as accounting, finance, marketing, or operations. This approach implies that partners are less likely to complain if they know what is going on, and that they have more incentive to perform than ordinary employees. Selection of a partner in business is nearly as important as selecting a mate. References and investigations should be conducted as a matter of principle even if the entrepreneur knows the individuals.

Sources of Capital

Let us assume that the entrepreneur has compiled all the capital he or she has saved or has borrowed from relatives. Partners have been selected or discarded as an alternative. Any additional capital must come from sources listed here.

1. *Leasing.* Instead of being bought, property and equipment are rented. The monthly fee plus interest is an expense.
2. *Trade credit.* Items for resale are purchased under terms that permit the entrepreneur to receive payment from customers before suppliers are paid.
3. *Loans from equipment sellers.* In a buyer's market it is possible to ask for three to five years to pay. This permits cash flow from operations to cover this capital expense.
4. *Mortgage loans.* Entrepreneurs frequently offer property as collateral, including their homes, as a means of borrowing.
5. *Commercial banks.* Some banks will work with entrepreneurs to complete the capital structure by assisting with partners and lending money, sometimes unsecured.

6. **Small Business Administration** *and other government agencies*. Some loans, or guarantees that facilitate bank loans, are available through this agency and other government sources. Exhausting paperwork and delays are usually involved.
7. **Regional Development Organizations**. Although often without the funding to lend or guarantee, many of these organizations will either help directly or indirectly by identifying private sources of equity or debt.
8. **Venture Capitalists**. Individuals and firms will complete the financial package of selected ventures with a combination of equity and loans.

Established businesses, which therefore have some financial history, will be able to borrow money more easily than new companies. Also, even if the entrepreneur forms a corporation to minimize personal liability, lenders will request that the individual pledge personal assets for security.

Estimates of Cash Inflow

This study is mostly a market analysis. However, it also estimates when the cash for the product or service, which has been sold, will be actually received.

The *first* step is to define as carefully as possible the goods and/or services to be offered. Usually this will not involve more than determining, for example, the type of store and quality of product rather than specific merchandise, or determining the product range rather than full specifications. Common sense will dictate the amount of detail needed to guide the market analysis.

The *second* step is to define the target market area for the business. Research may lead to modifying this area, but there must be a limit on the scope of the market. One extreme is to pick one section of a city; the other is to anticipate selling to much of the country because of the decision in the first step.

The *third* step is to conduct *desk research*. This means the entrepreneur collects all available information about the business and the geographic area selected. This information can come from U.S. government agencies (SBA, Bureau of Census, Bureau of Labor Statistics, and so on), state agencies, trade associations, chambers of commerce, magazine articles, and so on. Entrepreneurs who have a better than average chance of succeeding start collecting this information when the idea of starting a company becomes a serious possibility.

The *fourth* step is *field research*. Armed with some insight about the good and bad points of a business, the entrepreneur can ask intelligent questions of potential competitors, related businesses outside the selected geographic area, suppliers, banks, development agencies, and other sources. For example, an accountant might offer help with the intent of getting the business as a client. The purpose of field research is to get a picture of reality.

The *fifth* step is to analyze the information and make estimates of cash inflow. This requires objectivity and a market strategy that is detailed rather than general. The entrepreneur often does not have objectivity at this stage and may be overly enthusiastic unless the research uncovers very bad details. Therefore, estimates are often too optimistic. Nevertheless, the person should uncover the information shown in Table 19-1.

The *sixth* step is to show the estimates to two or three people in whom the entrepreneur has gained confidence during the course of the study, probably a market expert, a banker, or an accountant, who have little to gain from poor forecasts. This gives perspective that almost always leads to revisions. This step is frequently omitted by prospective business owners, and the result has been worrisome weeks of trying to refinance.

Table 19-1. *Determining the Sales Potential*

In the service business, your sales potential will depend on the area you serve. That is, how many customers in this area will need your products and/or services? Will your customers be industrial, commercial, consumer, or all of these?

When picking a site to locate your business, consider the nature of your product and/or service. If you pick up and deliver, you will want a site where the travel time will be low and you may later install a radio dispatch system. Or, if the customer must come to your place of business, the site must be conveniently located and easy to find.

You must pick *the site* that offers the best possibilities of being profitable. The following questions will help you think through this problem.

In selecting an area to serve, consider the following:

1. Population and its growth potential.
2. Income, age, occupation of population.
3. Number of competitive services in and around your proposed location.
4. Local ordinances and zoning regulations.
5. Type of trading area (commercial, industrial, residential, seasonal).

PRICING. In *setting prices* for your product and/or service, there are four main elements you must consider:

1. Materials and supplies.
2. Labor and operating expenses.
3. Planned profit.
4. Competition.

In estimating volume of products and/or services sold, you must consider:

1. Amounts sold by others of similar size.
2. Advantages and disadvantages of your position.
3. Seasonal or cyclical impact.

The critical element is timing. Entrepreneurs could be correct about the eventual percent of the total market, but it usually takes longer to achieve than the study indicates. While it is unrealistic to be too conservative, this mistake is better than misguided enthusiasm about sales in the early stages of the business. Specifically, if payments are scheduled to the bank, suppliers, and others on the basis of estimates for the cash inflow and there are delays, business owners may not be able to make the payments on time.

Estimates of Cash Outflow

The estimate of itemized expenses is dependent on completion of the sales forecast, mentioned in Chapter Eight. However, much insight can be gained from field research just mentioned. The more expenses are based on actual experience for similar businesses, the more accurate they will be.

The *first* step is to obtain an expense checklist from the SBA. This checklist gives broad categories of costs that must be determined. An example is given in Figure 19-2. Use of this checklist can prevent overlooking any of the standard items.

The *second* step is to obtain an expense profile for the type of business that has been selected. This supplements the first step and provides details on the average experience of small businesses in the entrepreneur's field by category of expense. Figure 19-3 gives an example. This information costs money, as much as $250 for reliable details for some businesses. However, the information is worth the cost to refine cash outflow estimates. The SBA has expense profiles for some businesses, and these would be a check against the purchased information. In summary, steps one and two identify the applicable expense items and provide an input for desk research.

The *third* step involves designing the organization, regardless of how simple the needs for personnel are. Each function is accounted for in this step. This assures that no personnel expense is overlooked. Some functions in the design can be given to services such as accounting or engineering. Preliminary salaries and wages are assigned to full-time employees, and the cost of services is also estimated. Part of this step is obtaining procedures and amounts for state and federal taxes, social security, unemployment, and other deductions, including any group insurance plan that will be offered.

The *fourth* step includes determining the local rates for electricity and other utilities, store and plant office rent, insurance, and other appropriate items given in the expense profile. In some cases, such rates will have to be based on volume, so comparisons are needed to estimate these costs.

The *fifth* step involves analysis of data obtained from the field work mentioned in the fourth step of cash inflow analysis. The purpose is to cross-check estimates derived from volume, and rates against the actual expenses of people in the business. Frequently, costs turn out to be substantially different because of inexperience and overlooked details. This information must be examined

Figure 19-2. *Worksheet No. 2*

Item	ESTIMATED MONTHLY EXPENSES Your estimate of monthly expenses based on sales of $_____ per year	Your estimate of how much cash you need to start your business (see column 3.)	What to put in column 2 (These figures are typical for one kind of business. You will have to decide how many months to allow for in your business.)
	Column 1	Column 2	Column 3
Salary of owner-manager	$	$	2 times column 1
All other salaries and wages			3 times column 1
Rent			3 times column 1
Advertising			3 times column 1
Delivery expense			3 times column 1
Supplies			3 times column 1
Telephone and telegraph			3 times column 1
Other utilities			3 times column 1
Insurance			Payment required by insurance company
Taxes, including Social Security			4 times column 1
Interest			3 times column 1
Maintenance			3 times column 1
Legal and other professional fees			3 times column 1
Miscellaneous			3 times column 1
STARTING COSTS YOU ONLY HAVE TO PAY ONCE			Leave column 2 blank
Fixtures and equipment			Fill in worksheet 3 on page 12 and put the total here
Decorating and remodeling			Talk it over with a contractor
Installation of fixtures and equipment			Talk to suppliers from who you buy these
Starting inventory			Suppliers will probably help you estimate this
Deposits with public utilities			Find out from utilities companies
Legal and other professional fees			Lawyer, accountant, and so on
Licenses and permits			Find out from city offices what you have to have
Advertising and promotion for opening			Estimate what you'll use
Accounts receivable			What you need to buy more stock until credit customers pay
Cash			For unexpected expenses or losses special purchases, etc.
Other			Make a separate list and enter total
TOTAL ESTIMATED CASH YOU NEED TO START WITH			Add up all the numbers in column

Reprinted through permission of the Small Business Administration.

Figure 19-3. Expenses Worksheet

	Sample Figures for Repair Services* Percent of Sales	% of Your Sales	Your Dollars JAN	Your Dollars FEB	Your Dollars MAR	Your Dollars APR	Your Dollars MAY	Your Dollars JUN	Your Dollars JUL	Your Dollars AUG	Your Dollars SEPT	Your Dollars OCT	Your Dollars NOV	Your Dollars DEC	Your Annual Sales Dollar
Sales	100%														
Cash receipts	–														
Cost of sales	47.51														
Gross profit	52.49														
Controllable expense															
Operating supplies	1.82														
Gross wages	16.98														
Repairs and maintenance	0.38														
Advertising	1.45														
Car and delivery	1.52														
Bad debts	0.04														
Administrative and legal	0.74														
Outside labor	1.21														
Miscellaneous expense	0.81														
Total controllable expense	24.95														
Fixed expense															
Rent	3.35														
Utilities	2.05														
Insurance	0.95														
Taxes and licenses	0.86														
Interest	0.12														
Depreciation	1.25														
Total fixed expenses	8.58														
Total expenses	33.58														
Net profit	18.96														

* These percentages are taken from Barometer of Small Business, Accounting Corporation of America. These figures are only a sample.

carefully. Potential competitors sometimes mislead researchers to discourage competition.

The *sixth* step is analysis, compilation, and preparation of final expense estimates. Outside sources to check the estimates are not likely to be available, unless the entrepreneur is willing to employ an expert for input on critical expense items.

This completes the "number stage," and a cash flow statement such as Figure 19-3 can be completed, along with a break-even analysis that reveals the minimum level of income required to meet all financial obligations. This analysis also leads to methods that can be used to lower costs in bad times. In addition, all financial statements can be prepared with final decisions on the capital requirements and the capital structure.

A careful entrepreneur will lay out a schedule for capital expenditures, payment of principal and interest on loans, and expected timing for construction and remodeling and/or penetration of the market. With each schedule change of any item, the entrepreneur can calculate the impact on finances, marketing strategy, purchasing, and other factors.

Nonfinancial Considerations

Several factors could be involved in one business and only a few in others. The principal considerations, including location, marketing strategy, labor unions, availability of personnel, and future potential, are given in the following paragraphs.

Location

The main criteria must be identified, and again, the field research will provide basic information. The SBA has prepared guides on the importance of location for many types of businesses. For example, visibility to and access by passing traffic may be critical to sales volume. Parking could be important. Transportation expenses and receiving and shipping facilities may affect selection of location. The list can be lengthy, and compromises are likely to be necessary. Both capital expenditures and operating expenses could be modified by the choice, as well as marketing factors. It must be emphasized that for some businesses a wrong decision could mean failure. Detailed studies must be conducted, often by consultants, to make the right decision.

Marketing Strategy

Some specific decisions are needed on how sales volume will be achieved after the selection of a certain location. Variables include advertising, promotion, training of sales people, use of commissions (sometimes to the extent of eliminating salaries or wages), and sales outside the location. A marketing strategy results from these decisions.

Labor Unions

It is a rare entrepreneur who does not have a natural dislike for unions. Inevitably, unions cost money and limit decision making. When given a choice, the owner will increase other costs to avoid organized employees.

Availability of Personnel

This could be a critical factor, even if special skills are not needed. For example, business owners have scheduled shifts around school dismissal times to permit working mothers to be home for the arrival of small children and to permit the employment of high school students. The primary point is the need for a flexible attitude in solving any personnel problems. Whenever the entrepreneur breaks with convention, there is a good possibility it will yield better talent for less expense

Future Potential

This book has discussed obsolescence and the short life of some products. The entrepreneur must determine whether the business has a long-range future or one with limited potential. A limited future could be acceptable if the entrepreneur recognizes that cash generated from the first operation must be invested in another venture.

The Go/No-Go Decision

Four situations exist at the conclusion of studies and judgments made by the entrepreneur:

1. *No-go.* The results clearly rule out going ahead. Even the person originally most enthusiastic recognizes that the business is a loser.
2. *Doubtful.* This is a dangerous situation. A backer of the proposal is likely to be providing excuses for any problem area, and an investment could go ahead that should have been dropped.
3. *Go.* The results support original feelings that profits would justify taking a risk and making the investment. No startling surprises or major worries cloud the decision.
4. *Excitement.* Results exceed expectations. The business is clearly superior to other investment alternatives. Enthusiasm is justified.

Comments on all four situations assume that there is adequate information for drawing conclusions. Consultants, bankers, and others regularly observing those establishing a small business claim that very few entrepreneurs (1) investigate the venture sufficiently or (2) fully use the free resources available to them. Therefore, in most cases any of the four possible conclusions could be wrong. It is this uncertainty that makes lenders skeptical about the forecasts of entrepreneurs.

PART 2: MANAGING THE SMALL BUSINESS

One way to identify success factors in managing a small business is to review studies of why many fail. The primary causes apparent in these studies are as follows:

1. *Incompetence in marketing.* It is possible that the sales potential never existed. However, a large percentage of those businesses that could succeed fail because of inadequate training, interest, and general ability in marketing.

2. *Inability to compete.* Another high percentage of failures stem from poor operating decisions. Side-by-side in a geographical area with a business seeking the same customers, some entrepreneurs do not have the managerial competence to identify differences between their companies and competitors and to make corrections. Some become so involved in solving the resulting problems that no attempts are made to correcting the basic causes.

3. *Record keeping.* Many businesses either have no system or do not use the system they have for knowing the status of important categories of information, such as inventories and condition of receivables. People get busy and do not take the time to do it themselves, and they fail to hire someone to do it for them. As a result, cash is used poorly, and mistakes are compounded due to lack of information.

4. *Inadequate capital.* This could result from: (a) undercapitalization at the beginning; (b) expansion of sales volume without increasing working capital; (c) poor use of original capital. Poor management of cash generated by the business could result in a downward spiral with banks owning the business. Occasionally, an entrepreneur will expand facilities for volume that never materializes, and is caught without funds to keep the operation going.

5. *Location.* The wrong decision was made, and correcting the error would be too costly.

6. *Miscellaneous.* Natural disasters have wiped out otherwise strong businesses. Events such as a super-highway or redevelopment zone could end a firm's operations. These and other similar causes are only related to poor management when the jeopardy was apparent and the owner/manager did nothing about it.

The symptoms of pending failure are deterioration in working capital and the status of ratios given in Chapter Thirteen, declining sales, and lower profits (or increasing losses). When these signs appear, management must take major steps toward identifying the causes and finding solutions.

Causes of Small Business Management Problems

Some people are incompetent and are natural "losers." Others have inadequate business experience and undertake ventures for which they are not prepared. This section concentrates on those who have a good chance for success.

The *primary cause* of poor management in small businesses is the level of talent expected from one or two people. In Part Three of this book the various functions necessary to run a company effectively are described. The jobs involved require some degree of specialization. These functions are necessary in small companies as well as in large corporations, and, while the scope of operations is obviously on a much smaller scale, each has to be handled adequately in order to be successful.

Some entrepreneurs are conscious of potential shortcomings and develop the following means to overcome them:

1. *Selection of partners.* The scope of the business sometimes justifies full-time owner/managers in order to secure talent needed. At other times the partners are only "watchdogs" in their area of expertise, such as reviewing accounts, marketing techniques, and so on, on a regular basis.

2. *Board of directors.* Talented people outside the ownership structure can be named to the board. For very small directors' fees a small company can gain a great deal of perspective about its problems and how to solve them most efficiently.

3. *Consultants.* Cost is a factor in retaining outside experts, yet the quality may depend on paying a reasonable fee. The entrepreneur concerned about balancing talent must identify people in the community who have what is required. Discussions determine those who will not charge beyond capacity to pay. Retired people, college professors with practical experience, and small consulting firms with low overhead expenses are possibilities.

4. *Employees.* Entrepreneurs try to avoid permanent obligations that add to their payroll expense. Sometimes the business cannot afford this approach and still yield an adequate return for investors. On the other hand, such an approach may be essential for survival.

The common mistake made in seeking outside talent is to "economize" by paying so little that the work is worthless or, worse, misleading.

The *second cause* is low quality of employees. Many people do not see a career in small business. Often, job applicants have less training and experience than ideally needed. This is because those applying consider it a "stepping stone" to something else, perhaps gaining valuable experience, since the employee must learn an entire business instead of only a specialized assignment as in a large company. Turnover is also part of this cause. In too many cases, the net result is that things are not done or that they are done poorly.

The entrepreneur can be the cause of quality problems with employees. The owner may select people on the wrong criteria, or the person's "people" skill may be low so that relations with qualified personnel are poor. This reputation precedes the owner, and, therefore, the quality of those applying may be affected. Finally, the small business owner often employs family members and relatives for important positions that could be filled by more qualified workers.

Types of Small Business Management

The following paragraphs cover management aspects of the four categories of small business: (1) retailing; (2) services; (3) wholesaling; and (4) manufacturing. Opportunities in franchising are included as a separate category.

Retailing

Each store develops a personality, and management must be conscious of the image to be projected. Physical characteristics, layout, and selection of fixtures are factors in creating this image. These three must be compatible with the store's mission: discount store, quality merchandise, full line, or some specialty such as stereophonic equipment or fabrics. A conscious effort to develop good customer relations, in combination with the correct "personality," will create the proper atmosphere for expected sales volume.

People who want to make a purchase must know the store exists in order to give it consideration. Location is important to sales in most businesses. However, advertising and promotion supplement exposure from a good location and can even compensate for a bad one in some cases. At the same time, advertising and promotion expenses must be justified by customer response and increased volume. Therefore, managers should make periodic analyses of changes in sales resulting from this type of spending.

Inventory control is critical because it leads to: (1) buying only what is in short supply; and (2) having available what the customer needs. A surprising number of managers order in regular patterns and do not adjust for changes in sales volume of specific items. Quantities of slow-moving merchandise accumulate, and good sellers will experience occasional stockouts. Systems are now available that relate each sale to the condition of inventory and alert the manager to order an item. These systems are not computerized for single locations, but they can be linked to a computer for multiple locations. Information is also provided on changing customer buying patterns.

Buying need not be in small volume if the retailer is part of a **cooperative** (independent retailers join to form a wholesaler to increase their buying strength) or a **voluntary** (an independent wholesaler acts on behalf of several retailers in the same lines).

Extending credit is always an important decision. It can be justified on the basis of increased sales volume and keeping up with key competitors. However, it adds to paperwork and creates the possibility of bad debts. Credit cards transfer the responsibility of collection at a cost to the retailer.

Retailers often have problems that are peculiar to their businesses. Common difficulties include:

1. Competition from chain stores operated by large corporations.
2. Shoplifting and theft by employees.
3. Infringement on parking space by new buildings or by local regulations.

4. Changes in the immediate environment of the store affecting the original reasons for choosing the location (particularly in downtown areas).
5. Fast, efficient delivery of goods at a reasonable price.

A variety of studies conducted in this country indicate that roughly half of the retailers survive the first two years and that about 20% continue in business after five years. This would indicate than many people are unprepared for managing a small retail operation and do not apply the principles outlined in this book.

Services

The number of services being offered is in the hundreds. Any business in which there is no tangible product provides a *service*. Motels, insurance brokers, consulting firms, building contractors, bowling alleys, repair shops, and accounting firms are examples. Almost 50% have less than 20 employees, but, interestingly, 30% have over 500 employees and billing that takes them outside the limits of the small business definition.

Repeat business is a key to success, as it is in most retail firms. This means a fair price for services, required quality, and prompt timing. It is difficult to measure fairness and quality in many instances. Some businesses emphasize reliability (a combination of quality and adherence to timing promises), but they inform the customer/client in advance of the high price compared to competitors who do not make such promises. The primary point is that the manager of a service business establishes policies for the three factors so that employees understand what is expected for the charges being billed.

Many of the comments under retailing for location and advertising apply to service businesses. Inventories may be less complicated or not even a factor. Credit is also less of a concern with many firms requiring cash or a reliable credit card. On the other hand, personnel can be a critical success factor. Special talents may be needed for a service business.

Manufacturing

The fundamentals discussed in previous chapters are broadly applicable to the small factory. Often, the primary problem facing the manager is marketing. The manager's talents are likely to be in industrial operations, perhaps with recognition of the need for records on inventories, budget controls, and similar operating information. One solution is the use of wholesalers in a variety of forms. These individuals and organizations are not employees or subsidiaries. They agree to sell the new line to round out the selection of products they can offer their customers. A primary consideration is getting these wholesalers to give the manufacturer's line sufficient attention. Usually they are already offering a number of other products, some of which may be competing.

Another serious problem is the cost of materials and components. A small factory does not have the volume to obtain large discounts. Moreover, there are very few cooperatives to join. In addition, less volume than many competitors means that control of overhead is critically important. Otherwise, unit costs are pushed upward by limited volume through both purchasing power and overhead expenses.

Credit terms from suppliers and the length of time between receipt of the goods and payments from customers for the finished product are probably highly sensitive factors. If working capital has to be increased to cover payments to suppliers because the time span is excessively long, the return on investment decreases. Small manufacturers are placed in this position when banks are reluctant to give a line of credit to substitute for increased capitalization.

Transportation is another concern. Damage en route is costly. Company owned vehicles driven by employees characteristically have a lower rate of damage. However, it is expensive to buy or lease the trucks, maintain them, and pay the drivers. Also, another union could be involved if a company decides to transport its own products. The manager has to list and analyze the specific costs and benefits to reach a profit-generating decision.

The personnel function is often overlooked in small factories. Employment is handled through agencies, advertising, and posted notices. Minimal training is conducted. Turnover is processed through the payroll department. However, the situation is getting more complicated for many manufacturers. OSHA (Occupational Safety and Health Agency) is administering the act passed in 1973 and mentioned in Chapter Twelve, and the "teeth" in this legislation could shut down a plant. With regulations on civil rights and increasing benefits negotiated with unions, the manager has more problems with administration of personnel than in the past.

Wholesalers

Most manufacturers attempt to have as few layers as possible between their firms and the ultimate customer. Each layer adds a mark-up to cover costs and earn a profit. The amount depends on the industry and the supply/demand position, but it is frequently 50% of the purchase price from the supplier (buys at $1.00 and sells at $1.50). The end result of using a wholesaler can be an overpriced product that is not competitive. Direct purchasing by large retail and manufacturing firms is an example of the customer trying to lower costs. Despite this trend there is a place for wholesalers. Their role is essential to: (1) small manufacturers; (2) foreign companies; (3) food and commodity transfers; and (4) independent retailers.

Sometimes wholesalers never see the goods that pass through their offices in the form of purchase orders with customers' addresses as delivery destinations, acknowledgments, and invoices. Wholesalers attempt to get exclusive territorial rights with suppliers to protect their positions and to avoid being by-passed by large customers whose orders could be handled directly by suppliers.

Some wholesalers provide warehousing, and this often secures their role between the producer and the consumer. Such facilities may be essential to the business, such as grain elevators and refrigerated storage. In other cases, storage is a supplementary service that involves charges for space.

The wholesaler has to be constantly concerned with earning an adequate profit, while avoiding mark-ups that motivate customers to buy direct. New concepts eliminate lines that were highly profitable in the past, and this necessitates building new customer relationships.

Franchises

A franchise involves a contract between an independent business person and a franchisor that supplies a name, goods, services, trademarks, patents, and similar items. For example, a Holiday Inn is often owned by an individual. However, this person follows the total system, including signs and exterior appearance used by all Holiday Inns. Most importantly, the owner has access to the worldwide reservation system and benefits from advertising campaigns. They increase business sufficiently to justify fees paid to Holiday Inn.

Over one in five independent businesses have a franchise agreement. There are more than 1,200 franchisors having contracts with nearly 700,000 franchisees.[1] The concepts of buying a "package" business has become appealing to the increasing number of people interested in small business. The cost of the package can range from a few thousand dollars for an ice cream store to $250,000 for a large fast-food service outlet such as McDonald's.

ADVANTAGES   The key attractions are summarized here.

1. The headaches of establishing a business are nearly eliminated. Cash inflows, budgets, location, and other success factors are provided to the best of the franchisor's ability.
2. Important management decisions and systems are provided, such as inventories, accounting systems, advertising formats and frequency, and so on.
3. Training and ongoing management assistance are offered by most franchisors. They work at minimizing the number of failures with which they are associated.
4. Credit ratings improve for a franchisee of a successful franchisor. Risk is substantially reduced, and some franchisors even cosign on loans. A few offer long-term loans to assure adequate capital.
5. The owner/manager has less than a 10% chance of failing as a new business as compared to a nearly 50% rate for other businesses.

These advantages are not universal to all franchisors, and considerable desk research is needed to get the best opportunity. Usually, there are at least three from which to choose. The important parts of each package should be listed side-by-side for comparison.

[1] National Federation of Independent Businessmen.

DISADVANTAGES   There are some drawbacks which are listed here.

1. The cost of association with the franchisor is high. The initial charge varies, but $10,000 is reasonably typical. The continuing fee is normally a percentage of gross sales, such as 5%.
2. The total package might include items that are successful in other locations but not in the area of a particular franchises. The contract might require the individual to retain this part of the line regardless of losses involved.
3. Controls maintained by the franchisor are often so strict that the independent business person turns out to be little more than a manager rather than an entrepreneur.

A wide range of differences exists for contracts of franchisors in the same business. The expectations of the investor are usually provided in accordance with the contract, but law suits and countersuits are prevalent in this approach to small business. Checklists are available for analysis of both the general terms and the details in the contract. A truism for franchising is that it is much less expensive to have a good lawyer at the beginning than later for a law suit.

FINDING THE FRANCHISE   There are two directories of franchising published each year:

The Franchise Annual by National Franchise Reports, 333 N. Michigan Avenue, Chicago, Illinois 60601

A *Franchise Directory* by International Franchise Opportunities, 421 Center Street, Lewiston, New York 14092

In addition to these sources, ideas can be found in trade journals of the industry, franchising magazines, exhibitions, and newspaper advertising.

CAREERS AND JOBS

In Chapter One the chairman and chief executive officer of EXXON indicated that the public had lost confidence in our major institutions. Rather than turn away from private enterprise, one of the reactions of the public has been to "start over." This has led to a general resurgence of interest in small business.

One of the problems with college education in business administration is the emphasis on training for large corporations. The greatest job market for graduates is from this source, and it is understandable that universities limit coverage of small business to one or two courses. However, specialization does not prepare entrepreneurs to perform all the functions described in

Part Three of this text. Moreover, individuals may not understand the importance of other fields nor the interrelationships of these fields that make for successful business.

Some steps are recommended here to assist young people interested in owning their own businesses.

First, look beyond the attraction of being your own boss and analyze whether you have the personal characteristics necessary to succeed. Self-analysis if fundamental before choosing any type of career, but it is particularly essential in small business. The entrepreneur is a special kind of individual, and most people would be happier working for a large company or the government.

Second, if you are convinced that small business is your way of life, investigate the types that appeal to you and that roughly fit your pocketbook. A sign that you are a true entrepreneur is that your estimate of the money you can raise might seem optimistic to others. Once you have narrowed the field to three or four possibilities, examine the success factors and lifestyles involved. Determine whether these are compatible with your self-analysis.

Third, make an investment in yourself. Spend a summer vacation working in your type of small business. It might pay less than other alternatives, but you will know whether you like the work or not. List the costs (things you give up) and the benefits (things you get) by being that type of small business person. This experience, perhaps repeated during the next vacation, will likely determine whether you are an entrepreneur. It is tragic that people wait until they have another career and, then, because of various frustrations, change to small business. Too often, it is a case of "leaping from the frying pan into the fire."

Fourth, now that you have identified one or two businesses that appeal to you, work on personal talents necessary for success. Prepare yourself. Study accounting! Learn about sales techniques! Study inventory control! Take the necessary courses and work on your personal characteristics which may not be the best for your business. Also, save some money. Do not depend on others if you can avoid it; you may need their help later.

Several years are advised for the process of determining "whether," "what," and "how" to be an entrepreneur. Those who compact the four steps into a few months are increasing the chance of failure. Being thorough in the process described for establishing a small business will increase the probability that your investment will work out.

CHAPTER SUMMARY

Small business is best defined as having independent owner/managers, capital supplied by an individual or small group, local operations, and a relatively small size as compared to other firms in the industry.

It is a special person who wants to run a small business. An entrepreneur must have energy, health, optimism, and thinking ability plus enthusiasm for the responsibilities of being the boss. There are major advantages and disadvantages in being a small business person, but even the disadvantages will seem minor to the natural entrepreneur. The individual's family plays an important part in achieving success.

Establishing a small business, Part 1 of the chapter, should start with the capital estimate and ownership structure. The entrepreneur must have cash reserves for times when things go wrong and the company needs more money. Therefore, the individual must know the scope of what is involved and whether he or she can have the amount of ownership that meets personal goals. Otherwise, studies on the operation of the business would be a waste of money and time. Several sources of capital are available to the entrepreneur, particularly if the person is buying an existing firm with a history of profits.

There are six steps to estimating cash inflow: (1) definition of goods and services to be offered; (2) definition of the market area; (3) accumulation and analysis of published material, or desk research; (4) field research, or interviews with people in the business or related to it; (5) preliminary estimates; and (6) exposure of conclusions to someone whose opinion was valuable during the field research, and revisions as required.

There are also six steps to estimating cash outflow: (1) obtain a checklist for expenses from the SBA; (2) obtain an expense profile for the business which might be available from the SBA or a commercial source; (3) design the organization and the assignment of each responsibility; (4) develop data on rates, fees, licenses and wages and salaries; (5) check estimates with other small businesses during field research for practical experience; and (6) compile the information, analyze it, and prepare the results.

Nonfinancial considerations of importance are location, marketing strategy, labor unions, availability of needed personnel and future potential, competition, and product life. With this information, cash flow estimates can be prepared. Capital estimates and ownership structure also permit completion of financial statements, and a go/no-go decision can be made.

Managing the small business, Part 2 of the chapter, involves most of the principles discussed earlier. The reasons cited most frequently for poor performance are: (1) marketing incompetence; (2) inability to compete through poor operating decisions; (3) lack of record keeping; (4) inadequate capital; (5) location; and (6) inability to anticipate serious problems. Some people are natural "losers," and others have inadequate training and experience. The remainder are often asked to perform too many functions in business, and people are bound to be weak in some areas. Partners, outside directors, consultants, and employees are sources of needed talent.

Another cause of poor performance or failure is inability to employ the required quality of personnel. The entrepreneur may complicate the problem through any shortcomings in "people" skill.

The image of a retail store must be compatible with its mission: discount store, quality merchandise, and so on. Location is important, but advertising and promotion are also critical in achieving sales potential. Inventory control has been made easier through new automated systems. Buying can be through cooperatives but is usually done by the individual store. Common problems that confront retailers are listed, and they contribute to the fact that only one independent retailer in two survives the first two years and only 20% last over five years.

Service businesses depend on the proper combination of fair price, required quality, and prompt timing. Policies will help employees know what is expected. Location and advertising are important, but inventory is less critical to success. Usually, service companies receive cash or take an acceptable credit card, and credit is not often a major factor.

Small factories are frequently faced with a marketing problem. The solution has been wholesalers in a variety of forms, such as sales representatives for specific territories who are not employees. Costs are adversely affected by small volume. Credit from suppliers and the terms of sale by the small business person affect working capital and return on investment. Transportation can be important to profits because of damage en route and service. Finally, the personnel function requires attention because of employee regulations.

Wholesalers have been by-passed in many instances, but they still have a role for small manufacturers, foreign companies, food and commodity transfers, and independent retailers. Some never see the goods and only handle the paperwork, while others provide warehousing services.

Franchising involves a contract between an independent business person and a large company offering a "packaged business." Normally, there are five advantages to this approach, the most important being a significantly lower failure rate. The disadvantages are cost, unwanted items included in the package, and rigidity in the system that converts the entrepreneur into a manager for the franchisor. Several alternatives are available, and comparisons should be made to get the "package" that best fits the individual.

Four steps are suggested for those interested in a small business. First, analyze whether you have the required characteristics. Second, look into the types that appeal to you. Third, work in a business similar to the one you have in mind. Finally, prepare yourself by taking the proper courses and developing needed skills.

PROVOCATIVE STATEMENT

Entrepreneurial Energy

1 "If there is any one coefficient of entrepreneurial success it is ENERGY. You may have all the ambition in the world, gobs of capital, a gambling man's soul, and business degrees covering an entire wall, but if you aren't virtually a human dynamo, forget it!

You've got to be able to go twenty-five hours a day, if need be, to make the business work, and that takes energy. If you don't have it, all the Wheaties and Ovaltine or little blue pills in the world aren't going to help."

                        Joseph Mancuso,
Fun and Guts: The Entrepreneur's Philosophy,
Reading, Massachusetts: Addison-Wesley
Publishing Company, 1973, p. 16.

PROVOCATIVE STATEMENT

Failure as a Part of Success

2 "When an entrepreneur is starting his business, the last thought to enter his head is that of failure. This is as it should be, but keep in mind the wise words of Henry Ford, America's premier entrepreneur, who said that 'Failure is the opportunity to begin again, more intelligently.'

One of the ingredients most necessary for success is failure.

Entrepreneurs nearly always pass through failure on the road to success. Most don't even try to avoid it, recognizing that it may be only a necessary detour on their way. Think of failure as a resting place, and you're in the proper frame of mind to start a business.

Remember, too, that success is relative. That is, you must measure it against a level of accomplishment: Such-and-such was more or less successful than something else. To express it another way, success (or lack of it) is what's left after you subtract your total failures from your total successes. It's the remainder that counts."

                        Joseph Mancuso,
Fun and Guts: The Entrepreneur's Philosophy,
Reading, Massachusetts: Addison-Wesley
Publishing Company, 1973, p. 41.

REVIEW QUESTIONS

1. Select a successful small business owner in your community. Do the characteristics cited for successful entrepreneurs at the beginning of the chapter match those of your business owner?
2. Analyze yourself. Would you make a good entrepreneur?
3. Name the advantages and disadvantages of being in business for yourself. Which are most important to you?
4. Pick a small business that appeals to you. Describe how you would estimate the amount of money you would need to start the business.
5. Using the same business as in Question 4, how would you find out whether it would be profitable?
6. Cite some factors that are important for success in retailing? Wholesaling? Service businesses? Manufacturing?
7. What are the typical reasons for small business failures?
8. Do you think a college education is needed for success in a small business?

Chapter Outline

Business Developments and Career Directions
    Changes in the Company
    Career Implications

Career Planning
    Self-analysis
    Career Directions
    Researching the Job
    Searching for a Job
        Résumés
        Cover Letters for Applications
    Interviews
        Preparation
        In the Interview
        Second and Third Interviews

Chapter Summary

Key Terms

Global competition	Realignment
Government intervention	Fee-paid positions
Technology	Cover letter
Automation	Résumé

Your Future Career in Business

"If you don't settle on a career direction, you will be still wondering what to do twenty years from now."
—Glenn L. Gardiner, *How You Can Get a Job*

This final chapter relates the basic principles and developments in business and numerous comments on careers and jobs to the reader's personal choices for a future career. Some major points are described from the viewpoint of an individual considering a specific company as a place to work, and the career implications are discussed. Then, the fundamentals of finding any kind of job are given as a guide to attaining your career goal.

BUSINESS DEVELOPMENTS AND CAREER DIRECTIONS

Companies are taking action to cope with or take advantage of the following:

1. **Global competition**. American companies have operations around the world, and investments by American firms based in foreign countries have increased significantly. In addition, trade between operations owned by foreigners and still other countries has increased. As a result, students with an interest in management must broaden the scope of their knowledge about other countries. A few will prepare for assignments abroad.

2. **Government intervention**. The latitude of privately owned companies to make operating decisions affecting profitability has been narrowed in recent years. Laws have been passed in several areas for the overall good of the public and social progress. Furthermore, there will be more government involvement in strategies to secure materials and components in short supply. In large corporations, these developments create interesting new areas of specialization, such as purchasing analysis, which provide future career opportunities.

3. *Technology.* New ways of satisfying customer needs, cutting costs, and improving managerial techniques, such as information systems, are motivated by the squeeze created by competition, government intervention, and developments in strategic variables, such as labor union demands and prices of commodities controlled by foreign governments. This creates opportunities for those with talents in the sciences, mathematics, computers, and systems analysis. Some people will have outstanding futures if care is used in selecting the most promising technical field.

4. *Inflation, finance, and monetary controls.* Concern about real profit growth has resulted in new ideas for adjusting prices with regard to rising costs. There is also concern about moving these profits across borders with minimum loss in value and maximum flexibility in their use. In addition, money management becomes critical in protecting profits from erosion and providing funds for growth. This is opening new areas of expertise in financial management, and careers will develop in this field for qualified people.

Actions being taken by companies to handle these developments are discussed in the following sections.

Changes in the Company

First, the need for information to make fast, accurate decisions has led to computerized systems that sort and refine information to meet specific needs. Many executives feel that laws, regulations, and policies of government, contracts with labor unions, and increasingly complex operating situations place tremendous importance on accuracy in decision making. There is resulting pressure to increase the percentage of correct decisions and to formulate a course of action in less time than in the past.

Second, tighter control of planning has been initiated. Each function is being asked to estimate its activities in specific future time periods as accurately as possible. Shortages are being countered with plans that balance the possibility of higher inventory costs with purchasing necessities. Pricing strategies must retain profit margins during inflation. Borrowing money requires careful consideration of timing and level of interest rates. In summary, the general manager and all company functions are finding it harder to carry out their responsibilities. Improved planning techniques are another part of the answer to this problem.

Third, the performance of individuals and departments is being monitored more carefully. The people who are not doing their jobs have to be transferred or fired. Competition and other factors are forcing management to pay more attention to: (1) selecting better qualified people; (2) "thinning" the organization to eliminate unnecessary jobs; and (3) investing in equipment to gain greater productivity from both blue- and white-collar workers. Such actions have resulted in emphasis on fewer and better people accomplishing more each day. Systems to monitor performance of individuals have become important.

Fourth, organizational design is going through adjustments. New concepts for reporting relationships are evolving. Also, specific developments are occurring in most companies. For example, responsibility for purchasing has shifted upward because this company function is no longer routine. Computers have eliminated many clerical activities and have forced consolidations of departments. Firms are struggling to find the best way of managing international operations. **Automation**—substituting machines others than the computer for people—has played a role in **realignment** of production, accounting, sales administration, and other areas where jobs are repetitive in nature.

Fifth, allocation of resources to projects involving social progress is continuing. However, investments for operating necessities stemming from energy and other shortages and for basic profit opportunities have gained in priority. Expansion and efficiency producing projects are important. As a result, performance is evaluated much more on the basis of profit contribution and cost reduction than in the early 1970s.

Career Implications

Changes occurring in many large companies are important indicators for career opportunities in the future. The primary conclusion is that any firm not responding to changes in the business environment has a high probability of becoming less competitive in future years. Within progressive firms career opportunities are developing for individuals willing to accept new techniques or to adjust to new routines.

Some type of training will be necessary to take full advantage of such situations. Some of the possibilities a student must consider are:

1. *Technical training, no college.* Examples include computer programmers, experts trained to service computers and peripheral equipment, electronic specialists to keep production equipment running, people trained to run or keep bookkeeping and inventory control machines operating, and workers for specific equipment, such as vacuum welding.

In this case, individuals offer skills that are currently in demand. If they are careful in selection of a career, their skill could be useful for most of their working lives. However, some might have to learn new skills as demand changes in future years.

This is not a route to management for the vast majority of people. There is reasonably good security and a respectable income. Responsibilities are focused on the quality of workmanship in specific assignments. Some people may eventually have the opportunity to supervise others doing similar jobs.

2. *College, no area of specialty.* Companies look for specific talents in their organizations. Some are willing to train generalists who have demonstrated intelligence and leadership capabilities in college, but competition for these jobs is intense. Graduates who do not have specialized skills may find themselves in positions such as sales or service representatives. However, a

few will be able to use their breadth of knowledge to recognize and obtain positions with a bright future.

It is acknowledged that generalists with a college degree have a chance to advance in management. Good performance is the road to success, and some individuals will pick up the basic knowledge about a job fast enough to compete with those having training in the field.

At one time companies wanted a generalist, and they molded the person into what they needed. This relieved the individual of any career decision at the college level. All the person had to do was to get the grades necessary to be accepted in the company training programs. This situation has changed in most corporations. They want to minimize training costs and get results as soon as possible.

3. *College, specialty, no graduate school.* A specialty gives a person something to offer a firm. If the individual has chosen wisely and not taken a field which is the preference of tens of others, there will be a demand for services. It is an axiom that easier courses attract the most people and that these fields will be more crowded than, for example, computer analysis where both quantitative techniques and mathematics are applied to business problems.

The dangers of specializing are: (a) advancement to jobs in general management can be blocked by either becoming too valuable in the specialty or developing an excessively narrow perspective about the business; and (b) the field of expertise can be by-passed by new technology or a shift in the company's plans. The specialist's alternatives are limited in comparison to those of a generalist when demand for the specialty declines, but this occurs infrequently. Consequently, early progress is likely to be better for the specialist.

In recent years, companies have been seeking college graduates to fit either specific openings or training programs designed for the specialty. The payoff is direct contributions to profit performance faster and more efficiently. This policy originates, in part, with the opinion of many executives that other approaches result in training ambitious young people for competitors. For example, one corporation found that 55% of the graduates of a general training program went to competing companies.

4. *College, specialty, graduate school.* A graduate degree can be used in two ways: expertise in one area can be developed to a point where the person is a highly trained specialist; or another field can be added to an undergraduate major to broaden, rather than narrow, the person's contributions to the company. In the first case, for example, an engineer could add rare capabilities in a specific field through a master's degree. In the second alternative the individual might choose business administration to improve the chances of advancing in management.

Students gamble when they elect to become highly specialized in certain fields. They accept the possibility that they might have little to offer employers if their specialties are no longer required. On the other hand, they could be extremely valuable, and their choice could lead to success and security. Also, specialists are more likely to enjoy what they are doing so that work becomes a pleasant experience.

A substantial investment is made by students and/or their parents to receive a college degree. At the end of four years, most are anxious to leave school behind. It takes determination to continue, especially if it is through one of the evening graduate degree programs. This effort lessens competition for many jobs and increases the chances of getting to the top.

Examples can be cited where entrepreneurs with no education have become millionaires and those with graduate degrees have had trouble earning a living. Experience, however, supports the conclusion implied in the four levels of education and specialization just discussed: the greater the investment in education, the better the chances of a successful, secure career.

CAREER PLANNING

The all-important job of selling your services to prospective employers is in your hands. The best record in job hunting is usually made by the person who carefully plans according to the following sequence of activities:

1. Self-analysis.
2. Selection of career direction.
3. Search for a job in the chosen field.
4. Interviews to secure the best available job.

Self-Analysis

The process of self-analysis should follow two steps. *First,* take a complete inventory of yourself. Define your strengths and weaknesses. Then ask yourself which characteristics are marketable qualities.

Second, put yourself down on paper—physical appearance, training, voice, habits, related experience, extracurricular activities, and so on. This step will enable you to see what qualities you have to sell and what you must do to add to your sales value.

To accomplish self-analysis successfully, determine your personality traits. There are several methods you can use to uncover the way others see you. One of these is the Sheldon Self-Rating Schedule shown in Table 20-1. In Sheldon's schedule, you call your desirable qualities "positives" and your undesirable ones "negatives." By checking the list, you can see your strong and weak traits (see p. 520).

Completing this schedule gives the student a self-profile as seen by the *individual.* It is critically important to have an understanding of yourself as others see you. Ask two or three people to give you the benefit of their judgment on the same basis. This will help you to anticipate and prepare to overcome weaknesses not apparent to you.

Table 20-1. *The Sheldon Self-Rating Schedule*

Positives	Negatives
Desire to serve	Self-interest
Earnestness	Indifference
Straightforwardness	Evasiveness
Ambition	Apathy
Sincerity	Insincerity
Unselfishness	Selfishness
Civility	Incivility
Refinement	Coarseness
Modesty	Vanity
Sensitivity	Callousness
Courage	Fear
Loyalty	Disloyalty
Moral uprightness	Moral crookedness
Optimism	Pessimism
Justice	Injustice
Honesty	Dishonesty
Hope	Despair
Faith	Doubt
Courtesy	Discourtesy
Contentment	Discontent
Politeness	Rudeness
Fidelity	Infidelity
Truthfulness	Lying
Temperance	Intemperance
Calmness	Rashness
Gratitude	Ingratitude
Sense of humor	Lack of humor
Reverence	Irreverence
Trustfulness	Suspicion
Generosity	Stinginess

Another approach to self-analysis is the rating schedule in Figure 20-1. In Column 1, rate yourself on the basis of 0–10, with 0 being the lowest possible entry and 10 being the highest. Then make five copies of the schedule and give them to five people who know you fairly well. Some of the people whose names you are planning to use as references would be good people to ask.

Be sure to explain to the people who are acting as judges that they should be as frank and honest as possible in all cases so that you can get as accurate an evaluation as possible. Ask them to return them to you in some manner so that you will not know who gave which ratings in case there are any uncomplimentary comments.

After you have received the schedules, enter the ratings in Columns 2 through 6 inclusive, average them, and put the averages in Column 7. You now can compare an analysis of yourself with how others see you to get a clearer picture of yourself.

Figure 20-1. *Personality Rating Schedule*

	1	2	3	4	5	6	7
Appearance							
Health							
Observation							
Concentration							
Memory							
Imagination							
Reasoning							
General knowledge							
Business knowledge							
Expression							
Ambition							
Confidence							
Loyalty							
Enthusiasm							
Cheerfulness							
Reliability							
Energy							
Persistence							
Initiative							
Self-control							
Efficiency							
Courtesy							
Sophistication							
Honesty							

Another important aspect of your self-analysis is educational background. Here, your aim should be to cover how far you have gone in school, major area of study, grade point average, subjects of most and least interests, honors received, and if and/or how much further you plan to continue your education. Grades are important because they are indicative of both potential and the will to use your abilities.

The next aspect of self-analysis covers work experience. In this area, you should list past employers and positions held, emphasizing accomplishments, responsibilities, and skills, Accordingly, ask yourself some of the following questions:

1. If you had an absolutely free choice, would you have chosen the job?
2. What features of that job did you like or dislike and why?
3. What qualities exhibited by you received praise and/or criticism?

The final aspect of the self-analysis should include personal accomplishments. In this area, include activities, interests, hobbies, recreations, and any honors or offices held.

Career Directions

The counsel of others will help you decide which type of job is best for you—industry, government, services, and so on. Tests are available to identify talents and weaknesses. Determine the degree of your ambitions. It is best to look ahead five years, determine where you want to be at the end of that time, and make every planning step needed to bring you closer to that realization. The end product of self-analysis and counseling is the selection of the most desirable career direction for you.

Your faculty can be of invaluable assistance as a start. They will raise questions about location, plans for a family, size of organization, and other considerations that narrow the number of possibilities.

Vocational counseling is an important part of the campus placement office's duties. The personnel are there to answer questions, offer suggestions, and give meaningful advice. Make proper use of this facility. You will find that placement directors are as interested in your success as you are because that is their job. The placement office's reputation depends on its ability to help you become a productive member of society.

Another alternative is personnel department employees of firms and agencies. Many are willing to offer insights on characteristics of the business, the techniques useful in impressing interviewers, and requirements for career success. You have nothing to lose by setting up two or three appointments to gain valuable perspective when you are still selecting the direction of your career.

Researching the Job

It is necessary to do some research on prospective employers, companies, government departments, and other pertinent sources. The following list gives many publications that can assist you in researching a company.

1. *College Placement Directory*, by Zimmerman and Lavine.
2. *College Placement Annual*, by the College Placement Publications Council.
3. Booklets and other materials at your campus placement office. (You may find detailed information printed by companies that is unavailable in general registers.)
4. *Thomas' Register of American Manufacturers.*
5. *Moody's Manuals.*
6. *Fitch Corporation Manuals.*
7. *MacRae's Bluebook.*
8. *Standard and Poor's Corporation Records.*
9. *Poor's Register of Directors and Executives.*
10. Dun and Bradstreet reference book.
11. Company annual reports.
12. The telephone book and yellow pages.
13. Department of Commerce publications.
14. Brokerage firm reports.
15. Chamber of Commerce directories.

Reference librarians can be very helpful. Hours of work can be saved by making use of their expertise. They need a clear statement of your career objectives to give you the most valuable assistance, but they can also help you get started. Names, titles, addresses, statistics, and so on are available. Write them down and put the information in your *career file* (see Chapter One).

This list will enable you to identify prospective employers and to prepare pertinent questions to ask during an interview. It also will give you data on the company's size, growth rate, locations, training programs, and positions available. From this you can see which organizations offer opportunities that coincide with your aspirations. Priorities can then be assigned to the ones that seem most attractive to you.

Searching for a Job

The first and most logical source is your *campus placement office*. Because of its constant contact with employer representatives, the placement office may be able to save you valuable time. It may know whether a vacancy such as the one you are seeking exists. On-campus interviewing is another aid it offers. Also, it may be able to give you other referrals or recommendations to put you in contact with potential employers.

Another source of employment is an *employment agency* in your locality. Check the agency and its reputation. When applying, be as specific as possible about the type of position you seek in order to avoid wasting time—yours and that of others. Determine the amount of the fee and who pays it. If you want the employer to pay the fee, be sure to let the agency know you are only interested in **fee-paid positions**.

Remember, you have just as much of a selling job with an agency as you have with a prospective employer to avoid being "just another applicant." After you have applied, recognize that it may be days, weeks, or even months before you are placed in the type of position you desire. Call the agency frequently to remind them you are still seeking employment. Also, if you should obtain a position through another source, you should notify the agency as soon as possible for two reasons. First, its search for you can stop. Secondly, it keeps good relations between you and the agency in the event you have to use its services again.

It is also worth your while to watch the *classified ads* in different publications. The local newspaper, papers with regional readership, such as the *New York Times*, and trade journals published for specific functions of business are examples. By choosing the publication that relates to your vocational interests, you may be able to discover openings not available through other means. The quality of the position offered, however, may be a direct function of the quality of the publication used.

Too many job seekers are hesitant to let *friends and acquaintances* know that they are looking for work. Those who could be of assistance to you are: friends, former teachers, relatives, neighbors, creditors, priest, minister, rabbi, fellow club members, merchants, and your banker. Approach these people, tell them your situation, and suggest that they keep you in mind if they hear of any job for which you may qualify.

After you have started the above sources in action, strike out on your own by using a mail campaign. "The more traps you set, the more likely you are to catch the fox." [1] A mail campaign consists of:

1. A mailing list of companies and other organizations employing people in your area of interest. Research to identify the names and titles of people in charge of the employment process is important because there is more certainty that your inquiry will be given consideration.

2. A **cover letter**. Normally, it is short and easy to read. You might consider investing in business-like stationery and automatic typing which makes each appear to be a personal letter by using the same machine to type the address and salutation as well as the body of the letter.

---

[1] Glenn L. Gardiner, *How You Can Get a Job*, New York: Harper & Brother, Inc., 1934, p. 12.

3. A copy of your résumé. Attention should be given to the printing quality and clarity in the method used for reproducing your background summary. The next section gives details on content.

Expectations for responses vary from 3 to 20% of the mailing. A general guide would be 10 interviews from 100 personally addressed letters and 2 to 3 job offers. The presentation of each item in the mailing will have a major impact on results.

Résumés

A **résumé** is a concise statement of your employment experience, educational training, personal details, interests, and vocational goals.

A recent graduate will probably have very little work experience. Your problem will be to impress the prospective employer with your potential, rather than with your experience. To accomplish this, it is best to make the most of scholastic and extracurricular activities and achievements. The personal inventory-taking process you have completed has the list of full- and part-time jobs, subjects of major interest and achievement, scholastic or athletic honors, and a list of extracurricular activities.

The content and format of résumés vary widely. Some basic points to keep in mind are:

1. A résumé should always be typed.
2. It should be neat, accurate, and concise.
3. It is generally best to make the résumé a maximum of two pages in length.
4. It should present a clean, pleasing impression. Sufficient spacing will help create an appearance of orderliness.

Figures 20-2 and 20-3, found on pp. 526 and 527, are samples of generally accepted résumés.

Cover Letters for Applications

When you answer a job advertisement, you are trying to sell yourself to whomever reads the replies. Your letter will have a great deal of stiff competition from others applying for the same position. Remember, this is your initial contact with the company.

The objective of the reply is to obtain an interview with the employer. Do *not* make the mistake of trying to make the letter get you the job. Your letter will be too long and probably will never be read.

Give only that information asked for in the advertisement. Your letter should be clear, concise, correct, and courteous, and it should have character. Your reply should contain definite statements—facts, not generalities—about what you have done, can do, and want to do. It should instill a sense of what you can do for the employer.

Figure 20-2. *Sample Résumé*

DOUGLAS G. WELLS

1971 Dermott Avenue
Wilmington, Delaware 19809   Telephone: (123) 456-7890

PERSONAL DATA

Age: 24   Birth Place: Houston, Texas
Height: 6' 2"   Weight: 198
Marital Status: Married, 1969   Children: 1, 7 months old
Health: Excellent

VOCATIONAL OBJECTIVES

To seek initial assignment in the commercial lending or trust department of a major banking institution with the ultimate goal of moving into an officer position.

EDUCATION

9/72 to 5/76	University of Delaware Newark, Delaware	BS in Business Admin. Concentration in Finance. Minor in Economics. Dean's List Junior and Senior Year. Class Rank: Upper Quarter.
Graduated 6/69	Long Horn High School Houston, Texas	Curriculum: Academic. Varsity Football, Baseball, and Wrestling Teams. Student Council, and President of Senior Class. Class Rank: Upper Quarter.

WORK EXPERIENCE

1/73 to Present	Bank of Delaware Wilmington, Delaware	Teller and Computer Operator.
4/66 to 6/69	Foot-Long Drive-in, Houston, Texas	Counter Worker and Cook.

MILITARY

6/69 to 5/72	United States Army	Airborne Ranger Team. Honorably Discharged at the Rank of Sgt. E-5. Specialization: Communications.

INTERESTS

Chess, tennis, golf, bridge, touch football, slow-pitch softball, running, boating, and reading.

Figure 20-3. *Sample Résumé*

BARBARA D. SWARTZ
#7 Payton Place
Boston, Massachusetts   Telephone: (098) 765-4321

Personal	Single	5'9"	150 pounds	25 years old

Professional
Objective   To begin a career in the retailing field. Prefer to obtain some exposure to both the buying and store management areas before advancing into managerial position and responsibilities.

Education   B.S., 1976, University of Massachusetts
Major: Business Administration, Concentration: Accounting.
Minor: Psychology.

Experience
1972 to 1976   Macy's, Amherst, Massachusetts
<u>Assistant Department Manager</u>. In charge of stocking and setting up displays in the women's clothing department. Other responsibilities were to follow-up purchasing orders of clothing for my department.

1969 to 1972   Harvey's Hardware Store
Boston, Massachusetts
<u>Bookkeeper</u>. Responsibility for keeping the book and all records for the store.

Military
1969 to Present   United States Army Reserve, Boston, Massachusetts.
<u>Personnel Clerk</u>: Specialist Fourth Class.

Background   Born in New York, but have been brought up in the Massachusetts area. Active in the Jewish League for Equality, presently Assistant Vice-President. Engaged and planning to marry after graduation. Have earned all my expenses since entering college. Willing to relocate.

Interests   Primarily interested in Butterfly Society of America and Bird Watchers. Also chess, bridge, and reading.

References   References will be furnished upon request.

January 1976

The first two paragraphs are the most important. The reader may be so harried that he won't have time to read the complete letter before turning to your resume. Figure 20-4 gives the form for a covering letter.[2]

---

[2] *Placement Manual. Indiana University 1972–1973*, Rahway, New Jersey: Placement Publications, Inc., 1972, p. 14.

Figure 20-4. *Cover Letter Form*

Your Address
City and State
Date of Writing

(inside address)

Dear Mr. _____:

<u>1st Paragraph</u>: Tell why you are writing, name and position for which you are applying, and if possible, how you heard of an opening.

<u>2nd Paragraph</u>: Statement of why you are interested in working for this company. Point out any work experience and achievements that relate to the position you are applying for.

<u>3rd Paragraph</u>: Refer to the attached résumé to show your qualifications for the position.

<u>4th Paragraph</u>: Use an appropriate closing statement to open the door for an interview by enclosing a return envelope, by asking for an application, by giving your telephone number, or by offering some similar suggestion for an immediate and favorable reply.

Very truly yours,

A general cover letter differs from a reply to a want ad only in the respect that you are taking the initiative. In this case, you do not know exactly what the employer's needs are. It is best for you to be as specific as possible in emphasizing the areas which are your strongest. You will be more likely to get the desired results from a quiet, dignified, business-like letter using a conversational tone, rather than trying to be clever (see Figure 20-5).

Interviews

Preparation

Obtaining the job may be solely dependent on how you handle the interview. This 30-minute conversation is the moment of truth. Your success may depend on your ability to adapt to the situation. A few suggestions are given here that are helpful in handling the interview.

1. Find out when and where the interview is to be held. Write this down; do not rely on your memory. Plan to arrive at the designated place at least 15 minutes early.

Figure 20-5. *Sample Cover Letter*

                                  Applicant's Address
                                  City and State
                                  Date of Writing

(Inside Address)

Dear Mr. Neal:

    I am attaching my résumé for you to consider my qualifications for employment with your firm.

    My experience is in sales and supervisory duties. However, I feel that any position in sales management which demands an alert, intelligent person who is willing to explore new avenues of growth is worth attention. The XYZ Company has long been known for its progressive and dynamic sales force, and I would be proud to join it.

    If, after reviewing my background, you wish to discuss the opportunity of employment with your firm, please write or call me at (123) 456-7890, to arrange an interview.

                                  Very truly yours,

---

    2. Do research on the company you are interviewing. Being knowledgeable about the employer's basic business impresses the interviewer and leaves you free to explore other possibilities during the time available. Find out the answers to such questions as:

    a. How big is the company?
    b. How old is it?
    c. What is its growth rate?
    d. What kind of reputation does it have?
    e. What are its products, and how diversified are they?
    f. Where are the company's plants and offices located?
    g. What are your chances of advancement within this firm?

    3. Know why you would like to work for this firm and how you could best benefit the organization by your employment there.

    4. Be prepared to ask at least two good questions concerning the company, its products, its policies, and so on.

    5. Establish all those points about yourself that you want presented during the interview. This requires a mental checklist.

    6. Dress in conservative good taste. Your physical appearance not only projects your personal attitude but is the single most important factor in creating a favorable first impression.

    7. Be sure to bring note paper and a pen or pencil to the interview. You may be asked to take something down.

8. Be confident. The final and most important step in preparing for the interview is your attitude. The more you believe in yourself, the more the interviewer will believe in you.

In the Interview

The following twenty DO'S & DON'TS can be used as a guide as to how to conduct yourself during an interview:

1. DO use a firm handshake if the interviewer offers his hand as a greeting. A "limp fish" handshake will create an impression of weak character.
2. DO act natural and present the attitude of assurance and interest throughout the interview.
3. DO ask relevant questions.
4. DO be a good listener, and use the interviewer's name throughout the interview.
5. DON'T talk and ramble. Stick to the point.
6. DO be courteous and cooperative. *Never* interrupt the interviewer.
7. DO maintain good posture and look alert.
8. DO let the interviewer take the initiative and set the pace, but DON'T be passive.
9. DO look the interviewer directly in the eye, and keep doing it throughout the encounter from time to time.
10. DO retain your poise, relax, and smile at appropriate occasions.
11. DO make sure your answers are consistent throughout the interview. Avoid self-contradictory statements.
12. DON'T ever plead for a job.
13. DO be frank and sincere, neither exaggerating nor discounting your qualifications.
14. DO speak distinctly in a normal conversational tone, neither too softly nor too boisterously.
15. DON'T ever criticize previous professors or employers.
16. DON'T discuss your weaknesses. Rather, emphasize your strengths.
17. DON'T smoke or chew gum during the interview.
18. DON'T drag out the interview.
19. DO be ready for surprise questions. You will be evaluated on how quickly and intelligently you respond.
20. DON'T ask about money or security unless the interviewer initiates it. Even then, try not to commit yourself on any salary or security issue.

Second and Third Interviews

If you are fortunate enough to receive an invitation for a second interview, you are being seriously considered for a job. It will probably be conducted at the company's facilities. The purpose of this visit is to give the company more time to evaluate you and to let you further assess the firm and its location. This is an invitation, and it should be acknowledged with a minimum of delay on your part.

Travel and hotel accommodations information will be provided in most instances. If you have any question regarding these or other expenses, clarify them in your reply letter. Most companies will require you to furnish them with an itemized list of the expenses which you incur as a result of your visit. You should use discretion in reporting your expenses.

The interviews at headquarters will be conducted in much the same manner as the initial interview. You will have the opportunity to meet a number of the company's executives, and these people are likely to decide your opportunities in their firm. Be careful that you do not "let down." Present your case completely, convincingly, and favorably. Do not contradict the attitude or actions you presented in the first interview. However, do adjust to the position and personalities involved in the second interview.

You should prepare for the visit in the same manner as you did for the initial interview. The only difference is that you will have a much longer interview period and will be able to ask much more specific questions concerning conditions of employment, salary, fringe benefits, job responsibilities, advancement, and the like.

If, after the follow-up interviews, you are interested in the opportunities with the company, you should let them know. A simple thank-you letter or follow-up letter is appropriate. You can use a letter format similar to the one which you sent after the initial interview.

CHAPTER SUMMARY

Business developments including global competition, increasing government intervention, new technology, and inflation are having direct effects on career opportunities. This results from changes occurring within many companies to handle these developments. The five cited are computerized information systems, tighter planning controls, more careful evaluation of performance by departments and individuals, organizational adjustments, and a temporary shift allocation of resources to projects earning attractive profits as compared to those increasing social progress.

The training necessary to take full advantage of the situation can be classified into four categories: (1) technical training, no college; (2) college; no area of specialty; (3) college, specialty, no graduate school; and (4) college, specialty, graduate school. Experience supports the conclusion that a greater investment in education increases the chances of a successful, secure career.

Career planning necessitates careful self-analysis involving a personal inventory of assets and drawbacks written down and checked with impartial observers. The successful choice of a career will depend on the amount of time and effort allocated to self-analysis and to investigations, counseling, and gathering of some experience in interesting fields.

Searching for a job can be carried out through the campus placement office, employment agencies, classified ads, friends and acquaintances, and a mailing campaign. Considerable work should go into preparation and presentation of résumés and covering letters.

Success in interviews will reflect preparation, adherence to the 20 "DO'S and DON'TS" for the interview itself, and consistency of performance in follow-up interviews.

REVIEW QUESTIONS

1. What is the value of self-analysis?
2. How do you relate the career file suggested in Chapter One and researching for a job?
3. Develop a résumé for yourself.

BIBLIOGRAPHY

Books

Beach, Dale S. *Personnel: The Management of People at Work.* New York: Macmillan Company, 1970.

Fancher, Albert. *Getting a Job and Getting Ahead.* New York: McGraw-Hill Book Company, 1934.

Fletcher, William L. *How to Get the Job You Want.* Norwood, Massachusetts: The Plimpton Press, 1925.

Gardiner, Glenn L. *How You Can Get a Job.* New York: Harper and Brothers, 1934.

Janis, J. Harold. *Writing and Communicating in Business.* New York: Macmillan Company, 1971.

Kitson, Harry Dexter. *Finding a Job During the Depression.* New York: Robert C. Cook Company, 1933.

Reader's Digest. Write Better, Speak Better. Pleasantville, New York: The Reader's Digest Association, Inc., 1972.

Booklets and Pamphlets

College Placement Annual 1973. Bethlehem, Pennsylvania: College Placement Council, Inc., 1972.

Job-Hunting (and Job Switching) Takes Planning. Midland, Michigan: Dow Chemical U.S.A., 1972.

Making the Most of Your Job Interview. New York: New York Life Insurance Company, n.d.

Placement Manual, Indiana University 1972–1973. Rahway, New Jersey: Placement Publications, Inc., 1972.

Glossary

Acceptance Sampling A procedure that controls quality of purchased items by examining a sample and deciding to accept or reject the shipment based on inspection of the sample.

Accessory Equipment Capital items such as typewriters, hand tools, small lathes, and adding machines. They are usually less expensive and shorter lived than installations.

Accounting Recording, classifying, summarizing, and interpreting of financial data.

Acquisitions and Mergers Department A department responsible for developing, evaluating, and coordinating actions necessary to complete acquisitions and mergers as a means of achieving company growth.

Advertising Agency A firm that produces and places advertisements in media and may arrange total programs of advertising for other businesses.

Advertising Media The different types of vehicles or devices by which advertising reaches its audience.

Agent Middleman A middleman who does not take title to the goods sold but earns a commission.

Airlines A mode of transportation that is fast but expensive.

Allied Lines By the addition to a fire insurance policy of a special agreement, the insuring company will cover such losses as wind or water damage.

Annuitant A person receiving an annuity or a fixed sum of money at regular intervals of time.

Antitrust Laws The Sherman Act, Clayton Act, and other laws designed to maintain competition.

Applied Research Research that has immediate practical application.

Apprentice System An employee works under the direct supervision of an experienced and skilled worker in order to learn the trade.

Arbitrator A neutral third party empowered to settle a dispute or grievance between labor and management.

Arithmetic-logic Element Performs the operations of addition, subtraction, multiplication, and division, as well as comparison operations.

Articles of Incorporation A document detailing the nature of a corporation's activities which, when filed in some state in which an aspect of the business will be conducted, becomes the corporation's charter.

Articles of Partnership A document detailing the nature of a partnership's ownership and business activities, which, when filed in some state, governs how the business will be conducted.

Audience Those who are reached through the communications media.

Audit The periodic checking of accounts and financial records to verify their correctness.

Auditing A formal, often periodic examination and checking of accounts or financial records to verify their correctness.

Automation The automatic control of mechanical equipment operations or processes by electronic devices, especially the computer.

Average A measure of central tendency; can be a mean, median, or mode.

Axiom A statement universally accepted as true.

Backward Integration Large corporations acquire companies to secure needed supplies such as raw materials or semiprocessed goods.

Bait and Switch Advertising A practice whereby a retailer advertises low prices on one product but tries to get the customer to buy higher priced products once the customer gets to the store.

Balance Sheet A dollar-and-cents picture of firm's assets, liabilities, and equities at one point in time.

Bargaining To negotiate the details of a transaction in an attempt to obtain the best possible terms.

Bargaining Unit All employees for whom the union negotiates, while required to pay dues to the union, they do not have to join it.

Base Pay Pay for normal working hours or standard performance.

Basic Research The study of underlying phenomena and relationships in order to gain a better understanding of fundamental principles, often without considering practical application.

Benefits of Information Management can plan operations better and control their plans if they have accurate, timely, and relevant information.

Bidding Offering a certain price or fee that one will pay or accept. This practice is often used when selling to the government.

Bill of Materials A detailed list of all the materials and components needed for the manufacture of a particular product.

Blue Collar Worker Worker who performs manual labor.

Bookkeeping The work of keeping a systematic record of business transactions.

Bottleneck A problem area through which work must be funneled causing a slowdown in progress.

Break-even Analysis An examination of the relationships between fixed costs, variable costs, volume, and price.

Broker An agent middleman who works for a buyer or seller and provides market information.

Budgeting A financial forecast showing expected income and expenditures for a given period of time.

Business Representative A person authorized to speak for a union in dealings with a company or firm.

Business Trust A form of business in which trustees manage business (usually real estate) for the benefit of beneficiaries or owners of the trust.

Buying Guides Publications listing different products, and their prices, and comparative quality as an aid in consumer purchasing.

Capital The properties or assets used in the conduct of business; financial resources of the firm.

Capital Budgeting The allocation of funds to fixed assets which will provide income flows for longer than one year.

Capital Contribution Resources contributed to a business by an owner or creditor.

Capital Gain Profit resulting from the sale of capital investments, such as stocks, real estate, and so forth.

Capital, Idle Capital that is not employed and, therefore, not earning any form of return such as interest or profits.

Capitalism An economic system based on private ownership and control of property and the sources of production and distribution.

Cash and Carry Wholesaler A limited service merchant middleman who accepts only cash purchases and does not provide delivery services.

Cash Flow The net income of a firm plus all expense charges that do not require an outlay of funds minus any income that does not generate cash.

Centralized Purchasing Large purchases, resulting from a single part of the company doing the buying for all parts of the company, for the purpose of lower prices and better supplier control.

Central Tendency A measure such as the mean, median, or mode which expresses the average of a group of numbers.

Certificate of Deposit A short-term debt obligation of a bank; a widely used investment in firm's marketable securities portfolio.

Chain Store One member of a group of stores, all centrally controlled and distributing similar lines of goods.

Channel of Distribution The network of business units through which title and goods are moved from their point of origin to their ultimate consumer.

Charter A document that must be filed by each corporation with the authorities that approves the creation of the corporation, specifies the areas of activity in which the corporation may engage, and spells out all of the constraints within which the corporation must operate.

C.I.F. Payment by the buyer in a lump sum covering the cost of the goods, insurance on them, and freight charges to their destination.

Class Action Suit A lawsuit by a single consumer that may result in recovery by a number of similarly injured parties.

Clayton Act A law which forbids persons engaged in interstate commerce to use price discrimination, tying contracts, exclusive dealing arrangements, or interlocking directorates if competition is lessened by these practices.

Closed loop Automation A computer system designed to monitor a production process and make automatic adjustments in the equipment to correct for errors.

Closed Shop A business or factory operated under a contractual arrangement between a labor union and an employer which denies employment to non-union applicants.

Coaching Instruction or training to develop a certain skill.

Coerce To restrain or constrain by force or by legal authority.

Coinsurance Clause Requirement that the insured buy coverage up to a stipulated percentage of the value of the property or assume a proportion of the loss.

Collateral Loan A debt secured by property deposited in addition to one's personal or contractual obligations; in case of default on the debt, such property is subject to forfeiture.

Collective Bargaining Representation of employees by union officers who bargain with management representatives over the terms and conditions of the labor contract.

Commercial Paper A short-term unsecured debt of a corporation. A common form of investment in a firm's marketable securities portfolio.

Commission Person A middleman who usually exercises physical control over and negotiates the sale of the goods he handles. He generally arranges delivery, extends necessary credit, collects, deducts its fees, and remits the balance to the principal.

Common Carriers A transportation unit that serves the general public and is required by law to provide uniform services to all at established rates.

Common Stock A certificate showing ownership in a corporation which entitles its owner to vote and to share in the assets of the corporation after all debts have been paid.

Communism An economic system characterized by government ownership and control of all sources of production.

Company Politics Relationship between individuals and/or portions of a company's organization which involve the goals and objectives of these individuals and/or portions of the organization rather than those of the company.

Competitive System The owners in each line of business compete with each other in the sale of their products or services; an alternate name for capitalism.

Compiler A completely mechanical translation process performed by the computer itself.

Component One of the parts of a whole; a constituent.

Computer Program The complete listing of the logical steps which the computer must take to obtain the desired results.

Computer Programmer One who writes the program that is to be fed into the computer.

Computer An electronic device which, by means of stored instruction and information, performs rapid, often complex calculations.

Computer Service Bureau A firm that sells the use of its computer to other firms.

Conflict of Interest A conflict between one's obligation to a company or the public good and one's own self-interest.

Consensus An opinion held by all or most.

Consolidation The organizing and strengthening of a smaller or nonprofitable firm into a larger or more profit-oriented one.

Consumer One who purchases goods and services for the satisfaction of his or her own needs and wants.

Consumer Cooperative A user-owned retail outlet of goods and services which is widespread in Denmark and Sweden but of little influence in the United States.

Consumer Credit Protection Act Requires businesses that lend money or sell goods on credit to tell customers what they will pay for the loan.

Consumerism A demand that marketers give greater attention to consumer wants and desires in making their decisions.

Consumerism Movement A movement to increase protection of consumers in the market place.

Consumer Price Index A figure that measures the dollar value of a selected group of goods and services against the same group in a specified base period; a measure of inflation.

Contingency An event whose occurrence depends on chance or uncertain conditions.

Contingency Funds Money set aside for use in the event an unforeseen event, such as a lawsuit or disaster, occurs against a firm.

Contingency Plans Actions that are taken in the event of accidental or unforeseen circumstances.

Continuous Production The application of labor and equipment to materials and components being processed or assembled without interruption.

Contract Carrier A transportation unit that provides service to one or several shippers under a contract arrangement.

Contract Period An agreement between two or more parties under law for a specific period of time.

Control Element A control unit that has the function of interpreting the program or instruction stored in the memory of a computer.

Controlled Feedback Preselected information received from specified sources at controlled intervals.

Controller A person in charge of the accounting function in a business, institution, or government.

Convenience Goods Goods that consumers like to be able to purchase conveniently, immediately, and with a minimum of effort.

Cooperative A collective business enterprise operated for the benefit of its members.

Corporation A legal entity separate and distinct from its owners, the stockholders, each of whom shares in ownership in proportion to individual shares of stock each of whom is liable for business losses only to the extent of the investment.

Corrective Advertising A regulation by the Federal Trade Commission or other governmental units requiring a firm to inform the public about previous advertisements which were deceptive.

Correlation The degree of relative correspondence between two sets of data.

Cost of Business Social Responsibility The cost incurred by a business for the welfare of the community.

Cost of Capital Minimum rate of return that must be earned on investment to justify raising funds to finance that investment.

Cost of Information The cost incurred to gather information; any cost incurred until information is gathered.

Cost of Living The price of goods and services in relation to wages, or the cost of commodities in terms of the work time required to earn purchases.

Cost–push Inflation High prices caused by an increase in the cost of resources.

Counterstrategy Plans made in opposition to or in retaliation to competitor actions, decisions by government or others outside the organization.

Countervailing Power A large power group which balances another, preventing extreme economic abuse by either.

CRAFT A computer program that provides five catagories of data for a solution:
1. Material component and product flow path
2. Material handling systems by designer priority
3. Floor area requirement of work station
4. Allowance for fixed work stations
5. Cost of material handling and total cost results.

Creditor A person who extends credit, or to whom money is owed.

Cumulative A feature of a stock which means that a dividend not paid becomes a future obligation.

Current Assets Assets that are converted into cash in the normal course of a firm's operating cycle, usually one year or less.

Current Liabilities Debts payable in the course of a firm's operating cycle, usually one year or less.

Custom Duties Taxes levied on the importation of foreign goods.

Data Processing The accumulation and storage of records followed by sorting, interpreting, and reporting of same at regular intervals.

Decentralized Purchasing Buying in smaller quantities by departments or other components of the company in order to have available the items required.

Deception Misrepresentation or fraud.

Decision, Go/No-Go The decision about whether a company should or should not go ahead with something such as an investment, organizational change, acquisition, and so forth.

Decision Making by Consensus A judgment or conclusion reached by the majority of a group.

Demand–pull Inflation High prices generated by an excess demand on society's productive capacity.

Demotion A lowering in rank or responsibility.

Department of Social Affairs A separate organization that handles social responsibilities and helps management make decisions.

Depreciation A reduction in asset value on the balance sheet and an expense on the income statement to indicate a decline in value of a fixed asset over time.

Deteriorate To decline in value over a period of time.

Devaluation A reduction in value of a country's monetary unit relative to gold or some other currency standard.

Direct Channel A method by which goods are sold from producer to consumer without the use of middlemen.

Direct Costs Those costs that can be specifically allocated to the production of a commodity, such as material and labor.

Direct Investment The direct placement of money in a firm through the purchase of stock or the investment of capital by a party in his own business.
Disability Insurance A policy designed to cover lost salary payments to employees unable to perform their jobs because of injury or illness.
Dispersion The variation or scattering of data around a central value.
Distribution The frequency or number of times each response is received.
Distributor One who distributes or sells merchandise.
Diversification The involvement of a firm in a variety of products or activities at the same time.
Divestiture To disencumber or be rid of something unwanted.
Dividend A payment made to stockholders by a corporation from its profits.
Documentary Stamp Taxes Taxes on documents or licenses.
Dormant Partner A partner who is inactive in management and keeps the status as a partner unknown.
Double-Counting In constructing the GNP, the act of adding a product's value more than once as it passes through the production process.
Double Standard A system, code, or criterion applied unequally.
Downside Out Analysis An analysis anticipating the worst developments which could occur and the consequences for the company under these adverse circumstances.
Downtime Time during which a computer or other type of machinery is unavailable for use.
Drop Shipper A middleman who takes ownership of the merchandise, but arranges direct shipment from the seller to the buyer.

Employee A person hired to work for a firm or organization.
Endowment Policy A form of insurance that emphasizes the savings element in a contract over the protective features. Face value of the policy is payable at insured's death or policy maturity, whichever comes first.
Entity An organization such as a company but also including labor unions, governments, departments, and so forth.
Entrepreneur A person who organizes and manages a business and assumes the risk of profit or loss.
Equal Opportunity Employer One who hires a job applicant without regard to race, sex, religion, or national origin.
Excise Tax A duty levied within a country on the manufacture, sale, or consumption of goods.
Exclusive Coverage The manufacturer grants exclusive rights to a wholesaler or retailer to sell in a geographic region.
Expediter One employed by an industry to dispatch urgent or involved projects.
External Policies Those policies concerning company actions involving outside parties such as the government, labor unions, and competitors.
Extrovert A very outgoing, gregarious person.

Fabricated Parts and Materials Industrial goods that become a part of the finished product and that have undergone processing beyond that required for raw materials.
Facilitating Agencies Those agencies that perform or assist in performing one

or a number of the marketing functions, but which neither take title to goods nor negotiate purchases or sales.

Factoring Outright sale of a company's receivables to raise cash.

Fair Labor Standards Act A law passed in 1938 that defines the normal work week and requires time-and-a-half pay for all hours worked by an employee over 40 during a given week.

Fair Packaging and Labeling Act A law that requires manufacturers to label a product and list its contents in order to protect the consumer.

Federal Cigarette Labeling and Advertising Act A law passed to regulate the sale, tax, and advertising of cigarettes.

Federal Reserve Banking System The central banking system of the United States of which the primary function is to control the money supply.

Federal Trade Commission An organization created in 1914 to regulate unfair methods of competition used in interstate commerce.

Federal Trade Commission Act A statute establishing an agency to enforce the prohibition of unfair methods of competition in interstate commerce.

Feedback A form of communication in which actual developments are relayed to decision makers for modification and correction of plans.

Fee-paid Position A position being filled from those candidates introduced to the company by an employment agency, the fees for this service being paid by the company rather than the person selected.

Feminist Movement The movement to equalize women's political, economic, and social rights.

Final Goods Finished goods that are placed in stock to await shipment to customers.

Fixed Assets Tangible assets of a permanent or long-term nature, usually financed on a long-range basis.

Fixed Cost Those costs incurred by a business firm which do not change in amount regardless of the level of output of the firm.

Flow Chart A graphic representation of the logical steps to be used in solving a problem.

Flow Process Charts Charts that are used to control the flow of goods and materials in the production process.

F.O.B. (Free on Board) A shipping agreement in which the seller customarily agrees to load the goods onto a transportation vehicle without charge.

F.O.B. Origin A shipping agreement in which the seller places goods on ship at the dock and all further transportation charges over and above the quoted price are to be paid by the buyer.

Foreman A person in charge of a department or group of workers in a factory.

Franchise A store outlet owned by a larger retail organization and operated on a contract basis by local independent retailers.

Franchise Organization A large retail organization whose stores or outlets are operated on a contract basis by a local independent retailer.

Full-line Product Concept A line of products designed to satisfy a very broad segment of the market.

Functional Layout An organizational pattern in which the firm is divided into functions, such as marketing and production.

Funds Cash resources of a firm.

General Accounting Area within the firm responsible for bookkeeping and other basic accounting functions.

General Partner One who associates with at least one other person as a co-owner of a business in the pursuit of profits; has unlimited liability for partnership debts.

General Public The overall population of a given area, characterized by certain wants and needs.

Global Competition The competing of firms on a worldwide basis.

Goods Products that satisfy needs.

Government The institution responsible for ensuring the well-being of the society it represents by providing those services that individuals cannot provide for themselves.

Government Intervention Interference by the government in the affairs of its constituents.

"Gozinto" Charts Charts that detail the materials and components needed for the production process including characteristics of the products, processes required, timing, and order of the operation.

Grievance A formal complaint about one's job that is brought to the attention of management.

Grievance Procedure The sequence of steps through which a grievance passes from lower to higher echelons of management and union officials.

Gross National Product The total value of a nation's annual output of goods and services.

Hazard A condition that makes the occurrence of a peril more likely.

Holding Company An organization formed for the sole purpose of controlling other companies through the purchase of their voting stock.

Household Consumers The ultimate consumers for whom businesses produce their goods and services.

Implement To carry out.

Income The money or other gain received in a given period by an individual or corporation; equals revenues less expenses.

Income Statement A financial statement showing revenues, expenses, and profits of a firm during a given period of time.

Income Taxes A tax that is levied against wages, salaries, commissions, dividends, interest, rents, and other similar sources of income of individuals and against net profits of corporations.

Incontestability A provision that specifies a period of time after which an insurer may not dispute a claim on the grounds of misrepresentation, fraud, or similar wrongful conduct on the part of the insured.

Independent Retailer An independently owned, single store which may offer any type of goods or services.

Industrial Traffic Manager The individual responsible for the flow of materials and products in and out of a company facility.

Industrial User A business institution that purchases goods for its operations or resale to consumers.

Inequality in Income Distribution An unequal dispersion of income across a country's population.
Inflation A rise in the general level of prices for goods and services.
Information Any data that helps decision makers make better decisions.
Innovative New, original, or unprecendented.
Input Data fed into an information system.
Inside Director One who plays an active role in the management of a corporation, usually an officer of the corporation.
Installation The firm's major capital assets such as factories and heavy machinery. They are relatively long-lived and are expensive.
In-store Retailing The selling of final goods and services in a "store" environment.
Intensive Coverage The sale of a product through any responsible and suitable wholesaler or retailer who will stock the product.
Interlocking Directorate A management situation wherein one or more persons serves on the board of directors of two or more companies that produce the same goods and services.
Intermediate Goods Goods that have been subjected to certain manufacturing processes and are held in storage until they are needed for assembly into finished products.
Intermittent Production The application of labor and equipment to the materials being processed on a periodic basis.
Internal Auditing On-going inspection of the financial control system of the firm by the company's own accountants.
Internal Policies Policies guiding the actions of company personnel on matters within the company.
International Business Trade and other business operations between entities of different nations.
Interview A face-to-face contact between a company representative and an applicant.
Introvert One who is chiefly concerned with his own thoughts.
Inventory The volume of goods on hand.

Job Description A formal statement describing the nature of a job.
Job Rotation The changing of duties in regular and recurring succession.
Joint Stock Company Ownership represented by transferable shares in which owners have unlimited liability.
Joint Venture A form of business ownership, essentially a limited partnership used for a specific business venture of limited duration. Also called a syndicate.

Lanham Act (1946) A law that established the procedures for registering brand names and trademarks of goods involved in interstate or foreign commerce.
Layoff Temporary separation of the employee from the job due to variation in the demand for the products marketed by the company.
Lead Time The period of time elapsed between the decision to make a product and the beginning of actual production.
Lease A contract for temporary use of property.
Leasing The use of equipment or facilities owned by another business unit in return for payment.

Leverage Use of borrowed money (debt) in the firm's capital structure.

License A formal document issued by a governmental body to a business or a person which authorizes the holder to engage in an activity that would otherwise be illegal.

Limited Liability The boundary placed on the obligations of a stockholder and his responsibility for a corporation's debts.

Limited Partner A partner whose liability for partnership debts is limited to the amount of investment. If the individual withdraws, the partnership is not automatically dissolved.

Limited Pay Life Insurance A policy in which premiums are paid for a stated number of years only. The annual payments are larger and the cash surrender values are higher than on a whole-life policy.

Line of Credit An informal arrangement between a bank and a borrower as to the maximum amount of funds which can be borrowed on short notice.

Liquidation The transfer of an asset into cash, usually when a business is dissolved.

Liquidity The ease with which an asset may be converted into cash.

Long-term Liabilities Bonds or other debts incurred by a firm that are not payable for at least one year.

Loss Leader Any article a store sells cheaply or below cost to attract customers.

Magnetic Spots Places on tapes where data are recorded by the presence and absence of magnetized areas arranged according to code.

Management by Objectives The process of setting specific goals for individuals and parts of the organization to measure performance and make corrections.

Manufacturer's Agent An agent middleman who generally operates on an extended contractual basis; often sells within an exclusive territory; handles noncompeting but related lines of goods; and possesses limited authority with regard to prices and terms of sale.

Market Economy An economic system in which relative prices determine how resources will be allocated and how the goods and services produced will be distributed.

Market Share The proportion of the total market held by a given seller for a particular product.

Marketing Activity That part of a firm's activity concerned with providing consumers with satisfying goods or services at a price they are willing to pay, at the place they want to buy them, and at the time they wish to buy or use them.

Marketing Manager One who supervises the marketing program as well as authorizes product research, development, and production.

Master Schedule Complete listing of the number of finished products that will come off the assembly each month or week until an order is completed.

Mean The sum of all the numbers in a distribution divided by the quantity of numbers in the distribution.

Mechanization The process of changing from manual to machine operation.

Median The middle number in a distribution.

Merchant Wholesaler One who takes title to the merchandise sold to other middlemen or industrial users.

Glossary

Merger A combination of formerly independent business firms operating under the name of one of the firms. $(A + B = A)$.

Middleman A business person acting in some capacity within the channel of distribution between the producer and the consumer of goods.

Mixed Economy A system that is neither purely capitalistic, nor purely socialistic, nor communistic.

Mode That number which occurs most often in a distribution.

Modes of Transportation Ways and means of sending and transporting merchandise, such as airlines, trucks, ships, and railroads.

Monopolistic Competition Many sellers trying to sell a differentiated product.

Multiregional The subdivision of a large corporation's activities into smaller centralized geographic areas.

Mutual Funds A trust or corporation that uses the funds it obtains from its shareholders to invest in diversified securities.

National Commission on Public Safety The government agency that sets safety standards for products such as lawnmowers.

National Environmental Policy Act A statute that provides for research into the effect of the environment upon people and the economy.

Nationalization To transfer ownership or control of land, resources, industries, and so forth to the national government or to private citizens of that country and away from foreign ownership.

National Traffic and Motor Vehicle Safety Act A statute requiring automobile manufacturers to notify every individual of all safety defects that come to light after a vehicle is on the market.

Net Scrap Generation Reuse of rejected materials for additional production and to prevent shortages.

Nonvoting Equity The stock owner, by contract, is restricted from voting, except on special matters.

Numerical Control A procedure by which machine tools are activated electronically by coded tapes to perform a number of predetermined tasks.

Obsolete No longer in use or practice; out of date.

Occupational Safety and Health Act Statute requiring employers to provide safe working conditions for employees.

Occupational Stamp Taxes Taxes placed on certain occupations such as retailers and lawyers.

Oligopoly Assumes a market situation in which only a few firms produce identical or similar products, these firms having the ability to influence price.

Operating Necessities The requirements for the process or action to work.

Operating Supplies Industrial goods that are considered regular expense items necessary in the daily operation of a firm, but do not become part of the final product.

Operating Variable A new entry that results in the higher utilization of facilities and personnel and the spreading of overhead and purchasing economies.

Order Getting A sales task that involves developing the need for a product and convincing the customer a product will satisfy that need.

Order Receiving A sales task that involves taking an order from a customer who already recognizes the need for a product.

Outside Directors   Directors of a corporation who are not employees of the corporation.
Overhead   The costs of the production facilities and supervisory personnel required for the manufacture of a product.

Parameter   A statistical measure of a population value.
Partnership   A form of business ownership in which two or more people agree to share in the profits and losses of the business in agreed upon proportions.
Paternalism   The principle or system of closely governing or controlling a group of employees by management.
Pension Funds   Monies set up by company and employee contributions to provide retirement benefits for the employees.
Per Capita   For each person.
Peril   A circumstance that may cause a loss.
Personal Property   All property excluding land and its permanent attachment.
Personal Selling   Direct contact of a prospective buyer by a sales representative in a face-to-face sales effort.
Peter Principle   People are promoted to a level within an organization at which they are no longer able to carry out their responsibilities.
Phantom Freight   A profit realized by a seller through charging a buyer higher transportation costs than are incurred to deliver the goods.
Pipeline   A specialized mode of transportation for the conveyance of natural gas and petroleum products in an uninterrupted flow through a system of long distance underground pipes.
Planning, Bottom-up   Planning in which personnel in lower levels of the organization make major contributions to the company's plan.
Planning, Top-down   Planning in which executives at the top of an organization make up the plan with little or no input from personnel at lower levels.
Predatory Pricing   A policy of charging less than the competition for a given product, in order to drive competition out.
Pre-emptive Right   The right of a shareholder to purchase enough new shares of a corporation's stock in order to maintain a proportionate ownership in the firm.
Preferred Stock   A certificate of ownership in a corporation whose holders maintain priority over common stockholders in the payment of dividends and claim to assets in the event of firm liquidation.
Price   A value expressed in dollars and cents.
Price Discrimination   The charging of different prices to different customers under similar conditions of sale with the possibility of violation of the antitrust statutes if it tends to create a monopoly or substantially lessen competition.
Price Fixing   The establishment and maintenance of a scale of prices agreed upon by specified groups of producers or distributors.
Price System   The determination of resource allocation and distribution of goods and services according to price.
Pricing Strategy   The science of planning a price in order to gain the best profit.
Private Carrier   A transport unit operated by a business for transport of goods it owns.
Private Warehouse   Storage facilities owned by a firm for the goods it produces.

Procedures Precise instructions to people or machines who process data into information.

Processor Part of an information system that changes data input into useful management information. It has a control element and an arithmetic-logic element.

Product A bundle of physical, service, and symbolic characteristics designed to produce consumer want satisfaction.

Production Cycle Smoothing Intelligently controlling production to minimize costs and maximize utilization of production facilities.

Product or Line Layout An arrangement of facilities that permits the flow of materials and components in an efficient manner to produce a product.

Profit Sharing A plan whereby an employee receives a portion of the profits earned by the company.

Proforma Statements Financial statements that show forecasted financial performance to acquire and employ funds during some future period.

Program A planned course of action to realize an objective.

Promissory Note A legally binding, written acknowledgement of indebtedness signed by the borrower.

Promotion All direct or indirect communication by a firm with its customers or potential customers for the purpose of sale.

Promotional Allowance The compensation granted to buyers for their costs in the performance of certain promotional functions for a product or service.

Promotional Balance General allocation of promotional budget to advertising, personal selling, and other methods of promotion.

Promotional Effectiveness A measurement of a promotion's success in reaching a specified market.

Promotion Budget Money allocated for promotion for the coming budgetary period.

Promotion Objective The purpose of promotion; inform, remind, or persuade.

Property Taxes Levies against the value of real estate, tangible personal property, and intangibles owned by the taxpayer.

Proprietorship The ownership of a business by one person.

Proxy A document that transfers the voting rights of a stockholder to another person.

Public Forces Opinions and organizations that influence the decisions made by a firm.

Public Warehouse An independent storage facility in which goods owned by others can be stored at a charge.

Purchase Requisition A document used to inform a supplier of the desire to purchase specified materials, which upon the supplier's acceptance, becomes a commitment to buy.

Purchasing Task Force People with expertise temporarily assigned especially to the task of procuring the materials required for production.

Pure Competition An economic system characterized by:
1. A large number of sellers in the market, all selling identical products.
2. Buyers and sellers are completely informed about the market and prices.
3. Free movement in and out of the market by buyers and sellers.
4. An inability of either buyer or seller to influence the price, which is determined by supply and demand.

Pure Monopoly   The complete control of the output of a product or service by one seller.
Pure Risk   A situation in which there is only a chance of loss with no opportunity for profit.
Puritan Ethic   Belief that success is achieved only through hard work.

Quality Control   A system of setting quality standards, determining actual quality, and taking corrective action if indicated.
Quantifiable   Able to be defined in mathematical terms.
Quantitative   Capable of being measured.
Quantitative Method   Application of mathematics and statistics to decision-oriented problems.

Railroad   A mode of transporting goods from one point to another on a system of rails.
Range   The difference between the largest value and the smallest value in a sample.
Ratio Analysis   A method of relating one piece of financial information to another in order to evaluate financial performance and position of a firm.
Raw Materials   Unprocessed materials used in the manufacturing of a product.
Realignment   The readjustment of alliances or working arrangements between companies.
Real Property   Land and its permanent attachment.
Reciprocity   A relationship between companies in which business with one leads to business with the other.
Regional Development Organization   An entity that tries to attract business to a specific geographic area.
Reporting Relationships   An accounting of relationships written for presentation to others for the purpose of coordinating communication.
Résumé   A short statement of one's qualifications for employment.
Retailer   Middleman who sells goods to the final consumer.
Retailer Cooperative Groups   Contractual agreements between a group of retailers where, in order to compete with chain stores, each retailer purchases stock in a retail-owned wholesaling operation and agrees to purchase a minimum percentage of his supplies from the operation.
Retained Earnings   Profits that are held for reinvestment.
Return on Invested Capital (ROI)   After-tax earnings from the investment of capital.
Revolving Credit Agreement   A contractual short-term source of funds where the borrower pays a fee on unborrowed as well as borrowed money that a lender agrees to extend.
Risk   The chance of loss.
Robinson–Patman Act   A federal law, an amendment to the Clayton Act, which prohibits price discrimination that harms small retailers and other competitors.
Routing   The order in which a product will be assembled and the physical arrangement of the various activities to insure the most efficient flow of materials.

Safety Stocks   Items which are kept for production or for sale in the event that demand is higher than usual or the delivery of goods is delayed.

Salary and Wages Payment to an employee for the job performed; wages are paid on an hourly basis while a salary is paid weekly or monthly.

Sales Branches A manufacturer does his own wholesaling by maintaining warehouses near customers.

Sales Forecast An estimate of the sales that will be made in some future time period.

Sales Offices Places of business separate from manufacturing plants, from which a sales force is directed but which do not maintain an inventory.

Sales Process The organizational procedure for selling a product.

Sales Results Tests A test run of an advertisement or campaign on a small scale to determine effectiveness before running the campaign over the entire marketing area with its attendant large costs.

Sales Taxes A tax on the sale of commodities or services or both that is paid by consumers.

Sales Supporting A basic sales task. It is an indirect type of selling that can be subclassified into those who sell the goodwill of a firm and those who provide the customer with technical or operational assistance.

Schedule Performance Reports Follow-up reports based on completed forms received from the operating departments.

Scheduling The allocation of time to plant equipment for various operations.

Scrambled Merchandising A practice of retailers adding new product lines that are different from previous lines carried.

Screening A system for separating job candidates on the basis of qualifications.

Secret Partner A partner who plays an active role in management of the partnership but who keeps his status as a partner anonymous.

Selective Coverage The choice or selection of only those middlemen who will do a good job with the product.

Self-Insurance Annual deposits into a special fund from which losses may be paid.

Selling Agent A middleman who sells the entire output of a product for one or more producers.

Seniority An employee's status based on the length of employment with the company; used as a basis for promotion.

Services Activities that are offered for sale or are offered in connection with sale of goods.

Sexual Complications Problems resulting from work relationships between people of opposite gender.

Shareholders People who own shares of stock in a corporation.

Sherman Act (1890) A law that forbids contracts, combinations, or conspiracies in restraint of trade or commerce.

Shopping Goods Products for which the consumer desires to compare the offering of competing stores on various bases, such as price, quality, and style.

Silent Partner A partner who does not desire to take an active role in the management of the company, but who is willing to let his/her name be used as one of the partners of the firm.

Small Business Administration A federal agency whose function is to aid the development of small business.

Social Audit A process that involves finding out how well business is satisfying its many publics.

Social Indicator A signal that shows the trend of public opinion and the quality of life.
Socialism An economic system in which basic industry and social services are controlled by the government.
Social Responsibility Accountability for one's dealings as they affect the common welfare.
Social Security Tax A tax on wages paid or received in order to provide old age, survivor's, disability, and medicare benefits.
Specialty Good A product for which consumers have developed loyalty to one brand; consumers will expend any effort necessary to get the desired brand.
Speculative Risk A situation characterized by a chance of loss and a chance of profit.
Spin-off The transfer of unwanted assets of a firm to another corporation in exchange for cash, stock, and/or other forms of payment.
Sponsor System A plan whereby a new employee learns the details of the job from another.
Standard Deviation The square root of the arithmetic average of the squares of the deviations from the mean in a frequency distribution.
Statistical Inference Process of making statements about a population on the basis of information contained in a sample.
Statistical Techniques The techniques used for collecting, organizing, summarizing, interpreting, and analyzing numerical data and making predictions and forecasts from this data.
Stock Certificate A certificate issued by a corporation to a shareholder as written evidence of ownership of shares of stock.
Stockholder A person owning stock in a given company.
Stockholders' Equity Stockholders' claim to the resources of the corporation. Equals corporation's assets less liabilities.
Stock Out A situation in which there is no product immediately available for sale or use.
Storage A place where information on products is accumulated for future use.
Strategic Planning Either a plan to control a strategy or planning for the long-range growth by forecasting strategic variables in the future and deciding on the best means of growth for a firm in this environment.
Strategic Variables Variables considered in planning which are out of the control of the company but which require forecasts to predict the environmental framework.
Strategies for Supply A forecast of the future size of all of the firm's present and potential consumption market and the attempts to identify its future needs and buying behavior.
Strategy A course of action to achieve a specific objective which has multiple components and a specified time period.
Subsidiary A company owned by a parent company.
Substandard Below an expectation stated either by law or by a standard established by the firm.
Supplier A person or firm that furnishes the necessary goods and services.
Suppliers of Information Internal and external sources who provide knowledge, data, and so forth.

Survey of Buyers' Intentions A study of customers' plans to buy products in the future.

Synergy The effect of elements joined together having a result greater than the sum of the elements.

System A number of independent elements or activities that are unified, organized, and coordinated to work for a common goal.

Systems Analyst One who interprets the computer's output and plans computerized information systems.

Tactics Actions which are intended to achieve goals within a plan or strategy.

Target Market A specific market or group or segment of customers that the company intends to serve.

Technology The application of knowledge in business to realize a marketable product or service.

Terminal A part of a computer system through which data are fed to the central processing unit.

Term Insurance A policy whereby the insurance company is obligated to pay if a loss occurs within the time limit covered by the policy.

Term Loan A source of intermediate-length financing usually repaid in installments.

Three-way Flow Refers to communications between the individuals being trained or developed, the trainer/developer, and the manager for whom the trainee works.

Title A document stating right of ownership.

Tolerances The leeway permitted in the measurement of manufactured parts.

Trade Credit A credit extended to a firm by its suppliers.

Trade Discount A discount given to middlemen on the basis of various marketing functions they perform.

Transaction A dealing or negotiation in business.

Transaction Loan A loan given for a specific business purpose.

Transfer Shifting an employee from one job to another that does not require the individual to possess greater skill or assume more duties.

Treasury Bills Short-term debt issue of the U.S. government; widely used as investments in marketable securities portfolios.

Truck Jobber A merchant middleman who takes orders and fills them simultaneously from the items carried in his truck. Only a limited line of fast-moving, perishable items are carried.

Trucks Motorized carriers that use the roads and highways to transport goods and people.

Trust A form of business organization that places the control of several companies in the hands of a group of people called trustees. This form of organization was used in the early 1900s to gain control of the oil industry.

Tying Arrangement An agreement wherein a buyer is required to take certain undesirable goods in order to secure more desirable merchandise.

Understudy Program A system designed to train a person in the duties of another so that he may substitute if necessary.

Uniform Delivered Pricing A policy that regards the entire nation as one physical zone and charges all purchasers, regardless of their location, the same delivered price.

Union An organization of workers formed to protect the economic rights of its members, through collective bargaining with its employer.

Users of Information Managers and other personnel who make use of the information provided by information systems.

Use Tax Sales tax on goods entering one state from another state.

Variable Costs Those costs whose magnitude changes with the level of output.

Variance The square of the standard deviation.

Venture Capitalists People who provide the funds for relatively risky operations and take their profit out of the subsequent profits, if they materialize.

Volume Maximization The objective of selling as much as possible to achieve full use of facilities.

Wage and Price Controls Limits placed by the government on the amounts of wages paid and prices demanded by business.

Water Carrier A ship or barge used in the transportation of goods.

Wheel of Retailing A cycle that retailers pass through and that results in gradual increases in the number of services offered and the prices demanded.

Whole-life Insurance An insurance plan combining protection and savings features wherein the insurer is obligated to make a payment at some point during the life of the policy or at its termination.

Wholesaler The middleman between the producer and the final consumer in the channel of distribution.

Wholesaler Sponsored, Voluntary Groups A group of retailers, each of whom owns and operates his own store and is associated with a wholesale organization to carry on joint merchandising activities; and who are characterized by some degree of group identity and uniformity of operation.

Word-of-Mouth Communication Verbal person-to-person communication including opinions and suggestions about products and sellers.

Working Capital Four types: net working capital equals current assets less current liabilities; gross working capital equals total current assets; permanent working capital is a base amount always on hand; temporary working capital varies with the firm's operating cycle.

Work Sampling A method of quality control.

Work Standard A predetermined level of performance in one's job.

Zone Pricing A policy of charging all purchasers within a geographic area the same price regardless of differences in transportation costs.

Index

AAIMS. *See* An Analytical Information Management System
Ability to pay, 315
Acceptance sampling, 204
Accessory equipment, 244
Accounting
  careers, 350–353
    government, 352
    industrial, 351, 352
    public, 350–351
    rewards, 352
  cost, 347, 351
  definition, 325–326
  equation, 328–329
  external use, 327–328
  financial, 333–343
  fundamentals, 328–333
  general, 348
  internal use, 327
  management, 343–348, 349
Accounts payable, 331
Accounts receivable, 330
  management, 362–363
Accrual, 331
Accrued expenses payable, 331
Acquisitions department, 304
Acquisitions and mergers, 472
  checklist, 472–473
Actuary, 400

Ad valorem, 53
Advertising, 255–258
  careers, 264–265
  choice of agency, 257–258
  direct mail, 256, 258
  message, 259
  selection of media, 256–257
Advertising agency, 257–258
Affirmative action programs, 303
Affluence, American, 12
AFL–CIO, 37, 38
Agent, 275
Aging of accounts, 341
Allied lines clause, 392
Allocation of resources, 469
Allowance for doubtful accounts, 335
American Airlines, 420
American College of Life Underwriters, 399
American Institute for Property and Liability Underwriting, 399
American Federation of Labor (AFL), 37
American Institute of Certified Public Accountants, 342
American Technological Foundation, 9
Analysis
  financial, 339
  historical, 339
  interfirm, 339
  ratio, 339

Analytical Information Management System, An, 420
Annuitants, 124
Antitrust laws, 60–62
Application form, 302
Applied research, 471
Apprentice system, 304
Arbitrator, 313
Arithmetic-logic element, 413
Arrearage, 371
Articles of incorporation, 165, 167–168
Articles of partnership, 162
Assembly, 190
Assembly line worker, 21–22
Assets, 328
   current, 330
   fixed, 330
   intangibles, 331
   net fixed, 337
   prepaid expenses, 331
   quick, 340
   turnover, 340
Audience, 242–245
   buying habits, 243–244
   geographic scope, 243
   size, 242
   type of customer, 243
Audit of accounts, 472
Auditing, 342
Automation, 190, 517
   closed loop, 191
Automatic vending, 281
Averages, 440

Backward integration, 11
Bait and switch advertising, 252
Balance sheet, 335
Bargaining, 20
Bargaining unit, 311
Base pay, 315
Basic research, 471
Beneficiaries of trust, 173
Benefits, 36
Benefits of information, 410
Better Business Bureau (BBB), 229
Bidding, 66
Bids, 181
Bill of materials, 200
Blocked currency, 480–481
Blue-collar workers, 315
Blue Cross and Blue Shield, 394
Board of directors, 170
   responsibilities, 170–172
Bottlenecks, 201

Bottom-up planning, 465
Bottom-up management, 146
Bonds, 475
Bookkeeping, 329–330
Boycotts, 311
Break-even analysis, 220, 345–346
Break-even sales volume, 346
Brokers, 279, 280
Budget, 345
Bureau of Labor, 37
Business, American
   advantages, 9–10
   careers, 13–15
   controls, 7
   developments affecting, 8–13
   energy shortages, 10–11
   improvements, 19–20
   long-range implications, 11
   nature, 5–6
   private, progress of, 7–8
Business audit, 472
Business statistics, 436
   descriptive, 439–443
   framework, 436–439
Business trust, 173–174. *See also* Massachusetts trust
Buying guides, 222

Campus placement office, 523–524
Canned computer operation, 422–423
Capital, 5, 35
   cost, 183
   idle, 184
Capital budgeting, 363–364
   examples, 364
   program, 364
Capital contribution, 162
Capital gain, 372, 473
Capital stock, 332
Capital surplus, 333
Capitalism, 104–106
   basic principles, 104
Careers
   choosing, 14–15
   directions, 522
   implications, 517–519
   planning, 519–522
   researching, 523
   searching for a job, 523–525
Career file, 14, 523
Carriers, 289
Cash consciousness, 138
Cash control, 361
Cash flow statement, 501

Cash inflow, 497
  estimating, 496–498
Cash manager, 375
Cash management, 360–361
Cash outflow
  estimating, 498–501
Cash planning, 360
Casualty Actuary Society, 400
Celler–Kefauver Act of 1950, 62
Centralization, 144
Central processing unit (CPU), 413
Central tendency, 440
Certificates of deposit, 362
Certified internal auditor (CIA), 352
Certified public accountant (CPA), 342–343
  career, 350–351
Chain stores, 281
Channel
  direct, 272, 274
  intermediate-length, 276
  long, 276
  short, 276
  two-level, 274, 275
Channel of distribution, 224
Charter, 165, 167
Chartered Life Underwriters (CLU), 399
Chartered Property and Casualty Underwriter (CPCU), 399
Chemical processes, 189
Civil Rights Act of 1964, 27, 58, 303, 314
Claims adjustment, 400
Class action suits, 230, 232
Classic capitalist system, 106. *See also* Pure competitive system
Classified ads, 524
Clayton Antitrust Act, 60–62, 285
Closed shop, 37
Coaching, 306
Cobol, 418
Coinsurance clause, 392
Collateral loan, 369
Collection period, 340
Collective bargaining, 311, 315
Collective demand, 104
Commercial paper, 362, 370
Commission person, 279, 280
Committee, 144–146
Committee for Economic Development of 1947, 489
Committee for Industrial Organization (CIO), 37
Common law, 60
Common stock, 168, 371
Common stockholders, 332
Communications, 222
  business controlled, 222, 223
  nonbusiness controlled, 222, 223
  word-of-mouth, 222, 223
Communism, 108–109
Company
  changes, 516–517
Company politics, 25
Competitive system, 104
Compiler, 418
Computers, 405
  future business use, 425
  jobs, 427–430
  problems, 422
  successful use, 419–425
Computer operator, 429–430
Computer program, 136, 428
Computer programmers, 418, 428–429
Computer service bureau, 424
Condition of the marketplace, 315
Conflict of interest, 464
Congress on Racial Equality (CORE), 28
Consensus, 447
Console operator, 429
Consolidation, 374
Consumers, 81–82
Consumer cooperative, 283
Consumer Credit Protection Act, 232
Consumer price index (CPI), 122
Consumer protection legislation, 63
Consumer's Research Bulletin, 222
Consumerism, 139
Consumerism movement, 228–230
  demands, 228
  reasons for beginning, 229
Contingency, 475
Contingency fund, 383
Contingency plans, 141
Contract, 311
Contractual relations, 282
Control
  setting standards, 409
  taking corrective action, 409–410
Control element, 413
Control systems, 347–348
Controlled feedback, 447
Controller, 23, 24, 348
  staff, 348–350
Convenience goods, 245
Convertible securities, 370
Cooperative, 505
Corporation, 163
  advantages, 175
  definition, 164–165
  disadvantages, 175
  formation, 165–168

Index

Correlation, 443
Costs, 219–220
   variable, 219
   fixed, 219
Cost, insurance and freight (C.I.F.), 183
Cost accounting, 347
Cost minimization, 138
Cost of business social responsibility, 90
Cost of capital, 365
Cost of goods sold, 338
Cost of information, 410
Cost of living, 20, 315
Council of Economic Advisors, 71
Counseling services, 319
Counterstrategy, 140
Countervailing power, 107
Cover letter, 524
   examples, 528, 529
CRAFT (Computerized Relative Allocation of Facilities Technique), 195
Credit manager, 375
Creditors, 79
Cumulative, 202
Cumulative preferred stock, 332
Current liabilities, 331
Custom duties, 53–54

Data processing, 349–350
Debentures, 370
Debugging, 428
Decentralization, 144
Deception, 252
   in advertising, 252
Decision by consensus, 146
Decision making, 134–136
Decision-making aids, 425–426
Defense Supply Agency, 64, 65
Delphi, The, 446–447
Department of Commerce, 68
Department of Defense, 66
Department of social affairs, 95, 97
   manager, 98
Departmentation, 143–144
Demotion, 303
Depreciation, 337, 338
Depreciation expense, 50
Desk research, 496
Detailed audit, 473
Deterioration, 188
Devaluation, 9
Direct costs, 183
Direct investment, 117
Direct-mail advertising, 256, 258
Director of taxes, 349

Disability benefits, 319
Disclaimer, 343
Dispersion, 441
Distribution, 223–224, 440
   careers, 291–293
Distributors, 81
District representatives, 310
Diversification, 469–470
Divestiture, 470
Dividends, 20, 139, 170
Dividend decision, 372–373
Documentary stamp taxes, 54
Dormant partner, 162
Double-counting, 109–110
Double standard, 28
Downside out analysis, 464
Downtime, 205
Dun and Bradstreet, 340

Earnings statement, 338
Ecology, 87
Economist, 126–127
Employees, 79
   needs of, 148–149
Employment Act of 1946, 71
Employment agency, 297, 301, 524
Employment, process of
   development, 305–306, 307
   discharging, 313–314
   job analysis, 299–301
   sequence, 302–303
   sources of candidates, 301
   training, 303–305, 307
Endowment policy, 389
Enterprise, forms of, 159
Entities, 136
Entrepreneur, 489–490
Entry into storage, 188
Environment Quality Council, 59–60
Equal opportunity employers, 113
Equal Pay Act of 1963, 27, 302–303
Equity, 328–329
   in corporations, 332
   in partnership, 332
   in proprietorship, 332
   stockholder's, 332
Evaluation, 307
Exception-basis, 326
Exclusive coverage, 285
Exclusive dealing agreement, 62
Exclusive dealing contract, 285
Executive programs, 318
Executive training, 304–305
Excise taxes, 52–53

Expediters, 146
Expenses, 160
External growth, 374
    consolidation, 374
    holding company, 374–375
    merger, 374
External policies, 139
Extrapolation, simple, 445
Extroverts, 14

Fabricated parts and materials, 244
Facilitating agencies, 288
Factor comparison system, 317
Factoring, 369–370
Fair Labor Standards Act, 58. *See also* Minimum Wage Law
Fair Packaging and Labeling Act, 232
Fair Trade Law, 221
False advertising, 252
Federal Career Directory, 1973: A Guide for College Students, 72
Federal Cigarette Labeling and Advertising Act, 231
Federal Communication Commission (FCC), 64
Federal Deposit Insurance Corporation (FDIC), 70
Federal income tax payable, 331
Federal Insurance Contribution (FICA), 52
Federal Power Commission, 64
Federal Reserve Banking System, 70
Federal Trade Commission (FTC), 221, 230–232, 251
Federal Trade Commission Acts, 60, 61, 62
Feedback, 150
Fee-paid positions, 524
Feminist movement, 28
Fidelity and surety bonds, 396
Field research, 496
Final goods, 109–110
Finance
    career opportunities, 375–376
        cash manager, 375
        credit manager, 375
        financial analyst, 376
        qualifications, 376
        treasurer, 376
    definition, 357–358
Financial accounting, 333
Financial analysis, 339
Financial analyst, 376
Financial ratio
    acid test ratio, 340
    annual net sales, 340
    asset turnover, 340
    coverage ratio, 341
    current ratio, 340
    debt equity ratio, 341
    gross profit margin, 341
    inventory turnover, 340
    net profit margin, 341
    return on tangible net worth, 341
Financial statements, 334–337
    analyzing, 339–340
    preparation of, 334–335
Finished goods, 330
Fiscal policies, 71
Fixed assets, 35, 330
Fixed costs, 219, 345
Flammable Fabrics Act, 230
Flow charts, 192, 428
Flow process chart, 193, 195
Food and Drug Administration (FDA), 230
Food, Drug, and Cosmetic Act of 1938, 230
Forecasting, 136
Foreign competition, 8
    problems, 8–9
Foreman, 22–23
Franchise, 508
    advantages, 508
    disadvantages, 509
    finding, 509
Franchise Annual, 509
Franchise Directory, 509
Franchise organizations, 282–283
Franchise tax, 166
Free on board (F.O.B.), 183, 290
Free enterprise, 127
Full-line product concept, 16
Full-resource planning, 465–466
Functional layout, 196
Funds, 358
    sources, 365
        debt, 365–371
        equity, 365–372
        liabilities, 365–372
Fur Products Labeling Act, 230

Galbraith, John Kenneth, 105
General accounting, 348
General accounting office (GAO), 352
General management
    careers and jobs, 483
    competence, 478
    factors affecting performance, 478–479
    growth sources, 469–477
    responsibilities, 462–465
    role in planning and strategy, 465–468
General partner, 161
General public, 82–84

Generally accepted accounting principles (GAAP), 333–335
Geographic structure, 144
Global competition, 515
Goldberg, Arthur, 172
Go/no-go decision, 473, 482, 502
Goods, 180
Government
  buyer role, 64–67
  careers, 71–73
  dispenser of funds, goods and services, 68–69
  regulator role, 48–64
  setting policy role, 70–71
Government intervention, 515
Gozinto charts, 192. *See also* Flow charts
Grievances, 311–313
Grievance procedure, 312
Gross National Product (GNP), 109–110, 446
Gross working capital, 358
Group bonuses, 317
Guaranteed renewable policy, 387

Hazard, 383
Health insurance, 319
Highway Safety Act, 229
Historical analysis, 339
Holding company, 374–375
Household consumers, 243, 245–246

Implementing, 137
Income, 160
Income statement, 338
Income taxes, 48–52
  acquiring money, 50
  buying, 50
  effect, 50
  producing, 50–51
  selling, 51–52
  state and local, 54–57
Incontestability clause, 391
Incorporators, 167
Independent agents, 399
Industrial accounting, 351–352
Industrial traffic manager, 291–293
Industrial users, 243–245
Industry, seasonal, 188–189
Inflation, 35, 120
  controls, 125
  effects, 122–123
  rate, 120
Inflation
  cost–push, 120, 122
  demand–pull, 120, 122, 125
Information, 405
  suppliers, 418–419
  systems to provide, 411–416
  types, 405–410
  users, 417–418
  value, 410–411
Input, 412–413
Innovative problem solving, 139
Inside directors, 172
Installations, 244
Institute of Internal Auditors, 352
Insurance
  accident and health, 394–395
  automobile, 393–394
  careers and jobs, 399–400
  casualty, 392–396
  disability, 395
  life and accident, 319
  major medical, 395
  marine, 396
  principles, 384–385
  product liability, 397
  property, 392, 393
    business interruption, 392
    fire insurance, 392, 393, 397
  theft, 394
  title, 396
Insurance, life
  cost, 389–390
  legalistic clauses, 391–392
  types
    endowment, 389
    limited pay life policy, 389
    term, 387, 388
    whole life, 388
Insurance agents and brokers, 399
Insurance companies, 386
  types
    mutual, 386
    stock, 386
Insurance policy, 384
Insurance underwriter, 399
Intensive coverage, 284
Interchangeability, 189
Interlocking directorates, 62
Intermediate goods, 109–110
Internal auditing, 349
Internal audit, 352
Internal development, 476
Internal policies, 139
International business, 20
International investment, 117–119
International operations, 480
  establishing, 481–482
  reasons for, 480–481

Index   559

International trade, 116–117
Interstate Commerce Commission, 64, 328
Interviews, 302, 528–531
Introverts, 14
Inventories, 184, 330
Inventory management, 363
Inventory systems, 185–187
Inventory, withdrawal from, 188
Investment decision, 358
Inequality in income distribution, 112–113

Jobs
    characteristics, 24–25
    description, 299–300
    security and income, 25–26
Job grade and ranking system, 317
Job rotation, 305
Joint stock company, 173
Joint venture, 173

Kaufman, Henry, 126

Labor laws, 57–59
Labor relations
    responsibilities, 309–310
Landrum–Griffin Act, 37, 58
Lanham Act, 63–64
Layoff, 303
Lead time, 184
Lease, 371
Leasing, 495
Legal contract, 161
Leverage, 367–369
Liabilities, 328
    current, 331
    long-term, 332
Licenses, 56
Licensing, 480
Life insurance. *See also* Insurance, life
Life Underwriting Training Council, 399
Limited liability, 162
Limited partner, 162, 163
Limited pay life policy, 389
Line layout, 197
Line of credit, 369
Line and staff, 142
Linear programming, 201
Liquidation, 170, 366
Liquidity, 358
Loans, 319
Logistics, 16
Long-range planning, 467–468
Long-term liabilities, 332
Loss leader, 274

Magnetic spots, 413–414
Maintenance, 204–205
    preventative, 205
    repair crews, 205
Management, 133
    autocratic, 146
    careers, 151–152
    democratic, 146
    laissez-faire, 146
Management by objectives (MBO), 307, 467
Management, industrial
    careers, 105–106
Management science, 451–453
    careers, 453–454
Management training programs, 304
Manager, scheduling, 201
Manpower and Development Training Act of 1962, 69
Manual, 316
Manufacturer's agents, 279, 280
Manufacturing, 506–507
Market economy, 104
Market share, 140
Merger, 374, 470
Marketable securities, 361–362
    examples, 361
Market basket, 120
Market value, 335
Marketing, 213–237
    career, 233–237
    function, 213–224
    historical change in importance, 226–228
    impact on firm, 224–225
Marketing activity, 213–214
Massachusetts trust, 173–174
Master schedule, 202
Mathematical programming, 448
Mean, 440
Meat Inspection Act, 230
Mechanization, 190
Median, 440
Medicare, 52
Middlemen, 243–245, 271
    categories of, 284–285
    choosing, 285–286
    elimination of, 273–274
    favorable characteristics, 286–287
    improving performance, 288
    motivation, 287
    performance evaluation, 287
    use of, 272–273
Minimum Wage Law, 58
Mixed economy, 106
Mode, 441

Model changeovers, 189
Monetary policy, 70, 71
Monopolistic competition, 106
Morris, Robert, Associates, 340
Motivation, 150
Multinational corporation (MNC), 482
Mutual funds, 19

Nader, Ralph, 228–229
National Aeronautics and Space Administration (NASA), 66
National Association of Accountants, 351
National Commission on Public Safety, 64
National Defense Education Act of 1958, 69
National Environment Policy Act, 59–60
National Highway Safety Bureau, 232
National Labor Relations Act, 37, 58
National Labor Relations Board, 37
National Traffic and Motor Vehicle Safety Act, 232
Nationalization, 12
Nazarevsky, Valentin A., 112
Near certainty, 444
Negotiation, 66
Nepotism, 301
Net sales, 338
Net scrap generation, 195
Net working capital, 358
Network models, 201
New York City's Department of Consumer Affairs, 232
Nonvoting equity, 475–476
Norris–LaGuardia Act of 1932, 37, 58
Note payable, 331
Noted score, 259
Numerical control, 191

Obsolete, 189
Obsolescence, rate of, 189
Occupational Safety and Health Act of 1973 (OSHA), 58, 59, 320
Occupational Safety and Health Agency (OSHA), 507
Occupational stamp taxes, 54
Oil trust, 61
Old Age, Survivors, and Disability Insurance (OASDI), 52
Oligopoly, 106–107
Operating necessities, 142
Operating supplies, 244–245
Operating variables, 144, 468
Optimizing skill, 148
Order getting, 253
Order receiving, 253
Output, 416
Overhead, 183, 297

Overruns, 477
Outside directors, 172

Parameter, 443
Par value, 332
Paternalism, 319
Partner's capital accounts, 332
Partnership, 161–163
    advantages, 174
    disadvantages, 175
    dissolving, 163
    forming, 162–163
Partnership capital, 162
Pay-premium days, 201
Pension funds, 19
People skill, 148
Per capita, 8
Percentage ownership, 494–495
Peril, 383
Perishability, rate of, 189
Personal property, 54–55
Personal selling, 251, 253
    compensating, 255
    hiring, 253
    organizing, 254–255
    training, 254
Personnel
    careers, 320–321
    function, 297–299
Personnel administration, 314
    responsibilities, 314
Personnel committee, 298
Peter Principle, 478
Phantom freight, 290
Piece work, 317–318
Planning, 136
Planning, long-range, 467–468
Planning, short-range, 466–467
Point system, 316–317
Policies, 138–139
Port of New York Authority, 69
Postproduction, 13
Predatory pricing, 220
Pre-emptive right, 169
Preferred stock, 332, 371
Premiums, 386
Preproduction, 13
Prevailing salaries and wages, 315
Price discrimination, 220, 221
Price fixing, 220–221
Price leader, 107
Price system, 104
Prior right, 332
Pro forma statements, 342

Procedures, 415
Processor, 413
Product, 215–218
　characteristics, 216
　consumer view, 216–217
　distribution, 223
　new, 218
　pricing, 217–218, 219
　planning, 215, 216
　promoting, 221–223
Product layout, 197
Product life, 189
Production
　continuous, 200
　intermittent, 200
Production bonus system, 318
Production cycle smoothing, 201
Production process
　management, 197–205
Productivity, 315–316
Professional insurance, 384
Profits, 3
Profit sharing, 318
Program, 140
Program director, 309
Promissory notes, 475
Promotion, 222–223, 303
　career
　　advertising, 264–265
　　selling, 260–264
　examples of specific objectives, 247
　goals, 246–247
　objectives, 241–247
Promotion activities, 253
　advertising, 255–258
　　choice of agency, 257–258
　　selection of media, 256–257
　personal selling
　　compensation, 254–258
　　hiring sales representatives, 253
　　organizing, 254–255
　　training, 254
Promotional allowance and services, 252
Promotional balance, 250–252
　customer characteristics, 251
　environmental considerations, 251–252
　firm considerations, 251
Promotional budget, 247
　available funds, 249
　competitive expenditures, 248
　objectives and tasks, 249–250
　sales, 248
Promotional effectiveness, 258–260
Property taxes, 54–55

Proprietorship, 159–161
　advantages, 174
　disadvantages, 174
　sole, 159
Proxy, 169
Public accounting, 350–351
Public forces, 77
Public Health Cigarette Smoking Act, 231
Public liability insurance, 395
Purchase requisition, 180
Purchasing, 180–183
　procedures, 185
Purchasing
　centralized, 181
　decentralized, 181–182
Purchasing ethics, 185
Purchasing task forces, 183
Pure competition, 106
Pure Food and Drug Act, 230
Pure monopoly, 106
Pure risk, 382–383
Puritan ethic, 85

Quality control, 192–193, 197, 203–204
Quality of the inventory, 341
Quantifiable, 133
Quantitative approach, 434
　consideration of alternatives, 435
　evaluation of course of action, 435
　problem definition, 434
　selection of course of action, 435
Quantitative methods, 201, 433
　techniques and terminology, 445–451
Queueing models, 449

Railroad Arbitration Act of 1963, 37
Range, 441
Ratio analysis, 339
Raw materials, 244, 330
Realignment, 517
Real property, 54
Reciprocity, 185
Recreation services, 319
Regional development organizations, 496
Release time, 310
Reporting relationships, 136
Research and development (R & D), 466, 471
Resource allocation, 447–451
Résumé, 302, 525
　examples, 526, 527
Retailer, 276–282
　contractual, 282
　independent, 281–282
　in-store, 279

full-service, 279
limited-service, 280
mail-order, 281
nonstore, 281
Retailer cooperative groups, 282
Retailing, 505
problems, 505–506
Retained earnings, 333, 372
Return on invested capital, 138
Return on investment (ROI), 474
Retirement benefits, 319
Revenue, 160, 329
Revolving credit agreement, 369
Risk, 381
business, 382
financial, 382
pure, 382–383
speculative, 381–382
Risk sharing, 12
Robber Barons, 85
Robinson–Patman Act of 1936, 61–62, 220, 221, 252
Routing, 202
Rural Electrification Administration, 68

Safety stocks, 184
Salaries and wages, prevailing, 315
Salary, 315
Sales branches, 277
Sales incentives, 318
Sales forecast, 180
Sales offices, 277
Sales process, 254
Sales representative, 24
career, 260–264
compensating, 255
hiring, 253
organizing, 254–255
performance, 259
training, 254
Sales results tests, 259
Sales supporting, 253
Sales taxes, 55
Schedule performance reports, 202–203
Scheduling, 200–201
Scheduling decisions, 202–203
Scrambled merchandising, 284
Screening, 135
Secret partner, 162
Securities and Exchange Commission, 342
Selective coverage, 285
Self-employment
advantages, 492
disadvantages, 492

Self-insurance, 383
Selling agents, 278, 280
Semiquartile range, 442
Seniority, 22
Sensitivity analysis, 451
Services, 180, 506
Sexual complications, 28
Shareholders, 168
Sheldon Self-Rating Schedule, 519–520
Sherman Act, 60, 61, 62, 85, 220
Shopping goods, 245
Short-range planning, 466–467
Silent partner, 162
Simulation, 451
Small business
careers and jobs, 509–510
definition, 489
establishing, 494–502
managing, 503–509
reasons for failure, 503
primary cause, 504
secondary cause, 504
Small Business Administration, 68, 489, 490, 496
Small Marketers Aid No. 71, 490
Social audit, 95
aspects, 96
Social indicators, 93–94
Social response
impact of new responsibilities on careers, 97–99
problems, 87–91
resolution of problems, 91–97
Social responsibility, 20, 85
Social security taxes, 52
Socialism, 108
Society of actuaries, 400
Span of control, 142–143
Specialty goods, 245–246
Speculative risk, 381–382
Spin-off, 470
Sponsor system, 304
Standard of living, 9
Start-up, 477
Standard deviation, 441, 442
Standardization, 189
Statement of financial position, 335
Statement of profit and loss, 338
Statistical inference, 443
Statistical techniques, 199
Stewards, 310
Stock certificate, 169
Stockholders, 78, 168
Stockholder's equity, 332
Stock out, 184
Stopwatch, 199